AFRICA 68-69

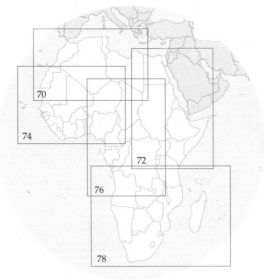

EUROPE 80-81

MACMILLAN
CONCISE
WORLD
ATLAS

MACMILLAN
CONCISE
WORLD
ATLAS

MACMILLAN

A DORLING KINDERSLEY BOOK

PROJECT CARTOGRAPHY AND DESIGN
Julia Lunn, Julie Turner

CARTOGRAPHERS
Roger Bullen, Bob Croser, Martin Darlison, Stephen Flanagan,
Sally Gable, Dieter Müller, John Plumer,
Andrew Thompson, Scott Wallace

DIGITAL CARTOGRAPHY CREATED IN DK CARTOPIA BY
Tom Coulson, Dan Gardiner, Phil Rowles, Rob Stokes

DESIGN
Katy Wall

INDEX-GAZETTEER
Debra Clapson, Natalie Clarkson, Ruth Duxbury,
Margaret Hynes, Simon Lewis

PRODUCTION
Hilary Stephens, David Proffit

CARTOGRAPHIC DIRECTOR
Andrew Heritage

ART DIRECTOR
Chez Picthall

First published in Australia by Pan Macmillan Australia Pty Limited
St Martins Tower, 31 Market Street, Sydney, NSW 2000, Australia

Copyright © 1997 Dorling Kindersley Limited, London
Visit us on the World Wide Web at http://www.dk.com

National Library of Australia cataloguing-in-publication data
Macmillan concise world atlas
ISBN 07 329 0889 2
1. Atlases I. Title: Macmillan concise world atlas
912

Film output by Colourpath, UK
Printed and bound by Graphicom Srl, Italy

KEY TO MAP SYMBOLS

BOUNDARIES

	Full international border
	Disputed *de facto* border
	Territorial claim border
	Ceasefire line
	Undefined boundary
	Internal administrative boundary

COMMUNICATION FEATURES

	Major road
	Minor road
	Railway
	International airport

DRAINAGE FEATURES

	Major perennial river
	Minor perennial river
	Seasonal river
	Canal
	Waterfall
	Perennial lake
	Seasonal lake
	Wetland

ICE FEATURES

	Permanent ice cap/ice shelf
	Winter limit of pack ice
	Summer limit of pack ice

LANDSCAPE FEATURES

	Sandy desert
∆	Spot height
∇	Spot depth
⌕	Volcano
)(	Pass/tunnel
+	Site of interest

POPULATED PLACES

○	Less than 50,000
○	50,000–100,000
◉	100,000–500,000
▣	Greater than 500,000
●	Capital
◉	Internal administrative capital

NAMES

TAIWAN	Country
JERSEY (to UK)	Dependent territory
PARIS	Capital
KANSAS	Administrative region
Dordogne	Cultural region
Sahara	Landscape feature
Mont Blanc 4807m	Mountain/pass
Blue Nile	Drainage feature
Sulu Sea	Ocean feature
Chile Rise	Underwater feature

INSET MAP SYMBOLS

	Urban area
	City
	Park
▪	Place of interest
▫	Suburb/district

CONTENTS

CONCISE WORLD ATLAS

The Political World 8-9
The Physical World 10-11
Time Zones 12-13
Geology & Structure 14-15
World Climate 16-17
Ocean Currents 18-19
Life Zones 20-21
Population 22-23
Languages 24-25
Religion 26-27
The Global Economy 28-29
Global Conflict 30-31

THE WORLD'S REGIONS

NORTH & CENTRAL AMERICA

North & Central America 34-35
Western Canada & Alaska 36-37
Eastern Canada 38-39
USA: The Northeast 40-41
  Bermuda
USA: The Southeast 42-43
USA: Central States 44-45
USA: The West 46-47
  Los Angeles & Hawaii
USA: The Southwest 48-49
Mexico 50-51
Central America 52-53
The Caribbean 54-55
  Jamaica, St Lucia & Barbados

SOUTH AMERICA

South America 56-57
Northern South America 58-59
Western South America 60-61
  Galapagos Islands
Brazil 62-63
Southern South America 64-65
The Atlantic Ocean 66-67

AFRICA

Africa 68-69
Northwest Africa 70-71
Northeast Africa 72-73
West Africa 74-75
Central Africa 76-77
  Sao Tome & Principe
Southern Africa 78-79

EUROPE

Europe 80-81
The North Atlantic 82-83
Scandinavia & Finland 84-85
The Low Countries 86-87
The British Isles 88-89
  London
France, Andorra & Monaco 90-91
  Paris, Andorra & Monaco

continued....

EUROPE *continued*

Spain & Portugal 92-93
  Azores & Gibraltar
Germany & the Alpine States 94-95
  Liechtenstein
Italy 96-97
  San Marino & Vatican City
Central Europe 98-99
The Western Balkans 100-101
  Bosnia & Herzegovina
The Mediterranean 102-103
  Malta & Cyprus
Bulgaria & Greece 104-105
The Baltic States & Belorussia . .106-107
Ukraine, Moldavia & Romania .108-109
European Russia 110-111

NORTH & WEST ASIA

North & West Asia 112-113
Russia & Kazakhstan 114-115
Turkey & the Caucasus 116-117
The Near East 118-119
The Middle East 120-121
  West Bank
Central Asia 122-123

SOUTH & EAST ASIA

South & East Asia 124-125
Western China & Mongolia 126-127

Eastern China & Korea 128-129
  Hong Kong
Japan .130-131
  Tōkyō & Nansei-Shotō
South India & Sri Lanka 132-133
North India, Pakistan &
  Bangladesh 134-135
Mainland Southeast Asia 136-137
Maritime Southeast Asia 138-139
  Singapore
The Indian Ocean 140-141

AUSTRALASIA & OCEANIA

Australasia & Oceania 142-143
The Southwest Pacific 144-145
Western Australia 146-147
Eastern Australia 148-149
  Sydney
New Zealand 150-151
The Pacific Ocean 152-153
Antarctica 154
The Arctic Ocean 155

INDEX – GAZETTEER

Overseas Territories &
  Dependencies 156-159
Glossary of Geographical
  Terms 160-161
Index-Gazetteer of Places &
  Countries 162-256

THE POLITICAL WORLD

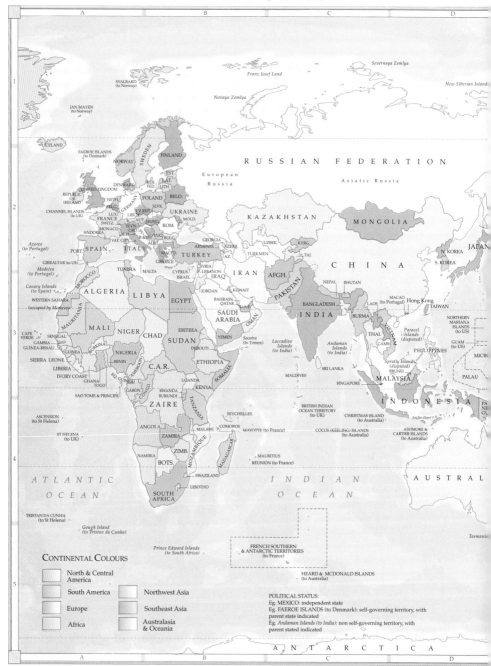

CONTINENTAL COLOURS

- North & Central America
- South America
- Europe
- Africa
- Northwest Asia
- Southeast Asia
- Australasia & Oceania

POLITICAL STATUS:
Eg. MEXICO: independent state
Eg. FAEROE ISLANDS (to Denmark): self-governing territory, with parent state indicated
Eg. *Andaman Islands (to India)*: non self-governing territory, with parent state indicated

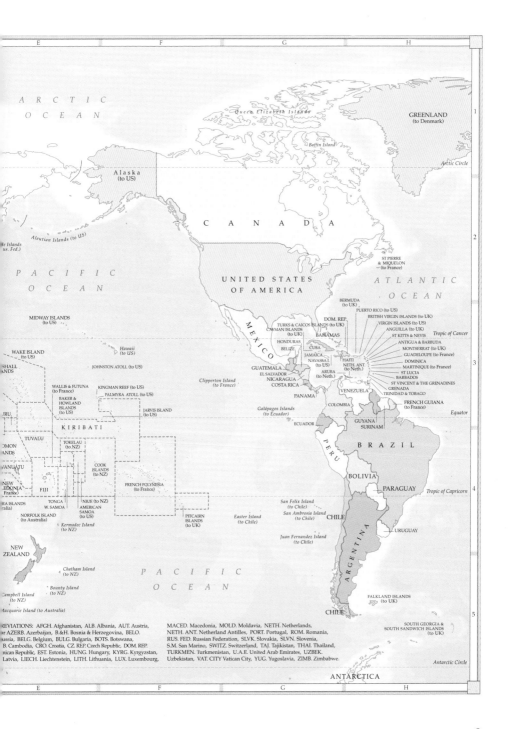

ABBREVIATIONS: AFGH. Afghanistan, ALB. Albania, AUT. Austria, AZERB. Azerbaijan, B.&H. Bosnia & Herzegovina, BELO. Russia, BELG. Belgium, BULG. Bulgaria, BOTS. Botswana, B. Cambodia, CRO. Croatia, CZ. REP. Czech Republic, DOM. REP. Dominican Republic, EST. Estonia, HUNG. Hungary, KYRG. Kyrgyzstan, Latvia, LIECH. Liechtenstein, LITH. Lithuania, LUX. Luxembourg, MACED. Macedonia, MOLD. Moldavia, NETH. Netherlands, NETH. ANT. Netherland Antilles, PORT. Portugal, ROM. Romania, RUS. FED. Russian Federation, SLVK. Slovakia, SLVN. Slovenia, S.M. San Marino, SWITZ. Switzerland, TAJ. Tajikistan, THAI. Thailand, TURKMEN. Turkmenistan, U.A.E. United Arab Emirates, UZBEK. Uzbekistan, VAT. CITY Vatican City, YUG. Yugoslavia, ZIMB. Zimbabwe.

THE PHYSICAL WORLD

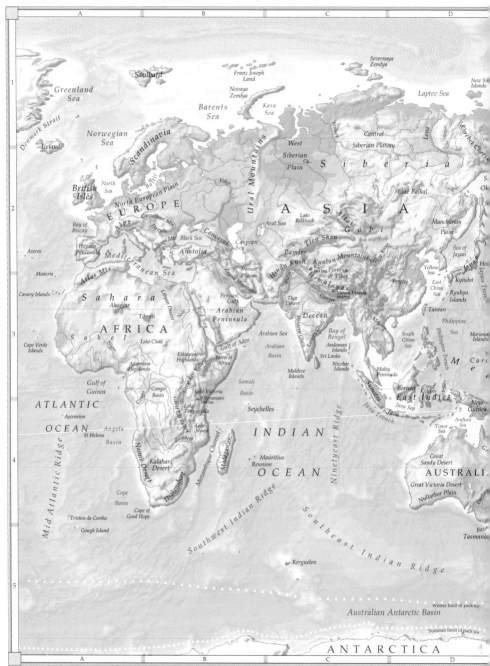

Greenland Sea

Svalbard

Franz Joseph Land

Novaya Zemlya

Severnaya Zemlya

New Si... Islands

Laptev Sea

Barents Sea

Kara Sea

Denmark Strait

Iceland

Norwegian Sea

Scandinavia

West Siberian Plain

Ob

Central Siberian Plateau

Lena

Kolyma

S i b e r i a

S...
Ok...

British Isles

North Sea

Baltic Sea

North European Plain

Ural Mountains

Volga

Yenisey

Lake Baikal

EUROPE

Alps

Carpathian Mts

Danube

Balkan Mts

Black Sea

Caucasus

A S I A

Lake Balkhash

Altai

Gobi

Manchurian Plain

Sea of Japan

Bay of Biscay

Azores

Iberian Peninsula

Aral Sea

Caspian Sea

Anatolia

Mediterranean Sea

Zagros Mountains

Iranian Plateau

Persian Gulf

Pamirs

Tien Shan

Hindu Kush

Kunlun Mountains

Himalayas

Plateau of Tibet

Yellow River

Yellow Sea

Kyushu

Japan Trench

Maderia

Atlas Mts

Canary Islands

Sahara

Ahaggar

Tibesti

Sahel

AFRICA

Niger

Lake Chad

Libyan Desert

Nile

Red Sea

Thar Desert

Arabian Peninsula

8611m Mount Everest 884m

Ganges

Deccan

Western Ghats

Eastern Ghats

Yangtze

East China Sea

Ryukyu Islands

Taiwan

Mekong

South China Sea

Philippine Sea

Philippine Trench

M... Ca... e...

Mariana Islands

Cape Verde Islands

Adamawa Highlands

Ethiopian Highlands

Gulf of Aden

Horn of Africa

Arabian Sea

Arabian Basin

Maldive Islands

Bay of Bengal

Andaman Islands

Sri Lanka

Nicobar Islands

Malay Peninsula

Gulf of Guinea

Congo

Congo Basin

Cabinda Plain

Great Rift Valley

Lake Victoria

Kilimanjaro 5895m

Somali Basin

Lake Tanganyika

Sumatra

Borneo

Celebes

Java Sea

East Indies

New Guinea

ATLANTIC

Ascension

OCEAN

St Helena

Angola Basin

Zambezi

Lake Nyasa

Seychelles

Java

Java Trench

Timor Sea

Arafura Sea

Mid Atlantic Ridge

Namib Desert

Kalahari Desert

Madagascar

Mozambique Channel

INDIAN

OCEAN

Mauritius

Reunion

Ninetyeast Ridge

Great Sandy Desert

AUSTRALI...

Great Victoria Desert

Nullarbor Plain

Cape Basin

Drakensberg

Cape of Good Hope

Tristan da Cunha

Gough Island

Southwest Indian Ridge

Kerguelen

Southeast Indian Ridge

Bass...

Tasmania

Winter limit of pack ice

Australian Antarctic Basin

Summer limit of pack ice

A N T A R C T I C A

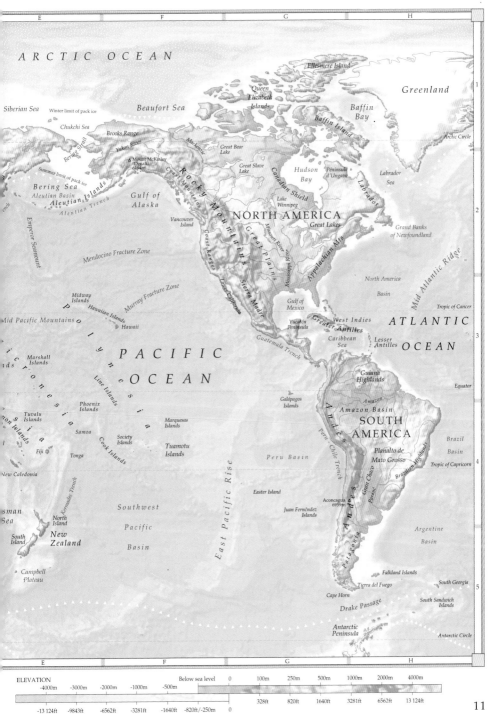

ARCTIC OCEAN

Siberian Sea

Winter limit of pack ice

Chukchi Sea

Beaufort Sea

Ellesmere Island

Queen
Elizabeth
Islands

Baffin Island

Baffin
Bay

Greenland

Arctic Circle

Brooks Range

Bering Strait

Yukon River

Mackenzie

Great Bear
Lake

Summer limit of pack ice

Bering Sea

Aleutian Basin

Aleutian Islands

Aleutian Trench

Mount McKinley
(Denali)
6194m

Coast Mountains

Rocky Mountains

Great Slave
Lake

Canadian Shield

Hudson
Bay

Península
d'Ungava

Labrador
Sea

Labrador

Lake
Winnipeg

NORTH AMERICA

Great Lakes

Grand Banks
of Newfoundland

Emperor Seamount

Gulf of
Alaska

Vancouver
Island

Coast Ranges

Great Plains

Missouri River

Mississippi River

Appalachian Mts

North America
Basin

Mid Atlantic Ridge

Mendocino Fracture Zone

Sierra Madre

Lower California

Gulf of
Mexico

Yucatán
Peninsula

Greater Antilles

West Indies

Tropic of Cancer

ATLANTIC

Midway
Islands

Murray Fracture Zone

Hawaiian Islands

Hawaii

Guatemala Trench

Caribbean
Sea

Lesser
Antilles

OCEAN

Mid Pacific Mountains

Marshall
Islands

PACIFIC

OCEAN

P o l y n e s i a

M i c r o n e s i a

Line Islands

Phoenix
Islands

Galápagos
Islands

Guiana
Highlands

Equator

Tuvalu
Islands

Samoa

Society
Islands

Marquesas
Islands

Amazon

Amazon Basin

SOUTH
AMERICA

Brazil
Basin

Fiji

Tonga

Cook Islands

Tuamotu
Islands

Peru Chile Trench

Andes

Planalto de
Mato Grosso

Brazilian Highlands

New Caledonia

Peru Basin

Tropic of Capricorn

East Pacific Rise

Easter Island

Aconcagua
6959m

Gran Chaco

Paraná

Tasman
Sea

North
Island

Southwest

Juan Fernández
Islands

Argentine
Basin

South
Island

New
Zealand

Pacific

Basin

Andes

Patagonia

Campbell
Plateau

Falkland Islands

South Georgia

Tierra del Fuego

South Sandwich
Islands

Cape Horn

Drake Passage

Antarctic
Peninsula

Antarctic Circle

ELEVATION

4000m   3000m   2000m   1000m   500m

Below sea level   0   100m   250m   500m   1000m   2000m   4000m

328ft   820ft   1640ft   3281ft   6562ft   13 124ft

13 124ft   9843ft   6562ft   3281ft   1640ft   820ft/-250m   0

11

TIME ZONES

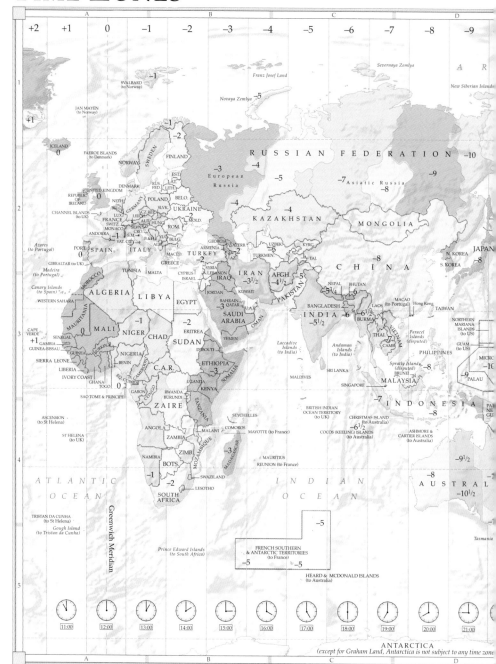

Numbers on the map indicate the number of hours which must be added or subtracted, as appropriate, in that time zone to reach GMT (Greenwich Mean Time).

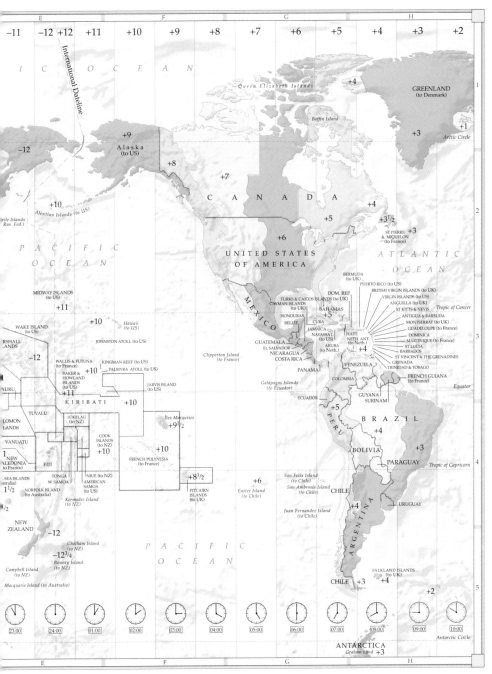

The clocks and 24 hour times given at the bottom of the map show the time in each time zone when it is 12:00 hours, or noon, at GMT.

GEOLOGY & STRUCTURE

EURASIAN PLATE

Ural Mountains

Alps

ANATOLIAN PLATE

IRANIAN PLATE

Himalayas

ARABIAN PLATE

PHILIPPINE PLATE

AFRICAN PLATE

INDO-AUSTRALIAN PLATE

ANTARCTIC PLATE

GEOLOGICAL REGIONS · continental shield · igneous rock types · MOUNTAIN RANGES · Hercynian (290 to 362 Ma) · Ma= milli... yea...

sedimentary rocks · coral formation · Alpine (5 to 23 Ma) · Caledonian (386 to 439 Ma)

earthquake zone   ▲ volcanic zone   PLATE BOUNDARIES   —— sliding plates   ▲▲ colliding plates

hot spot   ✕✕✕ rift valley   —— spreading plates   --- uncertain plate boundary

WORLD CLIMATE

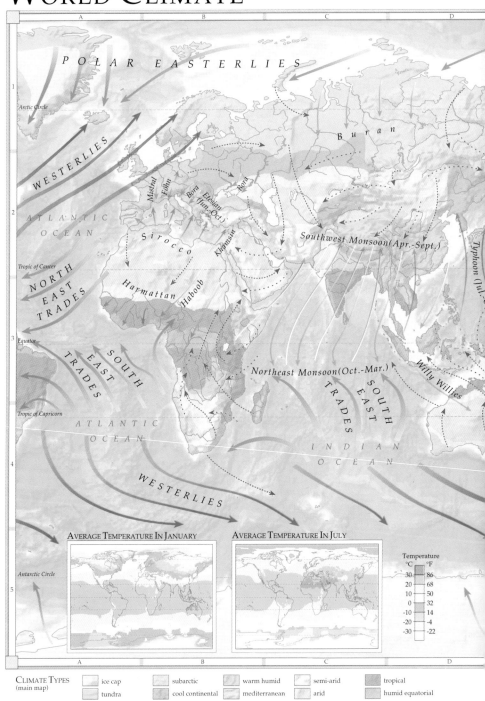

POLAR EASTERLIES

Arctic Circle

WESTERLIES

ATLANTIC
OCEAN

Buran

Mistral
Föhn
Biora
Etesian
(Jun.-Oct.)
Bora

Tropic of Cancer

NORTH
EAST
TRADES

Sirocco

Khamsin

Southwest Monsoon(Apr.-Sept.)

Typhoon (Jul.-

Harmattan
Haboob

Equator

SOUTH
EAST
TRADES

Northeast Monsoon(Oct.-Mar.)

SOUTH
EAST
TRADES

Willy Willies

Tropic of Capricorn

ATLANTIC
OCEAN

INDIAN
OCEAN

WESTERLIES

AVERAGE TEMPERATURE IN JANUARY

AVERAGE TEMPERATURE IN JULY

Antarctic Circle

Temperature	
°C	°F
30	86
20	68
10	50
0	32
-10	14
-20	-4
-30	-22

CLIMATE TYPES
(main map)

ice cap	subarctic	warm humid	semi-arid	tropical
tundra	cool continental	mediterranean	arid	humid equatorial

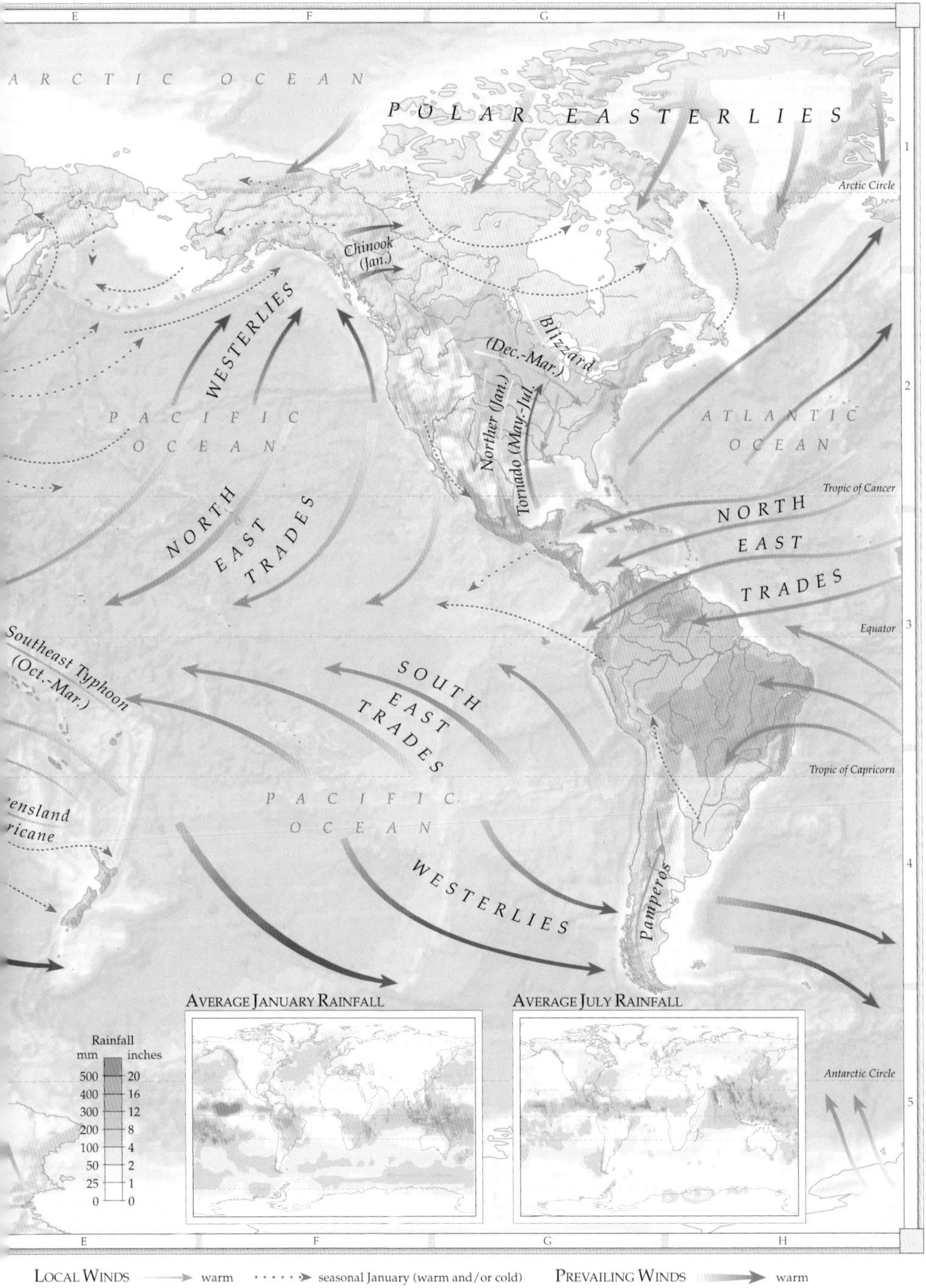
E
F
G
H
ARCTIC OCEAN
POLAR EASTERLIES
Arctic Circle
Chinook (Jan.)
WESTERLIES
Blizzard
(Dec.-Mar.)
Norther (Jan.)
Tornado (May-Jul.
PACIFIC OCEAN
ATLANTIC OCEAN
Tropic of Cancer
NORTH EAST TRADES
NORTH EAST TRADES
Equator
Southeast Typhoon (Oct.-Mar.)
SOUTH EAST TRADES
Tropic of Capricorn
PACIFIC OCEAN
ensland
ricane
WESTERLIES
Pamperos
Antarctic Circle
1
2
3
4
5
AVERAGE JANUARY RAINFALL
AVERAGE JULY RAINFALL
Rainfall
mm inches
500 20
400 16
300 12
200 8
100 4
50 2
25 1
0 0

LOCAL WINDS — warm; cold; seasonal January (warm and/or cold); seasonal July (warm and/or cold)

PREVAILING WINDS — warm; cold

OCEAN CURRENTS

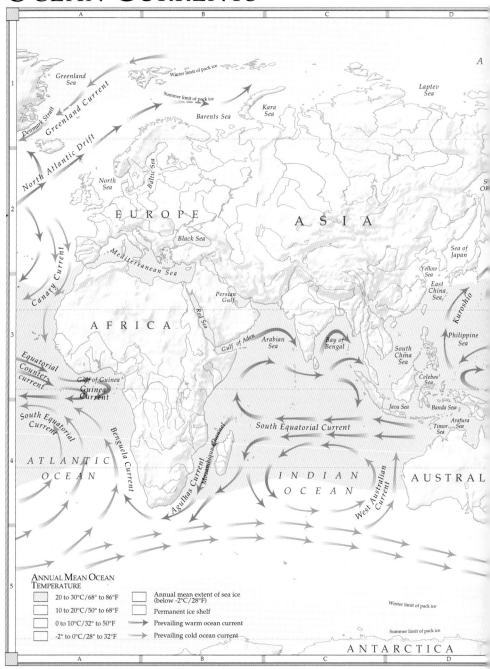

Greenland Sea

Winter limit of pack ice

Summer limit of pack ice

Laptev Sea

Denmark Strait

Greenland Current

Kara Sea

Barents Sea

North Atlantic Drift

North Sea

Baltic Sea

EUROPE

ASIA

Black Sea

Sea of Japan

Canary Current

Mediterranean Sea

Yellow Sea

East China Sea

Persian Gulf

Kuroshio

AFRICA

Red Sea

Gulf of Aden

Arabian Sea

Bay of Bengal

South China Sea

Philippine Sea

Equatorial Counter-current

Gulf of Guinea

Guinea Current

Celebes Sea

South Equatorial Current

Java Sea

Banda Sea

Benguela Current

South Equatorial Current

Timor Sea

Arafura Sea

ATLANTIC OCEAN

Agulhas Current

Mozambique Channel

INDIAN OCEAN

West Australian Current

AUSTRAL

ANTARCTICA

ANNUAL MEAN OCEAN TEMPERATURE

- 20 to 30°C/68° to 86°F
- 10 to 20°C/50° to 68°F
- 0 to 10°C/32° to 50°F
- -2° to 0°C/28° to 32°F

- Annual mean extent of sea ice (below -2°C/28°F)
- Permanent ice shelf
- → Prevailing warm ocean current
- → Prevailing cold ocean current

Winter limit of pack ice

Summer limit of pack ice

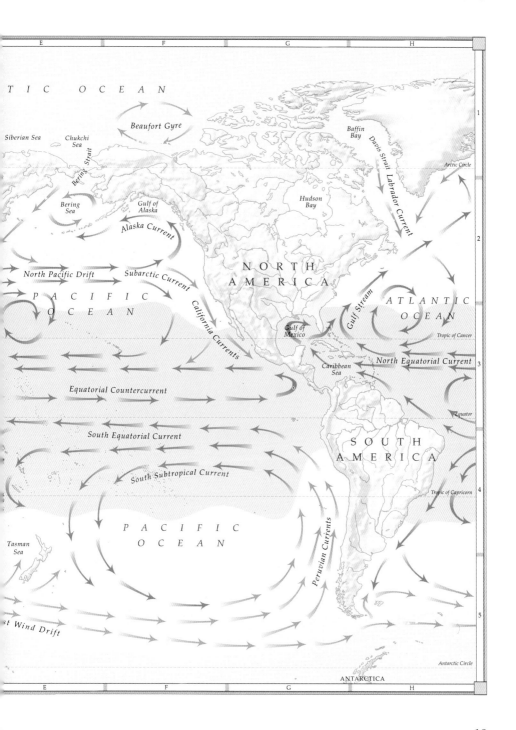

LIFE ZONES

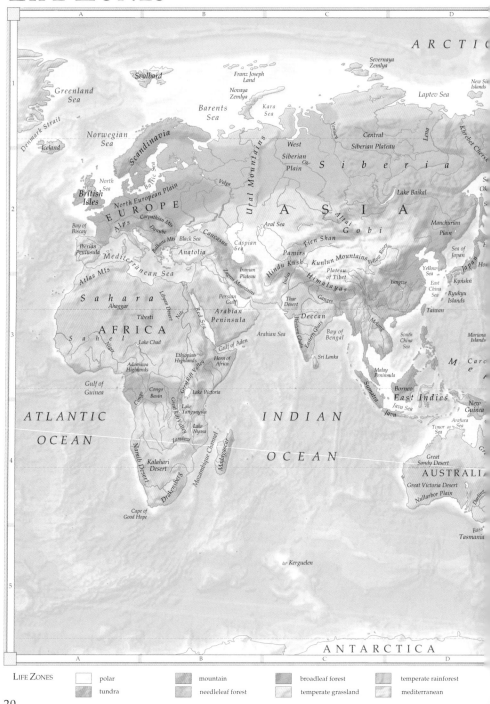

LIFE ZONES

polar	mountain
tundra	needleleaf forest

broadleaf forest	temperate rainforest
temperate grassland	mediterranean

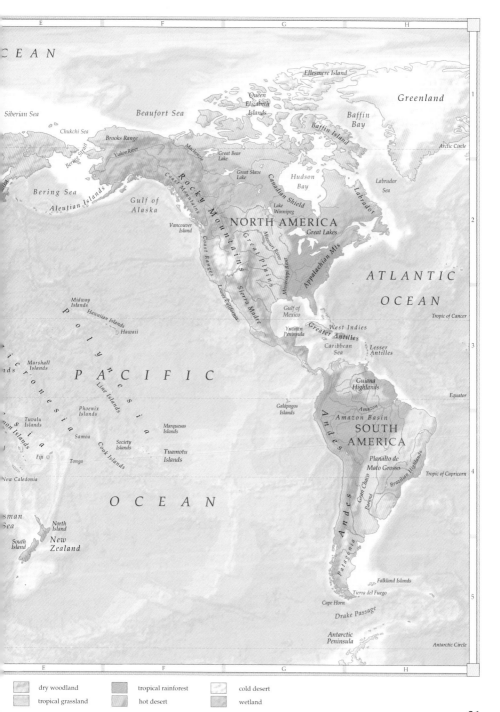

dry woodland

tropical grassland

tropical rainforest

hot desert

cold desert

wetland

POPULATION

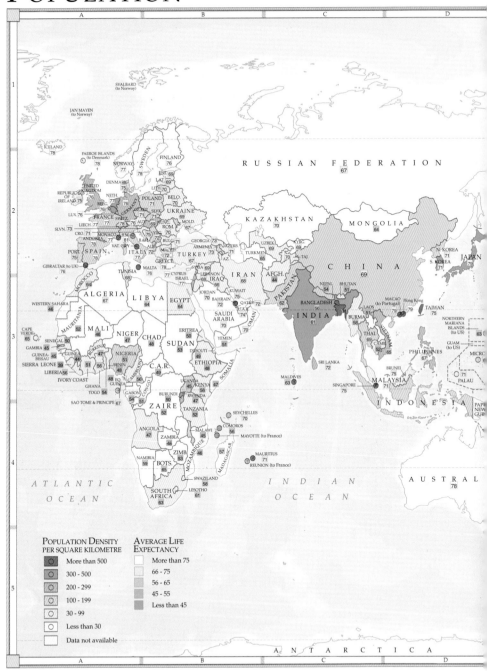

POPULATION DENSITY
PER SQUARE KILOMETRE

- More than 500
- 300 - 500
- 200 - 299
- 100 - 199
- 30 - 99
- Less than 30
- Data not available

AVERAGE LIFE
EXPECTANCY

- More than 75
- 66 - 75
- 56 - 65
- 45 - 55
- Less than 45

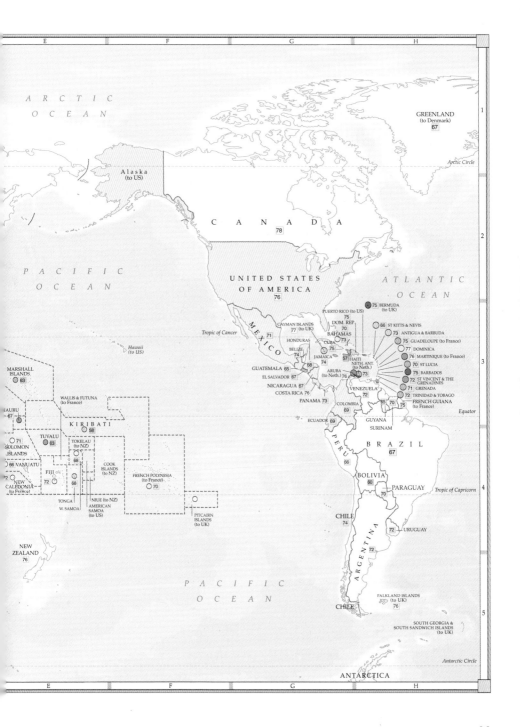

ARCTIC
OCEAN

GREENLAND
(to Denmark)
67

Arctic Circle

Alaska
(to US)

PACIFIC
OCEAN

C A N A D A
78

UNITED STATES
OF AMERICA
76

ATLANTIC
OCEAN

Tropic of Cancer

Hawaii
(to US)

M E X I C O
71

BERMUDA
(to UK)
75

PUERTO RICO (to US)
75
CAYMAN ISLANDS
(to UK) 77
DOM. REP.
70
BAHAMAS
CUBA 73
HONDURAS
70
BELIZE
74
JAMAICA
75
GUATEMALA 65
74
HAITI 57
NETH. ANT.
(to Neth.)
ARUBA
(to Neth.) 76 73
EL SALVADOR 67
NICARAGUA 67
COSTA RICA 76
VENEZUELA
72
PANAMA 73

ST KITTS & NEVIS 86
ANTIGUA & BARBUDA 73
GUADELOUPE (to France) 75
DOMINICA 77
MARTINIQUE (to France) 76
ST LUCIA 70
BARBADOS 75
ST VINCENT & THE
GRENADINES 72
GRENADA 71
TRINIDAD & TOBAGO 72
FRENCH GUIANA
(to France)

MARSHALL
ISLANDS
63

COLOMBIA
69
ECUADOR 69
GUYANA
SURINAM
65 70
75

Equator

WALLIS & FUTUNA
(to France)

NAURU
67

K I R I B A T I
58

TUVALU
83

TOKELAU
(to NZ)

SOLOMON
ISLANDS

71

VANUATU 66

COOK
ISLANDS
(to NZ)

FRENCH POLYNESIA
(to France)
70

FIJI
72

NEW
CALEDONIA
(to France)

68

68

PERU
66

BRAZIL
67

BOLIVIA
60

PARAGUAY
70

Tropic of Capricorn

TONGA
W. SAMOA

NIUE (to NZ)
AMERICAN
SAMOA
(to US)

PITCAIRN
ISLANDS
(to UK)

CHILE
74

ARGENTINA

URUGUAY
72

72

NEW
ZEALAND
76

PACIFIC
OCEAN

CHILE

FALKLAND ISLANDS
(to UK)
76

SOUTH GEORGIA &
SOUTH SANDWICH ISLANDS
(to UK)

Antarctic Circle

ANTARCTICA

23

LANGUAGES

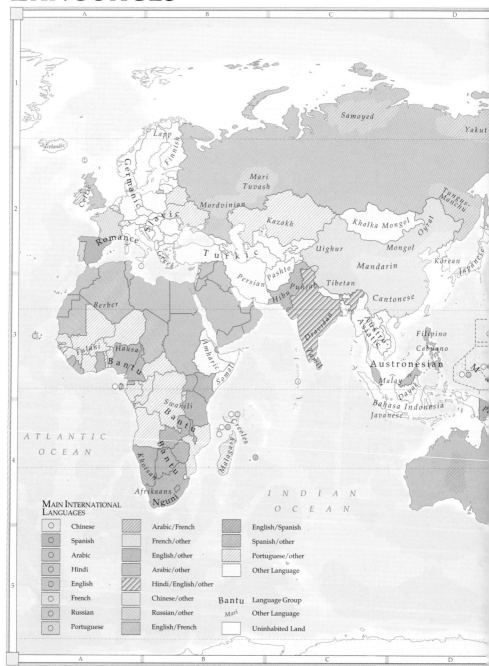

A B C D

1

Icelandic

Lapp

Finnish

Germanic

Celtic

Slavic

Samoyed

Yakut

Mari
Tuvash

Mordvinian

Tungus-
Manchu

Romance

Greek

Kazakh

Khalka Mongol

Oyrat

2

Turkic

Uighur

Mongol

Korean

Japanese

Persian *Pashto*

Mandarin

Hibu *Punjab* *Tibetan*

Cantonese

Berber

Dravidian

Austro-
Asiatic

Filipino

Cebuano

3

Fulani *Hausa*

Tamil

B a n t u

Amharic

Somali

Austronesian

Malay

Dayak

Bahasa Indonesia
Javanese

Swahili

B a n t u

ATLANTIC
OCEAN

Creoles

Madagasy

B a n t u

4

Khoisan

Afrikaans

Nguni

INDIAN

OCEAN

MAIN INTERNATIONAL LANGUAGES

○	Chinese	▨	Arabic/French	▨	English/Spanish
◉	Spanish	▨	French/other	▨	Spanish/other
◉	Arabic	▨	English/other	▨	Portuguese/other
◉	Hindi	▨	Arabic/other	☐	Other Language
◉	English	▨	Hindi/English/other		
◉	French	▨	Chinese/other	**Bantu**	Language Group
◉	Russian	▨	Russian/other	*Mari*	Other Language
◉	Portuguese	▨	English/French	☐	Uninhabited Land

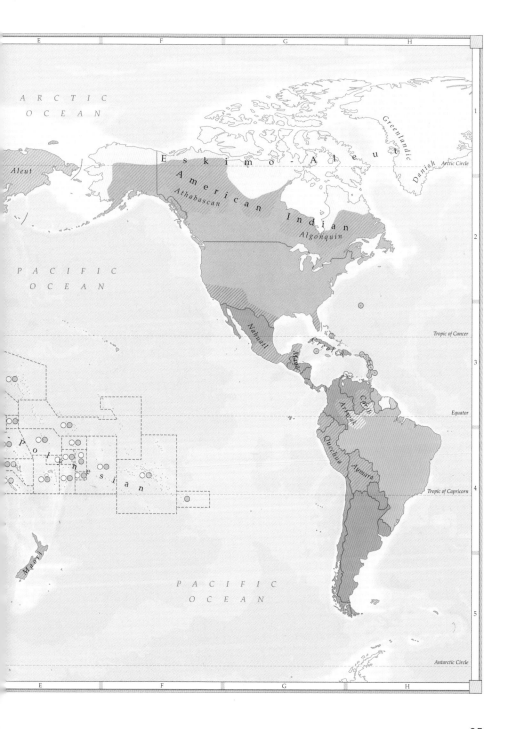

RELIGION

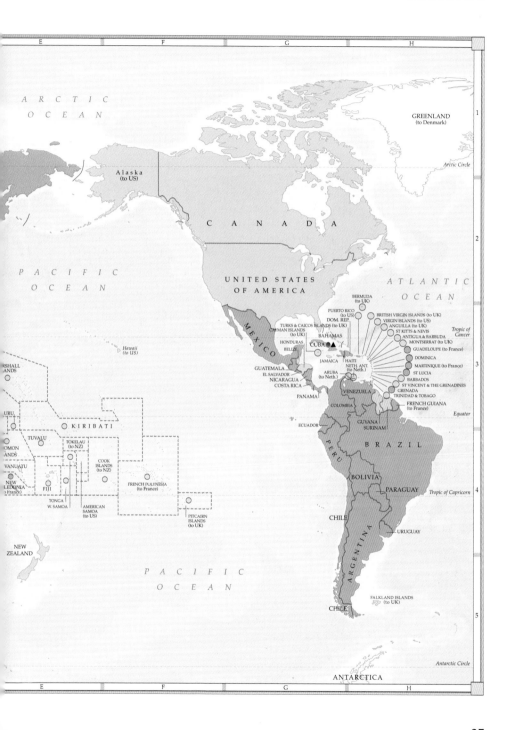

E   F   G   H

ARCTIC
OCEAN

GREENLAND
(to Denmark)

1

Arctic Circle

Alaska
(to US)

C A N A D A

2

PACIFIC
OCEAN

UNITED STATES
OF AMERICA

ATLANTIC
OCEAN

BERMUDA
(to UK)

Hawaii
(to US)

PUERTO RICO
(to US)
DOM. REP.

BRITISH VIRGIN ISLANDS (to UK)
VIRGIN ISLANDS (to US)
ANGUILLA (to UK)
ST KITTS & NEVIS
ANTIGUA & BARBUDA
MONTSERRAT (to UK)

Tropic of
Cancer

MEXICO

TURKS & CAICOS ISLANDS
(to UK)
CAYMAN ISLANDS
(to UK)

HONDURAS
BELIZE

BAHAMAS
CUBA

GUADELOUPE (to France)

MARSHALL
ISLANDS

JAMAICA

HAITI
NETH. ANT.
(to Neth.)

DOMINICA

MARTINIQUE (to France)
ST LUCIA

3

GUATEMALA
EL SALVADOR
NICARAGUA
COSTA RICA

ARUBA
(to Neth.)

BARBADOS
ST VINCENT & THE GRENADINES
GRENADA
TRINIDAD & TOBAGO

NAURU

PANAMA

VENEZUELA

FRENCH GUIANA
(to France)

TUVALU

KIRIBATI

COLOMBIA

Equator

SOLOMON
ISLANDS

TOKELAU
(to NZ)

ECUADOR

GUYANA
SURINAM

VANUATU

COOK
ISLANDS
(to NZ)

PERU

B R A Z I L

NEW
CALEDONIA
(to France)

FIJI

FRENCH POLYNESIA
(to France)

BOLIVIA

TONGA
W. SAMOA

AMERICAN
SAMOA
(to US)

PARAGUAY

Tropic of Capricorn

4

CHILE

PITCAIRN
ISLANDS
(to UK)

URUGUAY

NEW
ZEALAND

ARGENTINA

PACIFIC
OCEAN

FALKLAND ISLANDS
(to UK)

CHILE

5

Antarctic Circle

ANTARCTICA

E   F   G   H

THE GLOBAL ECONOMY

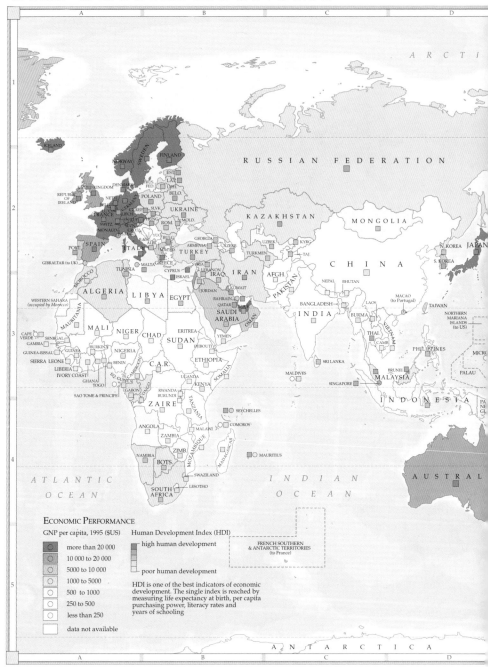

A R C T I

1

ICELAND

RUSSIAN FEDERATION

NORWAY SWEDEN FINLAND

EST
RUS. LAT.
FED. LITH.
DENMARK
UNITED KINGDOM
REPUBLIC OF IRELAND
NETH.
GERMANY
BEL. CZECH REP.
FRANCE
SWITZ.
MONACO
SPAIN
PORT.
GIBRALTAR (to UK)

BELO.
POLAND
SLVK
UKRAINE
AUST. HUNG.
CRO.
ROM.
MOLD.
YUGO
BULG.
MACED
GREECE
MALTA

KAZAKHSTAN

MONGOLIA

N. KOREA JAPAN
S. KOREA

GEORGIA
ARMENIA
AZER.
TURKMEN.
UZBEK
KYRG.
TAJ.

CHINA

2

TUNISIA
ITALY
CYPRUS
LEBANON
ISRAEL
JORDAN
TURKEY
SYRIA
IRAQ
IRAN
AFGH.

MOROCCO
ALGERIA
LIBYA
EGYPT
WESTERN SAHARA (occupied by Morocco)
MAURITANIA

KUWAIT
BAHRAIN
QATAR
U.A.E.
SAUDI ARABIA
OMAN

PAKISTAN
NEPAL
BHUTAN
BANGLADESH
INDIA
BURMA
LAOS
MACAO (to Portugal)
TAIWAN

NORTHERN MARIANA ISLANDS (to US)

MICRO

PALAU

3

CAPE VERDE
SENEGAL
GAMBIA
GUINEA-BISSAU
GUINEA
SIERRA LEONE
LIBERIA
IVORY COAST
GHANA
TOGO
BENIN
MALI
NIGER
CHAD
NIGERIA
BURKINA
CAMEROON
EQ. GUINEA
SAO TOME & PRINCIPE
GABON
CONGO
C.A.R.
ERITREA
YEMEN
DJIBOUTI
SUDAN
ETHIOPIA
SOMALIA
UGANDA
RWANDA
BURUNDI
KENYA
TANZANIA
ZAIRE

THAI
CAMB.
VIETNAM
PHILIPPINES

SRI LANKA
MALDIVES
SINGAPORE
BRUNEI
MALAYSIA

INDONESIA

PA
NE
GU

SEYCHELLES

ANGOLA
ZAMBIA
MALAWI
COMOROS
MOZAMBIQUE
ZIMB.
MADAGASCAR
NAMIBIA
BOTS.
SWAZILAND
SOUTH AFRICA
LESOTHO

MAURITIUS

4

ATLANTIC OCEAN

INDIAN OCEAN

AUSTRAL

ECONOMIC PERFORMANCE

GNP per capita, 1995 ($US)

- more than 20 000
- 10 000 to 20 000
- 5000 to 10 000
- 1000 to 5000
- 500 to 1000
- 250 to 500
- less than 250
- data not available

Human Development Index (HDI)

- high human development
- poor human development

FRENCH SOUTHERN & ANTARCTIC TERRITORIES (to France)

HDI is one of the best indicators of economic development. The single index is reached by measuring life expectancy at birth, per capita purchasing power, literacy rates and years of schooling

5

A N T A R C T I C A

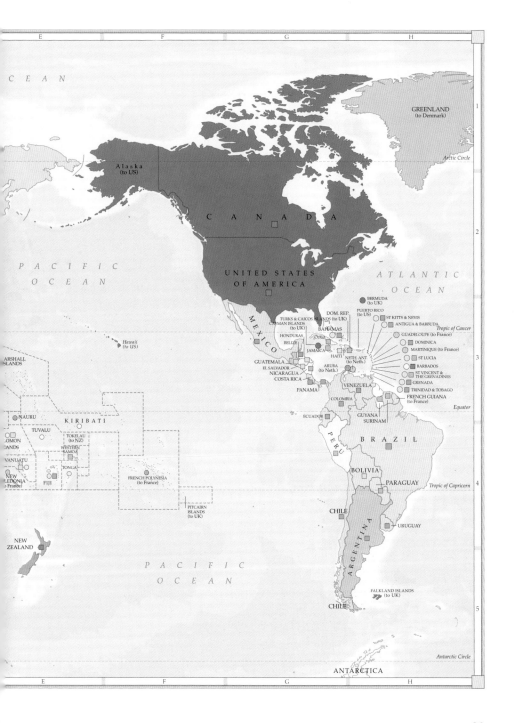

GREENLAND
(to Denmark)

Arctic Circle

Alaska
(to US)

C A N A D A

P A C I F I C
O C E A N

A T L A N T I C
OCEAN

UNITED STATES
OF AMERICA

BERMUDA
(to UK)

MEXICO

PUERTO RICO
(to US)

ST KITTS & NEVIS

TURKS & CAICOS ISLANDS
(to UK)

DOM. REP.

ANTIGUA & BARBUDA

Tropic of Cancer

CAYMAN ISLANDS
(to UK)

BAHAMAS

GUADELOUPE (to France)

HONDURAS

DOMINICA

BELIZE

CUBA

MARTINIQUE (to France)

JAMAICA

ST LUCIA

GUATEMALA

HAITI

BARBADOS

EL SALVADOR

NETH. ANT.
(to Neth.)

ST VINCENT &
THE GRENADINES

NICARAGUA

ARUBA
(to Neth.)

GRENADA

COSTA RICA

TRINIDAD & TOBAGO

PANAMA

VENEZUELA

FRENCH GUIANA
(to France)

MARSHALL
ISLANDS

Hawaii
(to US)

COLOMBIA

Equator

ECUADOR

GUYANA

NAURU

SURINAM

KIRIBATI

TUVALU

PERU

B R A Z I L

TOKELAU
(to NZ)

SOLOMON
ISLANDS

WESTERN
SAMOA

VANUATU

TONGA

BOLIVIA

NEW
CALEDONIA
(to France)

FIJI

FRENCH POLYNESIA
(to France)

PARAGUAY

Tropic of Capricorn

PITCAIRN
ISLANDS
(to UK)

CHILE

URUGUAY

NEW
ZEALAND

A R G E N T I N A

P A C I F I C
O C E A N

FALKLAND ISLANDS
(to UK)

CHILE

Antarctic Circle

ANTARCTICA

29

GLOBAL CONFLICT

KEY

International conflict since 1975

Civil unrest since 1975

Disputed territories

.... Disputed border

- - - - Undefined border

E   F   G   H

O C E A N

GREENLAND
(to Denmark)

1

Arctic Circle

Alaska
(to US)

C A N A D A

2

le Islands
us. Fed.)

P A C I F I C
O C E A N

UNITED STATES
OF AMERICA

A T L A N T I C
O C E A N

ST PIERRE
& MIQUELON
(to France)

BERMUDA
(to UK)

PUERTO RICO (to US)
BRITISH VIRGIN ISLANDS (to UK)
VIRGIN ISLANDS (to US)
ANGUILLA (to UK)
ST KITTS & NEVIS
ANTIGUA & BARBUDA
MONTSERRAT (to UK)
GUADELOUPE (to France)
DOMINICA
MARTINIQUE (to France)
ST LUCIA
BARBADOS
ST VINCENT & THE GRENADINES
GRENADA
TRINIDAD & TOBAGO

Tropic of Cancer

DOM. REP.

TURKS & CAICOS ISLANDS (to UK)
CAYMAN ISLANDS
(to UK)

BAHAMAS

HONDURAS
BELIZE

CUBA

JAMAICA
NAVASSA I.
(to US)

HAITI
NETH. ANT.
(to Neth.)

3

M E X I C O

GUATEMALA
EL SALVADOR
NICARAGUA

ARUBA
(to Neth.)

Hawaii
(to US)

SHALL
ANDS

WALLIS & FUTUNA
(to France)
BAKER &
HOWLAND
ISLANDS
(to US)

KINGMAN REEF (to US)
PALMYRA ATOLL (to US)

JARVIS ISLAND
(to US)

COSTA RICA

PANAMA

VENEZUELA

FRENCH GUIANA
(to France)

Equator

RU

K I R I B A T I

COLOMBIA

ECUADOR

GUYANA
SURINAM

TUVALU

TOKELAU
(to NZ)

OMON
NDS

P E R U

B R A Z I L

VANUATU

NEW
EDONIA
France)

COOK
ISLANDS
(to NZ)

FRENCH POLYNESIA
(to France)

BOLIVIA

PARAGUAY

Tropic of Capricorn

FIJI

TONGA
W. SAMOA

NIUE (to NZ)
AMERICAN
SAMOA
(to US)

PITCAIRN
ISLANDS
(to UK)

CHILE

URUGUAY

4

NEW
ZEALAND

A R G E N T I N A

P A C I F I C
O C E A N

FALKLAND ISLANDS
(to UK)

CHILE

5

Antarctic Circle

ANTARCTICA

E   F   G   H

ATLAS *of the*
WORLD'S
REGIONS

NORTH & CENTRAL AMERICA

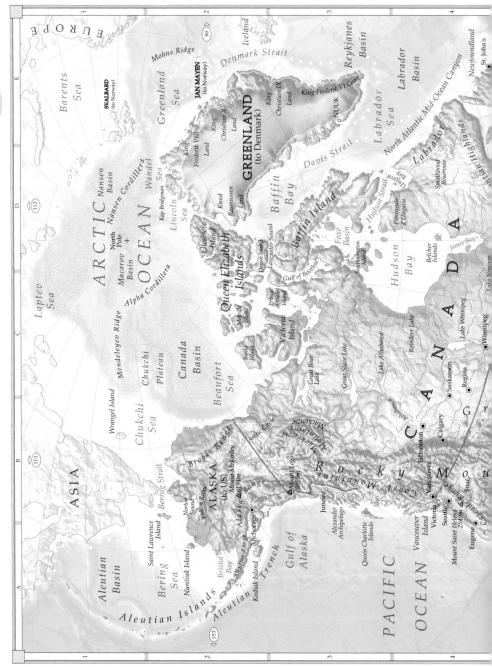

EUROPE

Barents
Sea

Mohns Ridge

Iceland

Denmark Strait

Reykjanes
Basin

Labrador
Basin

Newfoundland

St. John's

SVALBARD
(to Norway)

JAN MAYEN
(to Norway)

King
Christian IX
Land

King Frederik VI Coast

NUUK

Labrador
Sea

North Atlantic Mid-Ocean Canyon

Atlantic Highlands

Greenland
Sea

King
Christian X
Land

GREENLAND
(to Denmark)

King
Frederik VIII
Land

Davis Strait

Labrador

Smallwood
Reservoir

ARCTIC
OCEAN

Nansen
Basin

Nansen Cordillera

Wandel
Sea

Kap Brádgnun

Lincoln
Sea

Knud
Rasmussen
Land

Baffin
Bay

Hudson Strait

Peninsule
d'Ungava

Ungava
Bay

James Bay

North Pole

Macarov
Basin

Alpha Cordillera

Ellesmere
Island

Devon Island

Lancaster Sound

Foxe
Basin

Hudson

Bay

Belcher
Islands

Laptev
Sea

Mendeleyev Ridge

Chukchi
Plateau

Canada
Basin

Queen Elizabeth
Islands

Prince
of Wales
Island

Southampton
Island

Lake Nipigon

Baffin Island

Gulf of Boothia

Melville
Island

Victoria
Island

CANADA

Reindeer Lake

Wrangel Island

Chukchi
Sea

Beaufort
Sea

Banks
Island

Great Bear
Lake

Lake Athabasca

Lake Winnipeg

Winnipeg

Great Slave Lake

Athabasca

Saskatoon

Regina

Arctic Circle

Mackenzie
Mountains

Mackenzie

Edmonton

Calgary

Gr

ASIA

Bering Strait

Brooks Range

ALASKA
(to US)

Yukon Ridge

Norton
Sound

Saint Lawrence
Island

Nunivak Island

Mount McKinley
6194m

Alaska Range

Anchorage

Alaska
Range

Juneau

Rocky Mountains

Coast Range

Edmonton

Vancouver

Seattle

Mou

Aleutian
Basin

Bering
Sea

Bristol
Bay

Kodiak Island

Alexander
Archipelago

Queen Charlotte
Islands

Vancouver
Island

Victoria

Mount Saint Helens
2549m

Eugene

Mount Logan
5959m

Gulf of
Alaska

PACIFIC
OCEAN

Cascade Range

Snake

Aleutian Islands

Aleutian Trench

PACIFIC

OCEAN

POPULATION

○ Less than 50,000   ◔ 50,000 -100,000   ◉ 100,000 - 500,000   ■ Over 500,000

0 km   1000

0 miles   1000

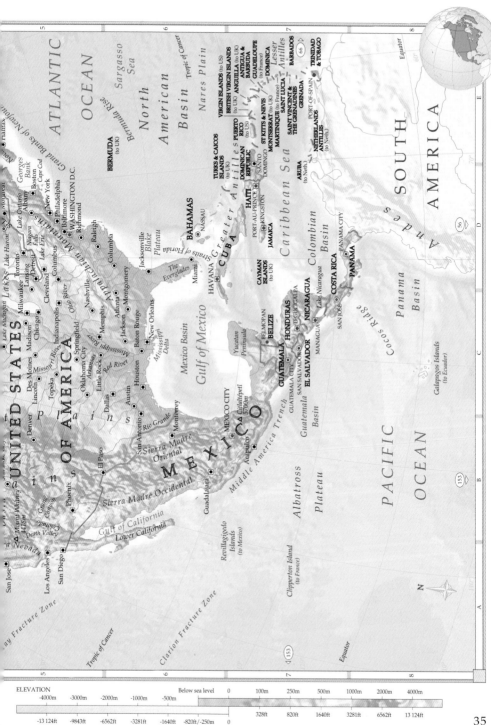

ATLANTIC OCEAN

Sargasso Sea

North American Basin

Nares Plain

Tropic of Cancer

Bermuda Rise

BERMUDA
(to UK)

Grand Banks of Newfoundland

Halifax

Georges Bank

Boston

Cape Cod

New York

Albany

Philadelphia

Baltimore

WASHINGTON D.C.

Richmond

Raleigh

Columbia

Appalachian Mountains

Nashville

Atlanta

Montgomery

Jacksonville

Blake Plateau

The Everglades

Miami

Straits of Florida

HAVANA

Gulf of Mexico

Mexico Basin

Yucatan Peninsula

CUBA

BAHAMAS

NASSAU

Greater Antilles

TURKS & CAICOS ISLANDS (to UK)

DOMINICAN REPUBLIC

SANTO DOMINGO

HAITI

PORT-AU-PRINCE

JAMAICA

KINGSTON

CAYMAN ISLANDS (to UK)

VIRGIN ISLANDS (to US)

BRITISH VIRGIN ISLANDS (to UK)

PUERTO RICO (to US)

ANGUILLA (to UK)

ANTIGUA & BARBUDA

ST KITTS & NEVIS

MONTSERRAT (to UK)

GUADELOUPE (to France)

DOMINICA

MARTINIQUE (to France)

SAINT LUCIA

SAINT VINCENT & THE GRENADINES

BARBADOS

GRENADA

TRINIDAD & TOBAGO

PORT-OF-SPAIN

ARUBA (to Neth.)

NETHERLANDS ANTILLES (to Neth.)

Lesser Antilles

Caribbean Sea

Colombian Basin

PANAMA CITY

PANAMA

COSTA RICA

SAN JOSÉ

NICARAGUA

MANAGUA

Lake Nicaragua

HONDURAS

TEGUCIGALPA

BELIZE

BELMOPAN

GUATEMALA

GUATEMALA CITY

SAN SALVADOR

EL SALVADOR

Guatemala Basin

MEXICO CITY

Citlaltepetl 5700m

Acapulco

Sierra Madre Oriental

Monterrey

MEXICO

Sierra Madre Occidental

Guadalajara

San Antonio

Austin

Dallas

Rio Grande

El Paso

Phoenix

San Diego

Los Angeles

San José

Grand Canyon

Colorado River

Death Valley

Nevada

Whitney 4418m

Lower California

Gulf of California

Revillagigedo Islands (to Mexico)

Clipperton Island (to France)

Albatross Plateau

Cocos Ridge

Panama Basin

Galápagos Islands (to Ecuador)

PACIFIC OCEAN

Middle America Trench

Clarion Fracture Zone

Tropic of Cancer

Equator

Fracture Zone

SOUTH AMERICA

Andes

UNITED STATES OF AMERICA

Great Plains

Denver

Des Moines

Lincoln

Topeka

Oklahoma City

Little Rock

Houston

Baton Rouge

New Orleans

Jackson

Memphis

Mississippi Delta

Mississippi River

Missouri River

Arkansas

Red River

Ohio River

Springfield

Indianapolis

Columbus

Cleveland

Detroit

Lansing

Chicago

Milwaukee

Madison

Lake Michigan

Lake Huron

Lake Ontario

Lake Erie

Niagara Falls

Toronto

Great Lakes

N

ELEVATION

-4000m	-3000m	-2000m	-1000m	-500m	Below sea level	0	100m	250m	500m	1000m	2000m	4000m

| -13 124ft | -9843ft | -6562ft | -3281ft | -1640ft | -820ft/-250m | 0 | 328ft | 820ft | 1640ft | 3281ft | 6562ft | 13 124ft |

35

WESTERN CANADA & ALASKA

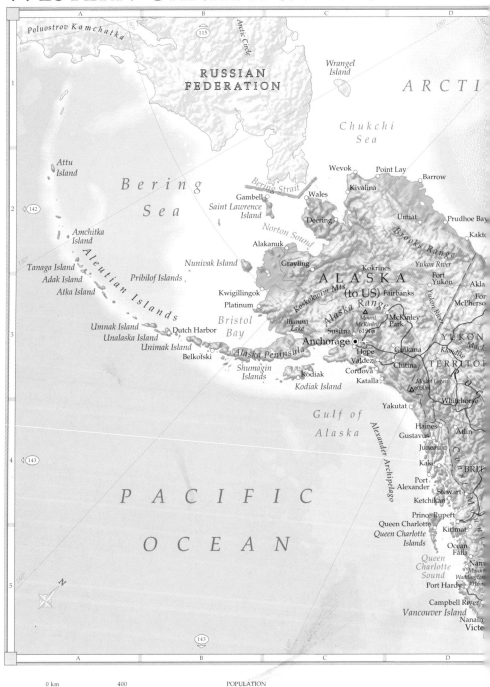

Poluostrov Kamchatka

Arctic Circle

RUSSIAN
FEDERATION

Wrangel
Island

ARCTI

Chukchi
Sea

Attu
Island

Bering
Sea

Wevok
Point Lay
Barrow
Kivalina
Gambell
Wales
Saint Lawrence
Island
Deering
Umiat
Prudhoe Bay
Kaktc

Amchitka
Island

Norton Sound

Alakanuk

Brooks Range

Tanaga Island
Adak Island
Atka Island

Aleutian Islands

Nunivak Island

Grayling

Kokrines

Yukon River

Fort
Yukon

Akla

ALASKA
(to US)

Kokokwim Mts

Fairbanks

For
McPherso

Pribilof Islands

Kwigillingok

Platinum

Yukon River

Umnak Island
Unalaska Island
Dutch Harbor
Unimak Island
Belkofski

Bristol
Bay

Iliamna
Lake

Alaska Range

Mount
McKinley
6194m

McKinley
Park

YUKON

Anchorage

Susitna

Klondike

Mack

Alaska Peninsula

Shumagin
Islands

Hope
Valdez
Cordova

Gulkana
Chitina

TERRITOI

Kodiak
Katalla

Mount Logan
6050m

Kodiak Island

Whitehorse

Yakutat

Gulf of
Alaska

Haines
Gustavus

Atlin

Juneau

Alexander Archipelago

Kake

BRI

PACIFIC

Port
Alexander
Ketchikan

Stewart

OCEAN

Prince Rupert
Queen Charlotte
Queen Charlotte
Islands

Kitimat

Ocean
Falls

Queen
Charlotte
Sound

Port Hardy

Mount
Waddington
4016m

Nan

Campbell River
Vancouver Island

Nanain
Victe

N

0 km   400

0 miles   400

POPULATION

○ Less than 50,000   ○ 50,000 -100,000   ● 100,000 - 500,000   ■ Over 500,000

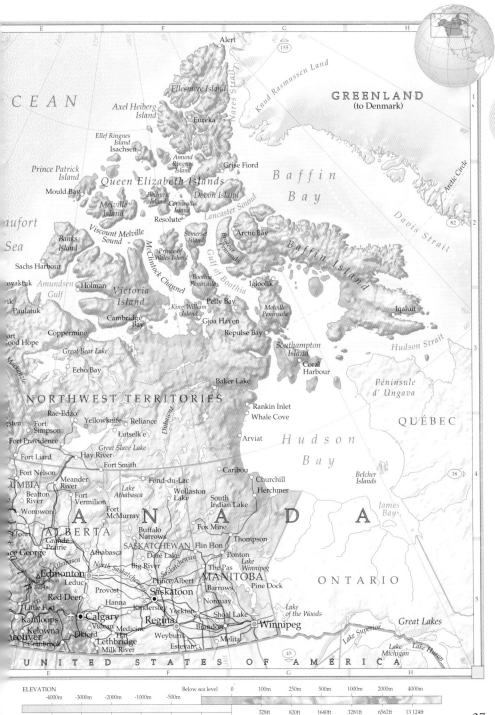

OCEAN

Alert

155

Ellesmere Island

Knud Rasmussen Land

GREENLAND
(to Denmark)

Axel Heiberg
Island

Eureka

Ellef Ringnes
Island
Isachsen

Amund
Ringnes
Island

Grise Fiord

Prince Patrick
Island

Queen Elizabeth Islands

Baffin

Mould Bay

Bathurst
Island

Devon Island

Melville
Island

Cornwallis
Island

Bay

Resolute

Lancaster Sound

Viscount Melville
Sound

Somerset
Island

Arctic Bay

Baffin Island

Davis Strait

Arctic Circle

82

Beaufort
Sea

Banks
Island

McClintock Channel

Prince of
Wales Island

Boothia
Peninsula

Gulf of Boothia

Sachs Harbour

Boothia
Peninsula

Igloolik

oyaktuk

Amundsen
Gulf

Holman

Victoria
Island

Iqaluit

Paulatuk

King William
Island

Pelly Bay

Melville
Peninsula

rik

Cambridge
Bay

Gjoa Haven

Coppermine

Repulse Bay

Hudson Strait

ort
ood Hope

Great Bear Lake

Southampton
Island

Péninsule
d' Ungava

Mackenzie

Echo Bay

Coral
Harbour

NORTHWEST TERRITORIES

Baker Lake

Rae-Edzo

Rankin Inlet

QUÉBEC

sten

Fort
Simpson

Yellowknife

Reliance

Whale Cove

Dubawnt

Fort Providence

Lutselk'e

Arviat

Hudson

Fort Liard

Great Slave Lake

Hay River

Bay

Fort Nelson

Fort Smith

Caribou

Churchill

Belcher
Islands

38

UMBIA

Meander
River

Fond-du-Lac

Herchmer

Beatton
River

Lake
Athabasca

Fort
Vermilion

Wollaston
Lake

South
Indian Lake

James
Bay

Wonowon

Fort
McMurray

Fox Mine

Grande
Prairie

ALBERTA

Buffalo
Narrows

ONTARIO

ce George

Athabasca

SASKATCHEWAN

Flin Flon

Thompson

CANADA

Mount Robson
3954m

Edmonton

North Saskatchewan

Doré Lake

Big River

Ponton

The Pas

Lake
Winnipeg

Leduc

Saskatchewan

MANITOBA

Provost

Prince Albert

Barrows

Pine Dock

Red Deer

Hanna

Saskatoon

Norquay

Little Fort

Kindersley

Yorkton

Shoal Lake

Lake
of the Woods

Calgary

Regina

Brandon

Winnipeg

Great Lakes

Kamloops

Vulcan

Medicine

Kelowna

Elkford

Lethbridge

Weyburn

Melita

Lake Superior

Lake
Michigan

Lake
Huron

ancouver

Cranbrook

Milk River

Estevan

45

UNITED   STATES   OF   AMERICA

ELEVATION

| -4000m | -3000m | -2000m | -1000m | -500m | Below sea level | 0 | 100m | 250m | 500m | 1000m | 2000m | 4000m |

| -13 124ft | -9843ft | -6562ft | -3281ft | -1640ft | -820ft/-250m | 0 | 328ft | 820ft | 1640ft | 3281ft | 6562ft | 13 124ft |

EASTERN CANADA

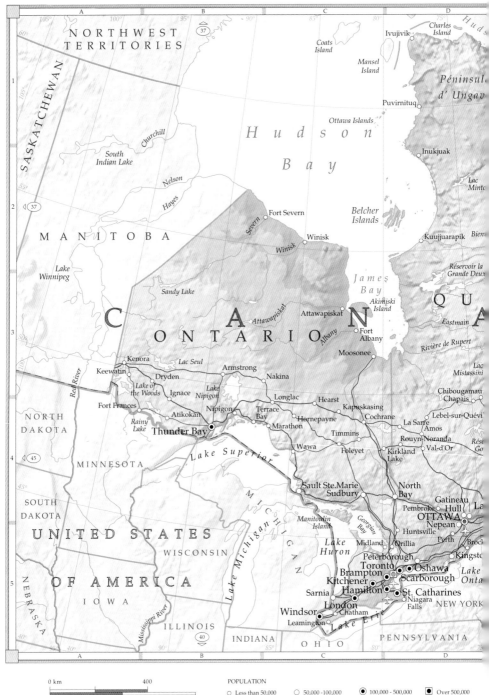

NORTHWEST TERRITORIES

SASKATCHEWAN

Charles Island

Ivujivik

Coats Island

Mansel Island

Péninsul d' Ungav

Puvirnituq

Churchill

South Indian Lake

Nelson

Hayes

Ottawa Islands

Inukjuak

Lac Minto

MANITOBA

Lake Winnipeg

Severn

Fort Severn

Winisk

Winisk

Hudson Bay

Belcher Islands

Kuujjuarapik

Bien

Réservoir la Grande Deux

Sandy Lake

CANADA

Attawapiskat

Attawapiskat

James Bay

Akimiski Island

QU

ONTARIO

Albany

Fort Albany

Eastmain

Rivière de Rupert

Kenora

Lac Seul

Armstrong

Nakina

Moosonee

Lac Mistassini

Keewatin

Dryden

Chibougamau
Chapais

Lake of the Woods

Ignace

Lake Nipigon

Longlac

Hearst

Kapuskasing

Lebel-sur-Quévi

Red River

Fort Frances

Atikokan

Nipigon

Terrace Bay

Hornepayne

Cochrane

La Sarre

Amos

Rainy Lake

Thunder Bay

Marathon

Timmins

Rouyn-Noranda

Val-d'Or

Rése
Go

Wawa

Foleyet

Kirkland Lake

NORTH DAKOTA

Lake Superior

MINNESOTA

MICHIGAN

Sault Ste.Marie

Sudbury

North Bay

Gatineau

Hull

La

Pembroke

OTTAWA

SOUTH DAKOTA

NEBRASKA

UNITED STATES

Manitoulin Island

Georgian Bay

Huntsville

Nepean

Perth

Broc

WISCONSIN

Lake Huron

Midland

Orillia

Kingst

OF AMERICA

IOWA

Lake Michigan

Peterborough

Toronto

Oshawa

Lake Onta

Brampton

Kitchener

Scarborough

Sarnia

Hamilton

St. Catharines

NEW YORK

Mississippi River

London

Niagara Falls

Windsor

Chatham

ILLINOIS

Leamington

Lake Erie

INDIANA

OHIO

PENNSYLVANIA

0 km 400

0 miles 400

POPULATION

○ Less than 50,000 ○ 50,000 -100,000 ◉ 100,000 - 500,000 ■ Over 500,000

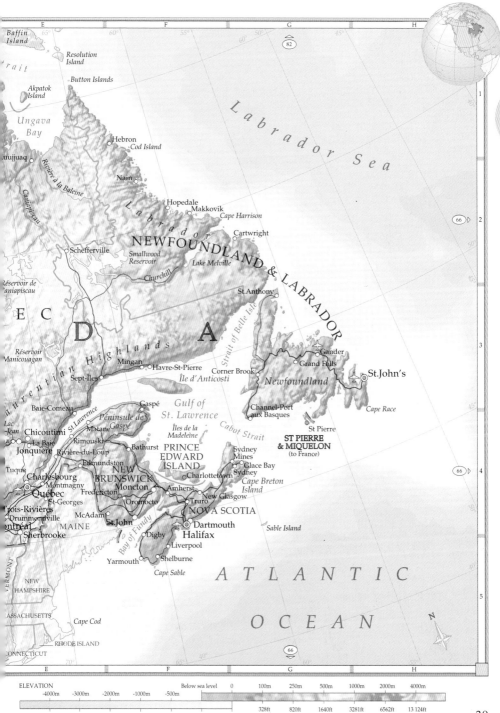

Baffin Island
Resolution Island
Akpatok Island
Button Islands
Ungava Bay
uujjuaq
Hebron
Cod Island
Rivière à la Baleine
Nain
Chinaupicau
Hopedale
Makkovik
Cape Harrison
Scheffervile
Cartwright
Labrador Sea
NEWFOUNDLAND & LABRADOR
Smallwood Reservoir
Lake Melville
Churchill
St.Anthony
Réservoir de 'anapiscau
Réservoir Manicouagan
E C D
A
Strait of Belle Isle
Mingan
Havre-St-Pierre
Île d'Anticosti
Sept-Îles
Gander
Grand Falls
Corner Brook
St.John's
Newfoundland
Cape Race
Baie-Comeau
Gaspé
Gulf of St. Lawrence
Îles de la Madeleine
Channel-Port aux Basques
St Pierre
Péninsule de Gaspé
Laurentian Highlands
Chicoutimi
Matane
St Lawrence
Rimouski
Cabot Strait
ST PIERRE & MIQUELON
(to France)
Lac-Jean
La Baie
Jonquière
Rivière-du-Loup
Bathurst
PRINCE EDWARD ISLAND
Sydney Mines
Glace Bay
Sydney
Tuque
Edmundston
NEW BRUNSWICK
Charlottetown
Cape Breton Island
Charlesbourg
Montmagny
Moncton
Amherst
New Glasgow
St-Georges
Fredericton
Truro
Québec
Oromocto
NOVA SCOTIA
Trois-Rivières
Drummondville
McAdam
St.John
Dartmouth
ntréal
MAINE
Bay of Fundy
Digby
Halifax
Sherbrooke
Liverpool
Sable Island
Yarmouth
Shelburne
Cape Sable
VERMONT
NEW HAMPSHIRE
A T L A N T I C
ASSACHUSETTS
Cape Cod
O C E A N
RHODE ISLAND
CONNECTICUT
N

ELEVATION

-4000m	-3000m	-2000m	-1000m	-500m	Below sea level	0	100m	250m	500m	1000m	2000m	4000m
-13 124ft	-9843ft	-6562ft	-3281ft	-1640ft	-820ft/-250m	0	328ft	820ft	1640ft	3281ft	6562ft	13 124ft

USA: THE NORTHEAST

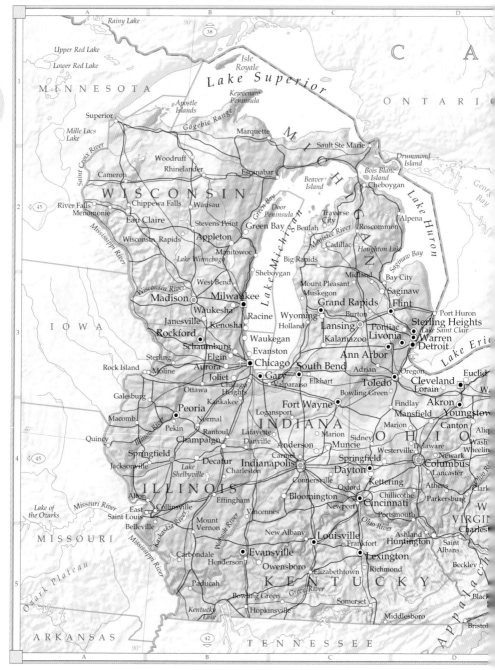

POPULATION

○ Less than 50,000   ○ 50,000 -100,000   ◉ 100,000 - 500,000   ■ Over 500,000

0 km   200

0 miles   200

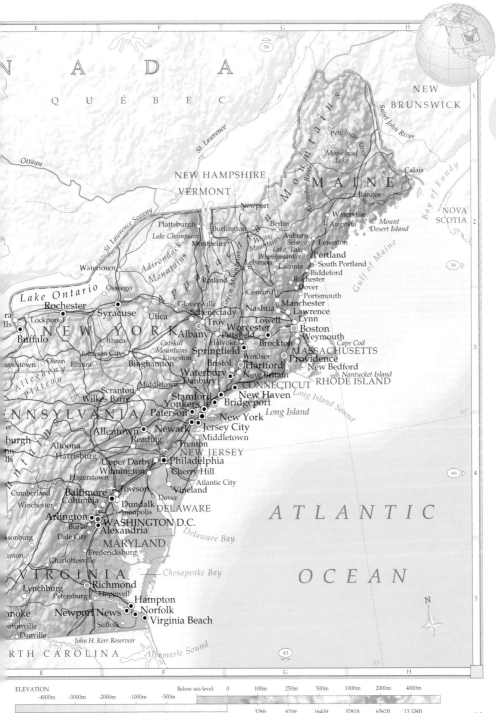

ELEVATION

| | | | | | Below sea level | 0 | 100m | 250m | 500m | 1000m | 2000m | 4000m |
| -4000m | -3000m | -2000m | -1000m | -500m | | | | | | | | |

| | | | | | | 0 | 328ft | 820ft | 1640ft | 3281ft | 6562ft | 13 124ft |
| -13 124ft | -9843ft | -6562ft | -3281ft | -1640ft | -820ft/-250m | 0 | | | | | | |

USA: THE SOUTHEAST

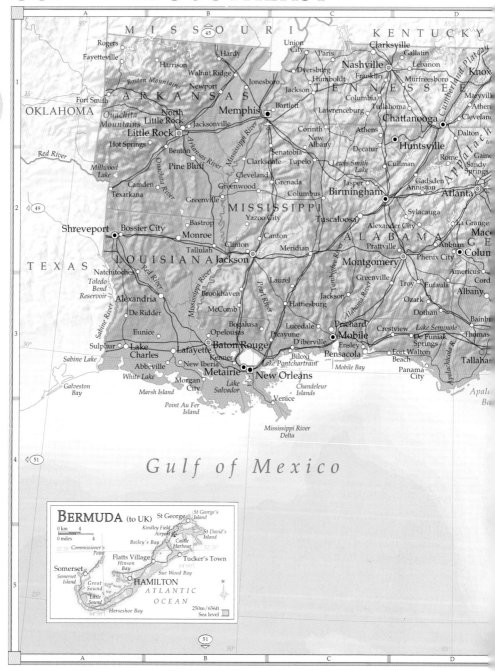

MISSOURI

45

Rogers
Fayetteville
Harrison
Walnut Ridge
Hardy
Newport
Jonesboro
Union City
Paris
Dyersburg
Humboldt
Jackson
Clarksville
Gallatin
Nashville
Franklin
Lebanon
Knox

KENTUCKY

Boston Mountains

Fort Smith

ARKANSAS

North
Little Rock
Jacksonville
Memphis
Bartlett
Columbia
Lawrenceburg
Tullahoma
Murfreesboro
Chattanooga
Cleveland
Maryvill
Athen

OKLAHOMA

Ouachita
Mountains
Little Rock
Hot Springs
Benton
Pine Bluff
Cleveland
Clarksdale
Tupelo
Senatobia
Corinth
New
Albany
Decatur
Athens
Huntsville
Cullman
Rome
Dalton
Gaine
Sandy
Springs

TENNESSEE

Red River
Millwood
Lake
Camden
Texarkana
Greenville
Greenwood
Grenada
Columbus
Lewis Smith
Lake
Jasper
Gadsden
Anniston
Birmingham
Sylacauga
Atlanta

MISSISSIPPI

Yazoo City
Tuscaloosa
Alexander City
La Grange
Mac
GE

Shreveport
Bossier City
Monroe
Bastrop
Canton
Clinton
Meridian

ALABAMA

Auburn
Colun

TEXAS

Natchitoches
Toledo
Bend
Reservoir
Alexandria
De Ridder
Eunice
Brookhaven
McComb
Laurel
Jackson
Hattiesburg
Montgomery
Greenville
Prattville
Phenix City
Troy
Eufaula
Ozark
Americus
Cord
Albany
Dothan
Bainbr

Sabine
Lake
Sulphur
Lake
Charles
Lafayette
Baton Rouge
Kenner
New Iberia
Bogalusa
Opelousas
Picayune
D'Iberville
Biloxi
Lucedale
Prichard
Mobile
Pensacola
Ensley
Crestview
De Funiak
Springs
Fort Walton
Beach
Lake Seminole
Thomas
Panama
City
Tallaha

Galveston
Bay
White Lake
Abbeville
Morgan
City
Marsh Island
Metairie
New Orleans
Lake
Salvador
Venice
Lake Pontchartrain
Mobile Bay
Chandeleur
Islands
Apala
Ba

Point Au Fer
Island

Mississippi River
Delta

Gulf of Mexico

BERMUDA (to UK)

0 km   4
0 miles   4

Commissioner's
Point
Somerset
Somerset
Island
Great
Sound
Little
Sound
Horseshoe Bay

St George
Kindley Field
Airport
Bailey's Bay
Flatts Village
Hinson
Bay
HAMILTON

St George's
Island
St David's
Island
Castle
Harbour
Tucker's Town
Sue Wood Bay

**ATLANTIC
OCEAN**

250m/656ft
Sea level

0 km   200
0 miles   200

POPULATION
○ Less than 50,000
○ 50,000 -100,000
◉ 100,000 - 500,000
◼ Over 500,000

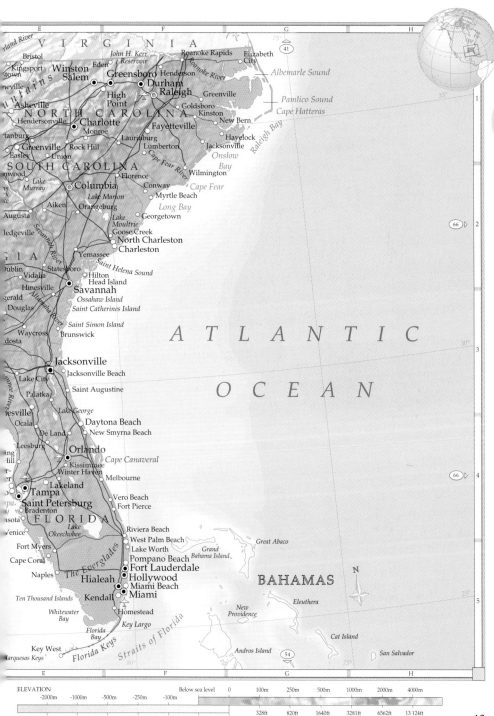

ELEVATION

					Below sea level	0	100m	250m	500m	1000m	2000m	4000m
-2000m	-1000m	-500m	-250m	-100m								
-6562ft	-3281ft	-1640ft	-820ft	-328ft	-164ft/-50m	0						
							328ft	820ft	1640ft	3281ft	6562ft	13 124ft

USA: Central States

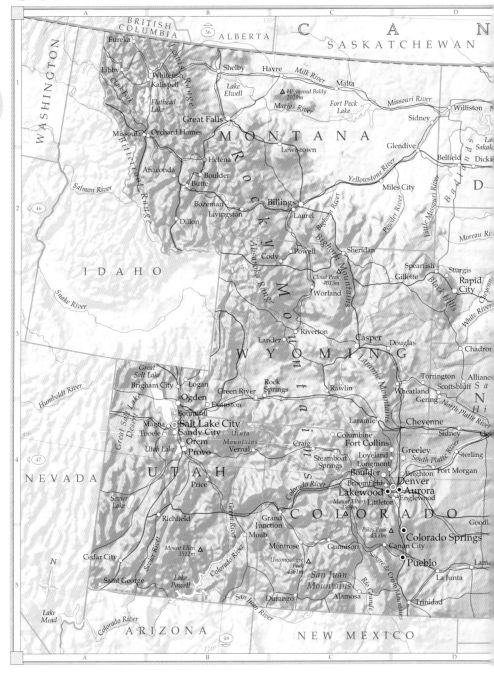

POPULATION

○ Less than 50,000 ○ 50,000 -100,000 ◉ 100,000 - 500,000 ◼ Over 500,000

0 km 200

0 miles 200

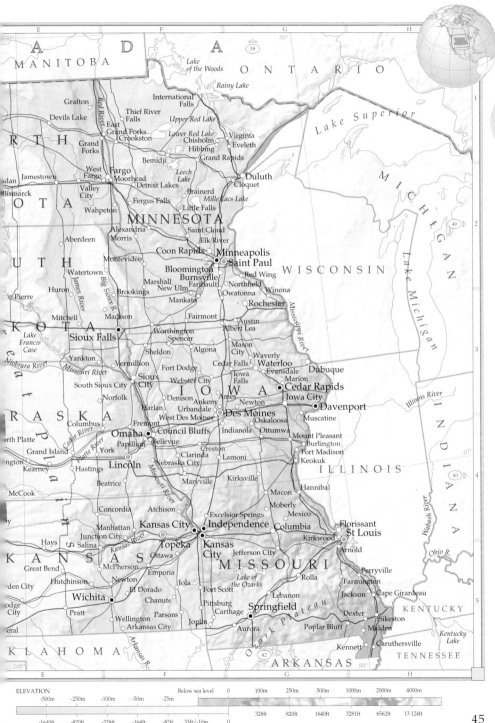

C A N A D A

MANITOBA

ONTARIO

Lake of the Woods

Rainy Lake

Lake Superior

MICHIGAN

Lake Michigan

38

90°

NORTH

Grafton

Devils Lake

East Grand Forks

Grand Forks

Red River

International Falls

Thief River Falls

Upper Red Lake

Crookston

Lower Red Lake

Chisholm

Virginia

Eveleth

Hibbing

Grand Rapids

Bemidji

Duluth

Cloquet

West Fargo

Fargo

Moorhead

Detroit Lakes

Leech Lake

DAKOTA

Jamestown

Bismarck

Valley City

Wahpeton

Fergus Falls

Brainerd

Mille Lacs Lake

Little Falls

MINNESOTA

WISCONSIN

SOUTH

Aberdeen

Alexandria

Morris

Saint Cloud

Elk River

Coon Rapids

Minneapolis

Saint Paul

Red Wing

Montevideo

Bloomington

Burnsville

Faribault

Northfield

Watertown

Marshall

New Ulm

Owatonna

Winona

Brookings

Mankato

Rochester

DAKOTA

Pierre

Huron

James River

Big Sioux R.

Madison

Fairmont

Austin

Albert Lea

Mitchell

Sioux Falls

Worthington

Spencer

Mason City

Lake Francis Case

Yankton

Sheldon

Algona

Waverly

Cedar Falls

Waterloo

Dubuque

Niobrara River

Vermillion

Fort Dodge

Iowa Falls

Evansdale

Marion

Cedar Rapids

Missouri River

South Sioux City

Sioux City

Webster City

IOWA

Iowa City

Davenport

Norfolk

Denison

Ames

Newton

Muscatine

Harlan

Urbandale

Des Moines

NEBRASKA

Columbus

Fremont

West Des Moines

Oskaloosa

Illinois River

INDIANA

North Platte

Grand Island

Omaha

Council Bluffs

Bellevue

Indianola

Ottumwa

Mount Pleasant

Burlington

Great Plains

Platte River

York

Papillion

Creston

Fort Madison

Kearney

Lincoln

Nebraska City

Lamoni

Keokuk

Hastings

Clarinda

ILLINOIS

Cedar River

Beatrice

Maryville

Kirksville

McCook

Concordia

Atchison

Macon

Moberly

Hannibal

Manhattan

Kansas City

Independence

Mexico

Columbia

Florissant

St Louis

Hays

Junction City

Salina

Topeka

Kansas City

Kirkwood

Arnold

Kansas River

Ottawa

Jefferson City

MISSOURI

Perryville

KANSAS

Great Bend

McPherson

Emporia

Lake of the Ozarks

Rolla

Farmington

Jackson

Cape Girardeau

Hutchinson

Newton

Iola

Fort Scott

Lebanon

KENTUCKY

Garden City

Pratt

El Dorado

Chanute

Pittsburg

Carthage

Springfield

Dexter

Sikeston

Wichita

Wellington

Parsons

Joplin

Aurora

Ozark Plateau

Poplar Bluff

Malden

Kentucky Lake

Liberal

Arkansas City

Arkansas R.

Kennett

Caruthersville

TENNESSEE

OKLAHOMA

42

ARKANSAS

90°

ELEVATION

| -500m | -250m | -100m | -50m | -25m | Below sea level | 0 | 100m | 250m | 500m | 1000m | 2000m | 4000m |

| -1640ft | -820ft | -328ft | -164ft | -82ft | 33ft/-10m | 0 | 328ft | 820ft | 1640ft | 3281ft | 6562ft | 13 124ft |

45

USA: THE WEST

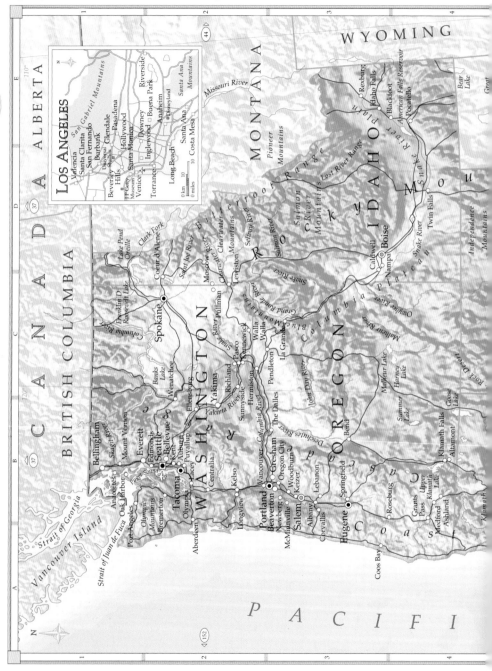

LOS ANGELES

San Gabriel Mountains
Valencia
Santa Clarita
San Fernando
Burbank
Universal Hollywood
City Glendale Pasadena
Beverley Hills
TP Getty Santa Monica
Museum
Venice Inglewood
Downey Riverside
Anaheim Disneyland
Buena Park
Santa Ana Mountains
Torrance Costa Mesa
Long Beach

0 km 10
0 miles 10

CANADA
ALBERTA
BRITISH COLUMBIA

WYOMING
MONTANA

Missouri River

IDAHO
ROCKY Mountains

Rexburg
Idaho Falls
Blackfoot
American Falls Reservoir
Pocatello
Twin Falls

Bear Lake

Pioneer Mountains
Salmon River
Clearwater Mountains
Salmon River
Snake River
Snake River Plain

Lost River Range

Boise
Caldwell
Nampa

Owyhee River

Malheur River

Independence Mountains

Lake Pend Oreille
Clark Fork
Coeur d'Alene

Pend Oreille River
Moscow
Clearwater
Lewiston
Grand Ronde River

Columbia Plateau

Spokane
Franklin D. Roosevelt Lake
Columbia River

WASHINGTON

Banks Lake
Wenatchee
Ellensburg
Yakima
Yakima River
Sunnyside
Richland
Kennewick
Pasco
Walla Walla
Pendleton
La Grande
Blue Mountains

John Day River

Malheur Lake
Harney Lake
Summer Lake

OREGON

Goose Lake
Klamath Falls
Altamont
Upper Klamath Lake

Rock Desert

Bellingham
Skagit River
Mount Vernon
Anacortes
Oak Harbor
Port Angeles
Olympic Mountains
Everett
Edmonds
Seattle
Bellevue
Kent
Auburn
Puyallup
Tacoma
Olympia
Bremerton
Puget Sound
Lacey

Centralia
Aberdeen
Kelso
Longview

Vancouver
Gresham
Portland
Beaverton
Oregon City
Woodburn
Newberg
McMinnville
Keizer
Salem
Albany
Lebanon
Corvallis
Springfield
Eugene
Coos Bay
Roseburg
Grants Pass
Medford
Ashland

Coast Range

Columbia River
Deschutes River
The Dalles
Bend
Cascade Range

Strait of Georgia
Vancouver Island
Strait of Juan de Fuca

P A C I F I C

POPULATION
○ Less than 50,000   ○ 50,000 -100,000   ◉ 100,000 - 500,000   ■ Over 500,000

0 km 200
0 miles 200

ELEVATION

					Below sea level	0	100m	250m	500m	1000m	2000m	4000m
-4000m	-3000m	-2000m	-1000m	-500m								
-13 124ft	-9843ft	-6562ft	-3281ft	-1640ft	-820ft/-250m	0	328ft	820ft	1640ft	3281ft	6562ft	13 124ft

47

USA: THE SOUTHWEST

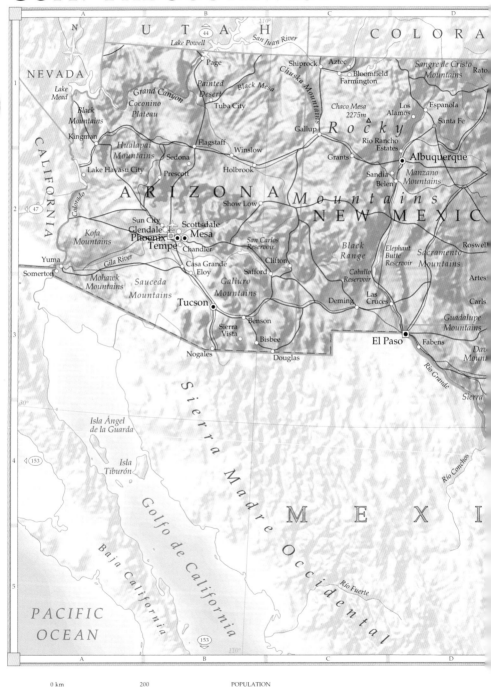

POPULATION

○ Less than 50,000   ○ 50,000 -100,000   ◉ 100,000 - 500,000   ■ Over 500,000

0 km   200

0 miles   200

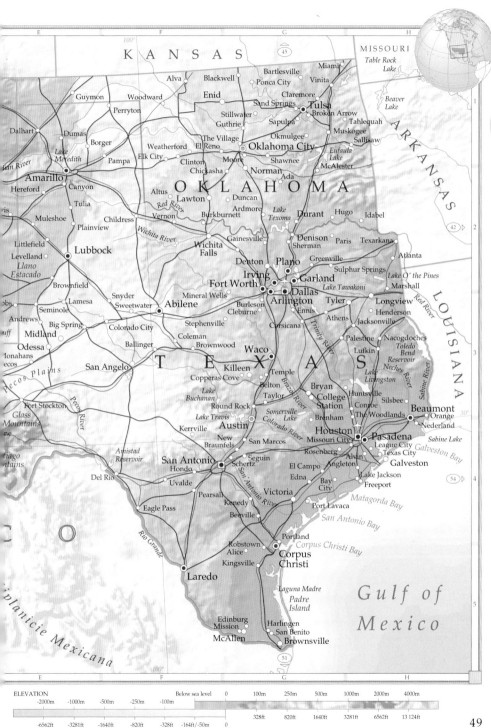

KANSAS

MISSOURI
Table Rock
Lake

Beaver
Lake

ARKANSAS

Guymon
Woodward
Alva
Blackwell
Bartlesville
Ponca City
Miami
Vinita

Perryton
Enid
Sand Springs
Tulsa
Broken Arrow

Dalhart
Dumas
Stillwater
Guthrie
Sapulpa
Claremore
Tahlequah

Borger
Weatherford
El Reno
Okmulgee
Muskogee
Sallisaw

Lake
Meredith
Pampa
Elk City
Clinton
Moore
Oklahoma City
Shawnee
Eufaula
Lake
McAlester

Amarillo
Canyon
Chickasha
Norman
Ada

Hereford
OKLAHOMA

Tulia
Lawton
Duncan
Altus
Ardmore
Hugo
Idabel

Muleshoe
Childress
Vernon
Burkburnett
Lake
Texoma
Durant

Plainview
Wichita River
Gainesville
Denison
Sherman
Paris
Texarkana

Littlefield
Wichita
Falls
Denton
Plano
Greenville
Atlanta

Lubbock
Levelland
Llano
Estacado
Irving
Garland
Sulphur Springs
Lake O' the Pines
Marshall

Brownfield
Fort Worth
Dallas
Lake Tawakoni
Longview
LOUISIANA

Lamesa
Mineral Wells
Arlington
Tyler
Henderson
Red River

Andrews
Seminole
Snyder
Sweetwater
Abilene
Burleson
Cleburne
Ennis
Athens
Jacksonville

Big Spring
Colorado City
Stephenville
Corsicana
Palestine
Nacogdoches

Midland
Coleman
Brownwood
Lufkin
Toledo
Bend
Reservoir

Odessa
Ballinger
TEXAS
Waco
Killeen
Neches River
Lake
Livingston
Sabine River

Monahans
San Angelo
Copperas Cove
Temple
Belton
Bryan
Huntsville
Silsbee

Pecos plains
Taylor
College
Station
Conroe
The Woodlands
Beaumont
Orange

Fort Stockton
Glass
Mountains
Lake
Buchanan
Round Rock
Somerville
Lake
Brenham
Houston
Nederland

Pecos River
Lake Travis
Austin
Colorado River
Missouri City
Pasadena
Sabine Lake

Kerrville
New
Braunfels
San Marcos
Rosenberg
Alvin
Texas City
Galveston Bay

Amistad
Reservoir
San Antonio
Hondo
Schertz
Seguin
El Campo
Angleton
Galveston

Del Rio
Uvalde
Pearsall
Edna
Bay
City
Lake Jackson
Freeport

Eagle Pass
Kenedy
Victoria
Port Lavaca
Matagorda Bay

Beeville
San Antonio Bay

Rio Grande
Robstown
Alice
Portland
Corpus Christi Bay

Laredo
Kingsville
Corpus
Christi

Laguna Madre
Padre
Island

Gulf of
Mexico

Edinburg
Mission
Harlingen
San Benito

McAllen
Brownsville

Planicie Mexicana

ELEVATION

-2000m	-1000m	-500m	-250m	-100m	Below sea level	0	100m	250m	500m	1000m	2000m	4000m
-6562ft	-3281ft	-1640ft	-820ft	-328ft	-164ft/-50m	0	328ft	820ft	1640ft	3281ft	6562ft	13 124ft

49

MEXICO

CALIFORNIA

A R I Z O N A

NEW MEXICO

UNITED STATES O

Rosarito
Mexicali
San Luis
Tijuana
Ensenada

48

110°

105°

115°

Colorado River

Desierto de Altar

Sierra San Pedro Mártir

Nogales
Cananéa
Caborca
Magdalena
Agua Prieta
Nuevo
Casas Grandes

Ciudad Juárez

Pecos River

Ojinaga

Ciudad Ac

Gulfo de

Bahía Sebastían Vizcaíno

Isla Ángel
de la Guarda
Isla
Tiburón

Isla Cedros

Guerrero Negro

Baja California

Hermosillo

Empalme
Guaymas
Esperanza
Ciudad
Obregón
Navojoa
Huatabampo

Sierra Madre Occidental

Chihuahua

Cuauhtémoc

Delicias
Ciudad Camargo

San Francisco
del Oro
Jiménez
Hidalgo del Parral
Santa Barbara

Nueva Rosi
Sab

Monclo

30°

152

2

152

Rio Conchos

Rio Yaqui

Rio Grande

Gómez Palacio
Torreón
Ciudad Lerdo

San Pe

Matamoros

Sierra de la Giganta

Isla Magdalena

Isla Santa Margarita

Loreto

San Blas
Los Mochis
Guasave
Guamúchil
Culiacán
Navolat

Durango

Miguel Asua

Juan Alda
Rio Gra

Bahía de La Paz

El Dorado

La Paz

M E X

25°

3

Tropic of Cancer

Mazatlán

Escuinapa

Acaponeta
Tuxpan

Fresnillo
Zacatecas
Guadalupe

Villanueva

20°

Islas Marías

Isla San Juanito
Isla Maria Madre
Isla Maria Magdalena
Isla Maria Cleofas

Tepic

Lagos de Mor
Yahualica

Aguascaliente:
Jalpa

Guadalajara
Tequila

Puerto Vallarta

Tlaquepaque

Chapala

Zamora de Hida

Ciudad Guzmán

Zap
Tux

4

152

Colima

Manzanillo
Tecomán

Aguili

PACIFIC OCEAN

Isla San Benedicto

Isla Socorro

Isla Roca Partida

Islas Revillagigedo

Isla Clarión

Lázaro Cárc

115°

110°

105°

5

N

153

A

B

C

D

0 km   400

0 miles   400

POPULATION

○ Less than 50,000   ○ 50,000 -100,000   ◉ 100,000 - 500,000   ■ Over 500,000

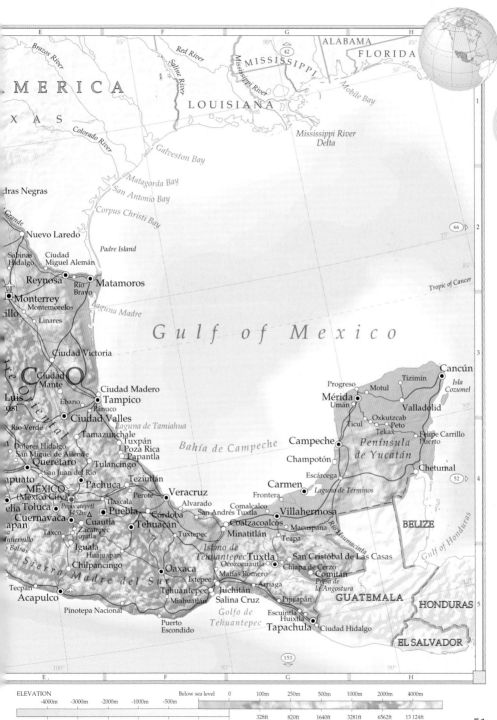

ELEVATION

-4000m	-3000m	-2000m	-1000m	-500m	Below sea level	0	100m	250m	500m	1000m	2000m	4000m

| -13 124ft | -9843ft | -6562ft | -3281ft | -1640ft | -820ft/-250m | 0 | 328ft | 820ft | 1640ft | 3281ft | 6562ft | 13 124ft |

CENTRAL AMERICA

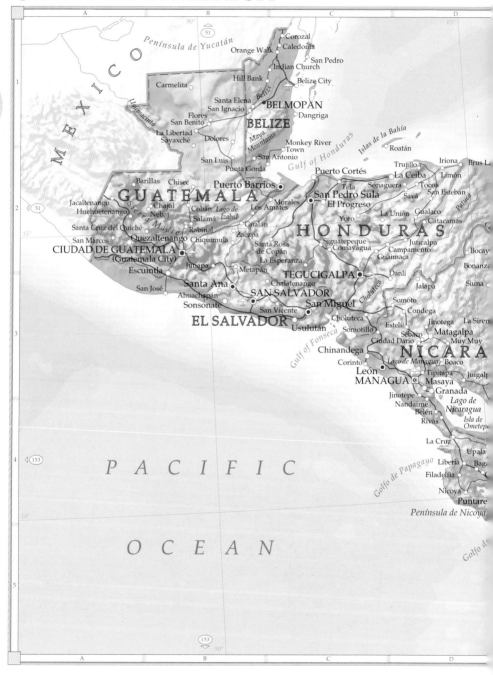

MEXICO

Península de Yucatán

Corozal
Caledonia
Orange Walk
San Pedro
Indian Church
Hill Bank
Carmelita
Belize City
Santa Elena
San Ignacio **BELMOPAN**
Flores
San Benito **BELIZE**
La Libertad Dangriga
Sayaxché
Dolores
Monkey River
Town
San Antonio
San Luis
Punta Gorda
Gulf of Honduras
Islas de la Bahía
Roatán

Barillas Chisec
Puerto Barrios
Trujillo Iriona Brus L.
La Ceiba Limón
Puerto Cortés
Jacaltenango
Huehuetenango Chajul
Nebaj Cobán *Lago de*
Santa Cruz del Quiché
San Marcos
Quezaltenango
GUATEMALA
Tela
San Pedro Sula Sonaguera
Tocón San Esteban
Savá
El Progreso
Yoro La Unión Gualaco Catacamas
Morales
Los Amates
Salamá *Izabal*
Rabinal Gualán
Chiquimula Zacapa
Santa Rosa
de Copán
La Esperanza
HONDURAS
Siguatepeque
Comayagua Campamento
Guaimaca
Juticalpa
Bocay
Bonanza

Sierra Madre

CIUDAD DE GUATEMALA
(Guatemala City)
Escuintla
San José
Jutiapa
Metapán
Santa Ana
Ahuachapán
Sonsonate
EL SALVADOR
Chalatenango
SAN SALVADOR
San Vicente
San Miguel
Usulután
TEGUCIGALPA
Danlí
Jalapa
Siuna
Somoto
Condega
Estelí
Jinotega La Siren
Matagalpa
Muy Muy
NICARA

Chalateca

Cholúteca
Somotillo
Chinandega
Corinto
MANAGUA
León
Ciudad Darío
Sébaco
Boaco
Lago de Managua
Tipitapa Juigalṛ
Masaya
Jinotepe Granada
Nandaime *Lago de*
Belén *Nicaragua*
Rivas *Isla de
Ometepe*

Gulf of Fonseca

La Cruz
Liberia Upala
Baga
Filadelfia
Nicoya
Puntare
Península de Nicoya
Golfo de Papagayo
Golfo d

P A C I F I C

O C E A N

0 km 200

0 miles 200

POPULATION
○ Less than 50,000   ○ 50,000 -100,000   ◉ 100,000 - 500,000   ◼ Over 500,000

N

Islas Santanilla
(to Honduras)

Bajo Nuevo
(to Colombia)

na de Caratasca

Puerto Lempira

spam

Cayos Miskitos

Tuapi
Puerto Cabezas

is

C a r i b b e a n

Prinzapolka

Isla de Providencia
(to Colombia)

Barra de Río Grande

S e a

Laguna de Perlas

Islas del Maíz

Isla de San Andrés
(to Colombia)

Rama

Bluefields

Punta Gorda

Bahía de San Juan del Norte

San Juan del Norte

uan

Puerto Viejo

sada

COSTA RICA

Alajuela

Siquirres

Istmo de Panamá

El Porvenir

Heredia

Limón

Portobelo

Gulf

SAN JOSÉ

Colón

of Darien

Cartago

Guabito

Cristóbal

Ailigandí

rro Chirripó

Almirante

Cordillera de San Blas

Grande

Cordillera de

Laguna

Chepo

Isla de Coiba

Panama Canal

Puerto Obaldía

3819m

Talmanca

de Chiriquí

Lago Gatún

San Miguelito

os

Golfo de los

PANAMÁ

Buenos Aires

Mosquitos

Balboa

Chimán

Cortés

Capira

Bahía de Panamá

Palmar Sur

Volcán Barú 3475m

Penonomé

La Palma

Yaviza

Bahía

Boquete

Serranía de Tabasará

Aguadulce

Archipiélago

Isla

El Real

oronado

La Concepción

P A N A M A

de las Perlas

del Rey

nínsula de Osa

Golfo Dulce

David

Santiago

Chitré

Garachiné

Golfo

Guarumal

Ocú

Las Tablas

Jaqué

de Chiriquí

Península de

Azuero

Golfo

Isla de Coiba

Isla
Cébaco

de Panamá

ELEVATION

Below sea level						0	100m	250m	500m	1000m	2000m	4000m
-4000m	-3000m	-2000m	-1000m	-500m		0						
-13 124ft	-9843ft	-6562ft	-3281ft	-1640ft	-820ft/-250m	0	328ft	820ft	1640ft	3281ft	6562ft	13 124ft

THE CARIBBEAN

N

UNITED STATES OF AMERICA

Gulf of Mexico

Tropic of Cancer

The Everglades

Grand Bahama Island

Freeport

Marsh Harbour

Great Abaco

Bimini Islands

Berry Islands

Nicholls Town

Northwest Providence

Spanish Wells

NASSAU

New Providence

Eleuthera Island

Rock Sound

Florida Keys

Straits of Florida

Andros Town

Andros Island

Exuma Cayes

Cat Island

The Bight

San Salvador

BAHAMAS

George Town

Rum Cay

Marianao

LA HABANA (Havana)

Cay Sal

Angila Isles

Great Exuma Island

Long Island

Artemisa

Guanabacoa

Cárdenas

Sagua la Grande

Clarence Town

Crooked Island

Pinar del Río

Consolación del Sur

Matanzas

Santa Clara

Placetas

Archipiélago de Camagüey

Acklins Island

Crooked Island Passage

La Fé

Golfo de Batabanó

Cienfuegos

Morón

Ragged Island Range

Mayaguana Passage

Yucatán Channel

Nueva Gerona

Key Largo

Sancti Spíritus

Ciego de Ávila

Nuevitas

Little Inagua

Caicos Passag

Isla de la Juventud

Archipiélago do los Canarreos

Bay of Pigs

CUBA

Camagüey

Las Tunas

Holguín

Lake Rosa

Matthew Town

Great Inas

Archipiélago de los Jardines de la Reina

Manzanillo

Bayamo

Guantánamo

Ca

Little Cayman

Cayman Brac

Palma Soriano

Santiago de Cuba

GUANTANAMO BAY (to US)

Haiti

Gonaïves

GEORGE TOWN

Grand Cayman

G

NAVASSA ISLAND (to US)

Île de la Gonâve

Windward Passag

HA

CAYMAN ISLANDS (to UK)

r

Jérémie

PORT-AU-PRINCE

Montego Bay

e

Jamaica Channel

Les Cayes

Jac

Spanish Town

Portmore

KINGSTON

a

JAMAICA

Pedro Cays

t

C

a

r

i

b

b

e

a

n

HONDURAS

JAMAICA

Montego Bay

Lucea

Falmouth

Runaway Bay

St Ann's Bay

Caribbean Sea

Cambridge

The Cockpit Country

Ocho Rios

Annotto Bay

Buff Bay

Savanna-la-Mar

Christiana

Spaldings

Ewarton

Port Antonio

Blue Mountain Peak △ 2256m

Mandeville

Spanish Town

Black River

May Pen

Old Harbour

KINGSTON

Portmore

N

Morant Bay

Portland Bight

2000m/6562ft
1000m/3281ft
500m/1640ft
200m/656ft
Sea level

0 km   20
0 miles   20

Caribbean Sea

COSTA RICA

COLOMBI

0 km   200
0 miles   200

POPULATION

○ Less than 50,000   ○ 50,000 -100,000   ◉ 100,000 - 500,000   ■ Over 500,000

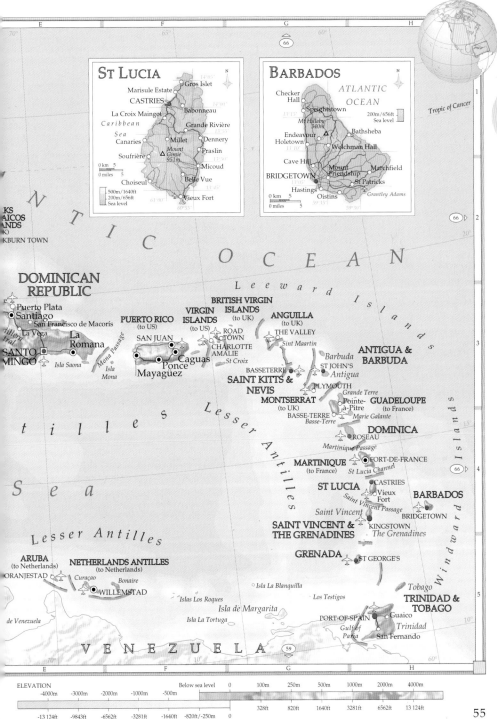

ST LUCIA

Gros Islet
Marisule Estate
CASTRIES
La Croix Maingot
Babonneau
Grande Rivière
Caribbean
Sea
Canaries
Millet
Dennery
Sou!rière
Praslin
Mount
Gimie
951m
Micoud
Choiseul
Belle Vue
Vieux Fort

0 km 5
0 miles 5

500m/1640ft
200m/656ft
Sea level

BARBADOS

ATLANTIC
OCEAN
Checker
Hall
Speightstown
Mt Hillaby
340m
Bathsheba
Endeavour
Holetown
Welchman Hall
Cave Hill
Mount
Friendship
Marchfield
BRIDGETOWN
St Patricks
Hastings
Oistins
Grantley Adams

200m/656ft
Sea level

0 km 5
0 miles 5

ATLANTIC OCEAN

Tropic of Cancer

KS
AICOS
NDS
K)
KBURN TOWN

DOMINICAN
REPUBLIC
Puerto Plata
Santiago
San Francisco de Macorís
La Vega
La
Romana
SANTO
MINGO
Isla Saona
Isla
Mona

Mona Passage

PUERTO RICO
(to US)
SAN JUAN
Ponce
Mayagüez
Caguas

VIRGIN
ISLANDS
(to US)
CHARLOTTE
AMALIE
St Croix

BRITISH VIRGIN
ISLANDS
(to UK)
ROAD
TOWN
Sint Maarten

ANGUILLA
THE VALLEY

Leeward Islands

Barbuda
ST JOHN'S
Antigua
ANTIGUA &
BARBUDA

BASSETERRE
SAINT KITTS &
NEVIS
PLYMOUTH
MONTSERRAT
(to UK)
BASSE-TERRE
Basse-Terre

Grande Terre
Pointe-
à-Pitre
GUADELOUPE
(to France)
Marie Galante

DOMINICA
ROSEAU
Martinique Passage

MARTINIQUE
(to France)
FORT-DE-FRANCE
St Lucia Channel

ST LUCIA
CASTRIES
Vieux
Fort
Saint Vincent Passage
BARBADOS
BRIDGETOWN

Saint Vincent
SAINT VINCENT &
THE GRENADINES
KINGSTOWN
The Grenadines

GRENADA
ST GEORGE'S

Lesser Antilles

ARUBA
(to Netherlands)
ORANJESTAD
NETHERLANDS ANTILLES
(to Netherlands)
Curaçao
Bonaire
WILLEMSTAD
Islas Los Roques
Isla La Blanquilla
Los Testigos
Tobago

de Venezuela
Isla de Margarita
Isla La Tortuga
PORT-OF-SPAIN
Guaico
Gulf of
Paria
Trinidad
San Fernando
TRINIDAD &
TOBAGO

VENEZUELA

tilles
Sea
Lesser Antilles
Windward Islands

ELEVATION

					Below sea level	0	100m	250m	500m	1000m	2000m	4000m
-4000m	-3000m	-2000m	-1000m	-500m								
								328ft	820ft	1640ft	3281ft	6562ft	13 124ft
-13 124ft	-9843ft	-6562ft	-3281ft	-1640ft	-820ft/-250m	0						

SOUTH AMERICA

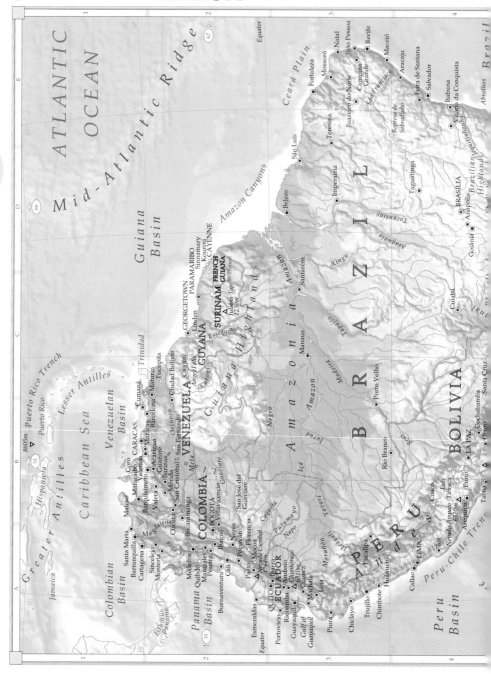

ATLANTIC OCEAN

Mid-Atlantic Ridge

Equator

Natal
João Pessoa
Recife
Maceió
Aracaju

Mossoró

Ceará Plain

Fortaleza

Juazeiro do Norte
Campina Grande
São Francisco

Feira de Santana
Salvador
Itabuna

Represa de Sobradinho

Vitória da Conquista
Abrolhos

Teresina

São Luís

Imperatriz

Taguatinga

Brazilian Highlands

Belém

BRASÍLIA
Anápolis
Goiânia

B R A Z I L

Guiana Basin

Amazon Canyons

PARAMARIBO
Sinnamary
Kourou
CAYENNE

GEORGETOWN
Linden
PARAMARIBO

SURINAM FRENCH GUIANA

Juliana Top 1230m

GUYANA

Essequibo

Guiana Highlands

Angel Falls

Tocantins

Araguaia

Cuiabá

Xingu

Santarém

Amazon

A m a z o n i a

Manaus

Madeira

Porto Velho

Negro

Tapajós

Juruá

Rio Branco

Içá

Iquitos

Tabatinga

BOLIVIA

Cochabamba
Santa Cruz

LA PAZ
Oruro

Lago Titicaca
Puno

Cusco

Nevado Ampato 6310m
Arequipa
Tacna

P E R U

LIMA
Callao

Huánuco
Pucallpa

Chimbote
Trujillo
Chiclayo

Piura

Andes

Peru-Chile Trench

Peru Basin

ATLANTIC OCEAN

Guiana Basin

Trinidad

Cumaná
Maturín
Barcelona
Tucupita
Ciudad Bolívar
Cuyuní
Caroní
Orinoco

VENEZUELA

Maracay
CARACAS
Maracaibo
Maracay
Valencia
Coro
Barquisimeto
Acarigua
Guanare
Valera
Barinas
San Cristóbal San Fernando

Mérida

COLOMBIA

Cúcuta
Bucaramanga
BOGOTÁ

Villavicencio

San José del Guaviare

Guaviare

Ibagué
Neiva
Popayán
Florencia

Putumayo

Napo

Medellín
Quibdó
Manizales
Pereira
Cali
Pasto
Mocoa

Caquetá

Marañón

Ucayali

Yavari

Purus

Madre de Dios

Magdalena

Cauca

Sincelejo
Montería
Santa Marta
Barranquilla
Cartagena

Caribbean Sea

Venezuelan Basin

Lesser Antilles

Puerto Rico Trench
Puerto Rico
8605m

Greater Antilles

Hispaniola

Jamaica

Colombian Basin

Panama Basin

Isthmus of Panama

Gulf of Guayaquil

Guayaquil

Equator

Esmeraldas
QUITO
ECUADOR
Portoviejo
Ambato
Riobamba
Guayaquil
Machala
Loja
Cuenca

Ibarra
Cayambe 5790m
Cotopaxi 5897m
Chimborazo 6310m

Buenaventura

Trinidad

0 km   500

0 miles   500

POPULATION

○ Less than 50,000   ◎ 50,000 -100,000   ◉ 100,000 - 500,000   ■ Over 500,000

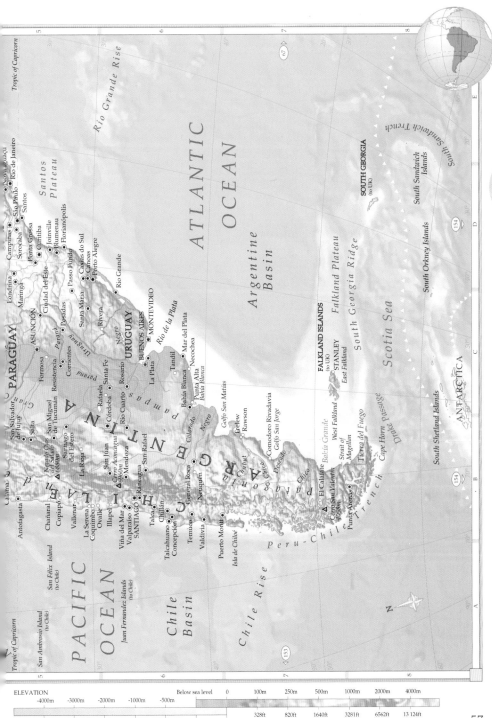

ELEVATION

-4000m	-3000m	-2000m	-1000m	-500m	Below sea level	0	100m	250m	500m	1000m	2000m	4000m

| -13 124ft | -9843ft | -6562ft | -3281ft | -1640ft | -820ft/-250m | 0 | | 328ft | 820ft | 1640ft | 3281ft | 6562ft | 13 124ft |

NORTHERN SOUTH AMERICA

Caribbean
Sea

Lesser Ant

Península
de la
Guajira

ARUBA
(to Netherlands)
Aruba

NETHERLANDS
ANTILLES
(to Netherlands)

Curaçao   Bonaire

Puerto López

Santa Marta   Riohacha

Golfo de
Venezuela

Punto Fijo   Puerto

Islas
Los Roques

La O

Barranquilla   Maicao   Coro   Cumarebo

Cienaga La Concepción   Dabajuro   Sabaneta
Cartagena   Soledad   Pico Cristóbal Colón   Maracaibo   Urumaco   Puerto Cabello   CARAC

Sabanalarga   △5775m   Maracaibo   Cabimas   San Felipe   Valencia

Malambo   Valledupar   Ciudad Ojeda   Carora   Maracay

El Carmen   Machiques   Lago de   Barquisimeto   San Juan
de Bolívar   Maracaibo   de los Mo

Sincelejo   Magangué   San Carlos   Valera   Val
del Zulia   Acarigua   Calabozo

Montería   Cereté   Mérida   Guanare   Corozo Par

Planeta Rica   Aguachica   El Vigía   Barinas   San Ferna

Necoclí   Caucasia   Ocaña   △Pico Bolívar
Apartadó   5007m

Dabeiba   Cúcuta   San Cristóbal   Santa M
del Orin

Yarumal   Pamplona   Arauca   Puerto Carre

Bello   Bucaramanga   Puerto Ayacu

Medellín   Barrancabermeja   Arauca   Meta

Quibdó   Itagüí   Puerto Berrío
Nuquí   Duitama   Sogamoso

Tunja   Yopal   Puerto Nuevo

Zipaquira   Manizales   Meta   Puerto Inírida

Pereira   BOGOTÁ
Armenia   Girardot   Villavicencio   Leticia

Tuluá   Ibagué
Buenaventura   Buga   Espinal

Palmira   COLOMBIA
Cali

Neiva   San José del Guaviare   Guaviare

Popayán   Garzón

Tumaco   Pitalito

Nevada de Cumbal   Mocoa   Florencia   Vaupés   Mitú
4764m△   Pasto
Ipiales   Orito

Equator   Napo   Putumayo   Caquetá   Japurá

ECUADOR

PERU   Icá

Içá

0 km   200

0 miles   200

POPULATION

○ Less than 50,000   ○ 50,000 -100,000   ◉ 100,000 - 500,000   ◼ Over 500,000

SAINT VINCENT &
THE GRENADINES

BARBADOS

GRENADA

Isla Blanquilla

Isla de
Margarita

Los Testigos

La Asunción
Porlamar

Tobago

tuga

naná

Carúpano

Cariaco

Gúira
Gulf of
Paria

The Dragon's Mouth

TRINIDAD &
TOBAGO

Puerto La Cruz

Barcelona

Trinidad

San Mateo

The Serpent's Mouth

Maturín

Anaco

Cantaura

za

El Tigre

Tucupita

Orinoco

Ciudad Guayana

Morawhanna

A T L A N T I C

O C E A N

S

Ciudad
Bolívar

Upata

Embalse de Guri

El Callao

Matthews
Ridge

Baramita

Baramanni

Charity

Suddie

Spring Garden

U E L A

El Dorado

Cuyuni

Parika

GEORGETOWN

New
Amsterdam

Aurora

Peters Mine

Bartica

Rockstone

Totness

PARAMARIBO

Nieuw Amsterdam

Salto Ángel
980m

Kamarang

Linden

Nieuw
Nickerie

Boskamp

Galibi

St-Laurent-du-Maroni

Sinnamary

Kourou

Paragua

Caroní

Serra Pacaraima

GUYANA

Apoera

W. J. van
Blommesteinmeer

Oreala

CAYENNE

Mount Roraima △
2810m

Kaaimanston

Maroni

Grand-
Santi

Montagnes
de la Trinité

Montagne
Tortue

Kurupukari

SURINAM

△*Juliana Top*
1230m

Cottica

Ouanary

St-Georges

Lethem

Kumaka

Teboe Top

FRENCH
GUIANA
(to France)

Camopi

Caura

Dadanawa

Courentyne

utana

Highla

Isherton

Acarai Mountains

Biloku

n d s

ro

Equator

Negro

B R A Z I L

a z o n i

Amazon

a

Purus

Tapajós

ELEVATION

					Below sea level	0	100m	250m	500m	1000m	2000m	4000m
-4000m	-3000m	-2000m	-1000m	-500m								
-13 124ft	-9843ft	-6562ft	-3281ft	-1640ft	-820ft/-250m	0		328ft	820ft	1640ft	3281ft	6562ft	13 124ft

WESTERN SOUTH AMERICA

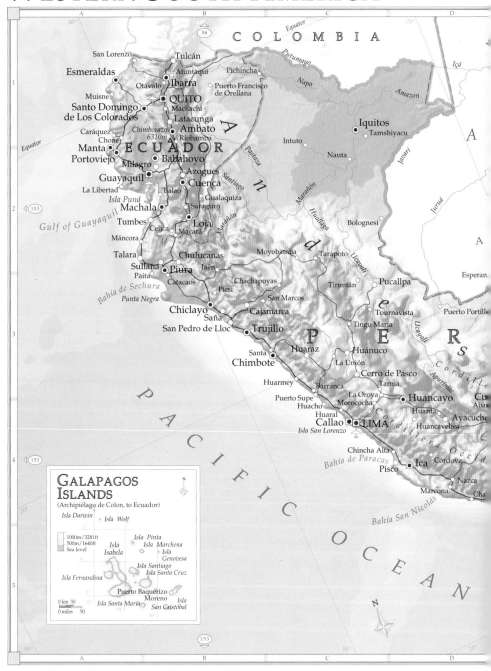

COLOMBIA

Equator

Putumayo

San Lorenzo
Tulcán
Esmeraldas
Atuntaqui
Pichincha
Napo
Otavalo Ibarra
Puerto Francisco
de Orellana
Muisne
QUITO
Santo Domingo
Machachi
de Los Colorados
Latacunga
Chimborazo Ambato
Caráquez *6310m* Riobamba
Chone
Manta ECUADOR
Portoviejo
Milagro Babahoyo
Guayaquil Azogues
La Libertad Balao Cuenca
Isla Puná Machala Gualaquiza
Saraguro
Machala
Gulf of Guayaquil
Tumbes
Celica Macará
Mańcora

Iquitos
Tamshiyacu

Intuto
Nauta

Javari

Bolognesi

Moyobamba
Talara
Chulucanas Tarapoto
Sullana Piura Jaén
Paita Chachapoyas Tiruntán
Catacaos
Piesi
Bahía de Sechura
Punta Negra San Marcos
Chiclayo Cajamarca
Saña
San Pedro de Lloc Trujillo
Santa Huaraz Huánuco
Chimbote La Unión
Huarmey Cerro de Pasco
Huaco Barranca Tarma
Puerto Supe La Oroya Huancayo
Huacho Morococha Huanta
Huaral Huancavelica
Callao LIMA
Isla San Lorenzo
Chincha Alta
Córdova
Bahía de Paracas Ica
Pisco
Nazca
Marcona

PACIFIC

Bahía San Nicolás

PERU

Pucallpa
Esperan
Tournavista
Puerto Portill
Tingo María

Cu
Aba

Ayacuch

OCEAN

GALAPAGOS ISLANDS
(Archipiélago de Colon, to Ecuador)

Isla Darwin • *Isla Wolf*

	1000m/3281ft
	500m/1640ft
	Sea level

Isla Isabela
Isla Pinta
Isla Marchena
Isla Genovesa
Isla Fernandina
Isla Santiago
Isla Santa Cruz

Puerto Baquerizo
Moreno
Isla Santa María *Isla San Cristóbal*

0 km 50
0 miles 50

0 km 400
0 miles 400

POPULATION
○ Less than 50,000   ○ 50,000 -100,000   ◉ 100,000 - 500,000   ◼ Over 500,000

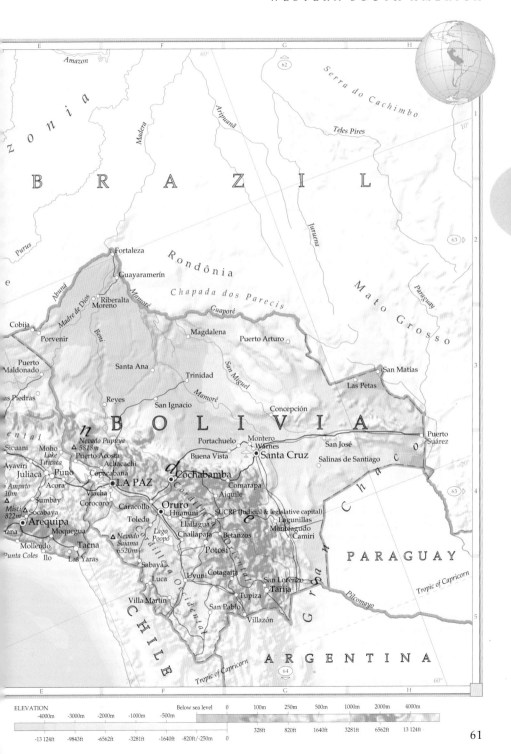

E   F   60°   G   62   H

Amazon

Aripuanā

Serra do Cachimbo

Teles Pires

1

10°

Z
O
n
i
a

Madera

Juruena

B   R   A   Z   I   L

Purus

63

2

Abunā

Fortaleza

Rondônia

Guayaramerín

Chapada dos Parecis

e

Madre de Dios

Riberalta
Moreno

Guaporé

Cobija

Porvenir

Beni

Mamoré

Magdalena

Puerto Arturo

Mato Grosso

San Matías

Paraguay

3

Puerto
Maldonado

Santa Ana

Trinidad

Las Petas

20°

as Piedras

Reyes

San Ignacio

Mamoré

San Miguel

Concepción

ental

B   O   L   I   V   I   A

Puerto
Suárez

Sicuani

Nevado Pupuya
△ 5818m

Portachuelo

Montero
Warnes

San José

Puerto
Suárez

Moho
Lake
Titicaca

Puerto Acosta

Buena Vista

Santa Cruz

Salinas de Santiago

63

Ayaviri

Achacachi

Juliaca
△ *Ampato*
10m

Copacabana

Cochabamba

Comarapa

C
h
a
c
o

4

Acora

Puno

LA PAZ

Aiquile

Lagunillas

Misti
△ 822m

Sumbay

Viacha
Corocoro

Oruro

Huanuni

SUCRE (Judicial & legislative capital)

Arequipa

Caracollo

Monteagudo
Camiri

Moquegua

Toledo

Llallagua

Betanzos

G
r
a
n

PARAGUAY

Nevado
△ *Sajama*
6520m

Lago
Poopó

Challapata

Potosí

Mollendo

Tacna

Cotagaita

Cordillera Occidental

Sabaya

Pilcomayo

Tropic of Capricorn

Punta Coles

Ilo

Las Yaras

Luca

Uyuni

San Lorenzo

Tarija

5

Villa Martín

San Pablo

Tupiza

Villazón

C   H   I   L   E

A   R   G   E   N   T   I   N   A

Tropic of Capricorn

64

60°

E   F   G   H

ELEVATION

| | | | | Below sea level | 0 | 100m | 250m | 500m | 1000m | 2000m | 4000m |
| -4000m | -3000m | -2000m | -1000m | -500m | | | | | | | |

| -13 124ft | -9843ft | -6562ft | -3281ft | -1640ft | -820ft/-250m | 0 | 328ft | 820ft | 1640ft | 3281ft | 6562ft | 13 124ft |

61

BRAZIL

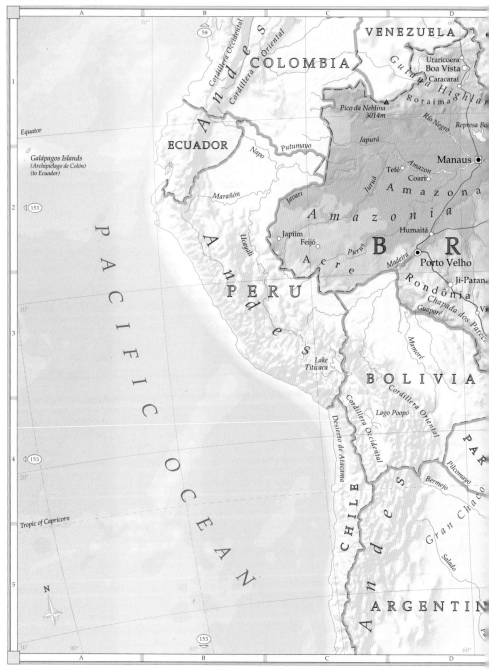

VENEZUELA

COLOMBIA

Cordillera Occidental

Cordillera Oriental

58

Guiana Highla

Uraricoera
Boa Vista
Caracaraí

Roraima

Pico da Neblina
3014m

Rio Negro

Represa Ba

A
n
d
e
s

ECUADOR

Napo

Putumayo

Japurá

Equator

Galápagos Islands
(Archipiélago de Colón)
(to Ecuador)

Marañón

Javari

Amazon

Manaus

Tefé
Coari

Amazona

153

Ucayali

Japiim
Feijó

A
m
a
z
o
n
i
a

Humaitá

B   R

Acre

Purus

Madeira

Porto Velho

Ji-Paran

A
n
d
e
s

PERU

Rondônia

Chapada dos Pareci

Guaporé

Vi

10°

Mamoré

PACIFIC OCEAN

Lake
Titicaca

BOLIVIA

Cordillera Oriental

Lago Poopó

Cordillera Occidental

153

20°

Desierto de Atacama

PAR

Bermejo

Pilcomayo

Tropic of Capricorn

N

Gran Chaco

Salado

C
H
I
L
E

A
n
d
e
s

153

ARGENTIN

30°

0 km   600

0 miles   600

POPULATION

○ Less than 50,000   ○ 50,000 -100,000   ◉ 100,000 - 500,000   ◼ Over 500,000

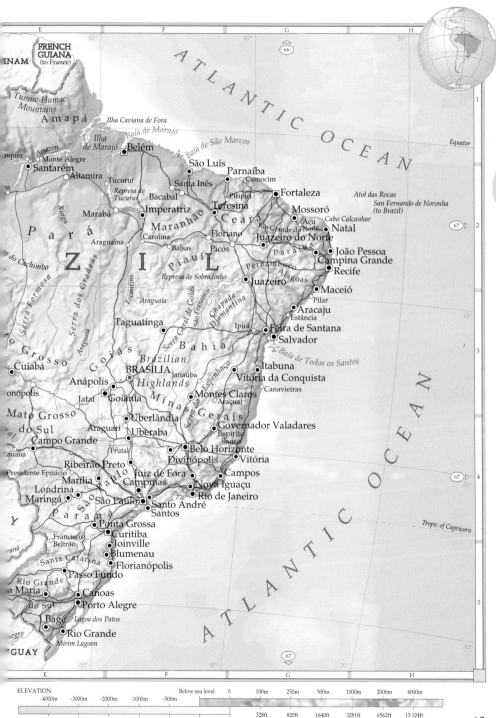

ELEVATION

					Below sea level	0	100m	250m	500m	1000m	2000m	4000m
-4000m	-3000m	-2000m	-1000m	-500m		0						
-13 124ft	-9843ft	-6562ft	-3281ft	-1640ft	-820ft/-250m	0	328ft	820ft	1640ft	3281ft	6562ft	13 124ft

63

0 km 200

0 miles 200

POPULATION

 Less than 50,000

 50,000 - 100,000

 100,000 - 500,000

 Over 500,000

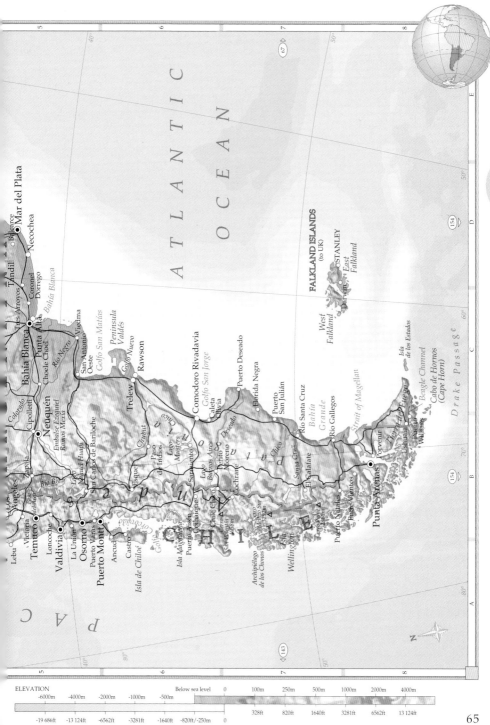

ATLANTIC

OCEAN

PACIFIC

FALKLAND ISLANDS
(to UK)

STANLEY
East
Falkland
West
Falkland
Darwin

Isla
de los Estados

Drake Passage

Cabo de Hornos
(Cape Horn)

Beagle Channel

Strait of Magellan

Mar del Plata
Necochea
Billkarce
Coronel
Dorrego
Las Arroyos
Tandil
Bahía Blanca
Punta Alta
Bahía Blanca
Cipoletti
Neuquén
Choele Choel
Río Negro
San Antonio
Oeste
Viedma
Golfo San Matías
Península Valdés
Golfo Nuevo
Rawson
Trelew
Comodoro Rivadavia
Golfo San Jorge
Caleta
Olivia
Puerto Deseado
Florida Negra
Puerto
San Julián
Río Santa Cruz
Bahía Grande
Río Gallegos
El Calafate
Porvenir
Ushuaia
Puerto
Williams
Punta Arenas
Puerto Natales
Puerto Montt
Osorno
Valdivia
Temuco
Puerto Varas
La Unión
Ancud
Castro
Isla de Chiloé
San Carlos de Bariloche
Esquel
Paso
de Indios
Río Chubut
Río Chico
Río Deseado
Río Chico
Río Santa Cruz
Lago
Musters
Lago
Buenos Aires
Cochrane
Chile Chico
Golfo Corcovado
Archipiélago de los Chonos
Isla Wellington
Tierra del Fuego
San Carlos de Bariloche

*Lago
Nahuel Huapi*

Colorado

Zapla

Río Bío

Victoria

Loncoche

Lebu
Los Ángeles

*Embalse Ezequiel
Ramos Mexia*

Esquel

ELEVATION

-6000m	-4000m	-2000m	-1000m	-500m	Below sea level	0	100m	250m	500m	1000m	2000m	4000m
-19 686ft	-13 124ft	-6562ft	-3281ft	-1640ft	-820ft/-250m	0	328ft	820ft	1640ft	3281ft	6562ft	13 124ft

THE ATLANTIC OCEAN

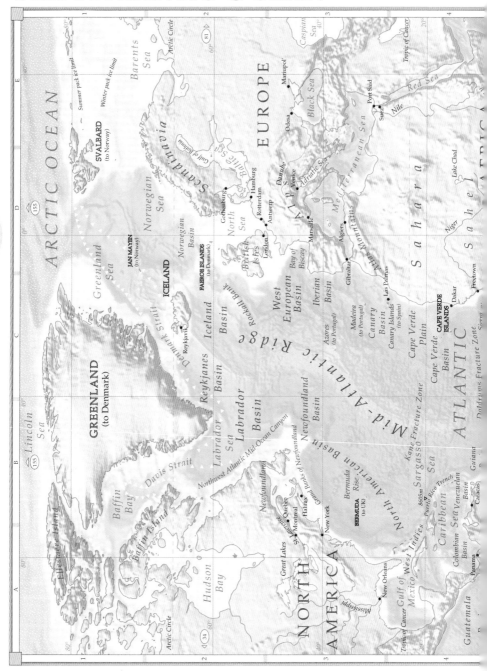

Major ports

0 km   1000

0 miles   1000

66

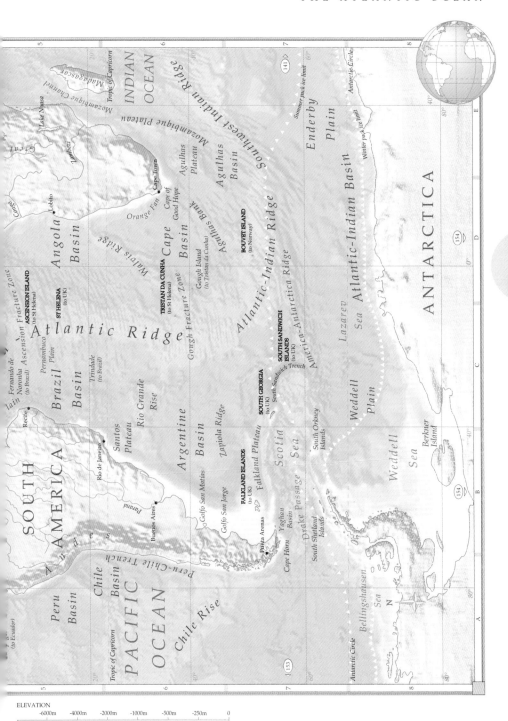

INDIAN OCEAN

Madagascar

Lake Nyasa

Mozambique Channel

Zambezi

Congo

Great

Mozambique Plateau

Southwest Indian Ridge

Cape Town

Cape of Good Hope

Agulhas Plateau

Agulhas Basin

Enderby Plain

Summer pack ice limit

Antarctic Circle

Winter pack ice limit

Lobito

Orange Fan

Cape Basin

Agulhas Bank

BOUVET ISLAND
(to Norway)

Atlantic–Indian Ridge

Atlantic–Indian Basin

ANTARCTICA

Angola Basin

Walvis Ridge

TRISTAN DA CUNHA
(to St Helena)

Gough Island
(to Tristan da Cunha)

Lazarev Sea

ASCENSION ISLAND
(to Brazil)

Ascension Fracture Zone

ST HELENA
(to UK)

Gough Fracture Zone

Fernando de Noronha
(to Brazil)

Atlantic Ridge

Pernambuco Plain

Brazil Basin

Trindade
(to Brazil)

Rio Grande Rise

SOUTH SANDWICH ISLANDS
(to UK)

South Sandwich Trench

America–Antarctica Ridge

Weddell Plain

Recife

SOUTH AMERICA

Santos Plateau

Argentine Basin

Zapiola Ridge

SOUTH GEORGIA
(to UK)

Scotia Sea

South Orkney Islands

Weddell Sea

Berkner Island

Rio de Janeiro

Paraná

Golfo San Matías

FALKLAND ISLANDS
(to UK)

Falkland Plateau

Buenos Aires

Golfo San Jorge

Yaghan Basin

Andes

Punta Arenas

Cape Horn

Drake Passage

South Shetland Islands

Bellingshausen Sea

N

Antarctic Circle

Chile Basin

Peru–Chile Trench

Peru Basin

PACIFIC OCEAN

Chile Rise

(to Ecuador)

Tropic of Capricorn

ELEVATION

-6000m	-4000m	-2000m	-1000m	-500m	-250m	0
-19 686ft	-13 124ft	-6562ft	-3281ft	-1640ft	-820ft	0

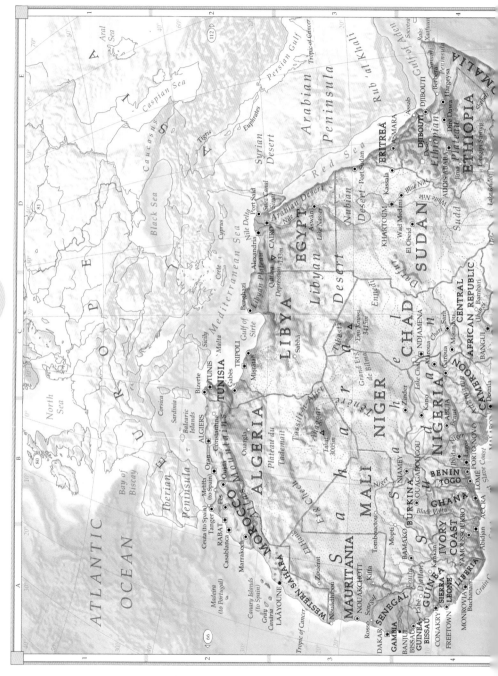

POPULATION

○ Less than 50,000 ○ 50,000 - 100,000 ◉ 100,000 - 500,000 ■ Over 500,000

0 km   1000

0 miles   1000

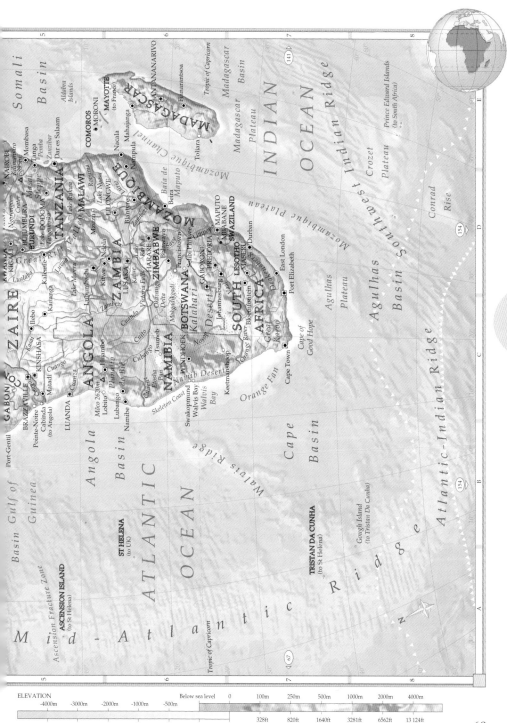

ELEVATION

-4000m	-3000m	-2000m	-1000m	-500m	Below sea level	0	100m	250m	500m	1000m	2000m	4000m
-13 124ft	-9843ft	-6562ft	-3281ft	-1640ft	-820ft/-250m	0	328ft	820ft	1640ft	3281ft	6562ft	13 124ft

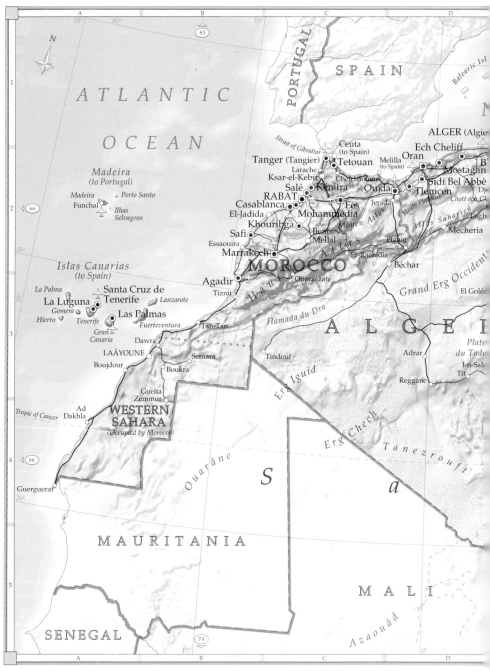

ATLANTIC

OCEAN

Madeira
(to Portugal)

Madeira • *Porto Santo*
Funchal
Ilhas
Selvagens

Islas Canarias
(to Spain)

La Palma
La Luguna *Lanzarote*
Gomera
Hierro *Tenerife* Las Palmas
Gran
Canaria *Fuerteventura*

Santa Cruz de
Tenerife

PORTUGAL

SPAIN

Balearic Isl

Strait of Gibraltar
Ceuta
(to Spain)
Tanger (Tangier) Tetouan
Larache Melilla
Ksar-el-Kebir *(to Spain)*
Chefchaouen
Salé Kenitra
RABAT Oujda
Casablanca Fès
El-Jadida Mohammedia Jerada
Khouribga *Moyen Atlas*
Beni-
Safi Mellal
Essaouira *Haut Atlas*
Marrakech Er-Rachidia
MOROCCO
Ouarzazate
Agadir
Tiznit

ALGER (Algie
Ech Cheliff
Oran
B
Mostagan
Sidi Bel Abbè
Tlemcen Dj
Haut Plateaux *Chott ech Ch*
Atlas Saharien Lagh
Mecheria

Figuig
Béchar

ALGEI

Grand Erg Occident El Gole

Plate
du Tade
Adrar
I-n-Sal
Reggane Tit

Tan-Tan
Hamada du Dra

Dawra
LAÂYOUNE
Boujdour Semara
Boukra

Guelta
Zemmur
Ad WESTERN
Dakhla SAHARA
(Occupied by Morocco)

Tropic of Cancer

Guerguerat

Erg Iguid

Tindouf

Erg Chech

Tanezrouft

S

a

Ouarâne

MAURITANIA

MALI

SENEGAL

Azaouâd

0 km   400

0 miles   400

POPULATION

○ Less than 50,000   ◎ 50,000 -100,000   ◉ 100,000 - 500,000   ◼ Over 500,000

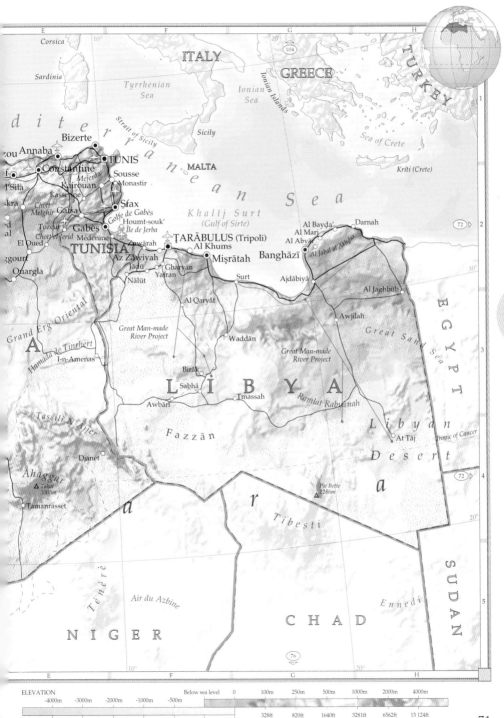

ELEVATION

-4000m	-3000m	-2000m	-1000m	-500m	Below sea level	0	100m	250m	500m	1000m	2000m	4000m
-13 124ft	-9843ft	-6562ft	-3281ft	-1640ft	-820ft/-250m	0	328ft	820ft	1640ft	3281ft	6562ft	13 124ft

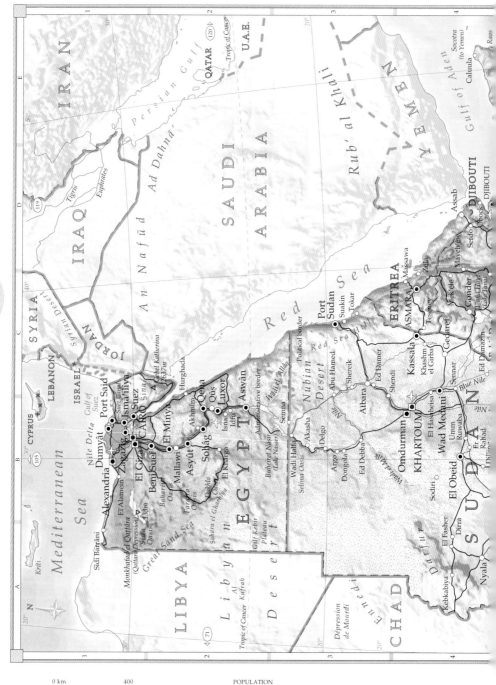

IRAN

IRAQ

SYRIA

JORDAN

LEBANON

CYPRUS

ISRAEL

SAUDI ARABIA

An Nafūd

Ad Dahna

Rub' al Khali

YEMEN

Persian Gulf

QATAR

U.A.E.

Tropic of Cancer

Socotra
(to Yemen)

Ras

Gulf of Aden

Calula

DJIBOUTI
DJIBOUTI

Assab

Docks

Serdo

Mayehew

ERITREA

ASMARA

Zula

Massawa

Mek'elē

Gonder

Lake Tana

Red Sea

Red Sea Hills

Port
Sudan

Suakin

Tokar

Teseney

Gedaref

Kassala

Khashm
el Girba

Sennar

Ed Damazin

Blue Nile

Nubian
Desert

Abu Hamed

Sherek

Ed Damer

Shendi

Atbara

Argo

Dongola

Ed Debba

Akasha

Delgo

Wadi Halfa

Selima Oasis

Buheiret Nasir
(Lake Nasser)

KHARTOUM

Omdurman

El Hasaheisa

Wad Medani

Umm
Ruwaba

El Obeid

Sodiri

Rahad

Dilling

Ed
Rahad

SUDAN

El Fasher

Dirra

Kebkabiya

Nyala

Darfur

CHAD

Ennedi

Dépression
de Mourdi

Mediterranean
Sea

Kriti

Sidi Barrâni

El Alamein

Alexandria

Dumyât

Port Said

Zagazig

Ismâ'ilîya

CAIRO

Suez

Gulf of Suez

Suez Canal

Gebel Katherina
2637m

Gebel Sinai

Hurghada

Nile Delta

El Giza

Benî Suef

El Minya

Mallawi

Asyût

Akhmim

Sohâg

Qena

Qûs

LUXOR

Isna

Idfû

Aswân

Esna

El Kharga

El Ghanayim

Farâfra
Oasis

Dâkhla
Oasis

Bahariya
Oasis

Sîwa
Oasis

Monkhafad el Qattâra
(Qattara Depression)
−133m

Gilf Kebir
Plateau

Sahara el Ghanâyim

Great Sand Sea

Tropic of Cancer

Al
Kufrah

LIBYA

Libyan
Desert

EGYPT

Wadi el 'Allâqi

Semna

Wadi al Mila

Nile

Political border

Administrative border

Red Sea

IRAN

N

0 km   400

0 miles   400

POPULATION

○ Less than 50,000   ○ 50,000 -100,000   ◉ 100,000 - 500,000   ◼ Over 500,000

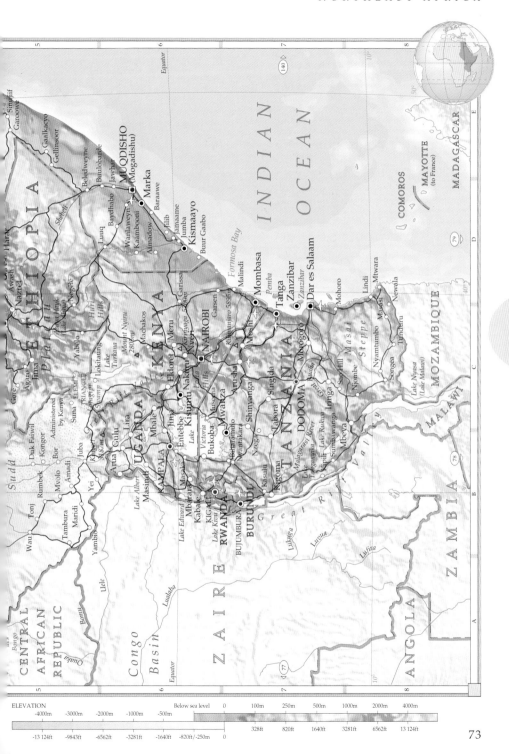

ELEVATION

-4000m	-3000m	-2000m	-1000m	-500m	Below sea level	0	100m	250m	500m	1000m	2000m	4000m

| -13 124ft | -9843ft | -6562ft | -3281ft | -1640ft | -820ft/-250m | 0 | | 328ft | 820ft | 1640ft | 3281ft | 6562ft | 13 124ft |

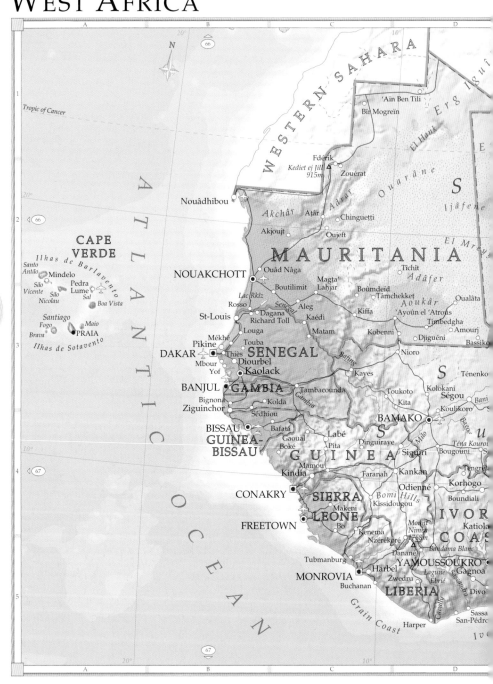

Tropic of Cancer

WESTERN SAHARA

'Aïn Ben Tili
Bir Mogreïn

Fdérik
Kediet ej Jill
915m
Zouérat

El Hank

Erg Iguîdi

Ouârâne

Ijâfene

Nouâdhibou
Akchâr
Atâr
Chinguetti

Akjoujt
Oujeft

MAURITANIA

Adâfer

Tîchît
Aoukâr

Ouâd Nâga
NOUAKCHOTT
Boutilimit
Magta'
Lahjar
Boûmdeïd
Tâmchekket
Oualâta

Lac Rkîz
Rosso
Aleg
Kiffa
'Ayoûn el 'Atroûs
Timbedgha
Amourj

St-Louis
Dagana
Richard Toll
Kaédi
Kobenni
Djiguéni
Bassiko

Louga
Matam
Nioro

Mékhé
Touba
Kayes
Ténenko

DAKAR
Pikine
Thiès
Diourbel
SENEGAL
Bafing
Kolokani
Ségou
Mbour
Yof
Kaolack
Toukoto
Kita
KouliKoro
Bani

BANJUL
GAMBIA
Tambacounda
BAMAKO

Bignona
Gambia
Kolda
Kayes

Ziguinchor
Sédhiou

BISSAU
Bafatá
Labé
Dinguiraye
Siguiri
Bougouni

GUINEA-
BISSAU
Gaoual
Boké
Pita
Téna Kourou
Tengréla

GUINEA
Mamou
Faranah
Kankan
Korhogo

Kindia
Odienné
Boundiali

CONAKRY
SIERRA
Bomi Hills
Kissidougou
IVOR

Makeni
LEONE
COAS
Katiola

FREETOWN
Bo
Kenema
Nzérékoré
*Mount
Nimba*
1768m
Bandama Blanc
YAMOUSSOUKRO

Tubmanburg
Danané
Gagnoa

MONROVIA
Harbel
Zwedru
*Laguna
Ébrié*
Divo

Buchanan
LIBERIA

*Grain
Coast*
Sassa
San-Pédro

Harper
Ivo

ATLANTIC

CAPE
VERDE

Ilhas de Barlavento

Santo
Antão
Mindelo
São
Vicente
São
Nicolau
Pedra
Lume
Sal
Boa Vista

Santiago
Maio
Fogo
Brava
PRAIA

Ilhas de Sotavento

OCEAN

0 km 250

0 miles 250

POPULATION

 Less than 50,000 50,000 -100,000 100,000 - 500,000 Over 500,000

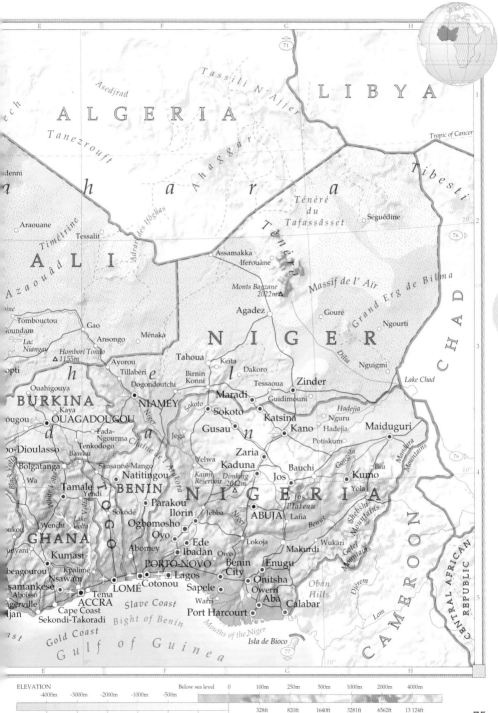

ELEVATION

					Below sea level	0	100m	250m	500m	1000m	2000m	4000m
-4000m	-3000m	-2000m	-1000m	-500m								

| -13 124ft | -9843ft | -6562ft | -3281ft | -1640ft | -820ft/-250m | 0 | 328ft | 820ft | 1640ft | 3281ft | 6562ft | 13 124ft |

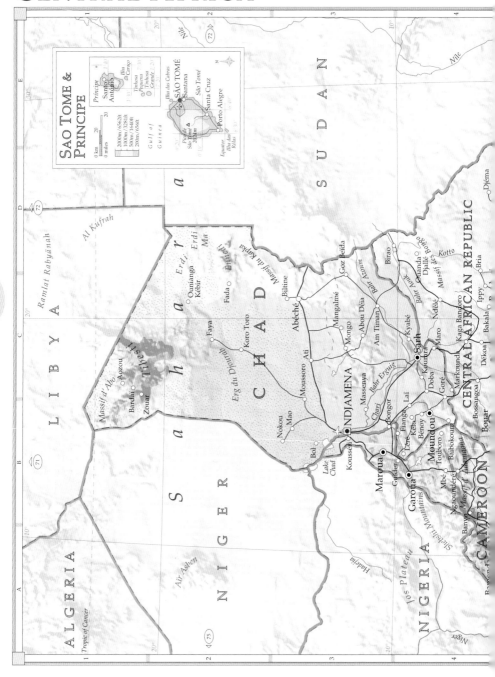

SAO TOME & PRINCIPE

Príncipe
Santo
António
Ilha
Cação

Ilha das Cabras
SÃO TOMÉ
Santana
São Tomé
Santa Cruz
Porto Alegre
Pico de São Tomé
2024m
Ilha das Rôlas
Equator

Gulf of Guinea

0 km   20
0 miles   20

2000m / 6562ft
1000m / 3281ft
50m / 164ft
20m / 65ft

LIBYA

Ramlat Rabyānah

Al Kūfrah

SUDAN

Nile

Djema

Sahara

Erdi Ma
Ennedi
Erdi

Ounianga Kébir
Fada
Biltine

Tibesti
Massif du Kapka

Massif a' Abo
Bardaï
Zouar

Faya
Koro Toro

Abéché

Goz Beïda
Birao

CHAD
Mangalmé
Mongo

Ati
Moussoro

Am Timan

Abou Déïa

CENTRAL AFRICAN REPUBLIC

Bria
Ippy
Bakala

Ndélé
Kaga Bandoro

NIGER

Nokou
Mao

Bol
Lake Chad

NDJAMENA

Massenya
Bousso

Bahr Erguig

Chari

Bongor
Fianga

Sarh
Koumra
Doba
Goré

Kyabé
Maro

Markounda
Dékoa
Bossangoa

Bouar

Kousséri
Maroua
Guider

Bénoye
Kélo
Léré

Lai

Toubouro
Babokoum

Garoua
Mbé

Ngaoundéré

CAMEROON

NIGERIA

Jos Plateau

Hadejia

Niger

Tropic of Cancer

ALGERIA

0 km   400
0 miles   400

POPULATION
○ Less than 50,000   ○ 50,000 -100,000   ◉ 100,000 - 500,000   ◼ Over 500,000

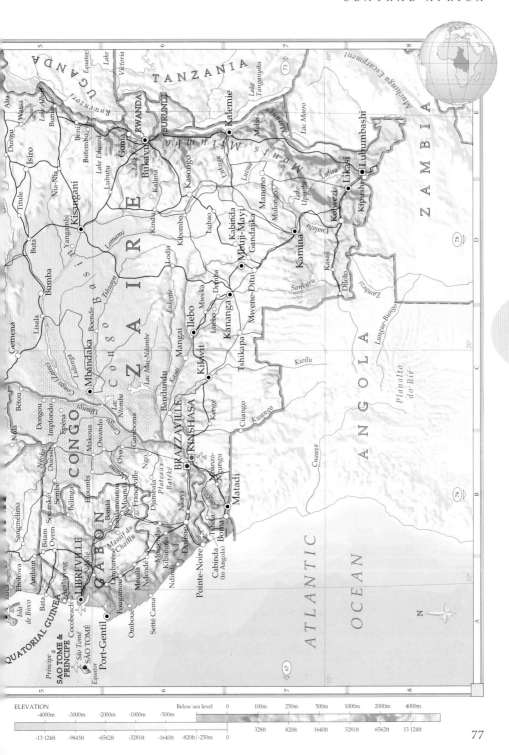

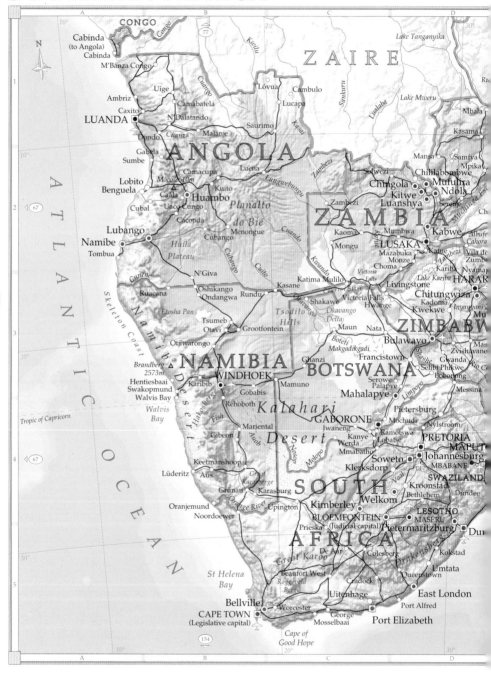

CONGO

Cabinda
(to Angola)
Cabinda

M'Banza Congo

Ambriz
Uíge
Caxito
LUANDA
Dondo
Gabela
Sumbe

Lobito
Benguela

Cubal

Lubango

Namibe
Tombua

Ruacana

Camabatela
N'Dalatando

Malanje

Camacupa
Moço 2510m
Caála
Uaco Cungo
Caconda

Cubango

N'Giva

Oshikango
Ondangwa

Lóvua
Cambulo
Lucapa

Saurimo

Luena

ANGOLA

Kuito
Huambo

*Planalto
do Bié*

Menongue

*Huíla
Plateau*

Cunene

Rundu

Cuanza

Z A I R E

Lake Tanganyika

Mbala
Kasama

Mansa
Solwezi
Chingola
Kitwe
Luanshya
Mumbwa

Mongu
Kaoma

Samfya
Mpika
Chililabombwe
Mufulira
Ndola
Serenje

Kabwe
LUSAKA
Mazabuka
Monze
Choma

Z A M B I A

Kasane

Katima Mulilo

Shakawe

Victoria Falls
Hwange

Maun

Nata

*Tsodilo
Hills*

*Okavango
Delta*

Ghanzi

Mbala

Rı

Mbala

Lake Mweru

Lualaba

Zambezi

Kwando

Cuando

Cuito

Livingstone

Lake Kariba
Kariba

*Albufe
Cahora*

Zambezi
Zumb
Nyama

HARAR

Chitungwiza
Kadoma
Kwekwe
Inyangani
Mu

ZIMBABW

Bulawayo
Francistown
Serowe
Palapye

Mahalapye

BOTSWANA

Makgadikgadi

Boteti

Gweru
Zvishavane
Gwanda
Selibi Phikwe
Bobonong

Mas

Messina

Limpopo

Pietersburg

Mochudi

PRETORIA

Brandberg
2573m

Karibib

WINDHOEK

Gobabis

Rehoboth

Kalahari

Desert

Mamuno

Jwaneng

GABORONE

Kanye
Werda
Mmabatho

Ramotswa
Lobatse

Hentiesbaai
Swakopmund
Walvis Bay

*Walvis
Bay*

Keetmanshoop

Lüderitz
Aus

Oranjemund
Noordoewer

Upington

Gibeon

Mariental

*Great
Karasberge*
Karasburg

Grünau

Orange River

Kimberley

Prieska

Klerksdorp

BLOEMFONTEIN
(Judicial capital)

S O U T H

De Aar

Colesberg

MAPUT

Nylstroom

Johannesburg

Soweto

MBABANE

SWAZILAND

Kroonstad
Bethlehem

Welkom

LESOTHO
MASERU

Dundee

Pietermaritzburg

Dur

Drakensberg

Kokstad

A F R I C A

Great Karoo

*Roggeveld
Berge*

Beaufort West

*St Helena
Bay*

Bellville
CAPE TOWN
(Legislative capital)

Worcester

George
Mosselbaai

*Cape of
Good Hope*

Cradock

Uitenhage

Port Elizabeth

Queenstown

Umtata

East London

Port Alfred

ATLANTIC OCEAN

Skeleton Coast

Namib Desert

Tropic of Capricorn

NAMIBIA

Otjiwarongo

Tsumeb
Otavi

Grootfontein

Etosha Pan

0 km   400

0 miles   400

POPULATION

 Less than 50,000

 50,000 -100,000

 100,000 - 500,000

 Over 500,000

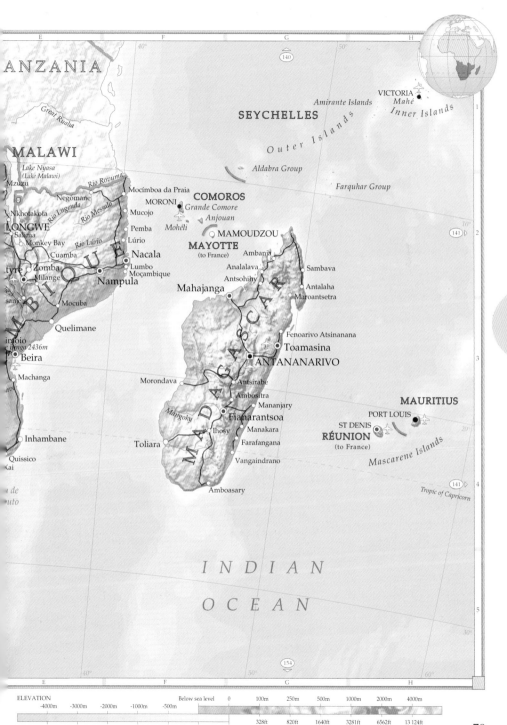

ELEVATION

				Below sea level	0	100m	250m	500m	1000m	2000m	4000m
-4000m	-3000m	-2000m	-1000m	-500m							
-13 124ft	-9843ft	-6562ft	-3281ft	-1640ft	-820ft/-250m	0	328ft	820ft	1640ft	3281ft	6562ft	13 124ft

155

Norwegian
Basin

REYKJAVÍK
ICELAND
Vatnajökull

Arctic Circle

Norwegian
Sea

Faeroe-Iceland
Ridge

FAEROE ISLANDS
(to Denmark)

Trondheim

Iceland
Basin

Faeroe-Shetland
Trough
Shetland Islands

Bergen

N
O
R

OSLO

Rockall Bank

Outer Hebrides

Orkney Islands

Stavanger

Gothenburg
Ålborg
Jylland

Jönk

MID-ATLANTIC RIDGE

Porcupine
Plain

British
Isles

Glasgow
Edinburgh
Belfast

North
Sea

DENMARK COPEN
Odense Ma

A T L A N T I C

REPUBLIC
OF
IRELAND
DUBLIN

UNITED
KINGDOM
Liverpool Manchester

O C E A N

Celtic
Sea
Cardiff

Birmingham

LONDON

NETHERLANDS
AMSTERDAM
Rotterdam

Hamburg
Elbe
Hannover

West
European
Basin

English Channel
Channel Islands
le Havre
Seine

BELGIUM BRUSSELS
Liège
LUXEMBOURG
LUXEMBOURG

Bonn

BERLIN

GERMANY
Frankfurt
am Main

Wroc
PF
CZE
REPU

Azores-Biscay Rise

Rennes

PARIS
Nantes *Loire* Orleans

Strasbourg
Stuttgart

Rhine

Biscay Plain
Bay of Biscay

FRANCE

Zürich
BERN
SWITZERLAND

Munich
LIECH.
Innsbruck

BRA
VIENN
Salzburg
AUSTRIA

Iberian
Plain

A Coruña

Bordeaux
Bilbao
Cordillera
Cantábrica

Lyon

Mont Blanc
4807m

Milan
SLOVENIA
Venice
Po
Turin

Trieste
HUB
CR

Porto

Douro

Massif
Central

Nice

PORTUGAL

Iberian
Zaragoza
Ebro

Toulouse
Pyrenees

ANDORRA

MONACO
Marseille

Bologna
Pisa

SAN
MARINO
SA
Mc

LISBON
MADRID
Tagus

Peninsula
Guadalquivir

Barcelona
Corsica

VATICAN CITY
ROME

Adriatic

Madeira
(to Portugal)

SPAIN

Seville

Valencia
Mallorca
Menorca

Naples
Bari

GIBRALTAR
(to UK)
Strait of Gibraltar
Málaga
Ceuta
(to Spain)

Eivissa
Palma
Balearic Islands

Sardinia

Tyrrhenian
Cagliari *Sea*

M e d i t e r
Balearic Plain

Cosenza

Canary Islands
(to Spain)

Melilla
(to Spain)

Palermo
Monti Et
4340m
Catani
Sicily

N

Atlas Mountains

A F R I C A

68

MALTA
VALLETTA

r a
n e
a

POPULATION

○ Less than 50,000   ○ 50,000 -100,000   ◉ 100,000 - 500,000   ■ Over 500,000

0 km   500

0 miles   500

Barents Sea

North Cape

Ostrov Kolguyev

Arctic Circle

Ob'

Irtysh

Murmansk

Kola
Peninsula

FINLAND

White
Sea

Archangel

Northern Dvina

Ural Mountains

R U S S I A N

112

Tampere

Lake Onega

Perm'

Turku HELSINKI

Lake Ladoga

Vologda

F E D E R A T I O N

sala

TALLINN

Saint Petersburg

Yaroslavl'

Ufa

OCKHOLM

ESTONIA

RĪGA

LATVIA

Kazan'

Nizhniy
Novgorod

MOSCOW

Ul'yanovsk

Orenburg

Samara

Ural

Vitsyebsk

LITHUANIA

ingrad Kaunas

VILNIUS

MINSK

nsk

Babruysk

Homyel'

Voronezh

Don

Volgograd

Astrakhan'

oszcz

WARSAW Brest

BELORUSSIA

Pripet
Marshes

Bug

AND

Kraków

L'viv

KIEV

Dnieper

Kharkiv

Dnipropetrovs'k

Rostov-na-Donu

Aral Sea

Sur Darya

Amu Darya

AKIA

Chernivtsi

Dniester

UKRAINE

Dnieper
Lowland

Donets'k

PEST

MOLDAVIA

CHIŞINĂU

Odesa

Sea of
Azov

Stavropol'

ARY Cluj-Napoca

ROMANIA

Braşov

Crimea

Caucasus

El'brus 5642m

Caspian Sea

112

BELGRADE

BUCHAREST

Constanţa

Simferopol'

GO-
AVIA

Danube

Black Sea

BULGARIA Varna

Mountains

SOFIA

Burgas

MACED

ANA

NIA

Aegean
Sea

Anatolia Plateau

Kūhhā-ye Zāgros

GREECE ATHENS

Piraeus

Tigris

e a

Irákleio

Crete

Cyprus

Syrian
Desert

118

Euphrates

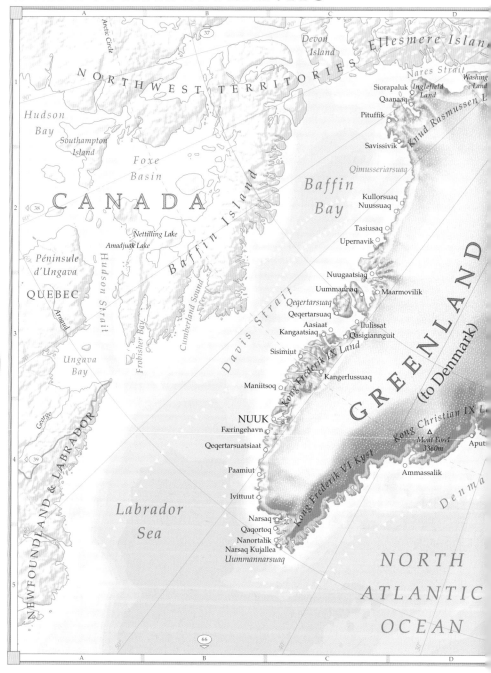

Arctic Circle

Devon
Island

Ellesmere Island

NORTHWEST TERRITORIES

Nares Strait

Washing
Land

Siorapaluk Inglefield
Land

Qaanaaq

Pituffik

Knud Rasmussen L.

Hudson
Bay

Southampton
Island

Savissivik

Qimusseriarsuaq

Foxe
Basin

Baffin
Bay

Kullorsuaq
Nuussuaq

CANADA

Nettilling Lake

Amadjuak Lake

Tasiusaq

Upernavik

Péninsule
d'Ungava

Nuugaatsiaq

Uummannaq   Maarmovilik

QUEBEC

Qeqertarsuaq
Qeqertarsuaq

Aasiaat   Ilulissat

Kangaatsiaq   Qasigianguit

Sisimiut

GREENLAND

Ungava
Bay

Maniitsoq   Kangerlussuaq

George

NUUK

Kong Christian IX L.

Mont Forel
3360m

Aput

Færingehavn

Qeqertarsuatsiaat

Ammassalik

Paamiut

Denma

Labrador
Sea

Ivittuut

NEWFOUNDLAND & LABRADOR

Narsaq
Qaqortoq
Nanortalik
Narsaq Kujallea
Uummannarsuaq

NORTH

ATLANTIC

OCEAN

0 km   400

0 miles   400

POPULATION

○ Less than 50,000   ○ 50,000 -100,000   ◉ 100,000 - 500,000   ◼ Over 500,000

ARCTIC
OCEAN

SVALBARD
(to Norway)

Lincoln
Sea

Peary
Land

Kap Bridgman

Wandel
Sea

Independence Fjord

Nord

Kong
Frederik VIII
Land

Danmark Havn

Greenland
Sea

Kong
Kristinn X
Land

Daneborg

Kangertittivaq

Ittoqqortoormiit

Zemlya
Frantsa-Iosifa

155

Kvitøya

Nordaustlandet

Novaya
Zemlya

Kong Karls Land

Spitsbergen
Pyramiden
LONGYEARBYEN
Barentsberg

Barentsøya

Edgeøya

Storfjorden

Barents
Sea

110

Bjørnøya
(to Norway)

Nordkapp
(North Cape)

FINLAND

Arctic Circle

84

JAN MAYEN
(to Norway)

Norwegian
Sea

Vestfjorden

SWEDEN

ICELAND

Bolungarvík
Siglufjördhur   Raufarhöfn
rdhur   Húsavík
        Akureyri
Stykkishólmur   Seydhisfjördhur
REYKJAVÍK   Neskaupstadhur
    Selfoss   Djúpivogur
Þlákshöfn   Vatnajökull
        Hvannadalshnúkur
        2119m
sey   Vestmannaeyjar

Gulf
of
Bothnia

FAEROE ISLANDS
(to Denmark)

N

TÓRSHAVN

NORWAY

Shetland
Islands

85

ELEVATION
-4000m   -3000m   -2000m   -1000m   -500m   Below sea level   0   100m   250m   500m   1000m   2000m   4000m

-13 124ft   -9843ft   -6562ft   -3281ft   -1640ft   -820ft/-250m   0   328ft   820ft   1640ft   3281ft   6562ft   13 124ft

SCANDINAVIA & FINLAND

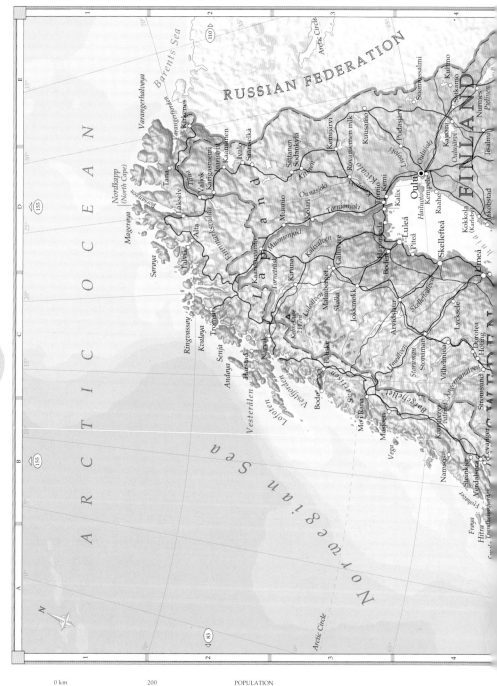

0 km	200
0 miles	200

POPULATION

○ Less than 50,000   ◎ 50,000 -100,000   ◉ 100,000 - 500,000   ■ Over 500,000

Barents Sea

RUSSIAN FEDERATION

FINLAND

Suomussalmi
Kuhmo
Nurmes
Kajaani
Oulujärvi
Iisalmi
Jakobstad
Kuusamo
Posjärvi
Leppäki
Oulu
Oulujoki
Kemijärvi
Salla
Raahe
Kokkola
(Karleby)
Pudasjärvi
Rovaniemen mlk
Kemijoki
Tornio
Kemi
Haukipudas
Kempele
Kalix
Skellefteå
Umeå
Kiruna
Sodankylä
Kitinen
Sättanen
Ounasjoki
Muonio
Kolari
Tornionjoki
Kaamanen
Kvarsjärvi
Ivalo
Saariselkä
Kaaresuvanto
Muonionjoki
Karigasniemi
Valjok
Kautokeino
Finnmarksvidda
Tanafjorden
Varangerfjorden
Kirkenes
Varangerhalvøya
Tana
Porsangen
Karasjok
Tärma
Lakselv
Alta
Talvik
Nordkapp
(North Cape)
Magerøya
Sørøya
Ringvassøy
Kvaløya
Senja
Tromsø
Andøya
Harstad
Narvik
Fauske
Bodø
Vesterålen
Lofoten
Vestfjorden
Saltfjorden
Mo i Rana
Mosjøen
Vega
Namsos
Steinkjer
Verdalsøra
Levanger
Frøya
Hitra
Kjerringøy
Borgefjell
Kvikkjokk
Jokkmokk
Skalka
Stalka
Luleälven
Kaitumälven
Kebnekaise 2117 m
Gällivare
Lansjärv
Malmberget
Haparanda
Boden
Luleå
Piteå
Älvsbyn
Arvidsjaur
Skellefteälven
Storuman
Sorsele
Storavan
Lycksele
Vilhelmina
Ångermanälven
Dorotea
Hoting
Strömsund
Vindelälven
Kalixälven
Överkalix
Jukkasjärvi
Kalaälven
Råneå

A R C T I C   O C E A N

L a p l a n d

Arctic Circle

N o r w e g i a n   S e a

Arctic Circle

N

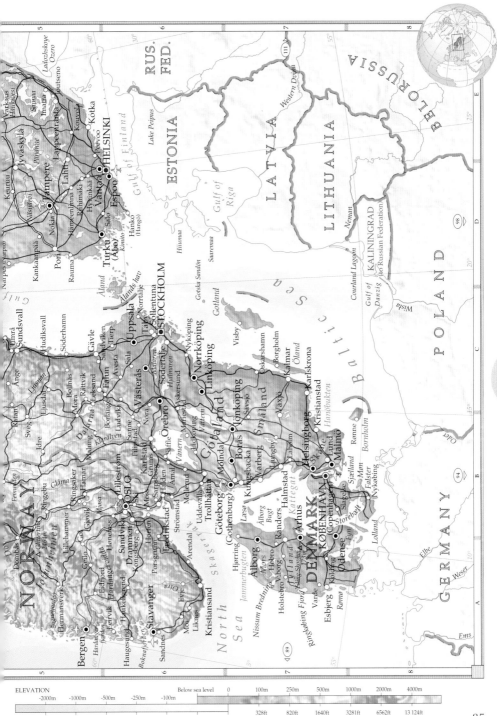

ELEVATION

					Below sea level	0	100m	250m	500m	1000m	2000m	4000m
-2000m	-1000m	-500m	-250m	-100m								
-6562ft	-3281ft	-1640ft	-820ft	-328ft	-164ft/-50m	0	328ft	820ft	1640ft	3281ft	6562ft	13 124ft

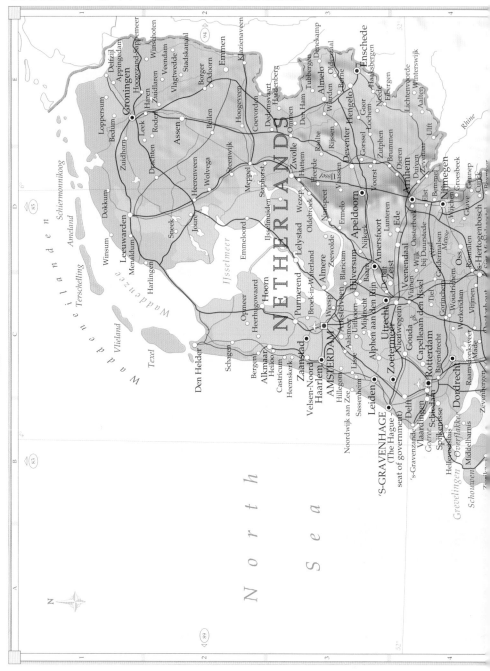

POPULATION

○ Less than 50,000 ○ 50,000 - 100,000 ◉ 100,000 - 500,000 ■ Over 500,000

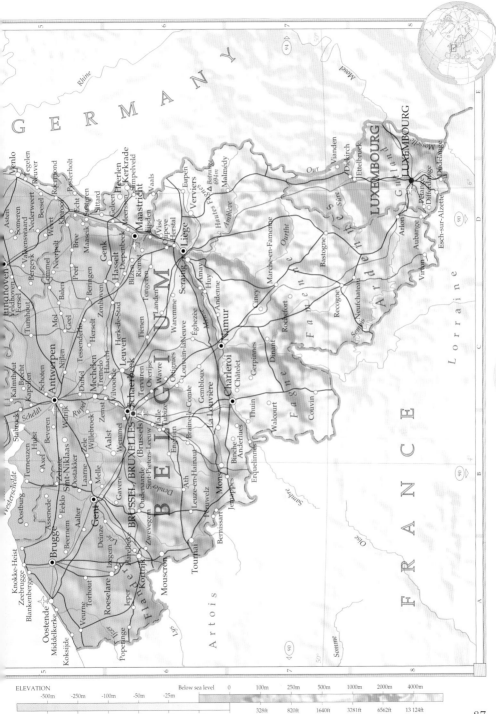

ELEVATION

					Below sea level	0	100m	250m	500m	1000m	2000m	4000m
-500m	-250m	-100m	-50m	-25m								
							328ft	820ft	1640ft	3281ft	6562ft	13 124ft
-1640ft	-820ft	-328ft	-164ft	-82ft	-33ft/-10m	0						

THE BRITISH ISLES

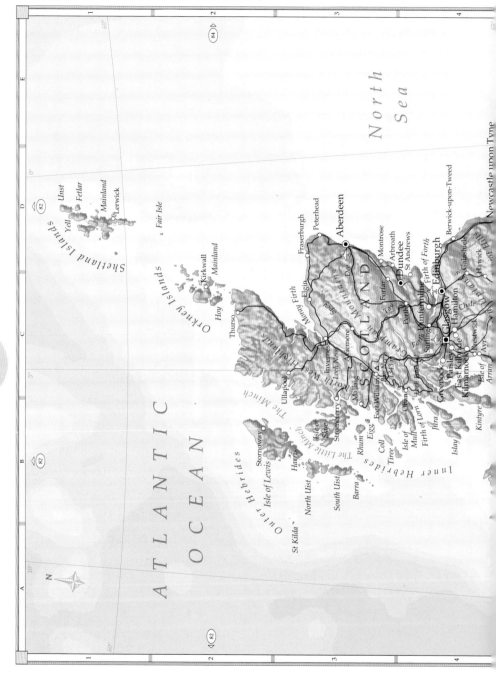

North Sea

ATLANTIC OCEAN

Shetland Islands

Unst
Fetlar
Yell
Mainland
Lerwick

Fair Isle

Orkney Islands

Kirkwall
Mainland
Hoy

Thurso

SCOTLAND

Peterhead
Fraserburgh
Aberdeen
Dee

Montrose
Arbroath
Dundee
St Andrews
Forfar
Firth of Forth
Edinburgh
Berwick-upon-Tweed

Elgin
Moray Firth
Nairn

Grampian Mountains
Tay
Perth

Newcastle upon Tyne
Galashiels
Hawick
Cheviot Hills

Glasgow
Hamilton
Clyde
Stirling
Kilmarnock
Prestwick
Ayr

Aviemore
Inverness
Loch Ness

North West Highlands

Ullapool

Malaig
Fort William
Ben Nevis 1343

Oban
Firth of Lorn
Isle of Mull
Jura
Islay

Kintyre
Arran
Isle of Arran

Inner Hebrides

The Minch
The Little Minch

Isle of Skye
Stromeferry
Rhum
Eigg
Coll
Tiree

Outer Hebrides

Stornoway
Isle of Lewis
Harris
North Uist
South Uist
Barra

St Kilda

N

0 km   100

0 miles   100

POPULATION

 Less than 50,000   ○ 50,000 -100,000   ● 100,000 - 500,000   ■ Over 500,000

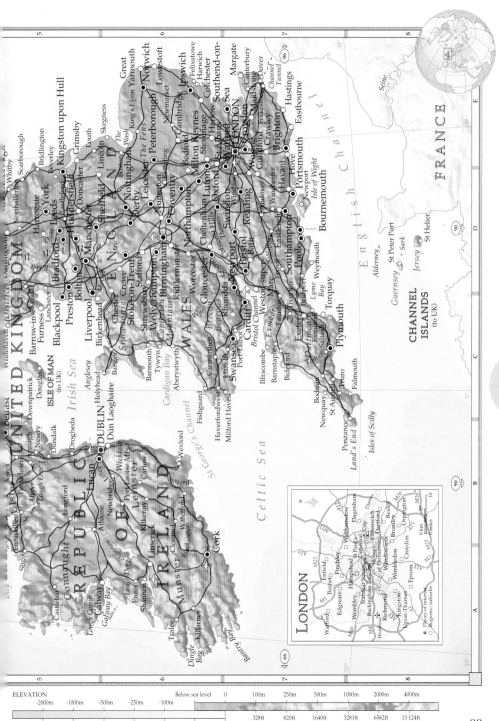

ELEVATION

-2000m	-1000m	-500m	-250m	-100m	Below sea level	0	100m	250m	500m	1000m	2000m	4000m
-6562ft	-3281ft	-1640ft	-820ft	-328ft	-164ft/-50m	0	328ft	820ft	1640ft	3281ft	6562ft	13 124ft

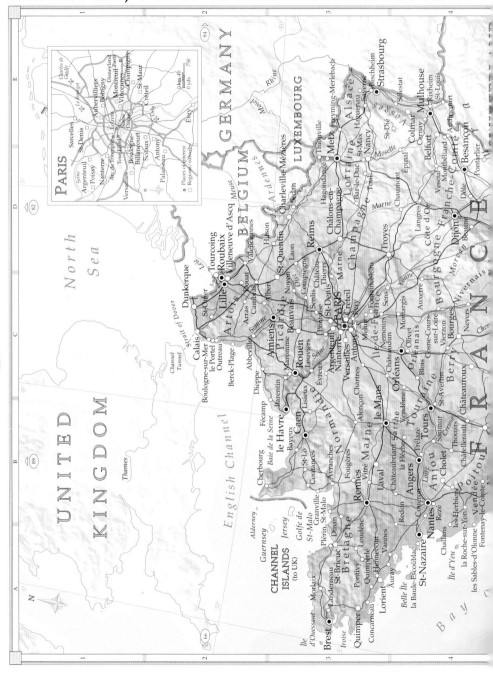

PARIS

Charles de Gaulle
Sarcelles
St-Denis
Argenteuil
Nanterre
Poissy
Versailles
Arc de Triomphe
Tour Eiffel
Boulogne-
Billancourt
Palaiseau
Disneyland
Bobigny
Montreuil Paris
Vincennes
St-Maur
Créteil
Antony
Sceaux
Orly
Evry

□ Places of interest
□ Regions/suburbs

□ km 10
0 yds 750

North Sea

UNITED KINGDOM

Thames

Channel Tunnel

English Channel

GERMANY

BELGIUM

LUXEMBOURG

Ardennes

Rhine

Moselle

Strasbourg
Bischheim
Mulhouse
St-Louis
Rixheim
Colmar
Sélestat
Cernay
Haguenau
Sarreguemines
St-Dié
Vosges
Épinal
St-Max
Nancy
Toul
Bar-le-Duc
Metz
Freyming-Merlebach
Thionville
Hagondange

Dunkerque
Calais
Boulogne-sur-Mer
le Portel
Outreau
Berck-Plage
St-Omer
Tourcoing
Roubaix
Lille
Villeneuve d'Ascq
Lys
Artois
Lens
Douai
Valenciennes
Hirson
Charleville-Mézières
Sedan
Meuse

Abbeville
Amiens
Arras
Cambrai
Albert
Picardie
Somme
Marquion
Beauvais
Noyon
St-Quentin
Laon
Oise
Compiègne
Senlis
Château-Thierry
St-Denis
Reims
Châlons-en-Champagne
Marne
Vitry-le-François
Bar-le-Duc
Lorraine
Alsace

Fécamp
Dieppe
Barentin
Rouen
Louviers
Évreux
Marne-la-Vallée
Pontoise
Argenteuil
Nanterre
PARIS
Versailles
Créteil
Antony
Île-de-France
Melun
Châteaudun
Nemours
Fontainebleau
Sens
Montargis
Auxerre
Troyes
Chaumont
Langres
Côte d'Or
Dijon
Morvan
Bourgogne
Franche-Comté
Vesoul
Montbéliard
Belfort
Besançon
Dôle
Pontarlier

Cherbourg
Baie de la Seine
le Havre
Caen
Bayeux
St-Lô
Coutances
Granville
Avranches
Fougères
Normandie
Lisieux
Alençon
Chartres
le Mans
Sarthe
la Flèche
Maine
Vendôme
Blois
Orléans
Orléanais
Olivet
Gien
Cosne-Cours-sur-Loire
Berry
Bourges
Vierzon
Cher
Nevers
Nivernais
Yonne

Channel Islands (to UK)
Alderney
Guernsey
Jersey
Golfe de St-Malo
St-Malo
Plérin
St-Brieuc
Dinan
Dinard
Loudéac
Bretagne
Landerneau
Morlaix
Brest
île d'Ouessant
Iroise
Quimper
Concarneau
Lorient
Quimperlé
Hennebont
Auray
Belle île
Pontivy
Vannes
Redon
Châteaubriant
Rennes
Vitré
Laval
Château-Gontier
Angers
Anjou
Cholet
Rezé
Nantes
St-Nazaire
la Baule-Escoublac
Challans
île d'Yeu
les Sables-d'Olonne
la Roche-sur-Yon
Vendée
Poitou
Fontenay-le-Comte
les Herbiers
Trélazé
Saumur
Loire
Tours
Touraine
Amboise
Chinon
Thouars
Châtellerault
Châteauroux
Creuse
Indre
la Flèche

FRANCE

Bay

0 km 100
0 miles 100

POPULATION
 Less than 50,000
 50,000 -100,000
○ 100,000 - 500,000
 Over 500,000

ELEVATION

					Below sea level	0	100m	250m	500m	1000m	2000m	4000m
-2000m	-1000m	-500m	-250m	-100m								
							328ft	820ft	1640ft	3281ft	6562ft	13 124ft
-6562ft	-3281ft	-1640ft	-820ft	-328ft	164ft/-50m	0						

SPAIN & PORTUGAL

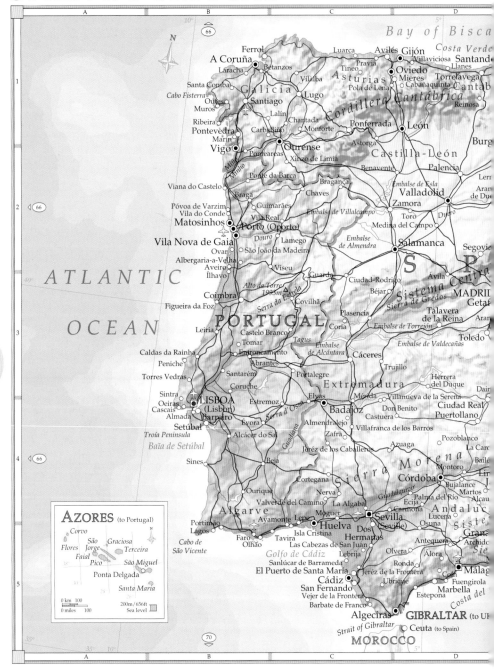

ATLANTIC

OCEAN

Bay of Biscay

Ferrol
A Coruña
Laracha
Betanzos
Luarca
Avilés
Gijón
Villaviciosa
Santand
Costa Verde
Tineo
Pravia
Oviedo
Mieres
Llanes
Torrelavega
Santa Comba
Vilalba
Asturias
Pola de Lena
Cabanaquinta
Reinosa
Outes
Santiago
Lugo
Cordillera Cantábrica
Cantab
Cabo Fisterra
Muros
Lalín
Chantada
Ponferrada
León
Burg
Ribeira
Carballino
Monforte
Astorga
Pontevedra
Marín
Castilla-León
Vigo
Ourense
Benavente
Palencia
Ponteareas
Xinzo de Limia
Embalse de Esla
Aran
de Due
Minho
Ponte da Barca
Bragança
Valladolid
Lerr
Viana do Castelo
Chaves
Zamora
Braga
Guimarães
Embalse de Villalcampo
Toro
Medina del Campo
Duero
Póvoa de Varzim
Vila Real
Vila do Conde
Matosinhos
Porto (Oporto)
Embalse de Almendra
Salamanca
Segovie
Vila Nova de Gaia
Douro
Lamego
São João da Madeira
S
P
Ovar
Albergaria-a-Velha
Viseu
Guarda
Ávila
Aveiro
Ciudad-Rodrigo
Sistema Central
Ílhavo
Alto da Torre
1993m
Béjar
Sierra de Gredos
MADRI
Coimbra
Serra da Estrela
Covilhã
Plasencia
Talavera
de la Reina
Getaf
Figueira da Foz
Coria
Embalse de Torrejón
Aran
PORTUGAL
Castelo Branco
Tagus
Toledo
Leiria
Cáceres
Caldas da Rainha
Tomar
Embalse
de Alcántara
Embalse de Valdecañas
Peniche
Entroncamento
Trujillo
Abrantes
Torres Vedras
Santarém
Portalegre
Herrera
del Duque
Sintra
Coruche
Extremadura
Dair
Oeiras
LISBOA
Elvas
Mérida
Villanueva de la Serena
Cascais
(Lisbon)
Estremoz
Badajoz
Ciudad Real
Almada
Barreiro
Serra d' Ossa
Don Benito
Puertollano
Setúbal
Évora
Castuera
Troía Peninsula
Alcácer do Sal
Almendralejo
Villafranca de los Barros
Pozoblanco
Baía de Setúbal
Zafra
Azuaga
La Car
Sines
Beja
Juréz de los Caballeros
Sierra Morena
Montoro
Baile
Cortegana
Córdoba
Lir
Ourique
Nerva
Bujalance
Martos
Alcau
Valverde del Camino
La Algaba
Guadalquivir
Ecija
Palma del Río
Algarve
Ayamonte
Lepe
Moguer
Carmona
Sevilla
Andaluc
Lucena
Osuna
Siste
Portimão
Faro
Tavira
Isla Cristina
Huelva
Dos
(Seville)
Antequera
Grana
Lagos
Olhão
Las Cabezas de San Juan
Hermanas
Olvera
Álora
Archido
Cabo de
São Vicente
Golfo de Cádiz
Lebrija
Ronda
Sie
Sanlúcar de Barrameda
El Puerto de Santa María
Jeréz de la Frontera
Ubrique
Cól
Málag
Cádiz
Fuengirola
San Fernando
Marbella
Vejer de la Frontera
Estepona
Barbate de Franco
Algeciras
Costa del
GIBRALTAR (to U
Ceuta (to Spain)
Strait of Gibraltar
MOROCCO

AZORES (to Portugal)

Corvo
Flores
São Jorge
Graciosa
Terceira
Faial
Pico
São Miguel
Cabo de
São Vicente
Ponta Delgada
Santa Maria

0 km 100
0 miles 100

200m/656ft
Sea level

0 km 100
0 miles 100

POPULATION
○ Less than 50,000   ○ 50,000 -100,000   ◉ 100,000 - 500,000   ▣ Over 500,000

ALGERIA

ELEVATION

					Below sea level	0	100m	250m	500m	1000m	2000m	4000m
-4000m	-3000m	-2000m	-1000m	-500m								
-13 124ft	-9843ft	-6562ft	-3281ft	-1640ft	-820ft/-250m	0	328ft	820ft	1640ft	3281ft	6562ft	13 124ft

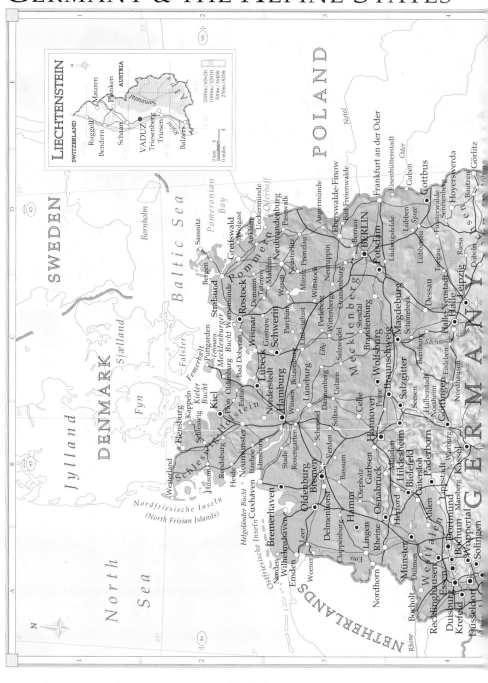

LIECHTENSTEIN

SWITZERLAND
AUSTRIA

Ruggell
Mauren
Bendern
Planken
Schaan
VADUZ
Triesenberg
Triesen
Balzers

2000m/6562ft
1000m/3281ft
500m/1640ft
250m/820ft

0 km   4
0 miles   4

SWEDEN

Bornholm

Baltic Sea

DENMARK

Sjælland

Falster

Jylland

Fyn

Fehmarn

Kieler Bucht

North Sea

Nordfriesische Inseln
(North Frisian Islands)

Helgolländer Bucht

Ostfriesische Inseln

NETHERLANDS

Pomeranian Bay

POLAND

Noteć

Oder

Frankfurt an der Oder
Eisenhüttenstadt
Guben
Cottbus
Görlitz
Hoyerswerda
Bautzen
Finsterwalde
Senftenberg
Lübben
Lübbenau
Torgau
Riesa
Döbeln
Spree

Angermünde
Eberswalde-Finow
Bad Freienwalde
Bernau
BERLIN
Potsdam
Ludwigsfelde
Dessau
Halle
Leipzig
Nauen-Neustadt

Uckermünde
Pasewalk
Prenzlau
Neubrandenburg
Neustrelitz
Oranienburg
Neuruppin
Wittstock
Perleberg
Wittenberge
Salzwedel
Stendal
Brandenburg
Magdeburg
Schönebeck
Bernburg
Eisleben
Sächsisch Saale
Nordhausen

Stralsund
Sassnitz
Bergen
Greifswald
Wolgast
Anklam
Demmin
Teterow
Waren
Güstrow
Malchin
Müritz
Rostock
Warnemünde
Schwerin
Parchim
Ludwigslust
Mecklenburg
Wolfsburg
Gifhorn
Braunschweig
Salzgitter
Seesen
Göttingen
Northeim
Halberstadt
Warburg

Wismar
Lübeck
Bad Doberan

Neumünster
Plön
Eutin
Kiel
Schleswig-Holstein
Norderstedt
Hamburg
Winsen
Boizenburg
Dannenberg
Uelzen
Celle
Hannover
Hildesheim

Flensburg
Kappeln
Schleswig
Rendsburg
Husum
Heide
Westerland

Itzehoe
Elmshorn
Stade
Rosengarten
Verden
Soltau
Schneverdingen
Lüneburg

Cuxhaven
Bremerhaven
Wilhelmshaven
Emden
Norden
Leer
Weener
Nordhorn

Bremen
Oldenburg
Delmenhorst
Cloppenburg
Lingen
Rheine
Bocholt

Bassum
Diepholz
Ham
Osnabrück
Herford
Bielefeld
Gütersloh
Münster
Dülmen
Recklinghausen
Bocholt

Minden
Hameln
Paderborn
Lippstadt
Marsberg
Kassel
Ahlen
Hamm
Dortmund
Bochum
Essen
Duisburg
Krefeld
Wuppertal
Solingen
Düsseldorf

GERMANY

Westfalen

Rhine
Ems

N

94

0 km   100

0 miles   100

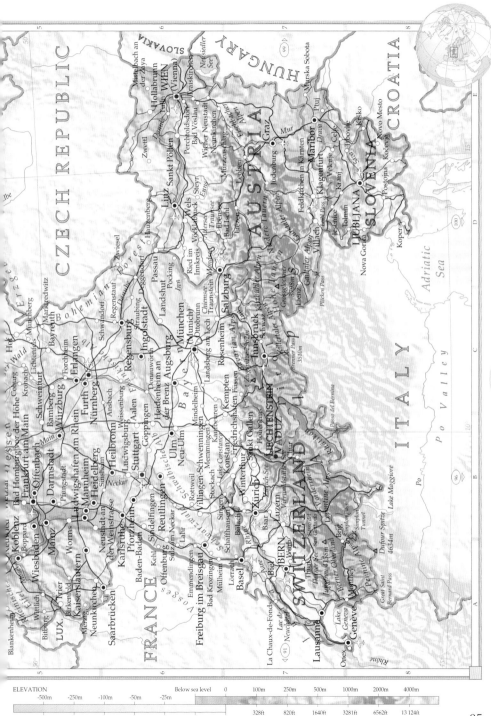

CZECH REPUBLIC

SLOVAKIA

HUNGARY

CROATIA

SLOVENIA

AUSTRIA

ITALY

FRANCE

SWITZERLAND

LIECHTENSTEIN
VADUZ

Erzgebirge
Bohmerwald
Bohmian Forest
Böhmerwald
Bayerischer Wald
Bayern
Schwäbische Alb
Jura suisse
Vosges
Eifel
Rheinisches
Hohe Tauern
Niedere Tauern
Po Valley
Adriatic Sea

Ilbe

WIEN
Vienna
Hollabrunn
Mistelbach an der Zaya
Neusiedler See
Wiener Neustadt
Neunkirchen
Wr. Neustadt
Perchtoldsdorf
Sankt Pölten
Linz
Wels
Steyr
Enns
Voitsberg
Leoben
Mürzzuschlag
Judenburg
Graz
Mur
Maribor
Ptuj
Murska Sobota
Celje
Velenje
Krško
Novo Mesto
Kočevje
Ljubljana
Kranj
Jesenice
Villach
Klagenfurt
Feldkirchen in Kärnten
Spittal
Tolmin
Nova Gorica
Postojna
Koper
Lienz
Plöcken Pass
Zwettl
Krems
Zwiesel
Schwandorf
Deggendorf
Passau
Regenstauf
Regensburg
Straubing
Landshut
Ingolstadt
Donauwörth
Eichstätt
Heidenheim an der Brenz
Aalen
Schwäbisch Gmünd
Göppingen
Augsburg
München
Munich
Freising
Dachau
Landsberg am Lech
Memmingen
Ottobrunn
Rosenheim
Traunstein
Bad Reichenhall
Salzburg
Bad Ischl
Bad Aussee
Ebensee
Gmunden
Vöcklabruck
Ried im Innkreis
Pocking
Inn
Mondsee
Traunsee
Attersee
Hallstätter See
Dachstein 2996m
Grossglockner 3798m
Grossvenediger 3666m
Zell am See
Schwaz
Innsbruck
Zugspitze 2962m
Füssen
Kempten
Kaufbeuren
Mindelheim
Wessling-Schwenningen
Kufstein
Premier Pass 3510m
Passo del Bernina
Passo del Stelvio
St Anton
Bludenz
Feldkirch
Bregenz
Dornbirn
Lindau
Friedrichshafen
Sankt Gallen
Konstanz
Lake Constance
Bodensee
Singen
Winterthur
Zürich
Baar
Luzern
Schaffhausen
Stein am Rhein
Frauenfeld
Rhein
Vorarlberger Alpen
Lechtaler Alpen
Ötztaler Alpen
Stubaier Alpen
Montafon
Chur
Davos
Arlberg
Rhätikon
Hof
Bayreuth
Bamberg
Schweinfurt
Würzburg
Nürnberg
Fürth
Erlangen
Forchheim
Ansbach
Lichtenfels
Kronach
Marktredwitz
Weiden
Münchberg
Hauzenberg
Coburg
Bad Homburg vor der Höhe
Frankfurt am Main
Offenbach
Darmstadt
Pirmasens
Mainz
Wiesbaden
Koblenz
Boppard
Worms
Ludwigshafen am Rhein
Mannheim
Neustadt an der Weinstrasse
Heidelberg
Sinsheim
Heilbronn
Ludwigsburg
Stuttgart
Pforzheim
Karlsruhe
Baden-Baden
Kehl
Offenburg
Lahr
Sulz am Neckar
Rottweil
Reutlingen
Sindelfingen
Villingen-Schwenningen
Stockach
Tuttlingen
Neckar
Main
Neu-Ulm
Ulm
Trier
Birkenfeld
Kaiserslautern
Neunkirchen
Saarbrücken
Bitburg
Wittlich
Blankenheim
Merzig
LUX.
Rheinisches
Emmendingen
Freiburg im Breisgau
Bad Krozingen
Lörrach
Basel
Biel
BERN
Worb
Thun
Brienzer See
Thuner See
Interlaken
Berner Oberland
Jungfrau 4158m
Lauterbrunnen
Lötschental
Wallis
Berner Alpen
Grindelwald
Sargans
Vaduz
Liechtensteiner
Säntis
Glärnisch
Pennine Alps
Great Saint Bernard Pass
Grand Combin
Mont Blanc
Simplon Pass
Simplon Tunnel
Dufour Spitze 4634m
Monte Rosa
La Chaux-de-Fonds
Lac de Neuchâtel
Neuchâtel
Lausanne
Genève
Lake Geneva
Lac Léman
Orbe
Rhône
Lake Maggiore
Lago Maggiore
Po
Vierwaldstätter See
Zürich See
Walen See
Lago di Lugano

ELEVATION

					Below sea level	0	100m	250m	500m	1000m	2000m	4000m
-500m	-250m	-100m	-50m	-25m								
-1640ft	-820ft	-328ft	-164ft	-82ft	-33ft/-10m	0	328ft	820ft	1640ft	3281ft	6562ft	13 124ft

95

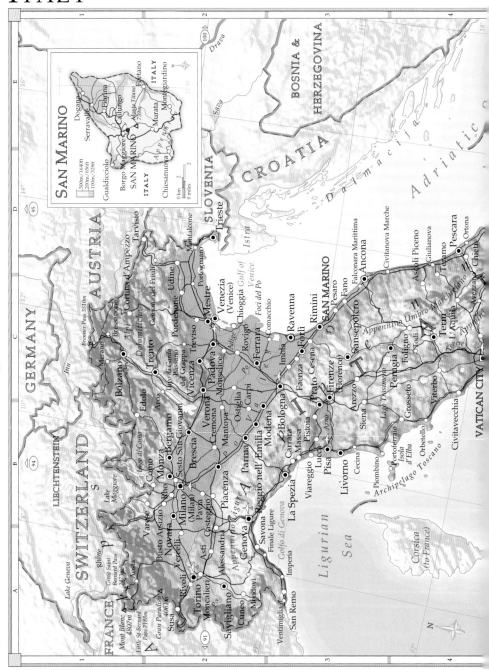

SAN MARINO

Dogana
Serravalle
Fiorina
Gualdicciolo
Borgo Maggiore
SAN MARINO
Chiesanuova
ITALY

Monte Titano
739m
Murata
Montegiardino
Faetano
ITALY

500m/1640ft
200m/656ft
100m/328ft

0 km   2
0 miles   2

GERMANY

LIECHTENSTEIN

SWITZERLAND

AUSTRIA

FRANCE

SLOVENIA

CROATIA

BOSNIA &
HERZEGOVINA

Adriatic Sea

Dalmacija

Lake Geneva
Mont Blanc
4807m
Little St-Bernard
Pass 2188m
Great Saint
Bernard Pass
Gran Paradiso
4061m
Rhône
Susa
Rivoli
Torino
Moncalieri
Savigliano
Cuneo
Mondovi
Ventimiglia
San Remo
Imperia
Finale Ligure
Savona
Genova
Alessandria
Asti
Novara
Busto Arsizio
Vercelli
Gattico
Pavia
Milano
(Milan)
Monza
Como
Varese
Lago di Como
Lake
Maggiore
Lago Maggiore
Inn
Merano
Bolzano
Edolo
Arco
Trento
Alpi
Dolomitiche
Bressanone
Brenner Pass 3510m
Tarvisio
Cortina d'Ampezzo
Cividale del Friuli
Udine
Portogruaro
Monfalcone
Trieste
Istra
Gulf of
Venice
Venezia
(Venice)
Mestre
Chioggia
Foci del Po
Comacchio
Ravenna
Rimini
Pesaro
Fano
Falconara Marittima
Ancona
Civitanova Marche
Ascoli Piceno
Giulianova
Teramo
Pescara
Ortona
Chieti
Avezzano
L'Aquila
Terni
Todi
Foligno
Perugia
Umbro-Marchetiano
Appennino
SAN MARINO
Sansepolcro
Forlì
Faenza
Imola
Cesena
Prato
Firenze
(Florence)
Arezzo
Siena
Lago Trasimeno
Viterbo
Grosseto
Orbetello
Civitavecchia
VATICAN CITY
Archipelago Toscano
Corsica
(to France)
Ligurian
Sea
Golfo di Genova
Appennino Ligure
La Spezia
Carrara
Massa
Viareggio
Lucca
Pisa
Livorno
Cecina
Piombino
Isola
d'Elba
Portoferraio
Reggio nell'Emilia
Parma
Piacenza
Cremona
Mantova
Bergamo
Brescia
Sesto San Giovanni
Vicenza
Padova
Monselice
Treviso
Pordenone
Cremona del Friuli
Ostiglia
Carpi
Modena
Bologna
Ferrara
Rovigo
Verona
Lago di Garda
Lugo di Bassano
del Grappa

POPULATION

○ Less than 50,000

○ 50,000 -100,000

◉ 100,000 - 500,000

■ Over 500,000

0 km   100

0 miles   100

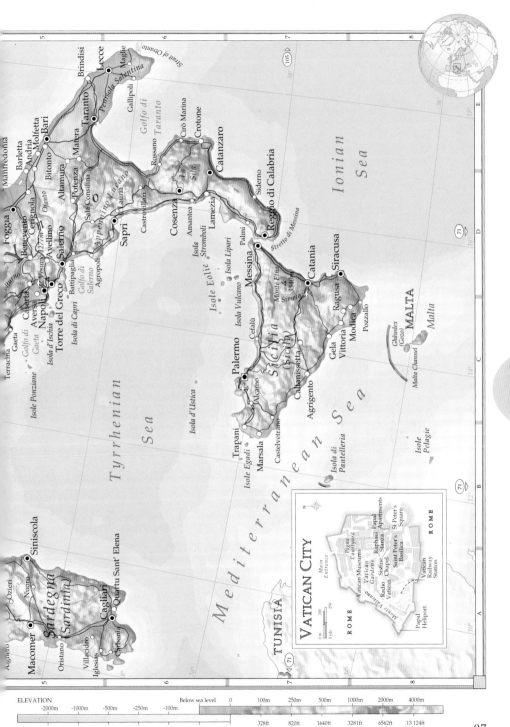

Strait of Otranto
Lecce
Brindisi
Maglie
Penisola Salentina
Taranto
Gallipoli
Golfo di Taranto
Manfredonia
Barletta
Molfetta
Andria
Bari
Bitonto
Matera
Ciro Marina
Rossano
Crotone
Altamura
Potenza
Lauria
Catanzaro
Foggia
Cerignola
Ofanto
Sala Consilina
Appennino Lucano
Castrovillari
La Sila
Benevento
Avellino
Sapri
Cosenza
Amantea
Siderno
Reggio di Calabria
Vesuvio 1277m
Salerno
Agropoli
Lamezia
Palmi
Ionian Sea
Caserta
Napoli
Golfo di Salerno
Isola Stromboli
Isola Lipari
Messina
Stretto di Messina
Aversa
Torre del Greco
Battipaglia
Isola di Capri
Isole Eolie
Isola Vulcano
Cefalù
Monte Etna 3340m
Catania
Siracusa
Gaeta
Golfo di Gaeta
Isola d'Ischia
Ragusa
Simeto
Terracina
Isole Ponziane
Modica
Pozzallo
MALTA
Gozo (Ghawdex)
Malta
Tyrrhenian Sea
Palermo
Sicilia (Sicily)
Gela
Vittoria
Malta Channel
Isola d'Ustica
Alcamo
Caltanissetta
Agrigento
Isole Pelagie
Trapani
Marsala
Castelvetrano
Isole Egadi
Isola di Pantelleria
Mediterranean Sea
Siniscola
Quartu Sant'Elena
Ozieri
Nuoro
Sardegna (Sardinia)
Cagliari
Macomer
Oristano
Villacidro
Carbonia
Iglesias
TUNISIA

Brindisi
Brindisi

VATICAN CITY

N
Pigna Courtyard
Vatican Museums
Vatican Gardens
Radio Vatican
Sistine Chapel
Raphael Stanza
Papal Apartments
St Peter's Square
Saint Peter's Basilica
Vatican Railway Station
Monte Paziano
Main Entrance
ROME
ROME
ROME
Papal Heliport
0 m   200
0 yds   200

ELEVATION

-2000m	-1000m	-500m	-250m	-100m	Below sea level	0	100m	250m	500m	1000m	2000m	4000m
-6562ft	-3281ft	-1640ft	-820ft	-328ft	-164ft/-50m	0	328ft	820ft	1640ft	3281ft	6562ft	13 124ft

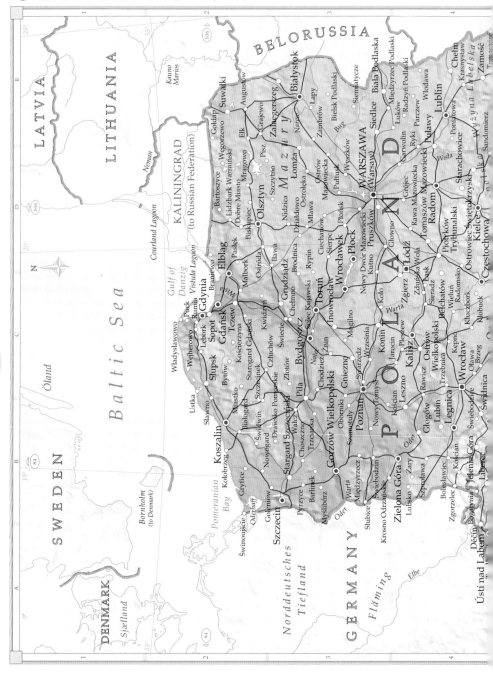

LATVIA

LITHUANIA

KALININGRAD
(to Russian Federation)

BELORUSSIA

POLAND

WARSZAWA
(Warsaw)

SWEDEN

DENMARK
Sjælland

Bornholm
(to Denmark)

Baltic Sea

Öland

GERMANY

Norddeutsches Tiefland

Fläming

Gulf of Danzig

Pomeranian Bay

Courland Lagoon

Białystok
Suwałki
Gdańsk
Gdynia
Szczecin
Poznań
Wrocław
Łódź
Radom
Lublin
Kielce
Częstochowa
Koszalin

0 km   100

0 miles   100

POPULATION

○ Less than 50,000   ○ 50,000 -100,000   ◉ 100,000 - 500,000   ◼ Over 500,000

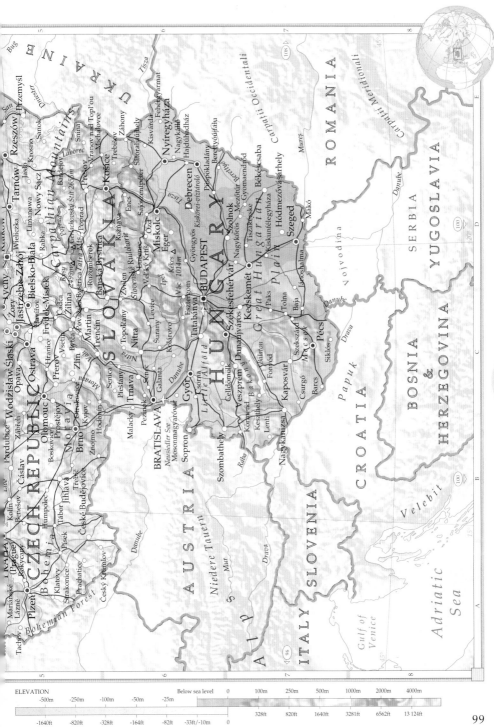

UKRAINE

ROMANIA

SERBIA

YUGOSLAVIA

BOSNIA & HERZEGOVINA

CROATIA

SLOVENIA

ITALY

AUSTRIA

CZECH REPUBLIC

SLOVAKIA

HUNGARY

Carpații Occidentali

Carpații Meridionali

Vojvodina

Velebit

Adriatic Sea

Gulf of Venice

Papuk

Great Hungarian Plain

Carpathian Mountains

Bohemia

Moravia

Bohemian Forest

Niedere Tauern

Alps

Little Alföld

Bakony

Kisalföld

Bug
San
Wisła
Dniester
Tisza
Mureş
Danube
Drava
Drau
Raba
Mur
Morava
Dunajec
Poprad
Latorica
Hornad
Bodrog
Váh
Nitra
Hron
Ipeľ
Labe
Vltava
Lužnice
Odra

Przemyśl
Rzeszów
Tarnów
Nowy Sącz
Krosno
Sanok
Bielsko-Biała
Żywiec
Jastrzębie-Zdrój
Wodzisław Śląski
Rabka
Limanowa
Sabinov
Bardejov
Snina
Humenné
Vranov nad Topľou
Michalovce
Stropkov
Svidník
Laborec
Prešov
Košice
Trebišov
Sátoraljaújhely
Kráľovský Chlmec
Sárospatak
Zápoľce
Záhony
Kisvárda
Nyíregyháza
Fehérgyarmat
Mátészalka
Nagykálló
Hajdúnánás
Hajdúböszörmény
Debrecen
Hajdúszoboszló
Berettyóújfalu
Püspökladány
Karcag
Kisújszállás
Mezőtúr
Gyomaendrőd
Békéscsaba
Orosháza
Gyula
Szarvas
Tiszaföldvár
Mezőberény
Szeged
Makó
Hódmezővásárhely
Szentes
Kiskunfélegyháza
Kecskemét
Szolnok
Nagykőrös
Cegléd
Gyöngyös
Eger
Miskolc
Ózd
Sajószentpéter
Kazincbarcika
Encs
Szerencs
Tiszaújváros
Jászberény

Rzeszów
Nowy Targ
Frýdek-Místek
Český Těšín
Karviná
Čadca
Žilina
Martin
Ružomberok
Liptovský Mikuláš
Banská Bystrica
Zvolen
Levice
Lučenec
Rimavská Sobota
Rožňava
Salgótarján
Gerlachovský štít 2655m
Vysoké Tatry
Kriváň
2494m
Poprad
Kráľova hoľa
1948m
Veľký Krtíš

BRATISLAVA
Trnava
Senec
Galanta
Nitra
Šaľa
Nové Zámky
Komárno
Štúrovo
Esztergom
Tatabánya
Tata
Vác
BUDAPEST
Dunakeszi
Gödöllő
Hatvan
Kőris
1014m
Kékes
Dunaújváros
Székesfehérvár
Veszprém
Ajka
Pápa
Celldömölk
Szombathely
Sárvár
Körmend
Zalaegerszeg
Keszthely
Lenti
Nagykanizsa
Csurgó
Barcs
Kaposvár
Balaton
Fonyód
Siófok
Marcali
Siklós
Pécs
Mohács
Szekszárd
Baja
Tolna
Paks
Dombóvár

Senica
Piešťany
Trenčín
Myjava
Skalica
Malacky
Pezinok
Modra
Bánovce nad Bebravou
Topoľčany
Partizánske
Prievidza
Sopron
Mosonmagyaróvár
Győr
Csorna
Neusiedler See

Praha
(Prague)
Kladno
Beroun
Kolín
Kutná Hora
Čáslav
Benešov
Tábor
Písek
Strakonice
Klatovy
Prachatice
České Budějovice
Jihlava
Humpolec
Třebíč
Znojmo
Brno
Blansko
Boskovice
Vyškov
Prostějov
Olomouc
Přerov
Kroměříž
Zlín
Uherské Hradiště
Hodonín
Kyjov
Břeclav
Ostrava
Opava
Nový Jičín
Valašské Meziříčí
Vsetín
Frýdek-Místek
Pardubice
Ústí nad Labem
Zábřeh
Šumperk

Tachov
Mariánské Lázně
Plzeň
 Český Krumlov

ELEVATION

| -500m | -250m | -100m | -50m | -25m | Below sea level | 0 | 100m | 250m | 500m | 1000m | 2000m | 4000m |

| -1640ft | -820ft | -328ft | -164ft | -82ft | -33ft/-10m | 0 | 328ft | 820ft | 1640ft | 3281ft | 6562ft | 13 124ft |

THE WESTERN BALKANS

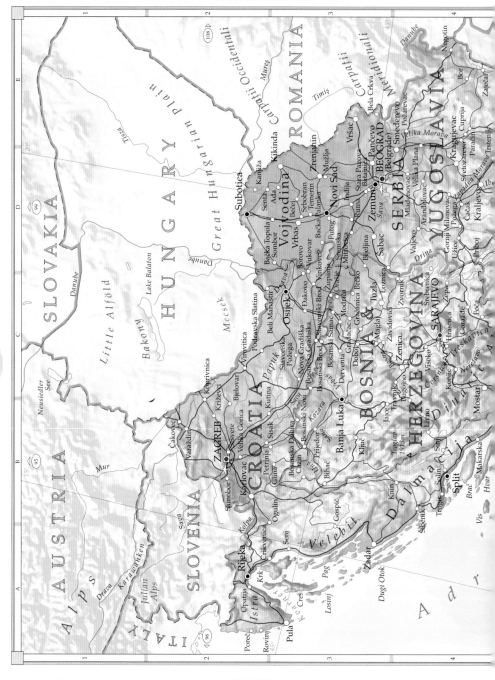

SLOVAKIA

AUSTRIA

ITALY

SLOVENIA

HUNGARY

ROMANIA

CROATIA

BOSNIA & HERZEGOVINA

SERBIA

YUGOSLAVIA

Vojvodina

Great Hungarian Plain

Carpaţii Occidentali

Carpaţii Meridionali

ZAGREB

BEOGRAD (Belgrade)

SARAJEVO

Novi Sad

Dalmacija

Julian Alps

Karawanken

Little Alföld

Bakony

Mecsek

Lake Balaton

Neusiedler See

A l p s

A d r i a t i c   S e a

A d r

POPULATION

○ Less than 50,000
◯ 50,000 - 100,000
◉ 100,000 - 500,000
◼ Over 500,000

0 km 75

0 miles 75

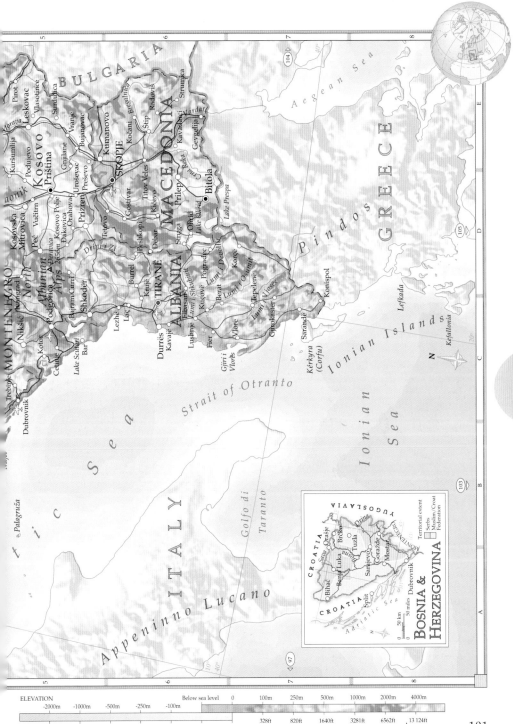

ELEVATION

-2000m	-1000m	-500m	-250m	-100m	Below sea level	0	100m	250m	500m	1000m	2000m	4000m
-6562ft	-3281ft	-1640ft	-820ft	-328ft	164ft/-50m	0	328ft	820ft	1640ft	3281ft	6562ft	13 124ft

THE MEDITERRANEAN

ATLANTIC OCEAN

Bay of Biscay

FRANCE

GERMANY

SWITZ.

LIECH.

Nantes

Loire

Seine

BERN

Lake Geneva

Lyon

△ Mont Blanc 4807m

Milan

Venice

Po

Po Valley

La Spezia

Genoa

SA MARI

Dordogne

Bordeaux

Garonne

Massif Central

Rhône

Nîmes

Montpellier

Toulouse

Marseille

Toulon

Nice

MONACO

Côte d'Azur

Golfo di Genova

Ligurian Sea

Perpignan

Golfe du Lion

Corsica

Isola d'Elba

VATICAN CITY

RO

Cordillera Cantábrica

A Coruña

Porto

Pyrenees

ANDORRA

Ebro

Zaragoza

Barcelona

Costa Brava

Sistema Ibérica

Iberian

Ajaccio

Isola Asinara

Tarragona

Costa Daurada

SPAIN

MADRID

Sierra de Guadarrama

Tagus

Sardinia

Monti del Gennargentu

△ 1835m

Tyrrhen

Gol Ga

LISBON

Peninsula

Valencia

Castelló de la Plana

Golfo de Valencia

Menorca

Isola di San Pietro

Sant'Antioco

Cagliari

Sea

Mallorca

Ibiza

Sierra Morena

Alicante

Murcia

Costa Blanca

Formentera

Islas Baleares

M

e

d

i

t

Pale

Guadalquivir

Sistema Penibético

Cartagena

Almería

Golfe de Tunis

Cap Bon

Isola Pant

Golfo de Cádiz

Cádiz

Málaga

Costa del Sol

Costa Cálida

ALGIERS

Cap Bougaroun

Annaba

TUNIS

Golfe de Hammamet

GIBRALTAR (to UK)

Ceuta (to Spain)

Oran

Mostaganem

Béjaïa

Skikda

Strait of Gibraltar

Tangier

Melilla (to Spain)

Cap des Trois Fourches

Ghazaouet

Chott el Hodna

Atlas Tellien

Massif de l'Aurès

Sfax

Tetouan

Île Cherg

Rif

Golfe de Gabès

RABAT

Chott ech Chergui

Chott Melghir

Chott el Jerid

Île de Jerbe

Casablanca

MOROCCO

Moyen Atlas

Atlas Mountains

ALGERIA

TUNISIA

TRIPO

Jabal Nafusah

S

a

h

a

r

Fazz

MALTA

Mediterranean Sea

Victoria (Gozo)

Għawdex (Gozo)

Kemmuna

Buġibba

St Julian's

Sliema

VALLETTA

Mellieħa

Msida

Qormi

Ħamrun

Mdina

Rabat

Luqa

Birżebbuġa

Malta

250m/3281ft

100m/1640ft

0 km 10

0 miles 10

CYPRUS

Mediterranean Sea

Dipkarpaz

Lapta

Girne

Çayirova

Güzelyurt

Değirmenlik

Gazimağusa Körfezi

NICOSIA

Gazimağusa

Troódos

Agía Nápa

Páfos

Lárnaca

Akrotíri

Lemesós

1000m/3281ft

500m/1640ft

250m/820ft

0m

0 km 25

0 miles 25

0 km 200

0 miles 200

POPULATION

○ Less than 50,000

○ 50,000 -100,000

◉ 100,000 - 500,000

◼ Over 500,000

ELEVATION

						Below sea level	0	100m	250m	500m	1000m	2000m	4000m
-4000m	-3000m	-2000m	-1000m	-500m									
-13 124ft	-9843ft	-6562ft	-3281ft	-1640ft	-820ft/-250m	0		328ft	820ft	1640ft	3281ft	6562ft	13 124ft

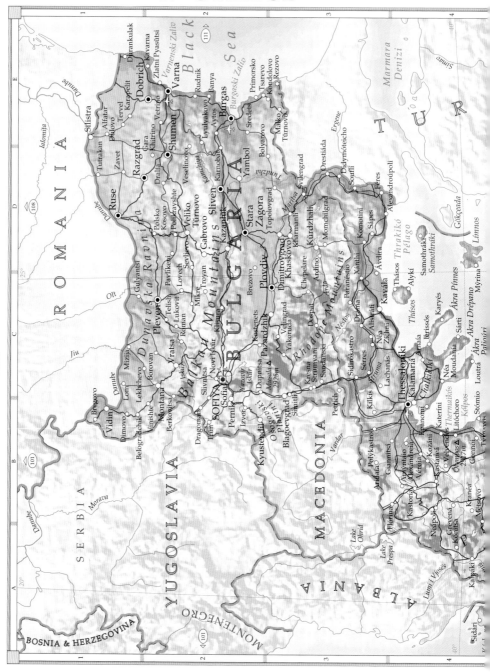

POPULATION

○ Less than 50,000   ○ 50,000 -100,000   ◉ 100,000 - 500,000   ⬤ Over 500,000

ELEVATION

				Below sea level	0	100m	250m	500m	1000m	2000m	4000m
-2000m	-1000m	-500m	-250m	-100m							
-6562ft	-3281ft	-1640ft	-820ft	-328ft	-164ft/-50m	0	328ft	820ft	1640ft	3281ft	6562ft	13 124ft

THE BALTIC STATES & BELORUSSIA

SWEDEN

FINLAND

RUSSIAN FEDERATION

ESTONIA

LATVIA

LITHUANIA

Gulf of Finland

Narva Bay

Lake Peipus

Lake Pskov

Baltic Sea

Gulf of Riga

Gulf of Aïnaži

TALLINN

RÍGA

Kaliningrad

KALININGRAD
(to Russian Federation)

Tartu

Panevėžys

Šiauliai

Klaipėda

Liepāja

Ventspils

POPULATION

○ Less than 50,000   ○ 50,000 -100,000   ◉ 100,000 - 500,000   ◼ Over 500,000

0 km   100

0 miles   100

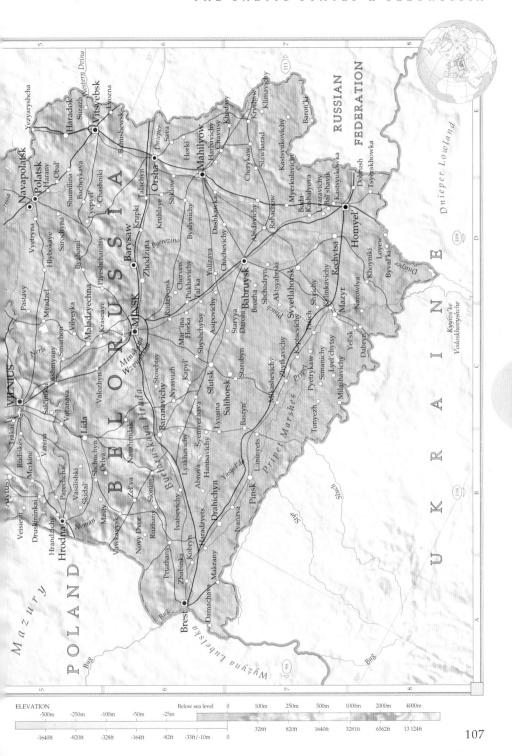

ELEVATION

				Below sea level	0	100m	250m	500m	1000m	2000m	4000m
-500m	-250m	-100m	-50m	-25m							
-1640ft	-820ft	-328ft	-164ft	-82ft	-33ft/-10m	328ft	820ft	1640ft	3281ft	6562ft	13 124ft
					0						

POPULATION

 Less than 50,000

 50,000 -100,000

 100,000 - 500,000

 Over 500,000

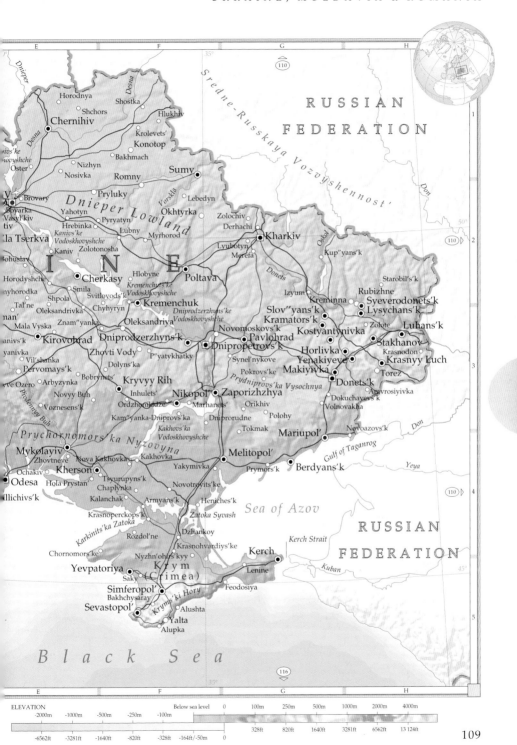

ELEVATION

					Below sea level	0	100m	250m	500m	1000m	2000m	4000m
-2000m	-1000m	-500m	-250m	-100m								
-6562ft	-3281ft	-1640ft	-820ft	-328ft	-164ft/-50m	0	328ft	820ft	1640ft	3281ft	6562ft	13 124ft

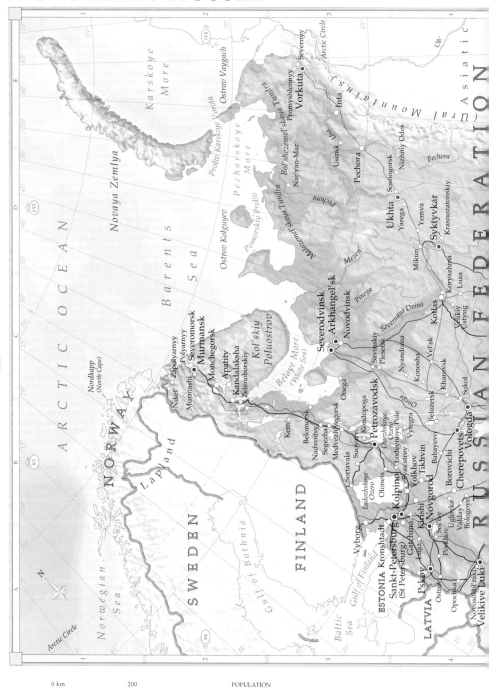

ELEVATION

					Below sea level	0	100m	250m	500m	1000m	2000m	4000m
-2000m	-1000m	-500m	-250m	-100m								
-6562ft	-3281ft	-1640ft	-820ft	-328ft	-164ft/-50m	0	328ft	820ft	1640ft	3281ft	6562ft	13 124ft

NORTH & WEST ASIA

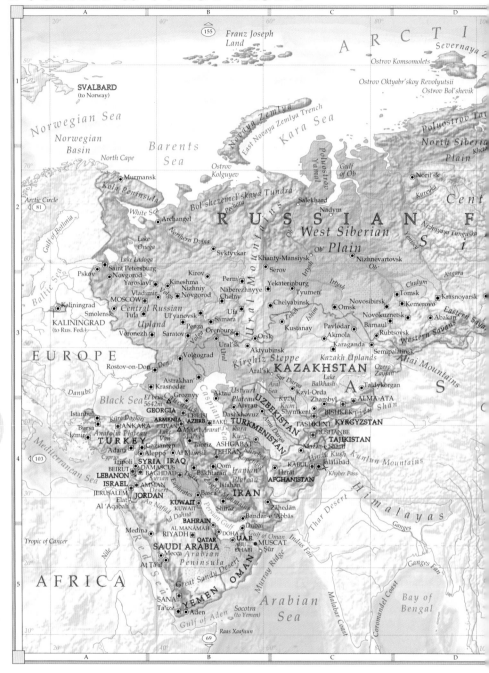

ARCTIC
Franz Joseph Land
155
Severnaya Z
Ostrov Komsomolets
SVALBARD
(to Norway)
Ostrov Oktyabr'skoy Revolyutsii
Ostrov Bol'shevik
Poluostrov Tai
Norwegian Sea
Norwegian Basin
Barents Sea
Kara Sea
North Siberia Plain
North Cape
Ostrov Kolguyev
Gulf of Ob
Khcha
Murmansk
Kola Peninsula
Poluostrov Yamal
Noril'sk
Bol'shezemel'skaya Tundra
Salekhard
Kureyka
Cent
Arctic Circle
81
White Sea
Archangel
Pechora
Nadym
R U S S I A N F
Lake Onega
Northern Dvina
West Siberian Plain
Nizhnyaya Tunguska
S
Lake Ladoga
Syktyvkar
Khanty-Mansiysk
Ob'
Yenisey
i
Saint Petersburg
Kirov
Serov
Nizhnevartovsk
Angara
Novgorod
Perm'
Yekaterinburg
Irtysh
Pskov
Yaroslavl'
Kineshma
Naberezhnyye Chelny
Tyumen'
Chulym
MOSCOW
Vladimir
Nizhniy Novgorod
Chelyabinsk
Tobol
Omsk
Novosibirsk
Tomsk
Kemerovo
Krasnoyarsk
Kaliningrad
Tula
Ufa
Ishim
Novokuznetsk
Abakan
Eastern Saya
Smolensk
Central Russian
Ul'yanovsk
Samara
Kustanay
Pavlodar
Barnaul
Rubtsovsk
KALININGRAD
Upland
Penza
Orenburg
Akmola
Karaganda
Western Sayans
(to Rus. Fed.)
Voronezh
Saratov
Orsk
Semipalatinsk
E U R O P E
Ural'sk
Aktyubinsk
Kazakh Uplands
Altai Mountains
Rostov-on-Don
Don
Volgograd
Kirghiz Steppe
KAZAKHSTAN
Ozero Zaysan
S
Astrakhan'
Aral'sk
Syr Darya
Lake Balkhash
Krasnodar
Aral Sea
Kyzl-Orda
Taldykorgan
A
Black Sea
El'brus 5642m
Groznyy
Aktau
Ustyurt Plateau
Kyzyl Kum
Zhambyl
ALMA-ATA
Istanbul
Caucasus
Atyrau
Dashkhovuz
Shymkent
Shan
Bursa
Kura Dağları
TBILISI
Caspian Sea
UZBEKISTAN
TASHKENT
KYRGYZSTAN
İzmir
ARMENIA
AZERB.
BAKU
Kara Kum
BISHKEK
Anatolia Plateau
YERIVAN
Amu Darya
TURKMENISTAN
DUSHANBE
TURKEY
Mount Ararat 5137m
Tabriz
Kopet Dag
TAJIKISTAN
ANKARA
Lake Van
Kara Kum
Mazar-e Sharif
Adana
Gaziantep
TEHRAN
Kunlun Mountains
Cyprus
Al Mawsil
Qom
KABUL
Jalalabad
Tripoli
SYRIA
IRAQ
Iranian
AFGHANISTAN
Khyber Pass
BEIRUT
Aleppo
Bakhtaran
Plateau
Herat
Himalayas
LEBANON
DAMASCUS
BAGHDAD
Isfahan
ISRAEL
AMMAN
Syrian
Basra
IRAN
JERUSALEM
JORDAN
Desert
Euphrates
Tigris
Elat
KUWAIT
Zahedan
Al 'Aqabah
KUWAIT
Shiraz
Thar Desert
An Nafud
Persian Gulf
Bandar-e Abbas
Ganges
BAHRAIN
Dubai
Gulf of Oman
Ganges Fan
Medina
AL MANAMAH
DOHA
U.A.E.
MUSCAT
Tropic of Cancer
RIYADH
QATAR
ABU DHABI
Sur
Mecca
SAUDI ARABIA
Arabian
OMAN
Coromandel Coast
At Ta'if
Peninsula
Indus Fan
Bay of
A F R I C A
Great Sandy Desert
Murray Ridge
Arabian Sea
Bengal
Red Sea
YEMEN
Malabar Coast
Nile
SANA
Socotra
(to Yemen)
Ta'izz
Aden
Gulf of Aden
Raas Xaafuun
69

0 km 800
0 miles 800

POPULATION
○ Less than 50,000   ◉ 50,000 -100,000   ◉ 100,000 - 500,000   ■ Over 500,000

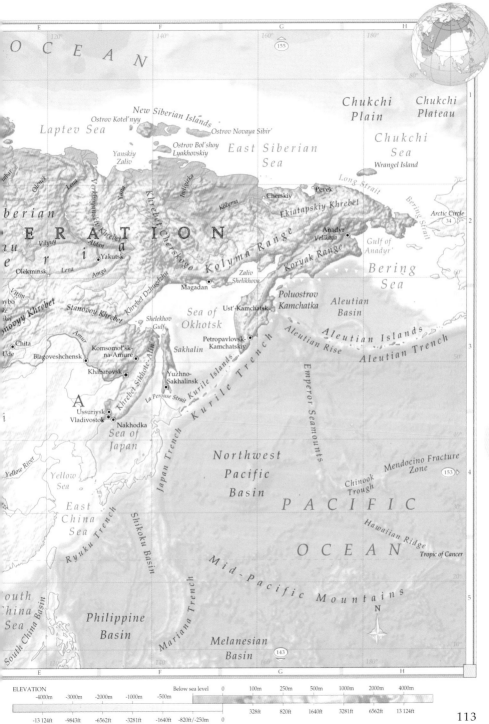

O C E A N

Laptev Sea

New Siberian Islands
Ostrov Kotel'nyy
Ostrov Novaya Sibir'
Ostrov Bol'shoy
Lyakhovskiy

Yanskiy
Zaliv

East Siberian
Sea

Chukchi
Plain

Chukchi
Plateau

Chukchi
Sea

Wrangel Island

Long Strait

Olenek
Lena
Verkhoyanskiy Khrebet

Khrebet Cherskogo

Indigirka
Kolyma
Cherskiy

Ekiatapskiy Khrebet
Pevek

Bering Strait

Arctic Circle
34

berian

ERATION

eria

Vilyuy
Yakutsk
Aldan
Khrebet

Kolyma Range

Zaliv
Shelikhova

Anadyr
Velikaya

Koryak Range

Gulf of
Anadyr'

Bering

Sea

Olekminsk
Lena
Amga
Magadan

Vitim
Stanovoy Khrebet
Khrebet Dzhugdzhur
Ust'-Kamchatsk
Poluostrov
Kamchatka

Aleutian
Basin

ybo
aybo
moyyy Khrebet
ikal
Shelekhov
Gulf
Sea of
Okhotsk

Chita
Ude
Amur
Komsomol'sk-
na-Amure
Khabarovsk
Khrebet Sikhote-Alin'
Sakhalin
Petropavlovsk-
Kamchatskiy

Aleutian Rise
Aleutian Islands

Aleutian Trench

A
Yuzhno-
Sakhalinsk
La Perouse Strait
Kurile Islands
Kurile Trench

Emperor Seamounts

Ussuriysk
Vladivostok
Nakhodka

i
Sea of
Japan

Japan Trench

Northwest
Pacific
Basin

Chinook
Trough
Mendocino Fracture
Zone
153

Yellow River
Yellow
Sea

P A C I F I C

East
China
Sea

Ryuku Trench

Shikoku Basin

O C E A N

Hawaiian Ridge
Tropic of Cancer

outh
hina
Sea

South China Basin

Philippine
Basin

Mariana Trench

Mid-Pacific Mountains

N

Melanesian
Basin
143

RUSSIA & KAZAKHSTAN

SVALBARD
(to Norway)

NORWAY

DENMARK

Zemlya Fran
Iosifa

SWEDEN

GERMANY

Nordkapp
(North Cape)

A R C T

Gulf of Bothnia

KALININGRAD
(to Rus. Fed.)

B a r e n t s

Kaliningrad

FINLAND

Murmansk

S e a

POLAND

Kandalaksha

Olenegorsk

Kola Poluostrov

Novaya Zemlya

LITH. LAT.

Sankt-Peterburg

EST.

Ladozhskoye

Ozero

Karskoye More

BELORUSSIA

Pskov

Petrozavodsk

Severodvinsk

Ostrov
Kolguyev

Ostrov Belyy

Novgorod

Onezhskoye

Arkhangel'sk

Dikson

Smolensk

Cherepovets

Ozero

Mezen

Nar'yan-Mar

Poluostrov Yamal

Tver

Vologda

Konosha

Pechora

Bol'shezemel'skaya Tundra

Obskaya Guba

MOSKVA

Vel'sk

Severnaya Dvina

(Moscow)

Yaroslavl'

Vorkuta

Salekhard

Noril'

Bryansk

Tula

Kineshma

Kotlas

UKRAINE

Vladimir

Nizhniy Novgorod

Syktyvkar

Nadym

Igarka

Belgorod

Ryazan'

G o r y

Voronezh

Tambov

Kotel'nich

Glazov

Zapadno-

Penza

Kazan'

Perm'

Serov

Khanty-Mansiysk

Sibirskaya

Sea of Azov

Mikhaylovka

Ul'yanovsk

Izhevsk

Rostov-na-

Saratov

Naberezhnyye

Ravnina

Donu

Balakovo

Tol'yatti Chelny

Yekaterinburg

Nizhnevartovsk

Krasnodar

Volgograd

Samara

Ufa

U r a l

Tobol'sk

RUSSIA

Sochi

Stavropol

Ural'sk

Sterlitamak

Tyumen'

Ob'

Chulym

El'brus

Orenburg

Chelyabinsk

5642m

Nal'chik

Astrakhan'

Magnitogorsk

Ishim

St

Vladikavkaz

Aktyubinsk

Orsk

Rudnyy

Petropavlovsk

Omsk

Tomsk

Groznyy

Atyrau

Alga

Dzhetygara

Kustanay

ARM.

Makhachkala

Emba

Kokshetau

Novosibirsk

Krasnoy

Fort-Shevchenko

Kazakhskiy Melkosopochnik

Shchuchinsk

AZERBAIJAN

Aktau

Chelkar

Atbasar

Kulundinskaya

Kemero

Novyy Uzen'

KAZAKHSTAN

Akmola

Yermak

Step

Barnaul

Ustyurt

Aral

Aral'sk

Temirtau

Karaganda

Novokuznetsk

Ab.

Plateau

Sea

Novokazalinsk

Saran'

Shakhtinsk

Kazakhskiy

Semipalatinsk

Zhezkazgan

Melkosopochnik

Charsk

Leninogorsk

Dzhusaly

Kzyl-Orda

Ust'-Kamenogorsk

Zyryanovsk

Syr Darya

Balkhash

Ayaguz

Gora Belukha

Kyzyl Kum

Ozero

Ozero

Altai Mountai

Balkhash

Zaysan

Turkestan

Kentau

Karatau

Taldykorgan

Shymkent

Arys'

Chu

Tekeli

IRAN

Zhambyl

ALMATY

CHINA

(Alma-Ata)

AFGHANISTAN

KYRGYZSTAN

Tien Shan

GEORGIA

C a u c a s u s

Caspian Sea

TURKMENISTAN

UZBEKISTAN

TAJIKISTAN

Black Sea

Don

Volga

Ural

Tobol

Irtysh

Ishim

Irtysh

Ob'

Yenisey

0 km   800

0 miles   800

POPULATION

○ Less than 50,000   ○ 50,000 -100,000   ◉ 100,000 - 500,000   ■ Over 500,000

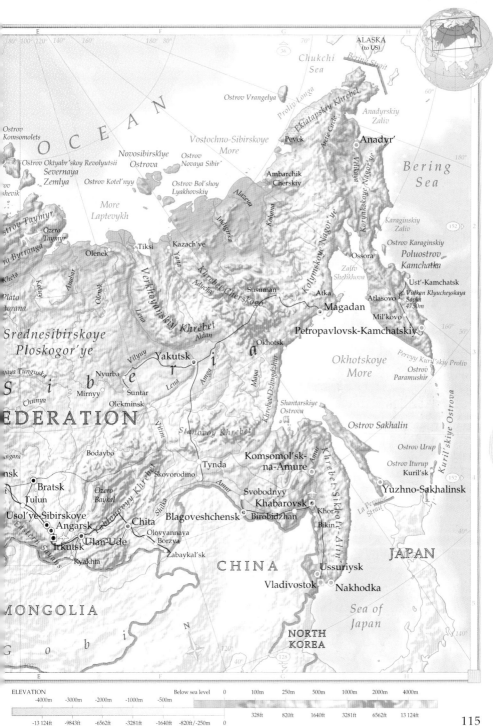

TURKEY & THE CAUCASUS

ROMANIA

Lacul Razim
Lacul Sinoie

N

BULGARIA

Danube

Maritsa

Varnenski Zaliv

Burgaski Zaliv

Black Sea

Kırklareli
Edirne
Ergene

Tekirdağ
Kağıthane
İstanbul
Marmara Deniz
Yalova
İznik Gölü

Bandırma

Çanakkale
Çanakkale Boğazı

Edremit

Ayvalık

Lésvos
Chíos

Menemen
Manisa
İzmir
Gediz

Torbalı
Sámos
Búyük Menderes
Nazilli
Söke
Aydın

Milas

Bodrum

Marmaris
Dalaman
Fethiye

Dodekánisos

Ródos (Rhodes)
Kas

Kárpathos

Zonguldak
Ereğli
Devrek

İzmit
Adapazarı

Bursa
Bilecik

Bozüyük
Eskişehir

Sinaw

Balıkesir
Kütahya

Simav
Gediz

Akhisar
Uşak

Alaşehir
Dinar
Denizli
Burdur
Burdur Gölü

Tavas

İsparta

Antalya
Manavgat

Afyon

Anatolia

Cihanbeyli

İstanbul Boğazı

Cide
İnebolu
Küre
Küre Dağları
Kastamonu

Karabük
Kargı
Ilgaz

Bolu
Gerede
Çankırı
Kızıl Irmak

ANKARA
Kalecik

Kırıkale

Kulu
Hirfanlı Barajı

Sinop
Gerze

Bafra
Samsun
Ün
Canik Dağları
Havza
O

Çorum
Alaca

Tokat
Yıldızeli

Sorgun

TURK

Şarkışla
Gemerek

Tuz Gölü
Nevşehir
Aksaray

İncesu

Bunyan

Kayseri

Siva

K

G

İskenderun

LEBANON

Konya

Ereğli

Beyşehir Gölü
Suğla Gölü

Karaman

Toros Dağları

Mut

Silifke

Gazipaşa
Anamur

Niğde
Göksun

Kahramanm

Osmaniye
Ceyhan
Adana
Mersin
Tarsus

Antakya

Gazia
Kilis
Kırıkhan

Oranı

Gün

TURKISH REPUBLIC OF NORTHERN CYPRUS

CYPRUS

Mediterranean Sea

Antalya Körfezi
Finike

0 km   200

0 miles   200

POPULATION

 Less than 50,000

 50,000 -100,000

 100,000 - 500,000

 Over 500,000

RUSSIAN
FEDERATION

Caucasus

RUSSIAN FEDERATION

Gagra
Gudaut'a
Sokhumi
Och'amch'ire
Abkhazia
Samtredia
P'ot'i
Ureki
K'obulet'i
Bat'umi
Hopa
Ajaria
Lesser Caucasus
Enguri
K'ut'aisi
South Ossetia
Gori
Kazbek 5047m
Alazani
Tsalka
Akhalts'ikhe
T'BILISI
Rust'avi
Zaqatala
Kura
Şäki
Greater Caucasus
Xaçmaz
Quba
Siyäzan
Şamaxı
Sumqayıt
BAKI

GEORGIA

Pazar
Rize
Of
Karadeniz Dağları
rabzon
iresun
oğu
Gümüşhane
Artvin
Gyumri
Kars
Vanadzor
Art'ik
Dilijan
Sevan
Sevana Lich
YEREVAN
Artashat
Gäncä
Yevlax
Mingäçevir
Xankändi
Nagornyy Karabakh
İmişli
Ali-Bayramll
Qazımämmäd

ARMENIA

AZERBAIJAN

Aşkale
Paşinler
Horasan
Sarıkamış
İspir
Çoruh Çayı
Aras
Goris
AZERB.
Naxçıvan
Biläsuvar
Länkäran

ye
Erzincan
Kemah
Tercan
Erzurum
Ağrı
Karaköse
Patnos
Bingöl
Erciş
Muradiye
Biŋ'ölkağrı Dağı 5123m

Y

Baraji Keban
eban
Elâzığ
latya
ğ u
iyaman
Diyarbakır
Silverek
Viranşehir
Şanlıurfa
Akçakale
Muş
Tatvan
Bitlis
Silvan
Siirt
Batman
Mardin
Nusaybin
Van Gölü
Van
Gevaş
Toroslar

Daryācheh-ye Orūmīyeh

Reshteh-ye Kühhä-ye Alborz

IRAN

Tigris
Jabal 'Abd al 'Azīz
rat
id
Euphrates
Jabal Bishrī
Nīnawé
Jabal Hamrīn
Kühhä-ye Zagros

RIA

IRAQ

ELEVATION

	-2000m	-1000m	-500m	-250m	-100m	Below sea level	0	100m	250m	500m	1000m	2000m	4000m
	-6562ft	-3281ft	-1640ft	-820ft	-328ft	-164ft/-50m	0	328ft	820ft	1640ft	3281ft	6562ft	13 124ft

117

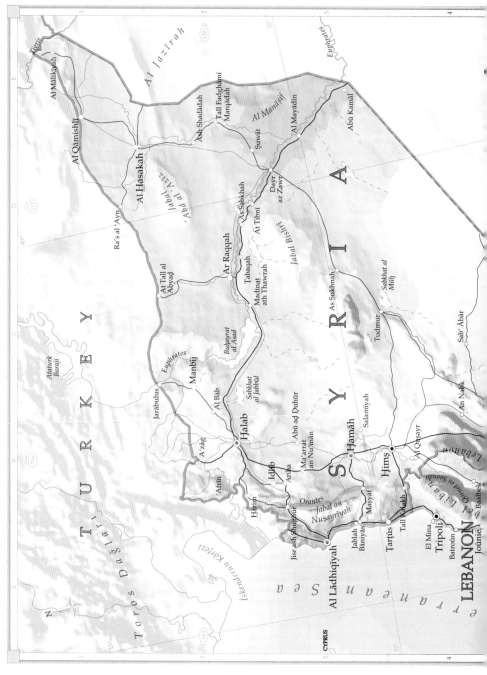

0 km 100

0 miles 100

POPULATION

○ Less than 50,000   ○ 50,000 -100,000   ◉ 100,000 - 500,000   ■ Over 500,000

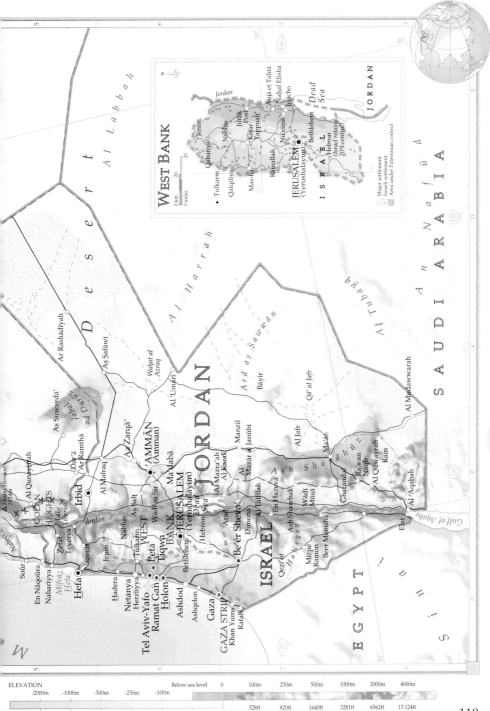

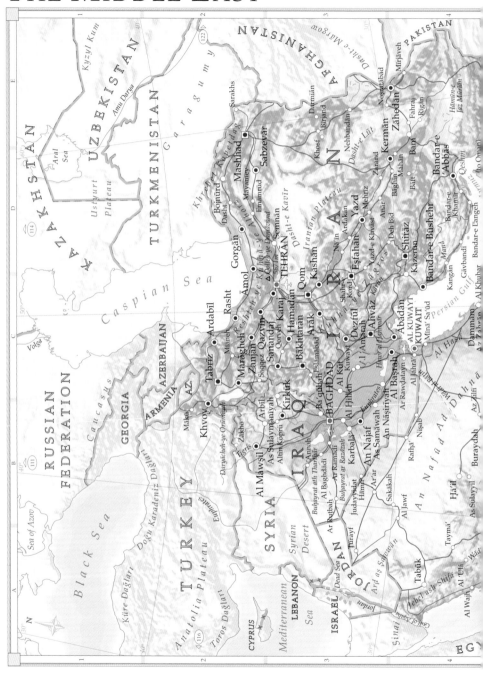

POPULATION

○ Less than 50,000   ○ 50,000 -100,000   ◉ 100,000 - 500,000   ◼ Over 500,000

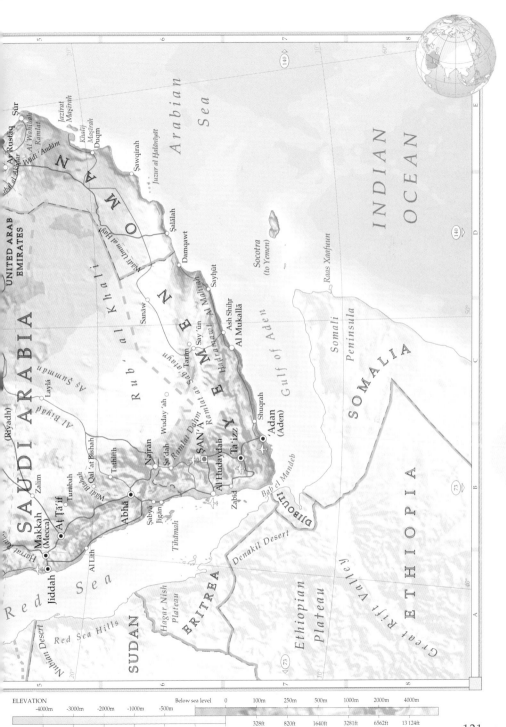

ELEVATION

					Below sea level	0	100m	250m	500m	1000m	2000m	4000m
-4000m	-3000m	-2000m	-1000m	-500m		0						
-13 124ft	-9843ft	-6562ft	-3281ft	-1640ft	-820ft/-250m	0	328ft	820ft	1640ft	3281ft	6562ft	13 124ft

CENTRAL ASIA

RUSSIAN
FEDERATION

GEORGIA

Caspian

AZERBAIJAN

Sea

Ustyurt
Plateau

Aral
Sea

Mŭynoq

Chimboy
Takhtakŭpir

Kēnetrgench
Nukus **UZBEKISTAN**
Gubadag
Takhiatosh
Ilyaly
Dashkhovuz
Urganch
Uchquduq
Khiwa
Tŭrtkŭl

Ky z y

Proliv Kara-
Bogaz-Gol
Zaliv
Kara-
Bogaz-Gol
Turkmenbashi
Dzhanak
Krasnovodskiy
Zaliv
Cheleken
Nebitdag
Gazandzhyk
Turkmenskiy
Zaliv

Gaz-Achak
Lebap
Zarafsho
Darvaza
Zaunguzskiye
Karakumy
Chjiduw
Gazli
Bukhoro
Seydi
Deynau

Amu Darya

TURKMENISTAN
Gyzylarbat
Kara-Kala
Bakharden
Geok-Tepe
Bruzmeyin
G a r a g u m y
Chardzhev
Sayat

Khrebet Kopetdag

Kelifs
Karakumskiy
ASHGABAT
Gora Reza
2942m
Tedzhen
Mary
Uzb
Kaakhka
Murgab
Bayramaly

Reshteh-ye Kŭhhā-ye Alborz

Serakhs
Kashaf Rŭd
Andkh
ozvyshennos
Karabil

Bālā Morghāb
Darya

Towraghoudi
Gushgy
ye Mor

Selseleh-ye Safīd K

Ghūriān
Herāt

I r a n i a n

P l a t e a u

IRAN

Kŭhhā-ye Zāgros

AFGHA
Shīndand

Farāh
Kŭh-e Chehel Abdalān
Delārām
Ger

Daryācheh-ye
Sīstān
Lashkar Gāh
Zarghūn Shahr
Zaranj
Kŭchna
Darvīsh
Dasht-e Mārgow
Chahār Borjak
Daryā-ye Helmand
Rīgesto
Bahrām Chāh

0 km   200

0 miles   200

POPULATION

○ Less than 50,000   ○ 50,000 -100,000   ◉ 100,000 - 500,000   ■ Over 500,000

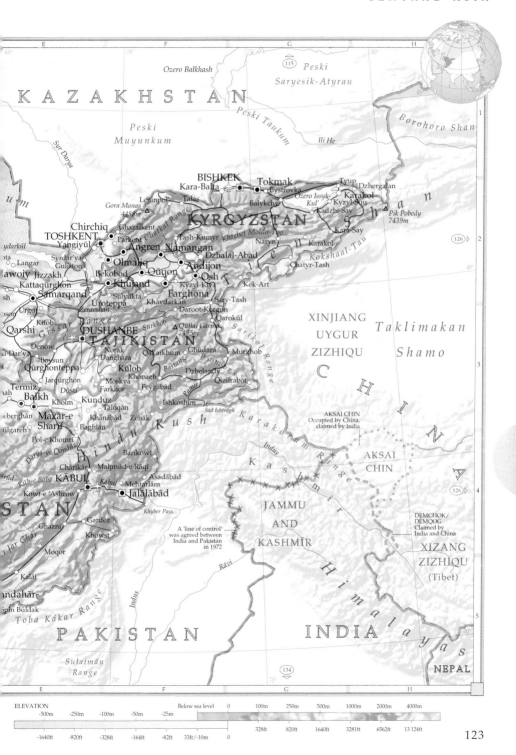

KAZAKHSTAN

Ozero Balkhash

Peski Saryesik-Atyrau

Peski Muyunkum

Peski Taukum

Syr Darya

Ili He

Borohoro Shan

BISHKEK
Kara-Balta
Tokmak
Bystrovka
Tyup
Dzhergalan
KYRGYZSTAN
Leninpol
Talas
Balykchy
Ozero Issyk-Kul'
Karakol
Kadzhi-Say
Kyzyl-Suu
Kara-Say
Gora Manas
4488m
Pik Pobedy
7439m

Chirchiq
Ghazalkent
Tash-Kumyr
Khrebet Molda-Too
TOSHKENT
Parkent
Naryn
Karakol
Yangiyul
Angren
Namangan
Dzhalal-Abad
Chatyr-Tash
Kokshaal-Tau
Syrdar'ya
Olmaliq
Osh
Guliston
Jizzakh
Bekobod
Andijon
Kattaqurghon
Khujand
Kyzyl-Kiya
Kök-Art
Samarqand
Farghona
Sülyükta
Khaydarkan
Sary-Tash
Uroteppa
Daroot-Korgon
Zeravshan
Surkhob
Range
Kitob
DUSHANBE
Qullai Garmo
7495m
Qarshi
TAJIKISTAN
Norak
Qal'aikhum
Ghudara
Murghob
Danghara
Sarikol Range
Boysun
Qürghonteppa
Kulob
Khorugh
Qizilrabot
Termiz
Jarqürghon
Moskva
Feyzabad
Dzhelandy
Balkh
Dusti
Farkhor
Kholm
Kunduz
Ishkoshim
Sad Ishtragh
Mazar-e
Sharif
Taloqan
Zebak
Karakoram Range
Khanabad
eberghan
Pol-e Khomri
Baghlan
AKSAI CHIN
Occupied by China,
claimed by India
ülgareh
Barikowt
AKSAI
CHIN
Darya-ye Qonduz
Charikar
Mahmud-e Raqi
KABUL
Asadabad
Mehtarlam
Kowt-e 'Ashrow
Jalalabad
DEMCHOK/
DEMQOG
Claimed by
India and China
Khyber Pass
Gardez
Ghazni
Khowst
JAMMU
AND
KASHMIR
XIZANG
ZIZHIQU
(Tibet)
Moqor
A 'line of control'
was agreed between
India and Pakistan
in 1972
Ravi
Kalat
Indus
Himalayas
Büldak
Toba Kakar Range
PAKISTAN
INDIA
*Sulaiman
Range*
NEPAL

XINJIANG
UYGUR
ZIZHIQU

*Taklimakan
Shamo*

CHINA

ELEVATION

-500m	-250m	-100m	-50m	-25m	Below sea level	0	100m	250m	500m	1000m	2000m	4000m
-1640ft	-820ft	-328ft	-164ft	-82ft	33ft/-10m	0	328ft	820ft	1640ft	3281ft	6562ft	13 124ft

SOUTH & EAST ASIA

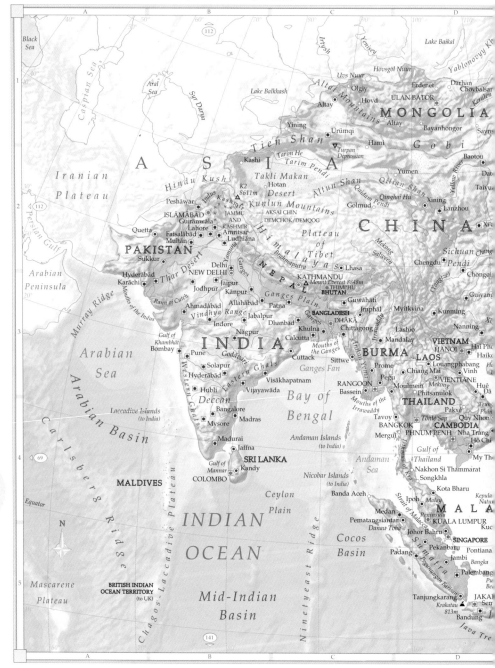

Black Sea

Aral Sea

Caspian Sea

Syr Darya

Lake Balkhash

Uvs Nuur

Hövsgöl Nuur

Lake Baikal

Yablonovyy Kh

Olgiy

Altay Mountains

Hovd

Altay

Yining

ULAN BATOR

Erdenet

Darhan

Choybalsan

Kerulen

MONGOLIA

Bayanhongor

Sayns

Baotou

Dat

Ürümqi

Turpan Depression

Hami

Gobi

Yumen

Taiyu

Iranian Plateau

Hindu Kush

Tien Shan

Kashi

Takli Makan Desert

Tarim He

Tarim Pendi

Altun Shan

Qaidam Pendi

Qilian Shan

Golmud

Qinghai Hu

Xining

Lanzhou

CHINA

Xi'a

Peshawar

K2 8611m

Kashmir

Hotan

Kunlun Mountains

AKSAI CHIN

DEMCHOK/DEMQOG

ISLĀMĀBĀD

JAMMU AND KASHMIR

Plateau of Tibet

Sichuan Pendi

Chang

Quetta

Gujranwala

Lahore

Amritsar

Ludhiāna

Himalaya

Lhasa

Chengdu

Chongqi

PAKISTAN

Faisalābād

Multan

Indus

Sukkur

Delhi

NEW DELHI

KATHMANDU

Mount Everest 8848m

THIMPHU

BHUTAN

Guyang

Hyderābād

Jodhpur

Jaipur

Kanpur

NEPAL

Ganges

Guwāhāti

Kunming

Nanning

Xi

Karāchi

Thar Desert

Ahmadābād

Allahābād

Patna

Ganges Plain

BANGLADESH

DHAKĀ

Imphāl

Myitkyina

Mouths of the Indus

Rann of Cutch

Vindhya Range

Jabalpur

Dhanbad

Khulna

Chittagong

Lashio

VIETNAM

Gulf of Khambāt

Bombay

Indore

Nāgpur

INDIA

Calcutta

Mouths of the Ganges

Mandalay

BURMA

HANOI

Hai Ph

Pune

Godāvari

Cuttack

Sittwe

Prome

LAOS

Louangphabang

Vinh

Arabian Sea

Solapur

Hyderābād

Eastern Ghats

Visākhapatnam

Ganges Fan

Pegu

Chiang Mai

VIENTIANE

Huê

Đà

Arabian Basin

Hubli

Vijayawāda

Bay of Bengal

Moulmein

Phitsanulok

THAILAND

Pakxé

Trun

Phan

Laccadive Islands (to India)

Bangalore

Madras

Mouths of the Irrawaddy

RANGOON

Basin

Tavoy

BANGKOK

Tônlé Sap

Quy Nhon

Carlsberg Ridge

Deccan

Mysore

Western Ghats

CAMBODIA

PHNUM PENH

Nha Trang

Madurai

Andaman Islands (to India)

Mergui

Hồ Chi

Jaffna

SRI LANKA

Gulf of Mannar

Kandy

Andaman Sea

Isthmus of Kra

Gulf of Thailand

My Th

MALDIVES

COLOMBO

Nicobar Islands (to India)

Nakhon Si Thammarat

Songkhla

Kota Bharu

Equator

Ceylon Plain

Banda Aceh

Ipoh

Malay

Kepula

Natu

Medan

Peninsula

MALA

Pematangsiantar

Danau Toba

Strait of Malacca

KUALA LUMPUR

Kuc

N

Chagos-Laccadive Plateau

INDIAN OCEAN

Cocos Basin

Johor Bahru

SINGAPORE

Mascarene Plateau

BRITISH INDIAN OCEAN TERRITORY (to UK)

Mid-Indian Basin

Ninetyeast Ridge

Padang

Sumatra

Pekanbaru

Jambi

Pontiana

Bangka

Palembang

Pu

Bee

Tanjungkarang

Krakatau 813m

JAKA

Sen

Bandung

Java Tre

0 km   1000

0 miles   1000

POPULATION

○ Less than 50,000   ◎ 50,000 -100,000   ◉ 100,000 - 500,000   ■ Over 500,000

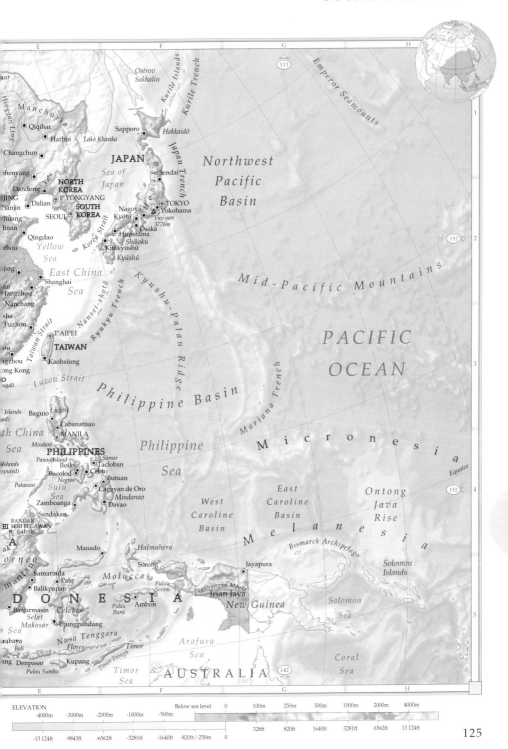

Manchuria

Ostrov
Sakhalin

Qiqihar

Kurile Islands

Kurile Trench

113

Harbin   Lake Khanka

Hsingan Ling

Changchun

Sapporo

Hokkaidō

Emperor Seamounts

JAPAN

*Northwest
Pacific
Basin*

shenyang

Sea of
Japan

NORTH
KOREA

Sendai

Dandong

Yalu

Japan Trench

JING

P'YONGYANG

TOKYO

Tianjin   Dalian   SOUTH

Nagoya

Yokohama

huang   SEOUL   KOREA

Kyōto   △ Fuji-san
3776m

Jinan

Osaka

1

Qingdao   Korea Strait   Hiroshima
Shikoku

zhou

Kitakyūshū

*Yellow
Sea*

Kyūshū

152

jing

East China

Shanghai

Mid-Pacific Mountains

angzhou

Sea

Nanchang

Nansei-shotō

sha   Fuzhou

PACIFIC

Kyushu-Palau Trench

Taiwan Strait

T'AIPEI

OCEAN

ou

TAIWAN

Ryukyu Trench

zhou   Kaohsiung

3

ng Kong

Kyushu-Palau Ridge

ugal)

Luzon Strait

Philippine Basin

Mariana Trench

Islands   Baguio   Luzon
ed)

Cabanatuan

th China   MANILA

M i c r o n e s

Sea   Mindoro

Equator

PHILIPPINES

Philippine

152

Islands   Panay Island   Samar
puted)   Iloilo   Tacloban

Sea

Palawan   Bacolod   Cebu
Negros   Butuan

*East
Caroline
Basin*

*Ontong
Java
Rise*

Cagayan de Oro

4

Sulu   Mindanao

*West
Caroline
Basin*

Zamboanga   Davao

Sea

Sandakan

BANDAR
El SERI BEGAWAN
Sabah

M e l a n e s i a

ak

orneo   Manado   Halmahera

Bismarck Archipelago

*Solomon
Islands*

mantan   Samarinda   Sorong

Jayapura

Palu

Balikpapan   *Moluccas*   Pulau
Seram   Pegunungan Maoke

*Solomon
Sea*

DONESIA

Irian Jaya

Banjarmasin   *Celebes*   Pulau
Buru   Ambon   *New Guinea*

5

Selat
Makasar

rabaya   Ujungpandang

*Arafura
Sea*

Sea   Bali   *Nusa Tenggara*
Flores   Timor

*Coral
Sea*

ng   Denpasar   Kupang
Pulau Sumba   Timor Trough

AUSTRALIA

142

Timor
Sea

E   F   G   H

ELEVATION

-4000m   -3000m   -2000m   -1000m   -500m   Below sea level   0   100m   250m   500m   1000m   2000m   4000m

-13 124ft   -9843ft   -6562ft   -3281ft   -1640ft   -820ft/-250m   0   328ft   820ft   1640ft   3281ft   6562ft   13 124ft

WESTERN CHINA & MONGOLIA

POPULATION

 Less than 50,000

 50,000 -100,000

 100,000 - 500,000

 Over 500,000

0 km   400
0 miles   400

zero Baykal

R A T I O N

Ergun Zuoqi
Xuguit Qi   Ergun   Oroqen Zizhiqi
Hailar   M a n c h u r i a
Manzhouli   HEILONGJIANG
Sühbaatar   Hulun   Butha Qi
Darhan   Nur
Sharingol
Dzüunharaa
ULAANBAATAR   Choybalsan
(Ulan Bator)   Menengiyn
Nalayh   Tal
Dzuunmod   Ondörhaan   Huolin Gol He
O L I A   Baruun-Urt   Tongliao   JILIN
Saynshand   Xilin Hot
Bulgan   Dzüünbayan   Erdenet   Erenhot   Laolia He   Sea
Dalandzadgad   Chifeng   LIAONING   of
Japan
Jining   NORTH
Yin Shan   BEIJING   KOREA
Hohhot   SOUTH
Tengger   Baotou   TIANJIN   Bo Hai   KOREA
Shamo   Wuhai   Korea
Ordos   Bay
NINGXIA   Desert   HEBEI
HUIZU   Great Wall of China   Yellow
ZIZHIQU   SHANXI   SHANDONG   Sea
N   A
GANSU   Huang He (Yellow River)   JIANGSU   East
SHAANXI   China
Han   HENAN   ANHUI   SHANGHAI   Sea
CHUAN   HUBEI   129
Chang Jiang (Yangtze)   ZHEJIANG
JIANGXI
YUNNAN   HUNAN   FUJIAN
GUIZHOU   TAIWAN

ELEVATION
-2000m   -1000m   -500m   -250m   -100m   Below sea level   0   100m   250m   500m   1000m   2000m   4000m

-6562ft   -3281ft   -1640ft   -820ft   -328ft   -164ft/-50m   0   328ft   820ft   1640ft   3281ft   6562ft   13 124ft

EASTERN CHINA & KOREA

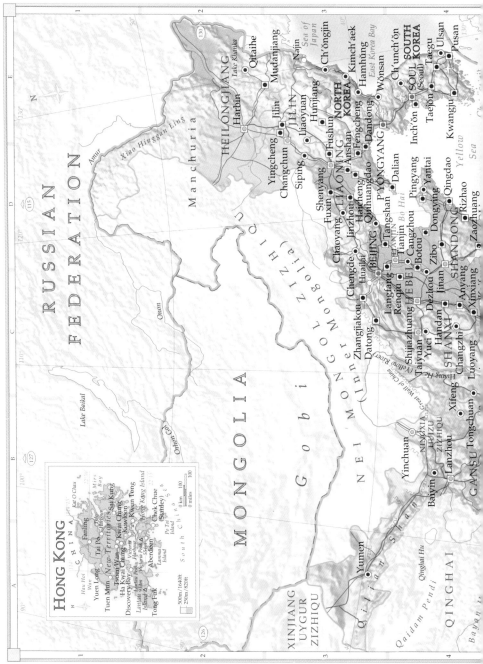

RUSSIAN FEDERATION

MONGOLIA

HEILONGJIANG

Manchuria

Xiao Hinggan Ling

Lake Khanka

Ottaihe

Mudanjiang

Naijin

Ch'ongjin

Sea of Japan

Harbin

Jilin

Yingcheng

Changchun

Liaoyuan

Hunjiang

Hamhŭng

Wŏnsan

Siping

JILIN

NORTH KOREA

Fengcheng

Kimch'aek

East Korea Bay

Ch'unch'ŏn

SOUTH KOREA

Taegu

Ulsan

Pusan

Shenyang

Fuxin

Fushun

Anshan

Dandong

LIAONING

Haicheng

P'YONGYANG

Inch'ŏn

SŎUL (Seoul)

Taejŏn

Kwangju

Yellow Sea

Chaoyang

Jinzhou

Qinhuangdao

Tangshan

Dalian

Pingyang

Yantai

Qingdao

Rizhao

Zaozhuang

Chengde

Huajiai

Tianjin

TIANJIN

Cangzhou

Botou

Dongying

Zibo

Anyang

Xinxiang

SHANDONG

Zhangjiakou

BEIJING

Langfang

Renqiu

HEBEI

Dezhou

Jinan

Datong

Shijiazhuang

Handan

SHANXI

Changzhi

Luoyang

Taiyuan

Yuci

Xifeng

Tongchuan

GANSU

Yinchuan

NINGXIA HUIZU ZIZHIQU

Baiyin

Lanzhou

Qilian Shan

Yumen

XINJIANG UYGUR ZIZHIQU

QINGHAI

Qinghai Hu

Qaidam Pendi

Bayan

NEI MONGOL (INNER MONGOLIA) ZIZHIQU

Gobi

Lake Baikal

Amur

Onon

Onon Gol

Orhon Gol

Huang He (Yellow River)

Great Wall of China

Bo Hai

HONG KONG

Hau Hoi Wan

Kat O Chau

Mirs Bay

Yuen Long

Fanling

Tai Po

Sha Tin

Sai Kung

Tuen Mun

Tsuen Wan

Kwai Chung

Kowloon

Kwun Tong

New Territories

Discovery Bay

Ha Kwai Chung

Victoria Harbour

Victoria Peak 554m

Lantau Island 934m

Hong Kong Island

Aberdeen

Po Toi Island

Lamma Island

Tong Fuk

Chek Chue (Stanley)

South China Sea

CHINA

0 km 100

0 miles 100

500m/1640ft

250m/820ft

POPULATION

○ Less than 50,000

○ 50,000 -100,000

◉ 100,000 - 500,000

■ Over 500,000

0 km 200

0 miles 200

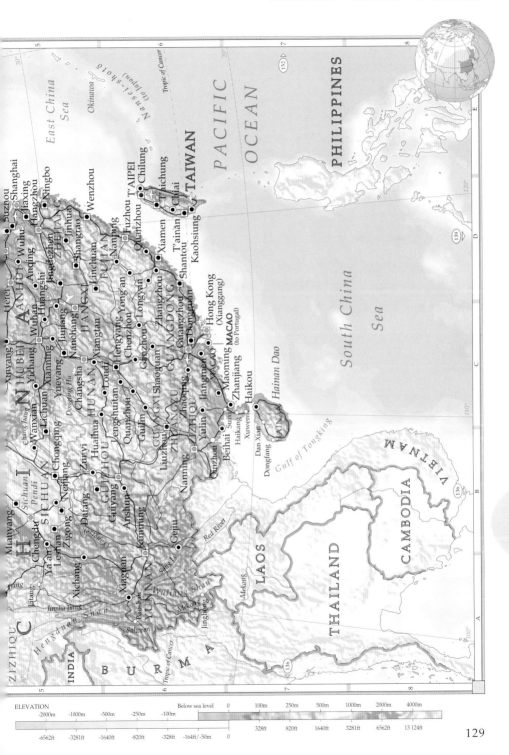

PACIFIC

OCEAN

East China
Sea

Okinawa

Nansei-shoto (to Japan)

Tropic of Cancer

PHILIPPINES

Shizou
Shanghai
Suzhou
Haxing
Wuhu
Hangzhou
Ningbo
Anqing
Wuhan
Huangshi
ZHEJIANG
Wenzhou
Shangrao
Jinhua
Jingdezhen

TAIPEI
Chilung
Taichung
Chiai
T'ainan
Kaohsiung
TAIWAN

South China
Sea

Xinyang
HUBEI
Yichang
ANHUI
N
HENAN
Hefei

JIANGXI
Nanchang
Jiujiang
FUJIAN
Nanping
Fuzhou
Yong'an
Quanzhou
Longyan
Xiamen
Shantou

Wanxian
Lichuan
Xianning
Yueyang
Dongting Hu
Changsha
Xiangtan
Toudi
HUNAN
Huaihua
Hengyang
Chenzhou
Ganzhou
Zhangzhou
GUANGDONG
Guangzhou
Dongguan
Hong Kong
(Xianggang)
MACAO
(to Portugal)

Chang Jiang
Wanzhou
Chongqing
SICHUAN
Nanning
Zunyi
GUIZHOU
Quanzhou
Guilin
GUANGXI
Shaoguan
Zhaoqing
Maoming
Zhanjiang
Haikou
HAINAN
Hainan Dao

Mianyang
HU
Chengdu
Yaan
Leshan
Zigong
Neijiang
Dafang
Guiyang
Anshun
Kunming
Yengshuitan
Liuzhou
ZHUANG
Yulin
Qinzhou
Beihai
Suixi
Haikang
Xuwen
Dan Xian
Gulf of Tongking
VIETNAM

ZIZHIQU
C
Litang
Xichang
INDIA
Jinsha Jiang
Xiangtan
Baoshan
YUNNAN
Wuliang Shan
Mekong
Jinghong
Salween
Tropic of Cancer
B U R M A
Red River
LAOS
Mekong
THAILAND
CAMBODIA

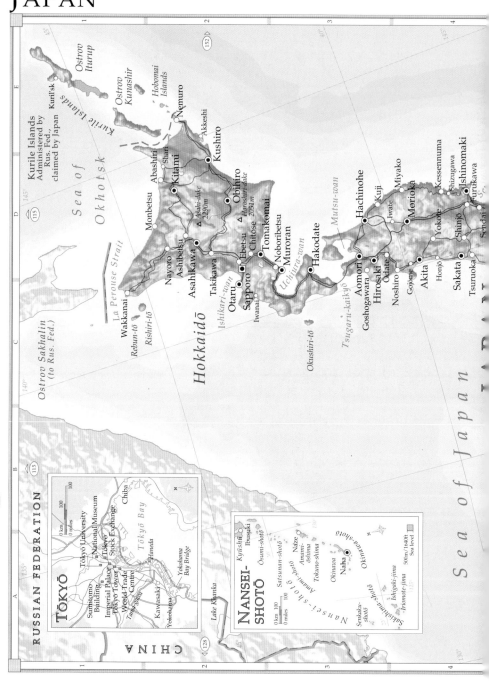

HONSHU

Iwaki
Hitachi
Sukagawa
Utsunomiya
Mito
Choshi
Oyama
TOKYO
Chiba
Kawagoe
Kawasaki
Yokohama
Omiya
Kofu
Bōsō-hantō
Maebashi
Nagano
Fuji
Matsumoto
Shizuoka
Hamamatsu
Joetsu
Ueda
Toyama
Hida-sanmyaku
Toyota
Ise-wan
Owase
Itoigawa
Takaoka
Gifu
Nagoya
Tsu
Shingū
Kanazawa
Ōgaki
Ōtsu
Wakayama
Tanabe
Komatsu
Tsuruga
Kyoto
Osaka
Gobō
Fukui
Kobe
Himeji
Kōchi
Shikoku
Tottori
Okayama
Tokushima
Nakamura
Matsue
Yonago
Kurashiki
Kure
Niihama
Matsuyama
Hamada
Hiroshima
Hōfu
Ōita
Nobeoka
Kyūshū
Miyazaki
Masuda
Iwakuni
Ube
Kurume
Miyakonojō
Yamaguchi
Fukuoka
Yatsushiro
Sendai
Kitakyūshū
Kumamoto
Kagoshima
Shimonoseki
Omuta
Saseb o
Nagasaki

Frji-san
3776m △

Sagami-nada
O-shima
Nii-jima
Miyake-jima
Mikura-shima
Hachijō-jima
Izu-shotō

P A C I F I C

O C E A N

SOUTH
KOREA

Korea Strait

East
China
Sea

Ōsumi-shotō
Kagoshima-wan
Tanega-shima
Yaku-shima

Liancourt Rocks
(claimed by Japan & South Korea)

Oki-shotō
Dōgo
Dōzen

Toyama-wan

Wakasa-wan

Kii-suidō

Tosa-wan

Bungo-suidō

Shibushi-wan

Tsushima
Ko-saki

Gotō-rettō
Amakusa-shotō
Koshikijima-rettō

Harima-nada
Awaji-shima

128

152

152

152

140

30

ELEVATION

-4000m	-3000m	-2000m	-1000m	-500m	Below sea level	0	100m	250m	500m	1000m	2000m	4000m
-13 124ft	-9843ft	-6562ft	-3281ft	-1640ft	-820ft/-250m	0		328ft	820ft	1640ft	3281ft	6562ft	13 124ft

SOUTH INDIA & SRI LANKA

Bombay (Mumbai) · Pune · Ahmadnagar · Nānded · Jagdalpur
Bārāmati · Nizāmābād · Karīmnagar
Solapur · Secunderābād · Vizianagaram
Sāngli · Gulbarga · Hyderābād · Visākhapatnam · Rajahmundry
Kolhāpur · Rāichūr · Kurnool · Kākināda
Belgaum · Dhārwād · Vijayawāda
Panaji (Goa) · Hubli · Nandyāl · Machilīpatnam
Chīrala · Ongole
Davangere · Tādpatri · Kāvali
Anantapur · Nellore
Shimoga · Bhadrāvati · Cuddapah
Udupi · Tumkūr
Mangalore · Bangalore · Vellore · Madras
Kāsaragod · Mandya · Krishnagiri · Kānchīpuram
Cannanore · Mysore · Tiruppattūr
Erode · Salem · Pondicherry
Calicut · Neyveli
Coimbatore
Trichūr · Tiruchchirāppalli
Ernākulam · Dindigul
Cochin · Madurai · Jaffna
Alleppey · Rājapālaiyam · Mannar · Vavuniya · Trincomalee
Quilon · Tuticorin · Anurādhapura · Eravur · Batticaloa
Trivandrum · Matale
Nāgercoil · Puttalam · Kandy
Negombo
COLOMBO · Kotte
Moratuwa · Ratnapura
Kalutara
Galle · Matara

Arabian Sea

I N D I A

Andhra Pradesh

Karnātaka

Eastern Ghāts

Western Ghāts

Malabar Coast

Coromandel Coast

Palk Strait

Gulf of Mannar

SRI LANKA

Godavari
Krishna
Tungabhadra Reservoir

Amīndīvi Islands
Kavaratti Island
Kalpeni Island

Lakshadweep
(Laccadive Islands)
(to India)

Nine Degree Channel
Minicoy Island
Eight Degree Channel

Ihavandippolhu Atoll

MALDIVES

Faadhippolhu Atoll
Horsburgh Atoll
Male'Atoll
Ari Atoll · MALE'
Felidhu Atoll
Mulaku Atoll
Hadhdhunmathi Atoll
Kolhumadulu Atoll
North Huvadhu Atoll
South Huvadhu Atoll
Gan
Addu Atoll

Equator

I N D I A N

0 km — 400
0 miles — 400

POPULATION
○ Less than 50,000   ○ 50,000 -100,000   ◉ 100,000 - 500,000   ■ Over 500,000

hmapur

Bay

of Bengal

BURMA

THAILAND

Mouths of the Irrawaddy

136

15°

1

Andaman Islands
(to India)

North Andaman

Middle Andaman

South Andaman

Little Andaman

Port Blair

Mergui Archipelago

137

10°

2

A n d a m a n

S e a

*Isthmus
of Kra*

Car Nicobar

Katchall Island

Nicobar Islands
(to India)

Little Nicobar

Great Nicobar

Strait of Malacca

5°

3

S u m a t e r a

138

4

INDONESIA

Kepulauan Banyak

Pulau
Simeulue

Pulau Nias

Equator

C E A N

Pulau Siberut

5

141

85°   90°   95°

E   F   G   H

ELEVATION

				Below sea level	0	100m	250m	500m	1000m	2000m	4000m
-4000m	-3000m	-2000m	-1000m	-500m							

328ft   820ft   1640ft   3281ft   6562ft   13 124ft

-13 124ft   -9843ft   -6562ft   -3281ft   -1640ft   -820ft/-250ft   0

NORTH INDIA, PAKISTAN & BANGLADES

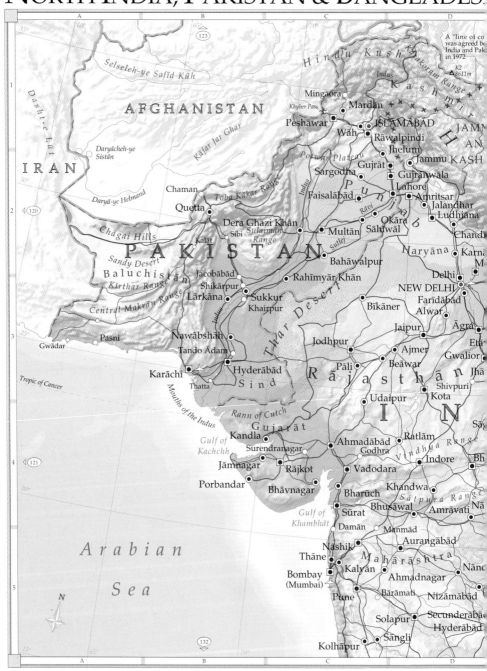

A "line of co
was agreed b
India and Pak
in 1972

AFGHANISTAN

Selseleh-ye Safīd Kūh

Hindu Kush

K2
△8611m

Indus

Kāsh m ī r

Mingāora

Khyber Pass

Mardān

Peshāwar

Wāh

ISLĀMĀBĀD

JAM

Dasht-e lūt

Daryācheh-ye
Sistān

Kāfir Jar Ghar

Rāwalpindi

AN

Jhelum

Jammu KASH

IRAN

Gujrāt

Gujrānwala

Sargodha

Kāfir Jar Ghar

Pothoha Plateau

Chaman

Toba Kākar Range

Faisalābād

Punjab

Lahore

Amritsar

Jalandhar

Ludhiāna

Quetta

Indus

Rāvi

Okāra

Chandī

Dera Ghazi Khān

Sibi

Sulaimān
Range

Multān

Sāhīwāl

M

Kalāt

Haryāna

Karna

PAKISTAN

Chāgai Hills

Baluchistān

Sutlej

Bahāwalpur

Sandy Desert

Kīrthar Range

Jacobābād

Shikārpur

Rahīmyār Khān

Delhi

NEW DELHI

Central Makrān Range

Lārkāna

Sukkur

Khairpur

Bīkāner

Farīdābād

Alwar

Pasni

Nawābshāh

Thar Desert

Jodhpur

Jaipur

Āgra

Etā

Gwādar

Tando Ādam

Indus

Pāli

Ajmer

Gwalior

Jha

Tropic of Cancer

Karāchi

Hyderābād

Sind

R ā j a s t h ā n

Beāwar

Thatta

Udaipur

Shivpuri

Kota

I

N

Rann of Cutch

Mouths of the Indus

Gujarāt

Sāg

Kandla

Ahmadābād

Ratlām

*Gulf of
Kachchh*

Surendranagar

Godhra

Indore

Bh

Jāmnagar

Rājkot

Vadodara

Vindhya Range

Porbandar

Bhāvnagar

Bharūch

Khandwa

Sātpura Range

Bhusāwal

Amrāvati

Na

Sūrat

Daman

Manmād

*Gulf of
Khambhāt*

Aurangābād

Nāshik

M a h ā r ā s h t r a

Nānc

A r a b i a n

Thāne

Kalyān

Ahmadnagar

S e a

Bombay
(Mumbai)

Pune

Bārāmati

Nizāmābād

N

Solapur

Secunderābā

Hyderābād

Sāngli

Kolhāpur

0 km   300
0 miles   300

POPULATION

 Less than 50,000   50,000-100,000   100,000 - 500,000   Over 500,000

XINJIANG
YGUR ZIZHIQU

Kunlun Mountains

AKSAI CHIN
Occupied by China,
claimed by India

DEMCHOK/
DEMQOG
Claimed by
India and China

QINGHAI

C H I N A

Tanggula Shan

Jinsha Jiang SICHUAN

Mekong

XIZANG ZIZHIQU

(Tibet)

Plateau of

Nyainqêntanglha Shan

126

Brahmaputra

Arunachal Pradesh

N E P A L
Annapurna
8091m △

Tibet

H i m a l a y a s

Mount Everest
8848m △
Kula Kangri
7554m △

Dibrugarh

Brahmaputra

reilly
Jaun
Sahraich
Lucknow

Salyan
Tansen

Pokhara

KATHMANDU
Bhaktapur
Lalitpur
Biratnagar

Gangtok
Darjiling

THIMPHU

BHUTAN

Shiliguri
Koch Bihar

Bongaigaon

Jorhāt

Kohima

Faizābād
Gorakhpur

Chhapra
Patna

Saidpur
Dinajpur

Guwāhāti
Rangpur

Dispur

A s s a m

Imphāl

Kānpur
Jaunpur

Mau
Varānasi
Sharif

Ganges

Bhāgalpur

Jamālpur

Sylhet
Silchar

Allahābād

Gaya

Rājshāhi
Dhanbād

BANGLADESH
Pābna

Brahmanbāria

Tropic of Cancer

Madhya Pradesh

Bokaro
Ranchi

Asansol
Bānkura

Ganges
Jessore

DHAKA
Comilla

B U R M A

Murwāra
Jabalpur

Chota Nagpur Plateau
Jamshedpur

West Bengal
Hāora

Khulna

Chittagong

136

Korba
Bilāspur

Raurkela

Kharagpur

Calcutta

Barisāl

Gondia
Raipur

Sambalpur

Bāleshwar

Mouths of the Ganges

Jāndgaon
Durg

O r i s s a

Cuttack
Bhubaneshwar

Puri

*Bay of
Bengal*

Jagdalpur

Brahmapur

Irrawaddy

imnagar
dhra Pradesh

Eastern Ghats

Srīkākulam
Vizianagaram
Visākhapatnam
Rājahmundry
Kākināda

Mouths of the Irrawaddy

133

ELEVATION

					Below sea level	0	100m	250m	500m	1000m	2000m	4000m
-2000m	-1000m	-500m	-250m	-100m								
						328ft	820ft	1640ft	3281ft	6562ft	13 124ft
-6562ft	-3281ft	-1640ft	-820ft	-328ft	-164ft/-50m	0						

MAINLAND SOUTHEAST ASIA

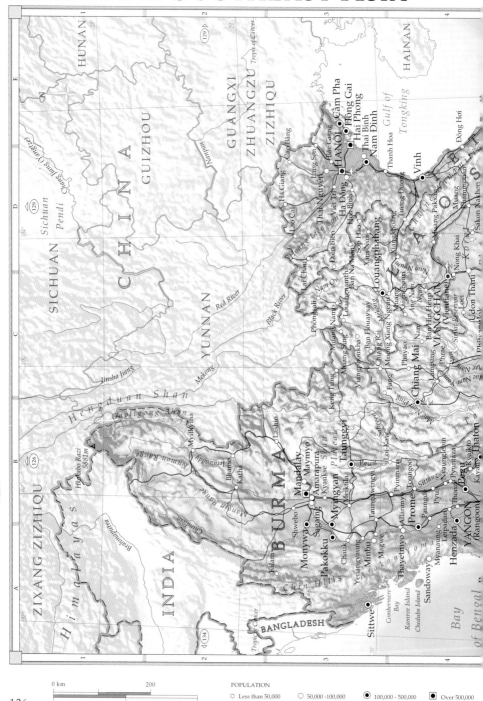

ZIXANG ZIZHIQU

HUNAN

GUIZHOU

Chang Jiang (Yangtze)

Sichuan
Pendi

SICHUAN

C H I N A

YUNNAN

Jinsha Jiang

Red River

Black River

Mekong

GUANGXI

ZHUANGZU

ZIZHIQU

Tropic of Cancer

Nanpan

HAINAN

Gulf of Tongking

Cầm Pha
Hồng Gai
HANOI
Hải Phòng
Thái Bình
Hà Đông
Nam Định

Đông Hới

Thanh Hoa

Vinh

Cao Bằng

Bắc Giang
Lạng Sơn
Việt Trì
Thái Nguyên
Ninh Bình

Hà Giang

Lào Cai

Điện Biên

Lai Châu

Nam Ou

Sơn Hạn
Sam Nua
Xam Nua

Phôngsali

Nam Nou

Muang Sing

Ban Houayxay

Chiang Rai

Muang Xiang Ngeun
Louabergamtha
Louangphabang

Kiang Khoang
Muang
Sam Neua

VIANGCHAN
(Vientiane)

L A O S

Mekong

Mường Sing

Vangviengkha

Phaya

Pak Sane
Ban Hin Heup
Lak Sao
Xaignabouri
Loei

Nong Khai

Udon Thani

Muang Pakxang
Nong Khai

Sirindit Reservoir

Chang Mai

Phrae

Lampang

Lae Nam Yom

Mae Nam Nan

Lae Nam Ping

Loi-Kaw

Kyaukse
Tawng
Pawn
Pyinmana
Toungoo
SHan

B U R M A

Lashio

Myitkyina

Bhamo

Katha

Myingyan
Meiktila
Taungdwingyi
Pyinmana
Nyaunglebin
Prome

Mandalay
Maymyo
Amarapura
Sagaing

Shwebo
Monywa

Pakokku

Chauk

Yenangyaung
Magwe
Minbu
Thayetmyo
Alanmyo
Thanraza
Prome
Myanaung
Henzada
Letpadan

YANGON
(Rangoon)

Pegu
Kavito
Thaton

Pyu

Chin Hills

Hkakabo Razi
5881m

Kumon Range

Irrawaddy

Chindwin

Hengduan Shan

Gaoligong Shan

Patkai Range

H i m a l a y a s

INDIA

Brahmaputra

BANGLADESH

Sittwe

Tropic of Cancer

Combermere
Bay

Ramree Island

Cheduba Island

Sandoway

Bay of Bengal

A r a k a n Y o m a

0 km   200

0 miles   200

POPULATION

O Less than 50,000   O 50,000 -100,000   ◉ 100,000 - 500,000   ■ Over 500,000

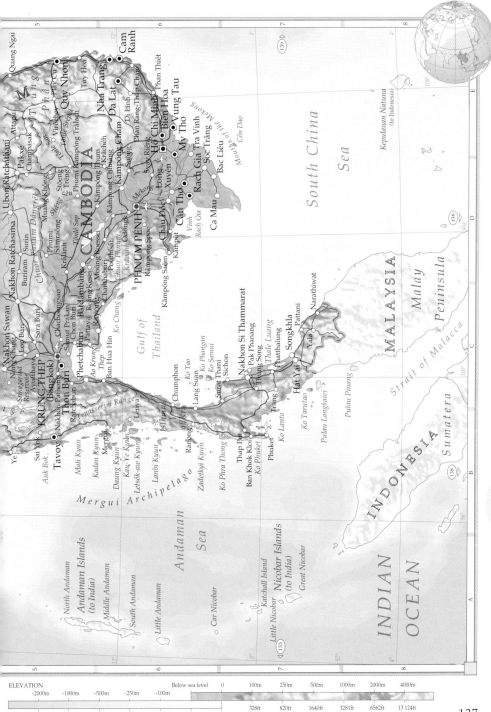

Quang Ngai

Cam Ranh

Quy Nhon

Tuy Hoa

Nha Trang

Da Lat

Phan Rang–Thap Cham

Phan Thiet

Bien Hoa

Vung Tau

Ho Chi Minh

My Tho

Con Dao

Tra Vinh

Soc Trang

Rach Gia

Can Tho

Bac Lieu

Ca Mau

South China Sea

Kepulauan Natuna
(to Indonesia)

Attapu

Ubon Ratchathani

Pakxe

Champasak

Stoeng

Treng

Krâchéh

Kâmpóng Cham

Suong

Long Xuyen

Chau Doc

Kampot

Vinh

Rach Gia

CAMBODIA

Phnum Dângrêk

Phumĭ

Sâmraông

Krâlănh

Siěm Réab

Bătdâmbâng

Bantéay Méanchey

Chhloŭ

Poŭthĭsăt

Kâmpóng Thum

Kâmpóng Chhnăng

Kâmpóng Spoe

PHNUM PENH

Kâmpóng Saôm

Kâ Chang

Nakhon Sawan

Nakhon Ratchasima

Lop Buri

Surin

Buriram

Sara Buri

Chon Buri

Chachoengsao

Pattaya

Ban Nong

Chang

Rayong

KRUNG THEP
(Bangkok)

Thon Buri

Nakhon Pathom

Samut Prakan

Phetchaburi

Hua Hin

Ban Hua Hin

Ratchaburi

Ayutthaya

Samut
Songkhram

Gulf of
Thailand

MALAYSIA

Malay

Peninsula

Strait of Malacca

Narathiwat

Nakhon Si Thammarat

Pak Phanang

Thale Luang

Phatthalung

Songkhla

Pattani

Yala

Hat Yai

Thung Song

Trang

Sichon

Surat Thani

Ko Samui

Ko Phangan

Ko Tao

Chumphon

Lang Suan

Thap Put

Ban Khok Kloi

Ko Phuket

Phuket

Ranong

Sumatera

INDONESIA

Pulau Pinang

Ko Tarutao

Pulau Langkawi

Ko Lanta

Phet

Ye

Tavoy

Sai Yok

Auk Bok

Mali Kyun

Kadan Kyun

Mergui

Daung Kyun

Kng Ye Kyun

Letsok-aw Kyun

Lenya

Limbi Kyun

Zadetkyi Kyun

Ko Phra Thong

Mergui Archipelago

Tenasserim Range

North Andaman

Andaman Islands
(to India)

Middle Andaman

South Andaman

Little Andaman

Andaman Sea

Car Nicobar

Katchall Island

Little Nicobar

Nicobar Islands
(to India)

Great Nicobar

INDIAN OCEAN

ELEVATION

					Below sea level	0	100m	250m	500m	1000m	2000m	4000m
-2000m	-1000m	-500m	-250m	-100m								
-6562ft	-3281ft	-1640ft	-820ft	-328ft	-164ft / -50m	0	328ft	820ft	1640ft	3281ft	6562ft	13 124ft

MARITIME SOUTHEAST ASIA

BURMA

SINGAPORE

MALAYSIA

0 km   10
0 miles   10

Johore Strait

Causeway
Lim Chu
Kang
Bukit Panjang Houngang
Choa Chu, New Town
Kang
Jurong City
Industrial
Estate
Selat Panda
Pulau Sudong
Pulau Pawai

*Pulau
Ubin*

*Pulau
Tekong*

Changi

Bedok
New Town

Telok Blangah
Sentosa

Strait of Singapore

Urban areas
Open areas
Nature reserves

Bukit Timah 176m

Queenstown

N

LAOS

VIETNAM

THAILAND

*Gulf of
Tongking*

Hainan
(to China)

Mekong

South Chin

Sea

Paracel Islands
(disputed)

CAMBODIA

Spratly Islands
(disputed)

Andaman

Sea

*Gulf of
Thailand*

Mouths of the Mekong

Nicobar Islands
(to India)

George
Town
Banda Aceh Sigli
Bireuen
Takengon
*Pulau
Pinang*

Butterworth
Taiping
Ipoh
Kampar

Kota Bharu

Kuala
Terengganu

Dungun
Cukai

Kota Kinabalu
**BANDAR SERI
BEGAWAN**
BRUNEI
Miri

Medan
Tebingtinggi
Pematangsiantar
Sibolga
*Danau
Toba*
Pulau Simeulue
Pulau Nias
Kepulauan Banyak

Teluk
Intan
Kelang
Seremban
Melaka
Muar
Batu Pahat

Kuantan

KUALA LUMPUR

Keluang
Johor Bahru
SINGAPORE

*Kepulauan Natuna
(to Indonesia)*

Bintulu
Bintang
Selat Serasan
Sibu
Kuching
Batang Rajang
Sri Aman

Sarawak

Balabac

Banjaran Crocker

Samarinda
Kawi

Muller

B o r n e o

Equator

Pekanbaru

Payakumbuh
Padang
Solok
Rengat
Kualatungkai
Jambi
Batang Hari
Simpang
Pangkalpinang
Palembang
Lahat
Baturaja
Kotabumi
Bengkulu
Kepulauan Mentawai
Pulau Siberut
Muarabungo
Pegunungan Barisan

*Kepulauan
Lingga*

Pontianak

Singkawang
Ngabang

Bangka

*Pulau
Belitung*

Selat Karimata

Sampit

Kapuas

Kalimatan

Barito

Balikpapan
Amunta
Kandan

Banjarmasin

Pegunungan

Sri Aman

Mahakam

I N D O

Sumatera
(Sumatra)
Tanjungkarang

INDIAN

OCEAN

Cirebon
Tegal
Laut Jawa
Pekalongan
Semarang
Kudus
Surabaya
Probolinggo
Jember
Madura
*Pulau
Laut*
Selat M

D

Jawa
(Java)
JAKARTA
Serang
Bogor
Sukabumi
Bandung
Cilacap
Tasikmalaya
Magelang
Yogyakarta
Surakarta
Selat Sunda
Cirebon
Malang
Kediri
Madiun
Bali
Denpa
*Pulau
Lombok*

138

POPULATION

 Less than 50,000
 50,000 -100,000
 100,000 - 500,000
 Over 500,000

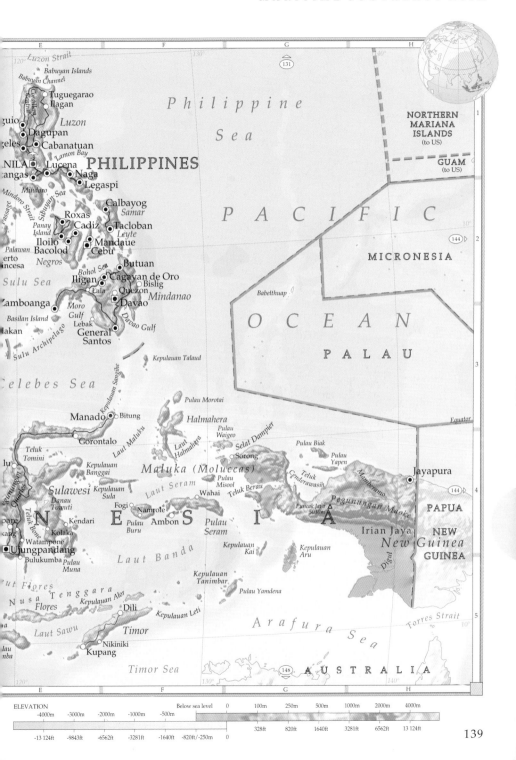

ELEVATION

-4000m	-3000m	-2000m	-1000m	-500m	Below sea level	0	100m	250m	500m	1000m	2000m	4000m
-13 124ft	-9843ft	-6562ft	-3281ft	-1640ft	-820ft/-250m	0	328ft	820ft	1640ft	3281ft	6562ft	13 124ft

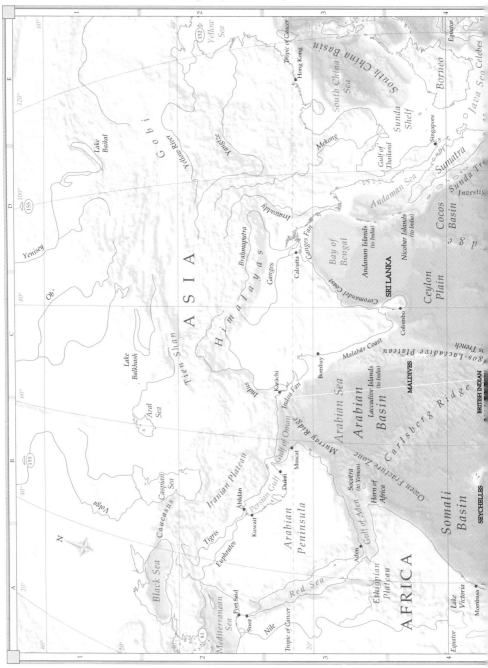

Yellow Sea

Hong Kong

South China Basin

South China Sea

Lake Baikal

Gobi

Yellow River

Yangtze

Sunda Shelf

Borneo

Java Sea

Celebes

Singapore

Sumatra

Gulf of Thailand

Mekong

Sunda Tre

Andaman Sea

Investig

Yenisey

Irrawaddy

Ganges Fan

Andaman Islands (to India)

Nicobar Islands (to India)

Cocos Basin

Ob'

Brahmaputra

Bay of Bengal

SRI LANKA

Ceylon Plain

Ganges

Calcutta

A S I A

Himalayas

Coromandel Coast

Colombo

Tien Shan

Lake Balkhash

Malabar Coast

MALDIVES

Laccadive Plateau

Trench

Aral Sea

Indus

Karachi

Bombay

Indus Fan

Laccadive Islands (to India)

Carlsberg Ridge

BRITISH INDIAN

Volga

Caspian Sea

Iranian Plateau

Persian Gulf

Gulf of Oman

Murray Ridge

Arabian Sea

Arabian Basin

Owen Fracture Zone

Somali Basin

SEYCHELLES

Caucasus

Black Sea

Abadan

Kuwait

Dubai

Muscat

Socotra (to Yemen)

Horn of Africa

Tigris

Euphrates

Arabian Peninsula

Gulf of Aden

Aden

Ethiopian Plateau

AFRICA

Lake Victoria

Mombasa

N

Mediterranean Sea

Port Said

Suez

Nile

Red Sea

Tropic of Cancer

Equator

60°

120°

100°

80°

60°

40°

20°

60°

20°

20°

155

155

155

152

81

E

D

C

B

A

1

2

3

4

0 km   1500

0 miles   1500

• Major ports

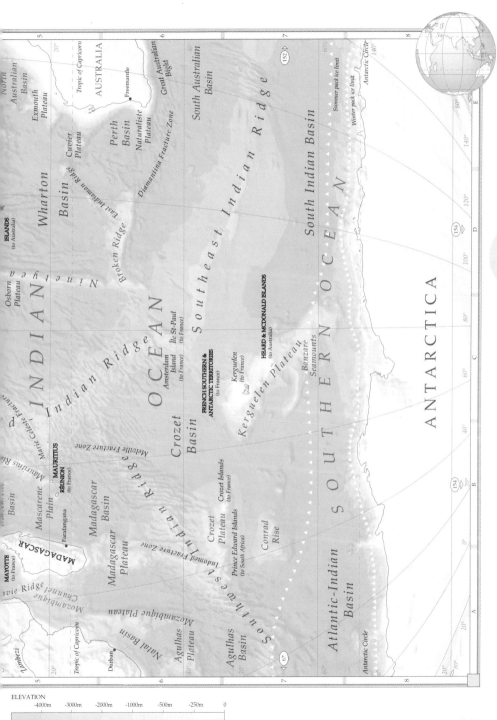

ELEVATION

-4000m	-3000m	-2000m	-1000m	-500m	-250m	0
-13 124ft	-9843ft	-6562ft	-3281ft	-1640ft	-820ft	0

141

AUSTRALASIA & OCEANIA

POPULATION

- ○ Less than 50,000
- ◎ 50,000 -100,000
- ◉ 100,000 - 500,000
- ◼ Over 500,000

0 km   1000

0 miles   1000

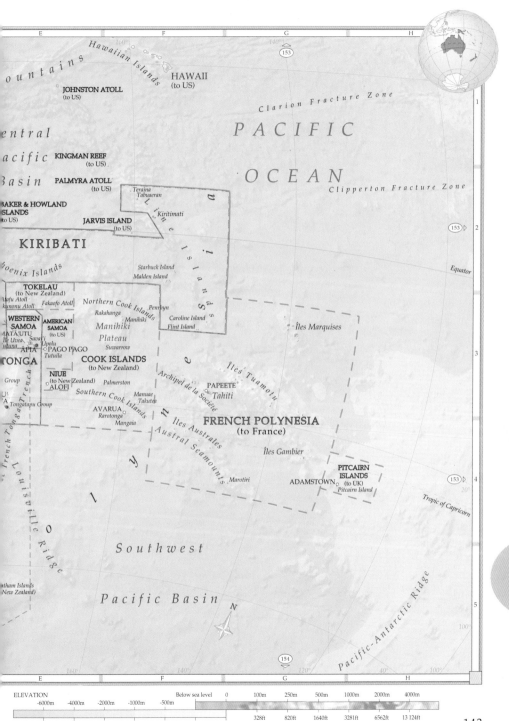

E · 160° · F · 140° · G · (153) · H

Hawaiian Islands

HAWAII
(to US)

JOHNSTON ATOLL
(to US)

ountains

entral

acific

Basin

KINGMAN REEF
(to US)

PALMYRA ATOLL
(to US)

BAKER & HOWLAND
ISLANDS
(to US)

JARVIS ISLAND
(to US)

KIRIBATI

Teraina
Tabuaeran

Kiritimati

Line Islands

PACIFIC

OCEAN

Clarion Fracture Zone

Clipperton Fracture Zone

153

1

153

2

Equator

hoenix Islands

TOKELAU
(to New Zealand)

afu Atoll
kunonu Atoll

Fakaofo Atoll

WESTERN
SAMOA
MATA'UTU
Ile Uvea
duna

Savai'i

AMERICAN
SAMOA
(to US)

Upolu
PAGO PAGO
Tutuila

Northern Cook Islands

Rakahanga

Manihiki

Manihiki
Plateau

Penrhyn

Caroline Island
Flint Island

Suwarrow

Starbuck Island
Malden Island

Îles Marquises

APIA

TONGA

NIUE
(to New Zealand)
ALOFI

COOK ISLANDS
(to New Zealand)

Palmerston

Southern Cook Islands

Manuae
Takutea

Archipel de la Société

Îles Tuamotu

PAPEETE
Tahiti

3

French Tonga Trench

Group

U

A

AVARUA
Rarotonga
Mangaia

Îles Australes

FRENCH POLYNESIA
(to France)

Austral Seamounts

Îles Gambier

Louisville Ridge

l

Marotiri

PITCAIRN
ISLANDS
ADAMSTOWN (to UK)
Pitcairn Island

153

4

20°

Tropic of Capricorn

Tongatapu Group

Southwest

o

atham Islands
New Zealand)

Pacific Basin

N

Pacific-Antarctic Ridge

100°

5

E · 160° · F · 140° · G · 120° · 40° · H · 100°

(154)

ELEVATION
Below sea level 0   100m   250m   500m   1000m   2000m   4000m
-6000m -4000m -2000m -1000m -500m
                                              328ft   820ft   1640ft   3281ft   6562ft   13 124ft
-19 686ft -13 124ft -6562ft -3281ft -1640ft -820ft/-250m 0

143

THE SOUTHWEST PACIFIC

NORTHERN MARIANA ISLANDS (to US)

Saipan
SAIPAN Tinian
Rota

GUAM (to US)
AGANA

MARSHALL ISLANDS

Micronesia

MICRONESIA

Yap

Enewetak Atoll
Bikini Atoll
Rongelap Atoll

Ratak Chain

Ujelang Atoll
Kwajalein Atoll
Ebeye Namu
Ailinglaplap Atoll
Jaluit Atoll Kili
Ebon Atoll

Ailuk A
Wotje A
Au
MA

Ratik Chain

Mi

KOROR
Babelthuap

Hall Islands
Chuuk

Oroluk Atoll

PALIKIR
Pohnpei

Kosrae

West Caroline Islands

East Caroline Islands

Caroline Islands

PALAU

Makin Ato
Tarawa
BAIRIK
Abemama A

Equator

PAPUA NEW GUINEA

Nauru Banaba

NAURU

Admiralty Islands

Mussau Island

Bismarck Archipelago

New Ireland

New Guinea

Bismarck Sea

New Britain

Bougainville Island

INDONESIA

Madang
Central Range
Mount Wilhelm 4509m
Lae

Choiseul
Santa Isabel

SOLOMON

Owen Stanley Range

Solomon Sea

Kiriwina Islands

New Georgia Islands

Malaita

ISLANDS

Arafura Sea

Gulf of Papua

HONIARA
Guadalcanal

San Cristobal
Rennell

Santa Cruz Islands

Torres Strait

PORT MORESBY

Louisiade Archipelago

Arnhem Land

Groote Eylandt

Gulf of Carpentaria

Cape York Peninsula

Coral Sea

VANUATU

Banks Islands

Espiritu Santo

Maewo
Pentecost
Ambrym
Épi

Barkly Tableland

Great Barrier Reef

CORAL SEA ISLANDS (to Australia)

Malekula

PORT-V
Éfaté

NORTHERN

NEW CALEDONIA (to France)

Erromang
Tanna
Anator

TERRITORY

Great Dividing Range

New Caledonia

Ouvéa
Lifou
Maré

Tropic of Capricorn

QUEENSLAND

NOUMÉA

Îles Loyauté

Macdonnell Ranges

AUSTRALIA

0 km   750
0 miles   750

POPULATION

 Less than 50,000
 50,000 -100,000
 100,000 - 500,000
 Over 500,000

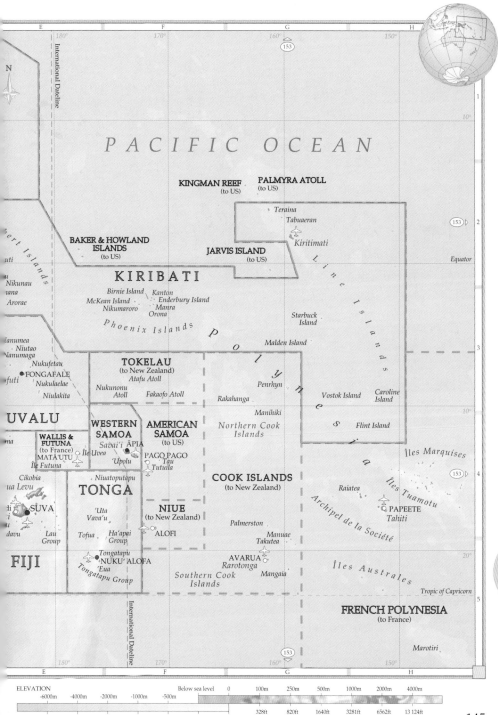

WESTERN AUSTRALIA

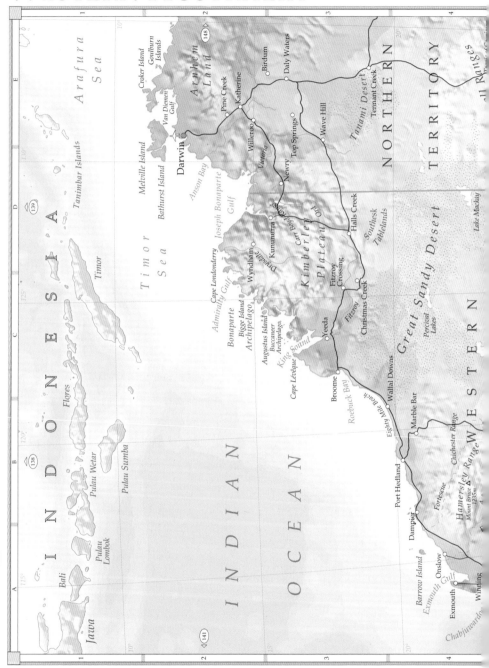

Arafura Sea

Timor Sea

Arnhem Land

Croker Island
Goulburn Islands

Birdum
Daly Waters

Pine Creek
Katherine

Wave Hill
Top Springs
Newry
Willeroo
Victoria

Darwin

Van Diemen Gulf

Melville Island

Bathurst Island

Joseph Bonaparte Gulf

Anson Bay

Tanimbar Islands

Timor

I N D O N E S I A

Flores

Pulau Wetar

Pulau Sumba

Pulau Lombok

Bali

Jawa

Tanami Desert

Tennant Creek

N O R T H E R N

T E R R I T O R Y

ll Ranges

Lake Mackay

Halls Creek
Southesk
Tablelands
Kimberley Plateau
Ord
Fitzroy Crossing
Christmas Creek

Kununurra
Drysdale
Wyndham

Cape Londonderry
Admiralty Gulf
Bonaparte Archipelago
Bigge Island
Augustus Island
Buccaneer Archipelago
Cape Lévêque
King Sound
Yeeda
Fitzroy

Great Sandy Desert
Percival Lakes

W E S T E R N

Wallal Downs
Broome
Roebuck Bay
Eighty Mile Beach
Marble Bar
Port Hedland

Chichester Range
Hamersley Range
Mount Bruce
1235m
Fortescue

Dampier
Barrow Island
Onslow
Exmouth
Exmouth Gulf
Winning

Chabjuwardoo

I N D I A N

O C E A N

0 km	400
0 miles	400

POPULATION

 Less than 50,000   50,000 -100,000   100,000 - 500,000   Over 500,000

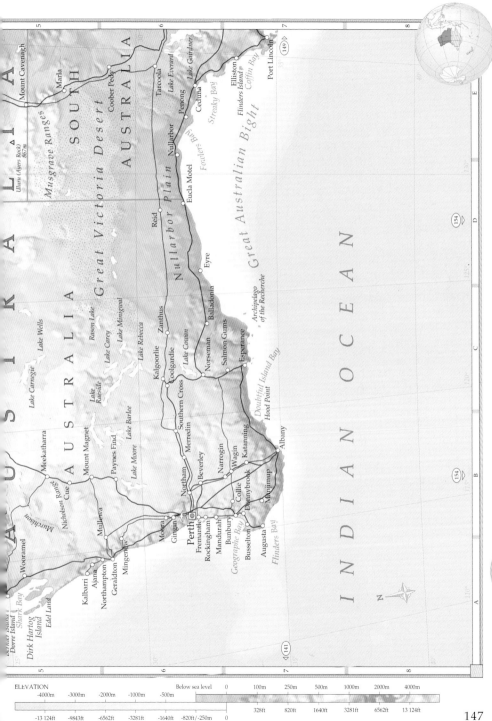

WESTERN AUSTRALIA

SOUTH AUSTRALIA

AUSTRALIA

Mount Cavenagh
Marla
Coober Pedy
Tarcoola
Lake Everard
Penong
Ceduna
Nullarbor
Eucla Motel
Reid
Eyre
Balladonia
Mount Everard
Lake Gairdner
Streaky Bay
Fowlers Bay
Elliston
Flinders Island
Coffin Bay
Port Lincoln

Uluru (Ayers Rock) 867m
Musgrave Ranges
Great Victoria Desert
Nullarbor Plain
Great Australian Bight

Archipelago of the Recherche
Zanthus
Kalgoorlie
Coolgardie
Lake Cowan
Norseman
Salmon Gums
Esperance
Doubtful Island Bay
Hood Point

Lake Wells
Lake Carnegie
Raeson Lake
Lake Carey
Lake Minigwal
Lake Rebecca
Southern Cross
Merredin

Meekatharra
Lake Raeside
Mount Magnet
Paynes Find
Lake Barlee
Lake Moore
Northam
Beverley
Narrogin
Wagin
Katanning
Albany

Cue
Nicholson Range
Mullewa
Mingenew
Moora
Gingin
Perth
Fremantle
Rockingham
Mandurah
Bunbury
Collie
Dardanup
Donnybrook
Manjimup

Wooramel
Murchison
Kalbarri
Ajana
Northampton
Geraldton
Busselton
Augusta
Geographe Bay
Flinders Bay

White Island
Dorre Island
Shark Bay
Dirk Hartog Island
Edel Land

INDIAN OCEAN

N

EASTERN AUSTRALIA

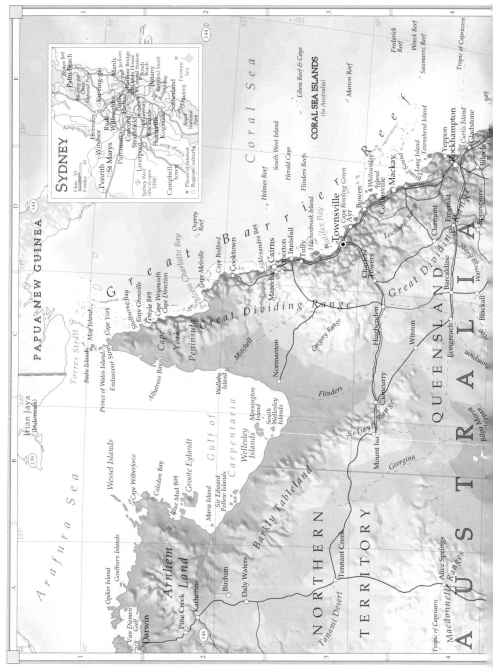

SYDNEY

Broken Bay
Palm Beach
Berowra-and-Chase
Manly
Warringah
Dee Why
Port Jackson
Mosman
Sydney Harbour Bridge
Opera House
Bondi
Botany Beach
Botany Bay
Bradfield Smith
Hornsby
Ryde Willoughby
Concord Drummoyne
Parramatta Strathfield
Liverpool Rockdale
Rockdale
Penrith Windsor
St Marys
Kogarah
Cronulla
Sutherland
Royal National Park
Port Hacking Bay
Kingsway
Campbelltown

Sydney West
(due to open 1998)

0 km 10
0 miles 10

■ Places of interest
□ Regions/suburbs

CORAL SEA ISLANDS
(to Australia)

Frederick Reef
Wreck Reef
Saumarez Reef
Lihou Reef & Cays
Marion Reef

Coral Sea
Holmes Reef
South West Island
Herald Cays
Flinders Reefs

Osprey Reef
Cape Bedford
Cooktown
Cape Melville
Princess Charlotte Bay
Cape Weymouth
Cape Direction
Shelburne Bay
Cape Grenville
Temple Bay
Cape York
Prince of Wales Island
Endeavour Strait
Badu Island
Mai Island

PAPUA NEW GUINEA

Irian Jaya
(Indonesia)

Torres Strait

Cape York Peninsula

Great Dividing Range

Mitchell

Normanton

Flinders

Gregory Range

Alexandra Bay
Cairns
Mareeba
Atherton
Innisfail
Tully
Hinchinbrook Island
Halifax Bay
Townsville
Cape Bowling Green
Ayr
Charters Towers

Whitsunday Island
Bowen
Collinsville
Mackay
Broad Sound
Long Island
Townsend Island
Curtis Island
Gladstone
Yeppoon
Rockhampton
Biloela

Leichhardt Range

Great Dividing Range

Clermont
Emerald
Barcaldine
Blackall
Springsure

Warrego River

Hughenden
Winton
Longreach

QUEENSLAND

Cloncurry
Selwyn Range
Mount Isa
Georgina

Barkly Tableland

Macdonnell Ranges
Alice Springs

NORTHERN TERRITORY

AUSTRALIA

Tennant Creek
Daly Waters
Birdum
Katherine
Pine Creek
Darwin
Van Diemen Gulf
Croker Island
Goulburn Islands

Arnhem Land

Arafura Sea

Wessel Islands
Cape Wilberforce
Caledon Bay
Blue Mud Bay
Groote Eylandt
Maria Island
Sir Edward Pellew Islands

Gulf of Carpentaria

Wellesley Islands
Mornington Island
South Wellesley Islands
Wallaby Island
Albatross Bay

Tanami Desert

Tropic of Capricorn

POPULATION

○ Less than 50,000 ○ 50,000 -100,000 ● 100,000 - 500,000 ■ Over 500,000

0 km — 400
0 miles — 400

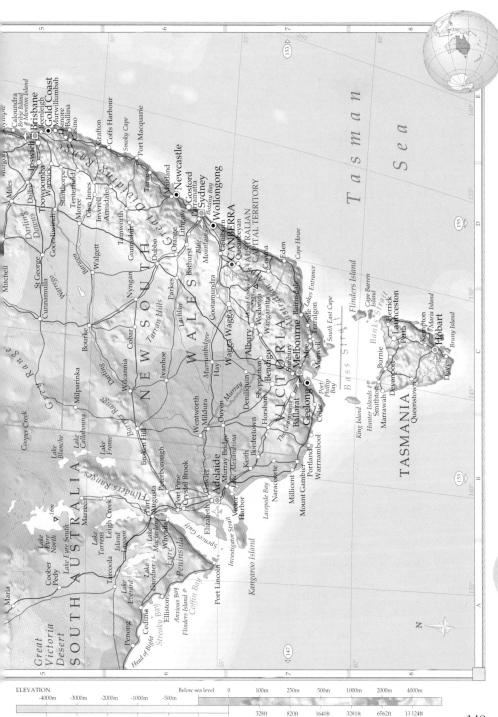

ELEVATION

-4000m	-3000m	-2000m	-1000m	-500m	Below sea level	0	100m	250m	500m	1000m	2000m	4000m

| -13 124ft | -9843ft | -6562ft | -3281ft | -1640ft | -820ft/-250m | 0 | 328ft | 820ft | 1640ft | 3281ft | 6562ft | 13 124ft |

NEW ZEALAND

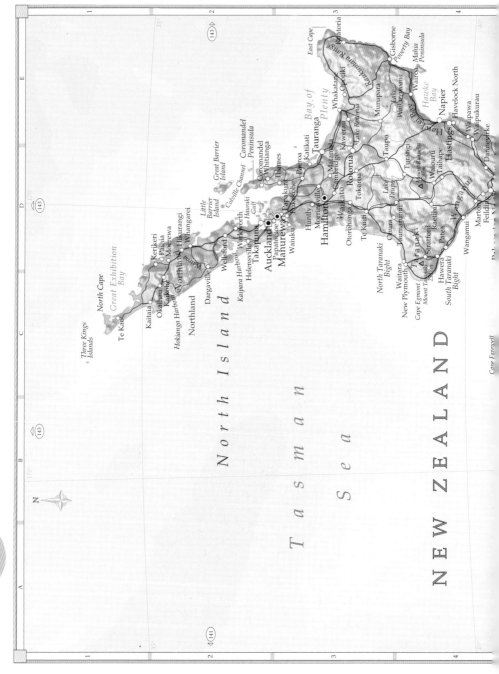

North Island

Tasman Sea

NEW ZEALAND

Three Kings Islands
North Cape
Great Exhibition Bay
Te Kao
Kaitaia
Okaihau
Kaikohe
Kerikeri
Paihia
Moerewa
Hokianga Harbour
Northland
Whangarei
Hikurangi
Northland
Dargaville
Kaipara Harbour
Wairoa
Wellsford
Warkworth
Helensville
Waiwera
Hauraki Gulf
Takapuna
Auckland
Papatoetoe
Mahurewa
Waiuku
Wanuku
Papakura
Waikato
Morrinsville
Huntly
Hamilton
Cambridge
Waikato
Te Awamutu
Otorohanga
Te Kuiti
Ohura
Taumarunui
North Taranaki Bight
Waitara
New Plymouth
Cape Egmont
Mount Taranaki
Taranaki
Stratford
Eltham
Hawera
Patea
South Taranaki Bight
Wanganui
Marton
Feilding

Little Barrier Island
Great Barrier Island
Colville Channel
Coromandel Peninsula
Coromandel
Whitianga
Thames
Paeroa
Te Aroha
Katikati
Tauranga
Bay of Plenty
Matamata
Putaruru
Tokoroa
Lake Rotorua
Rotorua
Kawerau
Lake Taupo
Taupo
Turangi
Mount Ruapehu
Waiouru
Raetihi
Ohakune
Taihape

Matatoria
East Cape
Matatoria
Whakatane
Opotiki
Raukumara Range
Gisborne
Poverty Bay
Mahia Peninsula
Wairoa
Murupara
Lake Waikaremoana
Hawke Bay
Napier
Hastings
Havelock North
Waipawa
Waipukurau
Dannevirke

Cape Farewell

0 km   100
0 miles   100

POPULATION
○ Less than 50,000   ○ 50,000 -100,000   ◉ 100,000 - 500,000   ◼ Over 500,000

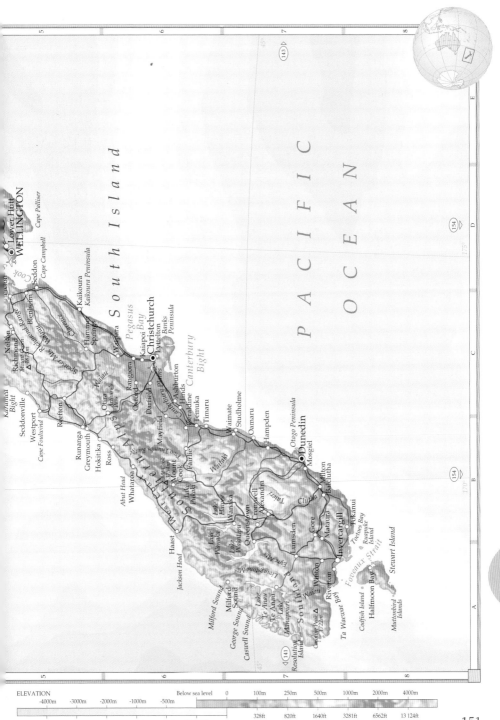

South Island

WELLINGTON
Lower Hutt
Cape Palliser
Cape Campbell
Seddon
Blenheim
Nelson
Richmond
Mount Cook Range
Kaikoura
Kaikoura Peninsula
Hammer Springs
Waiau
Amuri
Pegasus Bay
Christchurch
Kaiapoi
Lyttelton
Banks Peninsula
Rangiora
Oxford
Darfield
Ashburton
Mid Canterbury
Plains
Geraldine
Temuka
Timaru
Canterbury Bight
Waimate
Studholme
Oamaru
Hampden
Otago Peninsula
Dunedin
Mosgiel
Milton
Balclutha
Tokanui
Tai Tapu Bay
Ruapuke Island
Foveaux Strait
Stewart Island
Halfmoon Bay
Muttonbird Islands
Codfish Island
Reefton
Runanga
Greymouth
Hokitika
Ross
Whataroa
Abut Head
Haast
Jackson Head
Milford Sound
Milford Sound
George Sound
Caswell Sound
Resolution Island
Lake Te Anau
Te Anau
Manapouri
South West Point
Lake Manapouri
Livingstone Mts
Winton
Riverton
Invercargill
Gore
Mataura
Mataura
Lumsden
Cromwell
Alexandra
Clyde
Queenstown
Lake Hayes
Wanaka
Lake Wanaka
Lake Wakatipu
Lake Pukaki
Fairlie
Mayfield
Mount Cook
Westport
Seddonville
Cape Foulwind
Karamea Bight

Southern Alps

Pacific Ocean

ELEVATION

	Below sea level	0						
-4000m	-3000m	-2000m	-1000m	-500m				
					100m	250m	500m	1000m	2000m	4000m
-13 124ft	-9843ft	-6562ft	-3281ft	-1640ft	-820ft/-250m	0	328ft	820ft	1640ft	3281ft	6562ft	13 124ft

THE PACIFIC OCEAN

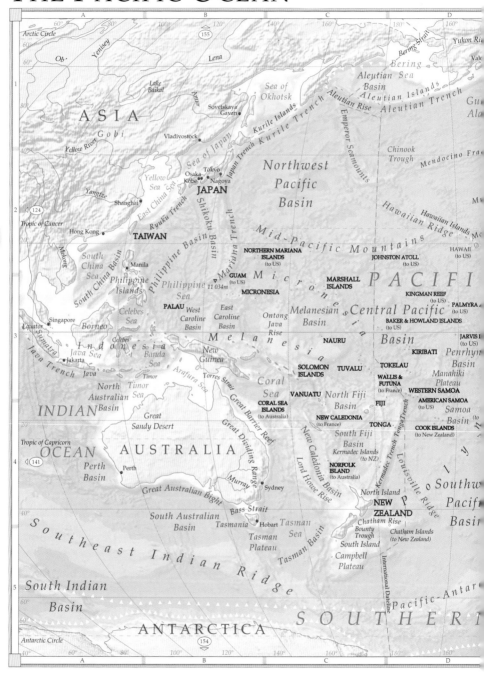

Arctic Circle
Yukon Ri
Yenisey
Ob
Lena
Bering
Aleutian Sea
Basin
Gu
Ala
Lake Baikal
Sea of Okhotsk
Aleutian Rise
Aleutian Islands
Aleutian Trench
ASIA
Gobi
Amur
Sovetskaya Gavan
Kurile Islands
Emperor Seamounts
Chinook Trough
Mendocino Fra
Vladivostock
Kurile Trench
Yellow River
Japan Trench
Northwest
Pacific
Basin
Sea of Japan
Osaka Tokyo
Kobe Nagoya
Yellow Sea
JAPAN
Hawaiian Ridge
M
Yangtze
East China Sea
Shanghai
Mc
Tropic of Cancer
Shikoku Basin
Mid-Pacific Mountains
Hawaiian Islands
Hong Kong
Ryuku Trench
TAIWAN
Ryukyu Trench
NORTHERN MARIANA ISLANDS (to US)
JOHNSTON ATOLL (to US)
HAWAII (to US)
South China Basin
Manila
Philippine Basin
Mariana Trench
GUAM (to US)
11 034m
Mi
cr
MARSHALL ISLANDS (to US)
PACIFI
South China Sea
Mekong
Philippine Islands
Philippine Sea
MICRONESIA
o
KINGMAN REEF (to US)
PALAU
West Caroline Basin
East Caroline Basin
Melanesian Basin
Central Pacific
PALMYRA (to US)
Singapore
Celebes Sea
Ontong Java Rise
n
e
s
BAKER & HOWLAND ISLANDS (to US)
Equator
Borneo
i
JARVIS I (to US)
Indonesia
Celebes
Me l a n e s i a
NAURU
Basin
Java Sea
Jakarta
Banda Sea
New Guinea
SOLOMON ISLANDS
TUVALU
KIRIBATI
Penrhyn Basin
Java Trench
Java
Arafura Sea
Torres Strait
TOKELAU
Manihiki Plateau
Sumatra
North Australian Basin
Timor
Timor Sea
Great Barrier Reef
Coral Sea
VANUATU
WALLIS & FUTUNA (to France)
WESTERN SAMOA
INDIAN
Great Sandy Desert
CORAL SEA ISLANDS (to Australia)
North Fiji Basin
FIJI
AMERICAN SAMOA (to US)
Samoa Basin (to
NEW CALEDONIA (to France)
TONGA
Tropic of Capricorn
Great Dividing Range
South Fiji Basin
Cook Islands (to New Zealand)
OCEAN
AUSTRALIA
New Caledonia Basin
Kermadec Islands (to NZ)
Kermadec Trench
Tonga Trench
Perth Basin
Perth
NORFOLK ISLAND (to Australia)
Lord Howe Rise
North Island
Louisville Ridge
Southw
Pacifi
Great Australian Bight
Murray
Sydney
NEW ZEALAND
P
Basir
Bass Strait
South Australian Basin
Tasmania
Hobart
Tasman Sea
Tasman Plateau
Chatham Rise
Bounty Trough
Chatham Islands (to New Zealand)
Southeast Indian Ridge
Tasman Basin
South Island
Campbell Plateau
South Indian
Basin
Pacific-Antar
International Dateline
Antarctic Circle
ANTARCTICA
SOUTHER

0 km   2000
0 miles   2000

• Major ports

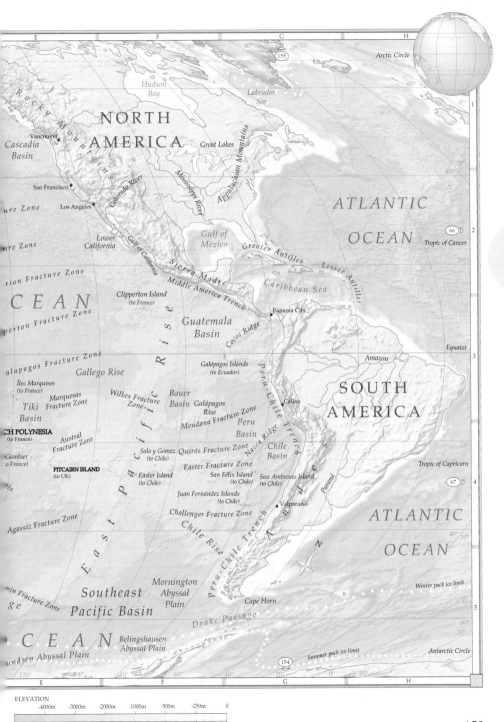

ELEVATION

| -4000m | -3000m | -2000m | -1000m | -500m | -250m | 0 |
| -13 124ft | -9843ft | -6562ft | -3281ft | -1640ft | -820ft | 0 |

ANTARCTICA

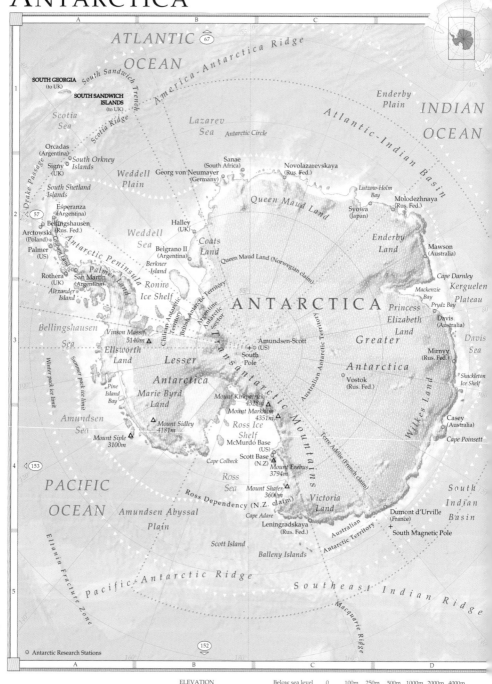

ATLANTIC OCEAN

America–Antarctica Ridge

INDIAN OCEAN

Enderby Plain

SOUTH GEORGIA
(to UK)

SOUTH SANDWICH ISLANDS
(to UK)

South Sandwich Trench

Scotia Sea

Lazarev Sea

Antarctic Circle

Atlantic–Indian Basin

Scotia Ridge

Orcadas
(Argentina)

South Orkney Islands

Signy
(UK)

Sanae
(South Africa)

Novolazarevskaya
(Rus. Fed.)

Lützow-Holm Bay

Molodezhnaya
(Rus. Fed.)

Georg von Neumayer
(Germany)

Weddell Plain

Queen Maud Land

Syowa
(Japan)

South Shetland Islands

Drake Passage

Esperanza
(Argentina)

Bellingshausen
(Rus. Fed.)

Arctowski
(Poland)

Palmer
(US)

Halley
(UK)

Weddell Sea

Coats Land

Belgrano II
(Argentina)

Queen Maud Land (Norwegian claim)

Enderby Land

Mawson
(Australia)

Cape Darnley

Kerguelen

Rothera
(UK)

San Martin
(Argentina)

Berkner Island

Ronne Ice Shelf

Mackenzie Bay

Prydz Bay

Plateau

Alexander Island

Palmer Land

ANTARCTICA

Princess Elizabeth Land

Davis
(Australia)

Davis Sea

Antarctic Peninsula

Chilean Antarctic Territory

British Antarctic Territory

Argentine Antarctic Sector

Australian Antarctic Territory

Bellingshausen Sea

Vinson Massif
5140m

Amundsen-Scott
(US)

South Pole

Greater Antarctica

Mirny
(Rus. Fed.)

Ellsworth Land

Lesser Antarctica

Vostok
(Rus. Fed.)

Shackleton Ice Shelf

Winter pack ice limit

Summer pack ice limit

Pine Island Bay

Marie Byrd Land

Transantarctic Mountains

Mount Kirkpatrick
4528m

Mount Markham
4351m

Ross Ice Shelf

Wilkes Land

Casey
(Australia)

Cape Poinsett

Amundsen Sea

Mount Sidley
4181m

Mount Siple
3100m

McMurdo Base
(US)

Scott Base
(N.Z.)

Mount Erebus
3794m

Terre Adélie (French claim)

South Indian Basin

PACIFIC OCEAN

Amundsen Abyssal Plain

Ross Sea

Cape Colbeck

Ross Dependency (N.Z. claim)

Mount Shafer
3600m

Cape Adare

Victoria Land

Dumont d'Urville
(France)

South Magnetic Pole

Leningradskaya
(Rus. Fed.)

Australian Antarctic Territory

Scott Island

Balleny Islands

Macquarie Ridge

Pacific–Antarctic Ridge

Southeast Indian Ridge

Eltanin Fracture Zone

⊙ Antarctic Research Stations

ELEVATION

Below sea level

-4000m -3000m -2000m -1000m -500m   0   100m 250m 500m 1000m 2000m 4000m

-13 124ft -9843ft -6562ft -3281ft -1640ft -820ft/-250m   328ft 820ft 1640ft 3281ft 6562ft 13 124ft

0 km 500

0 miles 500

ARCTIC OCEAN

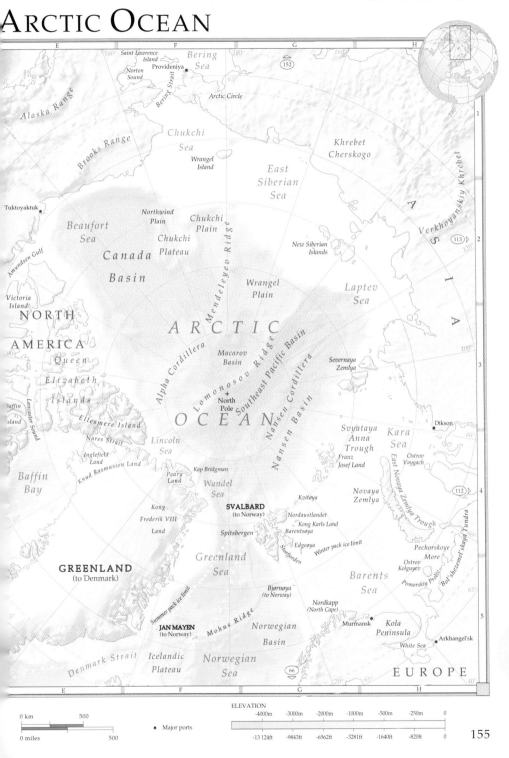

E · F · G · H

Bering Sea
Saint Lawrence Island
Norton Sound
Providenya
Bering Strait
152
Arctic Circle

Alaska Range
Brooks Range
Chukchi Sea
Wrangel Island
70
East Siberian Sea
Khrebet Cherskogo

Tuktoyaktuk
Beaufort Sea
Northwind Plain
Chukchi Plain
Chukchi Plateau
75
New Siberian Islands
Laptev Sea
Verkhoyanskiy Khrebet
A S I A
113
120°
100°

Canada Basin
Mendeleyev Ridge
Wrangel Plain

Amundsen Gulf
Victoria Island
NORTH
Queen
Elizabeth
Islands
A R C T I C
Macarov Basin
Alpha Cordillera
Lomonosov Ridge
Southeast Pacific Basin
North Pole
Nansen Cordillera
Nansen Basin
Severnaya Zemlya

AMERICA
Baffin Island
Lancaster Sound
Ellesmere Island
Nares Strait
Inglefield Land
Knud Rasmussen Land
Lincoln Sea
Peary Land
Kap Bridgman
O C E A N
Svyataya Anna Trough
Franz Josef Land
Kara Sea
Dikson
80°
Ostrov Vaygach
East Novaya Zemlya Trough
112

Baffin Bay
Kong Frederik VIII Land
Wandel Sea
SVALBARD (to Norway)
Kvitøya
Nordaustlandet
Spitsbergen
Kong Karls Land
Barentsøya
Edgeøya
Storfjorden
Winter pack ice limit
Novaya Zemlya
Pechorskoye More
Ostrov Kolguyev
Pomorskiy Proliv
Bol'shezemel'skaya Tundra
65°

GREENLAND (to Denmark)
Greenland Sea
Bjørnøya (to Norway)
Nordkapp (North Cape)
Barents Sea
Kola Peninsula
Murmansk
Arkhangel'sk
White Sea
40°

Summer pack ice limit
JAN MAYEN (to Norway)
Mohns Ridge
Norwegian Basin
Norwegian Sea
66
EUROPE

Denmark Strait
Icelandic Plateau
65°
20°

E · F · G · H

0 km	500		ELEVATION									
0 miles	500	● Major ports	-4000m	-3000m	-2000m	-1000m	-500m	-250m	0			
			-13 124ft	-9843ft	-6562ft	-3281ft	-1640ft	-820ft	0			

Despite the rapid process of decolonization since the Second World War, around 10 million people in 59 territories around the world continue to live under the protection of France, Australia, Denmark, Norway, Portugal, New Zealand, the UK, the USA, or the Netherlands. These remnants of former colonial empires may have persisted for economic, strategic or political reasons and are administered in a variety of ways.

AUSTRALIA

AUSTRALIA'S OVERSEAS TERRITORIES have not been an issue since Papua New Guinea became independent in 1975. Consequently there is no overriding policy towards them. Norfolk Island is inhabited by descendants of the HMS Bounty mutineers and more recent Australian migrants.

ASHMORE & CARTIER ISLANDS
Indian Ocean

STATUS: External territory
CLAIMED: 1978
CAPITAL: Not applicable
POPULATION: None
AREA: 5.2 sq km
(2 sq miles)

CHRISTMAS ISLAND
Indian Ocean

STATUS: External territory
CLAIMED: 1958
CAPITAL: Flying Fish Cove
POPULATION: 2,871
AREA: 134.6 sq km
(52 sq miles)

COCOS ISLANDS
Indian Ocean

STATUS: External territory
CLAIMED: 1955
CAPITAL: West Island
POPULATION: 555
AREA: 14.24 sq km
(5.5 sq miles)

CORAL SEA ISLANDS
South Pacific

STATUS: External territory
CLAIMED: 1969
CAPITAL: None
POPULATION: 8 (meteorologists)
AREA: Less than 3 sq km
(1.16 sq miles)

HEARD & McDONALD IS.
Indian Ocean

STATUS: External territory
CLAIMED: 1947
CAPITAL: Not applicable
POPULATION: None
AREA: 417 sq km
(161 sq miles)

NORFOLK ISLAND
South Pacific

STATUS: External territory
CLAIMED: 1913
CAPITAL: Kingston
POPULATION: 2,637
AREA: 34.4 sq km
(13.3 sq miles)

DENMARK

THE FAEROE ISLANDS have been under Danish administration since Queen Margreth I of Denmark inherited Norway in 1380. The Home Rule Act of 1948 gave the Faeroese control over all their internal affairs. Greenland first came under Danish rule in 1380. Today, Denmark remains responsible for the island's foreign affairs and defence.

FAEROE ISLANDS
North Atlantic

STATUS: External territory
CLAIMED: 1380
CAPITAL: Tórshavn
POPULATION: 47,310
AREA: 1,399 sq km
(540 sq miles)

GREENLAND
North Atlantic

STATUS: External territory
CLAIMED: 1380
CAPITAL: Nuuk
POPULATION: 55,385
AREA: 2,175,516 sq km
(840,000 sq miles)

FRANCE

FRANCE HAS DEVELOPED economic ties with its overseas territories, thereby stressing interdependence over independence. Overseas *départements*, officially part of France, have their own governments. Territorial *collectivités* and overseas *territoires* have varying degrees of autonomy.

CLIPPERTON ISLAND
East Pacific

STATUS: Dependency of French Polynesia
CLAIMED: 1930
CAPITAL: Not applicable
POPULATION: None
AREA: 7 sq km
(2.7 sq miles)

FRENCH GUIANA
South America

STATUS: Overseas department
CLAIMED: 1817
CAPITAL: Cayenne
POPULATION: 135,000
AREA: 90,996 sq km
(35,135 sq miles)

FRENCH POLYNESIA
South Pacific

STATUS: Overseas territory
CLAIMED: 1843
CAPITAL: Papeete
POPULATION: 211,000
AREA: 4,165 sq km
(1,608 sq miles)

GUADELOUPE
West Indies

STATUS: Overseas department
CLAIMED: 1635
CAPITAL: Basse-Terre
POPULATION: 413,000
AREA: 1,780 sq km
(687 sq miles)

MARTINIQUE

West Indies

STATUS: Overseas department
CLAIMED: 1635
CAPITAL: Fort-de-France
POPULATION: 371,000
AREA: 1,100 sq km
(425 sq miles)

MAYOTTE

Indian Ocean

STATUS: Territorial collectivity
CLAIMED: 1843
CAPITAL: Mamoudzou
POPULATION: 97,088
AREA: 374 sq km
(144 sq miles)

NEW CALEDONIA

South Pacific

STATUS: Overseas territory
CLAIMED: 1853
CAPITAL: Nouméa
POPULATION: 179,000
AREA: 19,103 sq km
(7,374 sq miles)

RÉUNION

Indian Ocean

STATUS: Overseas department
CLAIMED: 1638
CAPITAL: Saint-Denis
POPULATION: 632,000
AREA: 2,512 sq km
(970 sq miles)

ST PIERRE & MIQUELON

North America

STATUS: Territorial collectivity
CLAIMED: 1604
CAPITAL: Saint Pierre
POPULATION: 6,000
AREA: 242 sq km
(93.4 sq miles)

WALLIS & FUTUNA

South Pacific

STATUS: Overseas territory
CLAIMED: 1842
CAPITAL: Mata-Utu
POPULATION: 14,000
AREA: 274 sq km
(106 sq miles)

NETHERLANDS

THE COUNTRY'S TWO remaining overseas territories were formerly part of the Dutch West Indies. Both are now self-governing, but the Netherlands remains responsible for their defence.

ARUBA

West Indies

STATUS: Autonomous part of the Netherlands
CLAIMED: 1643
CAPITAL: Oranjestad
POPULATION: 69,000
AREA: 194 sq km
(75 sq miles)

NETHERLANDS ANTILLES

West Indies

STATUS: Autonomous part of the Netherlands
CLAIMED: 1816
CAPITAL: Willemstad
POPULATION: 195,000
AREA: 800 sq km
(308 sq miles)

NEW ZEALAND

NEW ZEALAND'S GOVERNMENT has no desire to retain any overseas territories. However, the economic weakness of its dependent territory Tokelau and its freely associated states, Niue and the Cook Islands, has forced New Zealand to remain responsible for their foreign policy and defence.

COOK ISLANDS

South Pacific

STATUS: Associated territory
CLAIMED: 1901
CAPITAL: Avarua
POPULATION: 19,000
AREA: 293 sq km
(113 sq miles)

NIUE

South Pacific

STATUS: Associated territory
CLAIMED: 1901
CAPITAL: Alofi
POPULATION: 2,000
AREA: 264 sq km
(102 sq miles)

TOKELAU

South Pacific

STATUS: Dependent territory
CLAIMED: 1926
CAPITAL: Not applicable
POPULATION: 2,000
AREA: 10.4 sq km
(4 sq miles)

NORWAY

IN 1920, 41 nations signed the Spitsbergen treaty recognizing Norwegian sovereignty over Svalbard. There is a Nato base on Jan Mayen. Bouvet Island is a nature reserve.

BOUVET ISLAND

South Atlantic

STATUS: Dependency
CLAIMED: 1928
CAPITAL: Not applicable
POPULATION: None
AREA: 58 sq km
(22 sq miles)

JAN MAYEN

North Atlantic

STATUS: Dependency
CLAIMED: 1929
CAPITAL: Not applicable
POPULATION: None
AREA: 381 sq km
(147 sq miles)

PETER I ISLAND

Southern Ocean

STATUS: Dependency
CLAIMED: 1931
CAPITAL: Not applicable
POPULATION: None
AREA: 180 sq km
(69 sq miles)

NORWAY *continued*

SVALBARD
Arctic Ocean
STATUS: Dependency
CLAIMED: 1920
CAPITAL: Longyearbyen
POPULATION: 3,431
AREA: 62,906 sq km
(24,289 sq miles)

PORTUGAL

AFTER A COUP in 1974, Portugal's overseas possessions were rapidly granted sovereignty. Macao is the only one remaining and it is to become a Special Administrative Region of China in 1999.

MACAO
South China
STATUS: Special territory
CLAIMED: 1557
CAPITAL: Macao
POPULATION: 388,000
AREA: 18 sq km
(7 sq miles)

UNITED KINGDOM

THE UK STILL has the largest number of overseas territories. Locally-governed by a mixture of elected representatives and appointed officials, they all enjoy a large measure of internal self-government, but certain powers, such as foreign affairs and defence, are reserved for Governors of the British Crown.

ANGUILLA
West Indies
STATUS: Dependent territory
CLAIMED: 1650
CAPITAL: The Valley
POPULATION: 8,960
AREA: 96 sq km
(37 sq miles)

ASCENSION
South Atlantic
STATUS: Dependency of St Helena
CLAIMED: 1673
CAPITAL: Not applicable
POPULATION: 1,099
AREA: 88 sq km
(34 sq miles)

BERMUDA
North Atlantic
STATUS: Crown colony
CLAIMED: 1612
CAPITAL: Hamilton
POPULATION: 60,686
AREA: 53 sq km
(20.5 sq miles)

BRITISH INDIAN OCEAN TERRITORY
STATUS: Dependent territory
CLAIMED: 1814
CAPITAL: Diego Garcia
POPULATION: 3,400
AREA: 60 sq km
(23 sq miles)

BRITISH VIRGIN ISLANDS
West Indies
STATUS: Dependent territory
CLAIMED: 1672
CAPITAL: Road Town
POPULATION: 16,644
AREA: 153 sq km
(59 sq miles)

CAYMAN ISLANDS
West Indies
STATUS: Dependent territory
CLAIMED: 1670
CAPITAL: George Town
POPULATION: 25,355
AREA: 259 sq km
(100 sq miles)

FALKLAND ISLANDS
South Atlantic
STATUS: Dependent territory
CLAIMED: 1832
CAPITAL: Stanley
POPULATION: 2,121
AREA: 12,173 sq km
(4,699 sq miles)

GIBRALTAR
South West Europe
STATUS: Crown colony
CLAIMED: 1713
CAPITAL: Gibraltar
POPULATION: 28,074
AREA: 6.5 sq km
(2.5 sq miles)

GUERNSEY
Channel Islands
STATUS: Crown dependency
CLAIMED: 1066
CAPITAL: St Peter Port
POPULATION: 58,000
AREA: 65 sq km
(25 sq miles)

HONG KONG (XIANGGANG)
South China
STATUS: Crown colony
CLAIMED: 1842
CAPITAL: Victoria
POPULATION: 5.9 million
AREA: 1,076 sq km
(415 sq miles)
Hong Kong will revert to China in June 1997, when the UK's 99-year lease on the New Territories expires.

ISLE OF MAN
British Isles
STATUS: Crown dependency
CLAIMED: 1765
CAPITAL: Douglas
POPULATION: 71,000
AREA: 572 sq km
(221 sq miles)

JERSEY
Channel Islands
STATUS: Crown dependency
CLAIMED: 1066
CAPITAL: St Helier
POPULATION: 84,082
AREA: 116 sq km
(45 sq miles)

MONTSERRAT
West Indies
STATUS: Dependent territory
CLAIMED: 1632
CAPITAL: Plymouth
POPULATION: 11,000
AREA: 102 sq km
(40 sq miles)

PITCAIRN ISLANDS
South Pacific
STATUS: Dependent territory
CLAIMED: 1887
CAPITAL: Adamstown
POPULATION: 66
AREA: 3.5 sq km (1.35 sq miles)

ST HELENA
South Atlantic
STATUS: Dependent territory
CLAIMED: 1673
CAPITAL: Jamestown
POPULATION: 6,000
AREA: 122 sq km (47 sq miles)

SOUTH GEORGIA & THE SANDWICH ISLANDS
South Atlantic
STATUS: Dependent territory
CLAIMED: 1775
POPULATION: No permanent residents
AREA: 3,592 sq km (1,387 sq miles)

TRISTAN DA CUNHA
South Atlantic
STATUS: Dependency of St Helena
CLAIMED: 1612
POPULATION: 297
AREA: 98 sq km (38 sq miles)

TURKS & CAICOS ISLANDS
West Indies
STATUS: Dependent territory
CLAIMED: 1766
CAPITAL: Cockburn Town
POPULATION: 13,000
AREA: 430 sq km (166 sq miles)

UNITED STATES OF AMERICA

AMERICA'S OVERSEAS TERRITORIES have been seen as strategically useful, if expensive, links with its 'backyards'. The US has, in most cases, given the local population a say in deciding their own status. A US Commonwealth territory, such as Puerto Rico has a greater level of independence than that of a US unincorporated or external territory.

AMERICAN SAMOA
South Pacific
STATUS: Unincorporated territory
CLAIMED: 1900
CAPITAL: Pago Pago
POPULATION: 51,000
AREA: 195 sq km (75 sq miles)

BAKER & HOWLAND ISLANDS
South Pacific
STATUS: Unincorporated territory
CLAIMED: 1856
CAPITAL: Not applicable
POPULATION: None
AREA: 1.4 sq km (0.54 sq miles)

GUAM
West Pacific
STATUS: Unincorporated territory
CLAIMED: 1898
CAPITAL: Agaña
POPULATION: 144,000
AREA: 549 sq km (212 sq miles)

JARVIS ISLAND
South Pacific
STATUS: Unincorporated territory
CLAIMED: 1856
CAPITAL: Not applicable
POPULATION: None
AREA: 4.5 sq km (1.7 sq miles)

JOHNSTON ATOLL
Central Pacific
STATUS: Unincorporated territory
CLAIMED: 1858
CAPITAL: Not applicable
POPULATION: 327
AREA: 2.8 sq km (1 sq mile)

KINGMAN REEF
Central Pacific
STATUS: Administered territory
CLAIMED: 1856
CAPITAL: Not applicable
POPULATION: None
AREA: 1 sq km (0.4 sq miles)

MIDWAY ISLANDS
Central Pacific
STATUS: Administered territory
CLAIMED: 1867
CAPITAL: Not applicable
POPULATION: 453
AREA: 5.2 sq km (2 sq miles)

NAVASSA ISLAND
West Indies
STATUS: Unincorporated territory
CLAIMED: 1856
CAPITAL: Not applicable
POPULATION: None
AREA: 5.2 sq km (2 sq miles)

NORTHERN MARIANA ISLANDS
West Pacific
STATUS: Commonwealth territory
CLAIMED: 1947
CAPITAL: Saipan
POPULATION: 47,000
AREA: 457 sq km (177 sq miles)

PALMYRA ATOLL
Central Pacific
STATUS: Unincorporated territory
CLAIMED: 1898
CAPITAL: Not applicable
POPULATION: None
AREA: 12 sq km (5 sq miles)

PUERTO RICO
West Indies
STATUS: Commonwealth territory
CLAIMED: 1898
CAPITAL: San Juan
POPULATION: 3.6 million
AREA: 8,959 sq km (3,458 sq miles)

VIRGIN ISLANDS
West Indies
STATUS: Unincorporated territory
CLAIMED: 1917
CAPITAL: Charlotte Amalie
POPULATION: 104,000
AREA: 355 sq km (137 sq miles)

WAKE ISLAND
Central Pacific
STATUS: Unincorporated territory
CLAIMED: 1898
CAPITAL: Not applicable
POPULATION: 302
AREA: 6.5 sq km (2.5 sq miles)

GLOSSARY OF GEOGRAPHICAL TERM

THE GLOSSARY FOLLOWING lists all geographical terms occuring on the maps and in the main-entry names in the Index–Gazetteer. These terms may precede, follow or be run together with the proper elements of the name; where they precede it the term is reversed for indexing purposes – thus Poluostov Yamal is indexed as Yamal, Poluostrov.

A

Å *Danish, Norwegian,* River
Alpen *German,* Alps
Altiplanicie *Spanish,* Plateau
Älv(en) *Swedish,* River
Anse *French,* Bay
Archipiélago *Spanish,* Archipelago
Arcipelago *Italian,* Archipelago
Arquipélago *Portuguese,* Archipelago
Aukštuma *Lithuanian,* Upland

B

Bahía *Spanish,* Bay
Baía *Portuguese,* Bay
Baḥr *Arabic,* River
Baie *French,* Bay
Bandao *Chinese,* Peninsula
Banjaran *Malay,* Mountain range
Batang *Malay,* Stream
-berg *Afrikaans, Norwegian,* Mountain
Birket *Arabic ,* Lake
Boğazı *Turkish,* Lake
Bucht *German,* Bay
Bugten *Danish,* Bay
Buḥayrat *Arabic,* Lake, reservoir
Buḥeiret *Arabic,* Lake
Bukit *Malay,* Mountain
-bukta *Norwegian,* Bay
bukten *Swedish,* Bay
Burnu *Turkish,* Cape, point
Buuraha *Somali,* Mountains

C

Cabo *Portuguese,* Cape
Cap *French,* Cape
Cascada *Portuguese,* Waterfall
Cerro *Spanish,* Mountain
Chaîne *French,* Mountain range
Chau *Cantonese,* Island
Chāy *Turkish,* River
Chhâk *Cambodian,* Bay
Chhu *Tibetan,* River
-chôsuji *Korean,* Reservoir

Chott *Arabic,* Salt lake, depression
Ch'ün-tao *Chinese,* Island group
**Cambodian,* Mountains
Cordillera *Spanish,* Mountain range
Costa *Spanish,* Coast
Côte *French,* Coast
Cuchilla *Spanish,* Mountains

D

Dağı *Azerbaijani, Turkish,* Mountain
Dağları *Azerbaijani, Turkish,* Mountains
-dake *Japanese,* Peak
Danau *Indonesian,* Lake
Đao *Vietnamese,* Island
Daryā *Persian,* River
Daryācheh *Persian,* Lake
Dasht *Persian,* Plain, desert
Dawḥat *Arabic,* Bay
Dere *Turkish,* Stream
Dili *Azerbaijani,* Spit
-do *Korean,* Island
Dooxo *Somali,* Valley
Düzü *Azerbaijani,* Steppe
-dwīp *Bengali,* Island

E

Embalse *Spanish,* Reservoir
Erg *Arabic,* Dunes
Estany *Catalan,* Lake
Estrecho *Spanish,* Strait
-ey *Icelandic,* Island
Ezero *Bulgarian, Macedonian,* Lake

F

Fjord *Danish,* Fjord
-fjorden *Norwegian,* Fjord
-fjørdhur *Faeroese,* Fjord
Fleuve *French,* River
Fliegu *Maltese,* Channel
-fljór *Icelandic,* River

G

-gang *Korean,* River
Ganga *Nepali, Sinhala,* River
Gaoyuan *Chinese,* Plateau
-gawa *Japanese,* River
Gebel *Arabic,* Mountain

-gebirge *German,* Mountains
Ghubbat *Arabic,* Bay
Gjiri *Albanian,* Bay
Gol *Mongolian,* River
Golfe *French,* Gulf
Golfo *Italian, Spanish,* Gulf
Gora *Russian, Serbian,* Mountain
Gory *Russian,* Mountains
Guba *Russian,* Bay
Gunung *Malay,* Mountain

H

Ḥadd *Arabic,* Spit
-haehyŏp *Korean,* Strait
Haff *German,* Lagoon
Hai *Chinese,* Sea, bay
Ḥammādat *Arabic,* Plateau
Hāmūn *Persian,* Lake
Hawr *Arabic,* Lake
Hāyk' *Amharic,* Lake
He *Chinese,* River
Helodrano *Malagasy,* Bay
-hegység *Hungarian,* Mountain range
Hka *Burmese,* River
-ho *Korean,* Lake
Hô *Korean,* Reservoir
Holot *Hebrew,* Dunes
Hora *Belorussian,* Mountain
Hrada *Belorussian,* Mountains, ridge
Hsi *Chinese,* River
Hu *Chinese,* Lake

I

Île(s) *French,* Island(s)
Ilha(s) *Portuguese,* Island(s)
Ilhéu(s) *Portuguese,* Islet(s)
Irmak *Turkish,* River
Isla(s) *Spanish,* Island(s)
Isola (Isole) *Italian,* Island(s)

J

Jabal *Arabic,* Mountain
Jāl *Arabic,* Ridge
-järvi *Finnish,* Lake
Jazīrat *Arabic,* Island
Jazīreh *Persian,* Island
Jebel *Arabic,* Mountain

Jezero *Serbo-Croatian,* Lake
Jiang *Chinese,* River
-joki *Finnish,* River
-jökull *Icelandic,* Glacier
Juzur *Arabic,* Islands

K

Kaikyō *Japanese,* Strait
-kaise *Lappish,* Mountain
Kali *Nepali,* River
Kalnas *Lithuanian,* Mountain
Kalns *Latvian,* Mountain
Kang *Chinese,* Harbour
Kangri *Tibetan,* Mountain(s)
Kaôh *Cambodian,* Island
Kapp *Norwegian,* Cape
Kavīr *Persian,* Desert
K'edi *Georgian,* Mountain range
Kediet *Arabic,* Mountain
Kepulauan *Indonesian, Malay,* Island group
Khalîg, Khalīj *Arabic,* Gulf
Khawr *Arabic,* Inlet
Khola *Nepali,* River
Khrebet *Russian,* Mountain range
Ko *Thai,* Island
Kolpos *Greek,* Bay
-kopf *German,* Peak
Körfäzi *Azerbaijani,* Bay
Körfezi *Turkish,* Bay
Kõrgustik *Estonian,* Upland
Koshi *Nepali,* River
Kowtal *Persian,* Pass
Kūh(hā) *Persian,* Mountain(s)
-kundo *Korean,* Island group
-kysten *Norwegian,* Coast
Kyun *Burmese,* Island

L

Laaq *Somali,* Watercourse
Lac *French,* Lake
Lacul *Romanian,* Lake
Lago *Italian, Portuguese, Spanish,* Lake
Laguna *Spanish,* Lagoon, Lake

160

Laht *Estonian*, Bay
Laut *Indonesian*, Sea
Lembalemba *Malagasy*, Plateau
Lerr *Armenian*, Mountain
Lerrnashght'a *Armenian*, Mountain range
Les *Czech*, Forest
Lich *Armenian*, Lake
Liqeni *Albanian*, Lake
Lumi *Albanian*, River
Lyman *Ukrainian*, Estuary

M

Mae Nam *Thai*, River
-mägi *Estonian*, Hill
Maja *Albanian*, Mountain
-man *Korean*, Bay
Marios *Lithuanian*, Lake
-meer *Dutch*, Lake
Melkosopochnik *Russian*, Plain
-meri *Estonian*, Sea
Mifraz *Hebrew*, Bay
Monkhafad *Arabic*, Depression
Mont(s) *French*, Mountain(s)
Monte *Italian*, *Portuguese*, Mountain
More *Russian*, Sea
Mörön *Mongolian*, River

N

Nagor'ye *Russian*, Upland
Nahal *Hebrew*, River
Nahr *Arabic*, River
Nam *Laotian*, River
Nehri *Turkish*, River
Nevado *Spanish*, Mountain (snow-capped)
Nisoi *Greek*, Islands
Nizmennost' *Russian*, Lowland, plain
Nosy *Malagasy*, Island
Nur *Mongolian*, Lake
Nuruu *Mongolian*, Mountains
Nuur *Mongolian*, Lake
Nyzovyna *Ukrainian*, Lowland, plain

O

Ostrov(a) *Russian*, Island(s)
Oued *Arabic*, Watercourse
-oy *Faeroese*, Island
-øy(a) *Norwegian*, Island
Oya *Sinhala*, River
Ozero *Russian*, *Ukrainian*, Lake

P

Passo *Italian*, Pass
Pegunungan *Indonesian*, *Malay*, Mountain range
Pelagos *Greek*, Sea
Penisola *Italian*, Peninsula
Peski *Russian*, Sands
Phanom *Thai*, Mountain
Phou *Laotian*, Mountain
Pic *Catalan*, Peak
Pico *Portuguese*, *Spanish*, Peak
Pik *Russian*, Peak
Planalto *Portuguese*, Plateau
Planina, Planini *Bulgarian*, *Macedonian*, *Serbo-Croatian*, Mountain range
Ploskogor'ye *Russian*, Upland
Poluostrov *Russian*, Peninsula
Potamos *Greek*, River
Proliv *Russian*, Strait
Pulau *Indonesian*, *Malay*, Island
Pulu *Malay*, Island
Punta *Portuguese*, *Spanish*, Point

Q

Qā' *Arabic*, Depression
Qolleh *Persian*, Mountain

R

Raas *Somali*, Cape
-rags *Latvian*, Cape
Ramlat *Arabic*, Sands
Ra's *Arabic*, Cape, point, headland
Ravnina *Bulgarian*, *Russian*, Plain
Rēcif *French*, Reef
Represa (Rep.) *Spanish*, *Portuguese*, Reservoir
-rettō *Japanese*, Island chain
Riacho *Spanish*, Stream
Riban' *Malagasy*, Mountains
Rio *Portuguese*, River
Río *Spanish*, River
Riu *Catalan*, River
Rivier *Dutch*, River
Rivière *French*, River
Rowd *Pashtu*, River
Rūd *Persian*, River
Rudohorie *Slovak*, Mountains
Ruisseau *French*, Stream

S

Sabkhat *Arabic*, Salt marsh
Ṣaḥrā' *Arabic*, Desert
Samudra *Sinhala*, Reservoir
-san *Japanese*, *Korean*, Mountain
-sanchi *Japanese*, Mountains
-sanmaek *Korean*, Mountain
Sarīr *Arabic*, Desert
Sebkha, Sebkhet *Arabic*, Salt marsh, depression
See *German*, Lake
Selat *Indonesian*, Strait
-selkä *Finnish*, Ridge
Selseleh *Persian*, Mountain range
Serra *Portuguese*, Mountain
Serranía *Spanish*, Mountain
Sha'īb *Arabic*, Watercourse
Shamo *Chinese*, Desert
Shan *Chinese*, Mountain(s)
Shan-mo *Chinese*, Mountain range
Shaṭṭ *Arabic*, Distributary
-shima *Japanese*, Island
Shui-tao *Chinese*, Channel
Sierra *Spanish*, Mountains
Sôn *Vietnamese*, Mountain
Sông *Vietnamese*, River
-spitze *German*, Peak
Štít *Slovak*, Peak
Stoeng *Cambodian*, River
Stretto *Italian*, Strait
Su Anbarı *Azerbaijani*, Reservoir
Sungai *Indonesian*, *Malay*, River
Suu *Turkish*, River

T

Tal *Mongolian*, Plain
Tandavan' *Malagasy*, Mountain range
Tangorombohitr' *Malagasy*, Mountain massif
Tao *Chinese*, Island
Tassili *Berber*, Plateau, mountain
Tau *Russian*, Mountain(s)
Taungdan *Burmese*, Mountain range
Teluk *Indonesian*, *Malay*, Bay

Terara *Amharic*, Mountain
Tog *Somali*, Valley
Tônlé *Cambodian*, Lake
Top *Dutch*, Peak
-tunturi *Finnish*, Mountain
Tur'at *Arabic*, Channel

V

Väin *Estonian*, Strait
-vatn *Icelandic*, Lake
-vesi *Finnish*, Lake
Vinh *Vietnamese*, Bay
Vodokhranilishche (Vdkhr.) *Russian*, Reservoir
Vodoskhovyshche (Vdskh.) *Ukrainian*, Reservoir
Volcán *Spanish*, Volcano
Vozvyshennost' *Russian*, Upland, plateau
Vrh *Macedonian*, Peak
Vysochyna *Ukrainian*, Upland
Vysočina *Czech*, Upland

W

Waadi *Somali*, Watercourse
Wādī *Arabic*, Watercourse
Wāḥat, Wâhat *Arabic*, Oasis
Wald *German*, Forest
Wan *Chinese*, Bay
Wyżyna *Polish*, Upland

X

Xé *Laotian*, River

Y

Yarımadası *Azerbaijani*, Peninsula
Yazovir *Bulgarian*, Reservoir
Yoma *Burmese*, Mountains
Yü *Chinese*, Island

Z

Zaliv *Bulgarian*, *Russian*, Bay
Zatoka *Ukrainian*, Bay
Zemlya *Russian*, Bay

GLOSSARY OF ABBREVIATIONS

THIS GLOSSARY provides a comprehensive guide to the abbreviations used in this Atlas, and in the Index-Gazetteer.

A
abbrev. abbreviation
Afr. Afrikaans
Alb. Albanian
Amh. Amharic
anc. ancient
Ar. Arabic
Arm. Armenian
Az. Azerbaijani

B
Basq. Basque
Bel. Belorussian
Ben. Bengali
Bibl. Biblical
Bret. Breton
Bul. Bulgarian
Bur. Burmese

C
Cam. Cambodian
Cant. Cantonese
Cast. Castilian
Cat. Catalan
Chin. Chinese
Cro. Croat
Cz. Czech

D
Dan. Danish
Dut. Dutch

E
Eng. English
Est. Estonian
est. estimated

F
Faer. Faeroese
Fij. Fijian
Fin. Finnish
Flem. Flemish
Fr. French
Fris. Frisian

G
Geor. Georgian
Ger. German
Gk. Greek
Guj. Gujarati

H
Haw. Hawaiian
Heb. Hebrew
Hind. Hindi
hist. historical
Hung. Hungarian

I
Icel. Icelandic
Ind. Indonesian
Inuit Inuit
Ir. Irish
It. Italian

J
Jap. Japanese

K
Kaz. Kazakh
Kir. Kirghiz
Kor. Korean
Kurd. Kurdish

L
Lao. Laotian
Lapp. Lappish
Lat. Latin

Latv. Latvian
Lith. Lithanian
Lus. Lusatian

M
Mac. Macedonian
Mal. Malay
Malg. Malagasy
Malt. Maltese
Mong. Mongolia

N
Nepali. Nepali
Nor. Norwegian

O
off. offically

P
Pash. Pashtu
Per. Persian
Pol. Polish
Port. Portuguese
prev. previously

R
Rmsch. Romansch
Roman. Romanian
Rus. Russian

S
SCr. Serbian and Croatian
Serb. Serbian
Slvk. Slovak
Slvn. Slovene
Som. Somali
Sp. Spanish
Swa. Swahili
Swe. Swedish

T
Taj. Tajik
Th. Thai
Tib. Tibetan
Turk. Turkish
Turkm. Turkmenistan

U
Uigh. Uighur
Ukr. Ukrainian
Uzb. Uzbek

V
var. variant
Vtn. Vietnamese

W
Wel. Welsh

X
Xh. Xhosa

Y
Yugo. Yugoslavia

Key to country factboxes within the index:

Date of formation
This denotes the country's date of independence or the date when its current borders were established.

Languages
Official language(s) are denoted by an asterisk.

INDEX

A

Aa *see* Gauja
Aachen 94 A 4 *Dut.* Aken, *Fr.* Aix-la-Chapelle; *anc.* Aquae Grani, Aquisgranum. W Germany
Aaiún *see* Laâyoune
Aalborg Bugt *see* Ålborg Bugt
Aalen 95 B 6 S Germany
Aalsmeer 86 C 3 C Netherlands
Aalst 87 B 6 *Fr.* Alost. C Belgium
Aalten 86 E 4 E Netherlands
Aalter 87 B 5 NW Belgium
Äänekoski 85 D 5 C Finland
Aar *see* Aare
Aare 95 A 7 *var.* Aar. River, W Switzerland
Aarhus *see* Århus
Aasiaat 82 C 3 *var.* Ausiait, *Dan.* Egedesminde. W Greenland
Aat *see* Ath
Aba 75 G 5 S Nigeria
Aba 77 E 5 NE Zaire
Abā as Su'ūd *see* Najrān
Abaco Island *see* Great Abaco
Ābādān 120 C 4 SW Iran
Abagnar Qi *see* Xilin Hot
Abakan 114 D 4 C Russian Federation
Abancay 60 D 4 SE Peru
Abashiri 130 D 2 *var.* Abasiri. Hokkaidō, NE Japan
Abasiri *see* Abashiri
Ābaya Hāyk' 73 C 5 *Eng.* Lake Margherita, *It.* Abbaia. Lake, SW Ethiopia
Abbatis Villa *see* Abbeville
Abbazia *see* Opatija
Abbeville 90 C 2 *anc.* Abbatis Villa. N France
Abbeville 42 B 3 Louisiana, S USA
'Abd al 'Azīz, Jabal 118 D 2 mountain range, NE Syria
Abéché 76 C 3 *var.* Abécher, Abeshr. SE Chad
Abellinum *see* Avellino
Abemama Atoll 144 D 2 *var.* Apamama; *prev.* Roger Simpson Island. Island, W Kiribati
Abengourou 75 E 5 E Ivory Coast
Aberbrothock *see* Arbroath
Abercorn *see* Mbala
Aberdeen 88 D 3 *anc.* Devana. E Scotland, UK
Aberdeen 128 A 2 S Hong Kong
Aberdeen 46 B 2 Washington, NW USA
Aberdeen 45 E 2 South Dakota, N USA
Abergwaun *see* Fishguard
Abertawe *see* Swansea
Aberystwyth 89 C 6 W Wales, UK
Abhā 121 B 6 SW Saudi Arabia
Abidavichy 107 D 7 *Rus.* Obidovichi. E Belorussia
Abidjan 75 E 5 S Ivory Coast
Abilene 49 F 3 Texas, S USA
Abingdon *see* Pinta, Isla
Abkhazia 117 F 2 region, NW Georgia
Åbo *see* Turku
Aboisso 75 E 5 SE Ivory Coast
Abo, Massif d' 76 B 1 mountain range, N Chad
Abomey 75 F 5 S Benin
Abou-Déïa 76 C 3 SE Chad
Aboudouhour *see* Abū aḍ Ḍuḩūr
Abou Kémal *see* Abū Kamāl
Abrantes 92 B 3 *var.* Abrántes. C Portugal

Abrántes *see* Abrantes
Abrashlare *see* Brezovo
Abrolhos Bank 57 E 4 undersea bank, W Atlantic Ocean
Abrova 107 B 6 *Rus.* Obrovo. SW Belorussia
Abrud 108 B 4 *Hung.* Abrudbánya. SW Romania
Abrudbánya *see* Abrud
Abruzzese, Appennino 96 C 4 mountain range, C Italy
Absaroka Range 44 B 2 mountain range, NW USA
Abū aḍ Ḍuḩūr 118 B 3 *Fr.* Aboudouhour. NW Syria
Abu Dhabi *see* Abū Ẓaby
Abu Hamed 72 C 3 N Sudan
Abuja 75 G 4 country capital, C Nigeria
Abū Kamāl 118 E 3 *Fr.* Abou Kémal. E Syria
Abuná 61 E 2 *var.* Río Abuná. River, Bolivia/Brazil
Abuná, Río *see* Abunã
Abut Head 151 B 6 headland, South Island, SW New Zealand
Ābuyē Mēda 73 D 5 mountain, C Ethiopia
Abū Ẓaby 121 D 5 *var.* Abū Ẓabī, *Eng.* Abu Dhabi. Country capital, C United Arab Emirates
Acalayong 77 A 5 SW Equatorial Guinea
Acaponeta 50 C 4 C Mexico
Acapulco 51 E 5 *var.* Acapulco de Juárez. S Mexico
Acapulco de Juárez *see* Acapulco
Acarai Mountains 59 F 4 *var.* Serra Acaraí. Mountain range, Brazil/Guyana
Acaraí, Serra *see* Acarai Mountains
Acarigua 58 D 2 N Venezuela
Acay, Abra del 64 C 2 pass, N Argentina
Accra 75 E 5 country capital, SE Ghana
Achacachi 61 F 4 W Bolivia
Acklins Island 54 D 2 island, SE Bahamas
Aconcagua, Cerro 64 B 4 mountain, W Argentina
Acora 61 E 4 SE Peru
A Coruña 92 B 1 *Cast.* La Coruña, *Eng.* Corunna; *anc.* Caronium. NW Spain
Acre 62 C 2 *off.* Estado do Acre. State, W Brazil
Acre 60 D 2 cultural region, W Brazil
Acre, Estado do *see* Acre
Açu 63 G 2 NE Brazil
Ada 49 G 2 Oklahoma, C USA
Ada 100 D 3 N Yugoslavia
Ada Bazar *see* Adapazarı
Adáfer 74 D 2 plateau, C Mauritania
Adak Island 36 A 3 island, Alaska, NW USA
Adamaoua, Massif d' 76 B 4 *Eng.* Adamawa Highlands. Mountain range, NW Cameroon
Adamawa 68 B 4 province, N Cameroon
Adamawa Highlands *see* Adamaoua, Massif d'
Adam-jo-Tando *see* Tando Ādam
Adamstown 143 G 4 dependent territory capital, Pitcairn Island, SW Pitcairn Islands
'Adan 121 B 7 *Eng.* Aden. SW Yemen
Adana 116 D 4 *var.* Seyhan. S Turkey

162

Adapazarı 116 B 3 *prev.* Ada Bazar. NW Turkey
Adare, Cape 154 B 4 headland, Antarctica
Ad Dahnā' 120 B 4 desert, E Saudi Arabia
Ad Dakhla 70 A 4 *var.* Dakhla; *prev.* Villa Cisneros. W Morocco
Ad Dalanj *see* Dilling
Ad Damazīn *see* Ed Damazin
Ad Dāmūr *see* Damoûr
Ad Dawḥah 120 D 4 *Eng.* Doha. Country capital, C Qatar
Aḍ Ḍiffah *see* Libyan Plateau
Addis Ababa *see* Ādīs Ābeba
Addu Atoll 132 B 5 island, S Maldives
Adelaide 149 B 6 South Australia, S Australia
Aden *see* 'Adan
Aden, Gulf of 121 C 7 *var.* Badyarada 'Adméd. Gulf, W Indian Ocean
Adige 96 C 2 *Ger.* Etsch. River, N Italy
Adirondack Mountains 41 F 2 mountain range, New York, NE USA
Ādīs Ābeba 73 C 5 *var.* Addis Ababa. Country capital, C Ethiopia
Adıyaman 117 E 4 SE Turkey
Adjud 108 C 4 E Romania
Admiralty Gulf 146 C 2 gulf, E Indian Ocean
Admiralty Islands 144 B 3 island group, N Papua New Guinea
Adra 93 E 5 S Spain
Adrar 74 C 2 mountainous region, W Mauritania
Adrar 70 D 3 mountain range, SE Algeria
Adrian 40 C 3 Michigan, N USA
Adriatic Sea 103 E 2 *Alb.* Deti Adriatik, *It.* Mare Adriatic, *SCr.* Jadransko More, *Slvn.* Jadransko Morje. Sea, N Mediterranean Sea
Adycha 115 F 2 river, NE Russian Federation
Aegean Sea 103 F 3 *Gk.* Aigaío Pélagos, Aigaion Pelagos, *Turk.* Ege Denizi. Sea, N Mediterranean Sea
Aegviidu 106 D 2 *Ger.* Charlottenhof. NW Estonia
Aelok *see* Ailuk Atoll

Afghanistan
122 D 4 *Per.* Dowlat-e Eslāmī-ye Afghānestān; *prev.* Republic of Afghanistan. Islamic state, C Asia

Official name: Islamic State of Afghanistan **Date of formation:** 1919 **Capital:** Kābul **Population:** 20.5 million **Total area:** 652,090 sq km (251,770 sq miles) **Languages:** Persian*, Pashtu* **Religions:** Sunni Muslim 84%, Shi'a Muslim 15%, other 1% **Ethnic mix:** Pashtun 38%, Tajik 25%, Hazara 19%, Uzbek 6%, other 12% **Government:** *Mujahideen* coalition **Currency:** Afghani = 100 puls

Afmadow 73 D 6 S Somalia
Africa 60 D 4 continent
'Afrīn 118 B 2 NW Syria
Afyon 116 B 3 *prev.* Afyonkarahisar. W Turkey
Afyonkarahisar *see* Afyon
Agadès *see* Agadez
Agadez 75 G 3 *prev.* Agadès. C Niger
Agadir 70 B 3 SW Morocco

Agana 144 B 1 *var.* Agaña. Dependent territory capital, NW Guam
Agaña *see* Agana
Āgaro 73 C 5 W Ethiopia
Agassiz Fracture Zone 153 E 4 fracture zone, S Pacific Ocean
Agatha *see* Agde
Agathónisi 105 D 6 island, Dodekánisos, SE Greece
Agde 91 C 6 *anc.* Agatha. S France
Agen 91 B 6 *anc.* Aginnum. SW France
Agiá 104 B 4 *var.* Ayiá. C Greece
Agía Marína 105 E 6 Leros, SE Greece
Aginnum *see* Agen
Ágios Nikólaos 105 D 8 *var.* Áyios Nikólaos. Kríti, SE Greece
Āgra 134 D 3 N India
Ağrı 117 F 3 *var.* Karaköse; *prev.* Karakılısse. NE Turkey
Agrigento 97 C 7 *Gk.* Akragas; *prev.* Girgenti . SW Italy
Agrínio 105 B 5 *prev.* Agrinion. W Greece
Agrinion *see* Agrínio
Agriovótano 105 C 5 C Greece
Agropoli 97 D 5 Italy
Aguachica 58 B 2 N Colombia
Aguadulce 53 F 5 S Panama
Agua Prieta 50 B 1 NW Mexico
Aguascalientes 50 D 4 C Mexico
Aguilas 93 E 5 SE Spain
Aguililla 50 D 4 SW Mexico
Agulhas Bank 67 D 6 undersea bank, SW Indian Ocean
Agulhas Basin 67 E 6 undersea basin, SW Indian Ocean
Agulhas Plateau 67 E 6 undersea plateau, SW Indian Ocean
Ahaggar 68 B 3 mountain range, SE Algeria
Ahlen 94 B 4 W Germany
Ahmadābād 134 C 4 *var.* Ahmedabad. W India
Ahmadnagar 134 C 5 *var.* Ahmednagar. W India
Ahmedabad *see* Ahmadābād
Ahmednagar *see* Ahmadnagar
Ahuachapán 52 B 3 W El Salvador
Ahvāz 120 C 3 *var.* Ahwāz; *prev.* Nāsiri. SW Iran
Aígina 105 C 6 *var.* Aíyina. C Greece
Aígio 105 B 5 *prev.* Aíyion. S Greece
Aiken 43 E 2 South Carolina, SE USA
Ailao Shan 129 A 6 mountain range, S China
Ailigandí 53 G 4 NE Panama
Ailinglaplap Atoll 144 D 2 *var.* Aelónlaplap, Ailinglapalap. Island, S Marshall Islands
Ailuk Atoll 144 D 1 *var.* Aelok. Island, NE Marshall Islands
Ainaži 106 C 3 *Est.* Heinaste, *Ger.* Hainasch. N Latvia
'Aïn Ben Tili 74 D 1 N Mauritania
Aiquile 61 F 4 C Bolivia
Air du Azbine *see* Aïr, Massif de l'
Aïr, Massif de l' 75 G 3 *var.* Aïr, Air du Azbine, Asben. Mountain range, NC Niger
Aiud 108 B 4 *Ger.* Strassburg, *Hung.* Nagyenyed; *prev.* Engeten. SW Romania
Aix-en-Provence 91 D 6 *var.* Aix; *anc.* Aquae Sextiae. SE France
Aizkraukle 106 C 4 S Latvia
Ajaccio 91 E 7 SE France

Ajana 147 A 5 W Australia
Ajaria 117 F 2 region, SW Georgia
Aj Bogd Uul 126 D 2 mountain, SW Mongolia
Ajdābiyā 71 G 2 *var.* Agedabia, Ajdābiyah. NE Libya
Ajmer 134 D 3 *var.* Ajmere. N India
Ajmere *see* Ajmer
Akasha 72 B 3 N Sudan
Akçakale 117 E 4 Turkey
Akchâr 74 C 2 desert, W Mauritania
Akdar, Jebel *see* Akhḍar al Jabal
Akhalts'ikhe 117 F 2 SW Georgia
Akhḍar, Jebel al 121 D 5 *var.* Jabal al Akhdar. Mountain range, NW Oman
Akhḍar, Jabal al *see* Akhḍar, Al Jabal al
Akhisar 116 A 3 W Turkey
Akhmīm 72 B 2 *anc.* Panopolis. C Egypt
Akhtubinsk 111 C 7 SW Russian Federation
Akhtyrka *see* Okhtyrka
Akimiski Island 38 C 3 island, Northwest Territories, C Canada
Akita 130 D 4 Honshū, C Japan
Akjoujt 74 C 2 *prev.* Fort-Repoux. W Mauritania
Akkeshi 130 E 2 Hokkaidō, NE Japan
Aklavik 36 D 3 North West Territories, NW Canada
Akmola 114 C 4 *Kaz.* Aqmola; *prev.* Akmolinsk, Tselinograd. N Kazakhstan
Akpatok Island 39 E 1 island, Northwest Territories, E Canada
Akron 40 D 4 Ohio, N USA
Akrotiri *see* Akrotírion
Aksai Chin 126 A 4 *Chin.* Aksayqin. Disputed region, China/India
Aksaray 116 C 4 C Turkey
Aksay *see* Toxkan He
Aksayqin *see* Aksai Chin
Aktash *see* Oqtosh
Aktau 114 A 4 *Kaz.* Aqtaü; *prev.* Shevchenko . W Kazakhstan
Aktsyabrski 107 D 7 *Rus.* Oktyabr'skiy; *prev.* Karpilovka. SE Belorussia
Aktyubinsk 114 B 4 *Kaz.* Aqtöbe. NW Kazakhstan
Akureyri 83 E 5 N Iceland
Akyab *see* Sittwe
Alabama 42 C 2 *off.* State of Alabama; nicknames Camellia State, Heart of Dixie, The Cotton State, Yellowhammer State. State, S USA
Alabama River 42 C 3 river, Alabama, S USA
Alagoas 63 G 2 *off.* Estado de Alagoas. State, E Brazil
Alagoas, Estado de *see* Alagoas
Alais *see* Alès
Alajuela 53 E 4 C Costa Rica
Alakanuk 36 D 2 Alaska, NW USA
Al 'Alamayn *see* El 'Alamein
Al 'Amārah 120 C 3 *var.* Amara. E Iraq
Alamosa 44 C 5 Colorado, C USA
Åland 85 C 6 *var.* Aland Islands, *Fin.* Ahvenanmaa. Island group, SW Finland
Aland Sea *see* Ålands hav
Ålands Hav 85 C 6 *var.* Aland Sea. Strait, C Baltic Sea

Al 'Aqabah 119 B 8 *var.* Akaba, Aqaba, 'Aqaba; *anc.* Aelana, Elath. SW Jordan
Alaşehir 116 A 4 W Turkey
Alaska 36 C 3 *off.* State of Alaska; nicknames Land of the Midnight Sun, Seward's Folly, The Last Frontier; *prev.* Russian America. State, NW USA
Alaska, Gulf of 152 D 1 gulf, NE Pacific Ocean
Alaska Peninsula 36 C 3 peninsula, Alaska, NW USA
Alaska Range 36 C 3 mountain range, Alaska, NW USA
Alattio *see* Alta
Alazani 117 G 2 *var.* Qanıx. River, Azerbaijan/Georgia
Alazeya 115 G 2 river, NE Russian Federation
Al Bāb 118 B 2 NW Syria
Albacete 93 E 4 C Spain
Al Baghdādī 120 B 3 *var.* Khān al Baghdādī. SW Iraq
Alba Iulia 108 B 4 *Ger.* Weissenburg, *Hung.* Gyulafehérvár; *prev.* Bălgrad, Karlsburg, Károly-Fehérvár. W Romania
Albania *see* Aubagne

Albania
101 C 6 *Alb.* Republika e Shqipërisë, Shqipëria; *prev.* People's Socialist Republic of Albania. Republic, SE Europe

Official name: Republic of Albania **Date of formation:** 1913 **Capital:** Tiranë **Population:** 3.3 million **Total area:** 28,750 sq km (11,100 sq miles) **Languages:** Albanian, Greek **Religions:** Muslim 70%, Greek Orthodox 20%, Roman Catholic 10% **Ethnic mix:** Albanian 96%, Greek 2%, other (inc. Macedonian) 2% **Government:** Multiparty republic **Currency:** Lek = 100 qindars

Albany 42 D 3 Georgia, SE USA
Albany 38 C 3 river, Ontario, S Canada
Albany 147 B 7 Western Australia, SW Australia
Albany 41 F 3 state capital, New York, NE USA
Albany 46 B 3 Oregon, NW USA
Al Başrah 120 C 4 *Eng.* Basra; *hist.* Busra, Bussora. SE Iraq
Albatross Bay 148 C 2 bay, SE Arafura Sea
Albatross Plateau 35 B 7 undersea plateau, E Pacific Ocean
Al Batrūn *see* Batroûn
Al Bayḍa' 71 G 2 *var.* Beida. NE Libya
Albemarle Island *see* Isabela, Isla
Albemarle Sound 43 G 1 inlet, W Atlantic Ocean
Albergaria-a-Velha 92 B 2 W Portugal
Albert 90 C 3 N France
Alberta 37 E 4 province, SW Canada
Albert, Lake 77 E 5 *var.* Albert Nyanza, Lac Mobutu Sese Seko. Lake, Uganda/Zaire
Albert Lea 45 G 3 Minnesota, N USA
Albertville *see* Kalemie
Albi 91 C 6 *anc.* Albiga. S France
Albiga *see* Albi
Al Biyāḍ 121 C 5 desert, C Saudi Arabia

Ålborg 85 B 7 *var.* Aalborg, Ålborg-Nørresundby; *anc.* Alburgum. N Denmark
Ålborg Bugt 85 B 7 *var.* Aalborg Bugt. Bay, E North Sea
Alborz, Reshteh-ye Kuhhā-ye 120 C 2 *Eng.* Elburz Mountains. Mountain range, N Iran
Albuquerque 48 D 2 New Mexico, SW USA
Albury 149 C 7 New South Wales, SE Australia
Alcácer do Sal 92 B 4 W Portugal
Alcalá de Henares 93 E 3 *Ar.* Alkal'a; *anc.* Complutim, Complutum. C Spain
Alcamo 97 C 7 SW Italy
Alcañiz 93 F 2 NE Spain
Alcántara, Embalse de 92 C 3 reservoir, W Spain
Alcaudete 92 D 4 S Spain
Alcoi *see* Alcoy
Alcoy 93 F 4 *var.* Alcoi. E Spain
Aldabra Group 79 G 2 island group, SW Seychelles
Aldan 115 F 3 river, E Russian Federation
al Dar al Baida *see* Rabat
Alderney 89 D 8 island, N Channel Islands
Aleg 74 C 3 SW Mauritania
Aleksandriya *see* Oleksandriya
Aleksandrovka *see* Oleksandrivka
Aleksin 111 B 5 W Russian Federation
Aleksinac 100 E 4 E Yugoslavia
Alençon 90 B 3 N France
Alenquer 63 E 2 NE Brazil
Aleppo *see* Ḥalab
Alert 37 F 1 Ellesmere Island, Canada
Alès 91 D 6 *prev.* Alais. S France
Aleşd 108 B 3 *Hung.* Élesd. SW Romania
Alessandria 96 B 2 *Fr.* Alexandrie. N Italy
Ålesund 85 A 5 S Norway
Aleutian Basin 152 C 1 undersea basin, SW Pacific Ocean
Aleutian Islands 36 A 3 island group, Alaska, NW USA
Aleutian Range 34 A 2 mountain range, Alaska, NW USA
Aleutian Rise 152 C 1 undersea rise, NW Pacific Ocean
Aleutian Trench 152 D 1 trench, SW Pacific Ocean
Alexander Archipelago 36 C 4 island group, Alaska, NW USA
Alexander City 42 D 2 Alabama, S USA
Alexander Island 154 A 3 island, Antarctica
Alexandra 151 B 7 South Island, SW New Zealand
Alexandra Bay 148 D 2 bay, NE Coral Sea
Alexándreia 104 B 4 *var.* Alexándria. N Greece
Alexandretta *see* İskenderun
Alexandretta, Gulf of *see* İskenderun Körfezi
Alexandria 42 B 3 Louisiana, S USA
Alexandria 41 E 4 Virginia, NE USA
Alexandria 108 C 5 S Romania
Alexandria 45 F 2 Minnesota, N USA
Alexandria 72 B 1 *Ar.* Al Iskandarīyah. N Egypt
Aléxandria *see* Alexándreia
Alexandrie *see* Alessandria

Alexandrina, Lake 149 B 7 lake, South Australia, SE Australia
Alexandroúpoli 104 D 3 *var.* Alexandroúpolis, *Turk.* Dedeagaç, Dedeagach. NE Greece
Al Fāshir *see* El Fasher
Alfatar 104 E 1 NE Bulgaria
Alfeiós 105 B 6 *prev.* Alfiós, *anc.* Alpheius, Alpheus. River, S Greece
Alga 114 B 4 *Kaz.* Algha. NW Kazakhstan
Algarve 92 B 4 cultural region, S Portugal
Algeciras 92 C 5 SW Spain
Algeciras, Bahía de *see* Gibraltar, Bay of
Algemesí 93 F 3 E Spain
Alger 70 D 1 *var.* Algiers, Al Jazair, El Djazaïr. Country capital, N Algeria

Algeria
70 C 3 NW Africa

Official name: Democratic and Popular Republic of Algeria **Date of formation:** 1962 **Capital:** Algiers **Population:** 27.1 million **Total area:** 2,381,740 sq km (919,590 sq miles) **Languages:** Arabic*, Berber, French **Religions:** Muslim 99%, Christian and Jewish 1% **Ethnic mix:** Arab and Berber 99% European 1% **Government:** Military regime **Currency:** Dinar = 100 centimes

Algerian Basin *see* Balearic Plain
Algha *see* Alga
Alghero 97 A 5 W Italy
Algiers *see* Alger
Al Golea *see* El Goléa
Algona 45 F 3 Iowa, C USA
Al Hasā 120 C 4 desert, NE Saudi Arabia
Al Ḥasakah 118 D 1 *var.* Al Hasijah, El Haseke, *Fr.* Hassetché. NE Syria
Al Ḥillah 120 B 3 *var.* Hilla. C Iraq
Al Hudaydah 121 B 6 *Eng.* Hodeida. W Yemen
Al Hufūf 121 C 5 *var.* Hofuf. NE Saudi Arabia
Alíartos 105 C 5 C Greece
Äli-Bayramlı 117 H 3 *Rus.* Ali-Bayramly. SE Azerbaijan
Ali-Bayramly *see* Äli-Bayramlı
Alicante 93 F 4 *Cat.* Alacant; *Lat.* Lucentum. SE Spain
Alice 49 G 5 Texas, S USA
Alice Springs 148 A 4 Northern Territory, C Australia
Aliki *see* Alykí
Alindao 76 C 4 S Central African Republic
Aliquippa 40 D 4 Pennsylvania, NE USA
Al Iskandarīyah *see* Alexandria
Alistráti 104 C 3 NE Greece
Alivéri 105 C 5 *var.* Alivérion. Évvoia, C Greece
Alivérion *see* Alivéri
Al Jabal al Akhḍar 71 G 2 *var.* Jebel Akdar. Mountain range, NE Libya
Al Jafr 119 B 7 S Jordan
Al Jaghbūb 71 H 3 NE Libya
Al Jahrā' 120 C 4 *var.* Al Jahrah, Jahra. C Kuwait
Al Jawf 120 B 4 *var.* Jauf. NW Saudi Arabia
Al Karak 119 B 7 *var.* El Kerak, Karak, Kerak; *anc.* Kir Moab, Kir of Moab. W Jordan

Al Khārijah *see* El Khârga
Al-Khobar *see* Al Khubar
Al Khubar 120 C 4 *var.* Al-Khobar. NE Saudi Arabia
Al Khums 71 F 2 *var.* Homs, Khoms, Khums. NW Libya
Alkmaar 86 C 3 NW Netherlands
Al Kufrah 72 A 2 *var.* Kufra Oasis, *It.* Cufra. Oasis, W Libya
Al Kūt 120 C 3 *var.* Kūt al 'Amārah, Kut al Imara. E Iraq
Al Kuwayt 120 C 4 *var.* Kuwait City, Al-Kuwait, *Eng.* Kuwait; *prev.* Qurein. Country capital, E Kuwait
Al Lādhiqīyah 118 A 3 *Eng.* Latakia, *Fr.* Lattaquié; *anc.* Laodicea, Laodicea ad Mare. W Syria
Allahābād 135 E 3 N India
Allanmyo 136 B 4 W Burma
'Allâq, Wâdi el 72 C 3 dry watercourse, Egypt/Sudan
Allegheny Plateau 41 E 3 mountain range, NE USA
Allenstein *see* Olsztyn
Allentown 41 F 4 Pennsylvania, NE USA
Alleppey 132 C 3 *var.* Alappuzha; *prev.* Alleppi. SW India
Alliance 44 D 3 Nebraska, C USA
Al Līth 121 B 5 SW Saudi Arabia
Alma 39 E 4 Québec, SE Canada
Alma-Ata *see* Almaty
Almada 92 B 4 W Portugal
Al Madīnah 121 B 5 *Eng.* Medina. W Saudi Arabia
Al Mafraq 119 B 6 *var.* Mafraq. N Jordan
Al Mahrah 121 C 6 mountain range, E Yemen
Al Majma'ah 120 C 4 C Saudi Arabia
Al Mālikīyah 118 E 1 *var.* Dayrīk, Malkiye, *Fr.* Malkieh. NE Syria
Almalyk *see* Olmaliq
Al Manāmah 120 C 4 *Eng.* Manama. Country capital, N Bahrain
Al Manāşif 118 E 3 mountain range, E Syria
Almansa 93 E 4 C Spain
Al Marj 71 G 2 *var.* Barka, *It.* Barce. NE Libya
Almaty 114 C 5 *var.* Alma-Ata. Country capital, SE Kazakhstan
Al Mawşil 120 B 2 *Eng.* Mosul. N Iraq
Al Mayādīn 118 E 3 *var.* Mayadin, *Fr.* Meyadine. E Syria
Al Mazār al Janūbī 119 B 7 *var.* Mazar. W Jordan
Al Mazra'ah 119 B 7 *var.* Al Mazra', Mazra'a. W Jordan
Almelo 86 E 3 E Netherlands
Almendra, Embalse de 92 C 2 reservoir, W Spain
Almendralejo 92 C 4 W Spain
Almere 86 C 3 *var.* Almere-stad. C Netherlands
Almere-stad *see* Almere
Almería 93 E 4 *Ar.* Al-Mariyya; *anc.* Unci, *Lat.* Portus Magnus. S Spain
Al Mīnā' *see* El Mina
Almirante 53 F 5 NW Panama
Al Mubarraz 120 C 4 E Saudi Arabia
Al Mudawwarah 119 B 8 SW Jordan
Al Mukallā 121 C 7 *var.* Mukalla. SE Yemen
Al Munastīr *see* Monastir

Alofi 145 F 5 dependent territory capital, W Niue
Aloja 106 D 3 N Latvia
Alónnisos 105 C 5 island, Vóreioi Sporádes, E Greece
Álora 92 D 5 S Spain
Alor, Kepulauan 139 E 5 island group, E Indonesia
Alost *see* Aalst
Alpena 40 D 2 Michigan, N USA
Alpha Cordillera 155 F 3 *var.* Alpha Ridge. Seamount range, Arctic Ocean
Alphen *see* Alphen aan den Rijn
Alphen aan den Rijn 86 C 3 *var.* Alphen. C Netherlands
Alpine 49 E 4 Texas, S USA
Alps 80 D 4 *Fr.* Alpes, *Ger.* Alpen, *It.* Alpi. Mountain range, C Europe
Al Qāmishlī 118 E 1 *var.* Kamishli, Qamishly. NE Syria
Al Qaryāt 71 F 3 NW Libya
Al Qaşrayn *see* Kasserine
Al Qayrawān *see* Kairouan
Al Qunayţirah 119 B 5 *var.* El Kuneitra, El Quneitra, Kuneitra, Qunaytra. SW Syria
Al Quşayr 118 B 4 *var.* El Quseir, Quayr, *Fr.* Kousseir. W Syria
Al Quwayrah 119 B 8 *var.* El Quweira. SW Jordan
Alsace 90 E 3 cultural region, NE France
Alsdorf 94 A 4 W Germany
Alta 84 D 2 *Fin.* Alattio. N Norway
Altai Mountains 124 C 1 *var.* Altay Shan. Mountain range, E Asia
AltaY Shan *see* Altai Mountains
Al Ṭalfilah 119 B 7 *var.* Et Tafila, Tafila. W Jordan
Altamaha River 43 E 3 river, Georgia, SE USA
Altamira 63 E 2 NE Brazil
Altamont 46 B 4 Oregon, NW USA
Altamura 97 E 5 *anc.* Lupatia. SE Italy
Altar, Desierto de 50 A 1 desert, Mexico/USA
Altay 126 D 2 W Mongolia
Altay 126 C 2 *Chin.* A-le-t'ai, Sharasume; *prev.* Ch'eng-hua, Chenghwa. NW China
Altin Köprü 120 B 3 *var.* Altun Kupri. Iraq
Alton 40 B 4 Illinois, N USA
Altoona 41 E 4 Pennsylvania, NE USA
Alto Paraná *see* Paraná
Alt-Schwanenburg *see* Gulbene
Altun Kupri *see* Altin Köprü
Altun Shan 126 C 4 *var.* Altyn Tagh. Mountain range, NW China
Altus 49 F 2 Oklahoma, C USA
Altyn Tagh *see* Altun Shan
Alūksne 106 D 3 *Ger.* Marienburg. NE Latvia
Al 'Ulá 120 A 4 NW Saudi Arabia
Al 'Umarī 119 C 6 E Jordan
Alupka 109 F 5 S Ukraine
Al Uqşur *see* Luxor
Alushta 109 F 5 S Ukraine
Alva 49 F 1 Oklahoma, C USA
Alvarado 51 F 4 E Mexico
Alvin 49 H 4 Texas, S USA
Al Waḥībah, Ramlat 121 E 5 *var.* Ramlat Ahl Wahībah, Ramlat Al Wahaybah, Wahībah Sands. Desert, N Oman
Al Wajh 120 A 4 NW Saudi Arabia
Alwar 134 D 3 N India

Alykí 104 C 4 *var.* Aliki. Thásos, N Greece
Alytus 107 B 5 *Pol.* Olita. S Lithuania
Amadeus, Lake 147 E 5 lake, South Australia, S Australia
Amadi 73 B 5 SW Sudan
Amadjuak Lake 82 A 2 lake, N Canada
Amakusa-shotō 131 A 8 island group, Japan
Åmål 85 B 6 S Sweden
Amami-ōshima 130 A 3 island, Nansei-shotō, S Japan
Amami-shotō 130 A 3 island group, Japan
Amantea 97 D 6 SW Italy
Amapá 63 E 1 *off.* Território de Amapá. State, NE Brazil
Amara *see* Al 'Amārah
Amarapura 136 B 3 C Burma
Amarillo 49 E 2 Texas, S USA
Amay 87 C 6 E Belgium
Amazon 56 C 3 *Sp.* Amazonas. River, Brazil/Peru
Amazonas 62 D 2 *off.* Estado do Amazonas. State, N Brazil
Amazonas *see* Amazon
Amazonas, Estado do *see* Amazonas
Amazon Canyons 56 D 2 trough, C Atlantic Ocean
Amazon Fan 67 B 5 undersea fan, W Atlantic Ocean
Amazonia 56 B 3 physical region, N South America
Ambam 77 A 5 S Cameroon
Ambanja 79 G 2 N Madagascar
Ambarchik 115 G 2 NE Russian Federation
Ambato 60 B 1 C Ecuador
Ambérieu-en-Bugey 91 D 5 E France
Amblève 87 D 7 river, E Belgium
Amboasary 79 F 4 S Madagascar
Ambon 139 F 4 *prev.* Amboina, Amboyna. Pulau Seram, E Indonesia
Ambositra 79 G 3 C Madagascar
Ambracia *see* Árta
Ambrim *see* Ambrym
Ambriz 78 A 1 NW Angola
Ambrym 144 D 4 *var.* Ambrim. Island, C Vanuatu
Amchitka Island 36 A 2 island, Alaska, NW USA
Amdo 126 C 5 W China
Ameland 86 D 1 *Fris.* It Amelân. Island, N Netherlands
America-Antarctica Ridge 67 C 7 undersea ridge, S Atlantic Ocean
American Falls Reservoir 46 E 4 reservoir, Idaho, NW USA
American Samoa 145 F 4 US unincorporated territory, S Pacific Ocean
Americus 42 D 3 Georgia, SE USA
Amersfoort 86 D 3 C Netherlands
Ames 45 F 3 Iowa, C USA
Amfilochía 105 B 5 *var.* Amfilokhía. C Greece
Amfilokhía *see* Amfilochía
Amga 115 F 3 river, C Russian Federation
Amherst 39 F 4 Nova Scotia, SE Canada
Amherst *see* Kyaikkami
Amiens 90 C 3 *anc.* Ambianum, Samarobriva. N France
Amīndīvi Islands 132 B 2 island group, Lakshadweep, SW India
Amirante Bank *see* Amirante Ridge
Amirante Islands 79 G 1 *var.* Amirantes Group. Island, C Seychelles

Amirantes Group *see* Amirante Islands
Amistad, Presa de la *see* Amistad Reservoir
Amistad Reservoir 49 F 4 *var.* Presa de la Amistad. Reservoir, Texas, S Mexico/USA
Amisus *see* Samsun
'Ammān 119 B 6 *var.* Amman; *anc.* Philadelphia, *Bibl.* Rabbah Ammon, Rabbath Ammon. Country capital, NW Jordan
Amman *see* 'Ammān
Ammassalik 82 D 4 *var.* Angmagssalik. SE Greenland
Amoentai *see* Amuntai
Āmol 120 D 2 *var.* Amul. N Iran
Amorgós 105 D 6 Amorgós, SE Greece
Amorgós 105 D 6 island, Kykládes, SE Greece
Amos 38 D 4 Québec, SE Canada
Amourj 74 D 3 SE Mauritania
Ampato, Nevado 61 E 4 mountain, S Peru
Amposta 93 F 3 NE Spain
Amraoti *see* Amrāvati
Amrāvati 134 D 4 *prev.* Amraoti. C India
Amritsar 134 D 2 N India
Amstelveen 86 C 3 C Netherlands
Amsterdam 86 C 3 country capital, C Netherlands
Amsterdam Island 141 C 6 island, NE French Southern & Antarctic Territories
Am Timan 76 C 3 SE Chad
Amu Darya 122 D 2 *Rus.* Amudar'ya, *Taj.* Dar"yoi Amu, *Turkm.* Amyderya, *Uzb.* Amudaryo; *anc.* Oxus. River, C Asia
Amu-Dar'ya 123 E 3 SE Turkmenistan
Amul *see* Āmol
Amund Ringnes Island 37 F 2 island, N Canada
Amundsen Abyssal Plain 154 B 4 abyssal plain, S Pacific Ocean
Amundsen Gulf 37 E 3 gulf, SE Beaufort Sea
Amundsen-Scott 154 B 3 research station, Antarctica
Amundsen Sea 154 A 4 sea, S Pacific Ocean
Amuntai 138 D 4 *prev.* Amoentai. Borneo, C Indonesia
Amur 128 D 1 *Chin.* Heilong Jiang. River, China/Russian Federation
Amvrosiyevka *see* Amvrosiyivka
Amvrosiyivka 109 H 3 *var.* Amvrosiyevka. SE Ukraine
Amýntaio 104 B 4 *prev.* Amíndaion. N Greece
Anabar 115 E 2 river, N Russian Federation
An Abhainn Mhór *see* Blackwater
Anaco 59 E 2 NE Venezuela
Anaconda 44 B 2 Montana, NW USA
Anacortes 46 B 1 Washington, NW USA
Anadolu Dağları *see* Doğu Karadeniz Dağları
Anadyr' 115 H 1 NE Russian Federation
Anadyr, Gulf of *see* Anadyrskiy Zaliv
Anadyrskiy Zaliv 115 H 1 *Eng.* Gulf of Anadyr. Gulf, N Bering Sea
Anáfi 105 D 7 *anc.* Anaphe. Island, Kykládes, SE Greece

'Ānah *see* 'Annah
Analalava 79 G 2 N Madagascar
Anamur 116 C 5 S Turkey
Anantapur 132 C 2 S India
Anaphe *see* Anáfi
Anápolis 63 F 3 C Brazil
Anār 120 D 3 C Iran
Anatolia *see* Anadolu
Anatolia Plateau 116 C 4 plateau, C Turkey
Anatom 144 D 5 *var.* Aneityum, *prev.* Kéamu. Island, S Vanuatu
An Bhearú *see* Barrow
Anchorage 36 C 3 Alaska, NW USA
Ancona 96 C 3 C Italy
Ancud 65 B 6 *prev.* San Carlos de Ancud. S Chile
Åndalsnes 85 A 5 S Norway
Andalucía 92 D 4 cultural region, S Spain
Andaman Islands 133 E 2 island group, SE India
Andaman Sea 133 G 2 sea, NE Indian Ocean
'Andām, Wādī 121 E 5 river, NE Oman
Andenne 87 C 6 SE Belgium
Anderlues 87 B 7 S Belgium
Anderson 40 C 4 Indiana, N USA
Andes 57 B 5 mountain range, South America
Andhra Pradesh 135 E 5 cultural region, E India
Andhra Pradesh 132 D 1 state, SE India
Andijon 123 F 2 *Rus.* Andizhan. E Uzbekistan
Andikíthira *see* Antikýthira
Andipaxi *see* Antípaxoi
Andípsara *see* Antípsara
Ándissa *see* Antissa
Andizhan *see* Andijon
Andkhvoy 122 D 3 N Afghanistan

Andorra 91 A 7 *Cat.* Valls d'Andorra, *Fr.* Vallée d'Andorra. Monarchy, SW Europe

Official name: Principality of Andorra **Date of formation:** 1278 **Capital:** Andorra la Vella **Population:** 58,000 **Total area:** 468 sq km (181 sq miles) **Languages:** Catalan*, Spanish **Religions:** Roman Catholic 86%, other 14% **Ethnic mix:** Catalan 61%, Spanish Castilian 30%, other 9% **Government:** Parliamentary democracy **Currency:** French franc, Spanish peseta

Andorra la Vella 91 B 7 *var.* Andorra, *Fr.* Andorre la Vielle, *Sp.* Andorra la Vieja. Country capital, C Andorra
Andover 89 D 7 S England, UK
Andøya 84 C 2 island, C Norway
Andrews 49 E 3 Texas, S USA
Andria 97 E 5 S Italy
Ándros 105 D 6 Ándros, SE Greece
Ándros 105 D 6 island, Kykládes, SE Greece
Andros Island 54 C 2 island, NW Bahamas
Andros Town 54 C 1 NW Bahamas
Angara 112 D 3 river, C Russian Federation
Angarsk 115 E 4 C Russian Federation

Ånge 85 C 5 C Sweden
Ángel de la Guarda, Isla 50 B 2 island, NW Mexico
Angeles 139 E 1 *off.* Angeles City. Luzon, N Philippines
Angeles City *see* Angeles
Angel Falls *see* Ángel, Salto
Ángel, Salto 59 E 3 *Eng.* Angel Falls. Waterfall, E Venezuela
Angerburg *see* Węgorzewo
Ångermanälven 84 C 4 river, N Sweden
Angermünde 94 D 3 NE Germany
Angers 90 B 4 *anc.* Juliomagus. NW France
Anglesey 89 C 5 island, NW England, UK
Anglet 91 A 6 SW France
Angleton 49 H 4 Texas, S USA
Anglia *see* England
Angmagssalik *see* Ammassalik
Ang Nam Ngum 136 C 4 lake, N Laos

Angola 78 B 2 *prev.* People's Republic of Angola, Portuguese West Africa. Republic, S Africa

Official name: Republic of Angola **Date of formation:** 1975 **Capital:** Luanda **Population:** 10.3 million **Total area:** 1,246,700 sq km (481,551 sq miles) **Languages:** Portuguese* **Religions:** Roman Catholic/Protestant 64%, traditional beliefs 34%, other 2% **Ethnic mix:** Ovimbundu 37%, Kimbundu 25%, Bakongo 13%, other 25% **Government:** Multiparty republic **Currency:** Kwanza = 100 lwei

Angola Basin 67 D 5 undersea basin, E Atlantic Ocean
Angostura *see* Ciudad Bolívar
Angostura, Presa de la 51 G 5 reservoir, SE Mexico
Angoulême 91 B 5 *anc.* Iculisma. W France
Angoumois 91 B 5 cultural region, W France
Angra Pequena *see* Lüderitz
Angren 123 F 2 E Uzbekistan
Anguilla 55 G 3 UK dependent territory, E Caribbean Sea
Anhui 129 C 5 *var.* Anhwei, Wan. Province, E China
Anina 108 A 4 *Ger.* Steierdorf, *Hung.* Stájerlakanina; *prev.* Staierdorf-Anina, Steierdorf-Anina, Steyerlak-Anina. SW Romania
Anjou 90 B 4 cultural region, NW France
Anjouan 79 F 2 *var.* Johanna Island, Nzwani. Island, Mozambique Channel/Pacific Ocean
Ankara 116 C 3 *prev.* Angora, *anc.* Ancyra. Country capital, C Turkey
Ankeny 45 F 3 Iowa, C USA
Anklam 94 D 2 NE Germany
An Longfort *see* Longford
An Mhuir Cheilteach *see* Celtic Sea
Annaba 71 E 1 *prev.* Bône. NE Algeria
An Nabk 118 B 4 *var.* El Nebk, Nabk, Nebk, Fr. Nébeck. SW Syria
An Nafūd 120 B 4 desert, NW Saudi Arabia
'Annah 120 B 3 *var.* 'Ānah. NW Iraq
An Najaf 120 B 3 *var.* S Iraq

Annamitique, Chaîne 136 D 4 mountain range, Laos
Annapolis 41 F 4 state capital, Maryland, NE USA
Annapurna 135 E 3 mountain, C Nepal
An Nāqūrah see En Nāqoûra
Ann Arbor 40 C 3 Michigan, N USA
An Nāṣirīyah 120 C 3 var. Nasiriya. SE Iraq
Anneciacum see Annecy
Annecy 91 D 5 anc. Anneciacum. E France
Anniston 42 D 2 Alabama, S USA
Annotto Bay 54 B 5 C Jamaica
An Ómaigh see Omagh
Anqing 129 D 5 E China
Ansbach 95 C 6 SE Germany
Anshan 128 D 3 NE China
Anshun 129 B 6 S China
Anson Bay 146 D 2 inlet, W Pacific Ocean
Ansongo 75 E 3 E Mali
An Srath Bán see Strabane
Antakya 116 D 5 anc. Antioch, Antiochia. S Turkey
Antalaha 79 G 2 NE Madagascar
Antalya 116 B 4 prev. Adalia, anc. Attaleia, Bibl. Attalia. SW Turkey
Antalya Körfezi 116 B 4 var. Gulf of Adalia, Eng. Gulf of Antalya. Gulf, NE Mediterranean Sea
Antananarivo 79 G 3 prev. Tananarive. Country capital, C Madagascar
Antarctica 154 B 3 continent, S
Antarctic Peninsula 154 A 2 peninsula, Antarctica
Antequera 92 D 5 anc. Anticaria, Antiquaria. S Spain
Antibes 91 E 6 anc. Antipolis. SE France
Anticosti, Île d' 39 F 3 Eng. Antiçosti Island. Island, Québec, E Canada
Antigua 55 G 3 island, S Antigua & Barbuda

Antigua & Barbuda
55 H 3 Commonwealth republic, E Caribbean Sea

Official name: Antigua & Barbuda Date of formation: 1981 Capital: St John's Population: 200,000 Total area: 440 sq km (170 sq miles) Languages: English*, English Creole Religions: Protestant 87%, Roman Catholic 10%, other 3% Ethnic mix: Black 98%, other 2% Government: Parliamentary democracy Currency: E. Caribbean $ = 100 cents

Antikýthira 105 C 7 var. Andikíthira. Island, S Greece
Anti-Lebanon 118 B 4 var. Jebel esh Sharqi, Ar. Al Jabal ash Sharqī, Fr. Anti-Liban. Mountain range, Lebanon/Syria
Antipaxoi 105 A 5 var. Andipaxi. Island, Iónioi Nísoi, W Greece
Antipodes Islands 142 D 5 island group, S New Zealand
Antipolis see Antibes
Antípsara 105 D 5 var. Andípsara. Island, E Greece
Ántissa 105 D 5 var. Ándissa. Lésvos, E Greece
An tIúr see Newry
Antivari see Bar
Antofagasta 64 B 2 N Chile
Antony 90 C 3 N France

An tSionainn see Shannon
Antsirabe 79 G 3 C Madagascar
Antsohihy 79 G 2 N Madagascar
Antwerp see Antwerpen
Antwerpen 87 C 5 Eng. Antwerp, Fr. Anvers. N Belgium
Anuradhapura 132 D 3 C Sri Lanka
Anxious Bay 149 A 6 bay, E Great Australian Bight
Anyang 128 C 4 NE China
A'nyêmaqên Shan 126 D 4 mountain range, C China
Anykščiai 106 C 4 E Lithuania
Anzio 97 C 5 C Italy
Aomori 130 D 3 Honshū, C Japan
Aosta 96 A 1 anc. Augusta Praetoria. NW Italy
Aoukâr 74 D 3 var. Aouker. Plateau, C Mauritania
Aouk, Bahr 76 C 4 river, Central African Republic/Chad
Aouker see Aoukâr
Aozou 76 C 1 N Chad
Apalachee Bay 42 D 3 bay, NE Gulf of Mexico
Apalachicola River 42 D 3 river, Florida, SE USA
Apartadó 58 B 2 NW Colombia
Apatity 110 C 2 NW Russian Federation
Ape 106 D 3 NE Latvia
Apeldoorn 86 D 3 E Netherlands
Apennines see Appennino
Àpia 145 F 4 country capital, Savai'i, E Western Samoa
Apoera 59 G 3 NW Surinam
Apollonopolis Parva see Qûs
Apostle Islands 40 B 1 island group, Wisconsin, N USA
Appalachian Mountains 35 C 5 mountain range, E USA
Appennino 96 C 3 Eng. Apennines. Mountain range, C Italy/San Marino
Appingedam 86 E 1 NE Netherlands
Appleton 40 B 2 Wisconsin, N USA
Apple Valley 47 C 7 California, W USA
Apsheronsk 111 A 7 SW Russian Federation
Apure 58 C 2 river, W Venezuela
Apurímac 60 D 3 river, S Peru
Aputiteeq 82 D 4 var. Aputitêq. Greenland
Aputitêq see Aputiteeq
Aqaba, Gulf of 120 A 4 var. Gulf of Elat, Sinus Aelaniticus, Ar. Khalīj al 'Aqabah. Gulf, Red Sea/Indian Ocean
Āqcheh 123 E 3 var. Ăqcheh. N Afghanistan
Ăqcheh see Āqcheh
Aquae Flaviae see Chaves
Aquidauana 63 E 4 S Brazil
Aquitaine 91 B 6 cultural region, SW France
Arabian Basin 140 B 3 undersea basin, N Indian Ocean
Arabian Desert 68 D 3 desert, E Egypt
Arabian Peninsula 140 A 3 peninsula, Iraq/Jordan
Arabian Sea 140 B 3 sea, NW Indian Ocean
Aracaju 63 G 3 E Brazil
Araçuai 63 F 3 SE Brazil
Arad 108 A 4 W Romania
'Arad 119 B 7 S Israel
Arafura Sea 152 B 3 sea, W Pacific Ocean

Aragón 93 E 2 cultural region, E Spain
Araguaia, Río 63 E 3 var. Araguaya. River, C Brazil
Araguaína 63 F 2 E Brazil
Araguari 63 F 4 SE Brazil
Araguaya see Araguaia, Río
Ara Jovis see Aranjuez
Arāk 120 C 3 prev. Sultānābād. W Iran
Arakan Yoma 136 A 3 mountain range, W Burma
Aral see Aral'sk
Aral Sea 122 D 1 Kaz. Aral Tengizi, Rus. Aral'skoye More, Uzb. Orol Dengizi. Inland sea, Kazakhstan/Uzbekistan
Aral'sk 114 B 4 Kaz. Aral. SW Kazakhstan
Aranda de Duero 92 D 2 N Spain
Arandelovac 100 D 4 prev. Arandjelovac. C Yugoslavia
Arandjelovac see Arandelovac
Aranjuez 92 D 3 anc. Ara Jovis. C Spain
Araouane 75 E 2 N Mali
'Ar'ar 120 B 3 N Saudi Arabia
Ararat, Mount see Büyükağrı Baği
Aras 117 F 3 Arm. Arak's, Az. Araz, Per. Rüd-e Aras, Rus. Araks, Turk. Aras Nehri; prev. Araxes. River, SW Asia
Arauca 58 C 2 NE Colombia
Arauca 58 D 2 river, Colombia/Venezuela
Arausio see Orange
Arbīl 120 B 3 var. Erbil, Irbîl, Kurd. Hawlêr; anc. Arbela. N Iraq
Arbroath 88 D 4 anc. Aberbrothock. E Scotland, UK
Arbuzinka see Arbyzynka
Arbyzynka 109 E 3 Rus. Arbuzinka. S Ukraine
Arcachon 91 A 5 SW France
Arcata 47 A 5 California, W USA
Archangel see Arkhangel'sk
Archidona 92 D 5 S Spain
Arco 96 C 2 N Italy
Arco, Paso del 65 B 5 pass, Argentina
Arctic Bay 37 G 2 Baffin Island, Canada
Arctic Ocean 155 F 3 ocean, Canada
Arctowski 154 A 2 research station, Antarctica
Arda 104 C 3 var. Ardhas, Gk. Ardas. River, Bulgaria/Greece
Ardabīl 120 C 2 var. Ardebil. NW Iran
Ardakān 120 D 3 C Iran
Ard aș Șawwān 119 C 7 var. Ardh es Suwwân. Plain, S Jordan
Ardebil see Ardabīl
Ardèche 91 C 5 cultural region, E France
Ardennes 87 D 8 plateau, W Europe
Ardh es Suwwân see Arḍ aș Șawwān
Ardino 104 D 3 S Bulgaria
Ard Mhacha see Armagh
Ardmore 49 G 2 Oklahoma, C USA
Arendal 85 A 6 S Norway
Arenys de Mar 93 G 2 NE Spain
Areópoli 105 B 7 prev. Areópolis. S Greece
Areópolis see Areópoli
Arequipa 61 E 4 SE Peru
Arezzo 96 C 3 anc. Arretium. C Italy
Argalastí 105 C 5 C Greece

Argenteuil 90 C 3 N France

Argentina
65 B 5 Republic, S South America

Official name: Argentine Republic Date of formation: 1850 Capital: Buenos Aires Population: 33.5 million Total area: 2,766,890 sq km (1,068,296 sq miles) Languages: Spanish*, Italian, English German, French, Indian languages Religions: Roman Catholic 90%, Jewish 2%, other 8% Ethnic mix: White 85%, other (including mestizo and Indian) 15% Government: Multiparty republic Currency: Peso = 100 centavos

Argentina Basin see Argentine Basin
Argentina, Republic of see Argentina
Argentine Antarctic Sector 154 B 3 Argentine territorial claim, Antarctica
Argentine Basin 67 B 6 var. Argentina Basin. Undersea basin, SW Atlantic Ocean
Argentine Rise see Falkland Plateau
Argo 72 B 3 N Sudan
Árgos 105 B 6 S Greece
Argostóli 105 A 5 var. Argostólion. Kefallinía, W Greece
Argostólion see Argostóli
Argun 111 B 8 SW Russian Federation
Århus 85 B 7 var. Aarhus. C Denmark
Ari Atoll 132 A 4 island, C Maldives
Arica 64 B 1 hist. San Marcos de Arica. N Chile
Aridaía 104 B 3 var. Aridhaía. N Greece
Ariha 118 B 3 var. Arīhā. W Syria
Arīhā see Ariha
Ariminum see Rimini
Arinsal 91 A 8 NW Andorra
Arizona 48 B 2 off. State of Arizona; nicknames Copper State, Grand Canyon State. State, SW USA
Arkansas 42 A 1 off. State of Arkansas; nickname Land of Opportunity. State, S USA
Arkansas City 45 F 5 Kansas, C USA
Arkansas River 42 B 2 river, C USA
Arkhangel'sk 110 C 3 var. Arcangelo, Eng. Archangel. NW Russian Federation
Arkoí 105 E 6 island, Dodekánisos, SE Greece
Arles 91 C 6 var. Arles-sur-Rhône; anc. Arelas, Arelate. SE France
Arlington 49 G 3 Texas, S USA
Arlington 41 E 4 Virginia, NE USA
Arlon 87 D 8 Dut. Aarlen, Ger. Arel; Lat. Orolaunum. SE Belgium
Armagh 89 B 5 Ir. Ard Mhacha. SE Northern Ireland, UK
Armagnac 91 B 6 cultural region, S France

Armenia
117 F 3 var. Ajastan, Arm. Hayastani Hanrapetut'yun; prev. Armenian Soviet Socialist Republic. Republic, SW Asia

Official name: Republic of Armenia Date of formation: 1991 Capital: Yerevan Population: 3.6 million Total area: 29,000 sq km (11,505 sq miles) Languages: Armenian*, Azerbaijani, Russian,

Kurdish **Religions:** Armenian Apostolic 90%, other Christian and Muslim 10% **Ethnic mix:** Armenian 93%, Azerbaijani 3%, Russian, Kurdish 4% **Government:** Multiparty republic **Currency:** Dram = 100 louma

Armenia 58 B 3 W Colombia
Armidale 149 D 6 New South Wales, SE Australia
Armstrong 38 B 3 Ontario, S Canada
Armyansk *see* Armyans'k
Armyans'k 109 F 4 *Rus.* Armyansk. S Ukraine
Arnaía 104 C 4 N Greece
Arnaud 82 A 3 river, E Canada
Arnea *see* Arnaía
Arnedo 93 E 2 N Spain
Arnhem 86 D 4 SE Netherlands
Arnhem Land 148 A 2 physical region, Northern Territory, N Australia
Arno 96 B 3 river, C Italy
Arno *see* Arno Atoll
Arnold 45 G 5 Missouri, C USA
Arnswalde *see* Choszczno
Arorae 145 E 3 island, W Kiribati
Ar Rahad *see* Er Rahad
Ar Ramādī 120 B 3 *var.* Ramadi, Rumadiya. SW Iraq
Ar Ramthā 119 B 5 *var.* Ramtha. N Jordan
Arran, Isle of 88 C 4 island, SW Scotland, UK
Ar Raqqah 118 C 2 *var.* Rakka; *anc.* Nicephorium. N Syria
Arras 90 C 2 *anc.* Nemetocenna. N France
Ar Rashādīyah 119 C 5 NE Jordan
Ar Rawḍatayn 120 C 4 *var.* Raudhatain. N Kuwait
Arretium *see* Arezzo
Arriaga 51 G 5 SE Mexico
Ar Riyāḍ 121 C 5 *Eng.* Riyadh. Country capital, C Saudi Arabia
Arroyo Grande 47 B 7 California, W USA
Ar Rustāq 121 E 5 *var.* Rostak, Rustaq. N Oman
Ar Ruṭbah 120 B 3 *var.* Rutba. SW Iraq
Árta 105 A 5 *anc.* Ambracia. W Greece
Artashat 117 G 3 S Armenia
Artemisa 54 B 2 W Cuba
Artesia 48 D 3 New Mexico, SW USA
Arthur's Pass 151 C 6 pass, South Island, C New Zealand
Artigas 64 D 3 *prev.* San Eugenio, San Eugenio del Cuareim. N Uruguay
Art'ik 117 F 2 W Armenia
Artois 90 C 2 cultural region, N France
Artsiz *see* Artsyz
Artsyz 108 D 4 *Rus.* Artsiz. SW Ukraine
Artvin 117 F 2 NE Turkey
Arua 73 B 6 NW Uganda
Aruba 55 E 5 *var.* Oruba. Dutch autonomous region, S Caribbean Sea
Aruba 58 C 1 island, SE Caribbean Sea
Aru, Kepulauan 139 G 4 *Eng.* Aru Islands; *prev.* Aroe Islands. Island group, E Indonesia
Arunāchal Pradesh 135 H 3 cultural region, NE India
Arusha 73 C 7 N Tanzania

Arviat 37 G 4 *prev.* Eskimo Point. North West Territories, C Canada
Arvidsjaur 84 C 4 N Sweden
Arys' 114 B 5 *Kaz.* Arys. S Kazakhstan
Arys *see* Arys'
Asadābād 123 F 4 *var.* Asaḏbād; *prev.* Chaghasarāy. E Afghanistan
Asad, Buḩayrat al 118 C 2 *Eng.* Lake Assad. Reservoir, N Syria
Asahi-dake 130 D 2 mountain, Hokkaidō, NE Japan
Asahikawa 130 D 2 Hokkaidō, NE Japan
Asamankese 75 E 5 SE Ghana
Āsānsol 135 F 4 NE India
Ascension Fracture Zone 67 C 5 fracture zone, C Atlantic Ocean
Ascension Island 69 A 5 island, E Atlantic Ocean
Ascoli Piceno 96 C 4 *anc.* Asculum Picenum. C Italy
Asculum Picenum *see* Ascoli Piceno
Ashburton 151 C 6 South Island, SW New Zealand
Ashburton 146 B 4 river, Western Australia, W Australia
Ashdod 119 A 6 *anc.* Azotos, *Lat.* Azotus. W Israel
Asheville 43 E 1 North Carolina, SE USA
Ashgabat 122 C 3 *prev.* Ashkhabad, Poltoratsk. Country capital, C Turkmenistan
Ashibetsu 130 D 2 *var.* Asibetu. Hokkaidō, NE Japan
Ashkelon *see* Ashqelon
Ashland 40 D 5 Kentucky, E USA
Ashland 46 B 4 Oregon, NW USA
Ashmore & Cartier Islands 142 A 3 Australian external territory, E Indian Ocean
Ashmyany 107 C 5 *Rus.* Oshmyany. W Belorussia
Ashqelon 119 A 6 *var.* Ashkelon. C Israel
Ash Shadādah 118 E 2 *var.* Ash Shaddādah, Jisr ash Shadadi Shaddādī, Shedadi, Tell Shedadi. NE Syria
Ash Sharāh 119 B 7 *var.* Esh Sharā. Mountain range, W Jordan
Ash Shawbak 119 B 7 W Jordan
Ash Shiḩr 121 C 7 SE Yemen
Asia 112 D 3 continent
Asibetu *see* Ashibetsu
Asipovichy 107 D 6 *Pol.* Mahilyowskaya Voblasts', *Rus.* Osipovichi. C Belorussia
Aşkale 117 E 3 NE Turkey
Askersund 85 C 6 C Sweden
Asmara 72 C 4 *Amh.* Āsmera. Country capital, C Eritrea
Āsmera *see* Asmara
Aspinwall *see* Colón
Assab 72 D 4 *Amh.* Āseb. SE Eritrea
As Sabkhah 118 D 2 *var.* Sabkha. NE Syria
Assad, Lake *see* Asad, Buḩayrat al
Aş Şafāwī 119 C 6 N Jordan
As Salamīyah *see* Salamīyah
As Salṭ 119 B 6 *var.* Salt. NW Jordan
Assam 135 G 3 cultural region, NE India
Assamaka *see* Assamakka
Assamakka 75 F 2 *var.* Assamaka. NW Niger
As Samāwah 120 B 3 *var.* Samawa. S Iraq
Assen 86 E 2 NE Netherlands
Assenede 87 B 5 NW Belgium

Assling *see* Jesenice
As Sukhnah 118 D 3 *var.* Sukhne, *Fr.* Soukhné. C Syria
As Sulaymānīyah 120 C 3 *var.* Sulaimaniya, *Kurd.* Slēmānī. NE Iraq
As Sulayyil 120 B 4 S Saudi Arabia
Aş Şummān 121 C 5 desert, N Saudi Arabia
As Suwaydā' 119 B 5 *var.* El Suweida, Es Suweida, Suweida, *Fr.* Soueida. SW Syria
Asten 87 D 5 SE Netherlands
Asti 96 A 2 *anc.* Asta Colonia, Asta Pompeia, Hasta Colonia, Hasta Pompeia. NW Italy
Astigi *see* Ecija
Astorga 92 C 2 *anc.* Asturica Augusta. N Spain
Astrakhan' 111 C 7 SW Russian Federation
Asturias 92 C 1 cultural region, NW Spain
Asturias *see* Oviedo
Asturica Augusta *see* Astorga
Astypálaia 105 D 7 *var.* Astipálaia, *It.* Stampalia. Island, Dodekánisos, SE Greece
Asunción 64 D 2 country capital, S Paraguay
Aswân 72 B 2 *var.* Assouan, Assuan; *anc.* Syene. SE Egypt
Asyût 72 B 2 *var.* Assiout, Assiut, Siut; *anc.* Lycopolis. C Egypt
Atacama Desert *see* Atacama, Desierto de
Atacama, Desierto de 64 B 1 *Eng.* Atacama Desert. Desert, N Chile
Atafu Atoll 145 F 3 island, NW Tokelau
Atakora, Chaîne de l' 75 F 4 *var.* Atakora Mountains. Mountain range, N Benin
Atakora Mountains *see* Atakora, Chaîne de l'
Atâr 74 C 2 NW Mauritania
Atas Bogd 126 D 3 mountain, SW Mongolia
Atascadero 47 B 7 California, W USA
Atbara 72 C 3 *var.* 'Aṭbārah. NE Sudan
'Aṭbārah *see* Atbara
Atbasar 114 C 4 N Kazakhstan
Atchison 45 F 4 Kansas, C USA
Ath 87 B 6 *var.* Aat. SW Belgium
Athabasca 37 E 5 Alberta, SW Canada
Athabasca 37 E 5 *var.* Athabaska. River, Alberta, SW Canada
Athabaska *see* Athabasca
Athabasca, Lake 37 F 4 lake, SW Canada
Athens 42 C 1 Alabama, S USA
Athens 42 D 1 Tennessee, S USA
Athens 43 E 2 Georgia, SE USA
Athens 39 G 3 Texas, S USA
Athens 40 D 4 Ohio, N USA
Athens *see* Athína
Atherton 148 D 3 Queensland, NE Australia
Athína 105 C 6 *Eng.* Athens; *prev.* Athínai, *anc.* Athenae. Country capital, C Greece
Athlone 89 B 6 *Ir.* Baile Átha Luain. C Ireland
Ath Thawrah *see* Madīnat ath Thawrah
Ati 76 C 3 C Chad
Atikokan 38 B 4 Ontario, S Canada
Atka 115 G 3 E Russian Federation
Atka Island 36 A 3 island, Alaska, NW USA

Atlanta 49 H 2 Texas, S USA
Atlanta 35 C 6 state capital, Georgia, SE USA
Atlantic City 41 F 4 New Jersey, NE USA
Atlantic-Indian Basin 67 D 8 undersea basin, SW Indian Ocean
Atlantic-Indian Ridge 67 D 7 undersea ridge, SW Indian Ocean
Atlantic Ocean 66 C 4 *var.* Atlantshaf. Ocean,
Atlantshaf *see* Atlantic Ocean
Atlas Mountains 68 B 2 mountain range, N Africa
Atlasovo 115 H 3 E Russian Federation
Atlas Saharien 70 D 2 *var.* Saharan Atlas. Mountain range, Algeria/Morocco
Atlin 36 D 4 British Columbia, W Canada
Aṭ Ṭā'if 121 B 5 W Saudi Arabia
Aṭ Ṭal al Abyaḍ 118 C 2 *var.* Tall al Abyaḍ, Tell Abyad, *Fr.* Tell Abiad. N Syria
Attapu 137 E 5 *var.* Attopeu. SE Laos
Attawapiskat 38 C 3 Ontario, C Canada
Attawapiskat 38 C 3 river, S Canada
Attersee 95 D 6 lake, N Austria
At Tibnī 118 D 2 *var.* Tibnī. N Syria
Attopeu *see* Samakhixai
Attu Island 36 A 2 island, Alaska, NW USA
Atuntaqui 60 B 1 N Ecuador
Atyrau 114 B 4 *prev.* Gur'yev. W Kazakhstan
Aubagne 91 D 6 *anc.* Albania. SE France
Aubange 87 D 8 SE Belgium
Auburn 42 D 2 Alabama, S USA
Auburn 41 G 2 Maine, NE USA
Auburn 46 B 2 Washington, NW USA
Auch 91 B 6 *Lat.* Augusta Auscorum, Elimberrum. S France
Auckland 150 D 2 North Island, N New Zealand
Auckland Islands 142 D 5 island group, S New Zealand
Aude 91 C 6 cultural region, S France
Audenarde *see* Oudenaarde
Audern *see* Audru
Audru 106 D 2 *Ger.* Audern. SW Estonia
Augila *see* Awjilah
Augsburg 95 C 6 *Fr.* Augsbourg; *anc.* Augusta Vindelicorum. S Germany
Augusta 43 E 2 Georgia, SE USA
Augusta 147 B 7 Western Australia, SW Australia
Augusta 41 G 2 state capital, Maine, NE USA
Augusta Emerita *see* Mérida
Augusta Praetoria *see* Aosta
Augusta Trajana *see* Stara Zagora
Augustobona Tricassium *see* Troyes
Augustodurum *see* Bayeux
Augustów 98 E 2 *Rus.* Avgustov. NE Poland
Augustus Island 146 C 3 island,
'Aujā et Tahtā 119 E 7 *var.* Khirbet el 'Aujā et Taḩtā. E West Bank

Auk Bok 137 B 5 *var.* South Island. Island, S Burma
Auob 78 B 4 *var.* Oup. River, E Namibia/South Africa
Aurangābād 134 D 5 W India
Aur Atoll 144 D 1 island, E Marshall Islands
Auray 90 A 4 NW France
Aurelia Aquensis *see* Baden-Baden
Aurelianum *see* Orléans
Aurillac 91 C 5 C France
Aurora 40 B 3 Illinois, N USA
Aurora 45 G 5 Missouri, C USA
Aurora 44 D 4 Colorado, C USA
Aurora 59 F 2 NW Guyana
Aurora *see* Maewo
Aus 78 B 4 SW Namibia
Aussig *see* Ústí nad Labem
Austin 35 C 6 state capital, Texas, S USA
Austin 45 G 3 Minnesota, N USA
Australes, Îles 145 H 5 island group, SW French Polynesia
Austral Fracture Zone 153 E 4 fracture zone, S Pacific Ocean

Australia 142 A 4 Commonwealth republic, Indian Ocean/Pacific Ocean

Official name: Commonwealth of Australia **Date of formation:** 1901 **Capital:** Canberra **Population:** 17.8 million **Total area:** 7,686,850 sq km (2,967,893 sq miles) **Languages:** English*, Greek, Italian, Malay, Aboriginal languages **Religions:** Protestant 60%, Roman Catholic 26%, other 14% **Ethnic mix:** Caucasian 95%, Asian 4%, Aboriginal, other 1% **Government:** Parliamentary democracy **Currency:** Australian $ = 100 cents

Australian Alps 149 C 7 mountain range, SE Australia
Australian Antarctic Territory 154 C 3 Australian territorial claim, Antarctica
Australian Capital Territory 149 D 7 *prev.* Federal Capital Territory. Territory, SE Australia
Australie, Bassin Nord de l' *see* North Australian Basin
Austral Seamounts 152 D 4 seamount range, S Pacific Ocean
Austrava *see* Ostrov

Austria 95 D 7 *Ger.* Österreich. Republic, C Europe

Official name: Republic of Austria **Date of formation:** 1920 **Capital:** Vienna **Population:** 7.8 million **Total area:** 83,850 sq km (32,375 sq miles) **Languages:** German*, Croatian, Slovene, Hungarian (Magyar) **Religions:** Roman Catholic 85%, Protestant 6%, other 9% **Ethnic mix:** German 99%, other (inc. Hungarian, Slovene, Croat) 1% **Government:** Multiparty republic **Currency:** Schilling = 100 groschen

Ausuitoq *see* Grise Fiord
Auvergne 91 C 5 cultural region, S France
Auxerre 90 C 4 *anc.* Autesiodorum, Autissiodorum. C France
Avaricum *see* Bourges
Avarua 145 G 5 dependent territory capital, Rarotonga, S Cook Islands
Ávdira 104 D 3 NE Greece

Aveiro 92 B 3 *anc.* Talabriga. W Portugal
Avellino 97 D 5 *anc.* Abellinum. S Italy
Avenio *see* Avignon
Aversa 97 D 5 S Italy
Avesta 85 C 6 C Sweden
Aveyron 91 C 6 river, S France
Avezzano 96 C 4 C Italy
Avgustov *see* Augustów
Aviemore 88 C 3 N Scotland, UK
Avignon 91 D 6 *anc.* Avenio. SE France
Ávila 92 D 3 *var.* Avila; *anc.* Abela, Abula, Abyla, Avela. C Spain
Avilés 92 C 1 NW Spain
Avranches 90 B 3 N France
Awaji-shima 131 C 6 island, Japan
Āwash 73 D 5 C Ethiopia
Awbārī 71 F 3 SW Libya
Awjilah 71 G 3 *It.* Augila. NE Libya
Awled Djellal *see* Ouled Djellal
Axel 87 B 5 SW Netherlands
Axel Heiberg Island 37 F 1 *var.* Axel Heiburg. Island, N Canada
Axel Heiburg *see* Axel Heiberg Island
Axiós *see* Vardar
Ayacucho 60 D 4 S Peru
Ayaguz 114 C 5 *Kaz.* Ayaköz; *prev.* Sergiopol. E Kazakhstan
Ayamonte 92 B 5 S Spain
Ayaviri 61 E 4 S Peru
Aydarkŭl 123 E 2 *Rus.* Ozero Aydarkul'. Lake, C Uzbekistan
Aydarkul', Ozero *see* Aydarkŭl
Aydın 116 A 4 *var.* Aïdin; *anc.* Tralles. SW Turkey
Ayers Rock *see* Uluru
Ayeyarwady *see* Irrawaddy
Ayiá *see* Agiá
Ayia Napa *see* Agía Nápa
Ayorou 75 F 3 W Niger
'Ayoûn el 'Atroûs 74 D 3 *var.* Aïoun el Atroûss, Aïoun el Atrous. SE Mauritania
Ayr 88 C 4 SW Scotland, UK
Ayr 148 D 3 Queensland, E Australia
Aytos 104 E 2 E Bulgaria
Ayutthaya 137 C 5 *var.* Phra Nakhon Si Ayutthaya. C Thailand
Ayvalık 116 A 3 W Turkey
A'zāg 118 B 2 NW Syria
Azahar, Costa del 93 F 3 coastal region, E Spain
Azaouâd 75 E 3 plateau, SW Mali

Azerbaijan 117 G 2 *Az.* Azärbaycan, Azärbaycan Respublikasi; *prev.* Azerbaijan SSR. Republic, SE Asia

Official name: Republic of Azerbaijan **Date of formation:** 1991 **Capital:** Baku **Population:** 7.3 million **Total area:** 86,600 sq km (33,436 sq miles) **Languages:** Azerbaijani*, Russian, Armenian **Religions:** Muslim 83%, Armenian Apostolic, Russian Orthodox 17% **Ethnic mix:** Azerbaijani 83%, Russian 6%, Armenian 6%, other 5% **Government:** Multiparty republic **Currency:** Manat = 100 gopik

Azimabad *see* Patna
Azogues 60 B 2 S Ecuador
Azores 2A 5 *var.* Açores, Ilhas dos Açores, *Port.* Arquipélago dos Açores. Island group, W Portugal
Azores-Biscay Rise 80 A 3 undersea rise, E Atlantic Ocean
Azoum, Bahr 76 C 3 river, SE Chad

Azov, Sea of 109 G 4 *Rus.* Azovskoye More, *Ukr.* Azovs'ke More. Sea, N Black Sea
Azraq, Waḥat al 119 C 6 oasis, N Jordan
Aztec 48 C 1 New Mexico, SW USA
Azuaga 92 C 4 W Spain
Azuero, Península de 53 F 5 peninsula, S Panama
Azul 65 D 5 E Argentina
Azur, Côte d' 91 C 6 coastal region, SE France
Aẕ Ẕahrān 120 C 4 *Eng.* Dhahran. NE Saudi Arabia
Az Zaqāzīq *see* Zagazig
Az Zarqā' 119 B 6 *var.* Zarqa. NW Jordan
Az Zāwiyah 71 F 2 *var.* Zawia. NW Libya
Az Zilfī 120 B 4 N Saudi Arabia
Æsernia *see* Isernia

B

Baabda 118 A 4 *var.* B'abdâ. C Lebanon
Baalbek 118 B 4 *var.* Ba'labakk; *anc.* Heliopolis. E Lebanon
Baar 95 B 7 N Switzerland
Baarle-Nassau 87 C 5 enclave, N Belgium
Baarn 86 C 3 C Netherlands
Babadag 108 D 5 SE Romania
Babahoyo 60 B 2 *prev.* Bodegas. C Ecuador
Babayevo *see* Babayevo
Bābā, Kūh-e 123 E 4 mountain range, C Afghanistan
Babayevo 110 B 4 *var.* Babajevo. NW Russian Federation
Bab el Mandeb 121 B 7 strait, Arabian Sea/Red Sea
Babelthuap 144 A 2 island, E Palau
Babonneau 55 F 1 N Saint Lucia
Babruysk 107 C 7 *Rus.* Bobruysk. E Belorussia
Babuyan Channel 139 E 1 channel, Philippine Sea/South China Sea
Babuyan Islands 139 E 1 island, N Philippines
Bacabal 63 F 2 E Brazil
Bacău 108 C 4 *Hung.* Bákó. NE Romania
Băc Giang 136 D 3 N Vietnam
Bacheykava 107 D 5 *Rus.* Bocheykovo. N Belorussia
Bačka Palanka 100 D 3 *prev.* Palanka. NW Yugoslavia
Bačka Topola 100 D 3 *Hung.* Topolya; *prev.* Bácstopolya. NW Yugoslavia
Bac Liêu 137 D 6 *var.* Vinh Loi. S Vietnam
Bacolod 139 E 2 *off.* Bacolod City. Negros, C Philippines
Bacolod City *see* Bacolod
Bactra *see* Balkh
Badain Jaran Shamo 126 D 3 desert, N China
Badajoz 92 C 4 *anc.* Pax Augusta. W Spain
Bad Doberan 94 C 2 N Germany
Baden-Baden 95 B 6 *anc.* Aurelia Aquensis. SW Germany
Bad Freienwalde 94 D 3 NE Germany
Bad Hersfeld 94 B 4 C Germany
Bad Homburg *see* Bad Homburg vor der Höhe
Bad Homburg vor der Höhe 95 B 5 *var.* Bad Homburg. W Germany
Bad Ischl 95 D 7 C Austria

Bad Krozingen 95 A 6 SW Germany
Badlands 44 D 2 physical region, North Dakota, N USA
Badu Island 148 C 1 island, Queensland, SW Australia
Bad Vöslau 95 E 6 NE Austria
Badyarada 'Admēd *see* Aden, Gulf of
Bafatá 74 C 4 C Guinea-Bissau
Baffin Bay 82 C 2 bay, NW Atlantic Ocean
Baffin Island 37 G 2 island, Northwest Territories, NE Canada
Bafing 74 C 3 river, NW Africa
Bafoussam 76 A 4 W Cameroon
Bafra 116 D 2 N Turkey
Bäft 120 D 4 S Iran
Bagaces 52 D 4 NW Costa Rica
Bagé 63 E 5 S Brazil
Baghdād 120 B 3 *var.* Bagdad, *Eng.* Baghdad. Country capital, C Iraq
Baghdad *see* Baghdād
Bāghīn 120 D 4 Iran
Baghlān 123 E 4 NE Afghanistan
Bago *see* Pegu
Bagoé 74 C 3 river, Ivory Coast/Mali
Bagratonovsk 106 A 4 *Ger.* Preussisch Eylau. W Russian Federation
Bagrax Hu *see* Bosten Hu
Baguio 139 E 1 *off.* Baguio City. Luzon, N Philippines
Baguio City *see* Baguio
Bagzane, Monts 75 G 3 mountain, N Niger
Bahama Islands *see* Bahamas

Bahamas 54 C 2 Commonwealth republic, N Caribbean Sea

Official name: The Commonwealth of the Bahamas **Date of formation:** 1973 **Capital:** Nassau **Population:** 300,000 **Total area:** 13,880 sq km (5,359 sq miles) **Languages:** English*, English Creole **Religions:** Protestant 76%, Roman Catholic 19%, other 5% **Ethnic mix:** Black 85%, White 15% **Government:** Parliamentary democracy **Currency:** Bahamian $ = 100 cents

Bahamas 35 D 6 *var.* Bahama Islands. Island group, W Atlantic Ocean
Bahariya Oasis 72 B 2 *var.* Wāhat el Bahariya. Oasis, C Egypt
Bahariya, Wāhat el *see* Bahariya Oasis
Bahāwalpur 134 C 2 E Pakistan
Bahia 63 F 3 *off.* Estado da Bahia. State, E Brazil
Bahía Blanca 65 C 5 E Argentina
Bahia, Estado da *see* Bahia
Bahía, Islas de la 52 C 1 *Eng.* Bay Islands. Island group, N Honduras
Bahir Dar 72 C 4 *var.* Bahr Dar, Bahrdar Giyorgis. NW Ethiopia
Bahraich 135 E 3 N India

Bahrain 120 C 4 *Ar.* Al Baḥrayn; *prev.* Bahrein, *anc.* Tylos or Tyros. Monarchy, SW Asia

Official name: State of Bahrain **Date of formation:** 1971 **Capital:** Manama **Population:** 500,000 **Total area:** 680 sq km (263 sq miles) **Languages:** Arabic*, English, Urdu

Religions: Muslim (Shi'a majority) 85%, Christian 7%, other 8% Ethnic mix: Arab 73%, South Asian 14%, Persian 8%, other 5% Government: Absolute monarchy (emirate) Currency: Dinar = 1,000 fils

Baḥr al Milḥ see Razāzah, Buḥayrat ar
Bahrām Chāh 122 D 5 SW Afghanistan
Bahushewsk 107 E 6 Rus. Bogushëvsk. NE Belorussia
Baia Mare 108 B 3 Ger. Frauenbach, Hung. Nagybánya; prev. Neustadt. NW Romania
Baia Sprie 108 B 3 Ger. Mittelstadt, Hung. Felsőbánya. NW Romania
Baïbokoum 76 B 4 SW Chad
Băicoi 108 C 5 SE Romania
Baie-Comeau 39 E 4 Québec, SE Canada
Baikal, Lake see Baykal, Ozero
Baile Átha Luain see Athlone
Bailén 92 D 4 S Spain
Baile na Mainistreach see Newtownabbey
Băileşti 108 B 5 SW Romania
Bailey's Bay 42 A 5 bay, W Atlantic Ocean
Bainbridge 42 D 3 Georgia, SE USA
Bā'ir see Bayir
Baireuth see Bayreuth
Bairiki 144 D 2 country capital, Tarawa, W Kiribati
Bairnsdale 149 C 7 Victoria, SE Australia
Baiyin 128 B 4 N China
Baja 99 C 7 S Hungary
Baja California 48 A 5 Eng. Lower California. Peninsula, NW Mexico
Baja California 50 A 2 state, NW Mexico
Bajo Boquete see Boquete
Bajram Curri 101 C 5 N Albania
Bakala 76 C 4 C Central African Republic
Baker & Howland Islands 145 F 2 US unincorporated territory, C Pacific Ocean
Baker Lake 37 F 3 C Canada
Bakersfield 47 C 7 California, W USA
Bakharden 122 C 3 Turkm. Bäherden; prev. Bakherden. C Turkmenistan
Bakhchisaray see Bakhchysaray
Bakhchysaray 109 F 5 Rus. Bakhchisaray. S Ukraine
Bakhmach 109 F 1 N Ukraine
Bākhtarān 122 C 4 var. Kermānshāh, Qahremānshahr. W Iran
Baki 117 H 2 Eng. Baku. Country capital, E Azerbaijan
Bákó see Bacău
Bakony 99 C 7 Eng. Bakony Mountains, Ger. Bakonywald. Mountain range, W Hungary
Baksan 111 B 8 SW Russian Federation
Baku see Baki
Baku 112 B 4 country capital, E Azerbaijan
Bakwanga see Mbuji-Mayi
Balabac, Selat see Balabac Strait
Balabac Strait 138 D 3 var. Selat Balabac. Strait, W Pacific Ocean
Balaguer 93 F 2 NE Spain
Balakovo 111 C 6 W Russian Federation
Bālā Morghāb 122 D 4 NW Afghanistan

Balao 60 B 2 S Ecuador
Balashov 111 B 6 W Russian Federation
Balasore see Bāleshwar
Balaton 99 C 7 var. Lake Balaton, Ger. Plattensee. Lake, W Hungary
Balbina, Represa 62 D 1 reservoir, NW Brazil
Balboa 53 G 5 C Panama
Balcarce 65 D 5 E Argentina
Balclutha 151 B 7 South Island, SW New Zealand
Baldy Mountain 44 C 1 mountain, Montana, NW USA
Baleares, Islas 93 H 4 Eng. Balearic Islands. Island group, E Spain
Balearic Islands see Baleares, Islas
Balearic Plain 80 C 5 var. Algerian Basin. Undersea basin, E Atlantic Ocean
Baleine, Rivière à la 39 E 2 river, Québec, E Canada
Balen 87 C 5 N Belgium
Bāleshwar 135 F 4 prev. Balasore. E India
Bali 138 D 5 island, C Indonesia
Balıkesir 116 A 3 W Turkey
Balikpapan 138 D 4 Borneo, C Indonesia
Balkan Mountains 104 C 2 Bul./SCr. Stara Planina. Mountain range, Bulgaria/Yugoslavia
Balkh 123 E 3 anc. Bactra. N Afghanistan
Balkhash 114 C 5 Kaz. Balqash. SE Kazakhstan
Balkhash, Lake see Balkhash, Ozero
Balkhash, Ozero 114 C 5 Eng. Lake Balkhash, Kaz. Balqash. Lake, SE Kazakhstan
Balladonia 147 C 6 Western Australia, S Australia
Ballarat 149 C 7 Victoria, SE Australia
Balleny Islands 154 B 5 island group, Antarctica
Ballina 149 E 5 New South Wales, SE Australia
Ballinger 49 F 3 Texas, S USA
Balls Pyramid 142 C 4 island, E Australia
Balqash see Balkhash
Balş 108 B 5 S Romania
Balsas 63 F 2 E Brazil
Balsas, Río 51 E 5 var. Río Mexcala. River, S Mexico
Bal'shavik 107 D 7 Rus. Bol'shevik. SE Belorussia
Balta 108 D 3 SW Ukraine
Bălţi 108 D 3 Rus. Bel'tsy. N Moldavia
Baltic Sea 66 D 2 Ger. Ostee, Rus. Baltiskoye More. Sea, NE Atlantic Ocean
Baltimore 41 F 4 Maryland, NE USA
Baluchistān 134 A 3 var. Balochistān, Beluchistan. Province, SW Pakistan
Balvi 106 D 4 NE Latvia
Balykchy 123 G 2 Kir. Ysyk-Köl; prev. Issyk-Kul', Rybach'ye. NE Kyrgyzstan
Balzers 94 E 2 S Liechtenstein
Bam 120 E 4 SE Iran
Bamako 74 D 4 country capital, SW Mali
Bambari 76 C 4 C Central African Republic
Bamberg 95 C 5 SE Germany
Bamenda 76 A 4 W Cameroon
Banaba 144 D 2 var. Ocean Island. Island, W Kiribati

Banc St.Lazarus see St.Lazarus Bank
Banda Aceh 138 A 3 var. Banda Atjeh; prev. Koetaradja, Kutaradja, Kutaraja. Sumatera, W Indonesia
Banda, Laut 139 F 5 Eng. Banda Sea. Sea, W Pacific Ocean
Bandama 74 D 5 var. Bandama Fleuve. River, S Ivory Coast
Bandama Blanc 74 D 5 river, C Ivory Coast
Bandama Fleuve see Bandama
Bandar-e 'Abbās 120 D 4 var. Bandar'Abbās; prev. Gombroon. S Iran
Bandar-e Būshehr 120 C 4 var. Būshehr, Eng. Bushire. S Iran
Bandar-e Khamīr 120 D 4 S Iran
Bandar-e Langeh 120 D 4 var. Bandar-e Lengeh, Lingeh. S Iran
Bandar Maharani see Muar
Bandar Penggaram see Batu Pahat
Bandar Seri Begawan 138 D 3 prev. Brunei Town. Country capital, N Brunei
Banda Sea see Banda, Laut
Bandırma 116 A 3 var. Penderma. NW Turkey
Bandjarmasin see Banjarmasin
Bandoeng see Bandung
Bandundu 77 C 6 prev. Banningville. SW Zaire
Bandung 138 C 5 prev. Bandoeng. Jawa, C Indonesia
Bangalore 132 C 2 state capital, S India
Bangassou 77 D 5 S Central African Republic
Banggai, Kepulauan 139 E 4 island group, C Indonesia
Banghāzī 71 G 2 Eng. Bengazi, Benghazi, It. Bengasi. NE Libya
Bangka 138 C 4 island, W Indonesia
Bangkok see Krung Thep
Bangkok, Bight of see Krung Thep, Ao

Bangladesh 135 F 3 prev. East Pakistan. Republic, S Asia

Official name: People's Republic of Bangladesh Date of formation: 1971 Capital: Dhaka Population: 122.2 million Total area: 143,998 sq km (55,598 sq miles) Languages: Bangla*, Urdu, Chakma Religions: Muslim 83%, Hindu 16%, 1% Ethnic mix: Bengali 98%, other 2% Government: Multiparty republic Currency: Taka = 100 paisa

Bangor 89 C 6 NW Wales, UK
Bangor 89 C 6 Ir. Beannchar. E Northern Ireland, UK
Bangor 41 H 2 Maine, NE USA
Bang Pla Soi see Chon Buri
Bangui 77 C 5 country capital, SW Central African Republic
Ban Hat Yai see Hat Yai
Ban Hin Heup 136 C 4 C Laos
Ban Houayxay 136 C 3 var. Ban Houei Sai. NW Laos
Ban Houei Sai see Houayxay
Ban Hua Hin 137 C 6 var. Hua Hin. C Thailand
Bani 74 D 3 river, S Mali
Banī Suwayf see Beni Suef
Bāniyās 118 A 3 var. Banias, Baniyas, Paneas. W Syria
Banjak, Kepulauan see Banyak, Kepulauan
Banja Luka 101 A 7 NW Bosnia & Herzegovina

Banjarmasin 138 D 4 prev. Bandjarmasin. Borneo, C Indonesia
Banjul 74 B 3 prev. Bathurst. Country capital, W Gambia
Ban Khok Kloi 137 B 7 S Thailand
Banks, Îles see Banks Islands
Banks Island 37 E 2 island, NW Canada
Banks Islands 144 D 4 Fr. Îles Banks. Island group, N Vanuatu
Banks Lake 46 C 2 reservoir, Washington, NW USA
Banks Peninsula 151 C 6 peninsula, South Island, C New Zealand
Banks Strait 149 C 8 strait, SW Tasman Sea
Bānkura 135 F 4 NE India
Banmo see Bhamo
Ban Na Môn 136 D 3 NE Laos
Banningville see Bandundu
Bañolas see Banyoles
Ban Pak Phanang see Pak Phanang
Banská Bystrica 99 C 6 Ger. Neusohl, Hung. Besztercebánya. C Slovakia
Bantry Bay 89 A 7 Ir. Bá Bheanntraí. Bay, NE Atlantic Ocean
Banya 101 E 2 E Bulgaria
Banyak, Kepulauan 138 A 3 prev. Kepulauan Banjak. Island group, NW Indonesia
Banyo 76 B 4 W Cameroon
Banyoles 93 G 2 var. Bañolas. NE Spain
Banzare Seamounts 141 C 7 seamount range, S Indian Ocean
Baoji 128 B 4 var. Pao-chi, Paoki. C China
Baoro 76 C 4 W Central African Republic
Baoshan 129 A 6 var. Pao-shan. SW China
Baotou 127 F 3 var. Pao-t'ou, Paotow. N China
Ba'qūbah 120 B 3 var. Qubba. C Iraq
Baquerizo Moreno see Puerto Baquerizo Moreno
Bar 101 C 5 It. Antivari. SW Yugoslavia
Baraawe 73 D 6 It. Brava. S Somalia
Baraji, Hirfanli 116 C 3 lake, Turkey
Baramanni 59 F 2 N Guyana
Bārāmati 134 C 5 W India
Baramita 59 F 2 N Guyana
Baranavichy 107 B 6 Pol. Baranowicze, Rus. Baranovichi. SW Belorussia

Barbados 55 G 1 Commonwealth republic, E Caribbean Sea

Official name: Barbados Date of formation: 1966 Capital: Bridgetown Population: 260,000 Total area: 430 sq km (166 sq miles) Languages: English*, English Creole Religions: Protestant 94%, Roman Catholic 5%, other 1% Ethnic mix: Black 80%, mixed 15%, White 4%, other 1% Government: Parliamentary democracy Currency: Barbados $ = 100 cents

Barbados 59 F 1 island, W Atlantic Ocean
Barbastro 93 F 2 NE Spain
Barbate de Franco 92 C 5 S Spain
Barbuda 55 G 3 island, N Antigua & Barbuda

Barcaldine 148 C 4 Queensland, E
Australia
Barcelona 93 G 2 *anc.* Barcino,
Barcinona. E Spain
Barcelona 59 E 2 NE Venezuela
Barcoo 148 C 4 river, E Australia
Barcs 99 C 7 SW Hungary
Bardaï 76 C 1 N Chad
Bardejov 99 D 5 *Ger.* Bartfeld,
Hung. Bártfa. NE Slovakia
Bardina, Gora *see* Bardin Seamount
Barduli *see* Barletta
Bareilly 135 E 3 *var.* Bareli. N India
Bareli *see* Bareilly
Barendrecht 86 C 4 SW
Netherlands
Barentin 90 B 3 N France
Barentsburg 83 G 2 W Svalbard
Barentsøya 83 G 2 island, E
Svalbard
Barents Sea 155 H 5 *Nor.* Barents
Havet, *Rus.* Barentsevo More. Sea,
Arctic Ocean
Bari 97 E 5 *var.* Bari delle Puglie;
anc. Barium. S Italy
Barikot *see* Barīkowṭ
Barīkowṭ 123 F 4 *var.* Barikot. NE
Afghanistan
Barillas 52 A 2 *var.* Santa Cruz
Barillas. NW Guatemala
Barinas 58 C 2 W Venezuela
Barisāl 135 G 4 S Bangladesh
Barisan, Pegunungan 138 B 4
mountain range, Sumatera, W
Indonesia
Barito 138 D 4 river, Borneo, C
Indonesia
Barkly Tableland 148 B 3 plateau,
N Australia
Bårlad 108 D 4 *prev.* Birlad. E
Romania
Barlavento, Ilhas de 74 A 2 *var.*
Windward Islands. Island group,
Cape Verde
Bar-le-Duc 90 D 3 *var.* Bar-sur-
Ornain. NE France
Barlee, Lake 147 B 6 lake, Western
Australia, W Australia
Barlee Range 146 B 4 mountain
range, Western Australia, W
Australia
Barletta 97 E 5 *anc.* Barduli. S Italy
Barlinek 98 B 3 *Ger.* Berlinchen. W
Poland
Barmen-Elberfeld *see* Wuppertal
Barmouth 89 C 6 W Wales, UK
Barnaul 114 D 4 C Russian
Federation
Barnstaple 89 C 7 SW England, UK
Baroda *see* Vadodara
Baron'ki 107 E 7 *Rus.* Boron'ki. E
Belorussia
Barquisimeto 58 C 2 NW
Venezuela
Barra 88 B 3 island, W Wales, UK
Barra de Río Grande 53 E 3 E
Nicaragua
Barranca 60 C 3 W Peru
Barrancabermija 58 B 2 N
Colombia
Barranquilla 58 B 1 N Colombia
Barreiro 92 B 4 W Portugal
Barrier Range 149 B 6 hill range,
New South Wales, SE Australia
Barrow 36 D 2 Alaska, NW USA
Barrow 91 A 6 *Ir.* An Bhearú. River,
SE Ireland
Barrow-in-Furness 89 C 5 NW
England, UK
Barrow Island 146 A 4 island, W
Australia

Barrows 37 F 5 Manitoba, S Canada
Bar-sur-Ornain *see* Bar-le-Duc
Bartang 123 F 3 river, SE Tajikistan
Bartenstein *see* Bartoszyce
Bartica 59 F 3 N Guyana
Bartlesville 49 G 1 Oklahoma, C
USA
Bartlett 42 C 1 Tennessee, S USA
Bartoszyce 98 D 2 *Ger.* Bartenstein.
N Poland
Baruun Huuray 126 C 2 wetland, E
Mongolia
Baruun-Urt 127 F 2 E Mongolia
Barú, Volcán 53 E 5 *var.* Volcán de
Chiriquí. Volcano, W Panama
Barwon 149 D 5 river, New South
Wales, SE Australia
Barysaw 107 D 6 *Rus.* Borisov. NE
Belorussia
Basarabeasca 108 D 4 *Rus.*
Bessarabka. SE Moldavia
Basel 95 A 7 *Eng.* Basle, *Fr.* Bâle.
NW Switzerland
Basilan Island 139 E 3 island, SW
Philippines
Basra *see* Al Başrah
Bassano del Grappa 96 C 2 NE
Italy
Bassein 136 A 4 *var.* Pathein SW
Burma
Basse-Terre 55 G 4 island, E
Guadeloupe
Basse-Terre 55 G 4 dependent
territory capital, SW Guadeloupe
Basseterre 55 G 3 country capital, C
Saint Kitts & Nevis
Bassikounou 74 D 3 SE Mauritania
Bass, Îlots de *see* Marotiri
Bass Strait 152 B 4 strait, Indian
Ocean/Pacific Ocean
Bassum 94 B 3 NW Germany
Bastia 91 E 7 SE France
Bastogne 87 D 7 SE Belgium
Bastrop 42 B 2 Louisiana, S USA
Bastyn' 107 C 7 *Rus.* Bostyn'. SW
Belorussia
Bata 77 A 5 NW Equatorial Guinea
Batabanó, Golfo de 54 B 2 gulf,
NW Caribbean Sea
Batae Coritanorum *see* Leicester
Batajnica 100 D 3 N Yugoslavia
Batangas 139 E 2 *off.* Batangas City.
Luzon, N Philippines
Batangas City *see* Batangas
Bataysk 111 B 7 SW Russian
Federation
Bâtdâmbâng 137 D 5 *prev.*
Battambang. NW Cambodia
Batéké, Plateaux 77 B 6 plateau, S
Congo
Bath 89 D 7 *hist.* Akermanceaster,
anc. Aquae Calidae, Aquae Solis.
S England, UK
Bathsheba 55 H 1 E Barbados
Bathurst 39 F 4 New Brunswick, SE
Canada
Bathurst 149 D 6 New South Wales,
SE Australia
Bathurst *see* Banjul
Bathurst Island 37 F 2 island, N
Canada
Bathurst Island 146 D 2 island,
Northern Territory, N Australia
Bāṭin, Wādī al 120 C 4 dry
watercourse, SW Asia
Batman 117 F 4 *var.* Iluh. SE Turkey
Baton Rouge 42 B 2 Louisiana, S
USA
Batroûn 118 A 4 *var.* Al Batrūn. N
Lebanon
Battambang *see* Bâtdâmbâng

Batticaloa 132 D 3 E Sri Lanka
Battipaglia 97 D 5 S Italy
Bat'umi 117 E 2 W Georgia
Batu Pahat 138 B 3 *prev.* Bandar
Penggaram. W Malaysia
Baturaja 138 B 4 W Indonesia
Bauchi 75 G 4 NE Nigeria
Bauer Basin 153 F 3 undersea
basin, E Pacific Ocean
Baumann, Pic *see* Agou, Mont
Bauru 57 D 5 S Brazil
Bauska 106 C 4 *Ger.* Bauske. S
Latvia
Bauske *see* Bauska
Bautzen 94 D 4 *Lus.* Budyšin. E
Germany
Bavarian Alps 95 C 7 *Ger.* Bayrische
Alpen. Mountain range,
Austria/Germany
Bawku 75 E 4 N Ghana
Bayamo 54 C 3 E Cuba
Bayan Har Shan 126 D 4 *var.* Bayan
Khar. mountain range, C China
Bayanhongor 126 D 2 C Mongolia
Bayan Khar *see* Bayan Har Shan
Bay City 49 G 4 Texas, S USA
Bay City 40 C 3 Michigan, N USA
Baydhabo 73 D 6 *var.* Baydhowa,
Isha Baydhabo, *It.* Baidoa. SW
Somalia
Bayern 95 C 6 cultural region, SE
Germany
Bayeux 90 B 3 *anc.* Augustodurum.
N France
Bāyir 119 C 7 *var.* Bā'ir. S Jordan
Bay Islands *see* Bahía, Islas de la
Baykal, Ozero 115 E 4 *Eng.* Lake
Baikal. Lake, S Russian
Federation
Baymak 111 D 6 W Russian
Federation
Bayonne 91 A 6 *anc.* Lapurdum.
SW France
Bayram-Ali *see* Bayramaly
Bayramaly 122 D 3 *prev.* Bayram-
Ali. S Turkmenistan
Bayreuth 95 C 5 *var.* Baireuth. SE
Germany
Bayrische Alpen *see* Bavarian Alps
Baysun *see* Boysun
Baza 93 E 4 S Spain
Beagle Channel 65 C 8 channel,
Atlantic Ocean/Pacific Ocean
Béal Feirste *see* Belfast
Beannchar *see* Bangor
Bear Island *see* Bjørnøya
Bear Lake 46 E 4 lake, NW USA
Beas de Segura 93 E 4 S Spain
Beata, Isla 55 E 3 island, SW
Dominican Republic
Beatrice 45 F 4 Nebraska, C USA
Beatton River 37 E 4 British
Columbia, W Canada
Beaucaire 91 C 6 S France
Beaufort-Wes *see* Beaufort West
Beaufort West 78 C 5 *Afr.* Beaufort-
Wes. SW South Africa
Beaumont 49 H 4 Texas, S USA
Beaune 90 D 4 C France
Beauvais 90 C 3 *anc.* Bellovacum,
Caesaromagus. N France
Beaver Island 40 C 2 island,
Michigan, N USA
Beaverton 46 B 3 Oregon, NW USA
Beāwar 134 C 3 N India
Bečej 100 D 3 *Ger.* Altbetsche,
Hung. Óbecse, Rácz-Becse; *prev.*
Magyar-Becse, Stari Bečej. N
Yugoslavia
Béchar 70 D 2 *prev.* Colomb-Béchar.
W Algeria

Beckley 40 D 5 West Virginia, NE
USA
Bedford 89 E 6 E England, UK
Bedford, Cape 148 D 2 headland,
Queensland, NE Australia
Bedum 86 E 1 NE Netherlands
Beenleigh 149 E 5 E Australia
Beer Menuha 119 B 7 S Israel
Beernem 87 A 5 NW Belgium
Be'ér Sheva' 119 A 7 *var.* Beersheba,
Ar. Bir es Saba. S Israel
Beesel 87 D 5 SE Netherlands
Beeville 49 G 4 Texas, S USA
Begoml' *see* Byahoml'
Behar *see* Bihār
Beida *see* Al Baydā'
Beihai 129 C 6 *var.* Peihai. S China
Beijing 128 D 3 *var.* Pei-ching, Eng.
Peking; *prev.* Pei-p'ing. Country
capital, China
Beilen 86 E 2 NE Netherlands
Beira 79 E 3 C Mozambique
Beirut *see* Beyrouth
Bei Shan 126 D 3 mountain range,
C China
Beiuş 108 B 3 *Hung.* Belényes. NW
Romania
Beja 92 B 4 *anc.* Pax Julia. SE
Portugal
Béjar 92 C 3 N Spain
Békás *see* Bicaz
Békéscsaba 99 D 7 *Rom.* Bichiş-
Ciaba. SE Hungary
Bekobod 123 E 2 *Rus.* Bekabad;
prev. Begovat. E Uzbekistan
Bela Crkva 100 E 3 *Ger.*
Weisskirchen, *Hung.*
Fehértemplom. E Yugoslavia
Belarus *see* Belorussia
Belau *see* Palau
Belaya Tserkov' *see* Bila Tserkva
Belchatow *see* Bełchatów
Bełchatów 98 C 4 *var.* Belchatow. C
Poland
Belcher, Îles *see* Belcher Islands
Belcher Islands 38 C 2 *Fr.* Îles
Belcher. Island group, Northwest
Territories, SE Canada
Beledweyne 73 D 5 *var.* Belet Huen,
It. Belet Uen. C Somalia
Belém 63 F 1 *var.* Pará. N Brazil
Belen 48 D 2 New Mexico, SW USA
Belén 52 D 4 SW Nicaragua
Belényes *see* Beiuş
Belfast 89 B 5 *Ir.* Béal Feirste. E
Northern Ireland, UK
Belfield 44 D 2 North Dakota, N
USA
Belfort 90 D 4 E France
Belgard *see* Białogard
Belgaum 132 B 1 W India

Belgium
87 B 6 *Dut.* België, *Fr.* Belgique.
Monarchy, W Europe

Official name: Kingdom of Belgium
Date of formation: 1830 **Capital:**
Brussels **Population:** 10 million
Total area: 33,100 sq km
(12,780 sq miles) **Languages:**
French*, Dutch*, Flemish **Religions:**
Roman Catholic 75%, other 25%
Ethnic mix: Flemish 58%, Walloon
32%, other European 6%, other 4%
Government: Constitutional
monarchy
Currency: Franc = 100 centimes

Belgorod 111 A 6 W Russian
Federation
Belgrade *see* Beograd
Belgrano II 154 B 2 research
station, Antarctica

Beli Manastir 100 C 2 *Hung.*
Pélmonostor; *prev.* Monostor. NE
Croatia
Bélinga 77 B 5 NE Gabon
Belitung, Pulau 138 C 4 island, W
Indonesia

Belize
52 B 1 *Sp.* Belice; *prev.* Colony of
Belize, British Honduras.
Commonwealth republic, Belize

Official name: Belize **Date of
formation:** 1981 **Capital:** Belmopan
Population: 200,000 **Total area:**
22,960 sq km (8,865 sq miles)
Languages: English*, English
Creole, Spanish **Religions:** Christian
87%, other 13% **Ethnic mix:** *mestizo*
44%, Creole 30%, Indian 11%,
Garifuna 8%, other 7% **Government:**
Parliamentary democracy **Currency:**
Belizean $ =100 cents

Belize 52 B 1 river,
Belize/Guatemala
Belize City 52 C 1 *var.* Belize, *Sp.*
Belice . NE Belize
Beljak *see* Villach
Belkofski 36 B 3 Alaska, NW USA
Belle Île 90 A 4 island, NW France
Belle Isle, Strait of 39 G 3 strait,
Newfoundland and Labrador,
NW Gulf of St.Lawrence
Belleville 40 B 5 Illinois, N USA
Belle Vue 55 F 2 S Saint Lucia
Bellevue 46 B 2 Washington, NW
USA
Bellevue 45 F 4 Nebraska, C USA
Bellingham 46 B 1 Washington,
NW USA
Belling Hausen Mulde *see*
Southeast Pacific Basin
Bellingshausen 154 A 2 research
station, Antarctica
Bellingshausen Abyssal Plain *see*
Bellingshausen Plain
Bellingshausen Sea 154 A 3 sea, SE
Pacific Ocean
Bello 58 B 2 W Colombia
Bello Horizonte *see* Belo Horizonte
Bellville 78 C 5 SW South Africa
Belmopan 52 C 1 country capital, C
Belize
Belogradchik 104 B 1 *var.*
Belogradčik. NW Bulgaria
Belogradčik *see* Belogradchik
Belo Horizonte 63 F 4 *prev.* Bello
Horizonte. SE Brazil
Belomorsk 110 B 3 NW Russian
Federation
Beloretsk 111 D 6 W Russian
Federation

Belorussia
107 C 6 *var.* Belarus, *Latv.*
Baltkrievija, *Rus.* Belorusskaya
SSR; *prev.* Belorussian SSR.
Republic, E Europe

Official name: Republic of Belarus
Date of formation: 1991 **Capital:**
Minsk **Population:** 10.3 million
Total area: 207,600 sq km (80,154 sq
miles) **Languages:** Belorussian*,
Russian **Religions:** Russian Orthodox
60%, Roman Catholic 8%, other 32%
Ethnic mix: Belorussian 78%, Russian
13%, Polish 4%, other 5%
Government: Multiparty republic
Currency: Rouble = 100 kopeks

Belorusskaya Gryada *see*
Byelaruskaya Hrada
Belovár *see* Bjelovar

Beloye More 110 C 3 *Eng.* White
Sea. Sea, Arctic Ocean/Barents
Sea
Belozersk 110 B 4 *var.* Beloz'orsk.
NW Russian Federation
Beloz'orsk *see* Belozersk
Belton 49 G 3 Texas, S USA
Bel'tsy *see* Bălţi
Belynichi *see* Byalynichy
Belyye Berega 111 A 5 W Russian
Federation
Belyy, Ostrov 114 D 2 island, N
Russian Federation
Bemidji 45 F 1 Minnesota, N USA
Bemmel 86 D 4 SE Netherlands
Benavente 92 C 2 N Spain
Bend 46 B 3 Oregon, NW USA
Bendern 94 E 1 NW Liechtenstein
Bendigo 149 C 7 Victoria, SE
Australia
Beneschau *see* Benešov
Benešov 99 B 5 *Ger.* Beneschau. W
Czech Republic
Benevento 97 D 5 *anc.* Beneventum,
Malventum. S Italy
Bengal, Bay of 133 E 1 bay, N
Indian Ocean
Bengbu 129 D 5 *var.* Peng-pu. E
China
Benghazi *see* Banghazi
Bengkulu 138 B 4 *prev.* Bengkoeloe,
Benkoelen, Benkulen. Sumatera,
W Indonesia
Benguela 78 B 2 *var.* Benguella. W
Angola
Benguella *see* Benguela
Beni 77 E 5 E Zaire
Beni 61 E 3 river, N Bolivia
Benidorm 93 F 4 SE Spain
Beni-Mellal 70 C 2 C Morocco

Benin
52 F 4 *prev.* Dahomey. Republic,
W Africa

Official name: Republic of Benin
Date of formation: 1960 **Capital:**
Porto-Novo **Population:** 5.1 million
Total area: 112,620 sq km
(43,480 sq miles) **Languages:**
French*, Fon, Bariba, Yoruba, Adja
Religions: Traditional beliefs 70%,
Muslim 15%, Christian 15%
Ethnic mix: Fon 39%, Yoruba 12%,
Adja 10%, other 39%
Government: Multiparty republic
Currency: CFA franc = 100 centimes

Benin, Bight of 75 F 5 bay, N Gulf
of Guinea
Benin City 75 G 5 SW Nigeria
Beni Suef 72 B 2 *var.* Bani Suwayf.
N Egypt
Ben Nevis 88 C 3 mountain, W
Scotland, UK
Bénoué *see* Benue
Bénoy 76 B 4 S Chad
Benson 48 B 3 Arizona, SW USA
Benton 42 B 2 Arkansas, C USA
Benue 68 B 4 *Fr.* Bénoué. River,
Cameroon/Nigeria
Beograd 100 D 3 *Eng.* Belgrade, *Ger.*
Belgrad; *anc.* Singidunum.
Country capital, N Yugoslavia
Berat 101 C 6 *var.* Berati, *SCr.*
Beligrad. C Albania
Berau, Teluk 139 G 4 *var.* MacCluer
Gulf. Gulf, W Pacific Ocean
Berbera 72 D 4 NW Somalia
Berbérati 77 B 5 SW Central
African Republic
Berck-Plage 90 C 2 N France
Berdichev *see* Berdychiv

Berdyans'k 109 G 4 *Rus.*
Berdyansk; *prev.* Osipenko. SE
Ukraine
Berdychiv 108 D 2 *Rus.* Berdichev.
N Ukraine
Berehove 108 B 3 *Cz.* Berehovo,
Hung. Beregszász, *Rus.* Beregovo.
W Ukraine
Berettyó 99 D 7 *Rom.* Barcău; *prev.*
Berătău, Beretău. River,
Hungary/Romania
Berettyóújfalu 99 E 6 E Hungary
Berezhany 108 C 2 *Pol.* Brzeżany W
Ukraine
Berezina *see* Byerezino
Berezniki 111 D 5 NW Russian
Federation
Berga 93 G 2 NE Spain
Bergamo 96 B 2 *anc.* Bergomum. N
Italy
Bergara 93 E 1 N Spain
Bergen 85 A 5 S Norway
Bergen 94 D 2 NE Germany
Bergen 86 C 2 NW Netherlands
Bergen *see* Mons
Bergerac 91 B 5 SW France
Bergeyk 87 D 5 S Netherlands
Bergomum *see* Bergamo
Beringen 87 C 5 NE Belgium
Beringov Proliv *see* Bering Strait
Bering Sea 152 D 1 sea, N Pacific
Ocean
Bering Strait 152 D 1 *Rus.* Beringov
Proliv. Strait, N Pacific Ocean
Berja 93 E 5 S Spain
Berkeley 47 B 6 California, W USA
Berkner Island 154 B 2 island,
Antarctica
Berkovitsa 104 C 2 NW Bulgaria
Berlin 94 D 3 country capital, NE
Germany
Berlin 41 G 2 Maine, NE USA
Berlinchen *see* Barlinek
Bermejo 64 C 2 river, N Argentina
Bermeo 93 E 1 N Spain
Bermuda 35 E 6 *var.* Bermuda
Islands, Bermudas; *prev.* Somers
Islands. UK crown colony, W
Atlantic Ocean
Bermuda Rise 66 B 3 undersea rise,
W Atlantic Ocean
Bern 95 A 7 *Fr.* Berne. Country
capital, W Switzerland
Bernau 94 D 3 NE Germany
Bernburg 94 C 4 C Germany
Berne *see* Bern
Berner Alpen 95 A 7 *var.* Berner
Oberland, *Eng.* Bernese Oberland.
Mountain range, SW Switzerland
Bernier Island 147 A 5 island, W
Australia
Bernina, Passo del 95 B 7 *Eng.*
Bernina Pass. Pass, SE
Switzerland
Bérnissart 87 B 6 SW Belgium
Berry 90 C 4 cultural region, C
France
Berry Islands 54 C 1 island group,
N Bahamas
Bertoua 77 B 5 C Cameroon
Beru 145 F 2 *var.* Peru. Island, W
Kiribati
Berwick-upon-Tweed 88 D 4 N
England, UK
Besançon 90 D 4 *anc.* Besontium,
Vesontio. E France
Beslan 111 B 8 SW Russian
Federation
Bessarabka *see* Basarabeasca
Betanzos 92 B 1 NW Spain

Betanzos 61 F 4 S Bolivia
Bethlehem 78 D 4 C South Africa
Bethlehem 119 E 7 *Ar.* Bayt Lahm,
Heb. Bet Lehem. C West Bank
Bético, Sistema 92 D 5 mountain
range, S Spain
Bétou 77 C 5 N Congo
Bette, Pic 71 G 4 *var.* Bikkū Bīttī, *It.*
Picco Bette. Mountain, S Libya
Beulah 40 C 2 Michigan, N USA
Beveren 87 B 5 N Belgium
Beverley 147 B 6 Western Australia,
W Australia
Beverley 89 D 5 NE England, UK
Beyrouth 118 A 4 *var.* Bayrūt, *Eng.*
Beirut; *anc.* Berytus. Country
capital, W Lebanon
Beyşehir Gölü 116 B 4 lake, C
Turkey
Béziers 91 C 6 *anc.* Baeterrae,
Baeterrae Septimanorum, Julia
Beterrae. S France
Bezwada *see* Vijayawāda
Bhadrāvati 132 C 2 SW India
Bhāgalpur 135 F 3 NE India
Bhaktapur 135 F 3 C Nepal
Bhamo 136 B 2 *var.* Banmo. N
Burma
Bharūch 134 C 4 W India
Bhaunagar *see* Bhāvnagar
Bhāvnagar 134 C 4 *prev.* Bhaunagar.
W India
Bheanntraí, Bá *see* Bantry Bay
Bhopāl 134 D 4 state capital, C
India
Bhubaneshwar 135 F 5 *prev.*
Bhubaneswar, Bhuvaneshwar.
State capital, E India
Bhusawal *see* Bhusāwal
Bhusāwal 134 D 4 *prev.* Bhusaval C
India

Bhutan
135 G 3 *var.* Druk-yul. Monarchy,
S Asia

Official name: Kingdom of Bhutan
Date of formation: 1865 **Capital:**
Thimphu **Population:** 1.7 million
Total Area: 47,000 sq km
(18,147 sq miles) **Languages:**
Dzongkha*, Nepali **Religions:**
Mahayana Buddhist 70%, Hindu 24%,
Muslim 5%, other 1% **Ethnic mix:**
Bhutia 61%, Gurung 15%, Assamese
13%, other 11% **Government:**
Constitutional monarchy
Currency: Ngultrum = 100 chetrum

Biak, Pulau 139 G 4 island, E
Indonesia
Biała Podlaska 98 E 3 E Poland
Białogard 98 B 2 *Ger.* Belgard. NW
Poland
Białystok 98 E 3 *Rus.* Belostok,
Bielostok. E Poland
Bianco, Monte *see* Blanc, Mont
Biarritz 91 A 6 SW France
Bicaz 108 C 4 *Hung.* Békás. NE
Romania
Bichiş-Ciaba *see* Békéscsaba
Biddeford 41 G 2 Maine, NE USA
Bideford 89 C 7 SW England, UK
Biel 95 A 7 *Fr.* Bienne. W
Switzerland
Bielefeld 94 B 4 NW Germany
Bielsko-Biała 99 C 5 *Ger.* Bielitz,
Bielitz-Biala. S Poland
Bielsk Podlaski 98 E 3 E Poland
Biên Hoa 137 E 6 S Vietnam
Bienne *see* Biel
Bienville, Lac 38 D 2 lake, Québec,
C Canada

Bié, Planalto do 69 C 6 *var.* Bié
Plateau. Plateau, C Angola
Bié Plateau *see* Bié, Planalto do
Bigge Island 146 C 2 island, W
Australia
Bighorn Mountains 44 C 2
mountain range, Wyoming, C
USA
Bighorn River 44 C 2 river, NW
USA
Bight, Head of 149 A 6 bay, NE
Great Australian Bight
Bight, The 54 C 1 C Bahamas
Bignona 74 B 3 SW Senegal
Bigorra *see* Tarbes
Bigosovo *see* Bihosava
Big Rapids 40 C 2 Michigan, N
USA
Big River 37 F 5 Saskatchewan, C
Canada
Big Sioux River 45 F 3 river, N
USA
Big Spring 49 E 3 Texas, S USA
Bihać 101 A 7 NW Bosnia &
Herzegovina
Bihār 135 F 4 *prev.* Behar. State, N
India
Biharamulo 73 B 7 NW Tanzania
Bihosava 107 D 5 *Rus.* Bigosovo.
NW Belorussia
Bijeljina 100 D 3 NE Bosnia &
Herzegovina
Bijelo Polje 101 D 5 W Yugoslavia
Bīkāner 134 C 3 NW India
Bikin 115 G 4 SE Russian
Federation
Bikini Atoll 144 D 1 *var.* Pikinni.
Island, NW Marshall Islands
Biläspur 135 E 4 C India
Biläsuvar 117 H 3 *Rus.* Bilyasuvar;
prev. Pushkino. SE Azerbaijan
Bila Tserkva 109 E 2 *Rus.* Belaya
Tserkov'. N Ukraine
Bilbao 93 E 1 *Basq.* Bilbo. N Spain
Bilbo *see* Bilbao
Bilecik 116 B 3 NW Turkey
Billings 44 C 2 Montana, NW USA
Biloela 148 D 4 Queensland, E
Australia
Biloku 59 G 4 S Guyana
Biloxi 42 C 3 Mississippi, S USA
Bilpa Morea Claypan 148 B 4 lake,
C Australia
Biltine 76 C 3 E Chad
Bilwi *see* Puerto Cabezas
Bilzen 87 D 6 NE Belgium
Bimini Islands 54 C 1 island group,
W Bahamas
Binche 87 B 7 S Belgium
Bindloe Island *see* Marchena, Isla
Binga, Monte 79 E 3 mountain, C
Mozambique
Bingerville 75 E 5 SE Ivory Coast
Binghamton 41 F 3 New York, NE
USA
Bingöl 117 E 3 E Turkey
Bintulu 138 D 3 Borneo, E Malaysia
Bío Bío 65 B 5 river, C Chile
Bioco, Isla de 77 A 5 *var.* Bioko,
Eng. Fernando Po, *Sp.* Fernando
Póo; *prev.* Macías Nguema
Biyogo. Island, NW Equatorial
Guinea
Birāk 71 F 3 *var.* Brak. C Libya
Birao 76 D 3 NE Central African
Republic
Biratnagar 135 F 3 E Nepal
Birdum 148 A 2 Northern Territory,
N Australia
Bireuen 138 A 3 W Indonesia
Bīrjand 120 E 3 E Iran

Birkenfeld 95 A 5 SW Germany
Birkenhead 89 C 6 NW England,
UK
Bîrlad *see* Bârlad
Birmingham 89 C 6 W England,
UK
Birmingham 42 C 2 Alabama, S
USA
Bîr Mogreïn 74 C 1 *var.* Bir
Moghrein; *prev.* Fort-Trinquet. N
Mauritania
Birnie Island 145 F 3 island, C
Kiribati
Birni-Nkonni *see* Birnin Konni
Birnin Konni 75 F 3 *var.* Birni-
Nkonni. SW Niger
Birobidzhan 115 G 4 SE Russian
Federation
Birsen *see* Biržai
Birsk 111 D 5 W Russian Federation
Biržai 106 C 4 *Ger.* Birsen. NE
Lithuania
Bisbee 48 B 3 Arizona, SW USA
Biscay, Bay of 66 D 3 *Fr.* Golfe de
Gascogne, *Sp.* Golfo de Vizcaya.
Bay, NE Atlantic Ocean
Biscay Plain 80 B 4 abyssal plain, E
Atlantic Ocean
Bischheim 90 E 3 NE France
Bischofsburg *see* Biskupiec
Bīshah, Wādī 121 B 5 dry
watercourse, W Saudi Arabia
Bishkek 123 G 2 *var.* Pishpek; *prev.*
Frunze. Country capital, N
Kyrgyzstan
Bishrī, Jabal 118 D 3 mountain
range, E Syria
Biskra 71 E 2 *var.* Beskra, Biskara.
NE Algeria
Biskupiec 98 D 2 *Ger.* Bischofsburg.
N Poland
Bislig 139 F 2 Mindanao, S
Philippines
Bismarck 45 E 2 state capital, North
Dakota, N USA
Bismarck Archipelago 144 C 3
island group, NE Papua New
Guinea
Bismarck Sea 144 B 3 sea, SW
Pacific Ocean
Bissau 74 B 4 country capital, W
Guinea-Bissau
Bistrița 108 B 3 *Ger.* Bistritz, *Hung.*
Besztercze; *prev.* Nösen. N
Romania
Bitam 77 B 5 N Gabon
Bitburg 95 A 5 SW Germany
Bitlis 117 F 4 SE Turkey
Bitoeng *see* Bitung
Bitola 101 D 6 *Turk.* Monastir; *prev.*
Bitolj. S Macedonia
Bitonto 97 E 5 *anc.* Butuntum. SE
Italy
Bitterroot Range 46 D 2 *Port.*
Cadeia Bitterroot. Mountain
range, NW USA
Bitung 139 F 3 *prev.* Bitoeng.
Celebes, C Indonesia
Biu 75 H 4 E Nigeria
Biwa-ko 131 C 6 lake, Honshū, SW
Japan
Biy-Khem *see* Bol'shoy Yenisey
Bizerte 71 E 1 *Ar.* Banzart, *Eng.*
Bizerta. N Tunisia
Bjelovar 100 B 2 *Hung.* Belovár. N
Croatia
Björneborg *see* Pori
Bjørnøya 83 G 3 *Eng.* Bear Island.
Island, N Norway
Blackall 148 C 4 Queensland, E
Australia
Blackfoot 46 E 4 Idaho, NW USA

Black Forest *see* Schwarzwald
Black Hills 44 D 3 mountain range,
N USA
Black Mesa 48 B 1 mountain,
Arizona, SW USA
Black Mountains 48 A 1 mountain
range, Arizona, SW USA
Blackpool 89 C 5 NW England, UK
Black Range 48 C 2 mountain
range, New Mexico, SW USA
Black River 54 A 5 W Jamaica
Black River 136 C 3 *Chin.* Lixian
Jiang, *Fr.* Rivière Noire, *Vtn.* Sông
Đa. River, China/Vietnam
Black Rock Desert 46 C 4 *Port.*
Deserto Black Rock. Desert,
Nevada, W USA
Blacksburg 40 D 5 Virginia, NE
USA
Black Sea 81 F 4 *Bul.* Cherno More,
Eng. Euxine Sea, *Rom.* Marea
Neagră, *Rus.* Chernoye More,
Turk. Karadeniz, *Ukr.* Chorne
More. Sea, SE Mediterranean Sea
Black Sea Lowland *see*
Prychornomors'ka Nyzovyna
Black Volta 75 E 4 *var.* Borongo,
Mouhoun, Moun Hou, *Fr.* Volta
Noire. River, NW Africa
Blackwater 89 B 6 *Ir.* An Abhainn
Mhór. River, S Ireland
Blackwell 49 G 1 Oklahoma, C
USA
Blagoevgrad 104 C 3 *prev.* Gorna
Dzhumaya. W Bulgaria
Blagoveshchensk 111 D 5 W
Russian Federation
Blagoveshchensk 115 G 4 SE
Russian Federation
Blake Plateau 35 D 6 *var.* Blake
Terrace. Undersea plateau, W
Atlantic Ocean
Blake Terrace *see* Blake Plateau
Blanca, Bahía 65 C 5 bay, SW
Atlantic Ocean
Blanca, Costa 93 F 4 physical
region, SE Spain
Blanche, Lake 149 B 5 lake, South
Australia, S Australia
Blanc, Mont 80 C 4 *It.* Monte
Bianco. Mountain, France/Italy
Blanes 93 G 2 NE Spain
Blankenberge 87 A 5 NW Belgium
Blankenheim 95 A 5 W Germany
Blanquilla, Isla 59 E 1 *var.* La
Blanquilla. Island, N Venezuela
Blantyre 79 E 2 *var.* Blantyre-Limbe.
S Malawi
Blantyre-Limbe *see* Blantyre
Blaricum 86 C 3 C Netherlands
Blenheim 151 D 5 South Island, C
New Zealand
Blesae *see* Blois
Blida 70 D 2 *var.* El Boulaida, El
Boulaïda. N Algeria
Bloemfontein 78 C 4 *var.*
Mangaung. C South Africa
Blois 90 C 4 *anc.* Blesae. C France
Bloomfield 48 C 1 New Mexico,
SW USA
Bloomington 40 C 4 Indiana, N
USA
Bloomington 45 F 2 Minnesota, N
USA
Bluefields 53 E 3 SE Nicaragua
Blue Mountain Peak 54 B 5
mountain, E Jamaica
Blue Mountains 149 D 6 mountain
range, New South Wales, SE
Australia
Blue Mountains 46 C 3 *Port.*
Montanha Azuis. Mountain
range, NW USA

Blue Mud Bay 148 B 2 bay, Gulf of
Carpentaria / Arafura Sea
Blue Nile 72 C 4 *var.* Bahr el Azraq,
Amh. Abai, Äbay Wenz, *Ar.* An
Nîl al Azraq. River,
Ethiopia/Sudan
Blumenau 63 F 5 S Brazil
Bo 74 C 4 S Sierra Leone
Boaco 52 D 3 W Nicaragua
Boa Vista 74 A 3 island, E Cape
Verde
Boa Vista 62 D 1 state capital, NW
Brazil
Bobo-Dioulasso 75 E 4 SW Burkina
Bobonong 78 D 3 E Botswana
Bobrinets *see* Bobrynets'
Bobruysk *see* Babruysk
Bobrynets' 109 E 3 *Rus.* Bobrinets.
C Ukraine
Bocay 52 D 2 N Nicaragua
Bocheykovo *see* Bacheykava
Bocholt 94 A 4 W Germany
Bochum 94 A 4 W Germany
Bocșca 108 A 4 *Ger.* Bokschen,
Hung. Boksánbanyá. SW Romania
Bodaybo 115 F 4 E Russian
Federation
Bodega Bay 47 A 6 bay, E Pacific
Ocean
Bodegas *see* Babahoyo
Boden 84 D 3 N Sweden
Bodensee *see* Lake Constance
Bodmin 89 C 7 SW England, UK
Bodø 84 C 3 C Norway
Bodrum 116 A 4 SW Turkey
Boeloekoemba *see* Bulukumba
Boende 77 C 5 C Zaire
Boeroe *see* Buru, Pulau
Bogale 137 B 5 S Burma
Bogalusa 42 B 3 Louisiana, S USA
Bogatynia 98 B 4 *Ger.* Reichenau.
SW Poland
Bogendorf *see* Łuków
Bogor 138 C 5 *Dut.* Buitenzorg.
Jawa, C Indonesia
Bogotá 58 B 3 *prev.* Santa Fe, Santa
Fe de Bogotá. Country capital, C
Colombia
Bogushëvsk *see* Bahushewsk
Boguslav *see* Bohuslav
Bo Hai 128 D 4 *var.* Gulf of Chihli.
Gulf, Yellow Sea/Pacific Ocean
Bohemia 99 A 5 *Cz.* Čechy, *Ger.*
Böhmen. Cultural region, W
Czech Republic
Bohemian Forest 95 C 5 *Cz.* Český
Les, Šumava, *Ger.* Böhmerwald.
Mountain range, C Europe
Bohol Sea 139 E 2 *var.* Mindanao
Sea. Sea, W Pacific Ocean
Bohoro Shan 126 B 2 mountain
range, NW China
Bohuslav 109 E 2 *Rus.* Boguslav. N
Ukraine
Bois Blanc Island 40 C 2 island,
Michigan, N USA
Boise 46 D 3 *var.* Boise City. State
capital, Idaho, NW USA
Boise City *see* Boise
Bois, Lac des *see* Woods, Lake of the
Boizenburg 94 C 3 N Germany
Bojador *see* Boujdour
Bojnūrd 120 D 2 *var.* Bujnurd. N
Iran
Bokåro 135 F 4 N India
Boké 74 C 4 W Guinea
Boknafjorden 85 A 6 fjord, NE
North Sea
Bol 76 B 3 W Chad
Bolesławiec 98 B 4 *Ger.* Bunzlau.
SW Poland

Bolgatanga 75 E 4 N Ghana
Bolgrad see Bolhrad
Bolhrad 108 D 4 *Rus.* Bolgrad. SW
  Ukraine
Bolívar, Pico 58 C 2 mountain, W
  Venezuela

Bolivia
  61 F 4 Republic, W South
  America

Official name: Republic of Bolivia
Date of formation: 1903 **Capital:**
La Paz **Population:** 7.8 million
Total area: 1,098,580 sq km
(424,162 sq miles) **Languages:**
Spanish*, Quechua*, Aymará*
Religions: Catholic 95%, other 5%
Ethnic mix: Indian 55%, *mestizo*
27%, White 10%, other 8%
Government: Multiparty republic
Currency: Boliviano = 100 centavos

Bollene 91 D 6 SE France
Bollnäs 85 C 5 C Sweden
Bologna 96 B 3 N Italy
Bolognesi 60 C 2 E Peru
Bologoye 110 B 4 W Russian
  Federation
Bol'sezemelskaja Tundra see
  Bol'shezemel'skaya Tundra
Bol'shevik see Bal'shavik
Bol'shevik, Ostrov 115 E 2 island,
  Severnaya Zemlya, N Russian
  Federation
Bol'shezemel'skaya Tundra 110 E 3
  var. Bol'sezemelskaja Tundra.
  Physical region, NW Russian
  Federation
Bol'shoy Lyakhovskiy, Ostrov 115 F
  2 island, N Russian Federation
Bolton 89 C 5 *prev.* Bolton-le-Moors.
  NW England, UK
Bolton-le-Moors see Bolton
Bolu 116 B 3 NW Turkey
Bolungarvík 83 E 4 NW Iceland
Bolyarovo 104 D 3 *prev.* Pashkeni.
  SE Bulgaria
Bolzano 96 C 1 *Ger.* Bozen; *anc.*
  Bauzanum. N Italy
Boma 77 B 7 W Zaire
Bombay 134 C 5 *Guj.* Mumbai.
  State capital, W India
Bomi Hills 74 D 4 hill range, NW
  Liberia
Bomu 76 D 4 *var.* M'Bomu,
  Mbomou, Mbomu. River, Central
  African Republic/Zaire
Bonaire 58 D 1 island, E
  Netherlands Antilles
Bonanza 52 D 2 NE Nicaragua
Bonaparte Archipelago 146 C 2
  island group, NW Australia
Bonda 77 B 6 C Gabon
Bondoukou 75 E 4 E Ivory Coast
Bone see Watampone
Bône see Annaba
Bone, Teluk 139 E 4 bay, W Pacific
  Ocean
Bongaigaon 135 G 3 NE India
Bongo, Massif des 76 D 4 *var.*
  Chaîne des Mongos. Mountain
  range, NE Central African
  Republic
Bongor 76 B 4 SW Chad
Bonifacio 91 E 7 SE France
Bonn 95 A 5 W Germany
Bononia see Vidin
Boothia Felix see Boothia Peninsula
Boothia, Gulf of 37 F 2 inlet, Arctic
  Ocean
Boothia Peninsula 37 F 2 *prev.*
  Boothia Felix. Peninsula,
  Northwest Territories, NE Canada

Boppard 95 A 5 W Germany
Boquete 53 F 5 *var.* Bajo Boquete. W
  Panama
Bor 100 E 4 E Yugoslavia
Bor 73 B 5 S Sudan
Borås 85 B 7 S Sweden
Bordeaux 91 B 5 *anc.* Burdigala. SW
  France
Bordertown 149 B 7 South
  Australia, S Australia
Borgå see Porvoo
Børgefjellet 84 C 4 mountain range,
  C Norway
Borger 49 E 1 Texas, S USA
Borger 86 E 2 NE Netherlands
Borgholm 85 C 7 S Sweden
Borgo Maggiore 96 E 1 NW San
  Marino
Borisoglebsk 111 B 6 W Russian
  Federation
Borisov see Barysaw
Borlänge 85 C 6 C Sweden
Borne 86 E 3 E Netherlands
Borneo 138 C 4 island, SE Asia
Bornholm 85 B 8 *var.* Bornholms
  Amt. Island group, E Denmark
Bornholm 90 D 2 island, E
  Denmark
Bornholms Amt see Bornholm
Boron'ki see Baron'ki
Borovan 104 C 2 NW Bulgaria
Borovichi 110 B 4 *var.* Boroviči W
  Russian Federation
Boroviči see Borovichi
Borovo 100 D 3 NE Croatia
Borşa 108 C 3 *Hung.* Borsa. N
  Romania
Borsa see Borşa
Bor Ul Shan 126 D 3 mountain
  range, N China
Boryslav 108 B 2 *Pol.* Boryslaw, *Rus.*
  Borislav. NW Ukraine
Borzya 115 F 5 S Russian
  Federation
Bosanska Dubica 100 B 3 NW
  Bosnia & Herzegovina
Bosanska Gradiška 100 C 3 N
  Bosnia & Herzegovina
Bosanski Brod 100 C 3 N Bosnia &
  Herzegovina
Bosanski Novi 100 B 3 NW Bosnia
  & Herzegovina
Bosanski Šamac 100 C 3 N Bosnia
  & Herzegovina
Boskamp 59 G 3 N Surinam
Boskovice 99 B 5 *Ger.* Boskowitz.
  SE Czech Republic
Boskowitz see Boskovice
Bosna 101 A 8 river, N Bosnia &
  Herzegovina

Bosnia & Herzegovina
  100 A 8 Republic, SE Europe

Official name: The Republic of
Bosnia and Herzegovina **Date of
formation:** 1992 **Capital:** Sarajevo
Population: 4.5 million **Total area:**
51,130 sq km (19,741 sq miles)
Languages: Serbian*, Croatian*
Religions: Muslim 40%, Orthodox
Catholic 31%, other 29% **Ethnic mix:**
Bosnian 44%, Serb 31%, Croat 17%,
other 8% **Government:** Multiparty
republic **Currency:** Dinar = 100 para

Bōsō-hantō 131 D 6 peninsula,
  Honshū, S Japan
Bossangoa 76 C 4 C Central African
  Republic
Bossembélé 76 B 4 C Central
  African Republic
Bossier City 42 A 2 Louisiana, S
  USA

Bosten Hu 126 C 3 *var.* Bagrax Hu.
  Lake, NW China
Boston 89 D 6 *prev.* St.Botolph's
  Town. E England, UK
Boston 41 G 3 state capital,
  Massachusetts, NE USA
Boston Mountains 42 B 1 mountain
  range, Arkansas, C USA
Bostyn' see Bastyn'
Botany Bay 149 D 6 bay, W Tasman
  Sea
Boteti 78 C 3 *var.* Botletle. River, N
  Botswana
Bothnia, Gulf of 66 D 2 *Fin.*
  Pohjanlahti, *Swe.* Bottniska Viken.
  Gulf, N Baltic Sea
Botletle see Boteti
Botoşani 108 C 3 *Hung.* Botosány.
  NE Romania
Botosány see Botoşani
Botou 128 D 4 NE China
Botrange 87 D 6 mountain, E
  Belgium

Botswana
  78 C 3 Republic, S Africa

Official name: Republic of
Botswana **Date of formation:** 1966
Capital: Gaborone **Population:**
1.4 million **Total area:** 581,730 sq km
(224,600 sq miles) **Languages:**
English*, Tswana, Shona, San
Religions: Traditional beliefs 50%,
Christian 50% **Ethnic mix:** Tswana
75%, Shona 12%, San 3%, other 10%
Government: Multiparty republic
Currency: Pula = 100 thebe

Bouar 76 B 4 W Central African
  Republic
Bougainville Island 144 C 3 island,
  NE Papua New Guinea
Bougouni 74 D 4 SW Mali
Boujdour 70 A 3 *var.* Bojador. W
  Western Sahara
Boukra 70 B 3 N Western Sahara
Boulder 44 B 2 Montana, NW USA
Boulder 44 C 4 Colorado, C USA
Boulogne-sur-Mer 90 B 2 *var.*
  Boulogne; *anc.* Bononia,
  Gesoriacum, Gessoriacum. N
  France
Boûmdeïd 74 C 3 *var.* Boumdeït. S
  Mauritania
Boumdeït see Boûmdeïd
Boundiali 74 D 4 N Ivory Coast
Bountiful 44 B 4 Utah, C USA
Bounty Basin see Bounty Trough
Bounty Islands 142 D 5 island
  group, S New Zealand
Bounty Trough 152 C 5 *var.* Bounty
  Basin. Trough, S Pacific Ocean
Bourbonnais 90 C 4 cultural region,
  C France
Bourgas see Burgas
Bourg-en-Bresse 91 D 5 *var.* Bourg,
  Bourge-en-Bresse. E France
Bourges 90 C 4 *anc.* Avaricum. C
  France
Bourgogne 90 C 4 *Eng.* Burgundy.
  Cultural region, E France
Bourke 149 C 5 New South Wales,
  SE Australia
Bournemouth 89 D 7 S England, UK
Boutilimit 74 C 3 SW Mauritania
Bowen 148 D 3 Queensland, NE
  Australia
Bowling Green 40 D 3 Ohio, N
  USA
Bowling Green 40 C 5 Kentucky, E
  USA

Bowling Green, Cape 148 D 3
  headland, Queensland, E
  Australia
Boxmeer 86 D 4 SE Netherlands
Boyarka 109 E 2 N Ukraine
Boysun 123 E 3 *Rus.* Baysun. S
  Uzbekistan
Bozeman 44 B 2 Montana, NW
  USA
Bozüyük 116 B 3 NW Turkey
Božava 100 B 4 *var.* Brach, *It.* Brazza;
  anc. Brattia. Island, S Croatia
Bracara Augusta see Braga
Bradenton 43 E 4 Florida, SE USA
Bradford 89 D 5 NW England, UK
Braga 92 B 2 *anc.* Bracara Augusta.
  NW Portugal
Bragança 92 C 2 *Eng.* Braganza; *anc.*
  Julio Briga. NE Portugal
Brahestad see Raahe
Brāhmanbāria 135 G 4 E
  Bangladesh
Brahmapur 135 F 5 E India
Brahmaputra 124 C 2 *var.* Tsangpo,
  Ben. Jamuna, *Chin.* Yarlung
  Zangbo Jiang. River, S Asia
Brăila 108 D 4 E Romania
Braine-le-Comte 87 B 6 SW
  Belgium
Brainerd 45 F 2 Minnesota, N USA
Brak see Birāk
Brampton 38 D 5 Ontario, S Canada
Brandberg 78 B 3 mountain, NW
  Namibia
Brandenburg 94 C 3 *var.*
  Brandenburg an der Havel. NE
  Germany
Brandenburg an der Havel see
  Brandenburg
Brandon 37 F 5 Manitoba, S Canada
Braniewo 98 C 2 *Ger.* Braunsberg. N
  Poland
Brasília 63 F 3 country capital, C
  Brazil
Braşov 108 C 4 *Ger.* Kronstadt,
  Hung. Brassó; *prev.* Oraşul Stalin.
  C Romania
Brasstown Bald 42 D 1 mountain,
  Georgia, SE USA
Bratislava 99 C 6 *Ger.* Pressburg,
  Hung. Pozsony. Country capital,
  SW Slovakia
Bratsk 115 E 4 C Russian
  Federation
Braunsberg see Braniewo
Braunschweig 94 C 4 *Eng./Fr.*
  Brunswick. N Germany
Brava 74 A 3 island, SW Cape
  Verde
Brava see Baraawe
Brava, Costa 93 H 2 coastal region,
  NE Spain
Bravo del Norte see Grande, Río
Brawley 47 D 8 California, W USA

Brazil
  62 C 2 *var.* República Federativa
  do Brasil, *Sp.* Brasil; *prev.* United
  States of Brazil. Federal republic,
  C Brazil

Official name: Federative Republic
of Brazil **Date of formation:** 1822
Capital: Brasília **Population:** 156.6
million **Total area:** 8,511,970 sq km
(3,286,472 sq miles) **Languages:**
Portuguese*, German, Italian
Religions: Roman Catholic 90%,
other 10% **Ethnic mix:** White
(Portuguese, Italian, German) 55%,
mixed 38%, Black 6%, other 1%
Government: Multiparty republic
Currency: Real = 100 centavos

Brazil Basin 67 C 5 *var.* Brazilian Basin, Brazil'skaya Kotlovina. Undersea basin, W Atlantic Ocean

Brazilian Highlands 63 F 3 *var.* Planalto Central. Mountain range, E Brazil

Brazos River 49 G 3 river, Texas, S USA

Brazzaville 77 B 6 country capital, S Congo

Brčko 101 B 7 NE Bosnia & Herzegovina

Brecht 87 C 5 N Belgium

Brecon Beacons 89 C 6 mountain range, S Wales, UK

Breda 86 C 4 S Netherlands

Bree 87 D 5 NE Belgium

Bregalnica 101 E 6 river, E Macedonia

Bregovo 104 B 1 NW Bulgaria

Brême *see* Bremen

Bremen 94 B 3 *Fr.* Brême. NW Germany

Bremerhaven 94 B 3 NW Germany

Bremerton 46 B 2 Washington, NW USA

Brenham 49 G 4 Texas, S USA

Brenner Pass 95 C 7 *var.* Col du Brenner, Brennero Sattel, *Ger.* Brennerpass, *It.* Passo del Brennero. Pass, Austria/Italy

Brescia 96 B 2 *anc.* Brixia. N Italy

Breslau *see* Wrocław

Bressanone 96 C 1 *Ger.* Brixen. Italy

Brest 90 A 3 NW France

Brest 107 A 6 *Pol.* Brześć nad Bugiem, *Rus.* Brest-Litovsk; *prev.* Brześć Litewski. SW Belorussia

Bretagne 90 A 3 *Eng.* Brittany; *Lat.* Britannia Minor. Cultural region, NW France

Brezhnev *see* Naberezhnyye Chelny

Brezovo 104 D 2 *prev.* Abrashlare. C Bulgaria

Bria 76 D 4 C Central African Republic

Briançon 91 D 5 *anc.* Brigantio. SE France

Bribie Island 149 E 5 island, Queensland, SE Australia

Bricgstow *see* Bristol

Bridgeport 41 F 3 Connecticut, NE USA

Bridgetown 55 G 2 country capital, SW Barbados

Bridgman, Kap 83 E 1 headland, NE Greenland

Bridlington 89 E 5 NE England, UK

Bridport 89 C 7 SW England, UK

Brig 95 B 7 *Fr.* Brigue, *It.* Briga. SW Switzerland

Brigantio *see* Briançon

Brigham City 44 B 3 Utah, W USA

Brighton 89 E 7 SE England, UK

Brighton 44 D 4 Colorado, C USA

Brindisi 97 E 5 *anc.* Brundisium, Brundusium, SE Italy

Brisbane 149 E 5 state capital, Queensland, E Australia

Bristol 89 D 7 *anc.* Bricgstow. S England, UK

Bristol 43 E 1 Tennessee, S USA

Bristol 40 D 5 Rhode Island, NE USA

Bristol 41 F 3 Connecticut, NE USA

Bristol Bay 36 B 3 bay, SE Bering Sea

Bristol Channel 89 C 7 inlet, Atlantic Ocean/Celtic Sea

British Antarctic Territory 154 B 3 UK territorial claim, Antarctica

British Columbia 36 D 4 *Fr.* Colombie-Britannique. Province, SW Canada

British Indian Ocean Territory 124 B 5 UK dependent territory, C Indian Ocean

British Indian Ocean Territory 140 C 4 *var.* Chagos Islands. Island group, C Indian Ocean

British Isles 66 D 2 island group, NE Atlantic Ocean

British Solomon Islands Protectorate *see* Solomon Islands

British Virgin Islands 55 G 3 *var.* Virgin Islands. UK dependent territory, Caribbean Sea

Brive-la-Gaillarde 91 C 5 *prev.* Brive, *anc.* Briva Curretia. C France

Brixen *see* Bressanone

Brixia *see* Brescia

Brno 99 B 5 *Ger.* Brünn. SE Czech Republic

Broad Sound 148 D 4 sound, SE Coral Sea

Broceni 106 B 3 SW Latvia

Brockton 41 G 3 Massachusetts, NE USA

Brockville 38 D 5 Ontario, SE Canada

Brodeur Peninsula 37 F 2 peninsula, Baffin Island, NE Canada

Brodnica 98 D 3 *Ger.* Buddenbrock. N Poland

Broek-in-Waterland 86 C 3 C Netherlands

Broken Arrow 49 G 1 Oklahoma, C USA

Broken Hill 149 B 6 New South Wales, SE Australia

Broken Ridge 141 D 6 undersea plateau, S Indian Ocean

Bromberg *see* Bydgoszcz

Brookhaven 42 B 3 Mississippi, S USA

Brookings 45 F 3 South Dakota, N USA

Brooks Range 36 D 2 mountain range, Alaska, NW USA

Broome 146 C 3 Western Australia, NW Australia

Broomfield 44 C 4 Colorado, C USA

Brovary 109 E 2 N Ukraine

Brownfield 49 E 2 Texas, S USA

Brownsville 49 G 5 Texas, S USA

Brownwood 49 F 3 Texas, S USA

Brozha 107 D 7 E Belorussia

Brozha *see* Brozha

Bruce, Mount 146 B 4 mountain, Western Australia, W Australia

Bruges *see* Brugge

Brugge 87 A 5 *Fr.* Bruges. NW Belgium

Brummen 86 D 4 E Netherlands

Brunei
138 D 3 *Mal.* Negara Brunei Darussalam. Monarchy, Borneo, SE Asia

Official name: The Sultanate of Brunei **Date of formation:** 1984 **Capital:** Bandar Seri Begawan **Population:** 300,000 **Total Area:** 5,770 sq km (2,228 sq miles) **Languages:** Malay*, English, Chinese **Religions:** Muslim 63%, Buddhist 14%, Christian 10%, other 13% **Ethnic mix:** Malay 69%, Chinese 18%, other 13% **Government:** Absolute monarchy **Currency:** Brunei $ = 100 cents

Brunei Town *see* Bandar Seri Begawan

Brünn *see* Brno

Brunswick 43 E 3 Georgia, SE USA

Brunswick *see* Braunschweig

Bruny Island 149 C 8 island, Tasmania, SE Australia

Brus Laguna 52 D 2 E Honduras

Brüx *see* Most

Bruxelles 87 C 6 *var.* Brussels, *Dut.* Brussel, *Ger.* Brüssel; *anc.* Broucsella. Country capital, C Belgium

Bryan 49 G 3 Texas, S USA

Bryansk 111 A 5 W Russian Federation

Brzeg 98 C 4 *Ger.* Brieg; *anc.* Civitas Altae Ripae. SW Poland

Brzeżany *see* Berezhany

Bucaramanga 58 B 2 N Colombia

Buccaneer Archipelago 146 C 3 island group, W Australia

Buchanan 74 C 5 *prev.* Grand Bassa. SW Liberia

Buchanan, Lake 49 F 3 reservoir, Texas, S USA

Bucharest *see* Bucuresti

Bu Craa *see* Bou Craa

Bucuresti 108 C 5 *Eng.* Bucharest, *Ger.* Bukarest, Gross Schlatten, *Hung.* Abrudbánya, *Rom.* Bucureti; *prev.* Altenburg, *anc.* Cetatea Dambovitei. Country capital, S Romania

Buda-Kashalyova 107 D 7 *Rus.* Buda-Koshelëvo. SE Belorussia

Buda-Koshelëvo *see* Buda-Kashalyova

Budapest 99 D 6 *off.* Budapest Fóváros, *SCr.* Budimpešta. Country capital, N Hungary

Budaun 135 E 3 N India

Buddenbrock *see* Brodnica

Budweis *see* České Budějovice

Budyšin *see* Bautzen

Buenaventura 58 A 3 W Colombia

Buena Vista 93 H 5 S Gibraltar

Buena Vista 61 G 4 C Bolivia

Buenos Aires 64 D 4 *hist.* Santa Maria del Buen Aire. Country capital, E Argentina

Buenos Aires 53 E 5 SE Costa Rica

Buenos Aires, Lago 65 B 6 *var.* Lago General Carrera. Lake, Argentina/Chile

Buffalo 41 E 3 New York, NE USA

Buffalo Narrows 37 F 4 Saskatchewan, C Canada

Buff Bay 54 B 4 E Jamaica

Buftea 108 C 5 S Romania

Bug 81 E 3 *Bel.* Zakhodni Buh, *Eng.* Western Bug, *Rus.* Zapadnyy Bug, *Ukr.* Zakhidnyy Buh. River, E Europe

Buga 58 B 3 W Colombia

Bughotu *see* Santa Isabel

Bugojno 100 B 4 C Bosnia & Herzegovina

Buhayrat ath Tharthar 120 B 3 lake, C Iraq

Buheiret Nâsir 72 B 3 *var.* Buíayrat Náir, *Eng.* Lake Nasser. Lake, Egypt/Sudan

Buitenzorg *see* Bogor

Bujalance 92 D 4 S Spain

Bujanovac 101 E 5 SE Yugoslavia

Bujnurd *see* Bojnürd

Bujumbura 73 B 7 *prev.* Usumbura. Country capital, W Burundi

Bukavu 77 E 6 *prev.* Costermansville. E Zaire

Bukhoro 122 D 2 *var.* Bokhara, *Rus.* Bukhara. C Uzbekistan

Bukit Panjang 138 A 1 C Singapore

Bukoba 73 B 6 NW Tanzania

Bülach 95 B 7 NW Switzerland

Bulawayo 78 D 3 *var.* Buluwayo. SW Zimbabwe

Buldur *see* Burdur

Bulgan 127 E 2 N Mongolia

Bulgaria
104 C 2 *var.* Bulgariya, *Bul.* Bŭlgariya; *prev.* People's Republic of Bulgaria. Republic, SE Europe

Official name: Republic of Bulgaria **Date of formation:** 1908 **Capital:** Sofia **Population:** 8.9 million **Total area:** 110,910 sq km (42,822 sq miles) **Languages:** Bulgarian*, Turkish, Macedonian, Romany **Religions:** Christian 85%, Muslim 13%, Jewish 1%, other 1% **Ethnic mix:** Bulgarian 85%, Turkish 9%, Macedonian 3%, Gypsy 3% **Government:** Multiparty republic **Currency:** Lev = 100 stoninki

Bulukumba 139 E 5 *prev.* Boeloekoemba. Celebes, C Indonesia

Buluwayo *see* Bulawayo

Bumba 77 D 5 N Zaire

Bunbury 147 B 7 Western Australia, SW Australia

Bundaberg 148 D 4 Queensland, E Australia

Bungo-suidō 131 B 7 strait, NW Pacific Ocean

Bunia 77 E 5 NE Zaire

Bunyan 116 D 3 C Turkey

Bunzlau *see* Bolesławiec

Buraida *see* Buraydah

Buraydah 120 B 4 *var.* Buraida. N Saudi Arabia

Burdigala *see* Bordeaux

Burdur 116 B 4 *var.* Buldur. SW Turkey

Burë 72 C 4 NW Ethiopia

Burgas 104 E 2 *var.* Bourgas. E Bulgaria

Burgaski Zaliv 104 E 2 gulf, W Black Sea

Burgos 92 D 2 N Spain

Burgundy *see* Bourgogne

Burhan Budai Shan 126 D 4 mountain range, C China

Buriram 137 D 5 *var.* Buri Ram, Puriramya. E Thailand

Burjassot 93 F 3 E Spain

Burkburnett 49 F 2 Texas, S USA

Burke 41 E 4 Virginia, NE USA

Burkina
75 E 3 *prev.* Upper Volta. Republic, NW Africa

Official name: Burkina Faso **Date of formation:** 1960 **Capital:** Ouagadougou **Population:** 9.8 million **Total area:** 274,200 sq km (105,870 sq miles) **Languages:** French*, Mossi, Fulani **Religions:** Traditional beliefs 65%, Muslim 25%, Christian 10% **Ethnic mix:** Mossi 45%, Mande 10%, Fulani 10%, other 35% **Government:** Multiparty republic **Currency:** CFA franc = 100 centimes

Burleson 49 G 3 Texas, S USA

Burlington 41 F 2 Maine, NE USA

Burlington 45 G 4 Iowa, C USA

Burma
136 B 3 *var.* Myanmar. Military dictatorship, SE Asia

Official name: Union of Myanmar
Date of formation: 1948 **Capital:**
Rangoon (Yangon) **Population:** 44.6
million **Total Area:** 676,550 sq km
(261,200 sq miles) **Languages:**
Burmese*, Karen, Mon **Religions:**
Buddhist 89%, Muslim 4%, other 7%
Ethnic mix: Burman 68%, Shan 9%,
Karen 6%, Rakhine 4%, other 13%
Government: Military regime
Currency: Kyat = 100 pyas

Burnie 149 C 8 Tasmania, SE
Australia
Burnsville 45 F 2 Minnesota, N
USA
Burrel 101 D 6 *var.* Burreli. C
Albania
Burreli *see* Burrel
Burriana 93 F 3 E Spain
Bursa 116 B 3 *var.* Brussa; *prev.*
Brusa, *anc.* Prusa. NW Turkey
Būr Sa'īd *see* Port Said
Burtnieks *see* Burtnieku Ezers
Burtnieku Ezers 106 D 3 *var.*
Burtnieks. Lake, N Latvia
Burton 40 C 3 Michigan, N USA

Burundi
73 B 7 *prev.* Kingdom of Burundi,
Urundi. Republic, NE Africa

Official name: Republic of Burundi
Date of formation: 1962
Capital: Bujumbura **Population:** 5.8
million **Total area:** 27,830 sq km
(10,750 sq miles) **Languages:**
Kirundi*, French*, Swahili
Religions: Christian 68%, traditional
beliefs 32% **Ethnic mix:** Hutu 85%,
Tutsi 13%, Twa pygmy 1%, other 1%
Government: Multiparty republic
Currency: Franc = 100 centimes

Buru, Pulau 139 F 4 *prev.* Boeroe.
Island, E Indonesia
Busselton 147 B 7 Western
Australia, SW Australia
Busto Arsizio 96 B 2 N Italy
Buta 77 D 5 N Zaire
Butembo 77 E 5 NE Zaire
Butha Qi 127 G 1 *var.* Zalantun. NE
China
Butler 41 E 4 Pennsylvania, NE
USA
Bütow *see* Bytów
Butte 44 B 2 Montana, NW USA
Butterworth 138 B 3 W Malaysia
Button Islands 39 E 1 island group,
Northwest Territories, NE Canada
Butuan 139 F 2 *off.* Butuan City.
Mindanao, S Philippines
Butuan City *see* Butuan
Butuntum *see* Bitonto
Buulobarde 73 D 6 *var.* Buulo
Berde. Somalia
Buulo Berde *see* Buulobarde
Buur Gaabo 73 D 6 S Somalia
Buynaksk 111 B 8 SW Russian
Federation
Büyükağrı Dağı 117 G 3 *var.* Aghri
Dagh, Agri Dagi, Koh I Noh,
Masis, *Eng.* Mount Ararat, Great
Ararat. Mountain, E Turkey
Buyuk Menderes 116 A 4 river, SW
Turkey
Buzău 108 C 5 SE Romania
Buzuluk 111 D 6 W Russian
Federation
Byahoml' 107 D 5 *Rus.* Begoml'. N
Belorussia
Byalynichy 107 D 6 *Rus.* Belynichi.
E Belorussia

Bydgoszcz 98 C 3 *Ger.* Bromberg. W
Poland
Byelaruskaya Hrada 107 B 6 *Rus.*
Belorusskaya Gryada. Ridge, N
Belorussia
Byerezino 107 D 6 *Rus.* Berezina.
River, E Belorussia
Byrranga, Gory 115 E 2 mountain
range, N Russian Federation
Bystrovka *see* Kemin
Bystrovka 123 G 2 N Kyrgyzstan
Bytča 99 C 5 NW Slovakia
Bytów 98 C 2 *Ger.* Bütow. NW
Poland
Byuzmeyin 122 C 3 *Turkm.*
Büzmeyin; *prev.* Bezmein. C
Turkmenistan
Byval'ki 107 D 8 SE Belorussia

C

Caála 78 B 2 *var.* Kaala, Robert
Williams, *Port.* Vila Robert
Williams. C Angola
Caazapá 64 D 3 S Paraguay
Caballo Reservoir 48 C 3 reservoir,
New Mexico, SW USA
Cabañaquinta 92 D 1 N Spain
Cabanatuan 139 E 1 *off.* Cabanatuan
City. Luzon, N Philippines
Cabanatuan City *see* Cabanatuan
Cabillonum *see* Chalon-sur-Saône
Cabimas 58 C 1 NW Venezuela
Cabinda 77 B 6 *var.* Kabinda.
Province, NW Angola
Cabinda 78 A 1 *var.* Kabinda NW
Angola
Cabora Bassa, Lake *see* Cahora
Bassa, Albufeira de
Caborca 50 B 1 NW Mexico
Cabot Strait 39 G 4 strait Atlantic
Ocean/Gulf of St.Lawrence
Cabras, Ilha das 76 E 2 island, E
Atlantic Ocean
Cabrera 93 G 3 *anc.* Capraria. E
Spain
Čačak 100 C 4 C Yugoslavia
Cáceres 92 C 3 *Ar.* Qazris. W Spain
Cachimbo, Serra do 63 E 2
mountain range, C Brazil
Caconda 78 B 2 C Angola
Čadca 99 C 5 *Hung.* Csaca. N
Slovakia
Cadillac 40 C 2 Michigan, N USA
Cadiz 139 E 2 *off.* Cadiz City.
Negros, C Philippines
Cádiz 92 C 5 *anc.* Gades, Gadier,
Gadir, Gadire. SW Spain
Cadiz City *see* Cadiz
Cádiz, Golfo de 92 B 5 *gulf,* NE
Atlantic Ocean
Cadiz, Gulf of *see* Cádiz, Golfo de
Cadurcum *see* Cahors
Caen 90 B 3 N France
Caerdydd *see* Cardiff
Caer Gybi *see* Holyhead
Caesena *see* Cesena
Cafayate 64 C 2 N Argentina
Cagayan de Oro 139 F 2 *off.*
Cagayan de Oro City. Mindanao,
S Philippines
Cagayan de Oro City *see* Cagayan
de Oro
Cagliari 97 A 6 *anc.* Caralis. W Italy
Caguas 55 F 3 E Puerto Rico
Cahora Bassa, Albufeira de 78 D 2
var. Lake Cabora Bassa. Reservoir,
NW Mozambique
Cahors 91 B 6 *anc.* Cadurcum. S
France
Cahul 108 D 4 *Rus.* Kagul. S
Moldavia

Caicos Passage 54 D 2 channel, N
Caribbean Sea
Cailungo 96 E 1 N San Marino
Cairns 148 D 3 Queensland, NE
Australia
Cairo 72 B 1 *Ar.* Al Qāhirah, El
Qāhira. Country capital, N Egypt
Caisleán an Bharraigh *see* Castlebar
Cajamarca 60 B 3 *prev.* Caxamarca.
NW Peru
Čajovskij *see* Chaykovskiy
Čakovec 100 B 2 *Ger.* Csakathurn,
Hung. Csáktornya; *prev. Ger.*
Tschakathurn. N Croatia
Calabar 75 G 5 S Nigeria
Calabozo 58 D 2 C Venezuela
Calafat 108 B 5 SW Romania
Calafate *see* El Calafate
Calahorra 93 E 2 N Spain
Calais 90 C 2 N France
Calais 41 H 2 Maine, NE USA
Calama 64 B 3 N Chile
Călărași 108 D 3 *var.* Călăras, *Rus.*
Kalarash. C Moldavia
Călărași 108 C 5 SE Romania
Calatayud 93 E 2 NE Spain
Calbayog 139 F 2 *off.* Calbayog City.
Samar, C Philippines
Calbayog City *see* Calbayog
Calcanhar, Cabo 63 G 2 headland,
NE Brazil
Calcutta 135 G 4 state capital, NE
India
Caldas da Rainha 92 A 3 W
Portugal
Caldera 64 B 3 N Chile
Caldwell 46 D 3 Idaho, NW USA
Caledon Bay 148 B 2 bay, Gulf of
Carpentaria/Arafura Sea
Caledonia 52 C 1 N Belize
Caleta *see* Catalan Bay
Caleta Olivia 65 B 6 SE Argentina
Calgary 37 E 5 Alberta, SW Canada
Cali 58 A 3 W Colombia
Calicut 132 C 2 *var.* Kozhikode. SW
India
Calida, Costa 93 F 5 physical
region, SE Spain
California 47 C 7 *off.* State of
California; *nicknames* El Dorado,
The Golden State. State, W USA
California, Golfo de *see* California,
Gulf of
California, Gulf of 153 F 2 *var.*
Golfo de California; *prev.* Sea of
Cortez. Gulf, E Pacific Ocean
Călimănești 108 B 4 SW Romania
Callabonna, Lake 149 B 5 lake,
South Australia, S Australia
Callao 60 C 4 W Peru
Callatis *see* Mangalia
Callosa de Segura 93 F 4 E Spain
Calmar *see* Kalmar
Caloundra 149 E 5 Queensland, E
Australia
Caltanissetta 97 C 7 SW Italy
Caluula 72 E 4 NE Somalia
Camabatela 78 B 1 NW Angola
Camacupa 78 B 2 *var.* General
Machado, *Port.* Vila General
Machado. C Angola
Camagüey 54 C 2 *prev.* Puerto
Principe. C Cuba
Camagüey, Archipiélago de 54 C 2
island group, C Cuba
Camana 61 E 4 *var.* Camaná. SW
Peru
Camaná *see* Camana
Camargue 91 D 6 physical region,
SE France

Ca Mau 137 D 6 *var.* Quan Long,
Quanlong; *prev.* Camau. S
Vietnam
Cambay, Gulf of *see* Khambhāt,
Gulf of
Camberia *see* Chambéry

Cambodia
137 D 5 *var.* Democratic
Kampuchea, Roat Kampuchea,
Cam. Kampuchea; *prev.* People's
Democratic Republic of
Kampuchea. Republic, SE Asia

Official name: State of Cambodia
Date of formation: 1953
Capital: Phnom Penh **Population:**
9 million **Total Area:** 181,040 sq km
(69,000 sq miles) **Languages:**
Khmer*, French **Religions:** Buddhist
88%, Muslim 2%, other 10% **Ethnic
mix:** Khmer 94%, Chinese 4%,
other 2% **Government:** Constitutional
monarchy **Currency:** Riel = 100 sen

Cambrai 90 C 2 *Flem.* Kambryk;
prev. Cambray, *anc.* Cameracum.
N France
Cambrian Mountains 89 C 6
mountain range, C Wales, UK
Cambridge 89 E 6 *Lat.* Cantabrigia.
E England, UK
Cambridge 54 A 5 W Jamaica
Cambridge 150 D 3 North Island, N
New Zealand
Cambridge Bay 37 F 3 Victoria
Island, Canada
Cambulo 78 C 1 NE Angola
Camden 42 B 2 South Carolina, SE
USA
Cameron 40 A 2 Wisconsin, N USA

Cameroon
76 B 4 *Fr.* Cameroun. Republic,
C Africa

Official name: Republic of Cameroon
Date of formation: 1961 **Capital:**
Yaoundé **Population:** 12.5 million
Total area: 475,440 sq km
(183,570 miles) **Languages:** English*,
French*, Fang, Bulu **Religions:**
Traditional beliefs 51%, Christian
33%, Muslim 16% **Ethnic mix:**
Bamileke and Manum 20%, Fang
19%, other 61% **Government:**
Multiparty republic **Currency:** CFA
franc = 100 centimes

Camiri 61 G 4 S Bolivia
Camocim 63 G 2 E Brazil
Camopi 59 H 3 E French Guiana
Campamento 52 C 2 C Honduras
Campbell, Cape 151 D 5 headland,
South Island, SW New Zealand
Campbell Island 142 D 5 island, S
New Zealand
Campbell Plateau 152 C 5 undersea
plateau, SW Pacific Ocean
Campbell River 36 D 5 Vancouver
Island, Canada
Campeche 51 G 4 SE Mexico
Campeche, Bahía de 51 F 4 *Eng.*
Bay of Campeche. Bay, S Gulf of
Mexico
Campeche, Bay of *see* Campeche,
Bahía de
Câm Pha 136 E 3 N Vietnam
Câmpina 108 C 5 *prev.* Cîmpina. SE
Romania
Campina Grande 63 G 2 E Brazil
Campinas 63 F 4 S Brazil
Campobasso 97 D 5 S Italy
Campo Criptana *see* Campo de
Criptana

Campo de Criptana 93 E 3 *var.*
Campo Criptana. C Spain
Campo dos Goitacazes *see* Campos
Campo Grande 63 E 4 state capital,
SW Brazil
Campos 63 F 4 *var.* Campo dos
Goitacazes. SE Brazil
Câmpulung 108 B 4 *prev.*
Câmpulung-Muşcel, Cîmpulung.
S Romania
Cam Ranh 137 E 6 SE Vietnam

Canada
34 C 4 Commonwealth republic,
N North America

Official name: Canada **Date of
formation:** 1949 **Capital:** Ottawa
Population: 27.8 million **Total area:**
9,976,140 sq km (3,851,788 sq miles)
Languages: English*, French*
Chinese, Italian, German, Inuit
Religions: Roman Catholic 46%,
Protestant 30%, other 24% **Ethnic
mix:** British origin 40%, French
origin 27%, other 33%
Government: Parliamentary state
Currency: Canadian $ = 100 cents

Canada Basin 155 F 2 undersea
basin, Arctic Ocean
Canadian River 49 E 2 river, S USA
Çanakkale 116 A 3 *var.* Dardanelli;
prev. Chanak, Kale Sultanie. W
Turkey
Çanakkale Boğazı 116 A 2 *Eng.*
Dardanelles. Strait, Marmara
Denizi/Mediterranean Sea
Cananea 50 B 1 NW Mexico
Canarias, Islas 70 A 2 autonomous
community, Spain
Canaries 55 F 1 W Saint Lucia
Canarreos, Archipiélago de los 54 B
2 island group, W Cuba
Canary Basin 66 C 3 *var.* Canaries
Basin, Monaco Basin. Undersea
basin, E Atlantic Ocean
Canary Islands 70 A 3 island
group, E Atlantic Ocean
Cañas 52 D 4 NW Costa Rica
Canaveral, Cape 43 F 4 headland,
Florida, SE USA
Canavieiras 63 G 3 E Brazil
Canberra 149 D 7 country/territory
capital, Australian Capital
Territory, SE Australia
Cancún 51 H 3 SE Mexico
Cangzhou 128 D 4 NE China
Caniapiscau 39 E 2 river, Québec, E
Canada
Caniapiscau, Réservoir de 39 E 2
reservoir, Québec, C Canada
Canik Dağları 116 D 2 mountain
range, N Turkey
Canillo 91 A 8 C Andorra
Çankırı 116 C 3 *var.* Chankiri; *anc.*
Gangra, Germanicopolis. N
Turkey
Cannanore 132 B 2 *var.* Kananur,
Kannur. SW India
Cannes 91 D 6 SE France
Canoas 63 E 5 S Brazil
Canon City 44 D 5 Colorado, C
USA
Cantabria 92 D 1 cultural region, N
Spain
Cantábrica, Cordillera 92 C 1
mountain range, N Spain
Cantabrigia *see* Cambridge
Cantaura 59 E 2 NE Venezuela
Canterbury 89 F 7 *hist.*
Cantwaraburh, *anc.* Durovernum,
Lat. Cantuaria. SE England, UK
Canterbury Bight 151 C 6 sea area,
S Pacific Ocean

Canterbury Plains 151 C 6 plain,
South Island, SW New Zealand
Cân Thơ 137 D 6 S Vietnam
Canton *see* Guangzhou
Canton 42 B 2 Mississippi, S USA
Canton 40 D 4 Ohio, N USA
Canyon 49 E 2 Texas, S USA
Cao Băng 136 D 3 *var.* Caobang. N
Vietnam
Caobang *see* Cao Băng
Cap-Breton, Île du *see* Cape Breton
Island
Cape Barren Island 149 C 8 island,
Tasmania, SE Australia
Cape Basin 67 D 6 undersea basin,
SW Atlantic Ocean
Cape Breton Island 39 G 4 *Fr.* Île
du Cap-Breton. Island, Nova
Scotia, SE Canada
Cape Coast 75 E 5 *prev.* Cape Coast
Castle. S Ghana
Cape Coast Castle *see* Cape Coast
Cape Coral 43 E 5 Florida, SE USA
Cape Fear River 43 F 2 river, North
Carolina, SE USA
Cape Girardeau 45 H 5 Missouri, C
USA
Capelle aan den IJssel 86 C 4 SW
Netherlands
Cape Palmas *see* Harper
Cape Town 78 B 5 *var.* Ekapa, *Afr.*
Kaapstad, Kapstad. SW South
Africa

Cape Verde
74 A 2 Port. Ilhas do Cabo Verde,
Cabo Verde. Republic, W Africa

Official name: Republic of Cape
Verde **Date of formation:** 1975
Capital: Praia **Population:** 400,000
(1,556 sq miles) **Languages:**
Portuguese*, Creole **Religions:**
Roman Catholic 98%, Protestant 2%
Ethnic mix: Creole (*mestiço*) 71%,
Black 28%, White 1%
Government: Multiparty republic
Currency: Escudo = 100 centavos

Cape Verde Basin 66 C 4 undersea
basin, SW Atlantic Ocean
Cape Verde Plain 66 C 4 abyssal
plain, E Atlantic Ocean
Cape York Peninsula 148 C 2
peninsula, N Australia
Cap-Haïtien 54 D 3 *var.* Le Cap. N
Haiti
Capira 53 G 5 C Panama
Capitán Bado 64 D 2 E Paraguay
Capitán Pablo Lagerenza 64 D 1
var. Mayor Pablo Lagerenza. N
Paraguay
Capri, Isola di 97 C 5 island, S Italy
Caprivi Strip 78 C 3 *Ger.*
Caprivizipfel; *prev.* Caprivi
Concession. Cultural region, NE
Namibia
Caquetá 58 C 5 *var.* Rio Japurá,
Yapurá. River, Brazil/Colombia
C A R *see* Central African Republic
Caracal 108 B 5 S Romania
Caracaraí 62 D 1 W Brazil
Caracas 58 D 1 country capital, N
Venezuela
Caracollo 61 F 4 W Bolivia
Caralis *see* Cagliari
Caráquez 60 A 1 *prev.* Bahía de
Caráquez. W Ecuador
Caráquez, Bahía de *see* Caráquez
Caraşova 108 A 4 *Hung.* Krassóvár.
SW Romania
Caratasca, Laguna de 53 E 2
lagoon, W Caribbean Sea

Carballiño 92 B 1 NW Spain
Carbondale 40 B 5 Illinois, N USA
Carbonia 97 A 6 *var.* Carbonia
Centro. S Italy
Carbonia Centro *see* Carbonia
Carcaso *see* Carcassonne
Carcassonne 91 B 6 *anc.* Carcaso. S
France
Cárdenas 54 B 2 W Cuba
Cardiff 89 C 7 *Wel.* Caerdydd. SE
Wales, UK
Cardigan Bay 89 C 6 bay, SE Irish
Sea
Carei 108 B 3 *Ger.* Gross-Karol,
Karol, *Hung.* Nagykároly; *prev.*
Careii-Mari. NW Romania
Carey, Lake 147 C 5 lake, Western
Australia, SW Australia
Cariaco 59 E 1 NE Venezuela
Caribbean Sea 66 B 4 sea, W
Atlantic Ocean
Caribou 37 H 4 Manitoba, C Canada
Carlisle 89 C 5 *anc.* Luguvallium,
Luguvallum, Caer Luel. NW
England, UK
Carlow 89 B 6 *Ir.* Ceatharlach. SE
Ireland
Carlsbad 48 D 3 New Mexico, SW
USA
Carlsberg Ridge 140 B 4 undersea
ridge, NW Indian Ocean
Carlsruhe *see* Karlsruhe
Carmarthen 89 C 6 SW Wales, UK
Carmaux 91 C 6 S France
Carmel 40 C 4 Indiana, N USA
Carmelita 52 B 1 N Guatemala
Carmen 51 G 4 *var.* Ciudad del
Carmen. SE Mexico
Carmona 92 D 4 S Spain
Carnarvon 147 A 5 Western
Australia, W Australia
Carnegie, Lake 147 C 5 salt lake,
Western Australia, W Australia
Car Nicobar 133 F 3 island, SW
India
Caroço, Ilha 76 E 1 island, E
Atlantic Ocean
Carolina 63 F 2 E Brazil
Caroline Island 145 H 3 *prev.*
Thornton Island. Island, E
Kiribati
Caroline Islands 144 B 2 island
group, S Micronesia
Caroline Peak 151 A 7 mountain,
South Island, S New Zealand
Caroní 59 E 3 river, E Venezuela
Carora 58 C 2 N Venezuela
Carpathian Mountains 81 E 4 *var.*
Carpathians, Cz./Pol. Karpaty,
Ger. Karpaten. Mountain range, E
Europe
Carpaţii Meridionali 108 B 4 *var.*
Alpi Transilvaniei, Carpaţii
Sudici, *Eng.* South Carpathians,
Transylvanian Alps, *Ger.*
Südkarpaten, Transsylvanische
Alpen, *Hung.* Déli-Kárpátok,
Erdélyi-Havasok. Mountain
Range, C Romania
Carpaţii Occidentali 108 B 4 *Eng.*
Western Carpathians. Mountain
range, W Romania
Carpentaria, Gulf of 148 B 2 gulf,
N Aurafua Sea
Carpi 96 B 2 N Italy
Carrara 96 B 3 C Italy
Carr Boyd Range 146 D 3 mountain
range, N Australia
Çarsk *see* Çarsk
Carson City 47 C 5 state capital,
Nevada, W USA
Carson Sink 47 C 5 salt flat,
Nevada, W USA

Cartagena 93 F 4 *anc.* Carthago
Nova. SE Spain
Cartagena 58 B 1 *var.* Cartagena de
los Indes. NW Colombia
Cartagena de los Indes *see*
Cartagena
Cartago 53 E 4 C Costa Rica
Carthage 45 F 5 Missouri, C USA
Carthago Nova *see* Cartagena
Cartwright 39 G 2 Newfoundland
and Labrador, E Canada
Carúpano 59 E 1 NE Venezuela
Carusbur *see* Cherbourg
Caruthersville 45 H 5 Missouri, C
USA
Casablanca 70 C 2 *Ar.* Dar-el-Beida.
NW Morocco
Casa Grande 48 B 2 Arizona, SW
USA
Cascade Range 46 B 4 mountain
range, NW USA
Cascadia Basin 153 E 1 undersea
basin, NE Pacific Ocean
Cascais 92 B 4 Portugal
Caserta 97 D 5 S Italy
Casey 154 D 4 research station,
Antarctica
Casino 149 E 5 New South Wales,
SE Australia
Časlav 99 B 5 *Ger.* Tschaslau. C
Czech Republic
Casper 44 C 3 Wyoming, C USA
Caspian Sea 114 A 4 *Az.* Xäzär
Dänizi, *Kaz.* Kaspiy Tengizi, *Per.*
Daryā-ye Khazar, Bạḥr-e Khazar,
Rus. Kaspiyskoye More. Inland
sea, Asia/Europe
Cassel *see* Kassel
Casteggio 96 B 2 N Italy
Castelló de la Plana 93 F 3 *var.*
Castellón. E Spain
Castellón *see* Castelló de la Plana
Castelnaudary 91 C 6 S France
Castelo Branco 92 B 3 C Portugal
Castelsarrasin 91 B 6 S France
Castelvetrano 97 C 7 SW Italy
Castilla-La Mancha 93 E 3 cultural
region, NE Spain
Castilla-León 92 C 2 cultural
region, NW Spain
Castlebar 89 A 5 *Ir.* Caisleán an
Bharraigh. W Ireland
Castleford 89 D 5 N England, UK
Castle Harbour 42 B 5 harbour, E
Bermuda
Castricum 86 C 3 W Netherlands
Castries 55 F 1 country capital, N
Saint Lucia
Castro 65 B 6 W Chile
Castrovillari 97 D 6 SW Italy
Castuera 92 D 4 W Spain
Caswell Sound 151 A 7 sound, S
Tasman Sea
Catacamas 52 D 2 C Honduras
Catacaos 60 B 3 NW Peru
Catalan Bay 93 H 4 *var.* Caleta. Bay,
W Mediterranean Sea
Catalan Bay 93 H 4 E Gibraltar
Catalina 62 B 2 N Chile
Cataluña 93 G 2 cultural region, N
Spain
Catamarca *see* San Fernando del
Valle de Catamarca
Catania 97 D 7 SW Italy
Catanzaro 97 E 6 SW Italy
Catarroja 93 F 3 E Spain
Cat Island 54 C 1 island, C
Bahamas
Catskill Mountains 41 F 3
mountain range, New York, NE
USA

Cattaro see Kotor
Cauca 58 B 2 river, N Colombia
Caucasia 58 B 2 NW Colombia
Caucasus 117 F 1 *Rus.* Kavkaz. Mountain range, Georgia/Russian Federation
Caura 59 E 3 river, C Venezuela
Cavally 74 D 5 *var.* Cavalla, Cavally Fleuve. River, Ivory Coast/Liberia
Cave Hill 55 G 2 W Barbdos
Caviana de Fora, Ilha 63 F 1 *var.* Ilha Caviana. Island, N Brazil
Caviana, Ilha see Caviana de Fora, Ilha
Cawnpore see Kānpur
Caxamarca see Cajamarca
Caxias do Sul 57 D 5 S Brazil
Caxito 78 B 1 NW Angola
Cayenne 59 H 3 dependent territory capital, NE French Guiana
Cayman Brac 54 B 3 island, E Cayman Islands
Cayman Islands 54 B 3 UK dependent territory, NW Cayman Islands
Cay Sal 54 B 2 island, SW Bahamas
Cazin 100 B 3 NW Bosnia & Herzegovina
Cazorla 93 E 4 S Spain
Ceará 63 G 2 *off.* Estado do Ceará. State, C Brazil
Ceará see Fortaleza
Ceara Abyssal Plain see Ceará Plain
Ceará, Estado do see Ceará
Ceará Plain 67 C 5 *var.* Ceara Abyssal Plain. Abyssal plain, W Atlantic Ocean
Ceatharlach see Carlow
Cébaco, Isla 53 F 5 island, SW Panama
Cebu 139 E 2 *off.* Cebu City. Cebu, C Philippines
Cebu City see Cebu
Cecina 96 B 3 Italy
Cedar City 44 A 5 Utah, W USA
Cedar Falls 45 G 3 Iowa, C USA
Cedar Rapids 45 G 3 Iowa, C USA
Cedar River 45 E 4 river, Nebraska, C USA
Cedros, Isla 50 A 2 island, W Mexico
Ceduna 149 A 6 South Australia, S Australia
Cefalù 97 C 7 *anc.* Cephaloedium. SW Italy
Celebes Sea 152 A 3 *Ind.* Laut Sulawesi. Sea, W Pacific Ocean
Celica 60 B 2 SW Ecuador
Celje 95 E 7 *Ger.* Cilli. C Slovenia
Čelkar see Chelkar
Celldömölk 99 C 7 W Hungary
Celle 94 B 3 *var.* Zelle. N Germany
Celovec see Klagenfurt
Celtic Sea 89 B 7 *Ir.* An Mhuir Cheilteach. Sea, NE Atlantic Ocean
Cenderawasih, Teluk 139 G 4 *var.* Teluk Cendrawasih. Bay, W Pacific Ocean
Cenon 91 B 5 SW France

Central African Republic 76 C 4 *var.* République Centrafricaine, *abbrev.* CAR; *prev.* Oubangui-Chari, Territoire de J'Oubangui-Chari, Ubangi-Shari. Republic, C Africa

Official name: Central African Republic **Date of formation:** 1960 **Capital:** Bangui **Population:** 3.3 million **Total area:** 622,980 sq km

(240,530 sq miles) **Languages:** French*, Sangho, Banda **Religions:** Christian 50%, traditional beliefs 27%, Muslim 15%, other 8% **Ethnic mix:** Baya 34%, Banda 27%, Mandjia 21%, other 18% **Government:** Multiparty republic **Currency:** CFA franc = 100 centimes

Central Group see Inner Islands
Centralia 46 B 2 Washington, NW USA
Central Indian Ridge see Mid-Indian Ridge
Central Makrān Range 134 A 3 mountain range, W Pakistan
Central Pacific Basin 152 D 3 undersea basin, C Pacific Ocean
Central Provinces and Berar see Madhya Pradesh
Central Range 144 B 3 mountain range, New Guinea, NW Papua New Guinea
Central Russian Upland see Central Russian Upland
Central Siberian Plateau see Srednesibirskoye Ploskogor'ye
Central, Sistema 92 D 3 mountain range, C Spain
Čepelare see Chepelare
Cephaloedium see Cefalù
Ceram Sea see Seram, Laut
Cereté 58 B 2 NW Colombia
Cerignola 97 D 5 SE Italy
Cernay 90 E 4 NE France
Cerro Chirripó see Chirripó Grande, Cerro
Cerro de Pasco 60 C 3 C Peru
Cervera 93 F 2 NE Spain
Cesena 96 C 3 *anc.* Caesena. N Italy
Cēsis 106 D 3 *Ger.* Wenden. C Latvia
Cette see Sète
Cettigne see Cetinje
Ceuta 70 D 5 Spanish enclave, N Morocco
Cévennes 91 C 6 mountain range, S France
Ceyhan 116 D 4 S Turkey
Ceylon Plain 140 C 4 abyssal plain, N Indian Ocean
Ceyre to the Caribs see Marie-Galante
Chabjuwardoo Bay 146 A 4 bay, E Indian Ocean
Chachapoyas 60 C 3 NW Peru
Chachevichy 107 D 6 *Rus.* Chechevichi. E Belorussia
Chachoengsao 137 C 5 *var.* Chaxerngsao. C Thailand
Chaco see Gran Chaco
Chaco Mesa 48 C 1 mountain, New Mexico, SW USA

Chad 76 C 2 *Fr.* Tchad. Republic, C Africa

Official name: Republic of Chad **Date of formation:** 1960 **Capital:** N'Djamena **Population:** 6 million **Total area:** 1,284,000 sq km (495,752 sq miles) **Languages:** French*, Sara, Maba **Religions:** Muslim 44%, Christian

33%, traditional beliefs 23% **Ethnic mix:** Bagirmi, Sara and Kreish 31%, Sudanic Arab 26%, Teda 7%, other 36% **Government:** Transitional **Currency:** CFA franc = 100 centimes

Chad, Lake 76 B 3 *Fr.* Lac Tchad. Lake, C Africa
Chadron 44 D 3 Nebraska, C USA
Chāgai Hills 134 A 2 *var.* Chāh Gay. Mountain range, Afghanistan/Pakistan
Chagos Islands see British Indian Ocean Territory
Chagos-Laccadive Plateau 140 C 4 undersea plateau, C Indian Ocean
Chagos Trench 140 C 4 trench, C Indian Ocean
Chāh Gay see Chāgai Hills
Chaillu, Massif du 77 B 6 mountain range, C Gabon
Chaîne Côtière see Coast Mountains
Chajul 52 B 2 W Guatemala
Chala 60 D 4 SW Peru
Chalatenango 52 C 3 N El Salvador
Chálki 105 E 7 island, Dodekánisos, SE Greece
Chalkidikí 104 C 4 *var.* Khalkidhikí; *anc.* Chalcidice. Peninsula, NE Greece
Challans 90 A 4 NW France
Challapata 61 F 4 SW Bolivia
Challenger Deep see Mariana Trench
Challenger Fracture Zone 153 F 4 fracture zone, SE Pacific Ocean
Châlons-en-Champagne 90 D 3 *prev.* Châlons-sur-Marne, *hist.* Arcae Remorum, *anc.* Carolopois. NE France
Chalon-sur-Saône 90 D 4 *anc.* Cabillonum. C France
Cha Mai see Thung Song
Chaman 134 B 2 SW Pakistan
Chambéry 91 D 5 *anc.* Camberia. E France
Champagne 90 D 3 cultural region, N France
Champaign 40 B 4 Illinois, N USA
Champasak 137 D 5 S Laos
Champlain, Lake 41 F 2 lake, Canada/USA
Champotón 51 G 4 SE Mexico
Chañaral 64 B 3 N Chile
Chanco 64 B 4 C Chile
Chandeleur Islands 42 C 3 island, S USA
Chandīgarh 134 D 2 state capital, N India
Chandler 48 B 2 Arizona, SW USA
Changane, Rio 78 D 3 river, S Mozambique
Changchun 128 E 3 *var.* Ch'angch'un, Ch'angch'un; *prev.* Hsinking. Province capital, NE China
Changi 138 B 1 E Singapore
Chang Jiang 129 C 5 *var.* Yangtze Kiang, *Eng.* Yangtze. River, C China
Chang, Ko 137 C 6 island, C Thailand
Changsha 129 C 5 *var.* Ch'angsha, Ch'ang-sha. Province capital, S China
Changzhi 128 C 4 C China
Chaniá 105 C 7 *var.* Khaniá, *Eng.* Canea; *anc.* Cydonia. SE Greece
Chañi, Nevado de 64 C 2 mountain, N Argentina
Channel Islands 89 C 8 *Fr.* Iles Normandes. British dependency, S England, UK

Channel-Port aux Basques 39 G 4 Newfoundland and Labrador, SE Canada
Channel Tunnel 89 E 7 tunnel, France/United Kingdom
Chantada 92 C 1 NW Spain
Chanthaburi 137 C 6 *var.* Chantabun, Chantaburi. C Thailand
Chanute 45 F 5 Kansas, C USA
Chaoyang 128 D 3 NE China
Chapais 38 D 4 Québec, SE Canada
Chapala 50 D 4 SW Mexico
Chapala, Lago de 50 D 4 lake, C Mexico
Chapayevsk 111 C 6 W Russian Federation
Chaplynka 109 F 4 S Ukraine
Chapra see Chhapra
Chardzhev 122 D 3 *prev.* Chardzhou, Chardzhui, Leninsk-Turkmenski, *Turkm.* Chärjew. E Turkmenistan
Charente 91 B 5 cultural region, W France
Charhār Borjak 122 D 5 SW Afghanistan
Chari 76 B 3 *var.* Shari. River, Central African Republic/Chad
Chārīkār 123 E 4 NE Afghanistan
Charity 59 F 2 NW Guyana
Charleroi 87 C 7 S Belgium
Charlesbourg 39 E 4 Québec, SE Canada
Charles Island 38 D 1 island, Northwest Territories, NE Canada
Charleston 43 F 2 South Carolina, SE USA
Charleston 40 B 4 state capital, Illinois USA
Charleston 40 D 5 West Virginia, N USA
Charleville 149 C 5 Queensland, E Australia
Charleville-Mézières 90 D 3 N France
Charlotte 43 E 1 North Carolina, SE USA
Charlotte Amalie 55 F 3 *prev.* Saint Thomas. Dependent territory capital, N Virgin Islands (US)
Charlottenhof see Aegviidu
Charlottesville 41 E 5 Virginia, NE USA
Charlotte Town see Roseau
Charlottetown 39 F 4 Prince Edward Island, SE Canada
Charsk 114 D 5 E Kazakhstan
Charters Towers 148 C 3 Queensland, NE Australia
Chartres 90 C 3 *anc.* Autricum, Civitas Carnutum. C France
Chashniki 107 D 5 N Belorussia
Chashniki see Chashniki
Châteaubriant 90 B 4 NW France
Châteaudun 90 C 4 C France
Châteauroux 90 B 4 *prev.* Indreville. C France
Château-Thierry 90 D 3 N France
Châtelet 87 C 7 S Belgium
Châtelherault see Châtellerault
Châtellerault 90 B 4 *var.* Châtelherault. W France
Chatham 38 C 5 New Brunswick, SE Canada
Chatham Island see San Cristóbal, Isla
Chatham Island Rise see Chatham Rise
Chatham Islands 152 D 5 island group, E New Zealand

Chatham Rise 152 C 4 *var.*
Chatham Island Rise. Undersea
rise, SW Pacific Ocean
Chatkal Range 123 F 2 *Rus.*
Chatkal'skiy Khrebet. Mountain
range, Kyrgyzstan/Uzbekistan
Chatkal'skiy Khrebet *see* Chatkal
Range
Chăttagăm *see* Chittagong
Chattanooga 42 D 1 Tennessee, S
USA
Chatyr-Tash 123 G 2 C Kyrgyzstan
Châu Độc 137 D 6 *var.* Chau Phu,
Chauphu. SW Vietnam
Chauk 136 A 3 W Burma
Chaumont 90 D 4 *prev.* Chaumont-
en-Bassigny. N France
Chaumont-en-Bassigny *see*
Chaumont
Chausy *see* Chavusy
Chaves 92 C 2 *anc.* Aquae Flaviae.
N Portugal
Chavusy 107 E 6 *Rus.* Chausy. E
Belorussia
Chaxerngsao *see* Chachoengsao
Chaykovskiy 111 D 5 *var.* Čajovskij
NW Russian Federation
Cheb 99 A 5 *Ger.* Eger. W Czech
Republic
Cheboksary 111 C 5 W Russian
Federation
Cheboygan 40 C 2 Michigan, N
USA
Chech, Erg 68 B 3 desert,
Algeria/Mali
Checker Hall 55 G 1 N Barbados
Cheduba Island 136 A 4 island, W
Burma
Chefchaouen 70 C 2 *var.* Chaouén,
Chaouèn, Chechaouén,
Chechaouèn, Chechaouen,
Chefchaouèn, *Sp.* Xauen. N
Morocco
Chehel Abdālān, Kūh-e 122 D 4
var. Chalap Dalam, *Pash.* Chalap
Dalan. Mountain range, C
Afghanistan
Cheju-do 128 E 4 *Jap.* Saishū; *prev.*
Quelpart. Island, S South Korea
Cheju Strait 128 E 4 strait, Yellow
Sea/Pacific Ocean
Chek Chue 128 B 2 *var.* Stanley. S
Hong Kong
Cheleken 122 B 2 W Turkmenistan
Chelkar 114 B 4 W Kazakhstan
Chełm 98 E 4 *Rus.* Kholm. SE
Poland
Chełmno 98 C 3 *Ger.* Culm, Kulm.
N Poland
Cheltenham 89 D 6 S England, UK
Chelyabinsk 114 C 3 C Russian
Federation
Chemnitz 94 D 4 *prev.* Karl-Marx-
Stadt. E Germany
Chengde 128 D 3 *var.* Jehol. SE
China
Chengdu 129 B 5 *var.* Ch'e.ng-tu,
Chengtu. Province capital, SW
China
Chenzhou 129 C 6 SE China
Chepelare 104 C 3 *var.* Čepelare. S
Bulgaria
Chepo 53 G 4 C Panama
Cher 90 C 4 river, C France
Cherbourg 90 B 3 *anc.* Carusbur. N
France
Cherepovets 110 B 4 *var.*
Cerepoveo, Cerepovec. NW
Russian Federation
Chergui, Chott ech 70 D 2 salt lake,
N Algeria
Cherikov *see* Cherykaw

Cherkassy *see* Cherkasy
Cherkasy 109 E 2 *Rus.* Cherkassy. C
Ukraine
Cherkessk 111 B 7 SW Russian
Federation
Chernigov *see* Chernihiv
Chernihiv 109 E 1 *Rus.* Chernigov.
NE Ukraine
Chernivtsi 108 C 3 *Ger.* Czernowitz,
Rom. Cernăuţi, *Rus.* Chernovtsy.
W Ukraine
Chernomorskoye *see*
Chornomors'ke
Chernyakhovsk 106 A 4 *Ger.*
Insterburg. W Russian Federation
Cherry Hill 41 F 4 New Jersey, NE
USA
Cherski *see* Cherskogo, Khrebet
Cherskogo, Khrebet 115 F 3 *var.*
Cherski. Mountain range, NE
Russian Federation
Cherson *see* Kherson
Cherven' 107 D 6 C Belorussia
Chervonograd *see* Chervonohrad
Chervonohrad 108 C 2 *Rus.*
Chervonograd. NW Ukraine
Cherykaw 107 E 7 *Rus.* Cherikov. E
Belorussia
Chesapeake Bay 41 F 5 bay, NE
Atlantic Ocean
Chester 89 C 6 *Wel.* Caerleon; *hist.*
Legaceaster, *Lat.* Deva, Devana
Castra. W England, UK
Chetumal 51 H 4 *var.* Payo Obispo.
SE Mexico
Cheviot Hills 88 D 4 hill range,
England/Scotland, UK
Cheyenne 44 D 4 state capital,
Wyoming, C USA
Cheyenne River 44 D 3 river, South
Dakota, N USA
Chhapra 135 F 3 *prev.* Chapra. N
India
Chiai 129 D 6 *var.* Chiayi, Kiayi, *Jap.*
Kagi. W Taiwan
Chiang Mai 136 C 4 *var.*
Chiangmai, Chiengmai,
Kiangmai. NW Thailand
Chiang Rai 136 C 3 *var.* Chianpai,
Chienrai, Muang Chiang Rai. N
Thailand
Chiapa *see* Chiapa de Cerzo
Chiapa de Cerzo 51 G 5 *var.*
Chiapa. SE Mexico
Chiba 131 D 5 *var.* Tiba. Honshū, S
Japan
Chibougamau 38 D 4 Québec, SE
Canada
Chicago 40 B 3 Illinois, N USA
Chicago Heights 40 B 3 Illinois, N
USA
Chichester Range 146 B 4 mountain
range, W Australia
Chickasha 49 G 2 Oklahoma, C
USA
Chiclayo 60 B 3 NW Peru
Chico 65 B 6 river, SE Argentina
Chico 47 B 5 California, W USA
Chicoutimi 39 E 4 Québec, SE
Canada
Chiemsee 95 C 6 lake, SE Germany
Chiesanuova 96 D 2 SW San
Marino
Chieti 96 D 4 *var.* Teate. C Italy
Chifeng 127 G 2 *var.* Ulanhad. N
China
Chigirin *see* Chyhyryn
Chihli, Gulf of *see* Bo Hai
Chihuahua 50 C 2 NW Mexico
Childress 49 F 2 Texas, S USA

Chile
64-65 B 6 Republic, S South
America

Official name: Republic of Chile
Date of formation: 1818
Capital: Santiago **Population:** 13.8
million **Total area:** 756,950 sq km
(292,258 sq miles) **Languages:**
Spanish*, Indian languages
Religions: Roman Catholic 89%,
Protestant 11% **Ethnic mix:** White
and *mestizo* 92%, Indian 6%, other 2%
Government: Multiparty republic
Currency: Peso = 100 centavos

Chilean Antarctic Territory 154 B 3
Chilean territorial claim,
Antarctica
Chile Basin 67 A 5 undersea basin,
E Pacific Ocean
Chile Chico 65 B 6 W Chile
Chile, Republic of *see* Chile
Chile Rise 67 A 6 undersea rise, SE
Pacific Ocean
Chilia-Nouă *see* Kiliya
Chililabombwe 78 D 2 C Zambia
Chillán 65 B 5 C Chile
Chillicothe 40 D 4 Ohio, N USA
Chiloé, Isla de 65 A 6 *var.* Isla
Grande de Chiloé. Island, W
Chile
Chiloé, Isla Grande de *see* Chiloé,
Isla de
Chilpancingo 51 E 5 *var.*
Chilpancingo de los Bravos. S
Mexico
Chilpancingo de los Bravos *see*
Chilpancingo
Chilung 129 D 6 *var.* Keelung, *Jap.*
Kirun, Kirun'; *prev.* *Sp.* Santissima
Trinidad. N Taiwan
Chimán 53 G 5 E Panama
Chimbay *see* Chimboy
Chimborazo 60 B 1 mountain, C
Ecuador
Chimbote 60 C 3 W Peru
Chimboy 122 D 1 *Rus.* Chimbay.
NW Uzbekistan
Chimoio 79 E 3 C Mozambique

China
124 D 2 *Chin.* Chung-hua Jen-min
Kung-ho-kuo, Zhonghua Renmin
Gonghe Guo; *prev.* Chinese
Empire. Republic, E Asia

Official name: People's Republic of
China **Date of formation:** 1912
Capital: Beijing **Population:**
1.2 billion **Total area:** 9,396,960 sq km
(3,628,166 sq miles) **Languages:**
Mandarin*, **Religions:** Confucianist
20%, Buddhist 6%, Taoist 2%, other
72% **Ethnic mix:** Han 93%, Zhuang
1%, Hui 1%, other 5% **Government:**
Single-party republic **Currency:**
Yuan = 10 jiao = 100 fen

Chinandega 52 C 3 NW Nicaragua
Chincha Alta 60 D 4 SW Peru
Chindwin 136 B 2 river, NW Burma
Chingola 78 D 2 C Zambia
Chinguetti 74 C 2 *var.* Chinguetti. C
Mauritania
Chinguetti *see* Chinguetti
Chin Hills 136 A 3 mountain range,
W Burma
Chinook Trough 152 D 2 trough, N
Pacific Ocean

Chíos 105 D 5 *var.* Khíos. Island, E
Greece
Chipata 78 D 2 *prev.* Fort Jameson.
E Zambia
Chippewa Falls 40 A 2 Wisconsin,
N USA
Chiquimula 52 B 2 SE Guatemala
Chīrāla 132 D 1 E India
Chirchik *see* Chirchiq
Chirchiq 123 F 2 *Rus.* Chirchik. E
Uzbekistan
Chiriquí, Golfo de 53 F 5 *Eng.*
Chiriquí Gulf. Inlet, E Pacific
Ocean
Chiriquí Gulf *see* Chiriquí, Golfo de
Chiriquí, Laguna de 53 F 5 inlet, E
Pacific Ocean
Chiriquí, Volcán de *see* Barú, Volcán
Chirripó Grande, Cerro 53 E 4 *var.*
Cerro Chirripó. Mountain, SE
Costa Rica
Chisec 52 B 2 C Guatemala
Chisholm 45 F 1 Minnesota, N USA
Chisinău 108 D 4 *Rus.* Kishinev. C
Moldavia
Chita 115 F 4 C Russian Federation
Chitangwiza *see* Chitungwiza
Chitina 36 D 3 Alaska, NW USA
Chitose 130 D 2 *var.* Titose.
Hokkaidō, NE Japan
Chitré 53 F 5 S Panama
Chittagong 135 G 4 *Ben.*
Chǎttagǎm. SE Bangladesh
Chitungwiza 78 D 3 *prev.*
Chitangwiza. NE Zimbabwe
Chkalov *see* Orenburg
Choa Chu Kang 138 A 1 W
Singapore
Chocolate Mountains 47 D 8
mountain range, California, W
USA
Chodzież 98 C 3 NW Poland
Choele Choel 65 C 5 C Argentina
Choiseul 55 F 2 SW Saint Lucia
Choiseul 144 C 3 *var.* Lauru. Island,
NW Solomon Islands
Ch'ok'ē 72 C 4 *var.* Choke
Mountains. Mountain range, NW
Ethiopia
Choke Mountains *see* Ch'ok'ē
Cholet 90 B 4 NW France
Choluteca 52 C 3 S Honduras
Choma 78 D 2 S Zambia
Chomutov 98 A 4 *Ger.* Komotau.
NW Czech Republic
Chon Buri 137 C 5 *prev.* Bang Pla
Soi. C Thailand
Chone 60 A 1 W Ecuador
Ch'ŏngjin 128 E 3 NE North Korea
Chongqing 129 B 5 *var.* Ch'ung-
ching, Ch'ung-ch'ing, Chungking,
Pahsien, Tchongking, Yuzhou. SW
China
Chonos, Archipiélago de los 65 A 7
island group, S Chile
Chornomors'ke 109 E 2 *Rus.*
Chernomorskoye. S Ukraine
Chortkiv 108 C 2 *Rus.* Chortkov. W
Ukraine
Chortkov *see* Chortkiv
Chorum *see* Çorum
Chorzów 99 C 5 *var.* Ger. Königshütte;
prev. Królewska Huta. S Poland
Chōshi 131 D 5 *var.* Tyôsi. Honshū,
S Japan
Choszczno 98 B 3 *Ger.* Arnswalde.
W Poland
Chota Nagpur Plateau 135 E 4
plateau, N India
Choybalsan 127 F 2 E Mongolia
Christchurch 151 C 6 South Island,
C New Zealand

Christiana 54 B 5 C Jamaica
Christiansand see Kristiansand
Christmas Creek 146 C 3 NW Australia
Christmas Island 141 D 5 Australian external territory, E Indian Ocean
Christmas Island see Kiritimati
Chu 114 C 5 *Kaz*. Shū. SE Kazakhstan
Chubut 65 B 6 river, SE Argentina
Chūgoku-sanchi 131 B 6 mountain range, Honshū, SW Japan
Chuí 64 E 4 *var*. Chuy E Uruguay
Chukchi Plain 155 F 2 abyssal plain, Arctic Ocean
Chukchi Plateau 155 F 2 undersea plateau, Arctic Ocean
Chukchi Sea 36 C 1 *Rus*. Chukotskoye More. Sea, Arctic Ocean
Chukotskoye More see Chukchi Sea
Chula Vista 47 C 8 California, W USA
Chulucanas 60 B 2 NW Peru
Chulym 114 D 4 river, C Russian Federation
Chumphon 137 C 6 *var*. Jumporn. S Thailand
Ch'unch'ŏn 128 E 4 *Jap*. Shunsen N South Korea
Chunya 115 E 3 river, C Russian Federation
Chuor Phnum Dângrêk 137 D 5 *var*. Phanom Dang Raek, Phanom Dong Rak, *Fr*. Chaîne des Dangrek. Mountain range, Cambodia/Thailand
Chuquicamata 64 B 2 N Chile
Chur 95 B 7 *Fr*. Coire, *It*. Coira, *Rmsch*. Cuera, Quera; *anc*. Curia Rhaetorum. E Switzerland
Churchill 37 G 4 Manitoba, C Canada
Churchill 39 F 2 river, E Canada
Chuska Mountains 48 C 1 mountain range, SW USA
Chusovoy 111 D 5 *var*. Čusovoj NW Russian Federation
Chuuk 144 B 2 *var*. Hogoley Islands. Island group, C Micronesia
Chyhyryn 109 E 3 *Rus*. Chigirin. N Ukraine
Ciadîr-Lunga 108 D 4 *var*. Ceadâr-Lunga, *Rus*. Chadyr-Lunga. S Moldavia
Cide 116 C 2 N Turkey
Ciechanów 98 D 3 *prev*. Zichenau. C Poland
Ciego de Ávila 54 C 2 C Cuba
Ciénaga 58 B 1 N Colombia
Cienfuegos 54 B 2 C Cuba
Cieza 93 E 4 SE Spain
Cihanbeyli 116 C 3 C Turkey
Cikobia 145 E 4 *prev*. Thikombia. Island, N Fiji
Cilacap 138 C 5 *prev*. Tjilatjap. Jawa, C Indonesia
Cill Airne see Killarney
Cill Chainnigh see Kilkenny
Cilli see Celje
Cîmpina see Câmpina
Cincinnati 40 C 4 Ohio, N USA
Ciney 87 C 7 SE Belgium
Cintra see Sintra
Cipolletti 65 B 5 C Argentina
Cirebon 138 C 4 *prev*. Tjirebon. Jawa, C Indonesia
Cirò Marina 97 E 6 Italy
Cisnădie 108 B 4 *Ger*. Heltau, *Hung*. Nagydisznód. SW Romania

Citharista see la Ciotat
Citlaltépetl 35 C 7 mountain, S Mexico
Citrus Heights 47 B 5 California, W USA
City of Manila see Manila
Ciudad Acuña 50 D 2 *var*. Villa Acuña. NE Mexico
Ciudad Bolívar 59 E 2 *prev*. Angostura. C Venezuela
Ciudad Camargo 50 D 2 N Mexico
Ciudad Cortés see Cortés
Ciudad Darío 52 D 3 *var*. Dario. W Nicaragua
Ciudad de Dolores Hidalgo see Dolores Hidalgo
Ciudad del Carmen see Carmen
Ciudad del Este 64 E 2 *prev*. Cuidad Presidente Stroessner, Presidente Stroessner, Puerto Presidente Stroessner. SE Paraguay
Ciudad Delicias see Delicias
Ciudad Guayana 59 E 2 *prev*. San Tomé de Guayana, Santo Tomé de Guayana. NE Venezuela
Ciudad Guzmán 50 D 4 SW Mexico
Ciudad Hidalgo 51 G 5 SE Mexico
Ciudad Juárez 50 C 1 N Mexico
Ciudad Lerdo 50 D 3 C Mexico
Ciudad Madero 51 E 3 *var*. Villa Cecilia. C Mexico
Ciudad Mante 51 E 3 C Mexico
Ciudad Miguel Alemán 51 E 2 C Mexico
Ciudad Obregón 50 B 2 NW Mexico
Ciudad Ojeda 58 C 1 NW Venezuela
Ciudad Porfirio Díaz see Piedras Negras
Ciudad Real 92 D 4 C Spain
Ciudad-Rodrigo 92 C 3 N Spain
Ciudad Trujillo see Santo Domingo
Ciudad Valles 51 E 4 C Mexico
Ciudad Victoria 51 E 3 C Mexico
Ciutadella see Ciutadella de Menorca
Ciutadella de Menorca 93 G 3 *var*. Ciutadella. E Spain
Civitanova Marche 96 D 4 C Italy
Civitas Eburovicum see Évreux
Civitavecchia 96 C 4 *anc*. Centum Cellae, Trajani Portus. C Italy
Claremore 49 G 1 Oklahoma, C USA
Clarence 151 C 5 river, South Island, C New Zealand
Clarence Town 54 D 2 C Bahamas
Clarinda 45 F 4 Iowa, C USA
Clarion Fracture Zone 153 E 2 fracture zone, NE Pacific Ocean
Clarión, Isla 50 A 5 island, W Mexico
Clark Fork 44 A 1 river, NW USA
Clark Hill Lake 43 E 2 *var*. J.Storm Thurmond Reservoir. Reservoir, SE USA
Clarksburg 40 D 4 West Virginia, NE USA
Clarksdale 42 B 2 Mississippi, S USA
Clarksville 42 C 1 Tennessee, S USA
Clearwater 43 E 4 Florida, SE USA
Clearwater Mountains 46 D 2 mountain range, Idaho, NW USA
Clearwater River 46 D 2 river, Idaho, NW USA
Cleburne 49 G 3 Texas, S USA
Clermont 148 D 4 Queensland, E Australia

Clermont-Ferrand 91 C 5 C France
Cleveland 42 D 1 Tennessee, S USA
Cleveland 42 B 2 Mississippi, S USA
Cleveland 40 D 3 Ohio, N USA
Clifton 48 C 2 Arizona, SW USA
Clinton 42 B 2 Mississippi, S USA
Clinton 49 F 1 Oklahoma, C USA
Clipperton Fracture Zone 153 E 3 fracture zone, E Pacific Ocean
Clipperton Island 153 F 3 island, E Pacific Ocean
Cloncurry 148 B 3 Queensland, C Australia
Clonmel 89 A 6 *Ir*. Cluain Meala. S Ireland
Cloppenburg 94 B 3 NW Germany
Cloquet 45 G 2 Minnesota, N USA
Cloud Peak 44 C 3 mountain, Wyoming, C USA
Clovis 49 E 2 New Mexico, SW USA
Clovis 47 C 6 California, W USA
Cluain Meala see Clonmel
Cluj-Napoca 108 B 3 *Ger*. Klausenburg, *Hung*. Kolozsvár; *prev*. Cluj. NW Romania
Clutha 151 B 7 river, South Island, SW New Zealand
Clyde 88 C 4 river, C Scotland, UK
Coari 62 D 2 N Brazil
Coast Mountains 36 D 4 *Fr*. Chaîne Côtière. Mountain range, Canada/USA
Coast Ranges 46 A 4 mountain range, W USA
Coats Island 38 C 1 island, Northwest Territories, NE Canada
Coats Land 154 B 2 physical region, Antarctica
Coatzacoalcos 51 F 4 *var*. Quetzalcoalco; *prev*. Puerto México. E Mexico
Cobán 52 B 2 C Guatemala
Cobar 149 C 6 New South Wales, SE Australia
Cobija 61 E 3 NW Bolivia
Coburg 95 C 5 SE Germany
Coca see Puerto Francisco de Orellana
Cocanada see Kākināda
Cochabamba 61 F 4 *hist*. Oropeza. C Bolivia
Cochin 132 C 3 *var*. Kochi. SW India
Cochrane 65 B 7 S Chile
Cochrane 38 C 4 Ontario, S Canada
Cockburn Town 55 E 2 dependent territory capital, E Turks & Caicos Islands
Cockpit Country, The 54 A 4 physical region, NW Jamaica
Coco 52 D 2 *var*. Río Wanki, Segoviao Wangkí. River, Honduras/Nicaragua
Cocobeach 77 A 5 NW Gabon
Coconino Plateau 48 B 1 plain, Arizona, SW USA
Cocos (Keeling) Islands 141 D 5 Australian external territory, E Indian Ocean
Cocos Basin 140 D 4 undersea basin, E Indian Ocean
Cocos Island Ridge see Cocos Ridge
Cocos Ridge 153 G 3 *var*. Cocos Island Ridge. Undersea ridge, E Pacific Ocean
Cod, Cape 41 G 3 headland, Massachusetts, NE USA
Codfish Island 151 A 8 island, South Island, SW New Zealand

Cod Island 39 F 1 island, Newfoundland and Labrador, E Canada
Codlea 108 C 4 *Ger*. Zeiden, *Hung*. Feketehalom. C Romania
Cody 44 C 2 Wyoming, C USA
Coeur d'Alene 46 C 2 Idaho, NW USA
Coevorden 86 E 2 NE Netherlands
Coffin Bay 149 A 6 South Australia, S Australia
Coffs Harbour 149 E 6 New South Wales, SE Australia
Cognac 91 B 5 *anc*. Compniacum. W France
Coiba, Isla de 53 F 5 island, SW Panama
Coihaique 65 B 6 *var*. Coyhaique. S Chile
Coimbatore 132 C 3 S India
Coimbra 92 B 3 *anc*. Conimbria, Conimbriga. W Portugal
Coín 92 D 5 S Spain
Coirib, Loch see Corrib, Lough
Colac 149 B 7 Victoria, SE Australia
Colbeck, Cape 154 B 4 headland, Antarctica
Colby 45 E 4 Kansas, C USA
Colchester 89 E 6 *hist*. Colneceaster, *anc*. Camulodunum. SE England, UK
Coleman 49 F 3 Texas, S USA
Coleraine 88 B 4 *Ir*. Cúil Raithin. N Northern Ireland, UK
Colesberg 78 C 5 C South Africa
Coles, Punta 61 E 5 headland, S Peru
Colima 50 D 4 S Mexico
Coll 88 B 3 island, W Scotland, UK
College Station 49 G 3 Texas, S USA
Collie 147 B 7 Western Australia, W Australia
Collinsville 148 D 3 Queensland, E Australia
Collinsville 40 B 4 Illinois, N USA
Collipo see Leiria
Colmar 90 E 4 *Ger*. Kolmar. NE France
Colomb-Béchar see Béchar

Colombia
58 B 3 . Republic, N South America

Official name: Republic of Colombia
Date of formation: 1903 **Capital:** Bogotá **Population:** 34 million
Total area: 1,138,910 sq km (439,733 sq miles) **Languages:** Spanish*, Indian languages, English Creole **Religions:** Roman Catholic 95%, other 5% **Ethnic mix:** *mestizo* 58%, White 20%, mixed 14%, other 8% **Government:** Multiparty republic **Currency:** Peso = 100 centavos

Colombian Basin 66 A 4 undersea basin, W Atlantic Ocean
Colombie-Britannique see British Columbia
Colombo 132 C 4 country capital, W Sri Lanka
Colón 53 G 4 *prev*. Aspinwall. C Panama
Colón, Archipiélago de see Galapagos Islands
Colonia see Kolonia
Colorado 65 B 5 river, E Argentina
Colorado 35 B 3 *var*. Río Colorado. River, Mexico/USA
Colorado 44 C 4 *off*. State of Colorado; *nicknames* Centennial State, Silver State. State, C USA

Colorado City 49 F 3 Texas, S USA
Colorado, Río see Colorado
Colorado Springs 44 D 5 Colorado, C USA
Columbia 43 E 2 state capital, South Carolina, SE USA
Columbia 42 C 1 Tennessee, S USA
Columbia 41 F 4 Maryland, NE USA
Columbia 45 G 4 Missouri, C USA
Columbia Plateau 46 C 3 plateau, NW USA
Columbia River 46 B 2 river, NW USA
Columbine 44 C 4 Colorado, C USA
Columbus 42 D 2 Georgia, SE USA
Columbus 42 C 2 Mississippi, S USA
Columbus 40 D 4 state capital, Ohio, N USA
Columbus 45 E 4 Nebraska, C USA
Colville Channel 150 D 2 channel, Bay of Plenty/Hauraki Gulf
Comacchio 96 C 3 var. Commachio; anc. Comactium. N Italy
Comalcalco 51 G 4 SE Mexico
Coma Pedrosa, Pic Alt de la see Coma Pedrosa, Pic de
Coma Pedrosa, Pic de 91 A 7 var. Pic Alt de la Coma Pedrosa. Mountain, NW Andorra
Comarapa 61 G 4 C Bolivia
Comarnic 108 C 4 SE Romania
Comayagua 52 C 2 W Honduras
Combermere Bay 136 A 4 bay, Bay of Bengal/Indian Ocean
Comilla 135 G 4 Ben. Kumillā. E Bangladesh
Comino see Comino
Comitán 51 G 5 var. Comitán de Domínguez. SE Mexico
Comitán de Domínguez see Comitán
Commissioner's Point 42 A 5 headland, W Bermuda
Como 96 B 2 anc. Comum. N Italy
Comodoro Rivadavia 65 B 6 SE Argentina
Como, Lago di 96 B 2 var. Lario, Eng. Lake Como, Ger. Comer See. Lake, N Italy

Comoros 79 F 2 Fr. République Fédérale Islamique des Comores. Republic, Indian Ocean

Official name: Federal Islamic Republic of the Comoros
Date of formation: 1975 **Capital:** Moroni **Population:** 600,000
Total area: 2,230 sq km (861 sq miles) **Languages:** Arabic*, French*
Religions: Muslim 86%, Roman Catholic 14% **Ethnic mix:** Comorian 96%, Makua 2%, other 2%
Government: Islamic republic **Currency:** Franc = 100 centimes

Compiègne 90 C 3 N France
Compniacum see Cognac
Comrat 108 D 4 Rus. Komrat. S Moldavia
Comum see Como
Conakry 74 C 4 country capital, SW Guinea
Conca see Cuenca
Concarneau 90 A 3 NW France
Concepción 65 B 5 C Chile
Concepción 64 D 2 var. Villa Concepción. C Paraguay
Concepción 61 G 3 E Bolivia

Concepción see La Concepción
Concepción de la Vega see La Vega
Conchos, Río 50 C 2 river, NW Mexico
Concord 41 G 3 state capital, New Hampshire, NE USA
Concordia 64 D 4 E Argentina
Concordia 45 E 4 Kansas USA
Condate see St-Claude
Condega 52 D 3 NW Nicaragua

Congo 77 B 5 Fr. Moyen-Congo; prev. Middle Congo. Republic, C Africa

Official name: The Republic of the Congo **Date of formation:** 1960
Capital: Brazzaville **Population:** 2.4 million **Total area:** 342,000 sq km (132,040 sq miles) **Languages:** French*, Kongo **Religions:** Roman Catholic 50%, traditional beliefs 48%, other 2% **Ethnic mix:** Bakongo 48%, Teke 17%, Mboshi 17%, other 18% **Government:** Multiparty republic **Currency:** CFA franc = 100 centimes

Congo 77 C 6 var. Kongo, Fr. Zaire. River, C Africa
Congo see Zaire
Congo Basin 77 C 6 basin, W Zaire
Congo Cone see Congo Fan
Coni see Cuneo
Conjeeveram see Kānchīpuram
Connaught 89 A 5 cultural region, W Ireland
Connecticut 41 G 3 off. State of Connecticut; nicknames Blue Law State, Constitution State, Land of Steady Habits, Nutmeg State. State, NE USA
Connersville 40 C 4 Indiana, N USA
Conrad Rise 141 B 7 undersea rise, SW Indian Ocean
Conroe 49 H 3 Texas, S USA
Consentia see Cosenza
Consolación del Sur 54 A 2 W Cuba
Con Son see Côn Đao
Con Son Island 137 E 7 Island, S Vietnam
Constance, Lake 95 B 6 Ger. Bodensee. Lake, Germany/Switzerland
Constanța 108 D 5 var. Küstendje, Eng. Constanza, Ger. Konstanza, Turk. Küstence. SE Romania
Constantia see Coutances
Constantine 71 E 2 var. Qacentina, Ar. Qoussantina. NE Algeria
Conway 43 F 2 South Carolina, SE USA
Coober Pedy 149 A 5 South Australia, S Australia
Cook Islands 145 F 4 territory in free association with New Zealand (defence, UN), S Pacific Ocean
Cook, Mount 151 B 6 prev. Aoraki, Aorangi. Mountain, South Island, SW New Zealand
Cook Strait 151 D 5 var. Raukawa. Channel, Pacific Ocean/Tasman Sea
Cooktown 148 D 2 Queensland, NE Australia
Coolgardie 147 C 6 Western Australia, W Australia
Cooma 149 D 7 New South Wales, SE Australia
Coomassie see Kumasi
Coon Rapids 45 F 2 Minnesota, N USA

Cooper Creek 149 B 5 var. Barcoo, Cooper's Creek. River, S Australia
Coos Bay 46 A 3 Oregon, NW USA
Cootamundra 149 C 6 New South Wales, SE Australia
Copacabana 61 E 4 W Bolivia
Copenhagen see København
Copiapó 64 B 3 hist. San Francisco de Selva . N Chile
Copiapó 57 B 5 N Chile
Copperas Cove 49 G 3 Texas, S USA
Coppermine 37 E 3 var. Qurlurtuuq. Northwest Territories, NW Canada
Coquilhatville see Mbandaka
Coquimbo 64 B 3 N Chile
Corabia 108 B 5 S Romania
Coral Harbour 37 G 3 Southampton Island, Canada
Coral Sea 144 B 4 sea, W Pacific Ocean
Coral Sea Islands 148 E 3 Australian external territory. NE Australia
Corcaigh see Cork
Corcovado, Golfo 65 B 6 gulf, SE Pacific Ocean
Cordele 42 D 3 Georgia, SE USA
Cordillera Central 55 E 3 mountain range, C Dominican Republic
Cordillera Central 58 B 3 mountain range, W Colombia
Cordillera Central 139 E 1 mountain range, Luzon, N Philippines
Cordillera Occidental 58 B 3 mountain range, W Colombia
Cordillera Occidental 61 F 5 mountain range, Bolivia/Chile
Cordillera Occidental 60 D 4 mountain range, W Peru
Córdoba 92 D 4 var. Cordoba, Eng. Cordova; anc. Corduba. SW Spain
Córdoba 64 C 4 C Argentina
Córdoba 51 F 4 E Mexico
Cordova 36 C 3 Alaska, NW USA
Córdova 60 D 4 SW Peru
Corfu see Kérkyra
Coria 92 C 3 W Spain
Corinth 42 C 1 Mississippi, S USA
Corinto 52 C 3 NW Nicaragua
Cork 89 A 6 Ir. Corcaigh. S Ireland
Corner Brook 39 G 3 Newfoundland and Labrador, E Canada
Corn Islands see Maíz, Islas del
Cornwallis Island 37 F 2 island, N Canada
Coro 58 C 1 prev. Santa Ana de Coro. NW Venezuela
Corocoro 61 F 4 W Bolivia
Coromandel 150 D 2 North Island, N New Zealand
Coromandel Coast 132 D 2 physical region, E India
Coromandel Peninsula 150 D 2 peninsula, North Island, N New Zealand
Coronado, Bahía de 53 E 5 inlet, E Pacific Ocean
Coronel Dorrego 65 C 5 E Argentina
Coronel Oviedo 64 D 2 SE Paraguay
Corozal 52 C 1 N Belize
Corozo Pando 58 D 2 C Venezuela
Corpus Christi 49 G 5 Texas, S USA
Corpus Christi Bay 49 G 5 bay, NW Gulf of Mexico
Corrib, Lough 89 A 5 Ir. Loch Coirib. Lake, W Ireland

Corrientes 64 D 3 NE Argentina
Corse 91 E 7 Eng. Corsica. Island, SE France
Corsica see Corse
Corsicana 49 G 3 Texas, S USA
Cortegana 92 C 4 S Spain
Cortés 53 E 5 var. Ciudad Cortés. SE Costa Rica
Cortina d'Ampezzo 96 C 1 NE Italy
Coruche 92 B 3 C Portugal
Çorum 116 D 3 var. Chorum. N Turkey
Çorum Çayı 117 E 3 river, NE Turkey
Corvallis 46 B 3 Oregon, NW USA
Corvo 92 A 5 var. Ilha do Corvo. Island, W Portugal
Corvo, Ilha do see Corvo
Cosenza 97 D 6 anc. Consentia. SW Italy
Cosne-Cours-sur-Loire 90 C 4 var. Cosne-sur-Loire; anc. Condate. C France
Costa Dorada see Daurada, Costa

Costa Rica 53 E 4 Republic, C Central America

Official name: Republic of Costa Rica **Date of formation:** 1821
Capital: San José **Population:** 3.3 million **Total area:** 51,100 sq km (19,730 miles) **Languages:** Spanish*, English Creole, Bribri, Cabecar **Religions:** Catholic 95%, other 5% **Ethnic mix:** White/mestizo (Euro-Indian) 96%, Black 2%, Indian 2% **Government:** Multiparty republic **Currency:** Colón = 100 centimos

Costermansville see Bukavu
Cotagaita 61 G 5 S Bolivia
Côte d'Ivoire see Ivory Coast
Côte d'Or 90 D 4 cultural region, E France
Cotonou 75 F 5 var. Kotonu. S Benin
Cotswold Hills 89 D 6 var. Cotswolds. Hill range, S England, UK
Cotswolds see Cotswold Hills
Cottbus 94 D 4 prev. Kottbus. E Germany
Cottica 59 H 3 E Surinam
Cotyora see Ordu
Couentrey see Coventry
Couëron 90 B 4 France
Council Bluffs 45 F 4 Iowa, C USA
Courantyne River 59 G 4 var. Corantijn Rivier, Corentyne River. River, Guyana/Surinam
Courland Lagoon 106 A 4 Ger. Kurisches Haff, Rus. Kurskiy Zaliv. Lagoon, SE Baltic Sea
Courtrai see Kortrijk
Coutances 90 B 3 anc. Constantia. N France
Couvin 87 C 7 S Belgium
Coventry 89 D 6 anc. Couentrey. C England, UK
Covilhã 92 C 3 E Portugal
Cowan, Lake 147 C 6 lake, Western Australia, SW Australia
Coyhaique see Coihaique
Cozumel, Isla 51 H 3 island, SE Mexico
Cradock 78 C 5 S South Africa
Craig 44 C 4 Colorado, C USA
Craiova 108 B 5 SW Romania
Cranbrook 37 E 5 Alberta. SW Canada
Crawley 89 E 7 SE England, UK
Cremona 96 B 2 N Italy

Cres 100 A 3 *It.* Cherso; *anc.* Crexa. Island, W Croatia

Creston 45 F 4 Iowa, C USA

Crestview 42 D 3 Florida, SE USA

Crete *see* Kriti

Créteil 90 C 3 N France

Creuse 90 B 4 river, C France

Crewe 89 C 6 W England, UK

Crikvenica 100 A 2 *It.* Cirquenizza; *prev.* Cirkvenica, Crjkvenica. NW Croatia

Crimea *see* Krym

Cristóbal 53 G 4 C Panama

Cristóbal Colón, Pico 58 B 1 mountain, N Colombia

Cristuru Secuiesc 108 C 4 *Ger.* Kreutz, *Hung.* Székelykeresztúr; *prev.* Cristur, Cristuru Săcuiesc, Sitaş Cristuru Szitás-Keresztúr, Szitás-Keresztúr. C Romania

Crna Gora *see* Montenegro

Crna Reka 101 E 6 river, S Macedonia

Croatia 100 B 2 *Ger.* Kroatien, *SCr.* Hrvatska. Republic, SE Europe

Official name: Republic of Croatia **Date of formation:** 1991 **Capital:** Zagreb **Population:** 4.9 million **Total area:** 56,540 sq km (21,830 sq miles) **Languages:** Croatian*, Serbian **Religions:** Roman Catholic 77%, Orthodox Catholic 11%, Protestant 1%, Muslim 1%, other 10% **Ethnic mix:** Croat 80%, Serb 12%, Hungarian, Slovenian, other 8% **Government:** Multiparty republic **Currency:** Kuna = 100 para

Crocker, Banjaran 138 D 3 *var.* Crocker Range. Mountain range, Borneo, E Malaysia

Crocker Range *see* Crocker, Banjaran

Crocodile *see* Limpopo

Croker Island 146 E 2 island, N Australia

Cromwell 151 B 7 South Island, SW New Zealand

Crooked Island 54 D 2 island, SE Bahamas

Crooked Island Passage 54 D 2 channel, N Caribbean Sea

Crookston 45 F 1 Minnesota, N USA

Crotone 97 E 6 *var.* Cotrone; *anc.* Crotona, Croton. SW Italy

Croydon 89 E 7 SE England, UK

Crozet Basin 141 B 6 undersea basin, S Indian Ocean

Crozet Islands 141 B 7 island group, W French Southern & Antarctic Territories

Crozet Plateau 141 B 6 *var.* Crozet Plateaus. Undersea plateau, SW Plateau

Crozet Plateaus *see* Crozet Plateau

Crystal Brook 149 B 6 South Australia, S Australia

Csaca *see* Čadca

Csorna 99 B 6 NW Hungary

Csurgó 99 C 7 SW Hungary

Cuamba 79 E 2 *prev.* Nova Freixo. N Mozambique

Cuando *see* Kwando

Cuango 77 C 7 NW Angola

Cuango *see* Kwango

Cuanza 69 C 5 *var.* Kwanza. River, C Angola

Cuauhtémoc 50 C 2 N Mexico

Cuautla 51 E 4 S Mexico

Cuba 54 B 2 Republic, N Caribbean Sea

Official name: Republic of Cuba **Date of formation:** 1902 **Capital:** Havana **Population:** 10.9 million **Total area:** 110,860 sq km (42,803 sq miles) **Languages:** Spanish*, English, French, Chinese **Religions:** Roman Catholic 85%, other 15% **Ethnic mix:** White 66%, Afro-European 22%, other 12% **Government:** Socialist republic **Currency:** Peso = 100 centavos

Cubal 78 B 2 W Angola

Cubango 78 B 2 *var.* Kuvango, *Port.* Vila Artur de Paiva, Vila da Ponte. C Angola

Cubango 78 B 2 *var.* Kavango, Kavengo, Kubango, Okavanggo, Okavango. River, S Africa

Cúcuta 58 C 2 *var.* San José de Cúcuta. N Colombia

Cuddapah 132 C 2 S India

Cue 147 B 5 Western Australia, W Australia

Cuenca 93 E 3 *anc.* Conca. C Spain

Cuenca 60 B 2 S Ecuador

Cuernavaca 51 E 4 S Mexico

Cuiabá 63 E 3 *prev.* Cuyabá. State capital, SW Brazil

Cuijck 86 D 4 SE Netherlands

Cúil Raithin *see* Coleraine

Cuito 78 B 2 *var.* Kwito. River, SE Angola

Cukai 138 B 3 *var.* Chukai, Kemaman. W Malaysia

Culiacán 50 C 3 *var.* Culiacán Rosales, Culiacán-Rosales. C Mexico

Cullera 93 F 3 E Spain

Cullman 42 C 2 Alabama, S USA

Culpepper Island *see* Darwin, Isla

Cumaná 59 E 1 NE Venezuela

Cumbal, Nevada de 58 A 4 mountain, SW Colombia

Cumberland 41 E 4 Maryland, NE USA

Cumberland Plateau 42 D 1 hill range, Maryland, E USA

Cumberland River 43 E 1 river, S USA

Cunene 78 A 3 *var.* Kunene. River, Angola/Namibia

Cuneo 96 A 2 *Fr.* Coni. NW Italy

Cunnamulla 149 C 5 Queensland, E Australia

Cuprija 100 D 4 C Yugoslavia

Curaçao 55 E 5 island, C Netherlands Antilles

Curicó 64 B 4 C Chile

Curitiba 63 F 4 *prev.* Curytiba. State capital, S Brazil

Curtea de Argeş 108 B 4 *var.* Curtea-de-Arges. S Romania

Curtea-de-Arges *see* Curtea de Argeş

Curtici 108 A 4 *Ger.* Kurtitsch, *Hung.* Kürtös. W Romania

Curtis Island 148 E 4 island, Queensland, SE Australia

Curuguaty 64 E 2 E Paraguay

Curytiba *see* Curitiba

Cusco 60 D 4 *var.* Cuzco. C Peru

Cusset 91 C 5 C France

Cutch, Rann of 134 B 4 *var.* Rann of Kachh, Rann of Kutch. Wetland, India/Pakistan

Cuttack 135 F 5 E India

Cuvier Plateau 141 E 5 undersea plateau, E Indian Ocean

Cuxhaven 94 B 2 NW Germany

Cuyabá *see* Cuiabá

Cuyuni 59 F 2 *var.* Río Cuyuni. River, Guyana/Venezuela

Cuyuni, Río *see* Cuyuni River

Cuzco *see* Cusco

Čvrsnica 100 C 4 mountain range, SW Bosnia & Herzegovina

Cyclades *see* Kykládes

Cymru *see* Wales

Cyprus 103 H4 Gk. Kypros, Turk. Kibris, Kibris Cumhuriyeti. Republic, SW Asia

Official name: Republic of Cyprus **Date of formation:** 1974 **Capital:** Nicosia **Population:** 700,000 **Total area:** 9,251 sq km (3,572 sq miles) **Languages:** Greek*, Turkish, other **Religions:** Greek Orthodox 77%, Muslim 18%, other 5% **Ethnic mix:** Greek 77%, Turkish 18%, other (mainly British) 5% **Government:** Multiparty republic **Currency:** Cypriot £/Turkish lira

Cyprus 103 H4 Gk. Kypros, Turk. Kibris, Kibris. Island, NE Mediterranean Sea

Czech Republic 99 B 5 *Cz.* Česká Republika. Republic, C Europe

Official name: Czech Republic **Date of formation:** 1993 **Capital:** Prague **Population:** 10.4 million **Total area:** 78,370 sq km (30,260 sq miles) **Languages:** Czech*, Slovak, Romany **Religions:** Roman Catholic 44%, Protestant 6%, other Christian 12%, other 38% **Ethnic mix:** Czech 85%, Moravian 13%, other 2% **Government:** Multiparty republic **Currency:** Koruna = 100 halura

Częstochowa 98 C 4 *Ger.* Czenstochau, Tschenstochau, *Rus.* Chenstokhov. S Poland

Człuchów 98 C 3 *Ger.* Schlochau. NW Poland

D

Dabajuro 58 C 1 NW Venezuela

Dabeiba 58 B 2 NW Colombia

Dąbrowa Tarnowska 99 D 5 SE Poland

Dabryn' 107 C 8 *Rus.* Dobryn'. SE Belorussia

Dacca *see* Dhākā

Dadanawa 59 F 4 SW Guyana

Dafang 129 B 5 E China

Dagana 74 B 3 N Senegal

Dagda 106 D 4 SE Latvia

Dagupan 139 E 1 *off.* Dagupan City. Luzon, N Philippines

Dagupan City *see* Dagupan

Da Hinggan Ling 127 G 1 *Eng.* Great Khingan Range. Mountain range, NE China

Dahm, Ramlat 121 B 6 desert, NW Yemen

Daimiel 92 D 3 C Spain

Daimoniá 105 B 7 S Greece

Daingin, Bá an *see* Dingle Bay

Dakar 74 B 3 country capital, W Senegal

Dakhla Oasis 72 A 2 *var.* Wāhat el Dākhla. Oasis, C Egypt

Dākhla, Wāhat el *see* Dakhla Oasis

Dakoro 75 G 3 S Niger

Đakovica 101 D 5 *var.* Djakovica, *Alb.* Gjakovë. SW Yugoslavia

Đakovo 100 C 3 *var.* Djakovo, *Hung.* Diakovár. E Croatia

Dakshin *see* Deccan

Dalaman 116 A 4 Turkey

Dalandzadgad 127 E 3 S Mongolia

Dalarna 85 C 5 *prev. Eng.* Dalecarlia. Cultural region, C Sweden

Dalecarlia *see* Dalarna

Dale City 41 E 4 Virginia, NE USA

Dalhart 49 E 1 New Mexico, SW USA

Dalian 128 D 4 *var.* Dairen, Dalien, Jay Dairen, Lüda,Ta-lien, *Rus.* Dalny. NE China

Dallas 49 G 3 Texas, S USA

Dalmacija 100 B 4 *Eng.* Dalmatia, *Ger.* Dalmatien, *It.* Dalmazia. Cultural region S Croatia

Dalton 42 D 1 Georgia, SE USA

Daly Waters 148 A 2 Northern Territory, N Australia

Damachava 107 A 6 *var.* Damachova, *Pol.* Domaczewo, *Rus.* Domachëvo. SW Belorussia

Damān 134 C 5 *Port.* Damão. W India

Damão *see* Damān

Damara 76 C 4 S Central African Republic

Damascus *see* Damascus

Damietta *see* Dumyât

Dammam 120 C 4 *var.* Ad Dammām. NE Saudi Arabia

Damoûr 119 A 5 *var.* Ad Dāmūr. W Lebanon

Dampier 146 B 4 Western Australia, W Australia

Dampier, Selat 139 G 4 strait, W Pacific Ocean

Damqawt 121 D 6 *var.* Damqut. E Yemen

Damqut *see* Damqawt

Damxung 126 C 5 W China

Danané 74 D 5 W Ivory Coast

Đà Nâng 137 E 5 *prev.* Touranc. C Vietnam

Danborg *see* Daneborg

Danbury 41 F 3 Connecticut, NE USA

Dandong 128 E 3 *var.* Tan-tung; *prev.* An-tung. NE China

Daneborg 83 E 3 *var.* Danborg. E Greenland

Dangara *see* Danghara

Danghara 123 E 3 *Rus.* Dangara. SW Tajikistan

Dangriga 52 C 1 *prev.* Stann Creek. E Belize

Danlí 52 D 3 S Honduras

Danmark Havn 83 E 2 E Greenland

Danmarksstraedet *see* Denmark Strait

Dannenberg 94 C 3 N Germany

Dannevirke 150 D 4 North Island, C New Zealand

Danube 81 E 4 *Bul.* Dunav, *Cz.* Dunaj, *Ger.* Donau, *Hung.* Duna, *Rom.* Dunărea. River, C Europe

Danube, Mouths of the 108 D 5 *Rom.* Delta Dunării. Delta, Romania/Ukraine

Danubian Plain *see* Dunavska Ravnina

Danum *see* Doncaster

Danville 41 E 5 Virginia, NE USA
Danville 40 B 4 Illinois, N USA
Dan Xian 129 C 7 *var.* Danxian,
 Nada. Hainan Dao, S China
Danzig, Gulf of 98 C 2 *var.* Gulf of
 Gdańsk, *Ger.* Danziger Bucht, *Pol.*
 Zakota Gdańska, *Rus.* Gdan'skaya
 Bukhta. Gulf, S Baltic Sea
Daqm *see* Duqm
Dar'ā 119 B 5 *var.* Der'a, *Fr.* Déraa.
 SW Syria
Darabani 108 C 3 NW Romania
Daraut-Kurgan *see* Daroot-Korgon
Darbénai 106 B 3 NW Lithuania
Dardanelles *see* Çanakkale Boğazı
Dar-el-Beida *see* Casablanca
Dar es Salaam 73 D 7 E Tanzania
Darfield 151 C 6 South Island, C
 New Zealand
Darfur 72 A 4 *var.* Darfur Massif.
 Mountain range, W Sudan
Darfur Massif *see* Darfur
Dargaville 150 D 2 North Island, N
 New Zealand
Darhan 127 E 2 N Mongolia
Darién, Golfo del *see* Darien, Gulf
 of
Darien, Gulf of 53 H 4 *Sp.* Golfo
 del Darién. Gulf, SE Caribbean
 Sea
Darién, Serranía del 53 H 5
 mountain range,
 Colombia/Panama
Dario *see* Ciudad Darío
Dariorigum *see* Vannes
Darjeeling *see* Darjiling
Darjiling 135 F 3 *prev.* Darjeeling.
 NE India
Darling 149 C 6 river, New South
 Wales, SE Australia
Darling Downs 149 D 5 hill range,
 Queensland, SE Australia
Darlington 89 D 5 N England, UK
Darmiān 120 E 3 E Iran
Darmstadt 95 B 5 SW Germany
Darnah 71 G 2 *var.* Dérna. NE Libya
Darnley, Cape 154 D 3 headland,
 Antarctica
Daroca 93 E 2 NE Spain
Daroot-Korgon 123 F 3 *var.* Daraut-
 Kurgan. SW Kyrgyzstan
Dartmoor 89 C 7 heathland, SW
 England, UK
Dartmouth 39 F 4 Nova Scotia, SE
 Canada
Darvaza 122 C 2 *Turkm.* Derweze. C
 Turkmenistan
Darwin 65 D 7 *var.* Darwin
 Settlement. Falkland Islands
Darwin 148 A 2 *prev.* Palmerston,
 Port Darwin. Territory capital,
 Northern Territory, N Australia
Darwin, Isla 60 A 4 *var.* Culpepper
 Island. Island, Galapagos Islands,
 E Pacific Ocean
Darwin Settlement *see* Darwin
Dashkawka 107 D 6 *Rus.*
 Dashkovka. E Belorussia
Dashkhovuz 122 C 2 *Turkm.*
 Dashhowuz; *prev.* Tashauz. N
 Turkmenistan
Dashkovka *see* Dashkawka
Dasht 120 D 2 N Iran
Datong 128 C 3 *var.* Tatung, Ta-
 t'ung. N China
Daugavpils 106 D 4 *Ger.* Dünaburg;
 prev. Rus. Dvinsk. SE Latvia
Daung Kyun 137 B 6 island, S
 Burma
Dauphiné 91 D 5 cultural region, E
 France
Daurada, Costa 93 G 2 *var.* Costa
 Dorada. Coastal region, E Spain

Dāvangere 132 C 2 W India
Davao 139 F 2 *off.* Davao City.
 Mindanao, S Philippines
Davao City *see* Davao
Davao Gulf 139 F 3 gulf, W Pacific
 Ocean
Davenport 45 G 3 Iowa, C USA
David 53 F 5 W Panama
Davie Ridge 141 A 5 undersea
 ridge, W Indian Ocean
Davis 154 D 3 research station,
 Antarctica
Davis 47 B 6 California, W USA
Davis Mountains 48 D 3 mountain
 range, Texas, S USA
Davis Sea 154 D 3 sea, S Indian
 Ocean
Davis Strait 82 B 3 strait, Baffin
 Bay/Labrador Sea
Davlekanovo 111 D 6 W Russian
 Federation
Dawei *see* Tavoy
Dawra 70 B 3 *var.* Daora, Daoura.
 NW Western Sahara
Dax 91 B 6 *var.* Ax; *anc.* Aquae
 Augustae, Aquae Tarbelicae. SW
 France
Dayr az Zawr 118 D 3 *var.* Deir ez
 Zor. E Syria
Dayton 40 C 4 Ohio, N USA
Daytona Beach 43 E 4 Florida, SE
 USA
De Aar 78 C 5 C South Africa
Dead Sea 119 B 7 *var.* Bahret Lut,
 Lacus Asphaltites, *Ar.* Al Baḥr al
 Mayyit, Baḥrat Lūṭ, *Heb.* Yam
 HaMelaḥ. Salt lake, Israel/Jordan
Deán Funes 64 C 3 C Argentina
Death Valley 47 D 6 valley,
 California, W USA
Debar 101 D 6 *Ger.* Dibra, *Turk.*
 Debre. W Macedonia
De Bildt *see* De Bilt
De Bilt 86 C 3 *var.* De Bildt. C
 Netherlands
Debrecen 99 D 6 *Ger.* Debreczin,
 Rom. Debrețin; *prev.* Debreczen. E
 Hungary
Decatur 42 C 2 Alabama, S USA
Decatur 40 B 4 Illinois, N USA
Deccan 132 C 1 *Hind.* Dakshin.
 Plateau, C India
Děčín 98 A 4 *Ger.* Tetschen. NW
 Czech Republic
Dedemsvaart 86 E 3 E Netherlands
Dee 88 C 3 river, E Scotland, UK
Deering 36 C 2 Alaska, NW USA
De Funiak Springs 42 D 3 Florida,
 SE USA
Deggendorf 95 D 6 SE Germany
Deh Bid 120 D 4 C Iran
Deinze 87 B 6 NW Belgium
Deir ez Zor *see* Dayr az Zawr
Deirgeirt, Loch *see* Derg, Lough
Dej 108 B 3 *Hung.* Dés; *prev.* Deés.
 NW Romania
De Jouwer *see* Joure
Dékoa 76 C 4 C Central African
 Republic
De Land 43 E 4 Florida, SE USA
Delano 47 C 7 California, W USA
Delārām 122 D 5 SW Afghanistan
Delaware 41 F 4 *off.* State of
 Delaware; *nicknames* Blue Hen
 State, Diamond State, First State.
 State, E USA
Delaware 40 D 4 Ohio, N USA
Delaware Bay 41 F 5 bay, W
 Atlantic Ocean
Delft 86 C 4 W Netherlands
Delfzijl 86 E 1 NE Netherlands

Delgo 72 B 3 N Sudan
Delhi 134 D 3 *var.* Dehli, *Hind.* Dilli;
 hist. Shahjahanabad. N India
Delicias 50 C 2 *var.* Ciudad
 Delicias. N Mexico
Delmenhorst 94 B 3 NW Germany
Del Rio 49 F 4 Texas, S USA
Demba 77 D 6 S Zaire
Dembia 76 D 4 SE Central African
 Republic
Demchok 126 A 4 *var.* Dêmqog.
 Disputed region, China/India
Deming 48 C 3 New Mexico, SW
 USA
Demmin 94 D 2 NE Germany
Dêmqog 126 A 4 *var.* Demchok.
 Disputed region, China/India
Denali *see* McKinley, Mount
Denau *see* Denow
Dender 87 B 6 *Fr.* Dendre. River, W
 Belgium
Dendre *see* Dender
Denekamp 86 E 3 E Netherlands
Den Ham 86 E 3 E Netherlands
Den Helder 86 C 2 NW
 Netherlands
Denia 93 F 4 E Spain
Deniliquin 149 C 7 New South
 Wales, SE Australia
Denison 49 G 2 Texas, S USA
Denison 45 F 3 Iowa, C USA
Denizli 116 B 4 SW Turkey

Denmark
 85 A 7 *Dan.* Danmark, *anc.*
 Hafnia. Monarchy, N Europe

 Official name: Kingdom of
 Denmark **Date of formation:**
 AD 960 **Capital:** Copenhagen
 Population: 5.2 million
 Total area: 43,069 sq km
 (16,629 sq miles) **Languages:**
 Danish* **Religions:** Evangelical
 Lutheran 91% other Christian 9%
 Ethnic mix: Danish 96%, Faeroese
 and Inuit 1%, other 3% **Government:**
 Constitutional monarchy
 Currency: Krone = 100 øre

Denmark Strait 82 D 4 *var.*
 Danmarksstraedet. Strait, N
 Atlantic Ocean
Dennery 55 F 1 E Saint Lucia
Denow 123 E 3 *Rus.* Denau. S
 Uzbekistan
Denpasar 138 D 5 *prev.* Paloe. Bali,
 C Indonesia
Denton 49 G 2 Texas, S USA
Denver 44 D 4 state capital,
 Colorado, C USA
Dera Ghāzi Khān 134 C 2 *var.* Dera
 Ghāzikhan. C Pakistan
Dera Ghāzikhān *see* Dera Ghāzi
 Khān
Đeravica 101 D 5 mountain, SW
 Yugoslavia
Derbent 111 C 8 SW Russian
 Federation
Derby 89 D 6 C England, UK
Dergachi *see* Derhachi
Derg, Lough 89 A 6 *Ir.* Loch
 Deirgeirt. Lake, W Ireland
Derhachi 109 G 2 *Rus.* Dergachi. E
 Ukraine
De Ridder 42 A 3 Louisiana, S USA
Dérna *see* Darnah
Dertosa *see* Tortosa
Derventa 100 C 3 N Bosnia &
 Herzegovina
Derweze *see* Darvaza
Deschutes River 46 B 3 river,
 Oregon, NW USA

Desē 72 D 4 *var.* Desse, *It.* Dessie. N
 Ethiopia
Deseado 65 B 7 river, S Argentina
Des Moines 45 F 4 state capital,
 Iowa, C USA
Desna 109 E 1 river, Russian
 Federation/Ukraine
Dessau 94 C 4 E Germany
Destêrro *see* Florianópolis
Detroit 40 D 3 Michigan, N USA
Detroit Lakes 45 F 2 Minnesota, N
 USA
Deurne 87 D 5 SE Netherlands
Deutsch-Eylau *see* Iława
Deutsch Krone *see* Wałcz
Deva 108 B 4 *Ger.* Diemrich, *Hung.*
 Déva. W Romania
Devana *see* Aberdeen
Deventer 86 D 3 E Netherlands
Devils Lake 45 E 1 Missouri, C
 USA
Devoll *see* Devollit, Lumi i
Devollit, Lumi i 101 D 6 *var.*
 Devoll. River, SE Albania
Devon Island 37 F 2 *prev.* North
 Devon Island. Island, NE Canada
Devonport 149 C 8 Tasmania, SE
 Australia
Devrek 116 C 2 N Turkey
Dexter 45 G 5 Missouri, C USA
Deynau 122 D 3 *var.* Dyanev, *Turkm.*
 Dänew. NE Turkmenistan
Dezfūl 120 C 3 *var.* Dizful. SW Iran
Dezhou 128 D 4 NE China
Dhahran *see* Az Ẓahrān
Dhākā 135 G 4 *prev.* Dacca. Country
 capital, C Bangladesh
Dhanbād 135 F 4 NE India
Dhārwād 132 B 1 *prev.* Dharwar.
 SW India
Dhíkti Ori *see* Dikti
Dhomokós *see* Domokós
Dhráma *see* Dráma
Dhrepanon, Akra *see* Drépano, Ákra
Dhún na nGall, Bá *see* Donegal Bay
Diamantina, Chapada 63 F 3
 mountain range, E Brazil
Diamantina Fracture Zone 141 E 6
 fracture zone, E Indian Ocean
D'Iberville 42 C 3 Mississippi, S
 USA
Dibio *see* Dijon
Dibrugarh 135 H 3 NE India
Dickinson 44 D 2 North Dakota, N
 USA
Didymóteicho 104 D 3 *var.*
 Dhidhimótikhon, Didimotiho. NE
 Greece
Diedenhofen *see* Thionville
Diekirch 87 D 8 C Luxembourg
Điên Biên 136 D 3 *var.* Bien Bien,
 Dien Bien Phu. NW Vietnam
Diepenbeek 87 D 6 NE Belgium
Diepholz 94 B 3 NW Germany
Dieppe 90 C 2 N France
Dieren 86 D 4 E Netherlands
Differdange 87 D 8 SW
 Luxembourg
Digne 91 D 6 *var.* Digne-les-Bains.
 SE France
Digne-les-Bains *see* Digne
Digoel *see* Digul, Sungai
Digoin 90 C 4 C France
Digul 139 H 5 *prev.* Digoel. River,
 New Guinea, E Indonesia
Dijon 90 D 4 *anc.* Dibio. C France
Dikhil 72 D 4 SW Djibouti
Dikson 114 D 2 N Russian
 Federation

Diktí 105 D 8 *var.* Dhíkti Ori. Mountain range, Krití, SE Greece
Dili 139 F 5 *var.* Dilli, Dilly. Timor, C Indonesia
Dilia 75 G 3 *var.* Dillia. River, SE Niger
Dilijan 117 G 2 *Rus.* Dilizhan. NE Armenia
Di Linh 137 E 6 S Vietnam
Dilizhan *see* Dilijan
Dillia *see* Dilia
Dilling 72 B 4 *var.* Ad Dalanj. C Sudan
Dillon 44 B 2 Montana, NW USA
Dilolo 77 D 8 S Zaire
Dimashq 119 B 5 *var.* Ash Shām, Esh Sham, *Eng.* Damascus, *Fr.* Damas, *It.* Damasco. Country capital, SW Syria
Dimitrovgrad 111 C 6 W Russian Federation
Dimitrovgrad 104 D 3 S Bulgaria
Dimitrovo *see* Pernik
Dimlang 75 G 4 *var.* Vogel Peak. Mountain, E Nigeria
Dimona 119 A 7 S Israel
Dimovo 104 B 1 NW Bulgaria
Dinājpur 135 G 3 NW Bangladesh
Dinan 90 A 3 NW France
Dinant 87 C 7 S Belgium
Dinar 116 B 4 SW Turkey
Dinara *see* Dinaric Alps
Dinaric Alps 100 C 4 *var.* Dinara. Mountain range, Bosnia & Herzegovina/Croatia
Dindigul 132 C 3 SE India
Dingle Bay 89 A 6 *Ir.* Bá an Daingin. Inlet, NE Atlantic Ocean
Dinguiraye 74 C 4 N Guinea
Diourbel 74 B 3 W Senegal
Direction, Cape 148 C 2 headland, Queensland, NE Australia
Dirē Dawa 73 D 5 E Ethiopia
Dirk Hartog Island 147 A 5 island, W Australia
Dirra 72 A 4 Sudan
Dirschau *see* Tczew
Disappointment, Lake 146 C 4 salt lake, Western Australia, W Australia
Discovery Bay 128 A 1 *Cant.* Tai Pak Wan. W Hong Kong
Dispur 135 G 3 NE India
Divinópolis 63 F 4 SE Brazil
Divo 74 D 5 S Ivory Coast
Diyarbakır 117 E 4 *var.* Diarbekr; *anc.* Amida. SE Turkey
Dızful *see* Dezfūl
Djambala 77 B 6 C Congo
Djambi *see* Hari, Batang
Djanet 71 E 4 *prev.* Fort Charlet. SE Algeria
Djelfa 70 D 2 *var.* El Djelfa. N Algeria
Djéma 76 D 4 E Central African Republic
Djember *see* Jember
Djérem 75 H 5 river, C Cameroon
Djibouti 72 D 4 *var.* Jibuti. Country capital, E Djibouti

Djibouti 72 D 4 *var.* Jibuti; *prev.* French Somaliland, French Territory of the Afars and Issas, *Fr.* Côte Française des Somalis, Territoire Français des Afars et des Issas. Republic, NE Africa

Official name: Republic of Djibouti
Date of formation: 1977
Capital: Djibouti **Population:**

500,000 **Total area:** 23,200 sq km (8,958 sq miles) **Languages:** Arabic*, French*, Somali : **Religions:** Christian 87%, other 13% **Ethnic mix:** Issa 35%, Afar 20%, Gadaboursis and Isaaks 28%, other 17% **Government:** Single-party republic **Currency:** Franc = 100 centimes

Djiguéni 74 D 3 SE Mauritania
Djisr el Choghour *see* Jisr ash Shughūr
Djourab, Erg du 76 C 2 desert, N Chad
Djúpivogur 83 E 5 SE Iceland
Dneprodzerzhinskoye Vodokhranilishche *see* Dniprodzerzhyns'ke Vodoskhovyshche
Dneprorudnoye *see* Dniprorudne
Dnieper 81 F 4 *Bel.* Dnyapro, *Rus.* Dnepr, *Ukr.* Dnipro. River, W Europe
Dnieper Lowland 109 F 2 *Bel.* Prydnyaprowskaya Nizina, *Ukr.* Prydniprovs'ka Nyzovyna. Lowlands, Belorussia/Ukraine
Dniester 108 D 3 *var.* Tyras, *Rom.* Nistru, *Rus.* Dnestr, *Ukr.* Dnister. River, Moldavia/Ukraine
Dniprodzerzhyns'k 109 F 3 *Rus.* Dneprodzerzhinsk; *prev.* Kamenskoye. C Ukraine
Dniprodzerzhyns'ke Vodoskhovyshche 109 F 3 *Rus.* Dneprodzerzhinskoye Vodokhranilishche. Reservoir, SE Ukraine
Dnipropetrovs'k 109 F 3 *Rus.* Dnepropetrovsk; *prev.* Yekaterinoslav. E Ukraine
Dniprorudne 109 F 3 *Rus.* Dneprorudnoye. SE Ukraine
Doba 76 C 4 S Chad
Döbeln 94 D 4 E Germany
Doboj 100 C 3 N Bosnia & Herzegovina
Dobre Miasto 98 D 2 *Ger.* Guttstadt. N Poland
Dobrich 104 E 2 *var.* Dobrič, *Rom.* Bazargic; *prev.* Tolbukhin. NE Bulgaria
Dobryn' *see* Dabryn'
Dodecanese *see* Dodekánisos
Dodekánisos 105 D 6 *var.* Nóties Sporádes, *Eng.* Dodecanese; *prev.* Dhodhekánisos. Island group, SE Greece
Dodge City 45 E 5 Kansas, C USA
Dodoma 73 C 7 country capital, C Tanzania
Dogana 96 E 1 NE San Marino
Dōgo 131 B 6 island, Oki-shotō, W Japan
Dogondoutchi 75 F 3 SW Niger
Dogrular *see* Pravda
Doğu Karadeniz Dağları 117 E 3 *var.* Anadolu Daĕlari. Mountain range, NE Turkey
Doha *see* Ad Dawḩah
Dokkum 86 D 1 N Netherlands
Dokuchayevs'k 109 G 3 *var.* Dokuchayevsk, SE Ukraine
Dokuchayevsk *see* Dokuchayevs'k
Doldrums Fracture Zone 66 C 4 fracture zone, W Atlantic Ocean
Dôle 90 D 4 E France
Dolina *see* Dolyna
Dolinskaya *see* Dolyns'ka
Dolisie 77 B 6 *prev.* Loubomo. S Congo

Dolomitiche, Alpi 96 C 1 *var.* Dolomiti, *Eng.* Dolomites. Mountain range, NE Italy
Dolores 64 D 4 W Uruguay
Dolores 64 D 4 E Argentina
Dolores 52 B 1 N Guatemala
Dolores Hidalgo 51 E 4 *var.* Ciudad de Dolores Hidalgo. C Mexico
Dolyna 108 B 2 *Rus.* Dolina. W Ukraine
Dolyns'ka 109 F 3 *Rus.* Dolinskaya. S Ukraine
Dombås 85 B 5 S Norway
Domesnes, Cape *see* Kolkasrags
Domeyko 64 B 3 N Chile

Dominica 55 H 4 Republic, E Caribbean Sea

Official name: Commonwealth of Dominica **Date of formation:** 1978 **Capital:** Roseau **Population:** 72,000 **Total area:** 750 sq km (290 sq miles) **Languages:** English*, French Creole, Carib, Cocoy **Religions:** Roman Catholic 77%, Protestant 15%, other 8% **Ethnic mix:** Black 98%, Indian 2% **Government:** Multiparty republic **Currency:** E. Caribbean $ = 100 cents

Dominican Republic 55 E 3 Republic, N Caribbean Sea

Official name: Dominican Republic **Date of formation:** 1865 **Capital:** Santo Domingo **Population:** 7.6 million **Total area:** 48,730 sq km (18,815 sq miles) **Languages:** Spanish*, French Creole **Religions:** Roman Catholic 95%, other 5% **Ethnic mix:** Afro-European 73%, White 16%, Black 11% **Government:** Multiparty republic **Currency:** Peso = 100 centavos

Domokós 105 B 5 *var.* Dhomokós. C Greece
Don 81 F 3 *var.* Duna, Tanais. River, SW Russian Federation
Donauwörth 95 C 6 S Germany
Don Benito 92 C 4 W Spain
Doncaster 89 D 5 *anc.* Danum. N England, UK
Dondo 78 B 1 NW Angola
Donegal 89 A 5 *Ir.* Dún na nGall. NW Ireland
Donegal Bay 89 A 5 *Ir.* Bá Dhún na nGall. Bay, E Atlantic Ocean
Donets 109 G 2 river, Russian Federation/Ukraine
Donets'k 109 G 3 *Rus.* Donetsk; *prev.* Stalino. E Ukraine
Dongfang 129 B 7 Hainan Dao, S China
Dôngha 136 E 4 C Vietnam
Dong Hai *see* East China Sea
Dông Hôi 136 E 4 C Vietnam
Dongola 72 B 3 *var.* Donqola, Dunqula. N Sudan
Dongou 77 C 5 NE Congo
Dongting Hu 129 C 5 *var.* Tung-t'ing Hu. Lake, SE China
Dongguan 129 C 6 SW China
Dongying 128 D 4 NE China
Donnybrook 147 B 7 SW Australia
Donostia-San Sebastián 93 E 1 N Spain
Door Peninsula 40 C 2 peninsula, Wisconsin, N USA
Dooxo Nugaaleed 73 E 5 *var.* Nogal Valley. Valley, E Somalia
Dordogne 91 B 5 cultural region, SW France
Dordogne 91 B 5 river, W France

Dordrecht 86 C 4 *var.* Dordt, Dort. SW Netherlands
Doré Lake 37 F 5 Saskatchewan, C Canada
Dorohoi 108 C 3 NE Romania
Dorotea 84 C 4 N Sweden
Dorre Island 147 A 5 island, W Australia
Dortmund 94 A 4 W Germany
Dos Hermanas 92 C 5 S Spain
Dospat 104 C 3 SW Bulgaria
Dothan 42 D 3 Alabama, S USA
Dotnuva 106 B 4 C Lithuania
Douai 90 C 2 *prev.* Douay, *anc.* Duacum. N France
Douala 77 A 5 *var.* Duala. W Cameroon
Doubtful Island Bay 147 C 7 bay, SE Indian Ocean
Douglas 89 C 5 dependent territory capital, E Isle of Man, British Isles
Douglas 43 E 3 Georgia, SE USA
Douglas 48 C 3 Arizona, SW USA
Douglas 44 C 3 Wyoming, C USA
Douma *see* Dūmā
Douro 92 B 2 *Sp.* Duero. River, Portugal/Spain
Douro, Rio *see* Duero
Dover 89 E 7 *Fr.* Douvres; *Lat.* Dubris Portus. SE England, UK
Dover 149 C 8 Tasmania, SE Australia
Dover 41 G 3 New Hampshire, NE USA
Dover 41 F 4 state capital, Delaware, NE USA
Dover, Strait of 90 C 2 *var.* Straits of Dover, *Fr.* Pas de Calais. Channel, NE Atlantic Ocean
Dovrefjell 85 B 5 mountain range, S Norway
Downpatrick 89 C 5 *Ir.* Dún Pádraig. SE Northern Ireland, UK
Dōzen 131 B 6 island, Oki-shotō, W Japan
Drachten 86 D 2 N Netherlands
Drăgăşani 108 B 5 SW Romania
Dragoman 104 B 2 W Bulgaria
Dragon's Mouth, The 59 F 1 strait, W Atlantic Ocean
Dra, Hamada du 70 C 3 *var.* Hammada du Drâa, Haut Plateau du Dra. Plateau, W Algeria
Drahichyn 107 B 6 *Pol.* Drohiczyn Poleski, *Rus.* Drogichin. SW Belorussia
Drakensberg 78 D 5 mountain range, Lesotho/South Africa
Drake Passage 153 F 5 passage, Atlantic Ocean/Pacific Ocean
Dralfa 104 D 2 N Bulgaria
Dráma 104 C 3 *var.* Dhráma. NE Greece
Dramburg *see* Drawsko Pomorskie
Drammen 85 B 6 S Norway
Drava 100 C 3 *var.* Drau, *Eng.* Drave, *Hung.* Dráva. River, C Europe
Drawsko Pomorskie 98 B 3 *Ger.* Dramburg. NW Poland
Drépano, Akra 104 C 4 *var.* Akra Dhrepanon. Headland, N Greece
Drepanum *see* Trapani
Dresden 94 D 4 E Germany
Drina 100 D 4 river, Bosnia & Herzegovina/Yugoslavia
Drini i Zi 101 D 5 *var.* Black Drin, *Alb.* Lumi i Drinit të Zi, *SCr.* Crni Drim. River, Albania/Macedonia
Drissa 107 D 5 *Bel.* Drysa. River, Belorussia/Russian Federation

Drobeta-Turnu Severin 108 B 5
prev. Turnu Severin. SW Romania
DroghEda 89 B 5 *Ir.* Droichead
Átha. NE Ireland
Drohobych 108 B 2 *Pol.* Drohobycz,
Rus. Drogobych. NW Ukraine
Droichead Átha *see* Drogheda
Drôme 91 D 6 cultural region,
France
Dronning Maud Land *see* Queen
Maud Land
Drug *see* Durg
Drummond Island 40 D 2 island,
Michigan, N USA
Drummondville 39 E 4 Québec, SE
Canada
Druskienniki *see* Druskininkai
Druskininkai 107 B 5 *Pol.*
Druskienniki. S Lithuania
Dryden 38 B 3 Ontario, C Canada
Drysa *see* Drissa
Drysdale 146 D 3 river, N Australia
Duala *see* Douala
Dubai *see* Dubayy
Dubăsari 108 D 3 *Rus.* Dubossary.
NE Moldavia
Dubawnt 37 F 4 river, Northwest
Territories, C Canada
Dubayy 120 D 4 *Eng.* Dubai. NE
United Arab Emirates
Dubbo 149 D 6 New South Wales,
SE Australia
Dublin 89 B 6 *Ir.* Baile Átha Cliath;
anc. Eblana. Country capital, E
Ireland
Dublin 43 E 2 Georgia, SE USA
Dubno 108 C 2 NW Ukraine
Dubossary *see* Dubăsari
Dubrovnik 101 A 8 *It.* Ragusa. SE
Croatia
Dubuque 45 G 3 Iowa, C USA
Dudelange 87 D 8 *var.* Forge du
Sud, *Ger.* Dudelingen. S
Luxembourg
D-U-D Municipality *see* Majuro
Duero 92 D 2 *Port.* Rio Douro.
River, Portugal/Spain
Duero *see* Douro
Duesseldorf *see* Düsseldorf
Duffel 87 C 5 C Belgium
Dufour Spitze 95 A 8 *var.* Punta
Dufour, *It.* Pizzo Dufour.
Mountain, Italy/Switzerland
Dugi Otok 100 A 3 *var.* Isola
Grossa, *It.* Isola Lunga. Island, W
Croatia
Duisburg 94 A 4 *prev.* Duisburg-
Hamborn. W Germany
Duisburg-Hamborn *see* Duisburg
Duitama 58 B 3 C Colombia
Duiven 86 D 4 E Netherlands
Duk Faiwil 73 B 5 Sudan
Dulan Xian 126 D 4 C China
Dulce, Golfo 53 E 5 gulf, E Pacific
Ocean
Dulce, Golfo *see* Izabal, Lago de
Dülmen 94 A 4 W Germany
Dulovo 104 E 1 NE Bulgaria
Duluth 45 G 2 Minnesota, N USA
Dūmā 119 B 5 *Fr.* Douma. SW Syria
Dumas 49 E 1 Texas, S USA
Dumfries 88 C 4 S Scotland, UK
Dumont d'Urville 154 D 4 research
station, Antarctica
Dumyât 72 B 1 *Eng.* Damietta. N
Egypt
Dunării, Delta *see* Danube, Mouths
of the
Dunaújváros 99 C 7 *prev.*
Dunapentele, Sztálinváros. C
Hungary

Dunavska Ravnina 104 C 2 *Eng.*
Danubian Plain. Plain, N Bulgaria
Duncan 49 G 2 Oklahoma, C USA
Dundalk 89 B 5 *Ir.* Dún Dealgan.
NE Ireland
Dundalk 41 F 4 Maryland, NE USA
Dún Dealgan *see* Dundalk
Dundee 88 C 4 E Scotland, UK
Dundee 78 D 4 E South Africa
Dunedin 151 B 7 South Island, SW
New Zealand
Dunfermline 88 C 4 C Scotland,
UK
Dungu 77 E 5 NE Zaire
Dungun 138 B 3 *var.* Kuala
Dungun. W Malaysia
Dunholme *see* Durham
Dunkerque 90 C 2 *Eng.* Dunkirk,
Flem. Duinekerke; *prev.*
Dunquerque. N France
Dún Laoghaire 89 B 6 *Eng.*
Dunleary; *prev.* Kingstown. E
Ireland
Dún na nGall *see* Donegal
Dún Pádraig *see* Downpatrick
Dupnitsa 104 C 2 *prev.* Stanke
Dimitrov, Marek. W Bulgaria
Duqm 121 E 5 *var.* Daqm. E Oman
Durance 91 D 6 river, SE France
Durango 50 D 3 *var.* Victoria de
Durango. W Mexico
Durango 44 C 5 Colorado, C USA
Durankulak 104 E 1 *Rom.* Răcari;
prev. Blatnitsa, Duranulac. NE
Bulgaria
Durant 49 G 2 Oklahoma, C USA
Durban 78 D 5 *var.* Port Natal. E
South Africa
Durbe 106 B 3 *Ger.* Durben. W
Latvia
Durben *see* Durbe
Durg 135 E 4 *prev.* Drug. C India
Durham 89 D 5 *hist.* Dunholme. N
England, UK
Durham 43 F 1 North Carolina, SE
USA
Durrës 101 C 6 *var.* Durrësi, Dursi,
It. Durazzo, *SCr.* Drač, *Turk.* Draç,
W Albania
Durrūz, Jabal ad 119 C 5 mountain ,
SW Syria
Dushanbe 123 E 3 *var.* Dyushambe,
Taj. Stalinobod; *prev.* Stalinabad.
Country capital, W Tajikistan
Düsseldorf 94 A 4 *var.* Duesseldorf.
W Germany
Dusti *see* Dŭsti
Dŭsti 123 E 3 *Rus.* Dusti. SW
Tajikistan
Dutch Harbor 36 B 3 Unalaska
Island, Alaska, USA
Dutch West Indies *see* Netherlands
Antilles
Dyersburg 42 C 1 Tennessee, S USA
Dzerzhinsk 111 C 5 W Russian
Federation
Dzhalal-Abad 123 F 2 *Kir.* Jalal-
Abad. W Kyrgyzstan
Dzhanak 122 C 2 physical region,
W Turkmenistan
Dzhankoy 109 F 4 S Ukraine
Dzharkurgan *see* Jarqŭrghon
Dzhelandy 123 F 3 SE Tajikistan
Dzhergalan 123 H 2 *Kir.* Jyrgalan.
NE Kyrgyzstan
Dzhetygara 114 B 4 *Kaz.* Zhetiqara.
NW Kazakhstan
Dzhizak *see* Jizzakh
Dzhugdzhur, Khrebet 115 G 3
mountain range, E Russian
Federation
Dzhusaly 114 B 4 *Kaz.* Zholsaly. SW
Kazakhstan

Działdowo 98 D 3 C Poland
Dzungaria 126 C 2 *var.* Sungaria,
Zungaria. Physical region, W
China
Dziünbayan 127 E 2 SE Mongolia
Dziünharaa 127 E 2 N Mongolia
Dzuunmod 127 E 2 C Mongolia

E

Eagle Lake 47 B 5 lake, California,
W USA
Eagle Pass 49 F 4 Texas, S USA
Easley 43 E 1 South Carolina, SE
USA
East Antarctica *see* Greater
Antarctica
East Australian Basin *see* Tasman
Basin
Eastbourne 89 E 7 SE England, UK
East Cape 150 E 3 region, North
Island, New Zealand
East Caroline Basin 152 B 3
undersea basin, SW Pacific Ocean
East Caroline Islands 144 C 2
island group, E Micronesia
East China Sea 152 B 2 *Chin.* Dong
Hai. Sea, NW Pacific Ocean
Easter Fracture Zone 153 F 4
fracture zone, E Pacific Ocean
Easter Island 153 F 4 island, E
Pacific Ocean
Eastern Ghats 124 B 3 mountain
range, SE India
Eastern Sayans 115 E 4 *Mong.*
Dzüün Soyoni Nuruu, *Rus.*
Vostochnyy Sayan. Mountain
range, Mongolia/Russian
Federation
Eastern Sierra Madre *see* Madre
Oriental, Sierra
East Falkland 65 D 8 *var.* Soledad.
Island, E Falkland Islands
East Frisian Islands *see* Ostfriesische
Inseln
East Grand Forks 45 F 1 Minnesota,
N USA
East Indiaman Ridge 141 D 5
undersea ridge, E Indian Ocean
East Kilbride 88 C 4 S Scotland, UK
East Korea Bay 128 E 3 bay, Sea of
Japan/Pacific Ocean
Eastleigh 89 D 7 S England, UK
East London 78 D 5 *Afr.* Oos-
Londen; *prev.* EMonti, Port Rex. S
South Africa
Eastmain 38 D 3 river, Québec, C
Canada
East Novaya Zemlya Trough 155 H
4 *var.* Novaya Zemlya Trough.
Trough, Arctic Ocean
East Pacific Rise 153 F 4 undersea
rise, E Pacific Ocean
East Saint Louis 40 B 4 Illinois, N
USA
East Siberian Sea *see* Vostochno-
Sibirskoye More
Eau Claire 40 A 2 Wisconsin, N
USA
Ébano 51 E 3 C Mexico
Ebensee 95 D 6 N Austria
Eberswalde-Finow 94 D 3 E
Germany
Ebetsu 130 D 2 *var.* Ebetu.
Hokkaidō, NE Japan
Ebetu *see* Ebetsu
Ebeye 144 D 1 island, C Marshall
Islands
Ebolowa 77 A 5 S Cameroon
Ebon Atoll 144 D 2 *var.* Epoon.
Island, S Marshall Islands

Ébrié, Lagune 74 D 5 lake, SW
Ivory Coast
Ebro 93 E 2 river, NE Spain
Ecbatana *see* Hamadān
Ech Cheliff 70 D 2 *var.* Chlef, Ech
Cheleff; *prev.* Al-Asnam, El
Asnam, Orléansville. NW Algeria
Echo Bay 37 E 3 Northwest
Territories, C Canada
Echt 87 D 5 SE Netherlands
Ecija 92 D 4 *anc.* Astigi. SW Spain
Eckengraf *see* Viesīte

Ecuador
60 A 2 Republic, NW South
America

Official name: Republic of Ecuador
Date of formation: 1830
Capital: Quito **Population:** 11.3
million **Total area:** 283,560 sq km
(109,483 sq miles) **Languages:**
Spanish*, Quechua*, eight other
Indian languages **Religions:** Roman
Catholic 95%, other 5% **Ethnic mix:**
mestizo (Euro-Indian) 55%, Indian
25%, Black 10%, White 10%
Government: Multiparty republic
Currency: Sucre = 100 centavos

Edd *see* Ed
Ed Da'ein 72 A 4 W Sudan
Ed Damazin 72 C 4 *var.* Ad
Damazīn. E Sudan
Ed Damer 72 C 3 *var.* Ad Damar,
Ad Dāmir. NE Sudan
Ed Debba 72 B 3 N Sudan
Ede 75 F 5 SW Nigeria
Ede 86 D 4 C Netherlands
Edéa 77 A 5 SW Cameroon
Edel Land 147 A 5 headland,
Western Australia, W Australia
Eden 43 F 1 North Carolina, SE
USA
Eden 149 D 7 New South Wales,
Australia
Edfu *see* Idfu
Edgeøya 83 G 2 island, S Svalbard
Edinburg 49 G 5 Texas, S USA
Edinburgh 88 C 4 SE Scotland, UK
Edingen *see* Enghien
Edirne 116 A 2 *var.* Adrianopolis,
Hadrianopolis. NW Turkey
Edmonds 46 B 2 Washington, NW
USA
Edmonton 37 E 5 province capital,
Alberta, SW Canada
Edmundston 39 E 4 New
Brunswick, SE Canada
Edna 49 G 4 Texas, S USA
Edolo 96 B 1 N Italy
Edremit 116 A 3 NW Turkey
Edward, Lake 77 E 6 *var.* Albert
Edward Nyanza, Edward
Nyanza, Lac Idi Amin, Lake
Rutanzige, Lake Edward/Zaire
Eeklo 87 B 5 *var.* Eekloo. NW
Belgium
Eekloo *see* Eeklo
Eems *see* Ems
Eersel 87 D 5 S Netherlands
Éfaté 144 D 4 *Fr.* Vaté; *prev.*
Sandwich Islands. Island group,
C Vanuatu
Effingham 40 B 4 Illinois, N USA
Eforie Sud 108 D 5 E Romania
Efstrátios, Ágios 104 D 4 *var.* Ayios
Evstrátios. Island, E Greece
Egadi, Isole 97 B 7 island group, S
Italy
Eger 99 D 6 *Ger.* Erlau. NE Hungary
Eger *see* Cheb
Éghezèe 87 C 6 C Belgium

Egiyn Gol 126 D 2 *var.* Egiyn Gul.
River, N Mongolia
Egiyn Gul *see* Egiyn Gol
Egmont *see* Taranaki, Mount
Egmont, Cape 150 C 4 headland,
North Island, C New Zealand

Egypt
72 B 2 *Ar.* Jumhūrīyah Miṣr al
'Arabīyah; *prev.* United Arab
Republic, *anc.* Aegyptus.
Republic, NE Africa

Official name: Arab Republic of
Egypt **Date of formation:** 1936
Capital: Cairo **Population:** 56.1
million **Total area:** 1,001,450 sq km
(386,660 sq miles) **Languages:**
Arabic*, French, English **Religions:**
Muslim 94%, other 6% **Ethnic mix:**
Eastern Hamitic 90%, other 10%
Government: Multiparty republic
Currency: Pound = 100 piastres

Eibar 93 E 1 N Spain
Eibergen 86 E 3 E Netherlands
Eidfjord 85 A 5 S Norway
Eifel 95 A 5 plateau, W Germany
Eigg 88 B 3 island, W Scotland, UK
Eight Degree Channel 132 B 3
channel, N Indian Ocean
Eighty Miles Beach 146 B 3 beach,
Western Australia, W Australia
Eijsden 87 D 6 SE Netherlands
Eindhoven 87 D 5 S Netherlands
Eisenhüttenstadt 94 D 4 E
Germany
Eisleben 94 C 4 C Germany
Eivissa 93 G 3 *var.* Iviza, *Cast.* Ibiza;
anc. Ebusus. Island, E Spain
Eivissa 93 G 4 *var.* Iviza, *Cast.* Ibiza;
anc. Ebusus. Island, E Spain
Ejea de los Caballeros 93 F 2 NE
Spain
Ekiatapskiy Khrebet 115 G 1
mountain range, NE Russian
Federation
El' Alamein 72 B 1 *var.* Al
'Alamayn. N Egypt
Elat 119 B 8 *var.* Eilat, Elath. S Israel
Elâzığ 117 E 3 *var.* Elâziz. E Turkey
Elâziz *see* Elâzığ
Elba, Isola d' 96 B 4 island, C Italy
Elbasan 101 C 6 *var.* Elbasani. C
Albania
Elbasani *see* Elbasan
Elbe 94 C 3 *Cz.* Labe River, Czech
Republic/Germany
Elbert, Mount 44 C 4 mountain,
Colorado, C USA
Elblag 98 D 2 *var.* Elblag, *Ger.*
Elbing. N Poland
El'brus 111 B 8 *var.* Gora El'brus.
Mountain, SW Russian Federation
El'brus, Gora *see* El'brus
El Burgo de Osma 93 E 2 C Spain
Elburz Mountains *see* Alborz,
Reshteh-ye Kūhhā-ye
El Calafate 65 B 7 *var.* Calafate. S
Argentina
El Callao 59 F 2 E Venezuela
El Campo 49 G 4 Texas, S USA
El Carmen de Bolívar 58 B 2 NW
Colombia
El Centro 47 D 8 California, W USA
Elche 93 F 4 *var.* Elx- Elche; *anc.*
Ilici, *Lat.* Illicis. E Spain
Elda 93 F 4 E Spain
El Djelfa *see* Djelfa
El Dorado 50 D 3 C Mexico
El Dorado 45 F 5 Kansas, C USA
El Dorado 59 F 2 E Venezuela
Eldorado 64 E 3 NE Argentina

Eldoret 73 C 6 W Kenya
Elektrostal' 111 B 5 W Russian
Federation
Elephant Butte Reservoir 48 C 2
reservoir, New Mexico, SW USA
Éleṣd *see* Aleṣd
Eleuthera Island 54 C 1 island, N
Bahamas
El Fasher 72 A 4 *var.* Al Fāshir. W
Sudan
Elgin 88 C 3 UK
Elgin 40 B 3 Illinois, N USA
El Giza 72 B 1 *var.* Al Jīzah, Gîza,
Gizeh. N Egypt
El Goléa 70 D 3 *var.* Al Golea. C
Algeria
El Hank 68 A 3 desert ,
Mali/Mauritania
El Hank 74 D 1 cliff, S Mauritania
El Hasaheisa 72 C 4 *var.* Al
Hasahisa, Al Ḥuṣayḥiṣah,
Hasaheisa. C Sudan
Élisabethville *see* Lubumbashi
Elista 111 B 7 SW Russian
Federation
Elizabeth 149 B 6 South Australia, S
Australia
Elizabeth City 43 G 1 North
Carolina, SE USA
Elizabethtown 40 C 5 Kentucky, E
USA
El-Jadida 70 C 2 *prev.* Mazagan. W
Morocco
Ełk 98 E 2 *Ger.* Lyck. NE Poland
Elk City 49 F 1 Oklahoma, C USA
Elkford 37 E 5 Alberta, SW Canada
El Khârga 72 B 2 *var.* Al Khārijah. C
Egypt
Elkhart 40 C 3 Indiana, N USA
Elk River 45 F 2 Minnesota, N USA
Ellef Ringnes Island 37 F 1 island,
N Canada
Ellen, Mount 44 B 5 mountain,
Utah, W USA
Ellensburg 46 B 2 Washington, NW
USA
Ellesmere Island 37 F 1 island, N
Canada
Ellice Islands, The *see* Tuvalu
Elliston 149 A 6 South Australia, S
Australia
Ellsworth Land 154 A 3 physical
region, Antarctica
El Mina 118 B 4 *var.* Al Mīnā'. N
Lebanon
El Minya 72 B 2 *var.* Al Minyā,
Minya. C Egypt
Elmira 41 E 3 New York, NE USA
El Mreyyé 74 D 2 desert, E
Mauritania
Elmshorn 94 B 3 N Germany
El Muglad 72 B 4 C Sudan
El Obeid 72 B 4 *var.* Al Obayyid, Al
Ubayyiḍ. C Sudan
El Oued 71 E 2 *var.* Al Oued, El
Ouâdi, El Wad. NE Algeria
Eloy 48 B 3 Arizona, SW USA
El Paso 48 D 3 Texas, S USA
El Porvenir 53 G 4 N Panama
El Progreso 52 C 2 NW Honduras
El Puerto de Santa María 92 B 5 S
Spain
El Quweira *see* Al Quwayrah
El Rama 53 E 3 SE Nicaragua
El Real 53 H 5 *var.* El Real de Santa
María. SE Panama
El Real de Santa María *see* El Real
El Reno 49 F 1 Oklahoma, C USA

El Salvador
52 B 3 Republic, W Central
America

Official name: Republic of El
Salvador **Date of formation:** 1856
Capital: San Salvador **Population:**
5.4 million **Total area:** 21,040 sq km
(8,124 sq miles) **Languages:**
Spanish*, Nahua **Religions:** Roman
Catholic 75%, other 25% **Ethnic mix:**
mestizo (Euro-Indian) 89%,
Indian 10%, White 1%
Government: Multiparty republic
Currency: Colón = 100 centavos

El Serrat 91 A 7 N Andorra
Elst 86 D 4 E Netherlands
Eltanin Fracture Zone 153 E 5
fracture zone, SE Pacific Ocean
El Tigre 59 E 2 NE Colombia
Elva 106 D 3 *Ger.* Elwa. SE Estonia
Elvas 92 C 4 C Portugal
El Vendrell 93 G 2 NE Spain
El Vigía 58 C 2 NW Venezuela
Elwa *see* Elva
Elwell, Lake 44 B 1 reservoir,
Montana, NW USA
El Yopal *see* Yopal
Emajõgi 106 D 3 *Ger.* Embach.
River, SE Estonia
Emámrúd 120 D 2 *prev.* Shāhrūd. N
Iran
Emba 114 B 4 *Kaz.* Embi. W
Kazakhstan
Embach *see* Emajõgi
Embi *see* Emba
Emden 94 A 3 NW Germany
Emerald 148 D 4 Queensland, E
Australia
Emerald Isle *see* Montserrat
Emi Koussi 68 C 3 mountain, N
Chad
Emmaste 106 C 2 Hiiumaa, W
Estonia
Emmeloord 86 D 2 N Netherlands
Emmen 86 E 2 NE Netherlands
Emmendingen 95 A 6 SW Germany
Empalme 50 B 3 NW Mexico
Emperor Seamounts 152 C 1
seamount range, NW Pacific
Ocean
Emporia 45 F 5 Kansas, C USA
Ems 94 A 3 *Dut.* Eems. River,
Germany
Encamp 91 A 8 C Andorra
Encarnación 64 D 3 S Paraguay
Encinitas 47 C 8 California, W USA
Encs 99 D 6 NE Hungary
Endeavour 55 G 1 NW Barbados
Endeavour Strait 148 C 1 strait,
Arafura Sea/Coral Sea
Enderbury Island 145 F 3 island, C
Kiribati
Enderby Land 154 D 2 physical
region, Antarctica
Enderby Plain 154 D 1 abyssal
plain, S Indian Ocean
Endersdorf *see* Jędrzejów
Enewetak Atoll 144 C 1 *var.*
Ānewetak, Eniwetok. Island, W
Marshall Islands
Enghien 87 B 6 *Dut.* Edingen. SW
Belgium
England 89 D 6 *Lat.* Anglia.
National region, UK
Englewood 44 D 4 Colorado, C
USA
English Channel 90 B 2 *var.* The
Channel, *Fr.* la Manche. Channel,
NE Atlantic Ocean
Engure 106 C 3 W Latvia
Engures Ezers 106 C 3 lake, NW
Latvia
Enguri 117 F 1 *Rus.* Inguri. River,
NW Georgia
En Hazeva 119 B 7 S Israel
Enid 49 F 1 Oklahoma, C USA

En Nâqoûra 119 A 5 *var.* An
Nāqūrah. SW Lebanon
Ennedi 76 D 2 plateau, E Chad
Ennis 89 A 6 *Ir.* Inis. W Ireland
Ennis 49 G 3 Texas, S USA
Enniskillen 89 A 5 *var.* Inniskilling,
Ir. Inis Ceithleann. S Northern
Ireland, UK
Enns 95 D 6 river, C Austria
Enschede 86 E 3 E Netherlands
Ensenada 50 A 1 NW Mexico
Ensley 42 C 3 Florida, SE USA
Entebbe 73 B 6 S Uganda
Entre Vientos 65 B 8 Chile
Entroncamento 92 B 3 C Portugal
Enugu 75 G 5 S Nigeria
Eolie, Isole 97 D 6 *var.* Isole Lipari,
Eng. Lipari Islands, Aeolian
Islands. Island group, S Italy
Epanomí 104 B 4 N Greece
Epéna 77 C 5 NE Congo
Épi 144 D 4 island, C Vanuatu
Épinal 90 D 4 NE France
Epoon *see* Ebon Atoll

Equatorial Guinea
77 A 5 Guinea. Republic, C
Africa

Official name: Republic of
Equatorial Guinea **Date of
formation:** 1968 **Capital:** Malabo
Population: 400,000 **Total area:**
28,050 sq km (10,830 sq miles)
Languages: Spanish*, Fang
Religions: Christian 89%, other 11%
Ethnic mix: Fang 72%, Bubi 14%,
Duala 3%, other 11% **Government:**
Multiparty republic **Currency:**
CFA franc = 100 centimes

Eravur 132 D 3 E Sri Lanka
Erciş 117 F 3 E Turkey
Erdenet 127 F 2 SE Mongolia
Erdenet 127 E 2 C Mongolia
Erdi 76 D 2 plateau, NE Chad
Erdi Ma 76 D 2 desert, NE Chad
Erebus, Mount 154 C 4 mountain,
Antarctica
Ereğli 116 B 2 NW Turkey
Ereğli 116 C 4 S Turkey
Erenhot 127 F 2 *var.* Erlian. NE
China
Erfurt 94 C 4 C Germany
Ergene 116 A 2 *var.* Ergene Irmaëi.
River, NW Turkey
Ergene Irmağı *see* Ergene
Erg Iguid 70 C 3 *var.* Erg Iguîdi.
Desert , Algeria/ Mauritania
Erg Iguîdi *see* Erg Iguid
Erguig, Bahr 76 C 3 river, SW Chad
Ergun 127 F 1 river, N China
Ergun Zuoqi 127 F 1 N China
Erie 41 E 3 Pennsylvania, NE USA
Érié, Lac *see* Erie, Lake
Erie, Lake 40 D 3 *Fr.* Lac Érié. Lake,
Canada/USA

Eritrea
72 C 4 Transitional government,
NE Africa

Official name: State of Eritrea **Date
of formation:** 1993 **Capital:** Asmara
Population: 3.5 million **Total area:**
93,680 sq km (36,170 sq miles)
Languages: Tigrinya*, Arabic*, Tigre
Religions: Coptic Christian 45%,
Muslim 45%, other 10% **Ethnic
mix:** Nine main Ethnic
groups **Government:** Provisional
military government
Currency: Ethiopian birr = 100 cents

Erivan *see* Yerevan

Erlangen 95 C 5 S Germany
Erlau see Eger
Erlian see Erenhot
Ermelo 86 D 3 C Netherlands
Ermióni 105 C 6 S Greece
Ermoúpoli 105 D 6 var.
Hermoupolis; prev. Ermoúpolis.
Kykládes, SE Greece
Ernākulam 132 C 3 SW India
Erode 132 C 2 SE India
Erquelinnes 87 B 7 S Belgium
Er-Rachidia 70 C 2 var. al Raudia,
Ksar al Soule. E Morocco
Er Rahad 72 B 4 var. Ar Rahad. C
Sudan
Erromango 144 D 4 island, S
Vanuatu
Erzerum see Erzurum
Erzgebirge 95 D 5 var. Krušné Hory,
Eng. Ore Mountains. Mountain
range, Czech Republic/Germany
Erzincan 117 E 3 var. Erzinjan. E
Turkey
Erzinjan see Erzincan
Erzurum 117 E 3 prev. Erzerum. NE
Turkey
Esbjerg 85 A 7 W Denmark
Esbo see Espoo
Escaldes 91 A 8 C Andorra
Escanaba 40 C 2 Michigan, N USA
Escárcega 51 G 4 SE Mexico
Esch-sur-Alzette 87 D 8 S
Luxembourg
Escondido 47 C 8 California, W
USA
Escuinapa 50 C 4 var. Escuinapa de
Hidalgo. C Mexico
Escuinapa de Hidalgo see Escuinapa
Escuintla 51 G 5 SE Mexico
Escuintla 52 B 3 S Guatemala
Eşfahān 120 D 3 Eng. Isfahan; anc.
Aspadana. C Iran
Esil see Ishim
Eskimo Point see Arviat
Eskişehir 116 B 3 var. Eskishehr. W
Turkey
Eskishehr see Eskişehir
Esla, Embalse de 92 C 2 var.
Embalse de Elsa. Reservoir, NW
Spain
Eslāmābād 120 C 3 var. Eslāmābād-
e Gharb; prev. Shāhābād,
Harunabad. W Iran
Esmeraldas 60 A 1 N Ecuador
Esna see Isna
Espanola 48 D 1 New Mexico, SW
USA
Esperance 147 C 7 Western
Australia, SW Australia
Esperanza 50 B 2 NW Mexico
Esperanza 154 A 2 research station,
Antarctica
Esperanza 60 D 3 E Peru
Espinal 58 B 3 C Colombia
Espinhaço, Serra do 63 F 3
mountain range, SE Brazil
Espírito Santo 63 G 4 off. Estado do
Espírito Santo. State, SE Brazil
Espírito Santo, Estado do see
Espírito Santo
Espiritu Santo 144 C 4 var. Santo.
Island, W Vanuatu
Espoo 85 D 6 Swe. Esbo. S Finland
Esquel 65 B 6 SW Argentina
Essaouira 70 B 2 prev. Mogador. W
Morocco
Es Semara see Smara
Essen 94 A 4 var. Essen an der
Ruhr. W Germany
Essen 87 C 5 N Belgium
Essen an der Ruhr see Essen

Essequibo 56 C 2 river, C Guyana
Estacado, Llano 49 E 2 plain, SW
USA
Estados, Isla de los 65 C 8 prev
Eng. Staten Island. Island, S
Argentina
Estância 63 G 3 E Brazil
Estelí 52 D 3 NW Nicaragua
Estella 93 E 1 N Spain
Estepona 92 D 5 S Spain
Estevan 37 F 5 Saskatchewan, S
Canada

Estonia
106 D 2 Est. Eesti Vabariik, Ger.
Estland, Latv. Igaunija; prev.
Estonian SSR, Rus. Estonskaya
SSR. Republic, E Europe

Official name: Republic of Estonia
Date of formation: 1991 **Capital:**
Tallinn **Population:** 1.6 million **Total
area:** 45,125 sq km (17,423 sq miles)
Languages: Estonian*, Russian
Religions: Evangelical Lutheran
98%, Eastern Orthodox, Baptist 2%
Ethnic mix: Estonian 62%, Russian
30%, Ukrainian 3%, other 5%
Government: Multiparty republic
Currency: Kroon = 100 cents

Estrela, Serra da 92 C 3 mountain
range, C Portugal
Estremoz 92 B 4 C Portugal
Esztergom 99 C 6 Ger. Gran; anc.
Strigonium. N Hungary
Etāwah 134 D 3 N India

Ethiopia
73 C 5 var. Abyssinia; prev.
People's Democratic Republic of
Ethiopia. Republic, NE Africa

Official name: Undetermined **Date
of formation:** 1993 **Capital:**
Addis Ababa **Population:** 51 million
Total area: 1,128,221 sq km
(435,605 sq miles) **Languages:**
Amharic*, English, Arabic
Religions: Muslim 43%, Christian
37%, traditional beliefs, other 20%,
Ethnic mix: Oromo 40%, Amhara
and Tigrean 32%, other 28%
Government: Multiparty republic
Currency: Birr = 100 cents

Ethiopian Highlands see Ethiopian
Plateau
Ethiopian Plateau 73 C 5 var.
Ethiopian Highlands. Plateau, N
Ethiopia
Etna, Monte 97 C 7 Eng. Mount
Etna. Volcano, SW Italy
Etna, Mount see Etna, Monte
Etosha Pan 78 B 3 salt lake, N
Namibia
Etoumbi 77 B 5 NW Congo
Etsch see Adige
Ettelbrück 87 D 8 C Luxembourg
'Eua 145 E 5 prev. Middleburg
Island. Island, S Tonga
Euboea see Évvoia
Eucla 147 D 6 Western Australia, S
Australia
Euclid 40 D 3 Ohio, N USA
Eufaula 42 D 3 Alabama, S USA
Eufaula Lake 49 G 1 var. Eufaula
Reservoir. Reservoir, Oklahoma,
C USA
Eufaula Reservoir see Eufaula Lake
Eugene 46 B 3 Oregon, NW USA
Eunice 42 B 3 Louisiana, S USA
Eupen 87 D 6 E Belgium
Euphrates 120 C 3 var. Firat Nehri,
Al-Furat. River, SW Asia

Eureka 37 F 1 Ellesmere Island,
Canada
Eureka 47 A 5 California, W USA
Eureka 44 A 1 Montana, NW USA
Europa Point 93 H 5 headland, S
Gibraltar
Europe 66 E 3 continent
Euskirchen 95 A 5 W Germany
Eutin 94 C 2 N Germany
Evansdale 45 G 3 Iowa, C USA
Evanston 40 B 3 Illinois, N USA
Evanston 44 B 4 Wyoming, C USA
Evansville 40 B 5 Indiana, N USA
Eveleth 45 G 1 Minnesota, N USA
Everard, Lake 149 A 6 salt lake, S
Australia
Everest, Mount 124 C 3 Chin.
Qomolangma Feng, Nep.
Sagarmatha. Mountain,
China/Nepal
Everett 46 B 2 Washington, NW
USA
Everglades, The 43 E 5 wetland,
Florida, SE USA
Evje 85 A 6 S Norway
Évora 92 B 4 Lat. Liberalitas Julia,
anc. Ebora. C Portugal
Évreux 90 C 3 anc. Civitas
Eburovicum. N France
Évry 90 C 3 N France
Evstratios, Ayios see Efstrátios,
Ágios
Évvoia 105 C 5 Lat. Euboea. Island,
Kykládes, C Greece
Ewarton 54 B 5 C Jamaica
Excelsior Springs 45 F 4 Missouri,
C USA
Exe 89 C 7 river, SW England, UK
Exeter 89 C 7 anc. Isca
Damnoniorum. SW England, UK
Exmoor 89 C 7 heathland, SW
England, UK
Exmouth 89 C 7 SW England, UK
Exmouth 146 A 4 Western
Australia, W Australia
Exmouth Gulf 146 A 4 gulf, W
Indian Ocean
Exmouth Plateau 141 E 5 undersea
plateau, E Indian Ocean
Extremadura 92 C 3 cultural region,
W Spain
Exuma Cayes 54 C 1 island group,
C Bahamas
Eyre 147 D 6 Western Australia, W
Australia
Eyre Mountains 151 A 7 mountain
range, South Island, SW New
Zealand
Eyre North, Lake 149 B 5 salt lake,
S Australia
Eyre Peninsula 149 A 6 peninsula,
S Australia
Eyre South, Lake 149 B 5 salt lake,
S Australia
Ezequiel Ramos Mexía, Embalse 65
B 5 lake, C Argentina

F

Faadhippolhu Atoll 132 B 4 var.
Fadiffolu, Lhaviyani Atoll. Island,
N Maldives
Fabens 48 D 3 Texas, S USA
Fada 76 C 2 E Chad
Fada-Ngourma 75 E 4 E Burkina
Fadghāmī see Tall Fadghāmī
Faenza 96 C 3 anc. Faventia. N Italy
Faeroe-Iceland Ridge 80 C 1
undersea ridge, NW Norwegian
Sea
Faeroe Islands 83 F 5 Dan.
Færøerne, Faer. Føroyar. Danish
external territory, N Atlantic
Ocean

Faeroe Islands 66 D 2 island group,
NE Atlantic Ocean
Faetano 96 E 2 E San Marino
Făgăraş 108 C 4 Ger. Fogarasch,
Hung. Fogaras. C Romania
Fagibina, Lake see Faguibine, Lac
Fagne 87 C 7 hill range, S Belgium
Faguibine, Lac 75 E 3 var. Lake
Fagibina. Lake, NW Mali
Fahlun see Falun
Fahraj 120 E 4 SE Iran
Faial 92 A 5 var. Ilha do Faial.
Island, W Portugal
Faial, Ilha do see Faial
Faifo see Hôi An
Fairbanks 36 C 3 Alaska, NW USA
Fairfield 47 B 6 California, W USA
Fair Isle 88 D 2 island, NE
Scotland, UK
Fairlie 151 B 6 South Island, SW
New Zealand
Fairmont 45 F 3 Minnesota, N USA
Faisalābād 134 C 2 prev. Lyallpur.
NE Pakistan
Faizābād 135 E 3 N India
Fakaofo Atoll 145 F 3 island, SE
Tokelau
Falam 136 A 3 NW Burma
Falconara Marittima 96 C 3 C Italy
Falkland Islands 65 C 7 island
group, SW Atlantic Ocean
Falkland Plateau 57 D 7 var.
Argentine Rise. Undersea plateau,
SW Atlantic Ocean
Fallbrook 47 C 8 California, W USA
Falmouth 89 C 8 SW England, UK
Falmouth 54 A 4 W Jamaica
Falster 85 B 8 island, SE Denmark
Fālticeni 108 C 3 Hung. Falticsén.
NE Romania
Falticsén see Fălticeni
Falun 85 C 5 var. Fahlun. C Sweden
Famenne 87 C 7 physical region, SE
Belgium
Fang 136 C 3 N Thailand
Fanling 128 A 1 N Hong Kong
Fanning Island see Tabuaeran
Fano 96 C 3 anc. Fanum Fortunae,
Colonia Julia Fanestris. C Italy
Farafangana 79 G 4 SE Madagascar
Farafra Oasis 72 B 2 var. Wāhat el
Faráfra. Oasis, C Egypt
Faráfra, Wāhat el see Farafra Oasis
Farāh 122 D 4 var. Farah, Fararud.
W Afghanistan
Faranah 74 C 4 S Guinea
Farewell, Cape 150 C 4 headland,
South Island, C New Zealand
Farghona 123 F 3 var. Fergana;
prev. Novyy Margilan . E
Uzbekistan
Fargo 45 F 2 North Dakota, N USA
Faribault 45 F 3 Minnesota, N USA
Farīdābād 134 D 3 N India
Farkhor 123 E 3 Rus. Parkhar. SW
Tajikistan
Farmington 48 C 1 New Mexico,
SW USA
Farmington 45 G 5 Missouri, C
USA
Faro 92 B 5 S Portugal
Farquhar Group 79 G 2 island
group, S Seychelles
Fastiv 109 E 2 Rus. Fastov. NW
Ukraine
Fastov see Fastiv
Fauske 84 C 3 C Norway
Faventia see Faenza
Faxa Bay see Faxaflói
Faxaflói 83 E 5 Eng. Faxa Bay. Bay,
N Atlantic Ocean

Faya 76 C 2 *prev.* Faya-Largeau, Largeau. N Chad
Fayetteville 42 A 1 Arkansas, SE USA
Fayetteville 43 F 1 North Carolina, SE USA
Fazzān 71 F 4 *Eng.* Fezzan. Cultural region, W Libya
Færingehavn 82 B 4 *var.* Kangerluarsoruseq. S Greenland
Fdérik 74 C 2 *var.* Fdérick, Fderik, *Fr.* Fort Gouraud. NW Mauritania
Fear, Cape 43 F 2 headland, North Carolina, SE USA
Fécamp 90 B 3 N France
Fédala *see* Mohammedia
Federal Capital Territory *see* Australian Capital Territory
Fehérgyarmat 99 E 6 E Hungary
Fehmarn 94 C 2 island, N Germany
Feijó 62 C 2 W Brazil
Feilding 150 D 4 North Island, C New Zealand
Feira *see* Feira de Santana
Feira de Santana 63 G 3 *var.* Feira. E Brazil
Felanitx 93 H 3 *anc.* Canati, Felaniche. E Spain
Feldkirchen in Kärnten 95 D 7 *Slvn.* Trg. S Austria
Félegyháza *see* Kiskunfélegyháza
Felidhu Atoll 132 B 4 island, C Maldives
Felipe Carrillo Puerto 51 H 4 SE Mexico
Felixstowe 89 E 6 E England, UK
Fellin *see* Viljandi
Femerbælt 94 C 2 *Dan.* Femer Bælt, *Ger.* Fehmarnbelt. Channel, SW Baltic Sea
Femunden 85 B 5 lake, S Norway
Fénérive *see* Fenoarivo Atsinanana
Fengcheng 128 D 3 *var.* Feng-ch eng, *Jap.* Fenghwangcheng. NE China
Fenoarivo Atsinanana 79 G 3 *prev.* Fénérive. NE Madagascar
Fens, The 89 E 6 wetland, E England, UK
Feodosiya 109 G 5 *var.* Kefe, *It.* Kaffa; *anc.* Theodosia. S Ukraine
Féres 104 D 3 NE Greece
Fergus Falls 45 F 2 Minnesota, N USA
Ferizaj *see* Uroševac
Fernandina, Isla 60 A 5 *var.* Narborough Island. Island, Galapagos Islands, E Pacific Ocean
Fernando de la Mora 64 D 2 S Paraguay
Fernando de Noronha 63 H 2 island, E Brazil
Ferrara 96 C 2 *anc.* Forum Alieni. N Italy
Ferrol 92 B 1 *var.* El Ferrol; *prev.* El Ferrol del Caudillo. NW Spain
Fertő *see* Neusiedler See
Fès 70 C 2 *Eng.* Fez. N Morocco
Fethiye 116 B 4 SW Turkey
Fetlar 88 D 1 island, NE Scotland, UK
Feyzābād 123 F 3 *var.* Faizabad, Faizābād, Feyzābād, Fyzabad. NE Afghanistan
Fez *see* Fès
Fezzan *see* Fazzān
Fianarantsoa 79 F 3 C Madagascar
Fianga 76 B 4 SW Chad
Fier 101 C 6 *var.* Fieri, SW Albania
Fieri *see* Fier
Figeac 91 C 5 S France

Figig *see* Figuig
Figueira da Foz 92 B 3 W Portugal
Figueres 93 G 2 E Spain
Figuig 70 D 2 *var.* Figig. E Morocco
Fiji
145 E 5 *Fij.* Viti. Republic, SW Pacific Ocean
Official name: Sovereign Democratic Republic of Fiji **Date of formation:** 1970 **Capital:** Suva **Population:** 700,000 **Total Area:** 18,270 sq km (7,054 sq miles) **Languages:** English*, Fijian, Hindu, Urdu, Tamil, Telugu **Religions:** Christian 52%, Hindu 8%, Muslim 8%, other 2% **Ethnic mix:** Native Fijian 49%, Indo-Fijian 46%, other 5% **Government:** Multiparty republic **Currency:** Fiji $ = 100 cents

Filadelfia 52 D 4 W Costa Rica
Filiaşi 108 B 5 SW Romania
Filipstad 85 B 6 C Sweden
Finale Ligure 96 A 3 Italy
Findlay 40 D 4 Ohio, N USA
Finike 116 B 4 SW Turkey
Finland
84 D 4 *Fin.* Suomen Tasavalta, Suomi. Republic, N Europe
Official name: Republic of Finland **Date of formation:** 1917 **Capital:** Helsinki **Population:** 5 million **Total Area:** 338,130 sq km (130,552 sq miles) **Languages:** Finnish*, Swedish, Lappish **Religions:** Evangelical Lutheran 89%, Greek Orthodox 1%, other 10% **Ethnic mix:** Finnish 93%, Swedish 6%, other (inc. Sami)1% **Government:** Multiparty republic **Currency:** Markka = 100 pennia

Finland, Gulf of 85 E 6 *Est.* Soome Laht, *Fin.* Suomenlahti, *Ger.* Finnischer Meerbusen, *Rus.* Finskiy Zaliv, *Swe.* Finska Viken. Gulf, Atlantic Ocean/Baltic Sea
Finnmarksvidda 84 D 2 physical region, N Norway
Finsterwalde 94 D 4 E Germany
Fiorina 96 E 1 NE San Marino
Firenze 96 C 3 *Eng.* Florence; *anc.* Florentia. C Italy
Fischbacher Alpen 95 E 7 mountain range, E Austria
Fischhausen *see* Primorsk
Fish 78 B 4 *var.* Vis. River, S Namibia
Fishguard 89 B 6 *Wel.* Abergwaun. SW Wales, UK
Fiskenæsset *see* Qeqertarsuatsiaat
Fisterra, Cabo 92 B 1 headland, NW Spain
Fitzgerald 43 E 3 Georgia, SE USA
Fitzroy 146 C 3 river, Western Australia, N Australia
Fitzroy Crossing 146 C 3 Western Australia, NW Australia
Flagstaff 48 B 2 Arizona, SW USA
Flanders 87 A 6 *Dut.* Vlaanderen, *Fr.* Flandre. Cultural region, Belgium/France
Flathead Lake 44 B 1 lake, Montana, NW USA
Flatts Village 42 B 5 *var.* The Flatts Village. C Bermuda
Flensburg 94 B 2 N Germany
Flinders 148 C 3 river, N Australia
Flinders Bay 147 A 7 bay, SE Indian Ocean

Flinders Island 149 C 8 island, Tasmania, SE Australia
Flinders Island 149 A 6 island, South Australia, S Australia
Flinders Ranges 149 B 6 mountain range, S Australia
Flinders Reefs 148 D 3 reef, W Coral Sea
Flin Flon 37 F 5 Manitoba, C Canada
Flint 40 D 3 Michigan, N USA
Flint Island 145 H 4 island, E Kiribati
Florence 43 F 2 South Carolina, SE USA
Florencia 58 B 4 S Colombia
Flores 92 A 5 island, W Portugal
Flores 52 B 1 N Guatemala
Flores 139 E 5 island, Nusa Tenggara, C Indonesia
Flores, Laut 139 E 5 *Eng.* Flores Sea. Sea, W Pacific Ocean
Flores Sea *see* Flores, Laut
Floriano 63 F 2 E Brazil
Florianópolis 63 F 5 *prev.* Destêrro. State capital, S Brazil
Florida 43 E 4 *off.* State of Florida; *nicknames* Peninsular State, Sunshine State. State, SE USA
Florida 64 D 4 S Uruguay
Florida Bay 43 E 5 bay, E Gulf of Mexico
Florida Keys 43 E 5 island, Florida, SE USA
Florida Negra 65 C 7 SE Argentina
Florida, Straits of 43 F 5 strait, W Atlantic Ocean
Flórina 104 B 4 *var.* Phlórina. N Greece
Florissant 45 G 4 Missouri, C USA
Floúda, Ákra 105 D 7 Headland, Astypálaia, SE Greece
Flylân *see* Vlieland
Foča 100 C 4 SE Bosnia & Herzegovina
Focşani 108 C 4 E Romania
Foggia 97 D 5 SE Italy
Fogi 139 F 4 E Indonesia
Fogo 74 A 3 island, SW Cape Verde
Foix 91 B 6 S France
Folégandros 105 C 7 island, Kykládes, SE Greece
Foleyet 38 C 4 Ontario, S Canada
Foligno 96 C 4 C Italy
Folkestone 89 E 7 SE England, UK
Folsom 47 B 5 California, W USA
Fond-du-Lac 37 F 4 Saskatchewan, C Canada
Fongafale 145 E 3 *var.* Funafuti. Country capital, Funafuti, C Tuvalu
Fonseca, Golfo de *see* Fonseca, Gulf of
Fonseca, Gulf of 52 C 3 *Sp.* Golfo de Fonseca. Gulf, E Pacific Ocean
Fontainebleau 90 C 3 N France
Fontenay-le-Comte 90 A 4 NW France
Fonyód 99 C 7 W Hungary
Forchheim 95 C 5 SE Germany
Forel, Mount 82 D 4 mountain, SE Greenland
Forfar 88 C 3 NE Scotland, UK
Forlì 96 C 3 *anc.* Forum Livii. N Italy
Formentera 93 G 4 *anc.* Ophiusa, *Lat.* Frumentum. Island, E Spain
Formosa 64 D 3 NE Argentina
Formosa Bay 73 D 7 *var.* Ungama Bay. Bay, NW Indian Ocean
Formosa, Serra 63 E 3 mountain range, C Brazil

Fort Albany 38 C 3 Ontario, C Canada
Fortaleza 63 G 2 *prev.* Ceará. State capital, NE Brazil
Fortaleza 61 F 2 N Bolivia
Fort-Archambault *see* Sarh
Fort Charlet *see* Djanet
Fort-Chimo *see* Kuujjuaq
Fort Collins 44 D 4 Colorado, C USA
Fort-Crampel *see* Kaga Bandoro
Fort-de-France 55 H 4 *prev.* Fort-Royal. Dependent territory capital, W Martinique
Fort Dodge 45 F 3 Iowa, C USA
Fortescue 146 B 4 river, W Australia
Fort Frances 38 B 4 Ontario, S Canada
Fort Good Hope 37 E 3 *var.* Good Hope. Northwest Territories, W Canada
Forth 88 C 4 river, S Scotland, UK
Forth, Firth of 88 D 4 estuary, NW North Sea
Fortín General Diaz 64 D 2 W Paraguay
Fort Jameson *see* Chipata
Fort Lauderdale 43 F 5 Florida, SE USA
Fort Liard 37 E 4 *var.* Liard. Northwest Territories, W Canada
Fort Madison 45 G 4 Iowa, C USA
Fort McMurray 37 F 4 Alberta, C Canada
Fort McPherson 36 D 3 *var.* McPherson. Northwest Territories, NW Canada
Fort Morgan 44 D 4 Colorado, C USA
Fort Myers 43 E 5 Florida, SE USA
Fort Nelson 37 E 4 British Columbia, W Canada
Fort Peck Lake 44 C 1 reservoir, Montana, NW USA
Fort Pierce 43 F 4 Florida, SE USA
Fort Providence 37 E 4 *var.* Providence. Northwest Territories, W Canada
Fort-Repoux *see* Akjoujt
Fort Rosebery *see* Mansa
Fort-Rousset *see* Owando
Fort-Royal *see* Fort-de-France
Fort St.John 37 E 5 British Columbia, W Canada
Fort Scott 45 F 5 Kansas, C USA
Fort Severn 38 C 2 Ontario, C Canada
Fort-Shevchenko 114 A 4 W Kazakhstan
Fort-Sibut *see* Sibut
Fort Simpson 37 E 4 *var.* Simpson. Northwest Territories, W Canada
Fort Smith 37 E 4 Northwest Territories, W Canada
Fort Smith 42 A 1 Arkansas, C USA
Fort Stockton 49 E 3 Texas, S USA
Fort Vermilion 37 E 4 Alberta, W Canada
Fort Walton Beach 42 D 3 Florida, SE USA
Fort Wayne 40 C 4 Indiana, N USA
Fort William 88 B 3 W Scotland, UK
Fort Worth 49 G 3 Texas, S USA
Fort Yukon 36 D 3 Alaska, NW USA
Forum Alieni *see* Ferrara
Forum Livii *see* Forlì
Fossa Claudia *see* Chioggia
Fougamou 77 A 6 C Gabon

Fougères 90 B 3 NW France
Foulwind, Cape 151 B 5 headland, South Island, C New Zealand
Foumban 76 A 4 NW Cameroon
Fouta Djallon 68 A 4 *var.* Futa Jallon. Mountain range, W Guinea
Foveaux Strait 151 A 8 strait, S Pacific Ocean
Fowlers Bay 147 E 6 bay, Great Australian Bight/Indian Ocean
Foxe Basin 82 B 2 undersea basin, NE Hudson Bay
Fox Mine 37 F 4 Manitoba, C Canada
Fraga 93 F 2 NE Spain

France
90 B 4 It./Sp. Francia; *prev.* Gaul, Gaule, *Lat.* Gallia. Republic, W Europe

Official name: The French Republic **Date of formation:** 1685 **Capital:** Paris **Population:** 57.4 million **Total area:** 551,500 sq km (212,930 sq miles) **Languages:** French*, Provençal, Breton, Catalan, Basque **Religions:** Roman Catholic 90%, Protestant 2%, Jewish 1%, other 7% **Ethnic mix:** French 92%, North African 3%, other 5% **Government:** Multiparty republic **Currency:** Franc = 100 centimes

Franceville 77 B 6 *var.* Massoukou, Masuku. E Gabon
Franche-Comté 90 D 4 cultural region, E France
Francis Case, Lake 45 E 3 reservoir, South Dakota, N USA
Francisco Beltrão 63 E 5 S Brazil
Francistown 78 D 3 NE Botswana
Frankfort 40 C 5 state capital, Kentucky, E USA
Frankfurt see Słubice
Frankfurt am Main 95 B 5 *var.* Frankfurt, *Fr.* Francfort; *prev. Eng.* Frankfort on the Main. SW Germany
Frankfurt an der Oder 94 D 3 E Germany
Fränkische Alb 95 C 6 *var.* Frankenalb, *Eng.* Franconian Jura. Mountain range, S Germany
Franklin 42 C 1 Tennessee, S USA
Franklin D.Roosevelt Lake 46 C 1 reservoir, Washington, NW USA
Frantsa-Iosifa, Zemlya 114 D 1 *Eng.* Franz Josef Land. Island group, N Russian Federation
Franz Josef Land see Frantsa-Iosifa, Zemlya
Fraserburgh 88 D 3 NE Scotland, UK
Fraser Island 148 E 4 *var.* Great Sandy Island island, E Australia
Frauenburg see Saldus
Frederick Reef 148 E 4 reef, W Coral Sea
Fredericksburg 41 E 5 Virginia, NE USA
Fredericton 39 F 4 New Brunswick, SE Canada
Frederiksdal see Narsaq Kujalleq
Fredrikshald see Halden
Fredrikstad 85 B 6 S Norway
Freeport 54 C 1 N Bahamas
Freeport 49 H 4 Texas, S USA
Freetown 74 C 4 country capital, W Sierra Leone
Freiburg im Breisgau 95 A 6 *var.* Freiburg, *Fr.* Fribourg-en-Brisgau. SW Germany

Fremantle 147 B 6 Western Australia, SW Australia
Fremont 47 B 6 California, W USA
Fremont 45 F 4 Nebraska, C USA
French Guiana 59 H 3 *var.* Guiana, Guyane. French overseas department, NE South America
French Polynesia 145 G 5 French overseas territory, S Pacific Ocean
French Southern & Antarctic Territories 141 C 6 *Fr.* Terres Australes et Antarctiques Françaises. French overseas territory, S Indian Ocean
Fresnillo 50 D 3 *var.* Fresnillo de Gonzales Echeverria, Fresnillo de González Echeverría. C Mexico
Fresno 47 C 6 California, W USA
Freyming-Merlebach 90 E 3 NE France
Frías 64 C 3 N Argentina
Friedek-Mistek see Frýdek-Místek
Friedrichshafen 95 B 7 S Germany
Frobisher Bay see Iqaluit
Frohavet 84 B 4 sound, SE Norwegian Sea
Frolovo 111 B 6 SW Russian Federation
Frome, Lake 149 B 6 salt lake, S Australia
Frontera 51 G 4 SE Mexico
Frontignan 91 C 6 S France
Frostviken see Kvarnbergsvattnet
Frøya 84 A 4 island, W Norway
Frutal 63 F 4 SE Brazil
Frýdek-Místek 99 C 5 *Ger.* Friedek-Mistek. SE Czech Republic
Fuengirola 92 D 5 S Spain
Fuerte Olimpo 64 D 2 *var.* Olimpo. NE Paraguay
Fuerteventura 70 B 3 island, Islas Canarias, SW Spain
Fuji 131 D 6 *var.* Huzi. Honshū, S Japan
Fujian 129 D 6 *var.* Fu-chien, Fuhkien, Fukien, Min. Province, SE China
Fuji-san 131 D 6 *var.* Fujiyama, Mount Fuji. Mountain, Honshū, SE Japan
Fukang 126 C 2 W China
Fukui 131 C 6 *var.* Hukui. Honshū, SW Japan
Fukuoka 131 A 7 *var.* Hukuoka; *hist.* Najima. Kyūshū, SW Japan
Fukushima 130 D 4 *var.* Hukusima. Honshū, C Japan
Fulda 95 B 5 C Germany
Funafuti 145 E 3 island, C Tuvalu
Funafuti see Fongafale
Funchal 70 A 2 Maderia, SW Portugal
Fundy, Bay of 39 F 5 inlet, NW Atlantic Ocean
Fünen see Fyn
Fung Wong Shan see Lantau Peak
Furnes see Veurne
Fürth 95 C 5 S Germany
Furukawa 130 D 4 *var.* Hurukawa. Honshū, C Japan
Fushun 128 D 3 *var.* Fou-shan, Fu-shun. NE China
Fuxin 128 D 3 *var.* Fou-hsin, Fu-hsin, Fusin. NE China
Fuzhou 129 D 6 *var.* Foochow, Fu-chou. Province capital, SE China
Fyn 85 B 8 *Ger.* Fünen. Island, C Denmark

G

Gaafu Alifu Atoll see North Huvadhu Atoll
Gaafu Dhaalu Atoll see South Huvadhu Atoll
Gaalkacyo 73 E 5 *var.* Galka'yo', *It.* Galcaio. C Somalia
Gabela 78 B 2 W Angola
Gaberones see Gaborone
Gabès 71 E 2 *var.* Qābis. E Tunisia
Gabès, Golfe de 71 F 2 *Ar.* Khalīj Qābis. Gulf, S Mediterranean Sea

Gabon
77 B 6 Republic, C Africa

Official name: The Gabonese Republic **Date of formation:** 1960 **Capital:** Libreville **Population:** 1.3 million **Total area:** 267,670 sq km (103,347 sq miles) **Languages:** French*, Fang **Religions:** Roman Catholic, other Christian 96%, Muslim 2%, other 2% **Ethnic mix:** Fang 36%, Mpongwe 15%, Mbete 14%, other 35% **Government:** Multiparty republic **Currency:** CFA franc = 100 centimes

Gaborone 78 C 4 *prev.* Gaberones. Country capital, SE Botswana
Gabrovo 104 D 2 C Bulgaria
Gadsden 42 D 2 Alabama, S USA
Gaeta 97 C 5 Italy
Gaeta, Golfo di 97 C 5 *var.* Gulf of Gaeta Gulf, E Tyrrhenian Sea
Gaeta, Gulf of see Gaeta, Golfo di
Gafsa 71 E 2 *var.* Qafşah. W Tunisia
Gagnoa 74 D 5 C Ivory Coast
Gagra 117 E 1 NW Georgia
Gaillac 91 C 6 *var.* Gaillac-sur-Tarn. S France
Gaillac-sur-Tarn see Gaillac
Gaillimh see Galway
Gaillimhe, Cuan na see Galway Bay
Gailtaler Alpen 95 D 7 mountain range, S Austria
Gainesville 42 D 2 Georgia, SE USA
Gainesville 43 E 3 Florida, SE USA
Gainesville 49 G 2 Texas, S USA
Gairdner, Lake 149 A 6 salt lake, S Australia
Gaiziņ see Gaizina Kalns
Gaizina Kalns 106 D 4 *var.* Gaiziņ. Mountain, E Latvia
Galán, Cerro 64 B 2 mountain, N Argentina
Galanta 99 C 6 *Hung.* Galánta. SW Slovakia
Galánta see Galanta
Galapagos Fracture Zone 153 E 3 fracture zone, E Pacific Ocean
Galapagos Islands 153 G 3 *var.* Archipiélago de Colón. island group, E Pacific Ocean
Galapagos Rise 153 F 3 undersea rise, E Pacific Ocean
Galashiels 88 D 4 SE Scotland, UK
Galaţi 108 D 5 *var.* Galatz. E Romania
Galatz see Galaţi
Galesburg 40 B 4 Illinois, N USA
Galibi 59 H 3 NE Surinam
Galicia 92 B 1 cultural region, NW Spain
Galiuro Mountains 48 B 3 mountain range, Arizona, SW USA
Gallatin 42 D 1 Tennessee, S USA
Galle 132 D 4 *prev.* Point de Galle. SW Sri Lanka

Gallego Rise 153 F 3 undersea rise, E Pacific Ocean
Gallipoli 97 E 6 SW Italy
Gällivare 84 D 3 N Sweden
Gallup 48 C 1 New Mexico, SW USA
Galveston 49 H 4 Texas, S USA
Galveston Bay 49 H 4 bay, N Gulf of Mexico
Galway 89 A 6 *Ir.* Gaillimh. W Ireland
Galway Bay 89 A 6 *Ir.* Cuan na Gaillimhe. Bay, NE Atlantic Ocean
Gámas see Kaamanen
Gambell 36 B 2 Saint Lawrence Island, Alaska, USA
Gambia 74 C 3 river, Gambia/Senegal

Gambia
74 B 3 Republic, W Africa

Official name: Republic of The Gambia **Date of formation:** 1965 **Capital:** Banjul **Population:** 900,000 **Total area:** 11,300 sq km (4,363 sq miles) **Languages:** English* **Religions:** Muslim 85%, Christian 9%, traditional beliefs 6% **Ethnic mix:** Mandinka 41%, Fulani 14%, Wolof 13%, other 32% **Government:** Military regime **Currency:** Dalasi = 100 butut

Gambier, Îles 153 E 4 island group, E French Polynesia
Gamboma 77 B 6 E Congo
Gan 132 B 5 Maldives
Gäncä 117 G 2 *Rus.* Gyandzha; *prev.* Kirovabad, Yelisavetpol. W Azerbaijan
Gandajika 77 D 7 S Zaire
Gander 39 G 3 Newfoundland and Labrador, SE Canada
Gandía 93 F 4 E Spain
Ganges 135 G 4 *Ben.* Padma. River, Bangladesh/India
Ganges Cone see Ganges Fan
Ganges Fan 140 D 3 *var.* Ganges Cone. Undersea fan, N Indian Ocean
Ganges, Mouths of the 135 G 4 delta, Bangladesh/India
Ganges Plain 124 C 3 plain, India/Pakistan
Gangtok 135 G 3 NE India
Gansu 128 B 4 *var.* Gan,Kansu. Province, N China
Ganzhou 129 C 6 S China
Gao 75 E 3 E Mali
Gaoligong Shan 136 B 1 mountain range, Burma/China
Gaoual 74 C 4 N Guinea
Gap 91 D 6 *anc.* Vapincum. SE France
Garabogazköl Bogazy see Kara-Bogaz-Gol, Proliv
Garachiné 53 G 5 SE Panama
Garagum Kanaly see Karakumskiy Kanal
Garagumy 122 C 3 *var.* Black Sand Desert, Qara Qum, *Eng.* Kara Kum, *Turkm.* Garagum; *prev.* Peski Karakumy. Desert, C Turkmenistan
Gara Khitrino 104 D 2 NE Bulgaria
Gárassavon see Kaaresuvanto
Garbsen 94 B 3 N Germany
Garda, Lago di 96 C 2 *var.* Benaco, *Eng.* Lake Garda, *Ger.* Gardasee. Lake, NE Italy

Garden City 45 E 5 Kansas, C USA
Gardēz 123 E 4 *var.* Gardeyz, Gardez, Gordiaz. E Afghanistan
Garegegasnjárga *see* Karigasniemi
Gargždai 106 B 3 W Lithuania
Garissa 73 D 6 E Kenya
Garland 49 G 2 Texas, S USA
Garmo, Qullai 123 F 3 *Eng.* Communism Peak, *Rus.* Kommunizma Pik; *prev.* Stalin Peak. Mountain, E Tajikistan
Garoe *see* Garoowe
Garonne 91 B 5 *anc.* Garumna. River, S France
Garoowe 73 E 5 *var.* Garoe. N Somalia
Garoua 76 B 4 *var.* Garua. N Cameroon
Garrygala *see* Kara-Kala
Garsen 73 D 6 SE Kenya
Garua *see* Garoua
Garumna *see* Garonne
Garwolin 98 D 4 E Poland
Gar Xincun 126 A 4 *var.* Gar. W China
Gary 40 B 3 Indiana, N USA
Garzón 58 B 4 S Colombia
Gascogne 91 B 6 *Eng.* Gascony. Cultural region, S France
Gascogne, Golfe de *see* Gascony, Gulf of
Gascony *see* Gascogne
Gascony, Gulf of 91 A 6 *var.* Golfe de Gascogne. Inlet, NE Atlantic Ocean
Gascoyne 147 B 5 river, W Australia
Gaspé 39 F 4 Québec, SE Canada
Gaspé, Péninsule de 39 F 4 *var.* Péninsule de la Gaspésie. Peninsula, Québec, SE Canada
Gaspésie, Péninsule de la *see* Gaspé, Péninsule de
Gastoúni 105 B 6 S Greece
Gatchina 110 B 4 *var.* Gatčina NW Russian Federation
Gatčina *see* Gatchina
Gatineau 38 D 4 Québec, SE Canada
Gatooma *see* Kadoma
Gatún, Lago 53 F 5 reservoir, C Panama
Gauhāti *see* Guwāhāti
Gauja 106 D 3 *Ger.* Aa. River, Latvia/Estonia
Gāvbandī 120 D 4 S Iran
Gavere 87 B 5 W Belgium
Gävle 85 C 5 *var.* Gäfle; *prev.* Gefle. C Sweden
Gawler 149 B 6 South Australia, S Australia
Gaya 135 F 4 N India
Gaya *see* Kyjov
Gaysin *see* Haysyn
Gaza 119 A 6 *Ar.* Ghazzah, *Heb.* 'Azza. NE Gaza Strip
Gaz-Achak 122 D 2 *Turkm.* Gazojak. NE Turkmenistan
Gazalkent *see* Ghazalkent
Gazandzhyk 122 B 2 *Turkm.* Gazanjyk; *prev.* Kazandzhik. W Turkmenistan
Gaza Strip 119 A 7 *Ar.* Qita Ghazzah. Disputed region, SW Asia
Gaziantep 116 D 4 *var.* Gazi Antep; *prev.* Aintab, Antep. S Turkey
Gazipaşa 116 C 5 Turkey
Gazli 122 D 2 C Uzbekistan
Gazojak *see* Gaz-Achak
Gdańsk 98 C 2 *Fr.* Dantzig, *Ger.* Danzig.

Gdynia 98 C 2 *Ger.* Gdingen. N Poland
Gedaref 72 C 4 *var.* Al Qadārif, El Gedaref. E Sudan
Gediz 116 A 3 river, W Turkey
Gediz 116 B 3 W Turkey
Geel 87 C 5 *var.* Gheel. N Belgium
Geelong 149 C 7 Victoria, SE Australia
Geilo 85 A 5 S Norway
Gejiu 129 B 6 *var.* Kochiu. S China
Gela 97 C 7 *prev.* Terranova di Sicilia. SW Italy
Geldermalsen 86 C 4 C Netherlands
Geleen 87 D 6 SE Netherlands
Gelib *see* Jilib
Gelinsoor *see* Gellinsoor
Gellinsoor 73 E 5 *var.* Gelinsoor. C Somalia
Gembloux 87 C 6 C Belgium
Gemena 77 C 5 NW Zaire
Gemerek 116 D 3 Turkey
Gemona del Friuli 96 D 2 NE Italy
Genck *see* Genk
General Alvear 64 B 4 W Argentina
General Carrera, Lago *see* Buenos Aires, Lago
General Eugenio A.Garay 64 C 1 NW Paraguay
General José F.Uriburu *see* Zárate
General Santos 139 F 3 *off.* General Santos City. Mindanao, SE Philippines
General Santos City *see* General Santos
Geneva, Lake 95 A 7 *var.* le Léman, *Fr.* Lac Léman, Lac de Genève, *Ger.* Genfer See. Lake, France/Switzerland
Genève 95 A 8 *Eng.* Geneva, *Ger.* Genf, *It.* Ginevra. SW Switzerland
Genichesk *see* Heniches'k
Genk 87 D 6 *var.* Genck. NE Belgium
Gennep 86 D 4 SE Netherlands
Genoa *see* Genova
Genoa, Gulf of *see* Genova, Golfo di
Genova 96 A 2 *Eng.* Genoa, *Fr.* Gênes, *anc.* Genua. NW Italy
Genova, Golfo di 96 A 3 *Eng.* Gulf of Genoa. Gulf, N Ligurian Sea
Genovesa, Isla 60 B 5 *var.* Tower Island. Island, Galapagos Islands, E Pacific Ocean
Gent 87 B 5 *Eng.* Ghent, *Fr.* Gand. NW Belgium
Geographe Bay 147 A 7 bay, E Indian Ocean
Geok-Tepe 122 C 3 *var.* Gökdepe, *Turkm.* Gökdepe. C Turkmenistan
George, Lake 43 E 4 lake, Florida, SE USA
George 78 C 5 S South Africa
George Sound 151 A 7 sound, S Tasman Sea
Georges Bank 35 D 5 undersea bank, W Atlantic Ocean
George Town 54 C 2 C Bahamas
George Town 54 B 3 *var.* Georgetown. Dependent territory capital, SW Cayman Islands
George Town 138 B 3 *var.* Penang, Pinang. Pulau Pinang, W Malaysia
Georgetown 43 F 2 South Carolina, SE USA
Georgetown 59 G 2 country capital, N Guyana
Georgetown *see* George Town
Georgia 42 D 3 *off.* State of Georgia; *nicknames* Empire State of the South, Peach State. State, SE USA

Georgia
117 F 2 *Geor.* Sak'art'velo, *Rus.* Gruzinskaya SSR, Gruziya; *prev.* Georgian SSR. Republic, SW Asia

Official name: Republic of Georgia **Date of formation:** 1991 **Capital:** Tbilisi **Population** 5.5 million **Total area:** 69,700 sq km (26,911 sq miles) **Languages:** Georgian*, Russian **Religions:** Georgian Orthodox 70%, Russian Orthodox 10%, other 20% **Ethnic mix:** Georgian 69%, Armenian 9%, Russian 6%, Azerbaijani 5%, other 11% **Government:** Republic **Currency:** Coupons

Georgian Bay 38 C 5 lake bay, Ontario, S Canada
Georgina 148 B 4 river, C Australia
Georgiu-Dezh *see* Liski
Georgiyevsk 111 B 7 SW Russian Federation
Georg von Neumayer 154 B 2 research station, Antarctica
Gera 94 C 4 E Germany
Geráki 105 B 6 S Greece
Geral de Goiás, Serra 63 F 3 mountain range, E Brazil
Geraldine 151 B 6 South Island, SW New Zealand
Geraldton 147 A 6 Western Australia, W Australia
Gerdauen *see* Zheleznodorozhnyy
Gerede 116 C 3 N Turkey
Gereshk 122 D 5 SW Afghanistan
Gering 44 D 4 Nebraska, C USA
Gerlachovský Štít 99 D 5 *var.* Gerlachovka, *Ger.* Gerlsdorfer Spitze, *Hung.* Gerlachfalvi Csúcs; *prev.* Stalinov Štít, *Ger.* Franz-Josef Spitze, *Hung.* Ferencz-József Csúcs. Mountain, N Slovakia

Germany
94 B 4 *Ger.* Deutschland. Federal republic, W Europe

Official name: Federal Republic of Germany **Date of formation:** 1990 **Capital:** Berlin **Population:** 80.6 million **Total area:** 356,910 sq km (137,800 sq miles) **Languages:** German*, Sorbian **Religions:** Protestant 45%, Roman Catholic 37%, other 18% **Ethnic mix:** German 92%, other 8% **Government:** Multiparty republic **Currency:** Deutsche Mark = 100 pfennigs

Geroliménas 105 B 7 S Greece
Gerpinnes 87 C 7 S Belgium
Gerze 116 D 2 N Turkey
Getafe 92 D 3 C Spain
Gevaş 117 F 4 SE Turkey
Gevgelija 101 E 6 *var.* Devdelija, Djevdjelija, *Turk.* Gevgeli. SE Macedonia

Ghana
75 E 5 Republic, W Africa

Official name: Republic of Ghana **Date of formation:** 1957 **Capital:** Accra **Population:** 16.4 million **Total area:** 238,540 sq km (92,100 sq miles) **Languages:** English,* Akan, Mossi **Religions:** Traditional beliefs 38%, Muslim 30%, Christian 24%, other 8% **Ethnic mix:** Akan 52%, Mossi 15%, Ewe 12%, Ga 8%, other 13% **Government:** Multiparty republic **Currency:** Cedi = 100 pesewas

Ghanzi 78 C 3 *var.* Khanzi. W Botswana

Gharandal 119 B 7 SW Jordan
Gharvān *see* Gharyān
Gharyān 71 F 2 *var.* Gharvān. NW Libya
Ghawdex 97 C 8 *var.* Gozo. Island, NW Malta
Ghazalkent 123 F 2 *Rus.* Gazalkent. E Uzbekistan
Ghazni 123 E 4 *var.* Ghazni. E Afghanistan
Ghazni *see* Ghazni
Gheel *see* Geel
Gheorgheni 108 C 4 *Ger.* Niklasmarkt, *Hung.* Gyergyószentmiklós; *prev. Ger.* Gheorghieni, Sîn-Miclăuş. C Romania
Gherla 108 B 3 *Ger.* Neuschliss, *Hung.* Szamosújvár; *prev. Ger.* Armenierstadt. NW Romania
Ghijduwon 122 D 2 *Rus.* Gizhduvan. C Uzbekistan
Ghūdara 123 F 3 *var.* Gudara, *Rus.* Kudara. SE Tajikistan
Ghūrīān 122 D 4 W Afghanistan
Giannitsá 104 B 4 *var.* Yiannitsá. N Greece
Gibeon 78 B 4 S Namibia
Gibraltar 93 G 4 UK dependent territory, S Gibraltar
Gibraltar, Bay of 93 G 5 *var.* Bahía de Algeciras. Bay, NE Atlantic Ocean
Gibraltar Harbour 93 H 4 W Gibraltar
Gibraltar, Strait of 92 C 5 *Fr.* Détroit de Gibraltar, *Sp.* Estrecho de Gibraltar. Strait, Atlantic Ocean/Mediterranean Sea
Gibson Desert 147 C 5 desert, Western Australia, W Australia
Giedraičiai 107 C 5 E Lithuania
Giessen 95 B 5 W Germany
Gifu 131 C 6 *var.* Gihu. Honshū, SW Japan
Giganta, Sierra de la 50 B 3 mountain range, W Mexico
Gihu *see* Gifu
Gijón 92 D 1 NW Spain
Gila River 48 A 2 river, Arizona, SW USA
Gilbert Islands 145 E 2 island group, W Kiribati
Gilf Kebir Plateau /2 A 2 *Ar.* Hadabat al Jilf al Kabīr. Plateau, SW Egypt
Gillette 44 D 3 Wyoming, C USA
Gilroy 47 B 6 California, W USA
Gimie, Mount 55 F 1 mountain, C Saint Lucia
Gingin 147 B 6 Western Australia, SW Australia
Gipeswic *see* Ipswich
Girardot 58 B 3 C Colombia
Giresun 117 E 2 *var.* Kerasunt; *anc.* Cerasus, Pharnacia. NE Turkey
Girona 93 G 2 *var.* Gerona; *anc.* Gerunda. E Spain
Gisborne 150 E 3 North Island, NE New Zealand
Gissar Range 123 E 3 *Rus.* Gissarskiy Khrebet. Mountain range, Tajikistan/Uzbekistan
Gissarskiy Khrebet *see* Gissar Range
Giulianova 96 D 4 C Italy
Giurgiu 108 C 5 S Romania
Gizhduvan *see* Ghijduwon
Gizo 144 C 3 NW Solomon Islands
Gjirokastër 101 C 7 *var.* Gjirokastra, *It.* Argirocastro, *Gk.* Argyrokastron; *prev.* Gjinokastër, Gjlrokastra. S Albania

Gjoa Haven 37 F 3 King William Island, Canada
Gjøvik 85 B 5 S Norway
Glace Bay 39 G 4 Nova Scotia, SE Canada
Gladstone 148 E 4 Queensland, E Australia
Glâma 85 B 5 river, E Norway
Glasgow 88 C 4 C Scotland, UK
Glass Mountains 49 E 4 mountain range, Texas, S USA
Glazov 111 D 5 NW Russian Federation
Gleiwitz see Gliwice
Glendale 48 B 2 Arizona, SW USA
Glendale 47 C 7 California, W USA
Glendive 44 D 2 Montana, NW USA
Glen Innes 149 D 5 New South Wales, SE Australia
Glina 100 B 3 NE Croatia
Glittertind 85 A 5 mountain, S Norway
Gliwice 99 C 5 Ger. Gleiwitz. S Poland
Globino see Hlobyne
Głogów 98 B 4 Ger. Glogau, Glogow. W Poland
Glommen see Glomma
Gloucester 89 C 6 hist. Caer Glou, Lat. Glevum. W England, UK
Gloversville 41 F 3 New York, NE USA
Głowno 98 D 4 var. Główno. C Poland
Główno see Glowno
Glubokiy 111 B 6 SW Russian Federation
Glubokoye see Hlybokaye
Glukhov see Hlukhiv
Gnesen see Gniezno
Gniezno 98 C 3 Ger. Gnesen. C Poland
Gnjilane 101 E 5 var. Gilani, Alb. Gjilan. S Yugoslavia
Goa 132 B 2 var. Old Goa, Port. Goa Velha. State, India
Gobabis 78 B 3 E Namibia
Gobi 124 D 1 desert, China/Mongolia
Gobō 131 C 7 Honshū, SW Japan
Godavari 135 E 5 river, S India
Godhra 134 C 4 W India
Göding see Hodonín
Godoy Cruz 64 B 4 W Argentina
Goeree 86 B 4 island, SW Netherlands
Goettingen see Göttingen
Gogebic Range 40 B 1 hill range, N USA
Goiânia 63 F 3 prev. Goyania. State capital, C Brazil
Goiás 63 E 3 off. Estado de Goiás; prev. Goiaz or Goyaz. State, C Brazil
Gojōme 130 D 4 Honshū, NW Japan
Göksun 116 D 4 C Turkey
Gol 85 A 5 S Norway
Golan Heights 119 B 5 Ar. Al Jawlān, Heb. HaGolan. Mountain range, SW Syria
Golaya Pristan see Hola Prystan'
Gołdap 98 E 2 Ger. Goldap. NE Poland
Goldap see Gołdap
Gold Coast 75 E 5 coastal region, S Ghana
Gold Coast 149 E 5 Queensland, E Australia
Golden Bay 150 C 4 bay, South Island, E Tasman Sea

Goldingen see Kuldīga
Goldsboro 43 F 1 North Carolina, SE USA
Goleniów 98 B 3 Ger. Gollnow. NW Poland
Gollnow see Goleniów
Golmud 126 D 4 var. Ge'e'mu, Golmo, Chin. Ko-erh-mu. C China
Golovanevsk see Holovanivs'k
Goma 77 E 6 NE Zaire
Gomel' see Homyel'
Gomera 70 A 3 island, Islas Canarias, SW Spain
Gómez Palacio 50 D 3 C Mexico
Gonaïves 54 D 3 var. Les Gonaïves. N Haiti
Gonâve, Île de la 54 D 3 island, C Haiti
Gondar see Gonder
Gonder 72 C 4 var. Gondar. NW Ethiopia
Gondia 135 E 4 C India
Gonggar X 126 C 5 W China
Gongola 75 G 4 river, E Nigeria
Gónnoi 104 B 4 var. Gónnos; prev. Dereli. C Greece
Good Hope see Fort Good Hope
Good Hope, Cape of 78 C 5 Afr. Kaap die Goeie Hoop; var. Kaap de Goede Hoop. Headland, SW South Africa
Goodland 44 D 4 Kansas, C USA
Goondiwindi 149 D 5 Queensland, E Australia
Goor 86 E 3 E Netherlands
Goose Creek 43 F 2 South Carolina, SE USA
Goose Lake 46 B 4 var. Lago dos Gansos. Lake, W USA
Göppingen 95 B 6 SW Germany
Gorakhpur 135 E 3 N India
Gorany see Harany
Goražde 101 A 8 SE Bosnia & Herzegovina
Gorbovichi see Harbavichy
Gore 151 B 7 South Island, SW New Zealand
Gorē 73 C 5 W Ethiopia
Goré 76 C 4 S Chad
Gorgān 120 D 2 var. Astarabad, Astrabad, Gurgan; prev. Asterābād, anc. Hyrcania. N Iran
Gori 117 F 2 C Georgia
Gorinchem 86 C 4 var. Gorkum. C Netherlands
Goris 117 G 3 SE Armenia
Gorki see Horki
Gor'kiy see Nizhniy Novgorod
Gorkum see Gorinchem
Görlitz 94 D 4 E Germany
Görlitz see Zgorzelec
Gorna Dzhumaya see Blagoevgrad
Gornji Milanovac 100 D 4 C Yugoslavia
Gorodets see Haradzyets
Gorodishche see Horodyshche
Gorodnya see Horodnya
Gorodok see Haradok
Gorontalo 139 E 4 Celebes, C Indonesia
Gorssel 86 D 3 E Netherlands
Gorzów Wielkopolski 98 B 3 Ger. Landsberg, Landsberg an der Warthe. W Poland
Gosford 149 D 6 New South Wales, SE Australia
Goshogawara 130 D 3 var. Gosyogawara. Honshū, C Japan
Gospić 100 A 3 C Croatia
Gostivar 101 D 6 W Macedonia
Gosyogawara see Goshogawara

Götaland 85 B 6 cultural region, S Sweden
Göteborg 85 B 7 Eng. Gothenburg. SW Sweden
Gotel Mountains 75 G 5 mountain range, E Nigeria
Gotha 94 C 4 C Germany
Gothenburg see Göteborg
Gotland 85 C 6 island, SE Sweden
Gotō-rettō 131 A 7 island group, Japan
Gotska Sandön 85 C 6 island, SE Sweden
Gōtsu 131 B 6 var. Gôtu. Honshū, SW Japan
Göttingen 94 B 4 var. Goettingen. C Germany
Gottschee see Kočevje
Gottwaldov see Zlín
Gôtu see Gōtsu
Gouda 86 C 4 C Netherlands
Gough Fracture Zone 67 C 6 fracture zone, S Atlantic Ocean
Gough Island 69 B 8 island, S Atlantic Ocean
Gouin, Réservoir 38 D 4 reservoir, Québec, SE Canada
Goulburn 149 D 7 New South Wales, SE Australia
Goulburn Islands 148 A 1 island group, Northern Territory, N Australia
Goundam 75 E 3 NW Mali
Gouré 75 G 3 SE Niger
Governador Valadares 63 F 4 SE Brazil
Goverla, Gora see Hoverla, Hora
Govĭ Altayn Nuru 127 E 3 mountain range, S Mongolia
Goya 64 D 3 NE Argentina
Goyania see Goiânia
Goz Beïda 76 D 3 SE Chad
Gozo see Gozo
Gračanica 100 C 3 NE Bosnia & Herzegovina
Graciosa 92 A 5 var. Ilha Graciosa. Island, W Portugal
Graciosa, Ilha see Graciosa
Gradačac 100 C 3 N Bosnia & Herzegovina
Gradaús, Serra dos 63 E 3 mountain range, C Brazil
Grafton 149 E 6 New South Wales, SE Australia
Grafton 45 E 1 North Dakota, N USA
Graham Land 154 A 2 physical region, Antarctica
Grain Coast 74 C 5 coastal region, S Liberia
Grajewo 98 E 2 NE Poland
Grampian Mountains 88 C 3 mountain range, C Scotland, UK
Grampians, The 149 B 7 mountain range, Victoria, SE Australia
Granada 92 D 5 S Spain
Granada 52 D 3 SW Nicaragua
Gran Canaria 70 A 3 var. Grand Canary. Island, Islas Canarias, SW Spain
Gran Chaco 61 G 4 var. Chaco. Physical region, W South America
Grand Bahama Island 54 C 1 island, N Bahamas
Grand Banks of Newfoundland 66 B 3 undersea basin, NW Atlantic Ocean
Grand Bassa see Buchanan
Grand Canary see Gran Canaria
Grand Canyon 48 B 1 valley, Arizona, SW USA
Grand Cayman 54 B 3 island, SW Cayman Islands

Grande, Bahía 65 C 7 bay, SW Atlantic Ocean
Grande Comore 79 F 2 var. Njazidja, Great Comoro. Island, NW Comoros
Grande Deux, Réservoir la 38 D 3 reservoir, Québec, E Canada
Grande Prairie 37 E 5 Alberta, W Canada
Grand Erg de Bilma 75 H 3 desert, NE Niger
Grand Erg Occidental 70 D 3 desert, W Algeria
Grand Erg Oriental 71 E 3 desert, Algeria/Tunisia
Grande, Rio 49 F 5 var. Rio Bravo, Río Bravo del Norte. River, Mexico/USA
Grande Rivière 55 F 1 C Saint Lucia
Grande Terre 55 G 3 island, E Guadeloupe
Grand Falls 39 G 3 New Brunswick, SE Canada
Grand Forks 45 E 1 North Dakota, N USA
Grandichi see Hrandzichy
Grand Island 45 E 4 Nebraska, C USA
Grand Junction 44 C 4 Colorado, C USA
Grand Lac de l'Ours see Great Bear Lake
Grand Lac des Esclaves see Great Slave Lake
Grand Paradis see Gran Paradiso
Grand Rapids 40 C 3 Michigan, N USA
Grand Rapids 45 F 1 Minnesota, N USA
Grand Ronde River 46 C 3 river, NW USA
Grand-Santi 59 H 3 W French Guiana
Gran Malvina see West Falkland
Granollers 93 G 2 var. Granollérs. NE Spain
Granollérs see Granollers
Gran Paradiso 96 A 2 Fr. Grand Paradis. Mountain, NW Italy
Gran Santiago see Santiago
Grantley Adams 55 H 2 international airport, SE Barbados
Grants 48 C 2 New Mexico, SW USA
Grants Pass 46 B 4 Oregon, NW USA
Granville 90 B 3 N France
Gratz see Graz
Graulhet 91 C 6 S France
Grave 86 D 4 SE Netherlands
Grayling 36 C 2 Alaska, NW USA
Graz 95 E 7 prev. Gratz. SE Austria
Great Abaco 54 C 1 var. Abaco Island. Island, N Bahamas
Great Australian Bight 152 B 4 bight, E Indian Ocean
Great Barrier Island 150 D 2 island, North Island, N New Zealand
Great Barrier Reef 148 D 2 reef W Pacific Ocean
Great Basin 47 C 5 basin, Nevada, W USA
Great Bear Lake 37 E 3 Fr. Grand Lac de l'Ours. Lake, Northwest Territories, NW Canada
Great Bend 45 E 5 Kansas, C USA
Great Dividing Range 148 C 2 mountain range, E Australia
Greater Antarctica 154 C 3 var. East Antarctica. Physical region, Antarctica

Greater Antilles 54 D 3 island group, NW Caribbean Sea
Greater Caucasus 117 G 2 *Az.* Ba Qafqaz Silsiläsi, *Geor.* Kavkasioni, *Rus.* Bol'shoy Kavkaz. Mountain range, N Azerbaijan/Georgia/Russian Federation
Great Exhibition Bay 150 C 1 inlet, S Pacific Ocean
Great Exuma Island 54 C 2 island, C Bahamas
Great Falls 44 B 1 Montana, NW USA
Great Grimsby *see* Grimsby
Great Hungarian Plain 99 D 7 *var.* Great Alföld, Plain of Hungary, *Hung.* Alföld. Plain, SE Europe
Great Inagua 54 D 2 *var.* Inagua Islands. Island, S Bahamas
Great Karoo 78 C 5 *var.* Great Karroo, High Veld, *Afr.* Groot Karoo, Hoë Karoo. Physical region, S South Africa
Great Khingan Range *see* Da Hinggan Ling
Great Lake *see* Tônlé Sap
Great Nicobar 133 G 3 island, SE India
Great Plains 45 E 3 physical region, C Canada/USA
Great Rift Valley 69 D 5 *var.* Rift Valley, Depression. Africa/Asia
Great Ruaha 73 C 7 river, S Tanzania
Great Saint Bernard Pass 95 A 8 *Fr.* Col du Grand-Saint-Bernard, *It.* Passo di Gran San Bernardo. Pass, Italy/Switzerland
Great Salt Desert *see* Kavîr, Dasht-e
Great Salt Lake 44 B 3 salt lake, Utah, W USA
Great Salt Lake Desert 44 A 4 plain, Utah, W USA
Great Sand Sea 72 A 2 desert, Egypt/Libya
Great Sandy Desert 146 C 4 desert, Western Australia, W Australia
Great Sandy Desert 112 B 5 desert, SW Asia
Great Sandy Island *see* Fraser Island
Great Slave Lake 37 E 4 *Fr.* Grand Lac des Esclaves. Lake, Northwest Territories, NW Canada
Great Sound 42 A 5 bay, W Atlantic Ocean
Great Victoria Desert 142 A 4 desert, SW Australia
Great Wall of China 127 E 4 ancient monument, C China
Great Yarmouth 89 E 6 *var.* Yarmouth. E England, UK
Grebenka *see* Hrebinka
Gredos, Sierra de 92 D 3 mountain range, C Spain

Greece
105 A 5 *Gk.* Ellás; *anc.* Hellas. Republic, SE Europe

Official name: Hellenic Republic
Date of formation: 1913
Capital: Athens **Population:** 10.2 million **Total area:** 131,990 sq km (50,961 sq miles) **Languages:** Greek*, Turkish, Albanian, Macedonian **Religions:** Greek Orthodox 98%, Muslim 1%, other 1% **Ethnic mix:** Greek 98%, other 2% **Government:** Multiparty republic **Currency:** Drachma = 100 lepta

Greeley 44 D 4 Colorado, C USA

Green Bay 40 B 2 N USA
Green Bay 40 B 2 lake bay, Wisconsin, N USA
Greeneville 43 E 1 Tennessee, S USA
Greenland 82 D 3 *Dan.* Grønland, *Inuit* Kalaallit Nunaat. Danish external territory, Arctic Ocean/Atlantic Ocean
Greenland Sea 83 F 2 sea, Arctic Ocean
Green Mountains 41 G 3 mountain range, Vermont, NE USA
Greenock 88 C 4 SW Scotland, UK
Green River 40 C 5 river, Kentucky, E USA
Green River 44 B 4 river, C USA
Greensboro 43 F 1 North Carolina, SE USA
Greenville 43 F 1 North Carolina, SE USA
Greenville 42 B 2 Arkansas, C USA
Greenville 42 D 3 Alabama, S USA
Greenville 43 E 1 South Carolina, SE USA
Greenville 49 G 2 Texas, S USA
Greenwood 42 B 2 Mississippi, S USA
Greenwood 43 E 2 South Carolina, SE USA
Gregory Range 148 C 3 mountain range, Queensland, E Australia
Greifswald 94 D 2 NE Germany
Grenada 42 C 2 Mississippi, S USA

Grenada
55 G 5 Commonwealth republic, E Caribbean Sea

Official name: Grenada
Date of formation: 1974 **Capital:** St George's **Population:** 91,000 **Total area:** 340 sq km (131 sq miles) **Languages:** English*, English Creole **Religions:** Roman Catholic 68%, Protestant 32% **Ethnic mix:** Black 84%, Afro-European 13%, South Asian 3% **Government:** Parliamentary democracy **Currency:** E. Caribbean $ = 100 cents

Grenadines, The 55 H 5 island group, E Caribbean Sea
Grenoble 91 D 5 *anc.* Cularo, Gratianopolis. E France
Grenville, Cape 148 C 2 headland, Queensland, NE Australia
Gresham 46 B 3 Oregon, NW USA
Grevelingen 86 B 4 estuary, S North Sea
Grevená 104 B 4 N Greece
Grey Range 149 C 5 mountain range, E Australia
Greytown *see* San Juan del Norte
Grimari 76 C 4 C Central African Republic
Grimsby 89 E 5 *prev.* Great Grimsby. NE England, UK
Grise Fiord 37 F 2 *var.* Ausuittoq. Ellesmere Island, Canada
Grobin *see* Grobiņa
Grobiņa 106 B 3 *Ger.* Grobin. W Latvia
Grodno *see* Hrodna
Groesbeek 86 D 4 SE Netherlands
Grójec 98 D 4 C Poland
Groningen 86 E 1 NE Netherlands
Groote Eylandt 148 B 2 island, N Australia
Grootfontein 78 B 3 N Namibia
Groot Karasberge 78 B 4 mountain range, S Namibia

Gros Islet 55 F 1 N Saint Lucia
Grosser Sund *see* Suur Väin
Grosseto 96 B 4 NW Italy
Grossglockner 95 D 7 mountain, Austria
Grosskanizsa *see* Nagykanizsa
Groznyy 111 B 8 SW Russian Federation
Grudziądz 98 C 3 *var.* Grudziädz, *Ger.* Graudenz. N Poland
Grums 85 B 6 C Sweden
Grünau 78 B 4 S Namibia
Gryazi 111 B 6 W Russian Federation
Gryfice 98 B 2 *Ger.* Greifenberg, Greifenberg in Pommern. NW Poland
Guabito 53 E 4 NW Panama
Guadalajara 93 E 3 *Ar.* Wad Al-Hajarah; *anc.* Arriaca. C Spain
Guadalajara 50 D 4 C Mexico
Guadalcanal 144 C 3 island, C Solomon Islands
Guadalquivir 92 D 4 river, W Spain
Guadalupe 50 D 3 C Mexico
Guadalupe Mountains 48 D 3 mountain range, SW USA
Guadeloupe 55 H 3 French overseas department, E Caribbean Sea
Guadiana 92 C 4 river, Portugal/Spain
Guadix 93 E 5 S Spain
Guaico 55 H 5 C Trinidad & Tobago
Guaimaca 52 C 2 C Honduras
Guajira, Península de la 58 C 1 peninsula, N Colombia
Gualaco 52 D 2 C Honduras
Gualán 52 B 2 C Guatemala
Gualaquiza 60 B 2 E Ecuador
Gualdicciolo 96 D 1 NW San Marino
Gualeguaychú 64 D 4 E Argentina
Guam 144 A 1 US unincorporated territory, W Pacific Ocean
Guamúchil 50 C 3 C Mexico
Guanabacoa 54 B 2 W Cuba
Guanare 58 C 2 N Venezuela
Guanare 58 D 2 river, NW Venezuela
Guangdong 129 C 6 *var.* Kuang-tung, Kwangtung, Yue. Province, SE China
Guangxi Zhuangzu Zizhiqu 129 B 6 *var.* Guangxi, Gui, Kuang-hsi, Kwangsi, *Eng.* Kwangsi Chuang Autonomous Region. Autonomous region, S China
Guangyuan 129 B 5 *var.* Kuang-yuan, Kwangyuan. SW China
Guangzhou 129 C 6 *var.* Kuang-chou, Kwangchow, *Eng.* Canton. Province capital, SE China
Guantánamo 54 D 3 SE Cuba
Guantanamo Bay 54 D 3 US military base, E Cuba
Guaporé 61 F 3 *var.* Río Iténez. River, Bolivia/Brazil
Guarda 92 C 3 E Portugal
Guarumal 53 F 5 S Panama
Guasave 50 C 3 C Mexico

Guatemala
52 A 2 Republic, NW Central America

Official name: Republic of Guatemala **Date of formation:** 1838 **Capital:** Guatemala City **Population:** 10 million **Total area:** 108,890 sq km (42,043 sq miles) **Languages:** Spanish*, Quiché, Mam, Kekchi **Religions:** Christian 99%,

other 1% **Ethnic mix:** Indian 55%, *ladino* (Euro-Indian, White) 45% **Government:** Multiparty republic **Currency:** Quetzal = 100 centavos

Guatemala Basin 153 F 3 undersea basin, E Pacific Ocean
Guatemala City *see* Guatemala, Ciudad de
Guatemala, Ciudad de 52 B 2 *Eng.* Guatemala City; *prev.* Santiago de los Caballeros. Country capital, C Guatemala
Guatemala, Republic of *see* Guatemala
Guaviare 58 C 3 river, E Colombia
Guayana, Macizo de las *see* Guiana Highlands
Guayaquil 60 B 2 *var.* Santiago de Guayaquil. SW Ecuador
Guayaquil, Gulf of 60 A 2 gulf, E Pacific Ocean
Guayaramerín 61 F 2 N Bolivia
Guaymas 50 B 2 NW Mexico
Gubadag 122 D 2 *Turkm.* Tel'man; *prev.* Tel'mansk. N Turkmenistan
Gubakha 111 D 5 *var.* Gubachaj, Gubaha. NW Russian Federation
Guben 94 D 4 *var.* Wilhelm-Pieck-Stadt. E Germany
Gubkin 111 B 6 W Russian Federation
Gudaut'a 117 E 1 NW Georgia
Guelta Zemmur 70 B 3 E Western Sahara
Guéret 91 C 5 C France
Guerguerat 70 A 4 SW Western Sahara
Guernsey 89 D 8 island, W Channel Islands
Guernsey, Bailiwick of *see* Guernsey
Guerrero Negro 50 A 2 NW Mexico
Guiana Basin 66 B 4 undersea basin, W Atlantic Ocean
Guiana Highlands 56 C 2 *var.* Macizo de las Guayana. Mountain range, N South America
Guidder *see* Guider
Guider 76 B 4 *var.* Guidder. N Cameroon
Guidimouni 75 G 3 S Niger
Guildford 89 D 7 SE England, UK
Guilin 129 C 6 *var.* Kuei-lin, Kweilin. C China
Guimarães *see* Guimarães
Guimarães 92 B 2 *var.* Guimarães. N Portugal

Guinea
74 C 4 *var.* Guinée; *prev.* French Guinea, People's Revolutionary Republic of Guinea. Republic, W Africa

Official name: Republic of Guinea **Date of formation:** 1958 **Capital:** Conakry **Population:** 6.3 million **Total area:** 245,860 sq km (94,926 sq miles) **Languages:** French*, Fulani, Malinke, Susu **Religions:** Muslim 85%, Christian 8%, traditional beliefs 7% **Ethnic mix:** Fulani 40%, Malinke 25%, Susu 12%, other 23% **Government:** Multiparty republic **Currency:** Franc = 100 centimes

Guinea Basin 67 D 5 undersea basin, E Atlantic Ocean

Guinea-Bissau
74 B 4 *Fr.* Guinée-Bissau, *Port.* Guiné-Bissau; *prev.* Portuguese

Guinea. Republic, W Africa

Official name: Republic of Guinea-Bissau **Date of formation:** 1974 **Capital:** Bissau **Population:** 1 million **Total area:** 36,120 sq km (13,940 sq miles) **Languages:** Portuguese*, local languages **Religions:** Traditional beliefs 54%, Muslim 38%, Christian 8% **Ethnic mix:** Balante 27%, Fulani 22%, Malinke 12%, other 39% **Government:** Multiparty republic **Currency:** Peso = 100 centavos

Guinea, Gulf of 69 B 5 *Fr.* Golfe de Guinée. Inlet, E Atlantic Ocean
Guinée, Golfe de *see* Guinea, Gulf of
Güiria 59 E 1 NE Venezuela
Guiyang 129 B 6 *var.* Kuei-Yang, Kuei-yang, Kueyang, Kweiyang; *prev.* Kweichu. Province capital, S China
Guizhou 129 B 6 *var.* Kuei-chou, Kweichow, Qian. Province, S China
Gujarāt 134 C 4 *var.* Gujerat. State, W India
Gujerat *see* Gujarāt
Gujrānwāla 134 D 2 NE Pakistan
Gujrāt 134 C 2 E Pakistan
Gulbarga 132 C 1 C India
Gulbene 106 D 3 *Ger.* Alt-Schwanenburg. NE Latvia
Gulistan *see* Guliston
Guliston 123 E 2 *Rus.* Gulistan. E Uzbekistan
Gulkana 36 D 3 Alaska, NW USA
Gulu 73 B 6 N Uganda
Gulyantsi 104 C 1 NW Bulgaria
Guma *see* Pishan
Gumbinnen *see* Gusev
Gümüşhane 117 E 3 *var.* Gumushkhane, Gümüşane. NE Turkey
Güney Doğu Toroslar 117 E 4 mountain range, SE Turkey
Gunnedah 149 D 6 New South Wales, SE Australia
Gunnison 44 C 5 Colorado, C USA
Gurbantünggüt Shamo 126 C 2 desert, NW China
Guri, Embalse de 59 E 2 reservoir, E Venezuela
Gurktaler Alpen 95 D 7 mountain range, S Austria
Gürün 116 D 3 C Turkey
Gur'yev *see* Atyrau
Gusau 75 G 4 N Nigeria
Gusev 106 B 4 *Ger.* Gumbinnen. W Russian Federation
Gushgy 122 D 4 *prev.* Kushka. S Turkmenistan
Gustavus 36 D 4 Alaska, NW USA
Güstrow 94 C 3 NE Germany
Gütersloh 94 B 4 W Germany
Guthrie 49 G 1 Oklahoma, C USA
Gutland 87 D 8 physical region, S Luxembourg
Guttstadt *see* Dobre Miasto
Guwāhāti 135 G 3 *prev.* Gauhāti. NE India

Guyana
59 F 3 *prev.* British Guiana. Republic, N South America

Official name: Cooperative Republic of Guyana **Date of formation:** 1966 **Capital:** Georgetown **Population:** 800,000 **Total area:** 214,970 sq km

(83,000 sq miles) **Languages:** English*, English Creole, other **Religions:** Christian 57%, Hindu 33%, Muslim 9%, other 1% **Ethnic mix:** South Asian 51%, Black and mixed 43%, other 6% **Government:** Multiparty republic **Currency:** Guyana $ =100 cents

Guymon 49 E 1 Oklahoma, C USA
Gvardeysk 106 A 4 *Ger.* Tapaiu. W Russian Federation
Gwādar 134 A 3 *var.* Gwadur. SW Pakistan
Gwadur *see* Gwādar
Gwalior 134 D 3 C India
Gwanda 78 D 3 SW Zimbabwe
Gwy *see* Wye
Gyangzê 126 C 5 W China
Gyaring Hu 126 C 5 lake, C China
Gympie 149 E 5 Queensland, E Australia
Gyomaendrőd 99 D 7 SE Hungary
Gyöngyös 99 D 6 NE Hungary
Győr 99 C 6 *Ger.* Raab; *Lat.* Arrabona. NW Hungary
Gýtheio 105 B 6 *prev.* Yíthion. S Greece
Gyumri 117 F 2 *var.* Giumri, *Rus.* Kumayri; *prev.* Leninakan, Aleksandropol'. W Armenia
Gyzylarbat 122 C 2 *prev.* Kizyl-Arvat. W Turkmenistan

H

Haabai *see* Ha'apai Group
Haacht 87 C 6 C Belgium
Haaksbergen 86 E 3 E Netherlands
Ha'apai Group 145 F 5 *var.* Haabai. Island group, C Tonga
Haapsalu 106 D 2 *Ger.* Hapsal. W Estonia
Haarlem 86 C 3 *prev.* Harlem. W Netherlands
Haast 151 B 6 South Island, SW New Zealand
Habomai Islands 130 E 2 island group, SE Russian Federation
Hachijō-jima 131 E 6 *var.* Hatizyô Zima. Island, Izu-shotō, E Japan
Hachinohe 130 D 3 Honshū, C Japan
Hadejia 75 G 4 N Nigeria
Hadejia 75 G 4 river, N Nigeria
Hadera 119 A 6 C Israel
Hadhdhunmati Atoll 132 A 5 *var.* Haddummati Atoll, Laamu Atoll. Island, S Maldives
Hadhramaut *see* Ḩaḑramawt
Ha Đông 136 D 3 *var.* Hadong. N Vietnam
Hadong *see* Ha Đông
Ḩaḑramawt 121 C 6 *Eng.* Hadhramaut. Mountain range, S Yemen
Hafren *see* Severn
Hagerstown 41 E 4 Maryland, NE USA
Ha Giang 136 D 3 NW Vietnam
Hagondange 90 D 3 NE France
Haguenau 90 E 3 NE France
Haicheng 128 D 3 NE China
Haidarabad *see* Hyderābād
Haifa, Bay of *see* Ḩefa, Mifraẕ
Haikang 129 C 7 *var.* Leizhou. S China
Haikou 129 C 7 *var.* Hai-k'ou, Hoihow, *Fr.* Hoï-Hao. Hainan Dao, S China
Ḩā'il 120 B 4 NW Saudi Arabia
Hailar 127 F 1 *var.* Hai-la-erh; *prev.* Hulun. N China

Hailuoto 84 D 4 *Swe.* Karlö. Island, W Finland
Hainan 129 B 7 *var.* Qiong. Province, S China
Hainan Dao 129 C 7 island, S China
Haines 36 D 4 Alaska, NW USA
Hainichen 94 D 4 E Germany
Hai Phong 136 E 3 *var.* Haifong, Haiphong. N Vietnam

Haiti
54 D 3 Republic, N Haiti

Official name: Republic of Haiti **Date of formation:** 1804 **Capital:** Port-au-Prince **Population:** 6.9 million **Total area:** 27,750 sq km (10,714 sq miles) **Languages:** French*, French Creole, English **Religions:** Roman Catholic 80%, Protestant 16%, Voodoo 4% **Ethnic mix:** Black 95%, Afro-European 5% **Government:** Multiparty republic **Currency:** Gourde = 100 centimes

Hajdúhadház 99 E 6 E Hungary
Hakodate 130 D 3 Hokkaidō, NE Japan
Hakosberge 78 B 4 mountain range, C Namibia
Ha Kwai Chung 128 A 1 W Hong Kong
Hal *see* Halle
Ḩalab 118 B 2 *Eng.* Aleppo, *Fr.* Alep; *anc.* Beroea. NW Syria
Ḩalāniyāt, Juzur al 121 D 6 *var.* Jazā'ir Bin Ghalfān, *Eng.* Kuria Muria Islands. Island group, S Oman
Halberstadt 94 C 4 C Germany
Halden 85 B 6 *prev.* Fredrikshald. S Norway
Halfmoon Bay 151 A 8 *var.* Oban. South Island, SW New Zealand
Halifax 39 F 4 Nova Scotia, SE Canada
Halifax Bay 148 D 3 bay, W Pacific Ocean
Halle 94 C 4 *var.* Halle an der Saale. C Germany
Halle 87 B 6 *Fr.* Hal. C Belgium
Halle an der Saale *see* Halle
Halle-Neustadt 94 C 4 C Germany
Halley 154 B 2 research station, Antarctica
Hall Islands 144 B 1 island group, C Micronesia
Halls Creek 146 D 3 Western Australia, NW Australia
Halmahera 139 F 3 *prev.* Djailolo, Gilolo, Jailolo. Island, E Indonesia
Halmahera, Laut 139 F 4 sea, W Pacific Ocean
Halmstad 85 B 7 S Sweden
Hälsingborg *see* Helsingborg
Hamada 131 B 6 Honshū, SW Japan
Hamadān 120 C 3 *anc.* Ecbatana. W Iran
Ḩamāh 118 B 3 *var.* Hama; *anc.* Epiphania, *Bibl.* Hamath. W Syria
Hamamatsu 131 D 6 *var.* Hamamatu. Honshū, S Japan
Hamamatu *see* Hamamatsu
Hamar 85 B 5 *prev.* Storhammer. S Norway
Hamburg 94 B 3 N Germany
Ḩamḑ, Wādī al 120 A 4 dry watercourse, W Saudi Arabia
Hämeenlinna 85 D 5 *Swe.* Tavastehus. SW Finland
Hamersley Range 146 B 4 mountain range, Western Australia, W Australia

Hamhŭng 128 E 3 C North Korea
Hami 126 C 3 *var.* Ha-mi, Uigh. Kumul, Qomul. NW China
Hamilton 88 C 4 S Scotland, UK
Hamilton 42 A 5 dependent territory capital, C Bermuda
Hamilton 150 D 3 North Island, N New Zealand
Hamilton 38 D 5 Ontario, S Canada
Hamm 94 B 3 *var.* Hamm in Westfalen. W Germany
Hamm in Westfalen *see* Hamm
Ḩammāmāt, Khalīj al *see* Hammamet, Golfe de
Ḩammār, Hawr al 120 C 3 lake, SE Iraq
Hammer Springs 151 C 5 South Island, C New Zealand
Hamm in Westfalen *see* Hamm
Hampden 151 B 7 South Island, SW New Zealand
Hampton 41 F 5 Virginia, NE USA
Handan 128 C 4 *var.* Han-tan. NE China
HaNegev 119 A 7 *Eng.* Negev. Desert, S Israel
Hanford 47 C 7 California, W USA
Hangayn Nuruu 126 D 2 mountain range, C Mongolia
Hangö *see* Hanko
Hangzhou 129 D 5 *var.* Hang-chou, Hangchow. Province capital, E China
Hanhöhiy Uul 126 C 2 mountain range, NW Mongolia
Hanko 85 D 6 *Swe.* Hangö. SW Finland
Hanna 37 E 5 Alberta, SW Canada
Hannibal 45 G 4 Missouri, C USA
Hannover 94 B 3 *Eng.* Hanover. NW Germany
Hanöbukten 85 B 7 bay, SW Baltic Sea
Ha Nôi 136 D 3 *var.* Ha Noi, Ha noi, *Eng.* Hanoi, *Fr.* Ha noï. Country capital, N Vietnam
Hanover *see* Hannover
Han-tan *see* Handan
Hantsavichy 107 B 6 *Pol.* Hancewicze, *Rus.* Gantsevichi. SW Belorussia
Hanzhong 129 B 5 C China
Hāora 135 G 4 *prev.* Howrah. NE India
Haparanda 84 D 3 N Sweden
Hapsal *see* Haapsalu
Haradok 107 E 5 *Rus.* Gorodok. N Belorussia
Haradzyets 107 B 6 *Rus.* Gorodets. SW Belorussia
Haramachi 131 D 5 Honshū, E Japan
Harany 107 D 5 *Rus.* Gorany. N Belorussia
Härar 73 D 5 Ethiopia
Harare 78 D 3 *prev.* Salisbury. Country capital, NE Zimbabwe
Harbavichy 107 E 6 *Rus.* Gorbovichi. E Belorussia
Harbel 74 C 5 NW Liberia
Harbin 128 E 2 *var.* Haerbin, Ha-erh-pin, Kharbin; *prev.* Haerhpin, Pinkiang, Pingkiang. Province capital, NE China
Hardanger-fjorden 85 A 5 fjord, E Norwegian Sea
Hardangervidda 85 A 6 mountain range, S Norway
Hardenberg 86 E 3 E Netherlands
Hardy 42 B 1 Arkansas, C USA
Harelbeke 87 A 6 *var.* Harlebeke. W Belgium
Harem *see* Ḩārim

Haren 86 E 2 NE Netherlands
Hargeisa *see* Hargeysa
Hargeysa 73 D 5 *var.* Hargeisa. NW Somalia
Hariana *see* Haryāna
Hari, Batang 138 B 4 *prev.* Djambi. River, Sumatera, W Indonesia
Hārim 118 B 2 *var.* Harem. W Syria
Harima-nada 131 B 6 sea, NW Pacific Ocean
Harīrūd 123 E 4 river, C Asia
Harlan 45 F 3 Iowa, C USA
Harlebeke *see* Harelbeke
Harlem *see* Haarlem
Harlingen 49 G 5 Texas, S USA
Harlingen 86 D 2 *Fris.* Harns. N Netherlands
Harlow 89 E 6 SE England, UK
Harmanli *see* Kharmanli
Harney Lake 46 C 4 lake, Oregon, NW USA
Härnösand 85 C 5 *var.* Hernösand. C Sweden
Harns *see* Harlingen
Har Nuur 126 C 2 lake, NW Mongolia
Harper 74 D 5 *var.* Cape Palmas. NE Liberia
Ḩarrat Raḩaṭ 121 B 5 lavaflow, W Saudi Arabia
Harris 88 B 3 physical region, NW Scotland, UK
Harrisburg 41 E 4 state capital, Pennsylvania, NE USA
Harrison 42 B 1 Arkansas, C USA
Harrisonburg 41 E 5 Virginia, NE USA
Harrison, Cape 39 F 2 headland, Newfoundland and Labrador, E Canada
Harrogate 89 D 5 N England, UK
Hârșova 108 D 5 *prev.* Hîrșova. SE Romania
Harstad 84 C 2 N Norway
Hartford 41 G 3 state capital, Connecticut, NE USA
Hartlepool 89 D 5 N England, UK
Har Us Nuur 126 C 2 lake, NW Mongolia
Harwich 89 E 6 E England, UK
Haryāna 134 D 2 *var.* Hariana. State, N India
Haskovo *see* Khaskovo
Hasselt 87 D 6 NE Belgium
Hastings 89 E 7 SE England, UK
Hastings 55 G 2 SW Barbados
Hastings 150 E 4 North Island, NE New Zealand
Hastings 45 E 4 Nebraska, C USA
Haţeg 108 B 4 *Ger.* Wallenthal, *Hung.* Hátszeg; *prev. Ger.* Hatzeg, Hötzing. SW Romania
Hattem 86 D 3 E Netherlands
Hatteras, Cape 43 G 1 headland, North Carolina, SE USA
Hattiesburg 42 C 3 Mississippi, S USA
Hat Yai 137 C 7 *var.* Ban Hat Yai. S Thailand
Haugesund 85 A 6 S Norway
Hau Hoi Wan 128 A 1 bay, NW Hong Kong
Haukeligrend 85 A 6 S Norway
Haukivesi 85 E 5 lake, SE Finland
Hauraki Gulf 150 D 2 gulf, N Pacific Ocean
Haut Atlas 70 C 3 *Eng.* High Atlas. Mountain range, C Morocco
Hautes Fagnes 87 D 6 *Ger.* Hohes Venn. Mountain range, E Belgium

Hauts Plateaux 70 D 2 *var.* Hauts-Plateaux. Plateau, Algeria/Morocco
Hauts-Plateaux *see* Hauts Plateaux
Hauzenberg 95 D 6 SE Germany
Havana 35 D 6 country capital, NW Cuba
Havana *see* La Habana
Havant 89 D 7 S England, UK
Havelock 43 F 1 North Carolina, SE USA
Havelock North 150 E 4 North Island, NE New Zealand
Haverfordwest 89 C 6 SW Wales, UK
Havířov 99 C 5 E Czech Republic
Havre 44 C 1 Montana, C USA
Havre-St-Pierre 39 F 3 Québec, E Canada
Havza 116 D 2 N Turkey
Hawaii 47 A 8 *off.* state of Hawaii; *nicknames* Aloha State, Paradise of the Pacific. State, W USA
Hawaii 47 B 8 *Haw.* Hawai'i. Island, W USA
Hawaiian Islands 152 D 2 *var.* The Hawaiian Islands; *prev.* The Sandwich Islands. Island group, C Pacific Ocean
Hawaiian Ridge 152 D 2 undersea ridge, N Pacific Ocean
Hawea, Lake 151 B 6 lake, South Island, SW New Zealand
Hawera 150 D 4 North Island, C New Zealand
Hawick 88 D 4 S Scotland, UK
Hawke Bay 150 E 4 bay, S Pacific Ocean
Hawkes Bay 150 E 4 cultural region, North Island, N New Zealand
Hay 149 C 6 New South Wales, SE Australia
Hay River 37 E 4 Northwest Territories, W Canada
Hays 45 E 5 Kansas, C USA
Haysyn 108 D 3 *Rus.* Gaysin. C Ukraine
Hay 119 A 5 *var.* Hattā; *hist.* Caiffa, Caiphas, *anc.* Sycaminum. N Israel
Hefa, Mifraz 119 A 5 *Eng.* Bay of Haifa. Bay, E Mediterranean Sea
Hefei 129 D 6 *var.* Hofei; *hist.* Luchow. E China
Heide 94 B 2 N Germany
Heidelberg 95 B 5 SW Germany
Heidenheim *see* Heidenheim an der Brenz
Heidenheim an der Brenz 95 B 6 *var.* Heidenheim. S Germany
Heilbronn 95 B 6 SW Germany
Heiligenbeil *see* Mamonovo
Heilong Jiang *see* Amur

Heilongjiang 128 D 2 *var.* Hei, Hei-lung-chiang, Heilungkiang. Province, NE China
Heiloo 86 C 3 NW Netherlands
Heilsberg *see* Lidzbark Warmiński
Heimdal 84 B 4 S Norway
Helan Shan 127 E 3 mountain range, N China
Helena 44 B 2 state capital, Montana, NW USA
Helensville 150 D 2 North Island, N New Zealand
Helgoländer Bucht 94 A 2 *var.* Helgoland Bay, Heligoland Bight. Bay, SE North Sea
Hellevoetsluis 86 B 4 SW Netherlands
Hellín 93 E 4 C Spain
Helmand, Daryā-ye 122 D 5 *var.* Hīrmand Rūd-e. River, Afghanistan/Iran
Helmond 87 D 5 S Netherlands
Helsingborg 85 B 7 *prev.* Hälsingborg. S Sweden
Helsingfors *see* Helsinki
Helsinki 85 D 5 *Swe.* Helsingfors. Country capital, S Finland
Henan 129 C 5 *var.* Honan, Yu. Province, C China
Henderson 43 F 1 North Carolina, SE USA
Henderson 49 H 3 Texas, S USA
Henderson 40 B 5 Kentucky, E USA
Henderson 47 D 7 Nevada, W USA
Hendersonville 43 E 1 North Carolina, SE USA
Hendū Kosh *see* Hindu Kush
Hengduan Shan 126 D 5 mountain range, SW China
Hengelo 86 E 3 E Netherlands
Hengyang 129 C 6 *var.* Hengnan, Heng-yang; *prev.* Hengchow. S China
Henichesk 109 F 4 *Rus.* Genichesk. S Ukraine
Hennebont 90 A 3 NW France
Hentiesbaai 78 B 3 W Namibia
Henzada 136 B 4 SW Burma
Herald Cays 148 D 3 island, E Australia
Herāt 122 D 4 *var.* Herat; *anc.* Aria. W Afghanistan
Herchmer 37 G 4 Manitoba, C Canada
Heredia 53 E 4 C Costa Rica
Hereford 49 E 2 Texas, S USA
Herford 94 B 4 NW Germany
Héristal *see* Herstal
Herk-de-Stad 87 C 6 NE Belgium
Hermansverk 85 A 5 S Norway
Hermiston 46 C 2 Oregon, NW USA
Hermon, Mount 119 B 5 *Ar.* Jabal ash Shaykh. Mountain, SW Syria
Hermosillo 50 B 2 NW Mexico
Hernösand *see* Härnösand
Herrera del Duque 92 D 3 W Spain
Herrick 149 C 8 Tasmania, SE Australia
Herselt 87 C 5 C Belgium
Herstal 87 D 6 *Fr.* Héristal. E Belgium
Hervey Bay 148 E 4 bay, SE Coral Sea
Herzliyya 119 A 6 *var.* Hertseliya, Herzeliyya. C Israel
Hessen 95 B 5 cultural region, C Germany
Heydekrug *see* Šilutė
Hialeah 43 F 5 Florida, SE USA
Hibbing 45 F 1 Minnesota, N USA

Hidalgo del Parral 50 C 2 *var.* Parral. N Mexico
Hida-sanmyaku 131 C 5 mountain range, Honshū, S Japan
Hierro 70 A 3 *var.* Ferro. Island, Islas Canarias, SW Spain
High Atlas *see* Haut Atlas
High Point 43 F 1 North Carolina, SE USA
Hiiumaa 106 C 2 *Ger.* Dagden, *Swe.* Dagö. Island, W Estonia
Hikurangi 150 D 2 North Island, N New Zealand
Hildesheim 94 B 4 N Germany
Hilla *see* Al Ḩillah
Hillaby, Mount 55 G 1 mountain, N Barbados
Hill Bank 52 C 1 N Belize
Hillegom 86 C 3 W Netherlands
Hilo 47 B 8 Hawaii, W USA
Hilton Head Island 43 E 2 South Carolina, SE USA
Hilversum 86 C 3 C Netherlands
Himalayas 124 C 2 *var.* Himalaya, *Chin.* Himalaya Shan. Mountain range, S Asia
Himeji 131 C 6 *var.* Himezi. Honshū, SW Japan
Himezi *see* Himeji
Ḩimş 118 B 4 *var.* Homs; *anc.* Emesa. C Syria
Hînceşti 108 D 4 *var.* Hâncești; *prev.* Kotovsk. C Moldava
Hinds 151 C 6 South Island, SW New Zealand
Hindu Kush 123 F 4 *Per.* Hendū Kosh. Mountain range, Afghanistan/Pakistan
Hinesville 43 E 3 Georgia, SE USA
Hinson Bay 42 A 5 bay, W Atlantic Ocean
Hīrmand Rūd-e *see* Helmand, Daryā-ye
Hirosaki 130 D 3 Honshū, C Japan
Hiroshima 131 B 7 *var.* Hirosima. Honshū, SW Japan
Hirosima *see* Hiroshima
Hirson 90 D 3 N France
Hîrşova *see* Hârșova
Hitachi 131 D 5 *var.* Hitati. Honshū, S Japan
Hitati *see* Hitachi
Hitchinbrook Island 148 D 3 island, Queensland, NE Australia
Hitra 84 A 4 *prev.* Hitteren. Island, S Norway
Hitteren *see* Hitra
Hjälmaren 85 C 6 *Eng.* Lake Hjalmar. Lake, C Sweden
Hjalmar, Lake *see* Hjälmaren
Hjørring 85 B 7 N Denmark
Hkakabo Razi 136 B 1 mountain, Burma/China
Hlobyne 109 F 2 *Rus.* Globino. NE Ukraine
Hlukhiv 109 F 1 *Rus.* Glukhov. NE Ukraine
Hlybokaye 107 D 5 *Rus.* Glubokoye, N Belorussia
Hoa Binh 136 D 3 N Vietnam
Hoang Liên Son 136 D 3 mountain range, N Vietnam
Hobart 149 C 8 *prev.* Hobart Town, Hobarton. State capital, Tasmania, SE Australia
Hobbs 49 E 3 New Mexico, SW USA
Hobro 85 A 7 N Denmark
Hô Chi Minh 137 E 6 *var.* Ho Chi Minh, Hồ Chi Minh City, Thanh Pho-Ho Chi Minh, Thanh Pho Ho Chi Minh, *prev.* Saigon, Sai Gon. S Vietnam

Hodeida *see* Al Ḥudaydah
Hódmezővásárhely 99 D 7 SE Hungary
Hodonín 99 B 6 *Ger.* Göding. SE Czech Republic
Hof 95 C 5 SE Germany
Hōfu 131 B 7 Honshū, SW Japan
Hofuf *see* Al Hufūf
Hohenems 95 B 7 W Austria
Hohenstadt *see* Zábřeh
Hohes Venn *see* Hautes Fagnes
Hohe Tauern 95 C 7 mountain range, W Austria
Hohhot 127 F 3 *var.* Huhehot, Huhohaot'e, *Mong.* Kukukhoto; *prev.* Kweisui, Kwesui. N China
Hôi An 137 E 5 *prev.* Faifo. C Vietnam
Hokianga Harbour 150 C 2 harbour, North Island, N New Zealand
Hokitika 151 B 5 South Island, SW New Zealand
Hokkaidō 130 C 2 territory, Hokkaidō, NE Japan
Hola Prystan' 109 E 4 *Rus.* Golaya Pristan. S Ukraine
Holbrook 48 B 2 Arizona, SW USA
Holetown 55 G 1 *prev.* Jamestown. W Barbados
Holguín 54 C 2 SE Cuba
Hollabrunn 95 E 6 NE Austria
Holland 40 C 3 Michigan, N USA
Hollywood 43 F 5 Florida, SE USA
Holman 37 E 3 Victoria Island, Canada
Holmes Reef 148 D 3 Reef, W Coral Sea
Holmsund 84 D 4 N Sweden
Holon 119 A 6 C Israel
Holovanivs'k 109 E 3 *Rus.* Golovanevsk. C Ukraine
Holstebro 85 A 7 W Denmark
Holyhead 89 C 6 *Wel.* Caer Gybi. NW Wales, UK
Holyoke 41 G 3 Massachusetts, NE USA
Hombori Tondo 75 E 3 mountain, E Mali
Homestead 43 F 5 Florida, SE USA
Homonsova, Khrebet *see* Lomonosov Ridge
Homr, Dar el 72 B 4 physical region, C Sudan
Homyel' 107 D 7 *Rus.* Gomel'. SE Belorussia
Hondo 49 F 4 Texas, S USA

Honduras 52 C 2 Republic, N Central America
Official name: Republic of Honduras **Date of formation:** 1821 **Capital:** Tegucigalpa **Population:** 5.6 million **Total area:** 112,090 sq km (43,278 sq miles) **Languages:** Spanish*, English Creole, Garifuna, Indian languages **Religions:** Roman Catholic 97%, other 3% **Ethnic mix:** *mestizo* 90%, Indian 7%, Garifuna (Black Carib) 2%, White 1% **Government:** Multiparty republic **Currency:** Lempira = 100 centavos

Honduras, Gulf of 52 C 2 *Sp.* Golfo de Honduras. Gulf, W Caribbean Sea
Honduras, Republic of *see* Honduras
Hønefoss 85 B 6 S Norway
Hông Gai 136 E 3 *var.* Hon Gai, Hongay. N Vietnam

Hong Kong 129 C 6 UK dependent territory to 1997, S. China
Hong Kong Island 128 B 2 island, S Hong Kong
Honiara 144 C 3 country capital, C Solomon Islands
Honjō 130 D 4 *var.* Honzyô. Honshū, C Japan
Honolulu 47 A 8 state capital, Hawaii, W USA
Honshū, 131 E 5 *var.* Hondo, Honsyû. Island, Japan
Honzyô *see* Honjō
Hood Point 147 B 7 headland, Western Australia, W Australia
Hoogeveen 86 E 2 NE Netherlands
Hoogezand-Sappemeer 86 E 2 NE Netherlands
Hoorn 86 C 2 NW Netherlands
Hopa 117 F 2 NE Turkey
Hope 36 C 3 Alaska, NW USA
Hopedale 39 F 2 Newfoundland and Labrador, NE Canada
Hopewell 41 E 5 Virginia, NE USA
Hopkinsville 40 B 5 Kentucky, E USA
Horasan 117 F 3 NE Turkey
Horki 107 E 6 *Rus.* Gorki. E Belorussia
Horlivka 109 G 3 *Rom.* Adâncata, *Rus.* Gorlovka. E Ukraine
Hormuz, Strait of 120 D 4 *var.* Strait of Ormuz; *Per.* Tangeh-ye Hormoz. Strait, Arabian Sea/Persian Gulf
Hornepayne 38 C 4 Ontario, S Canada
Hornos, Cabo de 65 C 8 *Eng.* Cape Horn. Headland, S Chile
Horodnya 109 E 1 *Rus.* Gorodnya. NE Ukraine
Horodok 108 B 2 *Pol.* Gródek Jagiello'nski, *Rus.* Gorodok, Gorodok Yagellonski. NW Ukraine
Horodyshche 109 E 2 *Rus.* Gorodishche. C Ukraine
Horoshiri-dake 130 D 2 *var.* Horosiri Dake. Mountain, Hokkaidō, NE Japan
Horosiri Dake *see* Horoshiri-dake
Horsburgh Atoll 132 B 4 island, N Maldives
Horseshoe Bay 42 A 5 bay, W Atlantic Ocean
Horsham 149 B 7 Victoria, SE Australia
Horst 87 D 5 SE Netherlands
Horten 85 B 6 S Norway
Hospitalet *see* L'Hospitalet de Llobregat
Hotan 126 B 4 *var.* Khotan, *Chin.* Ho-t'ien. NW China
Hoting 84 C 4 C Sweden
Hot Springs 42 B 1 Arkansas, C USA
Houghton Lake 40 C 2 lake, Michigan, N USA
Houilles 91 B 6 France
Houston 49 H 4 Texas, S USA
Hovd 126 C 2 *var.* Khovd. W Mongolia
Hove 89 D 7 S England, UK
Hoverla, Hora 108 B 3 *Rus.* Gora Goverla. Mountain, W Ukraine
Hovsgol, Lake *see* Hövsgöl Nuur
Hövsgöl Nuur 126 D 1 *var.* Lake Hovsgol. Lake, N Mongolia
Howe, Cape 149 D 7 headland, SE Australia
Howrah *see* Hāora
Hoy 88 C 2 island, N Scotland, UK

Hoyerswerda 94 D 4 E Germany
Hradec Králové 99 B 5 *Ger.* Königgrätz. NE Czech Republic
Hrandzichy 107 B 5 *Rus.* Grandichi. W Belorussia
Hranice 99 C 5 *Ger.* Mährisch-Weisskirchen. E Czech Republic
Hrasnica 100 C 4 SE Bosnia & Herzegovina
Hrebinka 109 E 2 *Rus.* Grebenka. NE Ukraine
Hrodna 107 B 5 *Pol.* Grodno. W Belorussia
Huacho 60 C 4 W Peru
Hua Hin *see* Ban Hua Hin
Huaihua 129 C 6 C China
Huailai 128 C 3 NE China
Huainan 129 D 5 *var.* Huai-nan, Hwainan. E China
Huajuapan 51 E 5 *var.* Huajuapan de León. SE Mexico
Huajuapan de León *see* Huajuapan
Hualapai Mountains 48 A 2 mountain range, Arizona, SW USA
Huallaga 60 C 2 river, N Peru
Huambo 78 B 2 *Port.* Nova Lisboa. C Angola
Huancavelica 60 D 4 SW Peru
Huancayo 60 D 4 C Peru
Huang He (Yellow River) 128 C 4 *var.* Yellow River. River, C China
Huangshi 129 C 5 *var.* Huang-shih, Hwangshih. E China
Huanta 60 D 4 C Peru
Huánuco 60 C 3 C Peru
Huanuni 61 F 4 W Bolivia
Huaral 60 C 4 W Peru
Huarás *see* Huaraz
Huaraz 60 C 3 *var.* Huarás. W Peru
Huarmey 60 C 3 W Peru
Huatabampo 50 B 2 NW Mexico
Hubei 129 C 5 *var.* E, Hupei. Province, C China
Hubli 132 B 2 SW India
Huddersfield 89 D 5 N England, UK
Hudiksvall 85 C 5 C Sweden
Hudson Bay 38 C 1 inlet, NW Atlantic Ocean
Hudson, Détroit d' *see* Hudson Strait
Hudson Strait 38 D 1 *Fr.* Détroit d'Hudson. Strait, Atlantic Ocean/Hudson Bay
Huê 136 E 4 C Vietnam
Huehuetenango 52 A 2 W Guatemala
Huelva 92 C 5 *anc.* Onuba. SW Spain
Huesca 93 F 2 *anc.* Osca. NE Spain
Huéscar 93 E 4 S Spain
Hughenden 148 C 3 NE Australia
Hugo 49 G 2 Oklahoma, C USA
Huíla Plateau 78 B 2 plateau, S Angola
Huixtla 51 G 5 SE Mexico
Hukui *see* Fukui
Hukusima *see* Fukushima
Hull 38 D 4 Québec, SE Canada
Hull *see* Kingston upon Hull
Hull Island *see* Orona
Hulst 87 B 5 SW Netherlands
Hulun Nur 127 F 1 *var.* Hu-lun Ch'ih; *prev.* Dalai Nor. Lake, NE China
Humaitá 62 D 2 N Brazil
Humboldt 42 C 1 Tennessee, S USA
Humboldt River 47 C 5 river, Nevada, W USA
Humpolec 99 B 5 *Ger.* Gumpolds, Humpoletz. C Czech Republic

Hunan 129 C 5 *var.* Xiang. Province, S China
Hunedoara 108 B 4 *Ger.* Eisenmarkt, *Hung.* Vajdahunyad. SW Romania
Hünfeld 95 B 5 C Germany

Hungary 99 D 6 *Ger.* Ungarn, *Hung.* Magyarország, *Rom.* Ungaria, *SCr.* Madarska, *Ukr.* Uhorshchyna; *prev.* Hungarian People's Republic. Republic, C Europe
Official name: Republic of Hungary **Date of formation:** 1918 **Capital:** Budapest **Population:** 10.5 million **Total area:** 93,030 sq km (35,919 sq miles) **Languages:** Hungarian (Magyar)*, German, Slovak **Religions:** Roman Catholic 68%, Protestant 25%, other 7% **Ethnic mix:** Hungarian (Magyar) 90%, German 2%, other 8% **Government:** Multiparty republic **Currency:** Forint = 100 fillér

Hunjiang 128 E 3 NE China
Hunter Islands 149 B 8 island group, Tasmania, NW Australia
Huntington 40 D 5 West Virginia, NE USA
Huntington Beach 47 C 8 California, W USA
Huntly 150 D 3 North Island, N New Zealand
Huntsville 42 D 1 Alabama, S USA
Huntsville 38 D 5 Ontario, S Canada
Huntsville 49 G 3 Texas, S USA
Huolin Gol He 127 F 2 NE China
Hurghada 72 C 2 *var.* Al Ghurdaqah, Ghurdaqah. E Egypt
Huri Hills 73 C 5 mountain range, NW Kenya
Huron 45 E 3 South Dakota, N USA
Huron, Lake 40 D 2 lake, Canada/USA
Hurukawa *see* Furukawa
Húsavík 83 E 4 NE Iceland
Husum 94 B 2 N Germany
Hutchinson 45 E 5 Kansas, C USA
Huy 87 C 6 *Dut.* Hoei, Hoey. E Belgium
Hvannadalshnúkur 83 E 5 mountain, S Iceland
Hvar 100 B 4 *It.* Lesina; *anc.* Pharus. Island, S Croatia
Hwange 78 D 3 *prev.* Wankie. W Zimbabwe
Hyargas Nuur 126 D 2 lake, W Mongolia
Hyderābād 134 D 5 *var.* Haidarabad. C India
Hyderābād 134 B 3 *var.* Haidarabad. SE Pakistan
Hyères 91 D 6 SE France
Hyères, Îles d' 91 D 6 island group, S France
Hyvinge *see* Hyvinkää
Hyvinkää 85 D 5 *Swe.* Hyvinge. S Finland

I

Ialomiţa 108 C 5 river, SE Romania
Iaşi 108 D 4 *Ger.* Jassy. NE Romania
Ibadan 75 F 5 SW Nigeria
Ibagué 58 B 3 C Colombia
Ibar 100 D 4 *Alb.* Ibër. River, C Yugoslavia
Ibarra 60 B 1 *var.* San Miguel de Ibarra. N Ecuador
Ibër *see* Ibar

Iberian Basin 66 C 3 undersea basin, E Atlantic Ocean
Iberian Peninsula 68 B 2 physical region, Portugal/Spain
Ibérico, Sistema 93 E 2 *var.* Cordillera Ibérica, *Eng.* Iberian Mountains. Mountain range, NE Spain
Ibiza *see* Eivissa
Ibusuki 130 B 2 Kyūshū, SW Japan
Ica 60 D 4 SW Peru
Içá *see* Putumayo

Iceland 83 E 4 *Dan.* Island, *Icel.* Ísland. Republic, NW Europe
Official name: Republic of Iceland **Date of formation:** 1944 **Capital:** Reykjavik **Population:** 300,000 **Total area:** 103,000 sq km (39,770 sq miles) **Languages:** Icelandic*, English **Religions:** Evangelical Lutheran 96%, other Christian 3%, other 1% **Ethnic mix:** Icelandic (Norwegian-Celtic descent) 98%, other 2% **Government:** Constitutional republic **Currency:** Krona = 100 aurar

Iceland Basin 66 C 2 undersea basin, N Atlantic Ocean
Icelandic Plateau 155 F 5 *var.* Iceland Plateau. Undersea plateau, Arctic Ocean/Atlantic Ocean
Iculisma *see* Angoulême
Idabel 49 H 2 Oklahoma, C USA
Idaho 46 D 3 *off.* State of Idaho; *nicknames* Gem State, Gem of the Mountains. State, NW USA
Idaho Falls 46 E 3 Idaho, NW USA
Idensalmi *see* Iisalmi
Idfu 72 B 2 *var.* Edfu. SE Egypt
Idlib 118 B 3 NW Syria
Idre 85 B 5 C Sweden
Iecava 106 C 3 S Latvia
Ieper 87 A 6 *Fr.* Ypres. W Belgium
Ierápetra 105 D 8 Kríti, SE Greece
Ierisós *see* Ierissós
Ierissós 104 C 4 *var.* Ierisós. N Greece
Iferouâne 75 G 2 N Niger
Ifôghas, Adrar des 75 F 2 *var.* Adrar des Iforas. Mountain range, NE Mali
Iforas, Adrar des *see* Adrar des Ifôghas
Igarka 114 D 3 N Russian Federation
Iglesias 97 A 5 W Italy
Igloolik 37 G 3 Northwest Territories, N Canada
Ignace 38 B 4 Ontario, S Canada
Igoumenítsa 104 A 4 W Greece
Iguala 51 E 5 *var.* Iguala de la Independencia. S Mexico
Iguala de la Independencia *see* Iguala
Ihavandiffulu Atoll *see* Ihavandippolhu Atoll
Ihavandippolhu Atoll 132 B 4 *var.* Ihavandiffulu Atoll. Island, N Maldives
Ihosy 79 F 4 S Madagascar
Iisalmi 84 E 4 *var.* Idensalmi. C Finland
Ijâfene 74 D 2 desert, Mauritania
IJssel 86 D 3 *var.* Yssel. River, Germany/Netherlands
IJsselmeer 86 C 2 *prev.* Zuider Zee. Lake, N Netherlands
IJsselmuiden 86 D 3 E Netherlands
Ijzer 87 A 6 river, W Belgium

Ikaría 105 D 6 *var.* Kariot, Nicaria, Nikaria; *anc.* Icaria. Island, SE Greece
Iki 131 A 7 island, Japan
Ilagan 139 E 1 Luzon, N Philippines
Iława 98 D 3 *Ger.* Deutsch-Eylau. N Poland
Ilebo 77 C 6 *prev.* Port-Francqui. W Zaire
Île-de-France 90 C 3 cultural region, N France
Ilfracombe 89 C 7 SW England, UK
Ilgaz 116 C 2 Turkey
Ílhavo 92 B 3 W Portugal
Iliamna Lake 36 C 3 lake, Alaska, NW USA
Il'ichevsk *see* Illichivs'k
Iligan 139 F 2 *off.* Iligan City. Mindanao, S Philippines
Iligan City *see* Iligan
Illapel 64 B 4 C Chile
Illichivs'k 109 E 4 *Rus.* Il'ichevsk. SW Ukraine
Illinois 40 B 4 *off.* State of Illinois; *nicknames* Prairie State, Sucker State. State, C USA
Illinois River 40 B 4 river, Illinois, N USA
Illuro *see* Mataró
Ilo 61 E 4 SW Peru
Iloilo 139 E 2 *off.* Iloilo City. Panay Island, C Philippines
Iloilo City *see* Iloilo
Ilorin 75 F 4 W Nigeria
Iluh *see* Batman
Ilulissat 82 C 3 *Dan.* Jakobshavn. W Greenland
Il'yaly 122 C 2 *var.* Yylanly. N Turkmenistan
Imatra 85 E 5 SE Finland
Imishli *see* İmişli
İmişli 117 H 3 *Rus.* Imishli. C˙ Azerbaijan
Imola 96 C 3 N Italy
Imperatriz 63 F 2 NE Brazil
Imperia 96 A 3 NW Italy
Impfondo 77 C 5 NE Congo
Imphāl 135 H 3 NE India
Inagua Islands *see* Great Inagua/Little Inagua
I-n-Amenas 71 E 3 *var.* In Aménas, In Amnas. E Algeria
Inarijärvi 84 D 2 *Lapp.* Aanaarjävri, *Swe.* Enareträsk. Lake, N Finland
Inawashiro-ko 131 D 5 *var.* Inawasiro Ko. Lake, Honshū, C Japan
Inawasiro Ko *see* Inawashiro-ko
İncesu 116 D 3 C Turkey
Inch'ŏn 128 E 4 *off.* Inch'ŏn-kwangyŏksi, *Jap.* Jinsen; *prev.* Chemulpo. NW South Korea
Independence 45 F 4 Missouri, C USA
Independence Fjord 83 E 1 fjord, W Wandell Sea
Independence Island *see* Malden Island
Independence Mountains 46 D 4 mountain range, Nevada, W USA

India 124 B 3 *var.* Indian Union, Union of India, *Hind.* Bhārat. Republic, S Asia
Official name: Republic of India **Date of formation:** 1947 **Capital:** New Delhi **Population:** 896.6 million **Total Area:** 3,287,590 sq km (1,269,338 sq miles) **Languages:** Hindi*, English* **Religions:** Hindu

83%, Muslim 11%, Christian 2%, Sikh 2%, other 2% **Ethnic mix:** Indo-Aryan 72%, Dravidian 25%, Mongoloid and other 3% **Government:** Multiparty republic **Currency:** Rupee = 100 paisa

Indiana 40 B 4 *off.* State of Indiana; nickname Hoosier State. State, C USA
Indianapolis 40 C 4 state captal, Indiana, N USA
Indian Church 52 C 1 N Belize
Indian Ocean 141 C 5 ocean, C USA
Indianola 45 F 4 Iowa, C USA
Indigirka 115 G 2 river, NE Russian Federation
Indija 100 D 3 *var.* Indija, *Hung.* India. N Yugoslavia
Indio 47 D 8 California, W USA
Indomed Fracture Zone 141 A 6 fracture zone, SW Indian Ocean

Indonesia 138 C 4 *Ind.* Republik Indonesia; *prev.* Dutch East Indies, Netherlands East Indies, United States of Indonesia. Republic, SE Asia
Official name: Republic of Indonesia **Date of formation:** 1949 **Capital:** Jakarta **Population:** 194.6 million **Total Area:** 1,904,570 sq km (735,555 sq miles) **Languages:** Bahasa Indonesia*, 250 (est.) languages or dialects **Religions:** Muslim 87%, Christian 10%, Hindu 2%, Buddhist 1% **Ethnic mix:** Javanese 45%, Sundanese 14%, Madurese 8%, other 33% **Government:** Multiparty republic **Currency:** Rupiah = 100 sen

Indonesian Borneo *see* Kalimantan
Indore 134 D 4 C India
Indreville *see* Châteauroux
Indus 134 C 2 *Chin.* Yindu He; *prev.* Yin-tu Ho. River, S Asia
Indus Cone *see* Indus Fan
Indus Fan 140 B 3 *var.* Indus Cone. Undersea fan, N Indian Ocean
Indus, Mouths of the 134 B 4 delta, S Pakistan
Inebolu 116 C 2 N Turkey
Ineu 108 A 4 *Hung.* Borosjenő; *prev.* Inău. W Romania
Infiernillo, Presa del 51 E 4 reservoir, S Mexico
Inglefield Land 82 D 1 physical region, NW Greenland
Ingolstadt 95 C 6 S Germany
Ingulets *see* Inhulets'
Inguri *see* Enguri
Inhambane 79 E 4 SE Mozambique
Inhulets' 109 F 3 *Rus.* Ingulets. E Ukraine
Inis *see* Ennis
Inn 95 C 6 river, C Europe
Inner Hebrides 88 B 4 island group, W Scotland, UK
Inner Islands 79 H 1 *var.* Central Group. Island group, Seychelles
Innisfail 148 D 3 Queensland, NE Australia
Innsbruch *see* Innsbruck
Innsbruck 95 C 7 *var.* Innsbruch. W Austria
Inowrocław 98 C 3 *Ger.* Hohensalza; *prev.* Inowrazlaw. C Poland
I-n-Salah 70 D 3 *var.* In Salah. C Algeria
In Salah *see* I-n-Salah
Insterburg *see* Chernyakhovsk

Inta 110 E 3 NW Russian Federation
Interamna *see* Teramo
Interamna Nahars *see* Terni
International Falls 45 F 1 Minnesota, N USA
Inukjuak 38 D 2 *var.* Inoucdjouac; *prev.* Port Harrison. Québec, NE Canada
Inuuvik *see* Inuvik
Inuvik 37 E 3 *var.* Inuuvik. Northwest Territories, NW Canada
Invercargill 151 A 7 South Island, SW New Zealand
Inverell 149 D 6 New South Wales, SE Australia
Inverness 88 C 3 N Scotland, UK
Investigator Ridge 140 D 4 undersea ridge, E Indian Ocean
Investigator Strait 149 A 7 strait, SE Indian Ocean
Inyangani 78 D 3 mountain, NE Zimbabwe
Ioánnina 104 A 4 *var.* Janina, Yannina. W Greece
Iola 45 F 5 Kansas, C USA
Ionia Basin *see* Ionian Basin
Ionian Basin 80 D 5 *var.* Ionia Basin. Undersea basin, C Mediterranean Sea
Ionian Islands *see* Iónioi Nísoi
Ionian Sea 103 E 3 *Gk.* Iónio Pélagos, *It.* Mar Ionio. Sea, C Mediterranean Sea
Iónioi Nísoi 105 A 5 *Eng.* Ionian Islands. Island group, W Greece
Íos 105 D 7 Íos, SE Greece
Íos 105 D 7 *var.* Nio. Island, Kykládes, SE Greece
Iowa 45 F 3 *off.* State of Iowa; nickname Hawkeye State. State, C USA
Iowa City 45 G 3 Iowa, C USA
Iowa Falls 45 G 3 Iowa, C USA
Ipel' 99 D 6 *var.* Ipoly, *Ger.* Eipel. River, Hungary/Slovakia
Ipiales 58 A 4 SW Colombia
Ipirá 63 G 3 E Brazil
Ipoh 138 B 3 W Malaysia
Ippy 76 C 4 C Central African Republic
Ipswich 89 E 6 *hist.* Gipeswic. E England, UK
Ipswich 149 E 5 Queensland, E Australia
Iqaluit 37 H 3 *prev.* Frobisher Bay. Baffin Island, NE Canada
Iquique 64 B 1 N Chile
Iquitos 60 C 1 N Peru
Irákleio 105 D 8 *var.* Herakleion, *Eng.* Candia; *prev.* Iráklion. Kríti, SE Greece

Iran 120 C 3 *prev.* Persia. Republic, SW Asia
Official name: Islamic Republic of Iran **Date of formation:** 1906 **Capital:** Tehran **Population:** 63.2 million **Total area:** 1,648,000 sq km (636,293 sq miles) **Languages:** Farsi (Persian)*, Azerbaijani, Kurdish **Religions:** Shi'a Muslim 95%, Sunni Muslim 4%, other 1% **Ethnic mix:** Persian 52%, Azerbaijani 24%, Kurdish 9%, other 15% **Government:** Islamic Republic **Currency:** Rial = 100 dinars

Iranian Plateau 120 D 3 *var.* Plateau of Iran. Plateau, C Iran

Iran, Plateau of *see* Iranian Plateau
Irapuato 51 E 4 C Mexico

Iraq
120 B 3 *Ar.* 'Irāq. Republic,
SW Asia

Official name: Republic of Iraq
Date of formation: 1932 **Capital:**
Baghdad **Population:**19.9 million
Total area: 438,320 sq km
(169,235 sq miles) **Languages:**
Arabic*, Kurdish, Turkish, Farsi
(Persian) **Religions:** Shi'a Muslim
63%, Sunni Muslim 34%, other 3%
Ethnic mix: Arab 79%, Kurdish 16%,
Persian 3%, Turkish 2%
Government: Single-party republic
Currency: Dinar = 1,000 fils

Irbid 119 B 5 NW Jordan

Ireland, Republic of
89 B 5 *var.* Ireland, *Ir.* Éire.
Republic, NW Europe

Official name: Republic of Ireland
Date of formation: 1921 **Capital:**
Dublin **Population:** 3.5 million **Total
area:** 70,280 sq km (27,155 sq miles)
Languages: English*, Irish Gaelic*
Religions: Roman Catholic 93%,
Protestant 5%, other 2% **Ethnic
mix:** Irish 95%, other 5%
Government: Multiparty republic
Currency: Irish pound = 100 pence

Irian Jaya 139 H 4 cultural region, E
Indonesia
Iringa 73 C 7 C Tanzania
Iriomote-jima 130 A 4 island,
Sakishima-shotō, SW Japan
Iriona 52 D 2 NE Honduras
Irish Sea 89 C 5 *Ir.* Muir Éireann.
Sea, NE Atlantic Ocean
Irkutsk 115 E 4 C Russian
Federation
Iroise 90 A 3 sea, NW France
Irrawaddy 136 B 2 *var.*
Ayeyarwady. River, C Burma
Irrawaddy, Mouths of the 137 A 5
delta area, SW Burma
Irtysh 114 C 3 *var.* Irtish, *Kaz.* Ertis.
River, C Asia
Irún 93 E 1 N Spain
Irving 49 G 2 Texas, S USA
Isabela, Isla 60 A 5 *var.* Albemarle
Island. Island, W Ecuador
Isaccea 108 D 5 E Romania
Isachsen 37 F 1 Ellef Ringnes
Island, Canada
Isbarta *see* Isparta
Isca Damnoniorum *see* Exeter
Ischia, Isola d' 97 C 5 island, S Italy
Ise 131 C 6 Honshū, SW Japan
Iseghem *see* Izegem
Isère 91 D 5 river, E France
Isernia 97 D 5 *var.* Æsernia. S Italy
Ise-wan 131 C 6 bay, NW Pacific
Ocean
Isfahan *see* Isfahan
Isherton 59 F 4 S Guyana
Ishigaki-jima 130 A 4 *var.* Isigaki
Zima. Island, Sakishima-shotō,
SW Japan
Ishikari-wan 130 C 2 bay, NE Sea of
Japan
Ishim 114 C 4 C Russian Federation
Ishim 114 C 4 *Kaz.* Esil. River,
Kazakhstan/Russian Federation
Ishimbay 111 D 6 W Russian
Federation
Ishinomaki 130 D 4 *var.* Isinomaki.
Honshū, C Japan

Ishkashim *see* Ishkoshim
Ishkoshim 123 F 3 *Rus.* Ishkashim.
S Tajikistan
Isinomaki *see* Ishinomaki
Isiro 77 E 5 NE Zaire
Iskăr *see* Iskŭr
İskenderun 116 D 4 *Eng.*
Alexandretta. S Turkey
Iskŭr 104 C 2 *var.* Iskăr. River, NW
Bulgaria
Iskŭr, Yazovir 104 C 2 *prev.* Stalin,
Yazovir. Reservoir, W Bulgaria
Isla Cristina 92 C 5 S Spain
Isla de León *see* San Fernando
Islāmābād 134 C 1 country capital,
NE Pakistan
Island Lagoon 149 B 6 lake, South
Australia, S Australia
Islay 88 B 4 island, SW Scotland,
UK
Isle 91 B 5 river, W France
Ismailia *see* Ismā'īlīya
Ismā'īlīya 72 B 1 *var.* Ismailia. N
Egypt
Isna 72 B 2 *var.* Esna. SE Egypt
Isoka 78 D 1 NE Zambia
İsparta 116 B 4 *var.* Isbarta. SW
Turkey
İspir 117 E 3 NE Turkey

Israel
119 A 7 *var.* Medinat Israel, *Heb.*
Yisrael, Yisra'el. Republic,
SW Asia

Official name: State of Israel
Date of formation: 1948
Capital: Jerusalem **Population**
5.4 million **Total area:** 20,700 sq km
(7,992 sq miles) **Languages:**
Hebrew*, Arabic, Yiddish
Religions: Jewish 83%, Muslim 13%,
Christian 2%, other 2% **Ethnic mix:**
Jewish 83%, Arab 17%
Government: Multiparty republic
Currency: New shekel = 100 agorat

Issoire 91 C 5 C France
Issyk-Kul', Ozero 123 G 2 *var.* Issiq
Köl, *Kir.* Ysyk-Köl. Lake, E
Kyrgyzstan
İstanbul 116 B 2 *Bul.* Tsarigrad, *Eng.*
Istanbul; *prev.* Constantinople,
anc. Byzantium. NW Turkey
Istanbul *see* Istanbul
İstanbul Boğazı 116 B 2 *var.*
Bosporus Thracius, *Eng.*
Bosporus, *Turk.* Karadeniz Boğazi.
Strait, Sea of Marmara/Black Sea
Istra 76 D 2 *Eng.* Istria. Peninsula,
Slovenia/Yugoslavia
Istra 100 A 2 *Eng.* Istria, *Ger.* Istrien.
Cultural region, NW Croatia
Istria *see* Istra
Itabuna 63 G 3 E Brazil
Itagüí 58 B 3 W Colombia
Itaituba 63 E 2 NE Brazil

Italy
96 C 3 *It.* Italia, Republica
Italiana. Republic, S Europe

Official name: Italian Republic
Date of formation: 1871 **Capital:**
Rome **Population:** 57.8 million **Total
area:** 301,270 sq km (116,320 sq miles)
Languages: Italian*, French,
Rhaeto-Romanic, Sardinian **Religions:**
Roman Catholic 99%, other 1%
Ethnic mix: Italian 98%, other 2%
Government: Multiparty republic
Currency: Lira = 100 centesimi

It Amelân *see* Ameland

Iténez, Río *see* Guaporé
Ithaca 41 F 3 New York, NE USA
It Hearrenfean *see* Heerenveen
Itoigawa 131 C 5 Honshū, C Japan
Ittoqqortoormiit 83 E 4 *var.*
Itseqqortoormiit, *Dan.*
Scoresbysund, *Eng.* Scoresby
Sound. SE Greenland
Iturup, Ostrov 115 H 4 island,
Kuril'skiye Ostrova, SE Russian
Federation
Itzehoe 94 B 2 N Germany
Ivalo 84 D 2 *Lapp.* Avvil, Avveel. N
Finland
Ivanava 107 B 7 *var.* Janów Poleski,
Pol. Janów, *Rus.* Ivanovo. SW
Belorussia
Ivangrad 101 D 5 *var.* Berane C
Yugoslavia
Ivanhoe 149 C 6 New South Wales,
SE Australia
Ivano-Frankivs'k 108 C 2 *Ger.*
Stanislau, *Pol.* Stanisławów, *Rus.*
Ivano-Frankivsk; *prev.* Stanislav.
W Ukraine
Ivanovo 111 C 5 W Russian
Federation
Ivatsevichy 107 B 6 *Pol.*
Iwacewicze, *Rus.* Ivantsevichi,
Ivatsevichi. SW Belorussia
Ivigtut *see* Ivittuut
Ivittuut 82 B 4 *var.* Ivigtut. SW
Greenland
Ivory Coast 74 D 5 *Fr.* Côte
d'Ivoire. Coastal region, S Ivory
Coast

Ivory Coast
74 D 4 *Fr.* République de la Côte
d'Ivoire, Côte d'Ivoire. Republic,
NW Africa

Official name: Republic of the Ivory
Coast **Date of formation:** 1960
Capital: Yamoussoukro **Population:**
13.4 million **Total area:** 322,463 sq
km (124,503 sq miles) **Languages:**
French*, Akran **Religions:**
Traditional beliefs 63%, Muslim
25%, Christian 12% **Ethnic mix:**
Baoule 23%, Bété 18%, Kru 17%,
Malinke 15%, other 27%
Government: Multiparty republic
Currency: CFA franc = 100 centimes

Ivujivik 38 D 1 Québec, NE Canada
Iwaki 131 D 5 Honshū, N Japan
Iwakuni 131 B 7 Honshū, SW Japan
Iwanai 130 C 2 Hokkaidō, NE
Japan
Iwate 130 D 4 Honshū, N Japan
Ixtapa 51 E 5 S Mexico
Ixtepec 51 F 5 SE Mexico
Iyo-nada 131 B 7 sea, NW Pacific
Ocean
Izabal, Lago de 52 B 2 *prev.* Golfo
Dulce. Lake, E Guatemala
Izberbash 111 B 8 SW Russian
Federation
Izegem 87 A 6 *prev.* Iseghem. W
Belgium
Izhevsk 111 D 5 *prev.* Ustinov. NW
Russian Federation
Izmail *see* Izmayil
Izmayil 108 D 4 *Rus.* Izmail. SW
Ukraine
İzmir 116 A 3 *prev.* Smyrna. W
Turkey
İzmit 116 B 3 *var.* Ismid; *anc.*
Astacus. NW Turkey
İznik Gölü 116 B 3 lake, NW
Turkey
Izúcar de Matamoros *see*
Matamoros

Izu-hantō 131 D 6 peninsula,
Honshū, S Japan
Izu-shotō 131 D 6 island group,
Japan
Izvor 104 B 2 W Bulgaria
Izyaslav 108 C 2 W Ukraine
Izyum 109 G 2 E Ukraine

J

Jabalpur 135 E 4 *prev.* Jubbulpore. C
India
Jabbūl, Sabkhat al 118 C 2 salt flat,
NW Syria
Jablah 118 B 3 *var.* Jeble, *Fr.* Djéblé.
W Syria
Jaca 93 F 1 NE Spain
Jacaltenango 52 A 2 W Guatemala
Jackson 42 B 2 Mississippi, S USA
Jackson 42 C 1 Alabama, S USA
Jackson 42 C 3 Tennessee, S USA
Jackson 45 H 5 Missouri, C USA
Jackson Head 151 A 6 headland,
South Island, SW New Zealand
Jacksonville 43 E 3 Florida, SE USA
Jacksonville 43 F 1 North Carolina,
SE USA
Jacksonville 42 B 1 Arkansas, SE
USA
Jacksonville 49 H 3 Texas, S USA
Jacksonville 40 B 4 Illinois, N USA
Jacksonville Beach 43 E 3 Florida,
SE USA
Jacmel 54 D 3 *var.* Jaquemel. S Haiti
Jacob *see* Nkayi
Jacobābād 134 B 3 SE Pakistan
Jadodina 0 Svetozarevo *see*
Jadotville *see* Likasi
Jādū 71 F 2 NW Libya
Jaén 92 D 4 SW Spain
Jaén 60 B 3 N Peru
Jaffna 132 D 3 N Sri Lanka
Jagdalpur 135 E 5 C India
Jaipur 134 D 3 *prev.* Jeypore. State
capital, N India
Jajce 100 B 3 W Bosnia &
Herzegovina
Jakarta 138 C 5 *Dut.* Batavia; *prev.*
Djakarta. Country capital, Jawa, C
Indonesia
Jakobshavn *see* Ilulissat
Jakobstad 84 D 4 *Fin.* Pietarsaari. W
Finland
Jakobstadt *see* Jēkabpils
Jalal-Abad *see* Dzhalal-Abad
Jalālābād 123 F 4 *var.* Jalalabad,
Jelalabad. E Afghanistan
Jalandhar 134 D 2 *prev.* Jullundur.
N India
Jalapa 52 D 3 NW Nicaragua
Jalpa 50 D 4 C Mexico
Jaluit Atoll 144 D 2 *var.* Jalwoj.
Island, S Marshall Islands
Jālwōj *see* Jaluit Atoll
Jamaame 73 D 6 *It.* Giamame; *prev.*
Margherita. S Somalia

Jamaica
54 A 4 Commonwealth republic,
N Caribbean Sea

Official name: Jamaica **Date of
formation:** 1962 **Capital:** Kingston
Population: 2.5 million **Total area:**
10,990 sq km (4,243 sq miles)
Languages: English*, English
Creole, other **Religions:** Christian
60% other 40% **Ethnic mix:** Black
75%, mixed 15%, South Asian 5%,
other 5% **Government:**
Parliamentary democracy **Currency:**
Jamaican $ = 100 cents

Jamaica Channel 54 D 3 channel, N Caribbean Sea
Jamālpur 135 G 3 N Bangladesh
Jambi 138 B 4 *var.* Telanaipura; *prev.* Djambi. Sumatera, W Indonesia
Jamdena *see* Yamdena, Pulau
James Bay 38 C 3 bay, S Hudson Bay
James River 45 E 3 river, N USA
Jamestown 41 E 3 New York, NE USA
Jamestown 45 E 2 North Dakota, N USA
Jamestown *see* Holetown
Jammerbugten 85 A 7 bay, E North Sea
Jammu 134 D 2 *prev.* Jummoo. State capital, NW India
Jammu and Kashmir 134 D 1 *var.* Jammu-Kashmir, Kashmir. State, NW India
Jammu and Kashmīr *see* Kashmīr
Jāmnagar 134 C 4 *prev.* Navanagar. W India
Jamshedpur 135 F 4 NE India
Janaúba 63 F 3 SE Brazil
Janesville 40 B 3 Wisconsin, N USA
Janischken *see* Joniškis
Jankovac *see* Jánoshalma
Jan Mayen 83 F 4 Norwegian territory, N Norwegian Sea
Jánoshalma 99 D 7 *SCr.* Jankovac. S Hungary

Japan 130 C 4 *var.* Nippon, *Jap.* Nihon. Monarchy, E Asia

Official name: Japan **Date of formation:** 1868 **Capital:** Toyko **Population:** 125 million **Total Area:** 377,800 sq km (145,869 sq miles) **Languages:** Japanese*, Korean, Chinese **Religions:** Shinto and Buddhist 76%, Buddhist 16%, other 8% **Ethnic mix:** Japanese 99.4%, other 0.6% **Government:** Constitutional monarchy **Currency:** Yen = 100 sen

Japan, Sea of 130 B 4 *Rus.* Yapanskoye More. Sea, SW Pacific Ocean
Japan Trench 152 B 2 trench, NW Pacific Ocean
Japen *see* Yapen, Pulau
Japiim 62 C 2 *var.* Máncio Lima. W Brazil
Japurá, Rio 62 C 1 *var.* Río Caquetá, Yapurá. River, Brazil/Colombia
Jaqué 53 G 5 SE Panama
Jaquemel *see* Jacmel
Jarābulus 118 C 2 *var.* Jarablos, Jerablus, *Fr.* Djérablous. N Syria
Jaransk *see* Yaransk
Jardines de la Reina, Archipiélago de los 54 B 2 island, group C Cuba
Jarega *see* Yarega
Jarīd, Shaṭṭ al *see* Jerid, Chott el
Jarocin 98 C 4 C Poland
Jaroslavl *see* Yaroslavl'
Jarosław 99 E 2 *Ger.* Jaroslau, *Rus.* Yaroslav. SE Poland
Jarqūrghon 123 E 3 *Rus.* Dzharkurgan. S Uzbekistan
Jarvis Island 145 F 2 US unincorporated territory, C Pacific Ocean
Jasło 99 D 5 SE Poland
Jasper 42 C 2 Alabama, S USA
Jassy *see* Iaşi

Jastrzębie-Zdrój 99 C 5 *var.* Jastrzebie Zdrój, Jastrzebie-Zdrój. S Poland
Jataí 63 E 3 C Brazil
Jauf *see* Al Jawf
Jaunpiebalga 106 D 3 NE Latvia
Jaunpur 135 E 3 N India
Java *see* Jawa
Javari 60 D 2 *var.* Yavarí. River, Brazil/ Peru
Javari *see* Yavarí
Java Sea *see* Jawa, Laut
Java Trench 141 E 5 trench, E Indian Ocean
Jawa 138 C 5 *Eng.* Java; *prev.* Djawa. Island, C Indonesia
Jawa, Laut 138 D 4 *Eng.* Java Sea. Sea, W Pacific Ocean
Jawhar 73 D 6 *var.* Jowhar, *It.* Giohar. S Somalia
Jaya, Puncak 139 G 4 *prev.* Puntjak Carstensz, Puntjak Sukarno. Mountain, New Guinea, E Indonesia
Jayapura 139 H 4 *var.* Djajapura, *Dut.* Hollandia; *prev.* Kotabaru, Sukarnapura. New Guinea, E Indonesia
Jaz Murian, Hamun-e 120 E 4 lake, SE Iran
Jebba 75 F 4 W Nigeria
Jebel ash Shifā 120 A 4 desert, NW Saudi Arabia
Jedda *see* Jiddah
Jędrzejów 98 D 4 *Ger.* Endersdorf. S Poland
Jefferson City 45 G 5 state capital, Missouri, C USA
Jega 75 F 4 NW Nigeria
Jehol *see* Chengde
Jēkabpils 106 D 4 *Ger.* Jakobstadt. S Latvia
Jelenia Góra 98 B 4 *Ger.* Hirschberg, Hirschberg im Riesengebirge, Hirschberg im Riesengebirge, Hirschberg in Schlesien. SW Poland
Jelgava 106 C 3 *Ger.* Mitau. C Latvia
Jemappes 87 B 7 S Belgium
Jember 138 D 5 *prev.* Djember. Jawa, C Indonesia
Jena 94 C 4 C Germany
Jenīn 119 E 6 N Israel
Jequitinhonha 56 E 4 river, E Brazil
Jerada 70 D 2 NE Morocco
Jerba, Île de 71 F 2 *var.* Djerba, Jazīrat Jarbah. Island, E Tunisia
Jérémie 54 D 3 SW Haiti
Jerez de la Frontera 92 C 5 *var.* Jerez; *prev.* Xeres. SW Spain
Jerez de los Caballeros 92 C 4 W Spain
Jericho 119 E 7 *Ar.* Arīḥā, *Heb.* Yeriẖo. E West Bank
Jerid, Chott el 71 E 2 lake, W Tunisia
Jersey 89 D 8 island, S Channel Islands
Jersey City 41 F 4 New Jersey, NE USA
Jerusalem 119 B 6 *var.* Al Quds ash Sharīf, *Ar.* Al Quds, *Heb.* Yerushalayim; *anc.* Hierosolyma. Country capital, NE Israel
Jesenice 95 D 7 *Ger.* Assling. NW Slovenia
Jesselton *see* Kota Kinabalu
Jessore 135 G 4 W Bangladesh
Jesús María 64 C 3 C Argentina
Jeypore *see* Jaipur
Jhānsi 134 D 3 N India
Jhelum 134 C 2 NE Pakistan

Jiangmen 129 C 6 SE China
Jiangsu 128 D 4 *var.* Chiang-su, Kiangsu, Su. Province, E China
Jiangxi 129 C 5 *var.* Chiang-hsi, Gan, Kiangsi. Province, SE China
Jiaxing 129 D 5 E China
Jibuti *see* Djibouti
Jiddah 121 A 5 *Eng.* Jedda. W Saudi Arabia
Jiftlik Post 119 E 7 E West Bank
Jīgān 121 B 6 *var.* Qīzān. SW Saudi Arabia
Jihlava 99 B 5 *Ger.* Iglau, *Pol.* Iglawa. S Czech Republic
Jilf al Kabīr, Haḍabat al *see* Gilf Kebir Plateau
Jilib 73 D 6 *It.* Gelib. S Somalia
Jilin 128 E 3 *var.* Chi-lin, Girin, Kirin; *prev.* Yunki, Yungki. NE China
Jilin 128 E 3 *var.* Chi-lin, Girin, Kirin, Ji. Province, NE China
Jill, Kediet ej 74 C 2 *var.* Kédia d'Idjil, Kediet Ijill. Mountain, NW Mauritania
Jīma 73 C 5 *var.* Jimma, *It.* Gimma. SW Ethiopia
Jimbolia 108 A 4 *Ger.* Hatzfeld, *Hung.* Zsombolya. W Romania
Jiménez 50 D 2 N Mexico
Jimsar 126 C 3 W China
Jinan 128 D 4 *var.* Chinan, Chi-nan, Tsinan. Province capital, E China
Jingdezhen 129 D 5 E China
Jinghong 129 A 6 S China
Jinhua 129 D 5 E China
Jining 128 D 3 N China
Jinja 73 C 6 S Uganda
Jinotega 52 D 3 NW Nicaragua
Jinotepe 52 D 3 SW Nicaragua
Jinsha 129 A 5 river, SW China
Jinzhou 128 D 3 *var.* Chin-chou, Chinchow; *prev.* Chinhsien. NE China
Ji-Paraná 62 D 3 W Brazil
Jisr ash Shughūr 118 B 3 *Fr.* Djisr el Choghour. NW Syria
Jiu 108 B 5 *Ger.* Schil, Schyl, *Hung.* Zsil, Zsily. River, S Romania
Jiujiang 129 D 5 E China
Jiulong *see* Kowloon
Jizl, Wādī al 120 A 4 dry watercourse, W Saudi Arabia
Jizzakh 123 E 2 *Rus.* Dzhizak. C Uzbekistan
João Pessoa 63 G 2 *prev.* Paraíba. State capital, E Brazil
Joazeiro *see* Juazeiro
Jodhpur 134 C 3 NW India
Joensuu 84 E 4 SE Finland
Jōetsu 131 C 5 *var.* Zyôetu. Honshū, C Japan
Johannesburg 78 D 4 *var.* Egoli, Erautini, Gauteng, *abbrev.* Jo'burg. NE South Africa
Johannisburg *see* Pisz
John Day River 46 B 3 river, Oregon, NW USA
John H.Kerr Reservoir 43 F 1 *var.* Buggs Island Lake, Kerr Lake. Reservoir, SE USA
Johnson City 41 F 3 New York, NE USA
Johor Bahru 138 B 3 *var.* Johor Baharu, Johore Bahru. W Malaysia
Johore Strait 138 A 1 *Mal.* Selat Johor. Strait, Indian Ocean/ Pacific Ocean
Joinvile *see* Joinville
Joinville 63 F 5 *var.* Joinvile. S Brazil

Jojutla 51 E 4 *var.* Jojutla de Juárez. S Mexico
Jojutla de Juárez *see* Jojutla
Jokkmokk 84 C 3 N Sweden
Joliet 40 B 3 Illinois, N USA
Jonava 106 B 4 *Ger.* Janow, *Pol.* Janów. C Lithuania
Jonesboro 42 B 1 Louisiana, S USA
Joniškis 106 C 4 *Ger.* Janischken. N Lithuania
Jönköping 85 B 7 S Sweden
Jonquière 39 E 4 Québec, SE Canada
Joplin 45 F 5 Missouri, C USA

Jordan 119 B 6 *Ar.* Al Mamlaka al Urduniya al Hashemiyah, Al Urdunn; *prev.* Transjordan. Monarchy, SW Asia

Official name: Hashemite Kingdom of Jordan **Date of formation:** 1949 **Capital:** Amman **Population:** 4.4 million **Total area:** 89,210 sq km (34,440 sq miles) **Languages:** Arabic*, Armenian **Religions:** Muslim 95%, Christian 5% **Ethnic mix:** Arab 98%, (Palestinian 49%), Armenian 1%, Circassian 1% **Government:** Constitutional monarchy **Currency:** Dinar = 1,000 fils

Jorhāt 135 H 3 NE India
Jos 75 G 4 C Nigeria
Joseph Bonaparte Gulf 146 D 2 gulf, S Timor Sea
Jos Plateau 75 G 4 plateau, C Nigeria
Jotunheimen 85 A 5 mountain range, S Norway
Joûnié 118 A 4 *var.* Junīyah. W Lebanon
Joure 86 D 2 *Fris.* De Jouwer. N Netherlands
Joutseno 85 E 5 SE Finland
J. Storm Thurmond Reservoir *see* Clark Hill Lake
Juan Aldama 50 D 3 C Mexico
Juan de Fuca, Strait of 46 A 1 strait, Canada/USA
Juan Fernández Islands 153 G 4 *Eng.* Juan Fernandez Islands. Island group, SE Pacific Ocean
Juazeiro 63 G 2 *prev.* Joazeiro. E Brazil
Juazeiro do Norte 63 G 2 E Brazil
Juba 73 B 5 *var.* Jūbā. S Sudan
Jūbā *see* Juba
Jubbulpore *see* Jabalpur
Jucar *see* Júcar
Júcar 93 E 3 *var.* Jucar. River, C Spain
Juchitán 51 F 5 *var.* Juchitán de Zaragosa. SE Mexico
Juchitán de Zaragosa *see* Juchitán
Judayidat Hāmir 120 B 3 S Iraq
Judenburg 95 D 7 C Austria
Juigalpa 52 D 3 S Nicaragua
Juiz de Fora 63 F 4 SE Brazil
Jujuy *see* San Salvador de Jujuy
Juliaca 61 E 4 SE Peru
Juliana Top 59 G 3 mountain, C Surinam
Julianehåb *see* Qaqortoq
Juliomagus *see* Angers
Jullundur *see* Jalandhar
Jumba 73 D 6 S Somalia
Jumilla 93 F 4 SE Spain
Jummoo *see* Jammu
Jumna *see* Yamuna
Jumporn *see* Chumphon

Junction City 45 F 4 Kansas, C USA
Juneau 36 D 4 state capital, Alaska, NW USA
Jungfrau 95 A 7 mountain, S Switzerland
Junín 64 C 4 E Argentina
Junīyah *see* Joûnié
Jura 88 B 4 island, SW Scotland, UK
Jura 95 A 7 *var.* Jura Mountains. Mountain range, France/Switzerland
Jura Mountains *see* Jura
Jurbarkas 106 B 4 *Ger.* Georgenburg, Jurburg. W Lithuania
Jūrmala 106 C 3 C Latvia
Juruá 62 C 2 *var.* Río Yuruá. River, Brazil/Peru
Jutiapa 52 B 2 S Guatemala
Juticalpa 52 D 2 C Honduras
Jutland *see* Jylland
Juvavum *see* Salzburg
Juventud, Isla de la 54 A 2 *var.* Isla de Pinos, *Eng.* Isle of Youth; *prev.* The Isle of the Pines. Island, W Cuba
Jwaneng 78 C 4 SE Botswana
Jylland 85 A 7 *Eng.* Jutland. Peninsula, W Denmark
Jyrgalan *see* Dzhergalan
Jyväskylä 85 D 5 C Finland

K

K2 134 D 1 *Chin.* Qogir Feng, *Eng.* Mount Godwin Austen. Mountain, China/Pakistan
Kaafu Atoll *see* Male' Atoll
Kaaimanston 59 G 3 N Surinam
Kaakhka 122 C 3 *var.* Kaka. S Turkmenistan
Kaamanen 84 D 2 *Lapp.* Gámas. N Finland
Kaambooni 73 D 6 S Somalia
Kaaresuvanto 84 D 2 *Lapp.* Gárassavon. N Finland
Kabale 73 B 6 SW Uganda
Kabinda 77 D 7 SE Zaire
Kabinda *see* Cabinda
Kabul 123 F 4 *var.* Daryā-ye Kābul. River, Afghanistan/Pakistan
Kābul 123 E 4 *var.* Kabul, *Per.* Kābol. Country capital, E Afghanistan
Kābul, Daryā-ye *see* Kabul
Kabwe 78 D 2 C Zambia
Kachchh, Gulf of 134 B 4 *var.* Gulf of Cutch, Gulf of Kutch. Gulf, N Arabian Sea
Kadan Kyun 137 B 6 *prev.* King Island. Island, S Burma
Kadavu 145 E 4 *prev.* Kandavu. Island, S Fiji
Kadoma 78 D 3 *prev.* Gatooma. C Zimbabwe
Kadugli 72 B 4 S Sudan
Kaduna 75 G 4 C Nigeria
Kadzhi-Say 123 G 2 *Kir.* Kajisay. NE Kyrgyzstan
Kaédi 74 C 3 S Mauritania
Kāfar Jar Ghar 123 E 5 mountain range, C Afghanistan
Kafue 78 C 2 river, C Zambia
Kafue 78 D 2 SE Zambia
Kaga Bandoro 76 C 4 *prev.* Fort-Crampel. C Central African Republic
Kagan *see* Kogon
Kâgithane 116 B 2 Turkey
Kagoshima 131 A 8 *var.* Kagosima. Kyūshū, SW Japan

Kagoshima-wan 131 A 8 bay, NW Pacific Ocean
Kagosima *see* Kagoshima
Kagul *see* Cahul
Kahramanmaraş 116 D 4 *var.* Kahraman Maraş, Maraş, Marash. S Turkey
Kaiapoi 151 C 6 South Island, C New Zealand
Kaifeng 128 C 4 C China
Kai, Kepulauan 139 G 4 *prev.* Kei Islands. Island group, Maluka, E Indonesia
Kaikohe 150 C 2 North Island, N New Zealand
Kaikoura 151 C 5 South Island, C New Zealand
Kaikoura Peninsula 151 C 5 peninsula, South Island, C New Zealand
Kainji Lake *see* Kainji Reservoir
Kainji Reservoir 75 F 4 *var.* Kainji Lake. Reservoir, W Nigeria
Kaipara Harbour 150 C 2 harbour, North Island, N New Zealand
Kairouan 71 E 2 *var.* Al Qayrawān. E Tunisia
Kaiserslautern 95 A 5 SW Germany
Kaišiadorys 107 B 5 S Lithuania
Kaitaia 150 C 2 North Island, N New Zealand
Kajaani 84 E 4 *Swe.* Kajana. C Finland
Kajan *see* Kayan, Sungai
Kajana *see* Kajaani
Kajisay *see* Kadzhi-Say
Kaka *see* Kaakhka
Kake 36 D 4 Alaska, NW USA
Kakhovka 109 F 4 S Ukraine
Kakhovs'ka Vodoskhovyshche 109 F 4 *Rus.* Kakhovskoye Vodokhranilishche. Reservoir, SE Ukraine
Kakhovskoye Vodokhranilishche *see* Kakhovs'ka Vodoskhovyshche
Kākīnāda 132 D 1 *prev.* Cocanada. E India
Ka-Krem *see* Malyy Yenisey
Kakshaal-Too, Khrebet *see* Kokshaal-Tau
Kaktovik 36 D 2 Alaska, NW USA
Kalach 111 B 6 W Russian Federation
Kalach-na-Donu 111 B 6 SW Russian Federation
Kalahari Desert 78 C 4 desert, S Africa
Kalaikhum *see* Qal'aikhum
Kalámai *see* Kalámata
Kalamariá 104 C 4 N Greece
Kalámata 105 B 6 *prev.* Kalámai. S Greece
Kalamazoo 40 C 3 Michigan, N USA
Kalambaka *see* Kalampáka
Kálamos 105 C 5 C Greece
Kalampáka 104 B 4 C Greece
Kalanchak 109 F 4 S Ukraine
Kalasin 136 D 4 *var.* Muang Kalasin. NE Thailand
Kalāt 134 B 2 *var.* Kelat, Khelat. SW Pakistan
Kalāt 123 E 5 *Per.* Qalāt. S Afghanistan
Kalbarri 147 A 5 Western Australia, W Australia
Kalecik 116 C 3 N Turkey
Kalemie 77 E 7 *prev.* Albertville. SE Zaire
Kalgoorlie 147 C 6 SW Australia
Kalima 77 D 6 E Zaire

Kalimantan 138 D 4 *Eng.* Indonesian Borneo. Geopolitical region, Borneo, C Indonesia
Kálimnos 105 D 6 island, W Greece
Kalinin *see* Tver'
Kaliningrad 106 A 4 Russian Federation
Kaliningrad 106 A 4 enclave, W Russian Federation
Kalinkavichy 107 C 7 *Rus.* Kalinkovichi. SE Belorussia
Kalinkovichi *see* Kalinkavichy
Kalispell 44 B 1 Montana, NW USA
Kalisz 98 C 4 *Ger.* Kalisch, *Rus.* Kalish; *anc.* Calisia. C Poland
Kalix 84 D 4 N Sweden
Kalixälven 84 D 3 river, N Sweden
Kallaste 106 E 3 *Ger.* Krasnogor. SE Estonia
Kallavesi 85 E 5 lake, SE Finland
Kalloní 105 D 5 Lésvos, E Greece
Kalmar 85 C 7 *var.* Calmar. S Sweden
Kalmthout 87 C 5 N Belgium
Kalpáki 104 A 4 W Greece
Kalpeni Island 132 B 3 island, Lakshadweep, SW India
Kaltdorf *see* Pruszków
Kaluga 111 B 5 W Russian Federation
Kalush 108 C 2 *Pol.* Kałusz. W Ukraine
Kałusz *see* Kalush
Kalutara 132 D 4 SW Sri Lanka
Kalvarija 107 B 5 *Pol.* Kalwaria. S Lithuania
Kalwaria *see* Kalvarija
Kalyān 134 C 5 W India
Kama 110 D 4 river, Russian Federation
Kamarang 59 F 3 W Guyana
Kamchatka *see* Kamchatka, Poluostrov
Kamchatka, Poluostrov 115 H 2 *Eng.* Kamchatka. Peninsula, NE Russian Federation
Kamchiya 104 D 2 river, E Bulgaria
Kamenets-Podol'skiy *see* Kam''yanets'-Podil's'kyy
Kamenka Dneprovskaya *see* Kam''yanka-Dniprovs'ka
Kamensk-Shakhtinskiy 111 B 6 SW Russian Federation
Kamina 77 D 7 S Zaire
Kamloops 37 E 5 British Columbia, SW Canada
Kampala 73 B 6 country capital, S Uganda
Kampar 138 B 3 W Malaysia
Kâmpóng Cham 137 D 6 *prev.* Kompong Cham. S Cambodia
Kâmpóng Chhnāng 137 D 6 *prev.* Kompong Chhnang. C Cambodia
Kâmpóng Saôm 137 D 6 *prev.* Kompong Som, Sihanoukville. SW Cambodia
Kâmpóng Spoe 137 D 6 *prev.* Kompong Speu. S Cambodia
Kâmpóng Thum 137 D 6 *prev.* Kompong Thom. C Cambodia
Kâmpôt 137 D 6 S Cambodia
Kam''yanets'-Podil's'kyy 108 C 3 *Rus.* Kamenets-Podol'skiy. W Ukraine
Kam''yanka-Dniprovs'ka 109 F 3 *Rus.* Kamenka Dneprovskaya. SE Ukraine
Kamyshin 111 C 6 W Russian Federation
Kananga 77 D 7 *prev.* Luluabourg. S Zaire
Kanash 111 C 5 W Russian Federation

Kanazawa 131 C 5 Honshū, SW Japan
Kānchīpuram 132 C 2 *prev.* Conjeeveram. SE India
Kandahār 123 E 5 *var.* Qandahār. S Afghanistan
Kandalaksha 110 C 2 *var.* Kandalakša, *Fin.* Kantalahti. NW Russian Federation
Kandangan 138 D 4 Borneo, C Indonesia
Kandau *see* Kandava
Kandava 106 C 3 *Ger.* Kandau. W Latvia
Kandavu *see* Kadavu
Kandla 134 C 4 W India
Kandy 132 D 3 C Sri Lanka
Kane Fracture Zone 66 B 4 fracture zone, NW Atlantic Ocean
Kaneohe 47 A 8 *Haw.* Kāne'ohe. Hawaii, W USA
Kāne'ohe *see* Kaneohe
Kanestron, Akra *see* Palioúri, Ákra
Kanëv *see* Kaniv
Kanevskoye Vodokhranilishche *see* Kaniv's'ke Vodoskhovyshche
Kangaatsiaq 82 C 3 *var.* Kangatsiak, Kangâtsiaq. W Greenland
Kangân 120 D 4 S Iran
Kangaroo Island 149 A.7 island, SW Australia
Kangerluarsoruseq *see* Færingehavn
Kangerlussuaq 82 C 3 *Dan.* Søndre Strømfjord. SW Greenland
Kangertittivaq 83 E 4 *Dan.* Scoresby Sund. Inlet, N Atlantic Ocean
Kaniv 109 E 2 *Rus.* Kanëv. C Ukraine
Kaniv's'ke Vodoskhovyshche 109 E 2 *Rus.* Kanevskoye Vodokhranilishche. Reservoir, C Ukraine
Kanjiža 100 D 2 *Ger.* Altkanischa, *Hung.* Magyarkanizsa, Ókanizsa; *prev.* Stara Kanjiža. N Yugoslavia
Kankaanpää 85 D 5 SW Finland
Kankakee 40 B 3 Illinois, N USA
Kankan 74 D 4 E Guinea
Kano 75 G 4 N Nigeria
Kānpur 135 E 3 *Eng.* Cawnpore. N India
Kansas 45 E 5 *off.* State of Kansas; *nicknames* Jayhawker State, Sunflower State. State, C USA
Kansas City 45 F 4 Kansas, C USA
Kansas City 45 F 4 Missouri, C USA
Kansas River 45 F 5 River, Kansas, C USA
Kansk 115 E 4 S Russian Federation
Kántanos 105 C 8 Kríti, SE Greece
Kantemirovka 111 B 6 W Russian Federation
Kantipur *see* Kathmandu
Kanton 145 F 3 *var.* Abariringa, Canton Island; *prev.* Mary Island. Island, C Kiribati
Kanye 78 C 4 SE Botswana
Kaohsiung 129 D 6 *var.* Gaoxiong, *Jap.* Takao, Takow. SW Taiwan
Kaolack 74 B 3 *var.* Kaolak. W Senegal
Kaolak *see* Kaolack
Kaoma 78 C 2 W Zambia
Kapelle 87 B 5 SW Netherlands
Kapellen 87 C 5 N Belgium
Kapka, Massif du 76 D 2 mountain range, E Chad
Kapoeas *see* Kapuas, Sungai
Kaposvár 99 C 7 SW Hungary
Kappeln 94 B 2 N Germany

Kaptsevichy 107 C 7 *Rus.*
Koptsevichi. SE Belorussia
Kapuas 138 C 4 *prev.* Kapoeas.
River, Borneo, C Indonesia
Kapuskasing 38 C 4 Ontario, S
Canada
Kapyl' 107 C 6 *Rus.* Kopyl'. C
Belorussia
Kara-Balta 123 F 2 N Kyrgyzstan
Karabil', Vozvyshennost' 122 D 3
mountain range, S Turkmenistan
Kara-Bogaz-Gol, Proliv 122 B 2
Turkm. Garabogazköl Bogazy.
Strait, E Caspian Sea
Kara-Bogaz-Gol, Zaliv 122 B 2 bay,
E Caspian Sea
Karabük 116 C 2 N Turkey
Karachev 111 B 5 W Russian
Federation
Karāchi 134 B 3 province capital, SE
Pakistan
Karácsonkő *see* Piţra-Neamt
Karaganda 114 C 4 *Kaz.*
Qaraghandy. C Kazakhstan
Karaginskiy, Ostrov 115 H 2 island,
E Russian Federation
Karaginskiy Zaliv 115 H 2 bay, W
Bering Sea
Karaj 120 C 3 N Iran
Kara-Kala 122 C 3 *var.* Garrygala.
W Turkmenistan
Karakax *see* Moyu
Karakol 123 G 2 *var.* Karakolka. NE
Kyrgyzstan
Karakol 123 G 2 *prev.* Przheval'sk.
NE Kyrgyzstan
Karakolka *see* Karakol
Karakoram Range 134 D 1
mountain range, India/Pakistan
Karaköse 117 F 3 Turkey
Karakul' *see* Qarokül
Kara Kum *see* Garagumy
Karakumskiy Kanal 122 D 3 *Turkm.*
Garagum Kanaly. Canal, C
Turkmenistan
Karaman 116 C 4 S Turkey
Karamay 126 B 2 *var.* Karamai,
Kelamayi, *Chin.* K'o-la-ma-i. NW
China
Karamea Bight 151 C 5 bight, South
Island, E Tasman Sea
Karapelit 104 E 1 *Rom.* Stejarul. NE
Bulgaria
Kara-Say 123 G 2 NE Kyrgyzstan
Karasburg 78 B 4 S Namibia
Kara Sea *see* Karskoye More
Karatau 114 C 5 *Kaz.* Qarataū. S
Kazakhstan
Karavanke *see* Karawanken
Karavás 105 B 7 Kýthira, S Greece
Karbalā' 120 B 3 *var.* Kerbala,
Kerbela. S Iraq
Kardhítsa *see* Kardítsa
Kardítsa 105 B 5 *var.* Kardhítsa. C
Greece
Kärdla 106 C 2 *Ger.* Kertel.
Hiiumaa, W Estonia
Kargı 116 C 2 N Turkey
Kargilik *see* Yecheng
Kariba 78 D 2 N Zimbabwe
Kariba, Lake 78 D 3 reservoir,
Zambia/Zimbabwe
Karibib 78 B 3 C Namibia
Karies *see* Karyés
Karigasniemi 84 D 2 *Lapp.*
Garegasnjárga. N Finland
Karimata, Selat 138 C 4 strait, Java
Sea/South China Sea
Karīmnagar 135 E 5 C India
Karin 72 D 4 N Somalia
Káristos *see* Kárystos

Karkinits'ka Zatoka 109 F 4 *Rus.*
Karkinitskiy Zaliv. Gulf, N Black
Sea
Karkinitskiy Zaliv *see* Karkinits'ka
Zatoka
Karl-Marx-Stadt *see* Chemnitz
Karlö *see* Hailuoto
Karlovac 100 B 2 *Ger.* Karlstadt,
Hung. Károlyváros. C Croatia
Karlovy Vary 99 A 5 *Ger.* Karlsbad;
prev. Eng. Carlsbad. W Czech
Republic
Karlskrona 85 C 7 S Sweden
Karlsruhe 95 B 6 *var.* Carlsruhe. SW
Germany
Karlstad 85 B 6 C Sweden
Karnāl 134 D 2 N India
Karnātaka 132 C 1 *var.* Kanara; *prev.*
Maisur, Mysore. State, W India
Karnobat 104 E 2 E Bulgaria
Karnul *see* Kurnool
Kárpathos 105 E 7 Kárpathos, SE
Greece
Kárpathos 105 E 7 *It.* Scarpanto;
anc. Carpathos, Carpathus. Island,
Dodekánisos, SE Greece
Karpenísi 105 B 5 *prev.*
Karpenísion. C Greece
Karpeníison *see* Karpenísi
Kars 117 F 3 *var.* Qars. NE Turkey
Kārsava 106 D 4 *Ger.* Karsau; *prev.*
Rus. Korsovka. E Latvia
Karskoye More 114 D 2 *Eng.* Kara
Sea. Sea, Arctic Ocean
Kārūn 120 C 3 *var.* Rúd-e Kárún.
River, SW Iran
Kārūn, Rūd-e *see* Kārūn
Karyés 104 C 4 *var.* Karies. N
Greece
Kárystos 105 C 6 *var.* Káristos.
Évvoia, C Greece
Kas 116 B 5 SW Turkey
Kasai 77 C 6 *var.* Cassai, Kassai.
River, Angola/Zaire
Kasaji 77 D 7 S Zaire
Kasama 78 D 1 N Zambia
Kasan *see* Koson
Kasane 78 C 3 NE Botswana
Kāsaragod 132 B 2 SW India
Kāshān 120 C 3 C Iran
Kashi 126 A 3 *Chin.* Kaxgar, K'o-
shih, *Uigh.* Kashgar. NW China
Kashmir 134 D 1 cultural region, N
India
Kaskaskia River 40 B 5 river,
Illinois, N USA
Kasongo 77 D 6 E Zaire
Kásos 105 E 7 island, S Greece
Kaspiysk 111 B 8 SW Russian
Federation
Kassala 72 C 4 E Sudan
Kassel 94 B 4 *prev.* Cassel. C
Germany
Kasserine 71 E 2 *var.* Al Qaşrayn.
W Tunisia
Kastamonu 116 C 2 *var.* Castamoni,
Kastamuni. N Turkey
Kastaneá 104 B 4 N Greece
Kastélli 105 C 7 Kríti, SE Greece
Kastoría 104 B 4 N Greece
Kástro 105 C 6 Sífnos, SE Greece
Kastsyukovichy 107 E 7 *Rus.*
Kostyukovichi. E Belorussia
Kastsyukowka 107 D 7 *Rus.*
Kostyukovka. SE Belorussia
Kasulu 73 B 7 W Tanzania
Kasumiga-ura 131 D 5 lake,
Honshū, S Japan
Katalla 36 C 3 Alaska, NW USA
Katana *see* Qaţanā
Katanning 147 B 7 Western
Australia, W Australia

Katchall Island 133 F 3 island, SW
India
Kateríni 104 B 4 N Greece
Katha 136 B 2 N Burma
Katherina, Gebel 72 C 2 *var.* Jabal
Katrínah, *Eng.* Mount Catherine.
Mountain, NE Egypt
Katherine 148 A 2 Northern
Territory, N Australia
Kathmandu 135 F 3 *prev.* Kantipur.
Country capital, C Nepal
Katikati 150 D 3 North Island, NE
New Zealand
Katima Mulilo 78 C 3 NE Namibia
Katiola 74 D 4 C Ivory Coast
Káto Achaïa 105 B 6 *var.* Káto
Akhaïa. S Greece
Kat O Chau 128 B 1 island, NE
Hong Kong
Katoúna 105 B 5 C Greece
Katowice 99 C 5 *Ger.* Kattowitz. S
Poland
Katsina 75 G 4 N Nigeria
Kattakurgan *see* Kattaqŭrghon
Kattaqŭrghon 123 E 2 *Rus.*
Kattakurgan. C Uzbekistan
Kattavía 105 E 7 Ródos, SE Greece
Kattegat 85 B 7 *Dan.* Kattegatt.
Strait, E North Sea
Kattegatt *see* Kattegat
Kattowitz *see* Katowice
Kauai 47 A 7 *Haw.* Kaua'i. Island,
Hawaii, W USA
Kaua'i *see* Kauai
Kaufbeuren 95 C 6 S Germany
Kaunas 106 B 4 *Ger.* Kauen, *Pol.*
Kowno; *prev. Rus.* Kovno. C
Lithuania
Kauno Marios 106 B 4 reservoir, S
Lithuania
Kau-Ye Kyun 137 B 6 *var.* Sir
Charles Forbes Island. Island, S
Burma
Kavadar *see* Kavadarci
Kavadarci 101 E 6 *Turk.* Kavadar. C
Macedonia
Kavajë 101 C 6 *It.* Cavaia, Kavaja.
W Albania
Kavakli *see* Topolovgrad
Kavála 104 C 3 *prev.* Kaválla. NE
Greece
Kaválla *see* Kavála
Kavaratti Island 132 B 3 island,
Lakshadweep, SW India
Kavarna 104 E 2 NE Bulgaria
Kavīr, Dasht-e 120 D 3 *var.* Dasht-e
Kavir. Salt lake, N Iran
Kavkaz *see* Caucasus
Kawagoe 131 D 5 Honshū, S Japan
Kawasaki 131 D 5 Honshū, S Japan
Kawerau 150 E 3 North Island, NE
New Zealand
Kaya 75 E 4 C Burkina
Kayan 136 B 4 S Burma
Kayan 138 D 3 *prev.* Kajan. River,
Borneo, C Indonesia
Kayes 74 C 3 W Mali
Kayseri 116 D 3 *var.* Kaisaria; *anc.*
Caesarea Mazaca, Mazaca. C
Turkey
Kazach'ye 115 F 2 N Russian
Federation
Kazakhskiy Melkosopochnik 114 B
4 *Eng.* Kazakh Uplands, Kirghiz
Steppe, *Kaz.* Saryarqa. Physical
region, C Kazakhstan

Kazakhstan
114 B 4 Qazaqstan Respublikasy,
var. Kazakstan, *Kaz.* Qazaqstan;
prev. Kazakh Soviet Socialist
Republic, *Rus.* Kazakhskaya SSR.
Republic, C Asia

Official name: Republic of
Kazakhstan **Date of formation:** 1991
Capital: Almaty **Population:** 17.2
million **Total Area:** 2,717,300 sq km
(1,049,150 sq miles) **Languages:**
Kazakh*, Russian **Religions:**
Muslim 47%, other 53% (mostly
Russian Orthodox, Lutheran) **Ethnic
mix:** Kazakh 40%, Russian 38%,
Ukrainian 6%, other 16%
Government: Multiparty republic
Currency: Tenge = 100 tein

Kazakh Uplands *see* Kazakhskiy
Melkosopochnik
Kazan' 111 D 5 W Russian
Federation
Kazan' 111 D 5 international
airport, W Russian Federation
Kazanlŭk 104 D 2 *var.* Kazanlŭk;
prev. Kazanlik. C Bulgaria
Kazatin *see* Kozyatyn
Kazbek 117 F 2 *Geor.* Mqinvartsveri.
Mountain, Armenia/Georgia
Kāzerūn 120 D 4 S Iran
Kazi Magomed *see* Qazimämmäd
Kazvin *see* Qazvīn
Kéa 105 C 6 Kéa, SE Greece
Kéa 105 C 6 *prev.* Kea. Ceos.
Island, Kykládes, SE Greece
Kearney 45 E 4 Nebraska, C USA
Keban 117 E 3 Turkey
Keban, Baraji 117 E 3 lake, C
Turkey
Kebkabiya 72 A 4 W Sudan
Kebnekaise 84 C 3 mountain, N
Sweden
Kecskemét 99 D 7 C Hungary
Kediri 138 D 5 Jawa, C Indonesia
Keetmanshoop 78 B 4 S Namibia
Keewatin 38 A 3 Ontario, S Canada
Kefallinía 105 A 5 *var.* Kefallonia.
Island, Iónioi Nísoi, W Greece
Kefallonia *see* Kefallinía
Kefar Tappuaḥ 119 E 7 C West
Bank
Kegel *see* Keila
Kehl 95 A 6 SW Germany
Kei Islands *see* Kai, Kepulauan
Keila 106 D 2 *Ger.* Kegel. NW
Estonia
Keita 75 F 3 C Niger
Keitele 84 D 4 lake, C Finland
Keith 149 B 7 South Australia, S
Australia
Keizer 46 B 3 Oregon, NW USA
Këk-Art 123 G 2 *prev.* Alaykel',
Alay-Kuu. SW Kyrgyzstan
Kékes 99 D 6 mountain, N
Hungary
Kelang 138 B 3 *var.* Kelang; *prev.*
Port Swettenham. W Malaysia
Kelifskiy Uzboy 122 D 3 wetland,
E Turkmenistan
Kelmë 106 B 4 C Lithuania
Kélo 76 B 4 SW Chad
Kelowna 37 E 5 British Columbia,
SW Canada
Kelso 46 B 3 Washington, NW USA
Keltsy *see* Kielce
Keluang 138 B 3 *var.* Kluang. W
Malaysia
Kem' 110 B 3 NW Russian
Federation
Kemah 117 E 3 E Turkey
Kemerovo 114 D 4 *prev.*
Shcheglovsk. C Russian
Federation
Kemi 84 D 3 NW Finland

Kemijärvi 84 D 3 *Swe.* Kemiträsk.
  N Finland
Kemijoki 84 D 3 river, NW Finland
Kemiö *see* Kimito
Kemiträsk *see* Kemijärvi
Kempele 84 D 4 C Finland
Kempten 95 C 7 S Germany
Kempton 149 C 8 Tasmania, SE
  Australia
Kendal 89 C 5 NW England, UK
Kendall 43 F 5 Florida, SE USA
Kendari 139 E 4 Celebes, C
  Indonesia
Kenedy 49 G 4 Texas, S USA
Kenema 74 C 4 SE Sierra Leone
Këneurgench 122 C 2 *Turkm.*
  Köneürgench; *prev.* Kunya-
  Urgench. N Turkmenistan
Kenge 77 C 6 SW Zaire
Keng Tung 136 C 3 *var.* Kentung.
  SE Burma
Kénitra 70 C 2 *prev.* Port-Lyautey.
  NW Morocco
Kennebec River 41 G 2 river,
  Maine, NE USA
Kenner 42 B 3 Louisiana, S USA
Kennett 45 H 5 Missouri, C USA
Kennewick 46 C 2 Washington,
  NW USA
Kenora 38 A 3 Ontario, S Canada
Kenosha 40 B 3 Wisconsin, N USA
Kent 46 B 2 Washington, NW USA
Kentau 114 B 5 S Kazakhstan
Kentucky 40 C 5 *off.*
  Commonwealth of Kentucky;
  nickname Bluegrass State. State, C
  USA
Kentucky Lake 40 B 5 reservoir, E
  USA
Kentung *see* Keng Tung

Kenya
  73 C 6 Republic, NE Africa

Official name: Republic of Kenya
Date of formation: 1963
Capital: Nairobi **Population:** 26.1
million **Total area:** 580,370 sq km
(224,081 sq miles) **Languages:**
Swahili*, English, Kikuyu, Luo,
Kamba **Religions:** Christian 66%,
traditional beliefs 26%, other 8%
Ethnic mix: Kikuyu 21%, Luhya
14%, Kamba 11%, other 54%
Government: Multiparty republic
Currency: Shilling = 100 cents

Kenya, Mount *see* Kirinyaga
Keokuk 45 G 4 Iowa, C USA
Kępno 98 C 4 C Poland
Kerala 132 C 2 state, S India
Keratea *see* Keratéa
Keratéa 105 C 6 *var.* Keratea. C
  Greece
Kerch 109 G 5 *Rus.* Kerch'. SE
  Ukraine
Kerch' *see* Kerch
Kerch Strait 109 G 4 *var.* Bosporus
  Cimmerius, Enikale Strait, *Rus.*
  Kerchenskiy Proliv, *Ukr.*
  Kerchens'ka Protska. Strait, Sea of
  Azov/Black Sea
Keremitlik *see* Lyulyakovo
Kerguelen 141 C 7 island, C French
  Southern & Antarctic Territories
Kerguelen Plateau 141 C 7
  undersea plateau, S Indian Ocean
Kerí 105 A 6 Zákynthos, W Greece
Kerikeri 150 D 2 North Island, N
  New Zealand
Kerki 123 E 3 E Turkmenistan
Kerkrade 87 D 6 SE Netherlands

Kérkyra 104 A 4 *var.* Kérkira, *Eng.*
  Corfu. Island, Iónioi Nísoi, W
  Greece
Kérkyra 104 A 4 *var.* Kérkira, *Eng.*
  Corfu. Kérkyra, W Greece
Kermadec Islands 152 C 4 island
  group, NE New Zealand
Kermadec Trench 152 D 4 trench, SE
  Pacific Ocean
Kermān 120 D 4 *var.* Kirman; *anc.*
  Carmana. C Iran
Kerrville 49 F 4 Texas, S USA
Kertel *see* Kärdla
Kerulen 127 E 2 *Chin.* Herlen He,
  Mong. Herlen Gol. River,
  China/Mongolia
Kessennuma 130 D 4 Honshū, C
  Japan
Keszthely 99 C 7 SW Hungary
Ketchikan 36 D 4 Alaska, NW USA
Kettering 89 D 6 C England, UK
Kettering 40 C 4 Ohio, N USA
Keupriya *see* Primorsko
Keuruu 85 D 5 C Finland
Keweenaw Peninsula 40 B 1
  headland, Michigan, N USA
Key Largo 54 B 2 island, W Cuba
Key West 43 E 5 Florida, SE USA
Khabarovsk 115 G 4 SE Russian
  Federation
Khachmas *see* Xaçmaz
Khairpur 134 B 3 SE Pakistan
Khambhāt, Gulf of 134 C 4 *Eng.*
  Gulf of Cambay. Gulf, NE
  Arabian Sea
Khānābād 123 E 3 NE Afghanistan
Khān al Baghdādī *see* Al Baghdādī
Khandwa 134 D 4 C India
Khanh Hung *see* Soc Trăng
Khanka, Lake 128 E 2 *var.* Hsing-
  K'ai Hu, Lake Hanka, *Chin.*
  Xingkai Hu, *Rus.* Ozero Khanka.
  Lake, China/Russian Federation
Khanty-Mansiysk 114 C 3 *prev.*
  Ostyako-Voguls'k. C Russian
  Federation
Khan Yums 119 A 7 S Israel
Khanzi *see* Ghanzi
Kharagpur 135 F 4 NE India
Khar'kov 109 G 2 *Rus.* Khar'kov. NE
  Ukraine
Khar'kov *see* Kharkiv
Kharmanli 104 D 3 *var.* Harmanli. S
  Bulgaria
Kharovsk 110 C 4 *var.* Charovsk,
  Harovsk. NW Russian Federation
Khartoum 72 B 4 *var.* El Khartûm,
  Khartum. Country capital, C
  Sudan
Khasavyurt 111 B 8 SW Russian
  Federation
Khashm el Girba 72 C 4 E Sudan
Khaskovo 104 D 3 *var.* Haskovo. S
  Bulgaria
Khaybar, Kowtal-e *see* Khyber Pass
Khaydarkan 123 F 2 *var.*
  Khaydarken. SW Kyrgyzstan
Khaydarken *see* Khaydarkan
Kherson 109 E 4 *var.* Cherson. S
  Ukraine
Kheta 115 E 2 river, N Russian
  Federation
Khíos *see* Chíos
Khiva *see* Khiwa
Khiwa 122 D 2 *Rus.* Khiva. W
  Uzbekistan
Khmel 'nyts'kyy 108 C 2 *Rus.*
  Khmel'nitskiy; *prev.* Proskurov. W
  Ukraine
Khodasy 107 E 7 *Rus.* Khodosy. E
  Belorussia
Khodoriv 108 C 2 *Pol.* Chodorów,
  Rus. Khodorov. NW Ukraine

Khodosy *see* Khodasy
Kholm 123 E 3 *var.* Tashqurghan,
  Pash. Khulm. N Afghanistan
Kholm *see* Chełm
Khong Sedone *see* Muang
  Khôngxédôn
Khon Kaen 136 D 4 *var.* Muang
  Khon Kaen. N Thailand
Khor 115 G 4 SE Russian Federation
Khorugh 123 F 3 *var.* Horog, *Rus.*
  Khorog. S Tajikistan
Kho Sawai Plateau *see* Korat
  Plateau
Khosf 120 E 3 E Iran
Khouribga 70 C 2 C Morocco
Khovd *see* Hovd
Khowst 123 F 4 E Afghanistan
Khoyniki 107 D 8 SE Belorussia
Khujand 123 F 2 *var.* Khodzhent,
  Khojend, *Rus.* Khudzhand, *Taj.*
  Leninobod; *prev.* Leninabad. N
  Tajikistan
Khulna 135 G 4 SW Bangladesh
Khust 108 B 3 *var.* Husté, *Cz.* Chust,
  Hung. Huszt. W Ukraine
Khvalynsk 111 C 6 W Russian
  Federation
Khvoy 120 C 2 *var.* Khoi, Khoy. NW
  Iran
Khyber Pass 123 F 4 *var.* Kowtal-e
  Khaybar. Pass,
  Afghanistan/Pakistan
Kiáto 105 B 6 *prev.* Kiáton. S Greece
Kiáton *see* Kiáto
Kibangou 77 B 5 SW Congo
Kibombo 77 D 6 E Zaire
Kičevo 101 D 5 SW Macedonia
Kidderminster 89 C 6 W England,
  UK
Kiel 94 B 2 N Germany
Kielce 98 D 4 *Rus.* Keltsy. SE
  Poland
Kieler Bucht 94 C 2 bay, W Baltic
  Sea
Kiev *see* Kyyiv
Kiffa 74 C 3 S Mauritania
Kigali 73 B 6 country capital, C
  Rwanda
Kigoma 73 B 7 W Tanzania
Kihnu 106 C 2 *var.* Kihnu Saar, *Ger.*
  Kühnö. Island, SW Estonia
Kihti *see* Skiftet
Kii-suidō 131 C 7 strait, NW Pacific
  Ocean
Kikinda 100 D 3 *Ger.* Grosskikinda,
  Hung. Nagykikinda; *prev.* Velika
  Kikinda. NE Yugoslavia
Kikwit 77 C 6 W Zaire
Kili 144 D 2 Island, S Marshall
  Islands
Kilien Mountains *see* Qilian Shan
Kilimanjaro 73 C 7 *var.* Vhuru
  Peak. Mountain, NE Tanzania
Kilingi-Nõmme 106 D 3 *Ger.*
  Kurkund. SW Estonia
Kilis 116 D 4 S Turkey
Kiliya 108 D 4 *Rom.* Chilia-Nouă.
  SW Ukraine
Kilkenny 89 B 6 *Ir.* Cill Chainnigh.
  S Ireland
Kilkís 104 B 3 N Greece
Killarney 89 A 6 *Ir.* Cill Airne. SW
  Ireland
Killeen 49 G 3 Texas, S USA
Kilmarnock 88 C 4 SW Scotland,
  UK
Kimberley 78 C 4 C South Africa
Kimberley Plateau 146 D 3 plateau,
  Western Australia, NW Australia
Kimch'aek 128 E 3 *prev.* Sŏngjin. E
  North Korea

Kími *see* Kými
Kimito 85 D 6 *Swe.* Kemiö. Island,
  SW Finland
Kimovsk 111 B 5 W Russian
  Federation
Kindersley 37 F 5 Saskatchewan, S
  Canada
Kindia 74 C 4 SW Guinea
Kindley Field Airport 42 B 5
  international airport, E Bermuda
Kindu 77 D 6 *prev.* Kindu-Port-
  Empain. C Zaire
Kindu-Port-Empain *see* Kindu
Kineshma 111 C 5 *var.* Kinešma. W
  Russian Federation
Kinešma *see* Kineshma
King Charles Islands *see* Kong
  Karls Land
King Christian IX Land *see* Kong
  Christian IX Land
King Christian X Land *see* Kong
  Christian X Land
King Frederik VI Coast *see* King
  Frederick VI Coast
King Frederik VIII Land *see* King
  Frederick VIII Land
King Frederik IX Land *see* King
  Frederik IX Land
King Frederik VI Coast *see* King
  Frederik VI Kyst
King Frederik VIII Land *see* Kong
  Frederik VIII Land
Kiáto 105 B 6 *prev.* Kiáton. S Greece
King George Island *see* King
  George Land
King I *see* Kadan Kyun
King Island 149 B 8 island,
  Tasmania, SE Australia
Kingman 48 A 2 Arizona, SW USA
Kingman Reef 145 G 2 reef, NE
  Australia
King's Lynn 89 E 6 *var.* Bishop's
  Lynn, Kings Lynn, Lynn, Lynn
  Regis. E England, UK
Kingston 54 B 5 country capital, SE
  Jamaica
Kingston 38 D 5 Ontario, SE
  Canada
Kingston 41 F 3 New York, NE
  USA
Kingston upon Hull 89 E 5 *var.*
  Hull. NE England, UK
Kingstown 55 H 4 country capital,
  N Saint Vincent & the Grenadines
Kingsville 49 G 5 Texas, S USA
King William Island 37 F 3 island,
  N Canada
Kinrooi 87 D 5 NE Belgium
Kinshasa 77 B 6 *prev.* Léopoldville.
  Country capital, W Zaire
Kinston 43 F 1 North Carolina, SE
  USA
Kintyre 88 B 4 peninsula, NE
  Scotland, UK
Kinyeti 73 B 5 mountain, S Sudan
Kiparissía *see* Kyparissía
Kipili 73 B 7 W Tanzania
Kipushi 77 E 8 SE Zaire
Kirghiz Range 114 C 5 *Rus.*
  Kirgizskiy Khrebet; *prev.*
  Alexander Range. Mountain
  range, Kazakhstan/Kyrgyzstan
Kirghiz Steppe *see* Kazakhskiy
  Melkosopochnik
Kırıkkale 116 C 3 C Turkey
Kırıkhan 116 D 4 S Turkey

Kiribati
  145 F 2 Republic, C Pacific Ocean

Official name: Republic of Kiribati
Date of formation: 1979 **Capital:**
Bairiki **Population:** 7,500 **Total Area:**
710 sq km (274 sq miles) **Languages:**
English*, Kiribati **Religions:** Roman
Catholic 53%, Protestant 40%, other
Christian 4%, other 3% **Ethnic mix:**
I-Kiribati 98%, other 2%
Government: Multiparty republic
Currency: Australian $ = 100 cents

Kiribati, Republic of see Kiribati
Kirinyaga 73 C 6 prev. Mount
Kenya. Volcano, C Kenya
Kirishi 110 B 4 var. Kirisi. NW
Russian Federation
Kirisi see Kirishi
Kiritimati 145 G 2 prev. Christmas
Island. Island, E Kiribati
Kiriwina Islands 144 C 3 var.
Trobriand Islands. Island group, S
Papua New Guinea
Kirkenes 84 E 2 var. Kirkkoniemi.
N Norway
Kirk-Kilissa see Kırklareli
Kirkkoniemi see Kirkenes
Kirkland Lake 38 D 4 Ontario, S
Canada
Kırklareli 116 A 2 prev. Kirk-Kilissa.
NW Turkey
Kirkpatrick, Mount 154 C 3
mountain, Antarctica
Kirksville 45 G 4 Missouri, C USA
Kirkûk 120 B 3 var. Karkûk,
Kerkuk. N Iraq
Kirkwall 88 C 2 island authority
area capital, NE Scotland, UK
Kirkwood 45 G 5 Missouri, C USA
Kirov 110 C 4 prev. Vyatka. NW
Russian Federation
Kirovakan see Vanadzor
Kirovo-Cepesk see Kirovo-Chepetsk
Kirovo-Chepetsk 111 D 5 var.
Kirovo-Čepeck. NW Russian
Federation
Kirovohrad 109 E 3 Rus.
Kirovograd; prev.
Kirovo,Yelizavetgrad,
Zinov'yevsk. C Ukraine
Kirsanov 111 B 6 W Russian
Federation
Kírthar Range 134 A 3 mountain
range, S Pakistan
Kiruna 84 C 3 N Sweden
Kisangani 77 D 5 prev. Stanleyville.
NE Zaire
Kishinev see Chişinău
Kiskörei-víztároló 99 D 6 reservoir,
E Hungary
Kiskunfélegyháza 99 D 7 var.
Félegyháza. C Hungary
Kislovodsk 111 B 7 SW Russian
Federation
Kismaayo 73 D 6 var. Chisimayu,
Kismayu, It. Chisimaio. S Somalia
Kissidougou 74 C 4 S Guinea
Kissimmee 43 E 4 Florida, SE USA
Kistna see Krishna
Kisumu 73 C 6 prev. Port Florence.
W Kenya
Kisvárda 99 E 6 Ger. Kleinwardein.
E Hungary
Kita 74 D 3 W Mali
Kitab see Kitob
Kitakyūshū 131 A 7 var.
Kitakyûsyû. Kyûshû, SW Japan
Kitakyûsyû see Kitakyūshū
Kitami 130 D 2 Hokkaidō, NE
Japan
Kitchener 38 C 5 Ontario, S Canada
Kitimat 36 D 5 British Columbia,
SW Canada

Kitinen 84 D 3 river, N Finland
Kitob 123 E 3 Rus. Kitab. S
Uzbekistan
Kitwe 78 D 2 var. Kitwe-Nkana. C
Zambia
Kitwe-Nkana see Kitwe
Kitzbühler Alpen 95 D 7 mountain
range, W Austria
Kivalina 36 C 2 Alaska, NW USA
Kivalo 84 D 3 ridge, C Finland
Kivertsi 108 C 1 Pol. Kiwerce, Rus.
Kivertsy. NW Ukraine
Kivu, Lac see Kivu, Lake
Kivu, Lake 77 E 6 Fr. Lac Kivu.
Lake, Rwanda/Zaire
Kiyevskoye Vodokhranilishche see
Kyyivs'ke Vodoskhovyshche
Kizel 111 D 5 NW Russian
Federation
Kızıl Irmak 116 C 3 river, C Turkey
Kizilyurt 111 B 8 SW Russian
Federation
Kizyl-Arvat see Gyzylarbat
Kjølen see Kölen
Kladno 99 A 5 NW Czech Republic
Klagenfurt 95 D 7 Slvn. Celovec. S
Austria
Klaipėda 106 B 3 Ger. Memel. NW
Lithuania
Klamath Falls 46 B 4 Oregon, NW
USA
Klamath Mountains 46 B 4
mountain range, W USA
Klarälven 85 B 6 river,
Norway/Sweden
Klatovy 99 A 5 Ger. Klattau. SW
Czech Republic
Klattau see Klatovy
Klazienaveen 86 E 2 NE
Netherlands
Kleinwardein see Kisvárda
Kleisoúra 105 A 5 W Greece
Klerksdorp 78 D 4 N South Africa
Klimavichy 107 E 7 Rus.
Klimovichi. E Belorussia
Klimovichi see Klimavichy
Klintsy 111 A 5 W Russian
Federation
Klisura 104 C 2 C Bulgaria
Ključ 100 B 3 NW Bosnia &
Herzegovina
Kłobuck 98 C 4 S Poland
Klondike 36 D 3 river, Yukon
Territory, W Canada
Kluang see Keluang
Kluczbork 98 C 4 Ger. Kreuzburg,
Kreuzburg in Oberschlesien. SW
Poland
Knin 100 B 4 S Croatia
Knjaževac 100 E 4 E Yugoslavia
Knokke-Heist 87 A 5 NW Belgium
Knoxville 42 D 1 Tennessee, S USA
Knud Rasmussen Land 82 D 1
physical region, N Greenland
Kōbe 131 C 6 Honshū, SW Japan
København 85 B 7 Eng.
Copenhagen; anc. Hafnia.
Country capital, E Denmark
Kobenni 74 D 3 S Mauritania
Koblenz 95 A 5 Fr. Coblence; prev.
Coblenz, anc. Confluentes. W
Germany
Kobryn 107 A 6 Pol. Kobryn, Rus.
Kobrin. SW Belorussia
K'obulet'i 117 F 2 W Georgia
Kočani 101 E 6 NE Macedonia
Kočevje 95 E 8 Ger. Gottschee. S
Slovenia
Koch Bihār 135 G 3 NE India
Kōchi 131 B 7 var. Kôti. Shikoku,
SW Japan

Kochi see Cochin
Kochiu see Gejiu
Kodiak 36 C 3 Kodiak Island,
Alaska, USA
Kodiak Island 36 C 3 island,
Alaska, NW USA
Koedoes see Kudus
Koepang see Kupang
Kofa Mountains 48 A 2 mountain
range, Arizona, SW USA
Kōfu 131 D 5 var. Kôhu. Honshū, S
Japan
Kogon 122 D 2 Rus. Kagan . C
Uzbekistan
Kohīma 135 H 3 var. Kohima. NE
India
Kohima see Kohīma
Kohtla-Järve 106 E 2 NE Estonia
Kokkola 84 D 4 Swe. Karleby; prev.
Swe. Gamlakarleby. W Finland
Kokrines 36 C 3 Alaska, NW USA
Kokshaal-Tau 123 G 2 Rus. Khrebet
Kakshaal-Too. Mountain range,
China/Kyrgyzstan
Kokshetau 114 C 4 Kaz. Kökshetaū;
prev. Kokchetav. N Kazakhstan
Koksijde 87 A 5 W Belgium
Kokstad 78 D 5 E South Africa
Kolaka 139 E 4 Celebes, C
Indonesia
Kola Peninsula see Kol'skiy
Poluostrov
Kolari 84 D 3 NW Finland
Kolárovo 99 C 6 Ger. Guta, Hung.
Gúta; prev. Guta. SW Slovakia
Kolberg see Kołobrzeg
Kolda 74 B 3 S Senegal
Kolding 85 A 7 C Denmark
Kôle see Kili Island
Kolguyev, Ostrov 110 D 2 island,
NW Russian Federation
Kolhāpur 132 B 1 SW India
Kolhumadulu Atoll 132 B 5 var.
Kolumadulu Atoll, Thaa Atoll.
Island, S Maldives
Kolín 99 B 5 Ger. Kolin. C Czech
Republic
Kolka 106 C 2 NW Latvia
Kolkasrags 106 C 2 prev. Eng. Cape
Domesnes. Headland, NW Latvia
Kolmar see Colmar
Köln 94 A 4 var. Koeln, Eng./Fr.
Cologne; prev. Cöln, anc. Colonia
Agrippina, Oppidum Ubiorum.
W Germany
Koło 98 C 3 C Poland
Kołobrzeg 98 B 2 Ger. Kolberg. NW
Poland
Kolokani 74 D 3 W Mali
Kolomea see Kolomyya
Kolomna 111 B 5 W Russian
Federation
Kolomyya 108 B 3 Ger. Kolomea. W
Ukraine
Kolonia 144 C 2 var. Colonia.
Pohnpei, E Micronesia
Kolpa 100 A 2 Ger. Kulpa, SCr.
Kupa. River, Croatia/Slovenia
Kolpino 110 B 4 NW Russian
Federation
Kol'skiy Poluostrov 110 C 2 Eng.
Kola Peninsula. Peninsula, NW
Russian Federation
Kolweżi 77 D 7 S Zaire
Kolyma 115 G 2 river, NE Russian
Federation
Kolyma Range 113 G 2 mountain
range, NE Russian Federation
Kolymskoye Nagor'ye 115 G 2 var.
Khrebet Kolymskiy, Eng. Kolyma
Range. Mountain range, NE
Russian Federation

Komatsu 131 C 5 var. Komatu.
Honshū, SW Japan
Komatu see Komatsu
Komoé 75 E 4 var. Komoé Fleuve.
River, E Ivory Coast
Komoé Fleuve see Komoé
Komotau see Chomutov
Komotiní 104 D 3 var. Gümüljina,
Turk. Gümülcine. NE Greece
Kompong see Kâmpóng Chhnăng
Kompong Cham see Kâmpóng
Cham
Kompong Speu see Kâmpóng Spoe
Kompong Thom see Kâmpóng
Thum
Komrat see Comrat
Komsomolets, Ostrov 115 E 1
island, Severnaya Zemlya, N
Russian Federation
Komsomol'sk-na-Amure 115 G 4
SE Russian Federation
Kondolovo 104 E 3 SE Bulgaria
Kondopoga 110 B 3 NW Russian
Federation
Kong Christian IX Land 82 D 4
Eng. King Christian IX Land.
Physical region, SE Greenland
Kong Christian X Land 83 E 3 Eng.
King Christian X Land. Physical
region, E Greenland
Kong Frederik IX Land 82 C 3 Eng.
King Frederik IX Land. Physical
region, SW Greenland
Kong Frederik VIII Land 83 E 2
Eng. King Frederik VIII Land.
Physical region, NE Greenland
Kong Frederik VI Kyst 82 C 4 Eng.
King Frederik VI Coast. Physical
region, SE Greenland
Kong Karls Land 83 G 2 Eng. King
Charles Islands. Island group, SE
Svalbard
Kongor 73 B 5 SE Sudan
Kongsberg 85 B 6 S Norway
Königgrätz see Hradec Králové
Konin 98 C 3 Ger. Kuhnau. C
Poland
Konispol 101 C 7 var. Konispoli. S
Albania
Konispoli see Konispol
Kónitsa 104 A 4 W Greece
Konjic 100 C 4 S Bosnia &
Herzegovina
Konoša see Konosha
Konosha 110 C 4 var. Konoša. NW
Russian Federation
Konotop 109 F 1 NE Ukraine
Konstantinovka see Kostyantynivka
Konstanz 95 B 7 var. Constanz, Eng.
Constance; hist. Kostnitz, anc.
Constantia. S Germany
Konya 116 C 4 var. Konieh; prev.
Konia, anc. Iconium. C Turkey
Kôohu see Kōfu
Kôotiô see Kōchi
Kopaonik 101 D 5 mountain range,
C Yugoslavia
Koper 95 D 8 It. Capodistria; prev.
Kopar. SW Slovenia
Kopetdag, Khrebet 122 C 3 Turkm.
Kopetdag Gershi, Per. Koppeh
Dāgh. Mountain range,
Iran/Turkmenistan
Koprivnica 100 C 2 Ger. Kopreinitz,
Hung. Kaproncza. N Croatia
Köprülü see Veles
Koptsevichi see Kaptsevichy
Kopyl' see Kapyl'
Korat Plateau 136 D 4 plateau, NE
Thailand
Korba 135 E 4 N India

Korçë 101 D 7 *var.* Korça, *Gk.*
Korytsa, *It.* Corriza; *prev.* Koritsa.
SE Albania
Korčula 100 B 4 *It.* Curzola; *anc.*
Corcyra Nigra. Island, S Croatia
Korea Strait 131 A 7 *Jap.* Chōsen-
kaikyō, *Kor.* Taehan-haehyŏp .
Strait, East China Sea/Sea of
Japan
Korhogo 74 D 4 N Ivory Coast
Korinthiakós Kólpos 105 B 5 *Eng.*
Gulf of Corinth; *anc.* Corinthiacus
Sinus. Gulf, E Ionian Sea
Kórinthos 105 B 6 *Eng.* Corinth;
anc. Corinthus. S Greece
Kōriyama 131 D 5 Honshū, C Japan
Korjazma *see* Koryazhma
Korla 126 B 3 *Chin.* K'u-erh-lo. NW
China
Körmend 99 B 7 W Hungary
Koróni 105 B 6 S Greece
Koror 144 A 2 country capital,
Babelthuap, C Palau
Korosten' 108 D 1 NW Ukraine
Koro Toro 76 C 2 N Chad
Kortrijk 87 A 6 *Fr.* Courtrai. W
Belgium
Koryak Range *see* Koryakskoye
Nagor'ye
Koryakskoye Nagor'ye 115 H 2 *var.*
Koryakskiy Khrebet, *Eng.* Koryak
Range. Mountain range, NE
Russian Federation
Koryazma 110 C 4 *var.* Korjazma.
NW Russian Federation
Kos 105 E 6 Kos, SE Greece
Kos 105 E 6 *It.* Coo; *anc.* Cos.
Island, Dodekánisos, SE Greece
Kō-saki 131 A 7 headland,
Tsushima, SW Japan
Kościan 98 B 4 *Ger.* Kosten. SW
Poland
Kościerzyna 98 C 2 NW Poland
Kosciusko, Mount 149 C 7
mountain, New South Wales, SE
Australia
Koshikijima-rettō 131 A 8 *var.*
Kosikizima Rettō. Island group,
Japan
Košice 99 D 6 *Ger.* Kaschau, *Hung.*
Kassa. E Slovakia
Kosikizima Rettō *see* Koshikijima-
rettō
Köslin *see* Koszalin
Koson 123 E 3 *Rus.* Kasan. S
Uzbekistan
Kosovo 101 E 5 *prev.* Autonomous
Province of Kosovo and Metohija.
Cultural region, S Yugoslavia
Kosovo Polje 101 D 5 S Yugoslavia
Kosovska Mitrovica 101 D 5 *Alb.*
Mitrovicë; *prev.* Mitrovica, Titova
Mitrovica. S Yugoslavia
Kosrae 144 D 2 *prev.* Kusaie. Island,
E Micronesia
Kostenets 104 C 2 *var.* Kostenec;
prev. Georgi Dimitrov. W Bulgaria
Kostroma 110 C 4 NW Russian
Federation
Kostyantynivka 109 G 3 *Rus.*
Konstantinovka. SE Ukraine
Kostyukovichi *see* Kastsyukovichy
Kostyukovka *see* Kastsyukowka
Koszalin 98 B 2 *Ger.* Köslin. NW
Poland
Kota 134 D 3 *prev.* Kotah. N India
Kota Bharu 138 B 3 *var.* Kota
Baharu, Kota Bahru. W Malaysia
Kotaboemi *see* Kotabumi
Kotabumi 138 B 4 *prev.* Kotaboemi.
W Indonesia
Kotah *see* Kota

Kota Kinabalu 138 D 3 *prev.*
Jesselton. Borneo, E Malaysia
Kota Kota *see* Nkhotakota
Kotelnič *see* Kotel'nich
Kotel'nich 114 B 3 *var.* Kotelnič.
NW Russian Federation
Kotel'nyy, Ostrov 115 F 2 island,
Novosibirskiye Ostrova, N
Russian Federation
Kotka 85 E 5 S Finland
Kotlas 110 C 4 NW Russian
Federation
Kotonu *see* Cotonou
Kotor 101 C 5 *It.* Cattaro. SW
Yugoslavia
Kotovs'k 108 D 3 *Rus.* Kotovsk. SW
Ukraine
Kotovsk *see* Kotovs'k
Kottbus *see* Cottbus
Kotte 132 D 4 W Sri Lanka
Kotto 76 D 4 river, Central African
Republic/Zaire
Kotuy 115 E 2 river, N Russian
Federation
Koudougou 75 E 4 C Burkina
Koulamoutou 77 B 6 C Gabon
Koulikoro 74 D 4 SW Mali
Koumra 76 C 4 S Chad
Kourou 59 H 3 N French Guiana
Kousséri 76 B 3 *prev.* Fort-Foureau.
NE Cameroon
Kouvola 85 E 5 S Finland
Kovel' 108 C 1 *Pol.* Kowel. NW
Ukraine
Kowel *see* Kovel'
Kowloon 128 A 1 *Chin.* Jiulong. SW
Hong Kong
Kowt-e 'Ashrow 123 E 4 E
Afghanistan
Kozáni 104 B 4 N Greece
Kozara 100 B 3 mountain range,
NW Bosnia & Herzegovina
Kozhikode *see* Calicut
Koz'modem'yansk 111 C 5 W
Russian Federation
Kōzu-shima 131 D 6 island, Izu-
shotō, E Japan
Kozyatyn 108 D 2 *Rus.* Kazatin. C
Ukraine
Kpalimé 75 E 5 *var.* Palimé. SW
Togo
Krâchéh 137 D 6 *prev.* Kratie. E
Cambodia
Kragujevac 100 D 4 C Yugoslavia
Krainburg *see* Kranj
Kra, Isthmus of 137 B 6 isthmus,
Malaysia/Thailand
Krakatau 124 D 5 volcano,
Indonesia
Kraków 99 D 5 *Eng.* Cracow, *Ger.*
Krakau; *anc.* Cracovia. S Poland
Krâlänh 137 D 5 NW Cambodia
Kraljevo 100 D 4 *prev.* Rankovićevo.
C Yugoslavia
Kramators'k 109 G 3 *Rus.*
Kramatorsk. SE Ukraine
Kramatorsk *see* Kramators'k
Kramfors 85 C 5 C Sweden
Kranéa 104 B 4 N Greece
Kranj 95 D 7 *Ger.* Krainburg. NW
Slovenia
Kräslava 106 D 4 SE Latvia
Krasnaye 107 C 5 *Rus.* Krasnoye. C
Belorussia
Krasnoarmeysk 111 C 6 W Russian
Federation
Krasnodar 111 A 7 *prev.*
Yekaterinodar. Kray capital, SW
Russian Federation
Krasnodon 109 H 3 E Ukraine
Krasnogor *see* Kallaste

Krasnogvardeyskoye *see*
Krasnohvardiys'ke
Krasnohvardiys'ke 109 F 4 *Rus.*
Krasnogvardeyskoye. S Ukraine
Krasnokamsk 111 D 5 W Russian
Federation
Krasnoperekops'k 109 F 4 *Rus.*
Krasnoperekopsk. S Ukraine
Krasnoperekopsk *see*
Krasnoperekops'k
Krasnostav *see* Krasnystaw
Krasnovodsk *see* Turkmenbashi
Krasnovodskiy Zaliv 122 B 2
Turkm. Krasnowodsk Aylagy.
Gulf, E Caspian Sea
Krasnoyarsk 114 D 4 C Russian
Federation
Krasnoye *see* Krasnaye
Krasnozatonskiy 110 D 4 *var.*
Krasnozatonski, Krasnozatonskij.
NW Russian Federation
Krasnystaw 98 E 4 *Rus.* Krasnostav.
SE Poland
Krasnyy Luch 109 H 3 *prev.*
Krindachevka. E Ukraine
Krassóvár *see* Caraşova
Kratie *see* Krâchéh
Krâvanh, Chuôr Phnum 137 D 6
Eng. Cardamom Mountains, *Fr.*
Chaîne des Cardaomes.
Mountain range, SW Cambodia
Krefeld 94 A 4 W Germany
Kremenchug *see* Kremenchuk
Kremenchuk 109 F 3 *Rus.*
Kremenchug. C Ukraine
Kremenchuts'ke Vodoskhovyshche
109 F 2 *Eng.* Kremenchuk
Reservoir, *Rus.* Kremenchugskoye
Vodokhranilishche. Reservoir, C
Ukraine
Kremenets' 108 C 2 *Pol.*
Krzemieniec, *Rus.* Kremenets. W
Ukraine
Kremennaya *see* Kreminna
Kreminna 109 H 2 *Rus.*
Kremennaya. E Ukraine
Kresena *see* Kresna
Kresna 104 C 3 *var.* Kresena. SW
Bulgaria
Kretinga 106 B 3 *Ger.* Krottingen.
NW Lithuania
Kreuz *see* Risti
Krichëv *see* Krychaw
Krindachevka *see* Krasnyy Luch
Krishna 132 C 1 *prev.* Kistna. River,
C India
Krishnagiri 132 C 2 SE India
Kristiansand 85 A 6 *var.*
Christiansand. S Norway
Kristiansted 85 B 7 S Sweden
Kristiansund 84 A 4 *var.*
Christiansund. S Norway
Kríti 105 D 8 *Eng.* Crete. Island, SE
Greece
Krivoy Rog *see* Kryvyy Rih
Krivyje Ozero *see* Kryve Ozero
Križevci 100 B 2 *Ger.* Kreuz, *Hung.*
Kőrös. NE Croatia
Krk 100 A 2 *It.* Veglia; *anc.* Curieta.
Island, NW Croatia
Krolevets' 109 F 1 *Rus.* Krolevets.
NE Ukraine
Krolevets *see* Krolevets'
Kronach 95 C 5 E Germany
Kronshtadt 110 B 4 *var.* Kronštadt
NW Russian Federation
Kronštadt *see* Kronshtadt
Kroonstad 78 D 4 C South Africa
Kropotkin 111 B 7 SW Russian
Federation

Krosno 99 E 5 *Ger.* Krossen. SE
Poland
Krosno Odrzańskie 98 B 3 *Ger.*
Crossen, Kreisstadt. W Poland
Krossen *see* Krosno
Krottingen *see* Kretinga
Krško 95 E 8 *Ger.* Gurkfeld; *prev.*
Videm-Krško. E Slovenia
Krugloye *see* Kruhlaye
Kruhlaye 107 D 6 *Rus.* Krugloye. E
Belorussia
Krujë 101 D 6 *var.* Kruja, *It.* Croia. C
Albania
Krung Thep 137 C 5 *var.* Krung
Thep Mahanakhon, *Eng.*
Bangkok. Country capital, C
Thailand
Krung Thep, Ao 137 C 5 bay, South
China Sea/Pacific Ocean
Krupki 107 D 6 C Belorussia
Kruševac 100 D 4 C Yugoslavia
Krychaw 107 E 7 *Rus.* Krichëv. E
Belorussia
Krym 109 F 5 *var.* Crimea. Cultural
region, Ukraine
Kryms'ki Hory 109 F 5 mountain
range, S Ukraine
Kryve Ozero 109 E 3 *Rus.* Krivyje
Ozero. SW Ukraine
Kryvyy Rih 109 F 3 *Rus.* Krivoy
Rog. SE Ukraine
Ksar-el-Kebir 70 C 2 *var.* Alcázar,
Ksar al Kabir, Ksar el Kebir, Ksar-
el-Kébir, *Ar.* Al-Kasr al-Kebir, Al-
Qsar al-Kbir, *Sp.* Alcazarquivir.
NW Morocco
Kstovo 111 C 5 W Russian
Federation
Kuala Dungun *see* Dungun
Kuala Lumpur 138 B 3 country
capital, W Malaysia
Kuala Terengganu 138 B 3 *var.*
Kuala Trengganu. W Malaysia
Kuala Trengganu *see* Kuala
Terengganu
Kualatungkai 138 B 4 W Indonesia
Kuantan 138 B 3 W Malaysia
Kuba *see* Quba
Kuching 138 C 3 *prev.* Sarawak.
Borneo, E Malaysia
Kūchnay Darvīshān 122 D 5 S
Afghanistan
Kuçovë 101 C 6 *var.* Kuçova; *prev.*
Qyteti Stalin. C Albania
Kudus 138 C 5 *prev.* Koedoes. Jawa,
C Indonesia
K'u-erh-lo *see* Korla
Kufra Oasis *see* Al Kufrah
Kuhmo 84 E 4 E Finland
Kuhnau *see* Konin
Kuito 78 B 2 *Port.* Silva Porto. C
Angola
Kuji 130 D 3 *var.* Kuzi. Japan
Kula Kangri 135 G 3 mountain,
Bhutan/China
Kuldīga 106 B 3 *Ger.* Goldingen. W
Latvia
Kullorsuaq 82 C 2 *var.*
Kuvdlorssuak, Kuvdlorssuaq.
NW Greenland
Kŭlob 123 F 3 *Rus.* Kulyab. SW
Tajikistan
Kulu 116 C 3 W Turkey
Kulundinskaya Step' 114 D 4
physical region, S Russian
Federation
Kulyab *see* Kŭlob
Kuma 111 B 7 river, SW Russian
Federation
Kumaka 59 F 3 SE Guyana
Kumamoto 131 A 7 Kyūshū, SW
Japan

Kumanova *see* Kumanovo
Kumanovo 101 E 5 *Turk.*
Kumanova. N Macedonia
Kumasi 75 E 5 *prev.* Coomassie. C
Ghana
Kumba 77 A 5 W Cameroon
Kumertau 111 D 6 W Russian
Federation
Kumillä *see* Comilla
Kumo 75 G 4 E Nigeria
Kumon Range 136 B 2 mountain
range, N Burma
Kunashir, Ostrov 130 E 1 *var.*
Kunashiri. Island, Kurile Islands,
SE Russian Federation
Kunda 106 E 2 NE Estonia
Kunduz 123 E 3 *var.* Kondoz,
Kundüz, Qondüz, *Per.* Kondüz.
NE Afghanistan
Kunene *see* Cunene
Kungsbacka 85 B 7 S Sweden
Kungur 111 D 5 NW Russian
Federation
Kunlun Mountains *see* Kunlun
Shan
Kunlun Shan 126 B 4 *var.* Kunlun
Mountains. Mountain range,
China/India
Kunming 129 B 6 *var.* K'un-ming;
prev. Yunnan. Province capital,
SW China
Kununurra 146 D 3 Western
Australia, N Australia
Kuopio 84 E 4 C Finland
Kupang 139 E 5 *prev.* Koepang.
Timor, C Indonesia
Kup"yans'k 109 G 2 *Rus.*
Kupyansk. E Ukraine
Kupyansk *see* Kup"yans'k
Kura 117 G 2 *Az.* Kür, *Geor.*
Mtkvari, *Turk.* Kura Nehri. River,
SW Asia
Kurashiki 131 B 6 *var.* Kurasiki.
Honshū, SW Japan
Kurasiki *see* Kurashiki
Kürdzhali 104 D 3 *var.* Kärdžali,
Kirdzhali. S Bulgaria
Kure 131 B 7 Honshū, SW Japan
Küre 116 C 2 Turkey
Küre Dağları 116 C 2 mountain
range, N Turkey
Kuressaare 106 C 2 *Ger.* Arensburg;
prev. Kingissepp. Saaremaa, W
Estonia
Kureyka 115 E 3 river, C Russian
Federation
Kurgan-Tyube *see* Qürghonteppa
Kuria Muria Bay *see* Ḥalānīyāt,
Khalīj al
Kurile Islands *see* Kuril'skiye
Ostrova
Kurile-Kamchatka Depression *see*
Kurile Trench
Kurile Trench 152 C 1 *var.* Kurile-
Kamchatka Depression. Trench,
NW Pacific Ocean
Kuril'sk 115 H 4 Kuril'skiye
Ostrova, SE Russian Federation
Kuril'skiye Ostrova 115 H 4 *Eng.*
Kurile Islands. Island group, E
Russian Federation
Kurkund *see* Kilingi-Nõmme
Kurnool 132 C 1 *var.* Karnul. S
India
Kursk 111 B 6 W Russian
Federation
Kuršumlija 101 D 5 SE Yugoslavia
Kuruktag 126 C 3 mountain range,
NW China
Kurume 131 A 7 Kyūshū, SW Japan
Kurupukari 59 F 3 C Guyana

Kurzeme 106 B 3 *Eng.* Courland,
Ger. Kurland. Cultural region, W
Latvia
Kusaie *see* Kosrae
Kushiro 130 D 2 *var.* Kusiro.
Hokkaidō, NE Japan
Kushka *see* Gushgy
Kusiro *see* Kushiro
Kuskokwim Mountains 36 C 3
mountain range, Alaska, NW
USA
Kustanay 114 C 4 *Kaz.* Qostanay. N
Kazakhstan
Kütahya 116 B 3 *prev.* Kutaia. W
Turkey
Kutaia *see* Kütahya
K'ut'aisi 117 F 2 W Georgia
Kutina 100 B 3 NE Croatia
Kutno 98 D 3 C Poland
Kuujjuaq 39 E 2 *prev.* Fort-Chimo.
Québec, E Canada
Kuujjuarapik 38 D 2 Québec, C
Canada
Kuusamo 84 E 3 E Finland

Kuwait
120 C 4 *var.* Dawlat al Kuwait,
Koweit, Kuwait. Monarchy,
SW Asia

Official name: State of Kuwait **Date
of formation:** 1961 **Capital:**
Kuwait City **Population:** 1.8 million
Total area: 17,820 sq km
(6,880 sq miles) **Languages:** Arabic*,
English **Religions:** Muslim 90%,
Christian 6%, other 2%
Ethnic mix: Arab 85%, South Asian
9%, Persian 4%, other 2%
Government: Constutional monarchy
Currency: Dinar = 1,000 fils

Kuwajleen *see* Kwajalein Atoll
Kuwayt 120 C 3 E Iraq
Kuybyshev *see* Samara
**Kuybyshevskoye
Vodokhranilishche** 111 C 5 *var.*
Kuibyshev, *Eng.* Kuybyshev
Reservoir. Reservoir, W Russian
Federation
Kuytun 126 B 3 NW China
Kuytun 126 B 2 NW China
Kuzi *see* Kuji
Kuznetsk 111 C 6 W Russian
Federation
Kvaløsa 84 C 2 island, N Norway
Kvarnbergs-vattnet 84 B 4 *var.*
Frostviken. Lake, N Sweden
Kvarner 100 A 3 *var.* Carnaro, *It.*
Quarnero. Gulf, Adriatic
Sea/Mediterranean Sea
Kvitøya 83 G 1 island, NE Svalbard
Kwai Chung 128 A 1 C Hong Kong
Kwajalein Atoll 144 D 1 *var.*
Kuwajleen. Island, C Marshall
Islands
Kwando *see* Cuando
Kwando 78 C 2 *var.* Cuando. River,
S Africa
Kwangju 128 E 4 *off.* Kwangju-
kwangyŏksi, *var.* Kwangchu, *Jap.*
Kōshū. SW South Korea
Kwango 77 C 7 *Port.* Cuango. River,
Angola/Zaire
Kwango *see* Cuango
Kwanza *see* Cuanza
Kwekwe 78 D 3 *prev.* Que Que. C
Zimbabwe
Kwidzyń 98 C 2 *Ger.* Marienwerder.
N Poland
Kwigillingok 36 B 3 Alaska, NW
USA
Kwilu 78 B 1 river, W Zaire

Kwito *see* Cuito
Kwun Tong 128 B 1 SE Hong Kong
Kyabé 76 C 4 S Chad
Kyaikkami 137 B 5 *prev.* Amherst.
SE Burma
Kyaiklat 136 B 4 S Burma
Kyaikto 136 B 4 S Burma
Kyakhta 115 E 5 S Russian
Federation
Kyaukse 136 B 3 C Burma
Kyjov 99 C 5 *Ger.* Gaya. SE Czech
Republic
Kykládes 105 D 6 *var.* Kikládhes,
Eng. Cyclades. Island group, SE
Greece
Kými 105 C 5 *prev.* Kími. Évvoia, C
Greece
Kyōto 131 C 6 Honshū, SW Japan
Kyparissía 105 B 6 *var.* Kiparissía. S
Greece
Kyrá Panagía 105 C 5 island,
Vóreioi Sporádes, E Greece

Kyrgyzstan
123 F 2 *var.* Kirghizia; *prev.*
Kirghiz SSR, Kirgizskaya SSR,
Republic of Kyrgyzstan. Republic,
C Asia

Official name: Kyrgyz Republic
Date of formation: 1991 **Capital:**
Bishkek **Population:** 4.6 million
Total Area: 198,500 sq km
(76,640 sq miles) **Languages:**
Kirghiz*, Russian, Uzbek **Religions:**
Muslim 60%, other (mostly Russian
Orthodox) 35% **Ethnic mix:** Kirghiz
52%, Russian 21%, Uzbek 13%, other
(mostly Kazakh and Tajik) 14%
Government: Multiparty republic
Currency: Som = 100 teen

Kýthira 105 B 7 *var.* Kíthira, *It.*
Cerigo; *Lat.* Cythera. S
Greece
Kýthira 105 B 7 *var.* Kíthira, *It.*
Cerigo; *Lat.* Cythera. Island, S
Greece
Kýthnos 105 C 6 Kýthnos, SE
Greece
Kýthnos 105 C 6 *var.* Kíthnos,
Thermiá, *It.* Termia; *anc.* Cythnos.
Island, Kykládes, SE Greece
Kythréa *see* Değirmenlik
Kyūshū 131 B 8 *var.* Kyúshyū. Island,
Japan
Kyustendil 104 B 2 *var.* Kjustendil;
anc. Pautalia. W Bulgaria
Kyusyu-Palau Ridge *see* Kyushu-
Palau Ridge
Kyyiv 109 E 2 *Eng.* Kiev, *Rus.* Kiyev.
Country capital, N Ukraine
Kyyivs'ke Vodoskhovyshche 109 E
1 *Rus.* Kiyevskoye
Vodokhranilishche. Reservoir, N
Ukraine
Kyzyl-Kiya 123 F 2 *Kir.* Kyzyl-
Kyya. SW Kyrgyzstan
Kyzyl Kum 122 D 2 *var.* Kizil Kum,
Qizil Qum, *Uzb.* Qizilqum.
Desert, Kazakhstan/Uzbekistan
Kyzyl-Kyya *see* Kyzyl-Kiya
Kyzylrabot *see* Qizilrabot
Kyzyl-Suu 123 G 2 *prev.* Pokrovka.
NE
KyKazakhstan/Uzbekistanrgyzyst
an
Kzyl-Orda 114 B 5 *var.* Qizil Orda,
Kaz. Qyzylorda; *prev.* Perovsk. S
Kazakhstan

L

Laaland *see* Lolland
La Algaba 92 C 4 S Spain
Laarne 87 B 5 NW Belgium
La Asunción 59 E 1 NE Venezuela
Laâyoune 70 A 3 *var.* Aaiún.
Country capital, NW Western
Sahara
Labe *see* Elbe
Labé 74 C 4 NW Guinea
La Baie 39 E 4 Québec, SE Canada
la Baule-Escoublac 90 A 4 NW
France
La Blanquilla *see* Blanquilla, Isla
Laborca *see* Laborec
Laborec 99 E 5 *Hung.* Laborca.
River, E Slovakia
Labrador 39 F 2 physical region,
Newfoundland and Labrador, SW
Canada
Labrador Basin 66 B 2 undersea
basin, NW Atlantic Ocean
Labrador Sea 39 G 1 sea, NW
Atlantic Ocean
Labutta 137 A 5 SW Burma
Laç 101 C 6 *var.* Laci. C Albania
La Calera 64 B 4 C Chile
La Carolina 92 D 4 S Spain
Laccadive Islands 132 A 3 island
group, SW India
La Ceiba 52 D 2 N Honduras
Lacepede Bay 149 B 7 bay, E Indian
Ocean
Lacey 46 B 2 Washington, NW USA
Lachanás 104 C 3 N Greece
La Chaux-de-Fonds 95 A 7 W
Switzerland
Lachlan 149 C 6 river, SE Australia
Laci *see* Laç
la Ciotat 91 D 6 *anc.* Citharista. SE
France
Lacobriga *see* Lagos
La Concepción 53 E 5 *var.*
Concepción. W Panama
La Concepción 58 C 1 NW
Venezuela
Laconia 41 G 2 New Hampshire,
NE USA
La Croix Maingot 55 F 1 NW Saint
Lucia
La Cruz 52 D 4 NW Costa Rica
Ladozhskoye Ozero 110 B 4 *var.*
Laa Tokka, *Eng.* Lake Ladoga, *Fin.*
Laatokka. Lake, NW Russian
Federation
Lae 144 B 3 New Guinea, W Papua
New Guinea
La Esperanza 52 C 2 SW Honduras
Lafayette 42 B 3 Louisiana, S USA
Lafayette 40 C 4 Indiana, N USA
La Fé 54 A 2 W Cuba
Lafia 75 G 4 C Nigeria
la Flèche 90 B 4 NW France
Laghouat 70 D 2 N Algeria
Lagos 92 B 5 *anc.* Lacobriga. S
Portugal
Lagos 75 F 5 SW Nigeria
Lagos de Moreno 50 D 4 SW
Mexico
La Grande 46 C 3 Oregon, NW
USA
La Grange 42 D 2 Georgia, SE USA
Lagunas 64 B 1 N Chile
Lagunillas 61 G 4 SE Bolivia
La Habana 54 B 2 *var.* Havana.
Country capital, W Cuba
Lahat 138 B 4 Sumatera, W
Indonesia
Laholm 85 B 7 S Sweden

Lahore 134 D 2 province capital, NE Pakistan
Lahr 95 A 6 S Germany
Lahti 85 E 5 *Swe.* Lahtis. S Finland
Lahtis *see* Lahti
Lai 76 B 4 *prev.* Behagle, De Behagle. S Chad
Lai Châu 136 D 3 NW Vietnam
Laila *see* Laylá
La Junta 44 D 5 Colorado, C USA
Lake Charles 42 A 3 Louisiana, S USA
Lake City 43 E 3 South Carolina, SE USA
Lake District 89 C 5 physical region, NW England, UK
Lake Havasu City 48 A 2 Arizona, SW USA
Lake Jackson 49 H 4 Texas, S USA
Lakeland 43 E 4 Florida, SE USA
Lakes Entrance 149 D 7 inlet, W Tasman Sea
Lakeside 47 D 8 California, W USA
Lakewood 44 C 4 Colorado, C USA
Lake Worth 43 F 5 Florida, SE USA
Lakhnau *see* Lucknow
Lakoníkós Kólpos 105 B 7 gulf, C Mediterranean Sea
Lakselv 84 D 2 N Norway
Lakshadweep 132 A 3 *prev.* the Laccadive, Minicoy and Amindivi Islands. Union territory, SW India
Lala 139 E 2 SW Philippines
La Laguna 70 A 3 Tenerife, SW Spain
La Libertad 52 B 1 N Guatemala
La Libertad 60 A 2 W Ecuador
La Ligua 64 B 4 C Chile
Lalín 92 C 1 NW Spain
Lalitpur 135 F 3 C Nepal
La Louvière 91 B 5 S Belgium
La Maçana *see* La Massana
La Maddalena 96 A 4 W Italy
Lamar 44 D 5 Iowa, C USA
La Massana 91 A 8 *var.* la Maçana. W Andorra
Lambaré 64 D 2 S Paraguay
Lambaréné 77 A 6 W Gabon
Lamego 92 C 2 N Portugal
Lamesa 49 E 3 Texas, S USA
Lamezia 97 D 6 SE Italy
Lamía 105 B 5 C Greece
Lamma Island 128 A 2 *Cant.* Pok Liu Chau. Island, S Hong Kong
Lamon Bay 139 E 1 bay, SW Philippine Sea
Lamoni 45 F 4 Wyoming, C USA
La Mosquitia 53 E 3 *var.* Miskito Coast, *Eng.* Mosquito Coast. Coastal region, E Nicaragua
Lampang 136 C 4 *var.* Muang Lampang. NW Thailand
Lámpeia 105 B 6 S Greece
Lanbi Kyun 137 B 6 *prev.* Sullivan Island. Island, S Burma
Lancaster 89 C 5 NW England, UK
Lancaster 40 D 4 Ohio, N USA
Lancaster 47 C 7 California, W USA
Lancaster Sound 37 F 2 channel, Arctic Ocean/Baffin Bay
Landen 87 C 6 C Belgium
Lander 44 C 3 Wyoming, C USA
Landerneau 90 A 3 NW France
Landes 91 B 5 cultural region, SW France
Landsberg am Lech 95 C 6 S Germany
Land's End 89 B 8 headland, SW England, UK
Landshut 95 C 6 SE Germany
Langar 123 E 2 *Rus.* Lyangar. C Uzbekistan

Langfang 128 D 4 NE China
Langres 90 D 4 N France
Lang Sơn 136 D 3 *var.* Langson. N Vietnam
Langson *see* Lang Sơn
Lang Suan 137 C 6 Thailand
Languedoc 91 C 6 cultural region, S France
Länkäran 117 H 3 *Rus.* Lenkoran'. S Azerbaijan
Lansing 40 C 3 state capital, Michigan, N USA
Lanta, Ko 137 B 7 island, S Thailand
Lantau Island 128 A 2 *Cant.* Tai Yue Shan. Island, SW Hong Kong
Lantau Peak 128 A 1 *Cant.* Fung Wong Shan. Mountain, Lantau Island, W Hong Kong
Lantung, Gulf of *see* Liaodong Wan
Lanzarote 70 B 3 island, Islas Canarias, SW Spain
Lanzhou 128 B 4 *var.* Lan-chou, Lanchow, Lan-chow; *prev.* Kaolan. Province capital, C China
Lao Cai 136 D 3 NW Vietnam
Laoet *see* Laut, Pulau
Laoha He 127 F 2 river, NE China
Laon 90 D 3 *var.* la Laon; *anc.* Laudunum. N France
Lao People's Democratic Republic *see* Laos
La Orchila, Isla 58 D 1 island, N Venezuela
La Oroya 60 C 3 C Peru

Laos
136 C 4 . Republic, SE Asia
Official name: Lao People's Democratic Republic **Date of formation:** 1953 **Capital:** Vientiane **Population:** 4.6 million **Total Area:** 236,800 sq km (91, 428 sq miles) **Languages:** Lao*, Miao, Yao **Religions:** Buddhist 85%, Christian 2%, other 13% **Ethnic mix:** Lao Loum 56%, Lao Theung 34%, Lao Soung 10% **Government:** Single-party republic **Currency:** Kip = 100 cents

La Palma 53 G 5 SE Panama
La Palma 70 A 3 island, Islas Canarias, SW Spain
La Paz 50 B 3 NW Mexico
La Paz 61 F 4 *var.* La Paz de Ayacucho. Country capital, W Bolivia
La Paz, Bahía de 50 B 3 bay, Golfo de California/Pacific Ocean
La Paz de Ayacucho *see* La Paz
La Perouse Strait 130 C 1 *Jap.* Sōya-kaikyō, *Rus.* Proliv Laperuza. Strait, Sea of Japan/Sea of Okhotsk
Lápithos *see* Lapta
Lapland 84 D 2 *Fin.* Lappi, *Swe.* Lappland. Cultural region, N Europe
Lappeenranta 85 E 5 *Swe.* Villmanstrand. SE Finland
Lappo *see* Lapua
Laptev Sea *see* Laptevykh, More
Laptevykh, More 115 F 2 *Eng.* Laptev Sea. Sea, Arctic Ocean
Lapua 85 D 5 *Swe.* Lappo. W Finland
La Puebla *see* Sa Pobla
Lapurdum *see* Bayonne
Łapy 98 E 3 E Poland
La Quiaca 64 C 2 N Argentina

L'Aquila 96 C 4 *var.* Aquila, Aquila degli Abruzzi. C Italy
Laracha 92 B 1 NW Spain
Larache 70 C 2 *var.* al Araïch, El Araïch, *Ar.* Al-Araish; *prev.* El Araïche, *anc.* Lixus. NW Morocco
Laramie 44 C 4 Wyoming, C USA
Laramie Mountains 44 C 3 mountain range, C USA
Laredo 93 E 1 N Spain
Laredo 49 F 5 Texas, S USA
La Réunion *see* Réunion
Largo 43 E 4 Florida, SE USA
La Rioja 93 E 2 cultural region, N Spain
La Rioja 64 C 3 NW Argentina
Lárisa 104 B 4 *var.* Larissa. C Greece
Larissa *see* Lárisa
Lārkāna 134 B 3 *var.* Larkhana. SE Pakistan
Larkhana *see* Lārkāna
la Rochelle 90 A 4 *anc.* Rupella. W France
la Roche-sur-Yon 90 A 4 *prev.* Bourbon Vendée, Napoléon-Vendée. NW France
La Roda 93 E 3 C Spain
La Romana 55 E 3 E Dominican Republic
La Sarre 38 D 4 Québec, SE Canada
Las Cabezas de San Juan 92 C 5 S Spain
Las Cruces 48 D 3 New Mexico, SW USA
La See d'Urgel 93 F 2 *var.* La Seu d'Urgell, Seo de Urgel. NE Spain
La Serena 64 B 3 N Chile
la Seyne-sur-Mer 91 D 6 SE France
Lashio 136 B 3 NE Burma
Lashkar Gāh 122 D 5 *var.* Lashkar Gah, Lash-Kar-Gar'. S Afghanistan
La Sila 97 E 6 mountain range, SW Italy
La Sirena 52 D 3 E Nicaragua
Łask 98 C 4 C Poland
Las Lomitas 64 D 2 N Argentina
La Solana 93 E 4 C Spain
Las Palmas 70 A 3 *var.* Las Palmas de Gran Canaria. Regional capital, Gran Canaria, SW Spain
Las Petas 61 H 3 NE Bolivia
La Spezia 96 B 3 NW Italy
Las Piedras 61 E 3 E Peru
Las Tablas 53 G 5 S Panama
Las Tunas 54 C 2 *var.* Victoria de las Tunas. E Cuba
Las Vegas 47 D 7 Nevada, W USA
Las Yaras 61 E 4 S Peru
Latacunga 60 B 1 C Ecuador
la Teste 91 A 5 SW France
Latgale 106 D 4 *Eng.* Latgallia. Cultural region, SE Latvia
Latgallia *see* Latgale
Latina 97 C 5 *prev.* Littoria. C Italy
La Tortuga, Isla 59 E 1 *var.* Isla Tortuga. Island, N Venezuela
La Tuque 39 E 4 Québec, SE Canada

Latvia
106 C 3 *Ger.* Lettland, *Latv.* Latvija, Latvijas Republika, *Rus.* Latviyskaya SSR; *prev.* Latvian SSR. Republic, NE Europe

Official name: Republic of Latvia **Date of formation:** 1991 **Capital:** Riga **Population:** 2.7 million **Total area:** 64,589 sq km (24,938 sq miles) **Languages:** Latvian*, Russian **Religions:** Evangelical Lutheran

85%, other Christian 15% **Ethnic mix:** Latvian 52%, Russian 34%, Belorussian 5%, other 9% **Government:** Multiparty republic **Currency:** Lats = 100 santimi

Lau Group 145 E 4 island group, E Fiji
Launceston 149 C 8 Tasmania, SE Australia
La Unión 93 F 4 SE Spain
La Unión 65 B 5 C Chile
La Unión 52 C 2 C Honduras
La Unión 60 C 3 C Peru
Laurel 42 C 3 Mississippi, S USA
Laurel 44 C 2 Montana, NW USA
Laurentian Highlands 39 E 3 *var.* Laurentian Mountains, *Fr.* Les Laurentides. Plateau, Canada/USA
Lauria 97 D 6 S Italy
Laurinburg 43 F 1 North Carolina, SE USA
Lauru *see* Choiseul
Lausanne 95 A 7 *It.* Losanna SW Switzerland
Laut, Pulau 138 D 4 *prev.* Laoet. Island, C Indonesia
Laval 90 B 3 NW France
Laval 38 D 4 Québec, SE Canada
La Vega 55 E 3 *var.* Concepción de la Vega. C Dominican Republic
La Vila Jojosa *see* Villajoyosa
Lávrio 105 C 6 *prev.* Lávrion. C Greece
Lávrion *see* Lávrio
Lawrence 41 G 3 Massachusetts, NE USA
Lawrenceburg 42 C 1 Tennessee, S USA
Lawton 49 F 2 Oklahoma, C USA
Laylá 121 C 5 *var.* Laila. C Saudi Arabia
Lazarev Sea 154 B 1 sea, S Atlantic Ocean
Lázaro Cárdenas 50 D 5 SW Mexico
Læsø 85 B 7 island, N Denmark
League City 49 H 4 Texas, S USA
Leal *see* Lihula
Leamhcán *see* Lucan
Leamington 38 C 5 Ontario, S Canada
Lebak 139 E 3 Mindanao, S Philippines
Lebanon 42 D 1 Tennessee, S USA
Lebanon 41 G 2 Kentucky, NE USA
Lebanon 46 B 3 Oregon, NW USA
Lebanon 45 G 5 Missouri, C USA

Lebanon
118 A 4 *Ar.* Al Lubnān, *Fr.* Liban. Republic, SW Asia

Official name: Republic of Lebanon **Date of formation:** 1944 **Capital:** Beirut **Population:** 2.9 million **Total area:** 10,400 sq km (4,015 sq miles) **Languages:** Arabic*, French, Armenian, Assyrian **Religions:** Muslim (mainly Sunni) 57%, Christian (mainly Maronite) 43% **Ethnic mix:** Arab 93% (Lebanese 83%, Palestinian 10%), other 7% **Government:** Multiparty republic **Currency:** Pound = 100 piastres

Lebap 122 D 2 NE Turkmenistan
Lebedin *see* Lebedyn
Lebedyn 109 F 2 *Rus.* Lebedin. NE Ukraine
Lebel-sur-Quévillon 38 D 4 Québec, SE Canada

Lębork 98 C 2 *var.* Lębórk, *Ger.*
Lauenburg, Lauenburg in
Pommern. NW Poland
Lebrija 92 C 5 S Spain
Lebu 65 A 5 C Chile
le Cannet 91 D 6 SE France
Le Cap *see* Cap-Haïtien
Lecce 97 E 6 SE Italy
Lechainá 105 B 6 *var.* Lekhainá. S
Greece
Ledo Salinarius *see* Lons-le-Saunier
Leduc 37 E 5 Alberta, SW Canada
Leech Lake 45 F 2 lake, Minnesota,
N USA
Leeds 89 D 5 N England, UK
Leek 86 E 2 NE Netherlands
Leer 94 A 3 NW Germany
Leesburg 43 E 4 Florida, SE USA
Leeuwarden 86 D 1 *Fris.* Ljouwert.
N Netherlands
Leeuwin, Cape 142 A 5 headland,
Western Australia, SW Australia
Leeward Islands 55 G 3 *var.* Society
Islands. Island group, E
Caribbean Sea
Leeward Islands *see* Sotavento, Ilhas
de
Lefkáda 105 A 5 *prev.* Levkás.
Lefkáda, W Greece
Lefkáda 105 A 5 *It.* Santa Maura;
prev. Levkás, *anc.* Leucas. Island,
Iónioi Nísoi, W Greece
Lefká Óri 105 C 7 mountain range,
Kríti, SE Greece
Lefkímmi 105 A 5 *var.* Levkímmi.
Kérkyra, W Greece
Legaspi 139 E 2 *off.* Legaspi City.
Luzon, N Philippines
Legaspi City *see* Legaspi
Leghorn *see* Livorno
Legnica 98 B 4 *Ger.* Liegnitz. W
Poland
le Havre 90 B 3 *Eng.* Havre; *prev.* le
Havre-de-Grâce. N France
Lehčevo *see* Lekhchevo
Leicester 89 D 6 *Lat.* Batae
Coritanorum. C England, UK
Leichhardt Range 148 D 4
mountain range, Queensland, NE
Australia
Leiden 86 C 3 *prev.* Leyden, *anc.*
Lugdunum Batavorum. W
Netherlands
Leie 87 B 6 *Fr.* Lys. River,
Belgium/France
Leigh Creek 149 B 6 South
Australia, S Australia
Leinster 89 B 6 cultural region, E
Ireland
Leipsoi 105 E 6 island,
Dodekánisos, SE Greece
Leipzig 94 C 4 *Pol.* Lipsk; hist. *Eng.*
Leipsic, *anc.* Lipsia. E Germany
Leiria 92 B 3 *anc.* Collipo. W
Portugal
Leirvik 85 A 6 S Norway
Leizhou *see* Haikang
Lek 86 C 4 river, SW Netherlands
Lekhchevo 104 C 2 *var.* Lehčevo.
NW Bulgaria
Leksand 85 C 5 C Sweden
Lel'chitsy *see* Lyel'chytsy
Lelystad 86 D 3 C Netherlands
le Mans 90 B 3 NW France
le Maroni Fleuve *see* Marowijne
Rivier
Lemnos *see* Limnos
Lena 115 F 3 river, E Russian
Federation
Lengshuitan 129 C 6 E China
Lenine 109 G 5 *Rus.* Lenino. S
Ukraine

Leningradskaya 154 C 4 research
station, Antarctica
Lenino *see* Lenine
Leninogorsk 114 D 5 *Kaz.* Leníngor.
E Kazakhstan
Leninogorsk 113 B 5 Russian
Federation
Leninpol' 123 F 2 NW Kyrgyzstan
Lenkoran' *see* Lenkeran
Lenti 99 B 7 SW Hungary
Lentia *see* Linz
Lenya 137 B 6 S Burma
Leoben 95 E 7 C Austria
León 92 D 1 NW Spain
León 51 E 4 *var.* León de los
Aldamas. C Mexico
León 52 C 3 NW Nicaragua
León de los Aldamas *see* León
Leonídi 105 B 6 S Greece
Léopold II, Lac *see* Mai-Ndombe,
Lac
Léopoldville *see* Kinshasa
Lepe 92 C 4 S Spain
Lepel' *see* Lyepyel'
Lepontine Alps 95 B 7 *Fr.* Alpes
Lépontiennes, *It.* Alpi Lepontine.
Mountain range,
Italy/Switzerland
le Portel 90 C 2 N France
le Puy 91 C 5 *prev.* le Puy-en-Velay,
hist. Anicium, Podium Anicensis.
C France
Léré 76 B 4 SW Chad
Lérida *see* Lleida
Lerma 92 D 2 N Spain
Léros 105 D 6 island, Dodekánisos,
SE Greece
Lerwick 88 D 1 island authority
area capital, NE Scotland, UK
Lesbos *see* Lésvos
Les Cayes 54 D 3 *var.* Cayes. SW
Haiti
Les Gonaïves *see* Gonaïves
Leshan 129 B 5 C China
les Herbiers 90 B 4 NW France
Leskovac 101 E 5 SE Yugoslavia

Lesotho
78 D 4 *prev.* Basutoland.
Monarchy, S Africa

Official name: Kingdom of Lesotho
Date of formation: 1966
Capital: Maseru **Population:**
1.9 million **Total area:** 30,350 sq km
(11,718 sq miles) **Languages:**
English*, Sesotho*, Zulu **Religions:**
Christian 93%, other 7%
Ethnic mix: Basotho 99%, other 1%
Government: Constitutional
monarchy **Currency:** Loti = 100 lisente

les Sables-d'Olonne 90 A 4 NW
France
Lesser Antarctica 154 B 3 *var.* West
Antarctica. Physical region,
Antarctica
Lesser Antilles 55 E 5 island group,
SE Caribbean Sea
Lesser Caucasus 117 F 2 *Rus.* Malyy
Kavkaz. Mountain range, SW
Asia
Lesser Khingan Range *see* Xiao
Hinggan Ling
Lesser Sunda Islands *see* Nusa
Tenggara
Lésvos 105 D 5 *anc.* Lesbos. Island,
E Greece
Leszno 98 B 4 *Ger.* Lissa. W Poland
Lethbridge 37 E 5 Alberta, SW
Canada
Lethem 59 F 3 S Guyana
Leticia 58 C 3 S Colombia
Leti, Kepulauan 139 F 5 island
group, E Indonesia

Letpadan 136 B 4 SW Burma
Letsôk-aw Kyun 137 B 6 *var.*
Letsutan Island; *prev.* Domel
Island. Island, S Burma
Leuven 87 C 6 *Fr.* Louvain, *Ger.*
Löwen. C Belgium
Leuze *see* Leuze-en-Hainaut
Leuze-en-Hainaut 87 B 6 *var.*
Leuze. SW Belgium
Levanger 84 B 4 C Norway
Levelland 49 E 2 Texas, S USA
Lévêque, Cape 146 C 3 headland,
Western Australia, W Australia
Leverkusen 94 A 4 W Germany
Levice 99 C 6 *var.* Lewentz, *Ger.*
Lewenz, *Hung.* Léva. SW Slovakia
Levin 150 D 4 North Island, C New
Zealand
Levkás *see* Lefkáda
Levkímmi *see* Lefkímmi
Lewis, Isle of 88 B 3 island, NW
Scotland, UK
Lewis Range 44 B 1 mountain
range, NW USA
Lewis Smith Lake 42 C 2 reservoir,
Alabama, S USA
Lewiston 41 G 2 Maine, NE USA
Lewiston 46 C 2 Idaho, NW USA
Lewistown 44 C 1 Montana, NW
USA
Lexington 40 C 5 Kentucky, E USA
Lexington 45 E 4 Nebraska, C USA
Leyte 139 F 2 island, Visayan
Islands, C Philippines
Leżajsk 99 E 5 SE Poland
Lezhë 101 C 6 *var.* Lezha; *prev.* Lesh,
Leshi. NW Albania
Lhasa 126 C 5 *var.* La-sa, Lassa. W
China
Lhazê 126 C 5 SW China
L'Hospitalet de Llobregat 93 G 2
var. Hospitalet. NE Spain
Liancourt Rocks 131 A 5 island
group, Japan/South Korea
Lianyungang 128 D 4 *var.* Xinpu. E
China
Liaoning 128 D 3 *var.* Liao,
Shengking; *hist.* Fengtien,
Fengtian. Province, NE China
Liao-yang *see* Liaoyang
Liaoyuan 128 E 3 *var.* Shuang-liao,
Jap. Chengchiatun. NE China
Liard *see* Fort Liard
Liban, Jebel 118 B 4 *var.* Jabal al
Gharbt, *Ar.* Jabal Lubnán, *Eng.*
Mount Lebanon. Mountain range,
C Lebanon
Libau *see* Liepája
Libby 44 A 1 Montana, NW USA
Liberal 45 E 5 Kansas, C USA
Liberec 98 B 4 *Ger.* Reichenberg. N
Czech Republic

Liberia
75 D 5 Republic, W Africa

Official name: Republic of Liberia
Date of formation: 1847 **Capital:**
Monrovia **Population:** 2.8 million
Total area: 111,370 sq km
(43,000 sq miles) **Languages:**
English*, Kpelle, Bassa Vai
Religions: Traditional beliefs 70%,
Muslim 20%, Christian 10% **Ethnic
mix:** Kpelle 20%, Bassa 14%,
Americo-Liberians 5%, other 61%
Government: Transitional
Currency: Liberian $ = 100 cents

Liberia 52 D 4 NW Costa Rica
Libourne 91 B 5 SW France
Libreville 77 A 5 country capital,
NW Gabon

Libya
71 F 3 *Ar.* Al Jamáhíríyah al
'Arabíyah al Líbíyah ash
Sha'bíyah al Ishtiråkíyah; *prev.*
Libyan Arab Republic. Islamic
state, N Africa

Official name: The Great Socialist
People's Libyan Arab *Jamahiriya*
Date of formation: 1951 **Capital:**
Tripoli **Population:** 5.5 million
Total area: 1,759,540 sq km
(679,358 sq miles) **Languages:**
Arabic*, Tuareg **Religions:** Muslim
97%, other 3% **Ethnic mix:** Arab
and Berber 97%, other 3%
Government: Socialist *jamahiriya*
(state of the masses)
Currency: Dinar = 1,000 dirhams

Libyan Desert 68 C 3 *var.* Libian
Desert, *Ar.* Aş Şahrå' al Líbíyah.
Desert, NE Africa
Libyan Plateau 68 C 2 plateau,
Egypt/Libya
Lichtenfels 95 C 5 SE Germany
Lichtenvoorde 86 E 4 E
Netherlands
Lichuan 129 C 5 C China
Lida 107 B 5 W Belorussia
Lidköping 85 B 6 S Sweden
Lidoríki 105 B 5 *prev.* Lidhorikíon,
Lidokhorikíon. C Greece
Lidzbark Warmiński 98 D 2 *Ger.*
Heilsberg. N Poland

Liechtenstein
94 D 1 Monarchy, C Europe

Official name: Principality of
Liechtenstein **Date of formation:**
1719 **Capital:** Vaduz **Population:**
29,000 **Total area:** 160 sq km
(62 sq miles) **Languages:** German*,
Alemannish **Religions:** Roman
Catholic 87%, Protestant 8%,
other 5% **Ethnic mix:**
Liechtensteiner 63%, Swiss 15%,
German 9%, other 13% **Government:**
Constitutional monarchy
Currency: Swiss franc = 100 centimes

Liechtenstein, Principality of *see*
Liechtenstein
Liège 87 D 6 *Dut.* Luik, *Ger.* Lüttich.
E Belgium
Liegnitz *see* Legnica
Lienz 95 D 7 W Austria
Liepája 106 B 3 *Ger.* Libau. W
Latvia
Lievenhof *see* Líváni
Liezen 95 D 7 C Austria
Liffey 89 B 6 river, E Ireland
Lifou 144 D 5 island, E New
Caledonia
Liger *see* Loire
Ligure, Appennino 96 A 2 *Eng.*
Ligurian Mountains. Mountain
range, NW Italy
Ligurian Mountains *see* Ligure,
Appennino
Ligurian Sea 102 D 2 *Fr.* Mer
Ligurienne, *It.* Mar Ligure. Sea, N
Mediterranean Sea
Lihou Reef & Cays 148 E 3 reef, C
Coral Sea
Lihue 47 A 8 *Haw.* Líhu'e. Hawaii,
W USA
Líhu'e *see* Lihue
Lihula 106 D 2 *Ger.* Leal. W Estonia
Likasi 77 D 8 *prev.* Jadotville. SE
Zaire
Liknes 85 A 6 S Norway

Lille 90 C 2 *var.* l'Isle, *Dut.* Rijssel, *Flem.* Ryssel; *prev.* Lisle, *anc.* Insula. N France
Lillehammer 85 B 5 S Norway
Lillestrøm 85 B 6 S Norway
Lilongwe 79 E 2 country capital, W Malawi
Lilybaeum *see* Marsala
Lima 60 C 4 country capital, W Peru
Limanowa 99 D 5 S Poland
Limassol *see* Lemesós
Lim Chu Kang 138 A 1 NW Singapore
Limerick 89 A 6 *Ir.* Luimneach. SW Ireland
Limín Vathéos *see* Sámos
Límnos 104 D 4 *anc.* Lemnos. Island, E Greece
Limoges 91 C 5 *anc.* Augustoritum Lemovicensium, Lemovices. C France
Limón 53 E 4 *var.* Puerto Limón. E Costa Rica
Limón 52 D 2 NE Honduras
Limousin 91 C 5 cultural region, C France
Limoux 91 C 6 S France
Limpopo 78 D 3 *var.* Crocodile. River, S Africa
Linares 92 D 4 S Spain
Linares 64 B 4 C Chile
Linares 51 E 3 NE Mexico
Linchuan 129 D 5 E China
Lincoln 89 D 6 *anc.* Lindum, Lindum Colonia. E England, UK
Lincoln 45 F 4 state capital, Nebraska, C USA
Lincoln Sea 83 E 1 sea, Arctic Ocean
Linden 59 G 3 E Guyana
Líndhos *see* Líndos
Lindi 73 D 8 SE Tanzania
Líndos 105 E 7 *var.* Líndhos. Ródos, SE Greece
Line Islands 145 H 3 island group, E Kiribati
Lingen 94 A 3 *var.* Lingen an der Ems. NW Germany
Lingen an der Ems *see* Lingen
Lingga, Kepulauan 138 B 4 island group, W Indonesia
Linköping 85 C 6 S Sweden
Linz 95 D 6 *anc.* Lentia. N Austria
Lion, Golfe du 91 C 7 *Eng.* Gulf of Lion, Gulf of Lions; *anc.* Sinus Gallicus. Inlet, NW Mediterranean Sea
Liozno *see* Lyozna
Lipari, Isola 97 D 7 island, S Italy
Lipetsk 111 B 5 W Russian Federation
Lipova 108 A 4 *Hung.* Lippa. W Romania
Lipovets *see* Lypovets'
Lippa *see* Lipova
Lippstadt 94 B 4 W Germany
Lira 73 B 6 N Uganda
Lisala 77 C 5 N Zaire
Lisboa 92 B 4 *var.* Lisbon; *anc.* Felicitas Julia, Olisipo. Country capital, W Portugal
Lisbon *see* Lisboa
Lisichansk *see* Lysychans'k
Lisieux 90 B 3 *anc.* Noviomagus. N France
Liski 111 B 6 *prev.* Georgiu-Dezh. W Russian Federation
Lismore 149 E 5 New South Wales, SE Australia
Lissa *see* Leszno

Lisse 86 C 3 W Netherlands
Litang 129 A 5 C China
Litani, Nahrel 119 B 5 *var.* Nahr al Litant. River, C Lebanon
Litant, Nahr al *see* Litani, Nahrel
Lithgow 149 D 6 New South Wales, SE Australia

Lithuania 106 B 4 *Ger.* Litauen, *Lith.* Lietuva, *Rus.* Litwa, *Rus.* Litva, Litovskaya SSR; *prev.* Lithuanian SSR. Republic, NE Europe

Official name: Republic of Lithuania **Date of formation:** 1991 **Capital:** Vilnius **Population:** 3.8 million **Total area:** 65,200 sq km (25,174 sq miles) **Languages:** Lithuanian*, Russian **Religions:** Roman Catholic 87%, Russian Orthodox 10%, other 3% **Ethnic mix:** Lithuanian 80%, Russian 9%, Polish 8%, other 3% **Government:** Multiparty republic **Currency:** Litas = 100 centas

Litóchoro 104 B 4 *var.* Litókhoron. N Greece
Little Alföld 99 C 6 *Ger.* Kleines Ungarisches Tiefland, *Hung.* Kisalföld, *Slvk.* Podunajská Rovina. Plain, Hungary/Slovakia
Little Andaman 133 F 2 island, SW India
Little Barrier Island 150 D 2 island, North Island, N New Zealand
Little Bay 93 H 5 bay, NE Atlantic Ocean
Little Cayman 54 B 3 island, E Cayman Islands
Little Falls 45 F 2 Minnesota, N USA
Littlefield 49 E 2 Texas, S USA
Little Fort 37 E 5 British Columbia, SW Canada
Little Inagua 54 D 2 *var.* Inagua Islands. Island, S Bahamas
Little Minch, The 88 B 3 strait, NE Atlantic Ocean
Little Missouri River 44 D 2 river, NW USA
Little Nicobar 133 G 3 island, SW India
Little Rock 42 B 1 state capital, Arkansas, C USA
Little St.Bernard Pass 96 A 2 *Fr.* Col du Petit St-Bernard, *It.* Colle di Piccolo San Bernardo. Pass, France/Italy
Little Sound 42 A 5 bay, W Atlantic Ocean
Littleton 44 C 4 Colorado, C USA
Littoria *see* Latina
Liuzhou 129 C 6 *var.* Liu-chou, Liuchow. S China
Livanátai *see* Livanátes
Livanátes 105 C 5 *prev.* Livanátai. C Greece
Līvāni 106 D 4 *Ger.* Lievenhof. SE Latvia
Liverpool 89 C 5 NW England, UK
Liverpool 39 F 5 Nova Scotia, SE Canada
Livingston 44 B 2 Montana, NW USA
Livingstone 78 C 3 *var.* Maramba. S Zambia
Livingstone Mountains 151 A 7 mountain range, South Island, SW New Zealand
Livingston, Lake 49 H 3 reservoir, Texas, S USA
Livno 100 B 4 SW Bosnia & Herzegovina

Livojoki 84 D 4 river, C Finland
Livonia 40 D 3 Michigan, N USA
Livonia *see* Vidzeme
Livorno 96 B 3 *Eng.* Leghorn. C Italy
Lixoúri 105 A 5 *prev.* Lixoúrion. Iónioi Nísoi, W Greece
Lixoúrion *see* Lixoúri
Ljouwert *see* Leeuwarden
Ljubljana 95 D 8 *Ger.* Laibach, *It.* Lubiana; *anc.* Aemona, Emona. Country capital, C Slovenia
Ljungby 85 B 7 S Sweden
Ljusdal 85 C 5 C Sweden
Ljusnan 85 C 5 river, C Sweden
Llallagua 61 F 4 SW Bolivia
Llanelli 89 C 7 *prev.* Llanelly. S Wales, UK
Llanelly *see* Llanelli
Llanes 92 D 1 N Spain
Llanos 58 D 2 physical region, Colombia/Venezuela
Lleida 93 F 2 *var.* Lérida; *anc.* Ilerda. NE Spain
Lluchmayor *see* Llucmajor
Llucmajor 93 G 3 *var.* Lluchmayor. E Spain
Lobatse 78 C 4 *var.* Lobatsi. SE Botswana
Lobatsi *see* Lobatse
Löbau 94 D 4 E Germany
Lobito 78 B 2 W Angola
Lobositz *see* Lovosice
Loburi *see* Lop Buri
Lochem 86 E 3 E Netherlands
Loch Garman *see* Wexford
Lockport 41 E 3 New York, NE USA
Lodeynoye Pole 110 B 4 *var.* Lodejnoje Pole, Lodeinoje Polje. NW Russian Federation
Lodi 47 B 6 California, W USA
Lodja 77 D 6 C Zaire
Lodz *see* Łódź
Łódź 98 D 4 *Rus.* Lodz. C Poland
Loei 136 C 4 *var.* Loey, Muang Loei. N Thailand
Lofoten 84 B 3 *var.* Lofoten Islands. Island group, C Norway
Lofoten Islands *see* Lofoten
Logan 44 B 3 Utah, W USA
Logan, Mount 36 D 3 mountain, Yukon Territory, W Canada
Logansport 40 C 4 Indiana, N USA
Logroño 93 E 2 *anc.* Vareia, *Lat.* Juliobriga. N Spain
Loibl Pass 95 D 7 *Ger.* Loiblpass, *Slvn.* Ljubelj. Pass, Austria/Slovenia
Loi-kaw 136 B 4 E Burma
Loire 90 B 4 *var.* Liger. River, C France
Loita Hills 73 C 6 hill range, SW Kenya
Loja 60 B 2 S Ecuador
Lokitaung 73 C 5 NW Kenya
Lokoja 75 G 5 C Nigeria
Loksa 106 E 2 *Ger.* Loxa. NW Estonia
Lolland 85 A 8 *prev.* Laaland. Island, S Denmark
Lom 75 H 5 river, Cameroon/Central African Republic
Lom 104 C 1 *prev.* Lom-Palanka. NW Bulgaria
Loma Mansa *see* Bintimani
Lomami 77 D 6 river, C Zaire
Lomas de Zamora 64 D 4 E Argentina
Lombok, Pulau 138 D 5 island, C Indonesia

Lomé 75 F 5 country capital, S Togo
Lommel 87 D 5 N Belgium
Lomond, Loch 88 C 4 lake, W Scotland, UK
Lomonsov Ridge 155 F 3 *var.* Harris Ridge, *Rus.* Khrebet Lomonsova. Undersea ridge, Arctic Ocean
Lom-Palanka *see* Lom
Lompoc 47 B 7 California, W USA
Lom Sak 136 C 4 *var.* Muang Lom Sak. N Thailand
Łomża 98 D 3 *Rus.* Lomzha. NE Poland
Lomzha *see* Łomża
Loncoche 65 B 5 C Chile
London 89 E 7 *anc.* Augusta, *Lat.* Londinium. Country capital, SE England, UK
London 38 C 5 Ontario, S Canada
Londonderry 88 A 4 *var.* Derry, *Ir.* Doire. N Northern Ireland, UK
Londonderry, Cape 146 C 2 headland, Western Australia, Australia
Londrina 63 E 4 S Brazil
Longa, Proliv 115 G 1 *Eng.* Long Strait. Strait, Chukchi Sea/East Siberian Sea
Long Bay 43 F 2 bay, NW Atlantic Ocean
Long Beach 47 C 8 California, W USA
Longford 89 B 5 *Ir.* An Longfort. C Ireland
Long Island 54 D 2 island, C Bahamas
Long Island 148 D 4 island, Queensland, E Australia
Long Island 41 G 4 island, New York, NE USA
Long Island Sound 41 G 3 sound, W Atlantic Ocean
Longlac 38 C 4 Ontario, S Canada
Longmont 44 C 4 Colorado, C USA
Longreach 148 C 4 Queensland, E Australia
Longview 49 H 3 Texas, S USA
Longview 46 B 2 Washington, NW USA
Long Xuyên 137 D 6 *var.* Longxuyen. SW Vietnam
Longxuyen *see* Long Xuyên
Longyan 129 D 6 SE China
Longyearbyen 83 G 2 dependent territory capital, W Svalbard
Lons-le-Saunier 90 D 4 *anc.* Ledo Salinarius. E France
Lop Buri 137 C 5 *var.* Loburi. C Thailand
Lop Nur 126 C 3 *var.* Lob Nor, Lop Nor, Lo-pu Po. Lake, NW China
Loppersum 86 E 1 NE Netherlands
Lorain 40 D 3 Ohio, N USA
Lorca 93 E 4 *Ar.* Lurka; *anc.* Eliocroca, *Lat.* Illur co. S Spain
Lord Howe Island 142 C 4 island, E Australia
Lord Howe Rise 152 C 4 undersea rise, SW Pacific Ocean
Loreto 50 B 3 W Mexico
Lorient 90 A 4 *prev.* l'Orient. NW France
l'Orient *see* Lorient
Lorn, Firth of 88 B 4 inlet, NE Atlantic Ocean
Lörrach 95 A 7 S Germany
Lorraine 90 D 3 cultural region, NE France
Los Alamos 48 D 1 New Mexico, SW USA
Los Amates 52 B 2 E Guatemala

Los Angeles 47 C 8 California, W USA

Los Ángeles 65 B 5 C Chile

Losanna see Lausanne

Los Banos 47 B 6 California, W USA

Losinj 100 A 3 var. Lošinj, Ger. Lussin, It. Lussino. Island, W Croatia

Loslau see Wodzisław Śląski

Los Mochis 50 C 3 C Mexico

Lô, Sông 128 A 1 var. Panlong Jiang. River, China/Vietnam

Los Roques, Islas 58 D 1 island group, N Venezuela

Los Testigos 59 E 1 island, NE Venezuela

Lost River Range 46 D 3 mountain range, Idaho, NW USA

Lot 91 B 5 cultural region, SW France

Lot 91 B 5 river, S France

Lotagipi Swamp 73 C 5 wetland, Kenya/Sudan

Loualaba see Lualaba

Louangnamtha 136 C 3 var. Luong Nam Tha. N Laos

Louangphabang 136 C 3 var. Louangphrabang, Luang Prabang. C Laos

Loubomo see Dolisie

Loudéac 90 A 3 NW France

Loudi 129 C 6 E China

Louga 74 B 3 NW Senegal

Louisiade Archipelago 144 C 4 island group, SE Papua New Guinea

Louisiana 42 A 2 off. State of Louisiana; nicknames Creole State, Pelican State. State, S USA

Louisville 40 C 5 Kentucky, E USA

Louisville Ridge 152 D 4 undersea ridge, SW Pacific Ocean

Lourdes 91 B 6 S France

Lourenço Marques see Maputo

Louth 89 E 5 E England, UK

Loutrá 104 C 4 N Greece

Louvain-la Neuve 87 C 6 C Belgium

Louviers 90 C 3 N France

Loveč see Lovech

Lovech 104 C 2 var. Loveč. NW Bulgaria

Loveland 44 C 4 Colorado, C USA

Lovosice 98 A 4 Ger. Lobositz. NW Czech Republic

Lóvua 78 C 1 NE Angola

Lowell 41 G 3 Massachusetts, NE USA

Lower California see Baja California

Lower Hutt 151 D 5 North Island, C New Zealand

Lower Lough Erne 89 A 5 lake, SW Northern Ireland, UK

Lower Red Lake 45 F 1 Lake, Minnesota, USA

Lower Tunguska see Nizhnyaya Tunguska

Lowestoft 89 E 6 E England, UK

Loxa see Loksa

Loyauté, Îles 144 D 5 island group, S New Caledonia

Loyev see Loyew

Loyew 107 D 8 Rus. Loyev. SE Belorussia

Loznica 100 D 3 W Yugoslavia

Lualaba 77 D 7 Fr. Loualaba. River, SE Zaire

Luanda 78 A 1 var. Loanda, Paulo de Loanda, Port. São. Country capital, NW Angola

Luang, Thale 137 C 7 lagoon, South China Sea/Pacific Ocean

Luanshya 78 D 2 C Zambia

Luarca 92 C 1 N Spain

Lubaczów 99 E 5 var. Lúbaczów. SE Poland

Lubānas Ezers see Lubāns

Lubango 78 B 2 Port. Sá da Bandeira. SW Angola

Lubāns 106 D 4 var. Lubānas Ezers. Lake, E Latvia

Lubao 77 D 6 C Zaire

Lübben 94 D 4 Ger. Germany

Lübbenau 94 D 4 E Germany

Lubbock 49 E 2 Texas, S USA

Lübeck 94 C 2 N Germany

Lubelska, Wyżyna 98 E 4 plateau, SE Poland

Lüben see Lubin

Lubin 98 B 4 var. Lüben. W Poland

Lublin 98 E 4 Rus. Lyublin. E Poland

Lubliniec 98 C 4 S Poland

Lubny 109 F 2 NE Ukraine

Lubsko 98 B 4 Ger. Sommerfeld. W Poland

Lubumbashi 77 E 8 prev. Élisabethville. SE Zaire

Lubutu 77 D 6 E Zaire

Luca 61 F 5 SW Bolivia

Luca see Lucca

Lucan 89 B 5 Ir. Leamhcán. E Ireland

Lucanian Mountains see Lucano, Appennino

Lucano, Appennino 97 D 6 Eng. Lucanian Mountains. Mountain range, S Italy

Lucapa 78 C 1 var. Lukapa. NE Angola

Lucca 96 B 3 anc. Luca. C Italy

Lucea 54 A 4 W Jamaica

Lucedale 42 C 3 Mississippi, S USA

Lucena 92 D 4 S Spain

Lucena 139 E 1 off. Lucena City. Luzon, N Philippines

Lucena City see Lucena

Lučenec 99 D 6 Ger. Losontz, Hung. Losonc. S Slovakia

Lucerne, Lake of see Vierwaldstätter See

Lucknow 135 E 3 var. Lakhnau. State capital, N India

Lüderitz 78 B 4 prev. Angra Pequena. SW Namibia

Ludhiāna 134 D 2 N India

Ludsan see Ludza

Luduş 108 B 4 Ger. Ludasch, Hung. Marosludas. C Romania

Ludvika 85 C 6 C Sweden

Ludwiglust 94 C 3 N Germany

Ludwigsburg 95 B 6 SW Germany

Ludwigsfelde 94 D 4 NE Germany

Ludwigshafen am Rhein. 95 B 5 var. Ludwigshafen. W Germany

Ludza 106 D 4 Ger. Ludsan. E Latvia

Luebo 77 C 6 SW Zaire

Luena 78 C 2 var. Lwena, Port. Luso. E Angola

Lufira 77 E 7 river, SE Zaire

Lufkin 49 H 3 Texas, S USA

Luga 110 A 4 NW Russian Federation

Lugenda, Rio 79 E 2 river, N Mozambique

Lugh Ganana see Luuq

Lugo 92 C 1 anc. Lugus Augusti. NW Spain

Lugoj 108 A 4 Ger. Lugosch, Hung. Lugos. W Romania

Lugus Augusti see Lugo

Luhans'k 109 H 3 Rus. Lugansk; prev. Voroshilovgrad. E Ukraine

Luimneach see Limerick

Lukapa see Lucapa

Lukenie 77 D 6 river, C Zaire

Lukovit 104 C 2 NW Bulgaria

Łuków 98 E 4 Ger. Bogendorf. E Poland

Lukuga 77 E 7 river, SE Zaire

Luleå 84 D 4 N Sweden

Luleälven 84 C 3 river, N Sweden

Lulonga 77 C 5 river, NW Zaire

Luluabourg see Kananga

Lumberton 43 F 1 North Carolina, SE USA

Lumbo 79 F 2 NE Mozambique

Lumi i Vjosës 104 A 4 var. Vijosa, Vijosë, Gk. Aóos. River, Albania/Greece

Lumsden 151 A 7 South Island, SW New Zealand

Lund 85 B 7 S Sweden

Lüneburg 94 B 3 N Germany

Lungué-Bungo see Lungwebungu

Lungwebungu 78 C 2 var. Lungué-Bungo. River, Angola/Zambia

Luninets 107 B 7 Pol. Łuniniec, Rus. Luninets. SW Belorussia

Lunteren 86 D 4 C Netherlands

Luong Nam Tha see Louangnamtha

Luoyang 128 C 4 var. Honan, Lo-yang. C China

Lupatia see Altamura

Lúrio 79 F 2 NE Mozambique

Lúrio, Rio 79 E 2 river, NE Mozambique

Lusaka 78 D 2 country capital, SE Zambia

Lushnja see Lushnjë

Lushnjë 101 C 6 var. Lushnja. C Albania

Lūt, Dasht-e 120 D 3 var. Kavír-e Lút. Desert, E Iran

Luton 89 D 6 S England, UK

Łutselk'e 37 F 4 prev. Snowdrift. Northwest Territories, C Canada

Luts'k 108 C 1 Pol. Łuck, Rus. Lutsk. NW Ukraine

Lutzow-Holm Bay 154 C 2 var. Lützow-Holmbukta. Bay, Atlantic Ocean/Indian Ocean

Lützow Holmbukta see Lutzow-Holm Bay

Luuq 73 D 6 It. Lugh Ganana. SW Somalia

Luvua 77 E 7 river, SE Zaire

Luxembourg 87 D 8 country capital, S Luxembourg

Luxembourg
87 D 8 var. Lëtzebuerg, Luxemburg. Monarchy, W Europe

Official name: Grand Duchy of Luxembourg **Date of formation:** 1867 **Capital:** Luxembourg **Population:** 400,000 **Total area:** 2,586 sq km (998 sq miles) **Languages:** Letzeburgish*, French, Portuguese, Italian **Religions:** Roman Catholic 97%, other 3% **Ethnic mix:** Luxemburger 72%, Portuguese 9%, Italian 5%, other 14% **Government:** Constitutional monarchy **Currency:** Franc = 100 centimes

Luxor 72 B 2 Ar. Al Uqşur. E Egypt

Luza 110 C 4 NW Russian Federation

Luzern 95 B 7 Fr. Lucerne, It. Lucerna. C Switzerland

Lugus Augusti see Lugo

Luhans'k 109 H 3 Rus. Lugansk; prev. Voroshilovgrad. E Ukraine

Luzon 139 E 1 island, N Philippines

Luzon Strait 139 E 1 strait, W Pacific Ocean

L'viv 108 B 2 Ger. Lemberg, Pol. Lwów, Rus. L'vov. W Ukraine

Lyakhavichy 107 D 6 Rus. Lyakhovichi. SW Belorussia

Lyakhovichi see Lyakhavichy

Lyallpur see Faisalābād

Lyangar see Langar

Lyck see Ełk

Lycksele 84 C 4 N Sweden

Lyel'chytsy 107 C 7 Rus. Lel'chitsy. SE Belorussia

Lyepyel' 107 D 5 Rus. Lepel'. N Belorussia

Lyme Bay 89 D 7 bay, Atlantic Ocean/English Channel

Lynchburg 41 E 5 Virginia, NE USA

Lynn 41 G 3 Massachusetts, NE USA

Lyon 91 D 5 Eng. Lyons; anc. Lugdunum. E France

Lyozna 107 E 6 Rus. Liozno. NE Belorussia

Lypovets' 108 D 2 Rus. Lipovets. C Ukraine

Lys see Leie

Lysychans'k 109 H 3 Rus. Lisichansk. E Ukraine

Lyttelton 151 C 6 South Island, C New Zealand

Lyublin see Lublin

Lyubotin see Lyubotyn

Lyubotyn 109 G 2 Rus. Lyubotin. E Ukraine

Lyulyakovo 104 E 2 prev. Keremitlik. E Bulgaria

Lyusina 107 C 6 Rus. Lyusino. SW Belorussia

Lyusino see Lyusina

M

Ma'ān 119 B 7 SW Jordan

Maardu 106 D 2 Ger. Maart. NW Estonia

Maarmovilik 82 C 3 var. Mârmorilik. W Greenland

Ma'arrat an Nu'mān 118 B 3 var. Ma'aret-en-Nu'man, Fr. Maarret enn Naamâne. NW Syria

Maart see Maardu

Maas see Meuse

Maaseik 87 D 5 prev. Maeseyck. NE Belgium

Maastricht 87 D 6 var. Maestricht; anc. Traiectum ad Mosam, Traiectum Tungorum. SE Netherlands

Macao 129 C 7 var. Macau, Chin. Aomen, Port. Mação. Portuguese territory, E Asia

Macao 129 C 6 var. Macau, Mação. Territory capital, N Macao

Macará 60 B 2 S Ecuador

Macarov Basin 155 G 3 undersea basin, Arctic Ocean

Macarsca see Makarska

Macāu see Makó

MacCluer Gulf see Berau, Teluk

Macdonnell Ranges 142 A 4 mountain range, Northern Territory, C Australia

Macedonia
101 D 6 abbrev. FYR Macedonia, Mac. Makedonija. Republic, SE Europe

Official name: Former Yugoslav Republic of Macedonia **Date of**

formation: 1991 **Capital:** Skopje
Population: 1.9 million **Total area:**
25,715 sq km (9,929 sq miles)
Languages: Macedonian, Albanian
Turkish (*no official language*)
Religions: Christian 80%, Muslim
20% **Ethnic mix:** Macedonian 67%,
Albanian 20%, Turkish 4%, other 9%
Government: Multiparty republic
Currency: Denar = 100 deni

Maceió 63 G 3 state capital, E Brazil
Macfarlane, Lake 149 B 6 *var.* Lake
Mcfarlane. Lake, South Australia,
S Australia
Machachi 60 B 1 C Ecuador
Machakos 73 C 6 S Kenya
Machala 60 B 2 SW Ecuador
Machanga 79 E 3 E Mozambique
Machattie, Lake 148 B 4 lake, C
Australia
Machilīpatnam 132 D 1 *var.* Bandar,
Masulipatnam. E India
Machiques 58 C 2 NW Venezuela
Măcin 108 D 5 SE Romania
Mackay 148 D 4 Queensland, NE
Australia
Mackay, Lake 146 D 4 salt lake, C
Australia
Mackenzie 37 E 3 river, Northwest
Territories, NW Canada
Mackenzie Bay 154 D 3 bay, C
Indian Ocean
Mackenzie Mountains 36 D 3
mountain range, Northwest
Territories, NW Canada
Macleod, Lake 146 A 4 lake, W
Australia
Macomb 40 A 4 Illinois, N USA
Macomer 97 A 5 W Italy
Macon 42 D 2 Georgia, SE USA
Macon 45 G 4 Missouri, C USA
Mâcon 91 D 5 *anc.* Matisco, Matisco
Ædourum. C France
Macquarie Ridge 154 C 5 undersea
ridge, SW Pacific Ocean
Macuspana 51 G 4 SE Mexico
Ma'dabā 119 B 6 *var.* Mādabā,
Madeba; *anc.* Medeba. NW Jordan

Madagascar
79° F 3 *Malg.* Madagasikara; *prev.*
Malagasy Republic. Republic,
E Africa

Official name: Democratic Republic
of Madagascar **Date of formation:**
1960 **Capital:** Antananarivo
Population: 13.3 million **Total area:**
587,040 sq km (226,660 sq miles)
Languages: Malagasy*, French*
Religions: Traditional beliefs 52%,
Christian 41%, Muslim 7% **Ethnic
mix:** Merina 26%, Betsimisaraka
15%, Betsileo 12%, other 47%
Government: Multiparty republic
Currency: Franc = 100 centimes

Madagascar Basin 141 B 5 undersea
basin, W Indian Ocean
Madagascar Plateau 141 A 6 *var.*
Madagascar Ridge, Madagascar
Rise, Madagaskarskiy Khrebet.
Undersea plateau, W Indian
Ocean
Madang 144 B 3 New Guinea, N
Papua New Guinea
Madanīy'ïn *see* Médenine
Made 86 C 4 S Netherlands
Madeira 62 D 2 *var.* Río Madera.
River, Bolivia/Brazil
Madeira 70 A 2 Portuguese
autonomous region, E Atlantic
Ocean
Madeira 70 A 2 *var.* Ilha de
Madeira. Island, E Atlantic Ocean

Madeira, Ilha de *see* Madeira
Madeleine, Îles de la 39 F 4 *Eng.*
Magdalen Islands. Island group,
Québec, E Canada
Madera 47 C 6 California, W USA
Madera, Río *see* Madeira
Madhya Pradesh 135 E 4 *prev.*
Central Provinces and Berar.
State, C India
Madīnat al Abyār *see* Al Abyār
Madīnat ath Thawrah 118 C 2 *var.*
Ath Thawrah. N Syria
Madioen *see* Madiun
Madison 40 B 3 state capital,
Wisconsin, N USA
Madison 45 F 3 South Dakota, N
USA
Madiun 138 D 5 *prev.* Madioen.
Jawa, C Indonesia
Madoera *see* Madura, Pulau
Madona 106 D 4 *Ger.* Modohn. E
Latvia
Madras 132 D 2 S India
Madras *see* Tamil Nādu
Madre de Dios 61 E 3 river,
Bolivia/Peru
Madre del Sur, Sierra 51 E 5
mountain range, S Mexico
Madre, Laguna 49 G 5 lake, Texas,
S USA
Madre, Laguna 51 F 3 lagoon, NW
Gulf of Mexico
Madre Occidental, Sierra 50 C 2
var. Western Sierra Madre.
Mountain range, C Mexico
Madre Oriental, Sierra 51 E 3 *var.*
Eastern Sierra Madre. Mountain
range, C Mexico
Madrid 92 D 3 country capital, C
Spain
Madura 138 D 5 *prev.* Madoera.
Island, C Indonesia
Madurai 132 C 3 *prev.* Madura,
Mathurai. S India
Maebashi 131 D 5 *var.* Maebasi,
Mayebashi. Honshū, S Japan
Maeikiai 106 B 3 NW Lithuania
Mae Nam Nan 136 C 4 river, S
Thailand
Mae Nam Yom 136 C 4 river, S
Thailand
Maeseyck *see* Maaseik
Maewo 144 D 4 *prev.* Aurora.
Island, C Vanuatu
Mafraq *see* Al Mafraq
Magadan 115 G 3 NE Russian
Federation
Magallanes *see* Punta Arenas
Magallanes, Estrecho de *see*
Magellan, Strait of
Magangué 58 B 2 N Colombia
Magdalena 50 B 2 NW Mexico
Magdalena 61 F 3 N Bolivia
Magdalena, Isla 65 A 6 island, S
Chile
Magdalena, Isla 50 B 3 island, W
Mexico
Magdalen Islands *see* Madeleine,
Îles de la
Magdeburg 94 C 4 C Germany
Magdelena 58 B 2 river, C
Colombia
Magelang 138 C 5 Jawa, C
Indonesia
Magellan, Strait of 65 C 8 *Sp.*
Estrecho de Magallanes. Strait,
Atlantic Ocean/Pacific Ocean
Magerøy *see* Magerøya
Magerøya 84 D 1 *var.* Magerøy.
Island, N Norway
Maggiore, Lago *see* Maggiore, Lake

Maggiore, Lake 96 B 1 *It.* Lago
Maggiore. Lake,
Italy/Switzerland
Maglaj 100 C 3 N Bosnia &
Herzegovina
Maglie 97 E 6 SE Italy
Magna 44 B 4 Utah, W USA
Magnitogorsk 114 B 4 C Russian
Federation
Magta' Lahjar 74 C 3 *var.* Magta'
Lahjar, Magtá Lahjar, Magta
Lahjar. SW Mauritania
Magway *see* Magwe
Magwe 136 A 3 *var.* Magway. W
Burma
Mahajanga 79 G 3 *var.* Majunga. N
Madagascar
**Mahakam, 138 D 4 *var.* Koetai,
Kutai. River, Borneo, C Indonesia
Mahalapye 78 D 3 *var.* Mahalatswe.
SE Botswana
Mahalatswe *see* Mahalapye
Mahān 120 D 4 E Iran
Mahārāshtra 134 D 5 state, W India
Mahé 79 H 1 island, NE Seychelles
Mahia Peninsula 150 E 4 peninsula,
North Island, E New Zealand
Mahilyow 107 E 6 *Rus.* Mogilëv. E
Belorussia
Mahmūd-e 'Erāqī *see* Maḥmūd-e
Rāqī
Maḥmūd-e Rāqī 123 E 4 *var.*
Mahmūd-e 'Erāqī. NE
Afghanistan
Mahón 93 H 3 *Cat.* Maó, *Eng.* Port
Mahon; *anc.* Portus Magonis. E
Spain
Mährisch-Weisskirchen *see* Hranice
Maicao 58 C 1 N Colombia
Maidstone 89 E 7 SE England, UK
Maiduguri 75 H 4 NE Nigeria
Main 95 B 5 river, C Germany
Mai-Ndombe, Lac 77 C 6 *prev.* Lac
Léopold II. Lake, W Zaire
Maine 90 B 3 cultural region, NW
France
Maine 41 G 2 *off.* State of Maine;
nicknames Lumber State, Pine Tree
State. State, NE USA
Maine, Gulf of 41 H 2 gulf, NW
Atlantic Ocean
Mainland 88 D 2 island, NE
Scotland, UK
Mainland 88 D 1 island NE
Scotland, UK
Mainz 95 B 5 *Fr.* Mayence. SW
Germany
Maio 74 A 3 *var.* Mayo. Island, SE
Cape Verde
Maisur *see* Mysore
Maitland 149 D 6 New South
Wales, SE Australia
Maizhokunggar X 126 C 5 W China
Maíz, Islas del 53 E 3 *var.* Corn
Islands. Island group, SE
Nicaragua
Majunga *see* Mahajanga
Majuro 142 D 2 *var.* D-U-D
Municipality. Country capital, S
Marshall Islands
Majuro 144 D 2 island, SE Marshall
Islands
Makale *see* Mek'elē
Makarikari Pans *see* Makgadikgadi
Makarska 100 B 4 *It.* Macarsca. SE
Croatia
Makasar, Selat 138 D 4 *Eng.*
Makassar Strait. Strait, Celebes
Sea/Java Sea
Makassar Strait *see* Makasar, Selat
Makeni 74 C 4 C Sierra Leone

Makgadikgadi 78 C 3 *var.*
Makarikari Pans. Salt lake, NE
Botswana
Makhachkala 111 B 8 *prev.*
Petrovsk-Port. SW Russian
Federation
Makin Atoll 144 D 2 *prev.* Pitt
Island. Island, W Kiribati
Makira *see* San Cristobal
Makiyivka 109 G 3 *Rus.*
Makeyevka; *prev.* Dmitriyevsk. E
Ukraine
Makkah 121 A 5 *Eng.* Mecca. W
Saudi Arabia
Makkovik 39 F 2 Newfoundland
and Labrador, NE Canada
Makó 99 D 7 *Rom.* Macău. SE
Hungary
Makoua 77 B 5 C Congo
Makran Coast 120 E 4 physical
region, SE Iran
Makrany 107 A 6 *Rus.* Mokrany.
SW Belorussia
Mākū 120 B 2 NW Iran
Makurdi 75 G 5 C Nigeria
Mala *see* Malaita
Malabār Coast 132 B 3 physical
region, SW India
Malabo 77 A 5 *prev.* Santa Isabel.
Country capital, NW Equatorial
Guinea
Malaca *see* Málaga
Malacca *see* Melaka
Malacca, Strait of 138 A 3 strait,
Indian Ocean/Pacific Ocean
Malacka *see* Malacky
Malacky 99 C 6 *Hung.* Malacka. W
Slovakia
Maladzyechna 107 C 5 *Pol.*
Molodeczno, *Rus.* Molodechno. C
Belorussia
Málaga 92 D 5 *anc.* Malaca. S Spain
Malagarasi River 73 B 7 river, SW
Tanzania
Malaita 144 C 3 *var.* Mala. Island, N
Solomon Islands
Malakal 73 B 5 S Sudan
Malambo 58 B 1 N Colombia
Malang 138 D 5 Jawa, C Indonesia
Malange *see* Malanje
Malanje 78 B 1 *var.* Malange. NW
Angola
Mälaren 85 C 6 lake, C Sweden
Malatya 117 E 4 *anc.* Melitene. SE
Turkey
Mala Vyska 109 E 3 *Rus.* Malaya
Viska. S Ukraine

Malawi
79 E 1 *prev.* Nyasaland,
Nyasaland Protectorate. Republic,
S Africa

Official name: Republic of Malawi
Date of formation: 1964 **Capital:**
Lilongwe **Population:** 10.7 million
Total area: 118,480 sq km
(45,745 sq miles) **Languages:** English*
Chewa **Religions:** Christian 66%,
traditional beliefs 18%,
other 16% **Ethnic mix:** Maravi 55%,
Lomwe 17%, Yao 13%, other 15%
Government: Multiparty republic
Currency: Kwacha = 100 tambala

Malaya Viska *see* Mala Vyska

Malaysia
138 B 3 *var.* Federation of
Malaysia; *prev.* the separate
territories of Federation of
Malaya, Sarawak and Sabah
(NorthBorneo) and Singapore.
Monarchy, SE Asia

Official name: Malaysia **Date of formation:** 1965 **Capital:** Kuala Lumpur **Population:** 19.2 million **Total Area:** 329,750 sq km (127,317 sq miles) **Languages:** Malay*, Chinese, Tamil **Religions:** Muslim 53%, Buddhist and Confucianist 30%, other 17% **Ethnic mix:** Malay and aborigine 60%, Chinese 30%, Indian 8%, other 2% **Government:** Federal constitutional monarchy **Currency:** Ringgit = 100 cents

Malbork 98 C 2 *Ger.* Marienburg, Marienburg in Westpreussen. N Poland
Malchin 94 C 3 N Germany
Malden 45 H 5 Missouri, C USA
Malden Island 145 G 3 *prev.* Independence Island. Island, E Kiribati

Maldives
132 A 4 Republic, Indian Ocean

Official name: Republic of Maldives **Date of formation:** 1965 **Capital:** Male' **Population:** 200,000 **Total Area:** 300 sq km (116 sq miles) **Languages:** Dhivehi (Maldivian)*, Sinhala, Tamil **Religions:** Sunni Muslim 100% **Ethnic mix:** Maldivian 99%, Sinhalese and other South Asian 1% **Government:** Republic **Currency:** Rufiyaa - 100 laari

Male' 132 B 4 country capital, C Maldives
Male' Atoll 132 B 4 *var.* Kaafu Atoll. Island, C Maldives
Malekula 144 D 4 *var.* Malakula; *prev.* Mallicolo. Island, W Vanuatu
Malesína 105 C 5 E Greece
Malheur Lake 46 C 3 lake, Oregon, NW USA
Malheur River 46 C 4 river, Oregon, NW USA

Mali
75 E 2 . *Fr.* République du Mali; *prev.* Sudanese Republic, French Sudan. Republic, W Africa

Official name: Republic of Mali **Date of formation:** 1960 **Capital:** Bamako **Population:** 10.1 million **Total area:** 1,240,190 sq km (478,837 sq miles) **Languages:** French*, Bambara, Fulani, Senufo **Religions:** Muslim 80%, traditional beliefs 18%, Christian 2% **Ethnic mix:** Bambara 31%, Fulani 13%, Senufo 12%, other 44% **Government:** Multiparty republic **Currency:** CFA franc = 100 centimes

Malik, Wadi al *see* Milk, Wadi el
Mali Kyun 137 B 5 *var.* Tavoy Island. Island, S Burma
Malin *see* Malyn
Malindi 73 D 7 SE Kenya
Malko Tŭrnovo 104 E 3 SE Bulgaria
Mallaig 88 C 3 W Scotland, UK
Mallawi 72 B 2 C Egypt
Mallorca 93 H 3 *Eng.* Majorca; *anc.* Baleares Major. Island, E Spain
Malmberget 84 C 3 N Sweden
Malmédy 87 D 7 E Belgium
Malmö 85 B 7 S Sweden
Malmyž *see* Malmyzh
Maloelap 144 D 1 *var.* Maoeap. Island, E Marshall Islands
Maloelap *see* Maloelap Atoll
Małopolska 98 D 4 plateau, S Poland
Malozemel'skaja Tundra *see* Malozemel'skaya Tundra

Malozemel'skaya Tundra 110 D 3 *var.* Malozemel'skaja Tundra. Physical region, NW Russian Federation

Malta
97 C 8 Republic, Mediterranean

Official name: Republic of Malta **Date of formation:** 1964 **Capital:** Valletta **Population:** 400,000 **Total area:** 320 sq km (124 sq miles) **Languages:** Maltese*, English **Religions:** Roman Catholic 98%, other (mostly Anglican) 2% **Ethnic mix:** Maltese (mixed Arab, Sicilian, Norman, Spanish, Italian, English) 98%, other 2% **Government:** Multiparty republic **Currency:** Lira = 100 cents

Malta 97 C 8 island, S Europe
Malta 106 D 4 SE Latvia
Malta 44 C 1 Montana, NW USA
Malta, Canale di *see* Malta Channel
Malta Channel 97 C 8 *It.* Canale di Malta. Channel, C Mediterranean Sea
Malta, Republic of *see* Malta
Maluka 139 F 4 *Eng.* Moluccas, *Dut.* Molukken; *prev.* Spice Islands. Island group, E Indonesia
Maluku, Laut 139 F 4 *Eng.* Molucca Sea. Sea, W Pacific Ocean
Malung 85 B 5 C Sweden
Malyn 108 D 2 *Rus.* Malin. N Ukraine
Malyy Kavkaz *see* Lesser Caucasus
Mamberamo 139 H 4 river, New Guinea, E Indonesia
Mamonovo 106 A 4 *Ger.* Heiligenbeil. W Russian Federation
Mamoré 61 F 3 river, Bolivia/Brazil
Mamou 74 C 4 W Guinea
Mamoudzou 79 F 2 dependent territory capital, N Mayotte
Mamuno 78 C 3 W Botswana
Manacor 93 H 3 E Spain
Manado 139 F 3 *prev.* Menado. Celebes, C Indonesia
Managua 52 D 3 country capital, W Nicaragua
Managua, Lago de 52 C 3 *var.* Xolotlán. Lake, W Nicaragua
Manahiki Plateau 152 D 3 undersea plateau, SW Pacific Ocean
Manakara 79 G 4 SE Madagascar
Manama *see* Al Manāmah
Mananjary 79 G 3 SE Madagascar
Manáos *see* Manaus
Manapouri, Lake 151 A 7 lake, South Island, SW New Zealand
Manar *see* Mannar
Manas, Gora 123 F 2 mountain, Kyrgyzstan/Uzbekistan
Manaus 62 D 2 *prev.* Manáos. State capital, NW Brazil
Manavgat 116 B 4 SW Turkey
Manbij 118 C 2 *var.* Mambij, *Fr.* Membidj. N Syria
Manchester 89 D 5 *Lat.* Mancunium. N England, UK
Manchester 41 G 3 New Hampshire, NE USA
Man-chou-li *see* Manzhouli
Manchuria 128 D 2 cultural region, NE China
Máncio Lima *see* Japiim
Máncora 60 B 2 NE Peru
Mancunium *see* Manchester
Mand 120 D 4 *var.* Rūd-e Mand. River, S Iran

Mandalay 136 B 3 N Burma
Mandan 45 E 2 North Dakota, N USA
Mandara Mountains 75 H 4 mountain range, E Nigeria
Mandaue 139 E 2 *off.* Mandaue City. Cebu, C Philippines
Mandaue City *see* Mandaue
Mandeville 54 B 5 C Jamaica
Mándra 105 C 6 C Greece
Mand, Rūd-e *see* Mand
Mandurah 147 B 6 Western Australia, SW Australia
Mandya 132 C 2 C India
Manfredonia 97 D 5 SE Italy
Mangai 77 C 6 W Zaire
Mangaia 145 G 5 island group, S Cook Islands
Mangalia 108 D 5 *anc.* Callatis. SE Romania
Mangalmé 76 C 3 SE Chad
Mangalore 132 B 2 W India
Manguang *see* Bloemfontein
Mangin Range 136 B 2 mountain range, C Burma
Mango *see* Sansanné-Mango
Mangoky 79 F 3 river, SW Madagascar
Manhattan 45 F 4 Kansas, C USA
Manicouagan, Réservoir 39 E 3 lake, Québec, E Canada
Manihiki 145 G 4 island, N Cook Islands
Maniitsoq 82 C 3 *var.* Manîtsoq, *Dan.* Sukkertoppen. SW Greenland
Manila 139 E 1 *off.* City of Manila. Country capital, Luzon, N Philippines
Manisa 116 A 3 *var.* Manissa; *prev.* Saruhan, *anc.* Magnesia. W Turkey
Man, Isle of 89 C 5 British dependency, W British Isles, UK
Manistee River 40 C 2 river, Michigan, N USA
Manitoba 37 F 5 province, S Canada
Manitoulin Island 38 C 5 island, Ontario, S Canada
Manitowoc 40 B 2 Wisconsin, N USA
Manizales 58 B 3 W Colombia
Manjimup 147 B 7 Western Australia, SW Australia
Mankato 45 F 3 Minnesota, N USA
Manlleu 93 G 2 NE Spain
Manmād 134 C 5 W India
Mannar 132 C 3 *var.* Manar. NW Sri Lanka
Mannar, Gulf of 132 C 3 gulf, N Indian Ocean
Mannheim 95 B 5 SW Germany
Manono 77 E 7 SE Zaire
Manosque 91 D 6 SE France
Manra 145 F 3 *prev.* Sydney Island. Island, C Kiribati
Mansa 78 D 2 *prev.* Fort Rosebery. N Zambia
Mansel Island 38 C 1 island, Northwest Territories, NE Canada
Mansfield 40 D 4 Ohio, N USA
Manta 60 A 2 W Ecuador
Manteca 47 B 6 California, W USA
Mantova 96 B 2 *Eng.* Mantua, *Fr.* Mantoue. NW Italy
Manuae 145 G 5 island, S Cook Islands
Manukau *see* Manurewa
Manurewa 150 D 3 *var.* Manukau. North Island, N New Zealand

Manzanares 93 E 4 C Spain
Manzanillo 54 C 3 E Cuba
Manzanillo 50 D 4 SW Mexico
Manzano Mountains 48 D 2 mountain range, New Mexico, SW USA
Manzhouli 127 F 1 *var.* Man-chou-li. N China
Manzil 119 B 7 W Jordan
Mao 76 B 3 W Chad
Maoke, Pegunungan 139 H 4 *Dut.* Sneeuw-gebergte, *Eng.* Snow Mountains. Mountain range, New Guinea, E Indonesia
Maoming 129 C 6 S China
Maputo 78 D 4 *prev.* Lourenço Marques. Country capital, S Mozambique
Maputo, Baía de 79 E 4 *var.* Baía de Lourenço Marques, *Eng.* Delagoa Bay. Bay, W Indian Ocean
Marabá 63 F 2 NE Brazil
Maracaibo 58 C 1 NW Venezuela
Maracaibo, Lago de 58 C 2 *var.* Lake Maracaibo. Lagoon, NW Venezuela
Maracaibo, Lake *see* Maracaibo, Lago de
Maracay 58 D 1 N Venezuela
Maradi 75 G 3 S Niger
Maragha *see* Marāgheh
Marāgheh 120 C 2 *var.* Maragha. NW Iran
Marajó, Baía de 63 F 1 bay, W Atlantic Ocean
Marajó, Ilha de 63 E 1 island, N Brazil
Maramba *see* Livingstone
Maranhão 63 F 2 *off.* Estado do Maranhão. State, E Brazil
Marañón 60 C 2 river, N Peru
Marathon 38 C 4 Ontario, S Canada
Marathón *see* Marathónas
Marathónas 105 C 5 *prev.* Marathón. C Greece
Marbella 92 D 5 S Spain
Marble Bar 146 B 4 Western Australia, W Australia
Marburg *see* Marburg an der Lahn
Marburg *see* Maribor
Marburg an der Lahn 94 B 4 *hist.* Eng. Marburg . W Germany
March *see* Morava
Marche 91 C 5 cultural region, C France
Marche-en-Famenne 87 D 7 SE Belgium
Marchena, Isla 60 B 5 *var.* Bindloe Island. Island, Galapagos Islands, E Pacific Ocean
Marchfield 55 H 2 SE Barbados
Mar Chiquita, Laguna 64 C 3 lake, C Argentina
Marcona 60 D 4 SW Peru
Marcounda *see* Markounda
Mardān 134 C 1 N Pakistan
Mar del Plata 65 D 5 E Argentina
Mardin 117 E 4 SE Turkey
Maré 144 D 5 island, E New Caledonia
Mareeba 148 C 3 Queensland, NE Australia
Marganets *see* Marhanets'
Margarita, Isla de 59 E 1 island, N Venezuela
Margate 89 E 7 *prev.* Mergate. SE England, UK
Marghita 108 B 3 *Hung.* Margitta. NW Romania
Margitta *see* Marghita**

Mārgow, Dasht-e 122 D 5 desert, SW Afghanistan
Marhanets' 109 F 3 *Rus.* Marganets. E Ukraine
Maria Cleofas, Isla 50 C 4 island, C Mexico
Maria Island 149 C 8 island, Tasmania, SE Australia
Maria Island 148 B 2 island, Northern Territory, NE Australia
Maria Madre, Isla 50 C 4 island, C Mexico
Maria Magdalena, Isla 50 C 4 island, C Mexico
Marianao 54 B 2 NW Cuba
Mariana Trench 152 B 2 *var.* Challenger Deep. Trench, W Pacific Ocean
Mariánské Lázně 99 A 5 *Ger.* Marienbad. W Czech Republic
Marías, Islas 50 C 4 island group, C Mexico
Marias River 44 C 1 river, Montana, NW USA
Maribor 95 E 7 *Ger.* Marburg. NE Slovenia
Maridi 73 B 5 SW Sudan
Marie Byrd Land 154 B 3 physical region, Antarctica
Marie Celeste Fracture Zone 141 C 5 fracture zone, C Indian Ocean
Marie Galante 55 H 4 *var.* Ceyre to the Caribs. Island, SE Guadeloupe
Marienbad *see* Mariánské Lázně
Marienburg *see* Alūksne
Marienhausen *see* Viš]aka
Mariental 78 B 4 SW Namibia
Marienwerder *see* Kwidzyń
Mariestad 85 B 6 S Sweden
Marília 63 E 4 S Brazil
Marín 92 B 2 NW Spain
Marina 47 B 6 California, W USA
Mar'ina Gorka *see* Mar"ina Horka
Mar"ina Horka 107 C 6 *Rus.* Mar'ina Gorka. C Belorussia
Maringá 63 E 4 S Brazil
Marion 40 C 4 Indiana, N USA
Marion 40 D 4 Ohio, N USA
Marion 45 G 3 Iowa, C USA
Marion, Lake 43 E 2 reservoir, South Carolina, SE USA
Marion Reef 148 E 3 reef, C Coral Sea
Mariscal Estigarribia 64 D 2 NW Paraguay
Marisule Estate 55 F 1 N Saint Lucia
Maritsa 104 D 3 *var.* Marica, *Gk.* Évros, *Turk.* Meriç; *anc.* Hebrus. River, SE Europe
Maritzburg *see* Pietermaritzburg
Mariupol' 109 G 4 *prev.* Zhdanov. SE Ukraine
Marka 73 D 6 *var.* Merca. S Somalia
Markham, Mount 154 C 4 mountain, Antarctica
Markounda 76 C 4 *var.* Marcounda. NW Central African Republic
Marktredwitz 95 C 5 E Germany
Marla 149 A 5 South Australia, S Australia
Marmande *see* Marmande
Marmande 91 B 5 *anc.* Marmanda. SW France
Marmara Denizi 116 A 2 *Eng.* Sea of Marmara. Sea, NE Mediterranean Sea
Marmara, Sea of *see* Marmara Denizi
Marmaris 116 A 4 SW Turkey
Mârmorilik *see* Maarmorilik

Marne 90 D 3 river, N France
Marne 90 D 3 cultural region, N France
Maro 76 C 4 S Chad
Maroantsetra 79 G 3 NE Madagascar
Maromme 90 C 3 N France
Maroni 59 H 3 *Dut.* Marowijne. River, French Guiana/Surinam
Marotiri 145 H 5 *var.* Îlots de Bass. Island group, SE French Polynesia
Maroua 76 B 3 N Cameroon
Marowijne 59 G 3 *var.* le Maroni Fleuve. River, French Guiana/Surinam
Marqādah 118 E 2 NE Syria
Marquesas Fracture Zone 153 E 3 fracture zone, E Pacific Ocean
Marquesas Islands *see* Marquises, Îles
Marquesas Keys 43 E 5 island, Florida, SE USA
Marquette 40 C 1 Michigan, N USA
Marquises, Îles 145 H 4 *Eng.* Marquesas Islands. Island group, N French Polynesia
Marrakech 70 C 2 *var.* Marakesh, *Eng.* Marrakesh; *prev.* Morocco. W Morocco
Marrawah 149 B 8 Tasmania, SE Australia
Marree 149 B 5 South Australia, S Australia
Marsala 97 B 7 *anc.* Lilybaeum. SW Italy
Marsberg 94 B 4 W Germany
Marseille 91 D 6 *Eng.* Marseilles; *anc.* Massilia. SE France
Marshall 49 H 3 Texas, S USA
Marshall 45 F 2 Minnesota, N USA

Marshall Islands 144 D 1. Republic, C Pacific Ocean

Official name: Republic of the Marshall Islands **Date of formation:** 1986 **Capital:** Majuro **Population:** 48,000 **Total Area:** 181 sq km (70 sq miles) **Languages:** English*, Marshallese* **Religions:** Protestant 80%, Roman Catholic 15%, other 5% **Ethnic mix:** Marshallese 90%, other Pacific Islanders 10% **Government:** Republic **Currency:** US $ = 100 cents

Marsh Harbour 54 C 1 W Bahamas
Marsh Island 42 A 3 island, S USA
Martaban 136 B 4 *var.* Moktama. SE Burma
Martigues 91 D 6 SE France
Martin 99 C 5 *Ger.* Sankt Martin, *Hung.* Turócszentmárton; *prev.* Svätý Martin, Turčiansky. NW Slovakia
Martinique 55 G 4 French overseas department, E Caribbean Sea
Martinique Passage 55 G 4 *var.* Dominica Channel, Martinique Channel. Channel, Atlantic Ocean/Caribbean Sea
Martinsville 41 E 5 Virginia, NE USA
Marton 150 D 4 North Island, C New Zealand
Martos 92 D 4 S Spain
Marungu 77 E 7 mountain range, SE Zaire
Mary 122 D 3 *prev.* Merv. S Turkmenistan
Maryborough 149 E 5 Queensland, E Australia

Maryland 41 F 5 *off.* State of Maryland; *nicknames* America in Miniature, Cockade State, Free State, Old Line State. State, E USA
Maryville 42 D 1 Tennessee, S USA
Maryville 45 F 4 Missouri, C USA
Masai Steppe 73 C 8 grassland, NW Tanzania
Masaka 73 B 6 SW Uganda
Masasi 73 C 8 SE Tanzania
Masaya 52 D 3 W Nicaragua
Mascarene Basin 141 B 5 undersea basin, W Indian Ocean
Mascarene Islands 79 H 4 island group, W Madagascar
Mascarene Plain 141 B 5 abyssal plain, W Indian Ocean
Mascarene Plateau 140 B 4 undersea plateau, W Indian Ocean
Maseru 78 D 4 country capital, W Lesotho
Mas-ha 119 D 7 W West Bank
Mashhad 120 E 2 *var.* Meshed. NE Iran
Maṣīrah, Jazīrat 121 E 5 *var.* Masira. Island, E Oman
Maṣīrah, Khalīj 121 E 5 *var.* Gulf of Masira. Gulf, E Oman
Masindi 73 B 6 W Uganda
Masira, Gulf of *see* Maṣīrah, Khal"ij
Mason City 45 G 3 Iowa, C USA
Masqaṭ 121 E 5 *var.* Maskat, *Eng.* Muscat. Country capital, NE Oman
Massa 96 B 3 C Italy
Massachusetts 41 G 3 *off.* Commonwealth of Massachusetts; *nicknames* Bay State, Old Bay State, Old Colony State. State, NE USA
Massawa 72 C 4 *Amh.* Mits'iwa. E Eritrea
Massenya 76 B 3 SW Chad
Massif Central 91 C 5 plateau, C France
Mastanli *see* Momchilgrad
Masterton 151 D 5 North Island, C New Zealand
Masty 107 B 5 *Rus.* Mosty. W Belorussia
Masuda 131 B 6 Honshū, SW Japan
Masvingo 78 D 3 *prev.* Victoria, Fort Victoria, Nyanda. SE Zimbabwe
Maşyāf 118 B 3 *Fr.* Misiaf. W Syria
Matadi 77 B 7 W Zaire
Matagalpa 52 D 3 C Nicaragua
Matagorda Bay 49 H 4 bay, Texas, S Gulf of Mexico
Matale 132 D 3 C Sri Lanka
Matam 74 C 3 NE Senegal
Matamata 150 D 3 North Island, N New Zealand
Matamoros 51 E 2 *var.* Izúcar de Matamoros. S Mexico
Matamoros 50 D 3 NE Mexico
Matane 39 E 4 Québec, SE Canada
Matanzas 54 B 2 NW Cuba
Matara 132 D 4 S Sri Lanka
Mataró 93 G 2 *anc.* Illuro. E Spain
Mataura 151 B 7 South Island, SW New Zealand
Mata Uta *see* Matā'utu
Matá'utu 145 E 4 *var.* Mata Uta. Dependent territory capital, S Wallis & Futuna
Matera 97 E 5 S Italy
Matías Romero 51 G 5 SE Mexico
Mato Grosso 63 E 3 *off.* Estado de Mato Grosso; *prev.* Matto Grosso. State, W Brazil

Mato Grosso do Sul 63 E 4 *off.* Estado de Mato Grosso do Sul. State, S Brazil
Mato Grosso do Sul, Estado de *see* Mato Grosso do Sul
Matosinhos 92 B 2 *prev.* Matozinhos. NW Portugal
Matozinhos *see* Matosinhos
Mătrăşeşti 108 C 4 E Romania
Matsue 131 B 6 *var.* Matsuye, Matue. Honshū, SW Japan
Matsumoto 131 C 5 *var.* Matumoto. Honshū, S Japan
Matsuyama 131 B 7 *var.* Matuyama. Shikoku, SW Japan
Matthews Ridge 59 F 2 N Guyana
Matthew Town 54 D 2 S Bahamas
Matumoto *see* Matsumoto
Maturín 59 E 2 NE Venezuela
Matuyama *see* Matsuyama
Mau 135 E 3 *var.* Maunāth Bhanjan. N India
Maui 47 B 8 island, Hawaii, W USA
Maun 78 C 3 C Botswana
Maunāth Bhanjan *see* Mau
Mauren 94 E 1 NE Liechtenstein

Mauritania 74 C 2 *Ar.* Mūrītānīyah. Republic, W Africa

Official name: Islamic Republic of Mauritania **Date of formation:** 1960 **Capital:** Nouakchott **Population:** 2.2 million **Total area:** 1,025,520 sq km (395,953 sq miles) **Language:** French*, Hassaniyah Arabic, Wolof **Religions:** Muslim 100% **Ethnic mix:** Maure 80%, Wolof 7%, Tukulor 5%, other 8% **Government:** Multiparty republic **Currency:** Ouguiya = 5 khoums

Mauritius 79 H 3 *Fr.* Maurice. Republic, E Africa

Official name: Mauritius **Date of formation:** 1968 **Capital:** Port Louis **Population:** 1.1 million **Total area:** 1,860 sq km (718 sq miles) **Languages:** English*, French Creole, Hindi **Religions:** Hindu 52%, Roman Catholic, 26%, Muslim 17%, other 5% **Ethnic mix:** Creole 55%, South Asian 40%, Chinese 3%, other 2% **Government:** Multiparty republic **Currency:** Rupee = 100 cents

Mauritius Ridge 141 B 5 undersea ridge, W Indian Ocean
Mawson 154 D 2 research station, Antarctica
Maya 115 G 3 river, E Russian Federation
Mayaguana 54 D 2 island, SE Bahamas
Mayaguana Passage 54 D 2 channel, N Caribbean Sea
Mayagüez 55 F 3 W Puerto Rico
Mayamey 120 D 2 N Iran
Maya Mountains 52 B 1 *Sp.* Montañas Mayas. Mountain range, Belize/Guatemala
Maych'ew 72 C 4 *var.* Mai Chio, *It.* Mai Ceu. N Ethiopia
Mayence *see* Mainz
Mayfield 151 C 6 South Island, SW New Zealand
Maykop 111 B 7 SW Russian Federation
Maymyo 136 B 3 N Burma
Mayo *see* Maio
Mayor Pablo Lagerenza *see* Capitán Pablo Lagerenza

Mayotte 79 F 2 French territorial collectivity, E Africa

May Pen 54 B 5 C Jamaica

Mazabuka 78 D 2 S Zambia

Mazagan *see* El-Jadida

Mazar *see* Al Mazār al Janūbī

Mazār-e Sharīf 123 E 3 *var.* Mazar-i-Sharif, Mazar-i Sharif. N Afghanistan

Mazatlán 50 C 3 C Mexico

Mazirbe 106 C 2 NW Latvia

Mazury 98 D 3 physical region, NE Poland

Mazyr 107 C 7 *Rus.* Mozyr'. SE Belorussia

Mbabane 78 D 4 country capital, NW Swaziland

M'Baïki *see* Mbaïki

Mbaïki 77 C 5 *var.* M'Baiki. SW Central African Republic

Mbala 78 D 1 *prev.* Abercorn. NE Zambia

Mbale 73 C 6 E Uganda

Mbandaka 77 C 5 *prev.* Coquilhatville. NW Zaire

M'Banza Congo 78 B 1 *var.* Mbanza Congo; *prev.* São Salvador do Congo, São Salvador. NW Angola

Mbanza-Ngungu 77 B 6 W Zaire

Mbarara 73 B 6 SW Uganda

Mbé 76 B 4 N Cameroon

Mbeya 73 C 8 SW Tanzania

Mbomou 77 C 5 *var.* Bomu, M'Bomu, Mbomu. River, Central African Republic/Zaire

Mbour 74 B 3 W Senegal

Mbuji-Mayi 77 D 7 *prev.* Bakwanga. S Zaire

McAdam 39 F 4 New Brunswick, SE Canada

McAlester 49 G 2 Oklahoma, C USA

McAllen 49 G 5 Texas, S USA

McClintock Channel 37 F 2 channel, Arctic Ocean

McComb 42 B 3 Mississippi, S USA

McCook 45 E 4 Nebraska, C USA

Mcfarlane, Lake *see* Macfarlane, Lake

McKean Island 145 E 3 island, C Kiribati

McKinley, Mount 36 C 3 *var.* Denali. Mountain, Alaska, NW USA

McKinley Park 36 D 3 Alaska, NW USA

McMinnville 46 B 3 Oregon, NW USA

McMurdo Base 154 C 4 research station, Antarctica

McPherson 45 F 5 Kansas, C USA

McPherson *see* Fort McPherson

Mead, Lake 48 A 1 reservoir, W USA

Meander River 37 E 4 Alberta, W Canada

Mecca *see* Makkah

Mechelen 87 C 5 *Eng.* Mechlin, *Fr.* Malines. C Belgium

Mecheria 70 D 2 *var.* Mechriyya. NW Algeria

Mechriyya *see* Mecheria

Mecklenberg 94 C 3 cultural region, N Germany

Mecklenburger Bucht 94 C 2 bay, SW Baltic Sea

Mecsek 99 C 7 mountain range, SW Hungary

Medan 138 B 3 Sumatera, E Indonesia

Medellín 58 B 3 NW Colombia

Médenine 71 F 2 *var.* Madanīyīn. SE Tunisia

Medeshamstede *see* Peterborough

Medford 46 B 4 Oregon, NW USA

Medgidia 108 D 5 SE Romania

Mediaş 108 B 4 *Ger.* Mediasch, *Hung.* Medgyes. C Romania

Medicine Hat 37 F 5 Alberta, SW Canada

Medina *see* Al Madīnah

Medinaceli 93 E 2 N Spain

Medina del Campo 92 C 2 N Spain

Mediolanum *see* Saintes

Mediterranean Sea 102 D 3 *Fr.* Mer Méditerranée. Sea, E Atlantic Ocean

Méditerranée, Mer *see* Mediterranean Sea

Médoc 91 B 5 cultural region, SW France

Medvezh'yegorsk 110 B 3 *var.* Medvežjegorsk, Medvezjegorsk. NW Russian Federation

Meekatharra 147 B 5 Western Australia, W Australia

Meemu Atoll *see* Mulaku Atoll

Meerssen 87 D 6 *var.* Mersen. SE Netherlands

Meerut 134 D 2 N India

Mehrīz 120 D 3 C Iran

Mehtarlām 123 F 4 *var.* Mehtar Lām, Meterlam, Methariam, Metharlam. E Afghanistan

Meiktila 136 B 3 C Burma

Mejerda 71 E 2 *var.* Oued Medjerda, Wādī Majardah. River, Algeria/Tunisia

Mejillones 64 B 2 N Chile

Mek'elē 72 C 4 *var.* Makale. N Ethiopia

Mékhé 74 B 3 NW Senegal

Mekong 124 D 3 *var.* Lan-ts'ang Chiang, *Cam.* Mékôngk, *Chin.* Lancang Jiang, *Lao.* Mènam Khong, *Th.* Mae Nam Khong, *Tib.* Dza Chu, *Vtn.* Sông Tiên Giang. River, E Asia

Mekong, Mouths of the 137 E 7 delta, S Vietnam

Melaka 138 B 3 *var.* Malacca. W Malaysia

Melanesia 144 D 3 island group, SW Pacific Ocean

Melanesian Basin 152 C 3 undersea basin, W Pacific Ocean

Melbourne 43 E 4 Florida, SE USA

Melbourne 149 C 7 state capital, Victoria, SE Australia

Melghir, Chott 71 E 2 *var.* Chott Melrhir. Salt lake, E Algeria

Melilla 68 B 2 *anc.* Rusaddir, Russadir. N Morocco

Melilla 70 C 2 Spanish enclave, N Morocco

Melita 37 F 5 Manitoba, S Canada

Melitene *see* Malatya

Melitopol' 109 G 4 SE Ukraine

Melle 87 B 5 NW Belgium

Mellerud 85 B 6 S Sweden

Meilzino Sur, Cerro 65 B 7 mountain, S Chile

Melo 64 E 4 E Uruguay

Melodunum *see* Melun

Melun 90 C 3 *anc.* Melodunum. N France

Melville, Cape 148 C 2 headland, Queensland, NE Australia

Melville Fracture Zone 141 B 6 fracture zone, C Indian Ocean

Melville Island 37 F 2 island, NW Canada

Melville Island 146 D 2 island, N Australia

Melville, Lake 39 F 2 lake, Newfoundland and Labrador, E Canada

Melville Peninsula 37 G 3 peninsula, Northwest Territories, NE Canada

Melville Sound *see* Viscount Melville Sound

Memel *see* Klaipėda

Memmingen 95 B 6 S Germany

Memphis 42 C 1 Tennessee, S USA

Menaam *see* Menaldum

Menado *see* Manado

Ménaka 75 F 3 E Mali

Menaldum 86 D 1 *Fris.* Menaam. N Netherlands

Mendaña Fracture Zone 153 F 4 fracture zone, E Pacific Ocean

Mende 91 C 6 *anc.* Mimatum. S France

Mendeleyev Ridge 155 F 2 undersea ridge, Arctic Ocean

Mendocino Fracture Zone 152 D 2 fracture zone, NE Pacific Ocean

Mendoza 64 B 4 W Argentina

Menemen 116 A 3 W Turkey

Menengiyn Tal 127 F 2 plain, E Mongolia

Menominee 40 A 2 Wisconsin, N USA

Menongue 78 B 2 *var.* Vila Serpa Pinto, *Port.* Serpa Pinto. C Angola

Menorca 93 H 3 *Eng.* Minorca; *anc.* Balearis Minor. Island, E Spain

Mentawai, Kepulauan 138 B 4 island group, W Indonesia

Meppel 86 D 2 NE Netherlands

Meran *see* Merano

Merano 96 C 1 *Ger.* Meran. N Italy

Merca *see* Marka

Mercedes 64 D 3 E Argentina

Mercedes 64 D 4 W Uruguay

Mercedes 64 C 4 NE Argentina

Meredith, Lake 49 E 1 reservoir, Texas, S USA

Merefa 109 G 2 E Ukraine

Mergate *see* Margate

Mergui 137 B 6 SE Burma

Mergui Archipelago 137 B 6 island group, S Burma

Mérida 92 C 4 *anc.* Augusta Emerita. W Spain

Mérida 51 H 3 SW Mexico

Mérida 58 C 2 W Venezuela

Mérida, Cordillera de 58 C 2 *var.* Sierra Nevada de Mérida. Mountain range, W Venezuela

Meridian 42 C 2 Mississippi, S USA

Mérignac 91 A 5 SW France

Merkinė 107 B 5 S Lithuania

Merkulovichi *see* Myerkulavichy

Merredin 147 B 6 Western Australia, SW Australia

Mersen *see* Meerssen

Mersey 89 D 6 river, NW England, UK

Mersin 116 C 4 S Turkey

Mērsrags 106 C 3 NW Latvia

Meru 73 C 6 C Kenya

Merv *see* Mary

Merzig 95 A 5 SW Germany

Mesa 48 B 2 Arizona, SW USA

Meseritz *see* Międzyrzecz

Meshed *see* Mashhad

Messalo, Rio 79 E 2 *var.* Mualo. River, NE Mozambique

Messana 97 D 7 *var.* Messana, Messene; *anc.* Zancle. SW Italy

Messina 78 D 3 NE South Africa

Messina, Strait of *see* Messina, Stretto di

Messina, Stretto di 97 D 7 *Eng.* Strait of Messina. Strait, C Mediterranean Sea

Messini 105 B 6 S Greece

Mestghanem *see* Mostaganem

Mestre 96 C 2 NE Italy

Meta 58 C 3 river, Colombia/Venezuela

Metairie 42 B 3 Louisiana USA

Metan 64 C 2 N Argentina

Metapán 52 B 2 NW El Salvador

Metković 100 B 4 SE Croatia

Métsovo 104 B 4 *prev.* Métsovon. C Greece

Métsovon *see* Métsovo

Metz 90 D 3 *anc.* Divodurum Mediomatricum, Mediomatrica, Metis. NE France

Meuse 86 D 4 *Dut.* Maas. River, W Europe

Mexcala, Río *see* Balsas, Río

Mexicali 50 A 1 NW Mexico

Mexicana, Altiplanicie 49 E 5 *Eng.* Mexican Plateau, Plateau of Mexico. Plateau, N Mexico

Mexico 50 C 3 *var.* Méjico, México, *Sp.* Estados Unidos Mexicanos. Federal republic, N North America

Official name: United Mexican States **Date of formation:** 1836 **Capital:** Mexico City **Population:** 90 million **Total area:** 1,958,200 sq km (756,061 sq miles) **Languages:** Spanish*, Mayan dialects **Religions:** Roman Catholic 89%, Protestant 6%, other 5% **Ethnic mix:** *mestizo* 55%, Indian 30%, White 6%, other 9% **Government:** Multiparty republic **Currency:** Peso = 100 centavos

Mexico 45 G 4 Missouri, C USA

México 51 E 4 *var.* Ciudad de México, *Eng.* Mexico City. Country capital, C Mexico

Mexico Basin 35 C 6 *var.* Sigsbee Deep. Undersea basin, N Gulf of Mexico

Mexico City *see* Mexico

México, Golfo de *see* Mexico, Gulf of

Mexico, Gulf of 66 A 4 *Sp.* Golfo de México. Gulf, N Atlantic Ocean

Mezen' 110 D 3 river, NW Russian Federation

Mezőtúr 99 D 7 E Hungary

Miahuatlán 51 F 5 *var.* Miahuatlán de Porfirio Díaz. SE Mexico

Miahuatlán de Porfirio Díaz *see* Miahuatlán

Miami 43 F 5 Florida, SE USA

Miami 49 G 1 Oklahoma, C USA

Miami Beach 43 F 5 Florida, SE USA

Miāneh 120 C 2 *var.* Miyáneh. NW Iran

Mianyang 129 B 5 C China

Miastko 98 C 2 *Ger.* Rummelsburg in Pommern. NW Poland

Michalovce 99 E 6 *Ger.* Grossmichel, *Hung.* Nagymihály. E Slovakia

Michigan 40 C 2 *off.* State of Michigan; *nicknames* Great Lakes State, Lake State, Wolverine State. State, N USA

Michigan, Lake 40 C 3 lake, N USA

Michurinsk 111 B 5 W Russian Federation

Micoud 55 F 2 SE Saint Lucia

Micronesia 144 C 1 island group, W Pacific Ocean

Micronesia 144 B 1 Federation, W Pacific Ocean

Official name: Federated States of Micronesia **Date of formation:** 1979 **Capital:** Kolonia **Population:** 101,000 **Total Area:** 2,900 sq km (1,120 sq miles) **Languages:** English*, Trukese, Pohnpeian, Mortlockese **Religions:** Catholic 50%, Protestant 48%, other 2% **Ethnic mix:** Micronesian 99%, other 1% **Government:** Republic **Currency:** US $ = 100 cents

Micronesia, Federated States of see Micronesia
Mid-Atlantic Ridge 67 C 5 var. Mid-Atlantic Cordillera, Mid-Atlantic Rise, Mid-Atlantic Swell. Undersea ridge, C Atlantic Ocean
Middelburg 87 B 5 SW Netherlands
Middelharnis 86 B 4 SW Netherlands
Middelkerke 87 A 5 W Belgium
Middle America Trench 153 F 3 trench, E Pacific Ocean
Middle Andaman 133 G 2 island, SE India
Middle Atlas see Moyen Atlas
Middlesboro 40 C 5 Kentucky, E USA
Middlesbrough 89 D 5 N England, UK
Middletown 41 F 4 New Jersey, NE USA
Middletown 41 F 3 Connecticut, NE USA
Mid-Indian Basin 140 C 4 undersea basin, C Indian Ocean
Mid-Indian Ridge 141 C 5 var. Central Indian Ridge. Undersea ridge, C Indian Ocean
Midland 38 D 5 Ontario, S Canada
Midland 49 E 3 Texas, S USA
Midland 40 C 3 Michigan, N USA
Mid-Pacific Mountains 152 C 2 var. Mid-Pacific Seamounts. Seamount range, NW Pacific Ocean
Mid-Pacific Seamounts see Mid-Pacific Mountains
Miechów 99 D 5 S Poland
Międzyrzec Podlaski 98 E 3 E Poland
Międzyrzecz 98 B 3 Ger. Meseritz. W Poland
Mielec 99 D 5 SE Poland
Miercurea-Ciuc 108 C 4 Ger. Szeklerburg, Hung. Csíkszereda. C Romania
Mieres 92 D 1 NW Spain
Mī'ēso 73 D 5 var. Meheso, Miesso. C Ethiopia
Miguel Asua 50 D 3 var. Miguel Auza. C Mexico
Miguel Auza see Miguel Asua
Mijdrecht 86 C 3 C Netherlands
Mikashevichy 107 C 7 Pol. Mikaszewicze, Rus. Mikashevichi. SW Belorussia
Mikhaylovka 111 B 6 SW Russian Federation
Míkonos see Mýkonos
Mikre 104 C 2 C Bulgaria
Mikun' 110 D 4 NW Russian Federation
Mikuni-sanmyaku 131 D 5 mountain range, Honshū, N Japan

Mikura-jima 131 D 6 island, Izu-shotō, E Japan
Milagro 60 B 2 SW Ecuador
Milan see Milano
Milange 79 E 2 NE Mozambique
Milano 96 B 2 Eng. Milan, Ger. Mailand; anc. Mediolanum. N Italy
Milas 116 A 4 SW Turkey
Milashavichy 107 C 7 Rus. Milashevichi. SE Belorussia
Milashevichi see Milashavichy
Mildura 149 B 6 Victoria, SE Australia
Mile see Mili Atoll
Miles 149 D 5 Queensland, E Australia
Miles City 44 C 2 Montana, NW USA
Milford see Milford Haven
Milford Haven 89 B 7 prev. Milford. SW Wales, UK
Milford Sound 151 A 7 South Island, SW New Zealand
Milford Sound 151 A 7 sound, E Tasman Sea
Mili Atoll 144 D 2 var. Mile. Island, SE Marshall Islands
Mil'kovo 115 H 3 E Russian Federation
Milk River 37 E 5 Alberta, SW Canada
Milk River 44 C 1 river, NW USA
Milk, Wadi el 72 B 4 var. Wadi al Malik. River, C Sudan
Milledgeville 43 E 2 Georgia, SE USA
Mille Lacs Lake 45 F 2 lake, Minnesota, N USA
Millerovo 111 B 6 SW Russian Federation
Millet 55 F 1 C Saint Lucia
Millicent 149 B 7 South Australia, S Australia
Millwood Lake 42 A 2 reservoir, Arkansas, C USA
Milo 74 D 4 river, E Guinea
Mílos 105 C 6 Mílos, SE Greece
Mílos 105 C 7 island, Kykládes, SE Greece
Milparinka 149 C 5 New South Wales, SE Australia
Milton 151 B 7 South Island, SW New Zealand
Milton Keynes 89 D 6 SE England, UK
Milwaukee 40 B 3 Wisconsin, N USA
Mimatum see Mende
Mīnā' Sa'ūd 120 C 4 var. Mīnā' Su'ūd. SE Kuwait
Minas Gerais 63 F 3 off. Estado de Minas Gerais. State, SE Brazil
Minas Gerais, Estado de see Minas Gerais
Minatitlán 51 F 4 E Mexico
Minbu 136 A 3 W Burma
Minch, The 88 B 3 var. North Minch. Strait, NE Atlantic Ocean
Mindanao 139 F 2 island, S Philippines
Mindanao Sea see Bohol Sea
Mindelheim 95 C 6 S Germany
Mindelo 74 A 2 var. Mindello; prev. Porto Grande. N Cape Verde
Minden 94 B 4 anc. Minthun. NW Germany
Mindoro 139 E 2 island, N Philippines
Mindoro Strait 139 E 2 strait, South China Sea/Sulu Sea
Mineral Wells 49 G 3 Texas, S USA

Mingäçevir 117 G 2 Rus. Mingechaur, Mingechevir C Azerbaijan
Mingan 39 F 3 Québec, E Canada
Mingāora 134 C 1 var. Mingora, Mongora. N Pakistan
Mingenew 147 B 6 W Australia
Minho 92 B 2 Sp. Miño. River, Portugal/Spain
Minho see Miño
Minicoy Island 132 A 3 island, Lakshadweep, SW India
Minigwal, Lake 147 C 6 lake, C Australia
Minneapolis 45 F 2 Minnesota, N USA
Minnesota 45 F 2 off. State of Minnesota; nicknames Gopher State, New England of the West, North Star State. State, N USA
Miño 92 B 2 var. Mino, Minius, Port. Minho. River, Portugal/Spain
Minot 44 D 1 North Dakota, N USA
Minsk 107 C 6 country capital, C Belorussia
Minskaya Wzvyshsha 107 C 6 mountain range, C Belorussia
Minthun see Minden
Minto, Lac 38 D 2 lake, Québec, C Canada
Miranda de Ebro 93 E 1 N Spain
Mirgorod see Myrhorod
Miri 138 D 3 Borneo, E Malaysia
Mirim Lagoon 63 E 5 var. Lake Mirim, Port. Lagoa Mirim, Sp. Laguna Merín. Lagoon, SW Atlantic Ocean
Mírina see Mýrina
Mīrjāveh 120 E 4 SE Iran
Mirnyy 115 F 3 C Russian Federation
Mirnyy 154 D 3 research station, Antarctica
Mirs Bay 128 B 1 bay, NE Hong Kong
Mirtóo Pelagos 105 C 6 Eng. Mirtoan Sea; anc. Myrtoum Mare. Sea, SW Aegean Sea
Misiaf see Maşyāf
Miskitos, Cayos 53 E 2 island group, NE Nicaragua
Miskolc 99 D 6 NE Hungary
Misool, Pulau 139 G 4 island, E Indonesia
Mişrātah 71 F 2 var. Misurata. NW Libya
Mission 49 G 5 Texas, S USA
Mississippi 42 B 2 off. State of Mississippi; nickname Bayou State, Magnolia State. State, SE USA
Mississippi Delta 35 C 6 delta, Mississippi, S USA
Mississippi River 35 C 6 river, C USA
Mississippi River Delta 42 C 4 river delta, Louisiana, S USA
Missoula 44 A 1 Montana, NW USA
Missouri 45 G 5 off. State of Missouri; nicknames Bullion State, Show Me State. State, C USA
Missouri City 49 H 4 Texas, S USA
Missouri River 45 F 4 river, N USA
Mistassini, Lac 38 D 3 lake, Québec, SE Canada
Mistelbach an der Zaya 95 E 6 NE Austria
Misti, Volcán 61 E 4 mountain, S Peru
Misurata see Mişrātah
Mitau see Jelgava

Mitchell 148 C 2 river, NE Australia
Mitchell 149 D 5 Queensland, E Australia
Mitchell 45 E 3 South Dakota, N USA
Mi Tho see My Tho
Mito 131 D 5 Honshū, S Japan
Mitú 58 C 4 SE Colombia
Mitumba, Monts 77 E 7 var. Chaîne des Mitumba, Mitumba Range. Mountain range, E Zaire
Miyake-jima 131 D 6 island, Sakishima-shotō, SW Japan
Miyako 130 D 4 Honshū, C Japan
Miyakonojō 131 B 8 var. Miyakonzyô. Kyūshū, SW Japan
Miyakonzyô see Miyakonojō
Miyāneh see Mīāneh
Miyazaki 131 B 8 Kyūshū, SW Japan
Mizija 104 C 1 NW Bulgaria
Mizil 108 C 5 SE Romania
Mizpé Ramon 119 A 7 S Israel
Mjøsa 85 B 5 var. Mjøsen. Lake, S Norway
Mjøsen see Mjøsa
Mladenovac 100 D 4 Yugoslavia
Mława 98 D 3 C Poland
Mljet 101 B 5 It. Meleda; anc. Melita. Island, S Croatia
Mmabatho 78 C 4 N South Africa
Moab 44 B 5 Utah, W USA
Moa Island 148 C 1 island, Queensland, NE Australia
Moanda 77 B 6 var. Mouanda SE Gabon
Moba 77 E 7 E Zaire
Mobay see Montego Bay
Mobaye 77 C 5 S Central African Republic
Moberly 45 G 4 Missouri, C USA
Mobile 42 C 3 Alabama, S USA
Mobile Bay 42 C 3 bay, N Gulf of Mexico
Moçambique 79 F 2 NE Mozambique
Mochudi 78 C 4 SE Botswana
Mocímboa da Praia 79 F 2 var. Vila de Mocímboa da Praia. N Mozambique
Môco 78 B 2 var. Morro de Môco. Mountain, W Angola
Mocoa 58 A 4 SW Colombia
Môco, Morro de see Môco
Mocuba 79 E 3 NE Mozambique
Modena 96 B 3 anc. Mutina. N Italy
Modesto 47 B 6 California, W USA
Modica 97 C 8 anc. Motyca. S Italy
Modohn see Madona
Modriča 100 C 3 N Bosnia & Herzegovina
Moe 149 C 7 Victoria, SE Australia
Möen see Møn
Moena see Muna, Pulau
Moerewa 150 D 2 North Island, N New Zealand
Moero, Lac see Mweru, Lake
Moeskroen see Mouscron
Mogadishu see Muqdisho
Mogador see Essaouira
Mogilëv see Mahilyow
Mogilev-Podol'skiy see Mohyliv-Podil's'kyy
Mogilno 98 C 3 C Poland
Moguer 92 C 4 S Spain
Mohammedia 70 C 2 prev. Fédala. NW Morocco
Mohave, Lake 47 D 7 lake, W USA
Mohawk Mountains 48 A 3 mountain range, Arizona, SW USA

Mohéli 79 F 2 island, S Comoros
Mohns Ridge 155 F 5 undersea ridge, Arctic Ocean
Moho 61 E 4 SW Peru
Mohoro 73 C 7 E Tanzania
Mohyliv-Podil's'kyy 108 C 3 *Rus.* Mogilev-Podol'skiy. C Ukraine
Moi 85 A 6 S Norway
Moincêr 126 B 5 SW China
Moíres 105 D 8 Kríti, SE Greece
Mõisaküla 106 D 3 *Ger.* Moiseküll. S Estonia
Moiseküll *see* Mõisaküla
Mo i Rana 84 C 3 C Norway
Moissac 91 B 6 S France
Mojácar 93 E 5 S Spain
Mojave Desert 47 D 7 plain, California, W USA
Mokrany *see* Makrany
Moktama *see* Martaban
Mol 87 C 5 *prev.* Moll. N Belgium

Moldavia 108 D 3 *var.* Moldova, *Rus.* Moldavskaya SSR; *prev.* Moldavian SSR. Republic, E Europe
Official name: Republic of Moldova
Date of formation: 1991 **Capital:** Chişinău **Population:** 4.4 million **Total area:** 33, 700 sq km (13,000 sq miles) **Languages:** Moldavian*, Ukrainian **Religions:** Romanian Orthodox 98%, Jewish 2%, other 1% **Ethnic mix:** Moldavian (Romanian) 65%, Ukrainian 14%, Russian 13%, other 8% **Government:** Multiparty republic **Currency:** Leu = 100 bani

Molde 85 A 5 S Norway
Moldotau, Khrebet *see* Moldo-Too, Khrebet
Moldo-Too, Khrebet 123 G 2 *prev.* Khrebet Moldotau. Mountain range, C Kyrgyzstan
Moldova *see* Moldavia
Moldova Nouă 108 A 4 *Ger.* Neumoldowa, *Hung.* Újmoldova. W Romania
Molfetta 97 E 5 SE Italy
Moline 40 B 3 Illinois, N USA
Moll *see* Mol
Mollendo 61 E 4 S Peru
Mölndal 85 B 7 S Sweden
Molochans'k 108 C 3 *Rus.* Molochansk. SE Ukraine
Molochansk *see* Molochans'k
Molodezhnaya 154 D 2 research station, Antarctica
Molokai 47 B 8 *Haw.* Moloka'i. Island, Hawaii, W USA
Moloka'i *see* Molokai
Molokai Fracture Zone 153 E 2 fracture zone, NE Pacific Ocean
Molopo 78 C 4 river, Botswana/South Africa
Mólos 105 B 5 C Greece
Molotov *see* Perm'
Moluccas *see* Maluku
Molucca Sea *see* Maluku, Laut
Mombasa 73 D 7 SE Kenya
Momchilgrad 104 D 3 *prev.* Mastanli. S Bulgaria
Møn 85 B 8 *prev.* Möen. Island, SE Denmark
Monaco 91 B 7 *var.* Monaco-Ville; *anc.* Monoecus. Country capital, C, Monaco

Monaco 91 B 7 Monarchy, W Europe

Official name: Principality of Monaco **Date of formation:** 1861 **Capital:** Monaco **Population:** 28,000 **Total area:** 1.95 sq km (0.75 sq miles) **Languages:** French*, Italian **Religions:** Roman Catholic 95%, other 5% **Ethnic mix:** French 47%, Monégasque 17%, Italian 16%, other 20% **Government:** Constitutional monarchy **Currency:** French franc = 100 centimes

Monaco, Principality of *see* Monaco
Monahans 49 E 3 Texas, S USA
Mona, Isla 55 F 3 island, W Puerto Rico
Mona Passage 55 F 3 channel, N Caribbean Sea
Monastir 71 F 2 *var.* Al Munastīr. NE Tunisia
Monbetsu 130 D 2 *var.* Mombetsu, Monbetu. Hokkaidō, NE Japan
Moncalieri 96 A 2 NW Italy
Mončegorsk *see* Monchegorsk
Monchegorsk 110 C 2 *var.* Mončegorsk. NW Russian Federation
Monclova 50 D 2 NE Mexico
Moncton 39 F 4 New Brunswick, SE Canada
Mondoví 96 A 2 NW Italy
Mondsee 95 D 6 lake, N Austria
Monfalcone 96 D 2 NE Italy
Monforte 92 C 1 NW Spain
Mongo 76 C 3 C Chad

Mongolia 126 C 2 *Mong.* Mongol Uls. Republic, Mongolia
Official name: Mongolia **Date of formation:** 1921 **Capital:** Ulan Bator **Population:** 2.4 million **Total Area:** 1,565,000 sq km (604,247 sq miles) **Languages:** Khalkha Mongol*, Turkic, Russian, Chinese **Religions:** Predominantly Tibetan Buddhist, with a Muslim minority **Ethnic mix:** Khalkha Mongol 90%, Kazakh 4%, Chinese 2%, other 4% **Government:** Multiparty republic **Currency:** Tughrik = 100 möngös

Mongos, Chaîne des *see* Bongo, Massif des
Mongu 78 C 2 W Zambia
Monkey Bay 79 E 2 SE Malawi
Monkey River *see* Monkey River Town
Monkey River Town 52 C 2 *var.* Monkey River. SE Belize
Mono Lake 47 C 6 lake, California, W USA
Monóvar 93 F 4 E Spain
Monroe 42 B 2 Louisiana, S USA
Monroe 43 E 1 North Carolina, SE USA
Monrovia 74 C 5 country capital, W Liberia
Mons 87 B 6 *Dut.* Bergen. S Belgium
Monselice 96 C 2 Italy
Montana 44 off. State of Montana; *nicknames* Mountain State, Treasure State. State, NW USA
Montana 104 C 2 *prev.* Ferdinand, Mikhaylovgrad. NW Bulgaria
Montañas Mayas *see* Maya Mountains
Montargis 90 C 4 C France
Montauban 91 B 6 S France
Montbéliard 90 D 4 E France
Montcalm, Lake *see* Dogai Coring
Mont Cenis, Col du 91 E 5 pass, E France

Mont-de-Marsan 91 A 6 SW France
Monteagudo 61 G 4 S Bolivia
Monte Alegre 63 E 2 N Brazil
Monte-Carlo 91 C 8 *var.* Monte Carlo. NE Monaco
Monte Carlo *see* Monte-Carlo
Monte Caseros 64 D 3 E Argentina
Monte Cristi 55 E 3 *var.* San Fernando de Monte Cristi. NW Dominican Republic
Montegiardino 96 E 2 SE San Marino
Montego Bay 54 A 4 *var.* Mobay. W Jamaica
Montélimar 91 C 6 *anc.* Acunum Acusio, Montilium Adhemari. E France
Montemorelos 51 E 3 NE Mexico
Montenegro 101 C 5 *Serb.* Crna Gora. Constituent republic of Yugoslavia, Yugoslavia. *See also* Yugoslavia
Monte Patria 64 B 3 N Chile
Monterey 47 B 6 California, W USA
Monterey *see* Monterrey
Monterey Bay 47 A 6 bay, E Pacific Ocean
Montería 58 B 2 NW Colombia
Montero 61 G 4 C Bolivia
Monterrey 51 E 3 *var.* Monterey. NE Mexico
Montes Claros 63 F 3 SE Brazil
Montevideo 64 D 4 country capital, S Uruguay
Montevideo 45 F 2 Minnesota, N USA
Montgenèvre, Col de 91 E 5 pass, France/Italy
Montgomery 42 D 2 state capital, Alabama, S USA
Montgomery *see* Sāhīwāl
Monthey 95 A 8 SW Switzerland
Montluçon 90 C 4 C France
Montmagny 39 E 4 Québec, SE Canada
Monto 148 D 4 Queensland, E Australia
Montoro 92 D 4 S Spain
Montpelier 41 G 2 state capital, Vermont, NE USA
Montpellier 91 C 6 S France
Montreal *see* Montréal
Montréal 39 E 4 *Eng.* Montreal. Québec, SE Canada
Montrose 88 D 3 E Scotland, UK
Montrose 44 C 5 Colorado, C USA
Montserrat 55 G 3 *var.* Emerald Isle. UK dependent territory, E Caribbean Sea
Monturaqui 64 B 2 NE Chile
Monywa 136 B 3 NW Burma
Monza 96 B 2 N Italy
Monze 78 D 2 S Zambia
Monzón 93 F 2 NE Spain
Moora 147 B 6 Western Australia, SW Australia
Moore 49 G 1 Oklahoma, C USA
Moore, Lake 147 B 6 lake, Western Australia, W Australia
Moorhead 45 F 2 North Dakota, N USA
Moosehead Lake 41 G 1 lake, Maine, NE USA
Moosonee 38 C 3 Ontario, SE Canada
Mopti 75 E 3 C Mali
Moqor 123 E 4 SE Afghanistan
Moquegua 61 E 4 SE Peru
Mora 85 C 5 C Sweden
Morales 52 C 2 E Guatemala
Morant Bay 54 B 5 E Jamaica

Moratalla 93 E 4 SE Spain
Moratuwa 132 D 4 SW Sri Lanka
Morava 99 C 5 *var.* March. River, C Europe
Morava 101 E 5 *var.* March. C Europe
Moravia 99 B 5 *Cz.* Morava, *Ger.* Mähren. Cultural region, E Czech Republic
Morawhanna 59 F 2 N Guyana
Moray Firth 88 C 3 inlet, NW North Sea
Moreau River 44 D 2 river, South Dakota, N USA
Moree 149 D 5 New South Wales, SE Australia
Morelia 51 E 4 S Mexico
Morena, Sierra 92 C 4 mountain range, SW Spain
Moreni 108 C 5 S Romania
Moreno 61 E 2 N Bolivia
Moreton Island 149 E 5 island, Queensland, SE Australia
Morgan City 42 B 3 Louisiana, S USA
Morghāb, Daryā-ye 122 D 4 *var.* Murgap Deryasy, *Rus.* Murgab. River, Afghanistan/Turkmenistan
Morioka 130 D 4 Honshū, C Japan
Morlaix 90 A 3 NW France
Mornington Abyssal Plain 153 F 5 abyssal plain, SE Pacific Ocean
Mornington Island 148 B 2 island, Queensland, NW Australia

Morocco 70 C 2 *Ar.* Al Mamlakah. Monarchy, NW Africa
Official name: Kingdom of Morocco **Date of formation:** 1956 **Capital:** Rabat **Population:** 27 million **Total area:** 698,670 sq km (269,757 sq miles) **Languages:** Arabic*, Berber, French **Religions:** Muslim 99%, other 1% **Ethnic mix:** Arab and Berber 99%, European 1% **Government:** Constitutional monarchy **Currency:** Dirham =100 centimes

Morococha 60 C 4 W Peru
Morogoro 73 C 7 E Tanzania
Moro Gulf 139 E 3 gulf, N Celebes Sea
Morón 54 C 2 C Cuba
Morón 64 D 4 E Argentina
Mörön 126 D 2 N Mongolia
Morondava 79 F 3 W Madagascar
Moroni 79 F 2 country capital, N Comoros
Morotai, Pulau 139 F 3 island, E Indonesia
Morrinsville 150 D 3 North Island, N New Zealand
Morris 45 F 2 Minnesota, N USA
Morristown 43 E 1 Tennessee, S USA
Mors 85 A 7 island, NW Denmark
Morvan 90 D 4 physical region, C France
Morwell 149 C 7 Victoria, SE Australia
Moscow 46 D 2 Idaho, NW USA
Moscow *see* Moskva
Mosel 95 A 5 *Fr.* Moselle. River, W Europe
Moselle *see* Mosel
Mosgiel 151 B 7 South Island, SW New Zealand
Moshi 73 C 7 NE Tanzania
Mosjøen 84 B 3 C Norway

Moskva 111 B 5 *Eng.* Moscow. Country capital, W Russian Federation
Moskva 123 E 3 *Rus.* Moskovskiy; *prev.* Chubek. SW Tajikistan
Mosonmagyaróvár 99 C 6 *Ger.* Wieselburg-Ungarisch-Altenburg; *prev.* Moson and Magyaróvár, *Ger.* Wieselburg and Ungarisch-Altenburg. NW Hungary
Mosquito Coast *see* La Mosquitia
Mosquito Gulf *see* Mosquitos, Golfo de los
Mosquitos, Golfo de los 53 F 5 *Eng.* Mosquito Gulf. Gulf, S Caribbean Sea
Moss 85 B 6 S Norway
Mosselbaai 78 C 5 *var.* Mosselbai, *Eng.* Mossel Bay. SW South Africa
Mossendjo 77 B 6 SW Congo
Mossoró 63 G 2 NE Brazil
Most 98 A 4 *Ger.* Brüx. NW Czech Republic
Mostaganem 70 D 2 *var.* Mestghanem. NW Algeria
Mostar 100 C 4 S Bosnia & Herzegovina
Mosty *see* Masty
Mosul *see* Al Mawşil
Mota del Cuervo 93 E 3 C Spain
Motril 92 D 5 S Spain
Motru 108 B 5 SW Romania
Motueka 151 C 5 South Island, C New Zealand
Motul 51 H 3 *var.* Motul de Felipe Carrillo Puerto. SE Mexico
Motul de Felipe Carrillo Puerto *see* Motul
Motyca *see* Modica
Mouanda *see* Moanda
Mouila 77 A 6 C Gabon
Mould Bay 37 E 2 Prince Patrick Island, Canada
Moulins 90 C 4 C France
Moulmein 136 B 4 *var.* Maulmain, Mawlamyine. SE Burma
Moultrie, Lake 43 F 2 reservoir, South Carolina, SE USA
Moundou 76 B 4 SW Chad
Moŭng Roessei 137 D 5 W Cambodia
Mount Cavenagh 147 E 5 C Australia
Mount Cook 151 B 6 South Island, SW New Zealand
Mount Desert Island 41 H 2 island, Maine, NE USA
Mount Friendship 55 G 2 SW Barbados
Mount Gambier 149 B 7 South Australia, S Australia
Mount Isa 148 B 3 Queensland, C Australia
Mount Magnet 147 B 5 Western Australia, W Australia
Mount Pleasant 40 C 3 Michigan, N USA
Mount Pleasant 45 G 4 Iowa, C USA
Mount Vernon 40 B 5 Illinois, N USA
Mount Vernon 46 B 1 Washington, NW USA
Mouscron 87 A 6 *Dut.* Moeskroen. W Belgium
Moussoro 76 C 3 W Chad
Moyen Atlas 70 C 2 *Eng.* Middle Atlas. Mountain range, N Morocco
Moyobamba 60 C 2 NW Peru
Moyu 126 B 4 *var.* Karakax. NW China
Moyynqum *see* Muyunkum, Peski

Mozambique 79 E 3 *off.* Republic of Mozambique; *prev.* People's Republic of Mozambique, Portuguese East Africa. Republic, S Africa
Official name: Republic of Mozambique **Date of formation:** 1975 **Capital:** Maputo **Population:** 15.3 million **Total area:** 801,590 sq km (309,493 sq miles) **Languages:** Portuguese* **Religions:** Traditional beliefs 60%, Christian 30%, Muslim 10% **Ethnic mix:** Makua-Lomwe 47%, Tsonga 23%, Malawi 12%, other 18% **Government:** Multiparty republic **Currency:** Metical = 100 centavos
Mozambique Basin *see* Natal Basin
Mozambique Channel 69 E 6 *Fr.* Canal de Mozambique, *Mal.* Lakandranon' i Mozambika, *Port.* Canal de Moçambique. Channel, W Indian Ocean
Mozambique Plateau 67 E 6 *var.* Mozambique Rise. Undersea plateau, SW Indian Ocean
Mozambique Rise *see* Mozambique Plateau
Mozambique Scarp *see* Mozambique Escarpment
Mozyr' *see* Mazyr
Mpama 77 B 6 river, C Congo
Mpika 78 D 2 NE Zambia
Mqinvartsveri *see* Kazbek
Mrągowo 98 D 2 *var.* Mragowo, *Ger.* Sensburg. NE Poland
M'Sila 71 E 2 *var.* Msila. N Algeria
Msila *see* M'Sila
Mtwara 73 D 8 SE Tanzania
Mualo *see* Messalo, Rio
Muang Kalasin *see* Kalasin
Muang Khammouan 136 D 4 *var.* Thakhek. S Laos
Muang Khanthabuli *see* Khanthabouli
Muang Không 137 D 5 S Laos
Muang Khôngxédôn 137 D 5 *var.* Khong Sedone. S Laos
Muang Khon Kaen *see* Khon Kaen
Muang Lampang *see* Lampang
Muang Lom Sak *see* Lom Sak
Muang Namo 136 C 3 N Laos
Muang Nan *see* Nan
Muang Pakxan 136 D 4 *var.* Pak Sane. C Laos
Muang Phalan 136 D 4 *var.* Muang Phalane. S Laos
Muang Phalane *see* Muang Phalan
Muang Phayao *see* Phayao
Muang Sing 136 C 3 NW Laos
Muang Xaignabouri 136 C 4 *var.* Sayaboury. W Laos
Muar 138 B 3 *var.* Bandar Maharani. W Malaysia
Muarabungo 138 B 4 Sumatera, W Indonesia
Muchinga Escarpment 78 D 2 mountain range, NE Zambia
Mucojo 79 F 2 N Mozambique
Mudanjiang 128 E 3 *var.* Mu-tan-chiang. NE China
Mudon 137 B 5 SE Burma
Mufulira 78 D 2 C Zambia
Mughla *see* Muğla
Muğla 116 A 4 *var.* Mughla. SW Turkey
Mŭh, Sabkhat al 118 C 3 lake, C Syria
Muir Éireann *see* Irish Sea

Muisne 60 A 1 NW Ecuador
Mukacheve 108 B 3 *Cz.* Mukačevo, *Hung.* Munkács, *Rus.* Mukachevo. W Ukraine
Mukalla *see* Al Mukallā
Mula 93 E 4 SE Spain
Mulaku Atoll 132 B 4 *var.* Meemu Atoll. Island, C Maldives
Muleshoe 49 E 2 Texas, S USA
Mulhacén 93 E 5 mountain, S Spain
Mülhausen *see* Mulhouse
Mülheim 95 A 6 SW Germany
Mulhouse 90 E 4 *Ger.* Mülhausen. NE France
Müller-gebergte *see* Muller, Pegunungan
Muller, Pegunungan 138 D 4 *Dut.* Müller-gebergte. Mountain range, Borneo, Indonesia
Mullewa 147 B 6 W Australia
Mull, Isle of 88 B 4 island, W Scotland, UK
Mulongo 77 D 7 SE Zaire
Multān 134 C 2 E Pakistan
Mumbai *see* Bombay
Mumbwa 78 D 2 C Zambia
Muna, Pulau 139 E 5 *prev.* Moena. Island, C Indonesia
Münchberg 95 C 5 E Germany
München 95 C 6 *var.* Muenchen, *Eng.* Munich, *It.* Monaco. SE Germany
Muncie 40 C 4 Indiana, N USA
Mu Nggava *see* Rennell
Munich *see* München
Munster 89 A 6 cultural region, S Ireland
Munster 94 A 4 NW Germany
Muong Xiang Ngeun 136 C 4 *var.* Xieng Ngeun. C Laos
Muonio 84 D 3 N Finland
Muonionjoki 84 D 3 *var.* Muoniojoki, *Swe.* Muonioälv. River, Finland/Sweden
Muqdisho 73 D 6 *Eng.* Mogadishu, *It.* Mogadiscio. Country capital, S Somalia
Mur 95 E 7 *SCr.* Mura. River, C Europe
Mura *see* Mur
Muradiye 117 F 3 E Turkey
Murapara *see* Murupara
Murata 96 E 2 S San Marino
Murchison 147 B 5 river, Western Australia, W Australia
Murcia 93 E 4 cultural region, SE Spain
Murcia 93 F 4 SE Spain
Mureş 108 A 4 *var.* Maros, Mureşul, *Ger.* Marosch, Mieresch. River, Hungary/Romania
Murfreesboro 42 D 1 Tennessee, S USA
Murgab 122 D 3 *var.* Murghab, *Pash.* Daryā-ye Morghāb, *Turkm.* Murgap Deryasy. River, Afghanistan/Turkmenistan
Murgab *see* Murghob
Murghob 123 G 3 *Rus.* Murgab. SE Tajikistan
Murgon 149 D 5 Queensland, E Australia
Müritz 94 C 3 *var.* Müritzee. Lake, NE Germany
Müritzee *see* Müritz
Murmansk 110 C 2 NW Russian Federation
Murmashi 110 C 2 *var.* Murmaši. NW Russian Federation
Murmaši *see* Murmashi
Murom 111 B 5 W Russian Federation

Muroran 130 D 3 Hokkaidō, NE Japan
Muros 92 B 1 NW Spain
Murray 149 C 7 river, SE Australia
Murray Bridge 149 B 7 South Australia, SE Australia
Murray Fracture Zone 153 E 2 fracture zone, NE Pacific Ocean
Murray, Lake 43 E 2 reservoir, South Carolina, SE USA
Murray Range *see* Murray Ridge
Murray Ridge 140 B 3 *var.* Murray Range. Undersea ridge, N Indian Ocean
Murrumbidgee 149 C 6 river, SE Australia
Murska Sobota 95 E 7 *Ger.* Olsnitz. NE Slovenia
Murupara 150 E 3 *var.* Murapara. North Island, NE New Zealand
Murwāra 135 E 4 N India
Murwillumbah 149 E 5 New South Wales, SE Australia
Mürzzuschlag 95 E 7 E Austria
Muş 117 F 3 *var.* Mush. E Turkey
Musala 104 C 3 mountain, W Bulgaria
Muscat *see* Masqaţ
Muscatine 45 G 4 Iowa, C USA
Musgrave Ranges 147 D 5 mountain range, South Australia, S Australia
Mush *see* Muş
Muskegon 40 C 3 Michigan, N USA
Muskogean *see* Tallahassee
Muskogee 49 G 1 Oklahoma, C USA
Musoma 73 C 6 N Tanzania
Mussau Island 144 B 3 island, NE Papua New Guinea
Mustafa-Pasha *see* Svilengrad
Musters, Lago 65 B 6 lake, S Argentina
Mut 116 C 4 S Turkey
Mu-tan-chiang *see* Mudanjiang
Mutare 78 D 3 *var.* Mutari; *prev.* Umtali. E Zimbabwe
Mutina *see* Modena
Mutsu-wan 130 D 3 bay, NW Pacific Ocean
Muttonbird Islands 151 A 8 island group, South Island, SW New Zealand
Mu Us Shamo *see* Ordos Desert
Muy Muy 52 D 3 C Nicaragua
Muynak *see* Mŭynoq
Mŭynoq 122 C 1 *Rus.* Muynak. NW Uzbekistan
Mužlja 100 D 3 *Hung.* Felsömuzslya; *prev.* Gornja Mužlja. N Yugoslavia
Mvolo 73 B 5 Sudan
Mwanza 73 C 7 NW Tanzania
Mweka 77 C 6 C Zaire
Mwene-Ditu 77 D 7 S Zaire
Mweru, Lake 77 E 7 *var.* Lac Moero. Lake, Zaire/Zambia
Myadzel 107 C 5 *Pol.* Miadzioł Nowy, *Rus.* Myadel'. N Belorussia
Myanaung 136 B 4 SW Burma
Myaungmya 136 A 4 SW Burma
Myerkulavichy 107 D 7 *Rus.* Merkulovichi. SE Belorussia
Myingyan 136 B 3 C Burma
Myitkyina 136 B 2 N Burma
Mykolayiv 109 E 4 *Rus.* Nikolayev. S Ukraine
Mýkonos 105 D 6 *var.* Míkonos. Ísland, Kykládes, SE Greece
Myrhorod 109 F 2 *Rus.* Mirgorod. NE Ukraine

Mýrina 104 D 4 *var.* Mírina. Límnos, SE Greece

Myrtle Beach 43 F 2 South Carolina, SE USA

Mýrtos 105 D 8 Kríti, SE Greece

Myślibórz 98 B 3 W Poland

Mysore 132 C 2 *var.* Maisur W India

My Tho 137 E 6 *var.* Mi Tho. S Vietnam

Mytilíni 105 D 5 *var.* Mitilíni; *anc.* Mytilene. Lésvos, E Greece

Mytishchi 111 B 5 W Russian Federation

Mzuzu 79 E 2 N Malawi

N

Naberezhnyye Chelny 111 D 5 *prev.* Brezhnev. W Russian Federation

Nablus 119 E 7 *var.* Nābulus, *Heb.* Shekhem; *anc.* Neapolis, *Bibl.* Shechem. N West Bank

Nacala 79 F 2 NE Mozambique

Nacogdoches 49 H 3 Texas, S USA

Nadi 145 E 4 *prev.* Nandi. Viti Levu, W Fiji

Nadvirna 108 B 3 *Pol.* Nadwóma, *Rus.* Nadvornaya. W Ukraine

Nadvoicy *see* Nadvoitsy

Nadvoitsy 110 B 3 *var.* Nadvoicy. NW Russian Federation

Nadym 114 D 3 N Russian Federation

Nadym 114 D 3 river, C Russian Federation

Náfpaktos 105 B 5 *var.* Návpaktos. C Greece

Náfplio 105 B 6 *prev.* Návplion. S Greece

Naga 139 E 1 *off.* Naga City; *prev.* Nueva Caceres. Luzon, N Philippines

Nagano 131 D 5 Honshū, S Japan

Nagaoka 131 D 5 Honshū, C Japan

Nagasaki 131 A 7 Kyūshū, SW Japan

Nagato 131 A 7 Honshū, SW Japan

Nāgercoil 132 C 3 SE India

Nagornyy Karabakh 117 G 3 *var.* Avtonomnaya Oblast Nagorno-Karabakhskaya, *Arm.* Lerrnayin Gharabakh, *Az.* Dağlıq Quarabaĕ. Former autonomous region, SW Azerbaijan

Nagoya 131 C 6 Honshū, SW Japan

Nāgpur 134 D 4 C India

Nagqu 126 C 5 *Chin.* Na-Ch'ii; *prev.* Hei-ho. W China

Nagykálló 99 E 6 E Hungary

Nagykanizsa 99 B 7 *Ger.* Grosskanizsa. SW Hungary

Nagykőrös 99 D 7 C Hungary

Nagysurány *see* Šurany

Nagyszalonta *see* Salonta

Nagytapolcsány *see* Topolčany

Naḥal Elisha 119 F 7 E West Bank

Nahariya *see* Nahariyya

Nahariyya 119 A 5 *var.* Nahariya. N Israel

Nahuel Huapi, Lago 65 B 5 lake, W Argentina

Nain 39 F 2 Newfoundland and Labrador, NE Canada

Nā'īn 120 D 3 C Iran

Nairobi 73 C 6 country capital, S Kenya

Najaf *see* An Najaf

Najin 128 E 3 NE North Korea

Najrān 121 B 6 *var.* Abā as Su'ūd. S Saudi Arabia

Nakamura 131 B 7 Shikoku, SW Japan

Nakatsugawa 131 C 6 *var.* Nakatugawa. Honshū, SW Japan

Nakatugawa *see* Nakatsugawa

Nakhichevan' *see* Naxçıvan

Nakhodka 115 G 5 SE Russian Federation

Nakhon Pathom 137 C 5 *var.* Nagara Pathom, Nakorn Pathom. C Thailand

Nakhon Ratchasima 137 C 5 *var.* Khorat, Korat. E Thailand

Nakhon Sawan 137 C 5 *var.* Muang Nakhon Sawan, Nagara Svarga. W Thailand

Nakhon Si Thammarat 137 C 7 *var.* Nagara Sridharmaraj, Nakhon Sithammaraj. SW Thailand

Nakina 38 C 3 British Columbia, W Canada

Nakuru 73 C 6 W Kenya

Nalayh 127 E 2 C Mongolia

Nal'chik 111 B 8 SW Russian Federation

Nālūt 71 F 2 NW Libya

Namangan 123 F 2 E Uzbekistan

Nam Co 126 C 5 lake, W China

Nam Đinh 136 D 3 N Vietnam

Namen *see* Namur

Namib Desert 78 B 3 desert, W Namibia

Namibe 78 A 2 *Port.* Moçâmedes, Mossâmedes. SW Angola

Namibia 78 B 3 *Afr.* Suidwes-Afrika, *Eng.* South West Africa, *Ger.* Deutsch-Südwestafrika; *prev.* German Southwest Africa, South-West Africa. Republic, S Africa

Official name: Republic of Namibia
Date of formation: 1990
Capital: Windhoek **Population:** 1.6 million **Total Area:** 824,290 sq km (318,260 sq miles) **Languages:** English*, Afrikaans, Ovambo **Religions:** Christian 90%, other 10% **Ethnic mix:** Ovambo 50%, Kavango 9%, Herero 7%, Damara 7%, other 27% **Government:** Multiparty republic **Currency:** Rand = 100 cents

---

Nam Ngum 136 D 4 river, C Laos

Namo *see* Namu Atoll

Nam Ou 136 C 3 river, N Laos

Nampa 46 D 3 Idaho, NW USA

Nampula 79 E 2 NE Mozambique

Namrole 139 F 4 E Indonesia

Namsos 84 B 4 C Norway

Namu 36 D 5 British Columbia, SW Canada

Namu 144 D 2 island, C Marshall Islands

Namur 87 C 6 *Dut.* Namen. SE Belgium

Nan 136 C 4 *var.* Muang Nan. N Thailand

Nanaimo 36 D 5 Vancouver Island, Canada

Nanchang 129 C 5 *var.* Nan-ch'ang, Nanch'ang-hsien. Province capital, SE China

Nancy 90 D 3 NE France

Nandaime 52 D 4 SW Nicaragua

Nānded 134 D 5 C India

Nandi *see* Nadi

Nandyāl 132 C 2 E India

Naniwa *see* Ōsaka

Nanjing 129 D 5 *var.* Nan-ching, Nanking; *prev.* Chian-ning, Chianning, Kiang-ning. Province capital, E China

Nanning 129 B 6 *var.* Nan-ning; *prev.* Yung-ning. Autonomous region capital, S China

Nanortalik 82 C 5 S Greenland

Nanping 129 D 6 *var.* Nan-p'ing; *prev.* Yenping. E China

Nansei-shotō 130 A 2 *var.* Ryukyu Islands. Island group, Japan

Nansei Syotō Trench *see* Ryukyu Trench

Nansen Basin 155 G 4 undersea basin, Arctic Ocean

Nansen Cordillera 155 G 3 seamount range, Arctic Ocean

Nansha Qundao *see* Spratly Islands

Nanterre 90 C 3 N France

Nantes 90 A 4 *Bret.* Naoned; *anc.* Condivincum, Namnetes. NW France

Nantucket Island 41 G 3 island, Massachusetts, NE USA

Nanumaga 145 E 3 *var.* Nanumanga. Island, NW Tuvalu

Nanumanga *see* Nanumaga

Nanumea 145 E 3 island, NW Tuvalu

Nanyang 129 C 5 *var.* Nan-yang. C China

Nan-yang *see* Nanyang

Napa 47 B 6 California, W USA

Napier 150 E 4 North Island, N New Zealand

Naples 43 E 5 Florida, SE USA

Naples *see* Napoli

Napo 60 C 1 river, Ecuador/Peru

Napoli 97 D 5 *Eng.* Naples, *Ger.* Neapel; *anc.* Neapolis. S Italy

Naracoorte 149 B 7 South Australia, S Australia

Naradhivas *see* Narathiwat

Narathiwat 137 C 7 *var.* Naradhivas. S Thailand

Narbo Martius *see* Narbonne

Narbonne 91 C 6 *anc.* Narbo Martius. S France

Narborough Island *see* Fernandina, Isla

Nares Abyssal Plain *see* Nares Plain

Nares Plain 35 E 6 *var.* Nares Abyssal Plain. Abyssal plain, NW Atlantic Ocean

Nares Strait 82 D 1 *Dan.* Nares Stræde. Strait, S Lincoln Sea

Nares Stræde *see* Nares Strait

Narew 98 E 3 river, E Poland

Narova *see* Narva

Narovlya *see* Narowlya

Narowlya 107 C 8 *Rus.* Narovlya. SE Belorussia

Närpes 85 D 5 *Fin.* Närpiö. W Finland

Närpiö *see* Närpes

Narrogin 147 B 7 SW Australia

Narsaq 82 C 4 *var.* Narssaq. SW Greenland

Narsaq Kujallea 82 C 5 *Dan.* Frederiksdal. S Greenland

Narssaq *see* Narsaq

Narva 106 E 2 NE Estonia

Narva 106 E 2 *prev.* Narova. River, Estonia/Russian Federation

Narva Bay 106 E 2 *Est.* Narva Laht, *Ger.* Narwa-Bucht, *Rus.* Narvskiy Zaliv. Bay, E Baltic Sea

Narva Reservoir 106 E 2 *Est.* Narva Veehoidla, *Rus.* Narvskoye Vodokhranilishche. Reservoir, Estonia/Russian Federation

Narvik 84 C 3 C Norway

Nar'yan-Mar 110 D 3 *var.* Narjan-Mar, Nar'jan-Mar; *prev.* Dzerzhinskiy, Beloshchel'ye. NW Russian Federation

Naryn 123 G 2 C Kyrgyzstan

Năsăud 108 B 3 *Ger.* Nussdorf, *Hung.* Naszód. N Romania

Nashik 134 C 5 *prev.* Nāsik. W India

Nashua 41 G 3 New Hampshire, NE USA

Nashville 42 C 1 state capital, Tennessee, S USA

Näsijärvi 85 D 5 lake, SW Finland

Nāsik *see* Nashik

Nasiriya *see* An Nāsirīyah

Nassau 54 C 1 country capital, C Bahamas

Nasser, Lake 68 D 3 lake, Egypt/Sudan

Nata 78 C 3 NE Botswana

Natal 63 G 2 state capital, E Brazil

Natal Basin 141 A 6 *var.* Mozambique Basin. Undersea basin, SW Indian Ocean

Natchitoches 42 A 3 Louisiana, S USA

National City 47 C 8 California, W USA

Natitingou 75 F 4 NW Benin

Natuna, Kepulauan 138 C 3 island group, W Indonesia

Naturaliste Plateau 141 E 6 undersea plateau, E Indian Ocean

Naujamiestis 106 C 4 C Lithuania

Nauru 144 D 2 Island, W Pacific Ocean

Nauru 144 D 3 *prev.* Pleasant Island. Republic, W Pacific Ocean

Official name: Republic of Nauru
Date of formation: 1968
Capital: No official Capital
Population: 10,000 **Total Area:** 21.2 sq km (8.2 sq miles)
Languages: Nauruan*, English
Religions: Christian 95%, other 5%
Ethnic mix: Nauruan 58%, other Pacific Islanders 26%, Chinese 8%, European 8% **Government:** Parliamentary democracy
Currency: Australian $ = 100 cents

Nauta 60 C 2 N Peru

Navahrudak 107 C 6 *Pol.* Nowogródek, *Rus.* Novogrudok. W Belorussia

Navanagar *see* Jāmnagar

Navapolatsk 107 D 5 *Rus.* Novopolotsk. N Belorussia

Navarra 93 E 2 cultural region, N Spain

Navassa Island 54 D 3 US unincorporated territory, N Caribbean Sea

Navoi *see* Navoiy

Navojoa 50 B 2 NW Mexico

Navolat 50 C 3 *var.* Navolato. C Mexico

Navolato *see* Navolat

Návpaktos *see* Náfpaktos

Návplion *see* Náfplio

Nawabashah *see* Nawābshāh

Nawābshāh 134 B 3 *var.* Nawabashah. S Pakistan

Nawoiy 123 E 2 *Rus.* Navoi. C Uzbekistan

Naxçıvan 117 G 3 *Rus.* Nakhichevan'. SW Azerbaijan

Naxos *see* Náxos

Náxos 105 D 6 *var.* Naxos. Náxos, SE Greece

Náxos 105 D 6 island, Kykládes, S Greece

Nayoro 130 D 2 Hokkaidō, NE Japan

Nazca 60 D 4 S Peru
Nazca Ridge 57 A 5 undersea ridge, E Pacific Ocean
Naze 130 B 3 Nansei-shotō, S Japan
Nazerat 119 A 5 *Ar.* En Nazira, *Eng.* Nazareth. N Israel
Nazilli 116 A 4 SW Turkey
Nazrēt 73 C 5 *var.* Adama, Hadama. C Ethiopia
N'Dalatango 78 B 1 *var.* Salazar, *Port.* Vila Salazar. NW Angola
Ndélé 76 C 4 N Central African Republic
Ndendé 77 A 6 S Gabon
Ndindi 77 A 6 S Gabon
Ndjamena 76 B 3 *var.* N'Djamena, *prev.* Fort-Lamy. Country capital, W Chad
Ndjolé 77 A 5 C Gabon
Ndola 78 D 2 C Zambia
Neagh, Lough 89 B 5 lake, E Northern Ireland, UK
Néa Moudanía 104 C 4 *var.* Néa Moudhaniá. N Greece
Néa Moudhaniá *see* Néa Moudanía
Neápoli 104 B 4 *prev.* Neápolis. N Greece
Neápoli 105 C 7 SE Greece
Neápoli 105 D 8 Kríti, SE Greece
Neápolis *see* Neápoli
Néa Zíchni 104 C 3 *var.* Néa Zíkhni; *prev.* Néa Zíkhna. NE Greece
Nebaj 52 B 2 W Guatemala
Nebitdag 122 B 2 W Turkmenistan
Neblina, Pico da 62 D 1 mountain, NW Brazil
Nebraska 44 D 4 *off.* State of Nebraska; *nicknames* Blackwater State, Cornhusker State, Tree Planters State. State, C USA
Nebraska City 45 F 4 Nebraska, C USA
Neches River 49 H 3 river, Texas, S USA
Neckar 95 B 6 river, SW Germany
Necochea 65 D 5 E Argentina
Necocli 58 A 2 NW Colombia
Nederland 49 H 4 Texas, S USA
Nederweert 87 D 5 SE Netherlands
Neede 86 E 3 E Netherlands
Neerpelt 87 D 5 NE Belgium
Neftekamsk 111 D 5 W Russian Federation
Neftezavodsk *see* Seydi
Negēlē 73 D 5 *var.* Negelli, *It.* Neghelli. S Ethiopia
Negev *see* HaNegev
Negomane 79 E 2 *var.* Negomano. N Mozambique
Negomano *see* Negomane
Negombo 132 C 3 SW Sri Lanka
Negotin 100 E 4 E Yugoslavia
Negra, Punta 60 A 3 headland, NW Peru
Negreşti-Oaş 108 B 3 *Hung.* Avasfelsőfalu; *prev.* Negreşti. NE Romania
Negro, Río 65 C 5 river, Brazil/Uruguay
Negro, Río 62 D 1 river, N South America
Negros 139 E 2 island, Visayan Islands, C Philippines
Nehbandān 120 E 3 E Iran
Neijiang 129 B 5 C China
Nei Mongol Zizhiqu 127 F 3 *var.* Nei Mongol, *Eng.* Inner Mongolian Autonomous Region, Inner Mongolia; *prev.* Nei Monggol Zizhiqu. Autonomous region, N China

Neiva 58 B 3 S Colombia
Nellore 132 D 2 E India
Nelson 151 C 5 South Island, C New Zealand
Neman 106 B 4 *Bel.* Nyoman, *Ger.* Memel, *Lith.* Nemunas, *Pol.* Niemen. River, NE Europe
Neman 106 B 4 *Ger.* Ragnit. W Russian Federation
Neméa 105 B 6 S Greece
Nemetocenna *see* Arras
Nemours 90 C 4 N France
Nemuro 130 E 2 Hokkaidō, NE Japan
Neochóri 105 B 5 C Greece

Nepal
135 E 3 . Monarchy, S Asia

Official name: Kingdom of Nepal **Date of formation:** 1769 **Capital:** Kathmandu **Population:** 21.1 million (54,363 sq miles) **Languages:** Nepali*, Maithili **Religions:** Hindu 90%, Buddhist 5%, Muslim 3%, other 2% **Ethnic mix:** Nepalese 58%, Bihari 19%, Tamang 6%, other 17% **Government:** Constitutional monarchy **Currency:** Rupee = 100 paisa

---

Nepean 38 D 5 Ontario, SE Canada
Nereta 106 C 4 S Latvia
Neretava 100 C 4 river, Bosnia & Herzegovina/Croatia
Neringa 106 A 3 *Ger.* Nidden; *prev.* Nida. SW Lithuania
Neris 107 C 5 *Bel.* Viliya, *Pol.* Wilia; *prev. Pol.* Wilja. River, Belorussia/Lithuania
Nerva 92 C 4 S Spain
Neskaupstadhur 83 E 5 E Iceland
Ness, Loch 88 C 3 lake, N Scotland, UK
Néstos 104 C 3 *Bul.* Mesta, *Turk.* Kara Su. River, Bulgaria/Greece
Netanya 119 A 6 *var.* Natanya, Nathanya. C Israel

Netherlands
86 C 3 *var.* Holland, *Dut.* Koninkrijk der Nederlanden, Nederland. Monarchy, W Europe

Official name: Kingdom of the Netherlands **Date of formation:** 1815 **Capitals:** Amsterdam, The Hague **Population:** 15.3 million **Total area:** 37,330 sq km (14,410 sq miles) **Languages:** Dutch*, Frisian **Religions:** Roman Catholic 36%, Protestant 27%, other 37% **Ethnic mix:** Dutch 96%, other 4% **Government:** Constitutional monarchy **Currency:** Guilder = 100 cents

---

Netherlands Antilles 55 F 5 *prev.* Dutch West Indies. Autonomous region of Netherlands, S Caribbean Sea
Nettilling Lake 82 A 2 lake, N Canada
Netze *see* Noteć
Neu Amerika *see* Puławy
Neubrandenburg 94 D 3 NE Germany
Neuchâtel, Lac de 95 A 7 *Ger.* Neuenburger See. Lake, W Switzerland
Neuenburger See *see* Neuchâtel, Lac de
Neufchâteau 87 D 8 SE Belgium
Neukuhren *see* Pionerskiy

Neumünster 94 B 2 N Germany
Neunkirchen 95 A 5 SW Germany
Neunkirchen 95 E 6 *var.* Neunkirchen am Steinfeld E Austria
Neunkirchen am Steinfeld *see* Neunkirchen
Neuquén 65 B 5 SE Argentina
Neuruppin 94 C 3 NE Germany
Neu Sandec *see* Nowy Sącz
Neusiedler See 95 E 6 *Hung.* Fertő. Lake, Austria/Hungary
Neustadt an der Weinstrasse 95 B 5 *prev.* Neustadt an der Haardt; *hist.* Niewenstat, *anc.* Nova Civitas. SW Germany
Neustettin *see* Szczecinek
Neustrelitz 94 D 3 NE Germany
Neu-Ulm 95 B 6 S Germany
Neuwied 95 A 5 W Germany
Neuzen *see* Terneuzen
Nevada 47 C 5 *off.* State of Nevada; *nicknames* Battle Born State, Sagebrush State, Silver State. State, W USA
Nevada, Sierra 92 D 5 mountain range, S Spain
Nevers 90 C 4 *anc.* Noviodunum. C France
Nevinnomyssk 111 B 7 SW Russian Federation
Nevşehir 116 C 3 *var.* Nevshehr. C Turkey
Nevshehr *see* Nevşehir
Newala 73 D 8 SE Tanzania
New Albany 42 C 2 Mississippi, S USA
New Albany 40 C 5 Indiana, N USA
New Amsterdam 59 G 3 E Guyana
Newark 41 F 4 New Jersey, N USA
Newark 40 D 4 Ohio, NE USA
New Bedford 41 G 3 Massachusetts, NE USA
Newberg 46 B 3 Oregon, NW USA
New Bern 43 F 1 North Carolina, SE USA
New Braunfels 49 G 4 Texas, S USA
Newbridge 89 B 6 *Ir.* An Droichead Nua. C Ireland
New Britain 41 G 3 Connecticut, NE USA
New Britain 144 B 3 island, E Papua New Guinea
New Brunswick 39 F 4 *Fr.* Nouveau-Brunswick. Province, SE Canada
New Caledonia 144 C 4 *var.* Kanaky, *Fr.* Nouvelle-Calédonie. French overseas territory, S Pacific Ocean
New Caledonia 144 C 5 island, S New Caledonia
New Caledonia Basin 152 C 4 undersea basin, W Pacific Ocean
Newcastle 149 D 6 New South Wales, SE Australia
Newcastle upon Tyne 88 D 4 *var.* Newcastle; *hist.* Monkchester, *Lat.* Pons Aelii. N England, UK
New Delhi 134 D 3 country capital, N India
Newfoundland 39 G 3 *Fr.* Terre-Neuve. Island, Newfoundland and Labrador Canada
Newfoundland & Labrador 39 F 2 *Fr.* Terre Neuve. Province, E Canada
Newfoundland Basin 66 B 3 undersea basin, NW Atlantic Ocean

New Georgia Islands 144 C 3 island group, NW Solomon Islands
New Glasgow 39 F 4 Nova Scotia, SE Canada
New Guinea 144 A 3 *Dut.* Nieuw Guinea, *Ind.* Irian. Island, Indonesia/Papua New Guinea
New Hampshire 41 F 2 *off.* State of New Hampshire; nickname Granite State. State, NE USA
New Haven 41 G 3 Connecticut, NE USA
New Iberia 42 B 3 Louisiana, S USA
New Ireland 144 C 3 island, NE Papua New Guinea
New Jersey 41 F 4 *off.* State of New Jersey; nickname Garden State. State, E USA
Newman 146 B 4 Western Australia, W Australia
Newmarket 89 E 6 E England, UK
New Mexico 48 C 2 *off.* State of New Mexico; *nicknames* Land of Enchantment, Sunshine State. State, SW USA
New Orleans 42 B 3 Louisiana, S USA
New Plymouth 150 D 4 North Island, C New Zealand
Newport 89 D 7 S England, UK
Newport 89 D 7 SE Wales, UK
Newport 42 B 1 Arkansas, C USA
Newport 40 C 4 Kentucky, E USA
Newport 41 G 2 Maine, NE USA
Newport News 41 F 5 Virginia, NE USA
New Providence 54 C 1 island, N Bahamas
Newquay 89 B 7 SW England, UK
Newry 89 B 5 *Ir.* An tIúr. SE Northern Ireland, UK
Newry 146 D 3 N Australia
New Sarum *see* Salisbury
New Siberian Islands *see* Novosibirskiye Ostrova
New Smyrna Beach 43 E 4 Florida, SE USA
New South Wales 149 C 6 state, SE Australia
New Territories 128 A 1 geopolitical region, N Hong Kong
Newton 45 F 5 Iowa, C USA
Newton 45 G 3 Kansas, C USA
Newtownabbey 89 B 5 *Ir.* Baile na Mainistreach. E Northern Ireland, UK
New Ulm 45 F 3 Minnesota, N USA
New York 41 F 3 New York, NE USA
New York 41 E 3 state, NE USA

New Zealand
150 A 4 Commonwealth republic, SW Pacific Ocean

Official name: The Dominion of New Zealand **Date of formation:** 1947 **Capital:** Wellington **Population:** 3.5 million **Total Area:** 268,680 sq km (103,730 sq miles) **Languages:** English*, Maori **Religions:** Protestant 62%, Roman Catholic 18%, other 20% **Ethnic mix:** European 88%, Maori 9%, other 3% **Government:** Constitutional monarchy **Currency:** NZ $ = 100 cents

---

Neyveli 132 C 2 SE India
Nezhin *see* Nizhyn
Ngabang 138 C 4 Borneo, C Indonesia

Ngangzê Co 126 B 5 lake, W China
N'Gaoundéré *see* Ngaoundéré
Ngaoundéré 76 B 4 *var.*
N'Gaoundéré. N Cameroon
N'Giva 78 B 3 *var.* Ondjiva, *Port.*
Vila Pereira de Eça. S Angola
Ngo 77 B 6 SE Congo
Ngoko 77 B 5 river,
Cameroon/Congo
Ngorongoro Crater 69 D 5 crater, N
Tanzania
Ngourti 75 H 3 E Niger
N'Guigmi *see* Nguigmi
Nguigmi 75 H 3 *var.* N'Guigmi. SE
Niger
Nguru 75 G 4 NE Nigeria
Nha Trang 137 E 6 SE Vietnam
Niagara Falls 38 D 5 Ontario, S
Canada
Niagara Falls 41 E 3 New York, NE
USA
Niagara Falls 35 D 5 waterfall,
Canada/USA
Niamey 75 F 3 country capital, SW
Niger
Niangay, Lac 75 E 3 lake, E Mali
Nia-Nia 77 D 5 NE Zaire
Nias, Pulau 138 A 3 island, W
Indonesia

Nicaragua
52 D 3 Republic, C Central
America

Official name: Republic of
Nicaragua **Date of formation:** 1838
Capital: Managua **Population:** 4.1
million **Total area:** 130,000 sq km
(50,193 sq miles) **Languages:**
Spanish*, English Creole, Miskito
Religions: Roman Catholic 95%,
other 5% **Ethnic mix:** *mestizo* 69%,
White 17%, Black 9%, Indian 5%
Government: Multiparty republic
Currency: Córdoba = 100 pence

Nicaragua, Lago de 52 D 4 *var.*
Cocibolca, Gran Lago, *Eng.* Lake
Nicaragua. Lake
Nicaragua, Lake *see* Nicaragua,
Lago de
Nicaragua, Republic of *see*
Nicaragua
Nice 91 D 6 *It.* Nizza; *anc.* Nicaea.
SE France
Nicholas II Land *see* Severnaya
Zemlya
Nicholls Town 54 C 1 NW
Bahamas
Nicholson Range 147 B 5 mountain
range, W Australia
Nicobar Islands 133 F 3 island
group, SE India
Nicoya 52 D 4 W Costa Rica
Nicoya, Golfo de 52 D 5 gulf, E
Pacific Ocean
Nicoya, Península de 52 D 4
peninsula, NW Costa Rica
Nidzica 98 D 3 *Ger.* Niedenburg. N
Poland
Niedenburg *see* Nidzica
Niedere Tauern 95 D 7 mountain
range, C Austria
Nieuw Amsterdam 59 G 3 NE
Surinam
Nieuw-Bergen 86 D 4 SE
Netherlands
Nieuwegein 86 C 4 C Netherlands
Nieuw Nickerie 59 G 3 NW
Surinam
Niğde 116 C 4 C Turkey
Niger 75 F 4 river, W Africa

Niger
75 F 3 Republic, W Africa

Official name: Republic of Niger
Date of formation: 1960 **Capital:**
Niamey **Population:** 8.5 million
Total area: 1,267,000 sq km
(489,188 sq miles) **Languages:**
French*, Hausa, Djerma, Fulani
Religions: Muslim 85%, traditional
beliefs 14%, Christian 1% **Ethnic mix:**
Hausa 56%, Djerma 22%, Fulani 9%,
other 13% **Government:** Multiparty
republic **Currency:** CFA franc =
100 centimes

Nigeria
75 F 4 Nigeria. Federal republic,
W Africa

Official name: Federal Republic of
Nigeria **Date of formation:** 1960
Capital: Abuja **Population:** 119
million **Total area:** 923,770 sq km
(356,668 sq miles) **Languages:**
English*, Hausa, Yoruba, Ibo
Religions: Muslim 50%, Christian
40%, traditional beliefs 10%
Ethnic mix: Hausa 21%, Yoruba
20%, Ibo 17%, Fulani 9%, other 33%
Government: Military regime
Currency: Naira = 100 kobo

Niger, Mouths of the 75 G 5 delta,
S Nigeria
Niigata 131 D 5 Honshū, C Japan
Niihama 131 B 7 Japan
Niihau 47 A 7 island, Hawaii, W
USA
Nii-jima 131 D 6 island, Izu-shotō,
E Japan
Nijkerk 86 D 3 C Netherlands
Nijlen 87 C 5 N Belgium
Nijmegen 86 D 4 *Ger.* Nimwegen;
anc. Noviomagus. SE Netherlands
Nikel' 110 C 2 NW Russian
Federation
Nikiniki 139 E 5 Timor, S Indonesia
Nikólaos, Ágios *see* Ágios Nikólaos
Nikolayev *see* Mykolayiv
Nikopol' 109 F 3 SE Ukraine
Nikšić 101 C 5 SW Yugoslavia
Nikumaroro 145 F 3 *prev.* Gardner
Island, Kemins Island. Island, C
Kiribati
Nikunau 145 E 3 *var.* Nukunau;
prev. Byron Island. Island, W
Kiribati
Nile 72 B 3 *Ar.* Nahr an Nīl. River,
NE Africa
Nile Delta 72 B 1 delta, N Egypt
Nīl, Nahr an *see* Nile
Nimba, Mount 74 D 4 mountain, W
Africa
Nîmes 91 C 6 *anc.* Nemausus,
Nismes. S France
Nînawé 117 F 5 N Iraq
Nine Degree Channel 132 B 3
channel, N Indian Ocean
Ninetyeast Ridge 141 D 5 undersea
ridge, E Indian Ocean
Ningbo 129 D 5 *var.* Ning-po, Yin-
hsien; *prev.* Ninghsien. E China
Ningxia Huizu Zizhiqu 128 B 4
autonomous region, N China
Nio *see* Íos
Niobrara River 45 E 3 river, C USA
Nioro 74 D 1 *var.* Nioro du Sahel. N
Mali
Nioro du Sahel *see* Nioro
Niort 90 B 4 W France
Nipigon 38 B 4 Ontario, S Canada
Nipigon, Lake 38 B 3 lake, Ontario,
S Canada

Niš 101 E 5 *Eng.* Nish, *Ger.* Nisch;
anc. Naissus. SE Yugoslavia
Niṣab 120 B 4 N Saudi Arabia
Nisibin *see* Nusaybin
Nisiros *see* Nísyros
Nisko 98 E 4 SE Poland
Nissan Islands *see* Green Islands
Nissum Bredning 85 A 7 inlet, E
North Sea
Nísyros 105 E 7 *var.* Nisiros. Island,
Dodekánisos, SE Greece
Nitra 99 C 6 *Ger.* Neutra, *Hung.*
Nyitra. River, Slovakia
Nitra 99 C 6 *Ger.* Neutra, *Hung.*
Nyitra. SW Slovakia
Niuatoputapu 145 E 4 *var.*
Niuatobutabu; *prev.* Keppel
Island. Island, N Tonga
Niue 145 F 4 self-governing
territory, S Pacific Ocean
Niulakita 145 E 3 *var.* Nurakita.
Island, S Tuvalu
Niutao 145 E 3 island, NW Tuvalu
Nivernais 90 C 4 cultural region, C
France
Nizāmābād 134 D 5 C India
Nizhnegorskiy *see* Nyzhn'ohirs'kyy
Nizhnekamsk 111 C 5 W Russian
Federation
Nizhnevartovsk 114 D 3 C Russian
Federation
Nizhniy Novgorod 111 C 5 *prev.*
Gor'kiy. W Russian Federation
Nizhniy Odes 110 D 4 *var.* Nižni
Odes, Nižnij Odes. NW Russian
Federation
Nizhnyaya Tunguska 115 E 3 *Eng.*
Lower Tunguska. River, C
Russian Federation
Nizhyn 109 E 1 *Rus.* Nezhin. NE
Ukraine
Njombe 73 C 8 S Tanzania
Nkayi 77 B 6 *var.* Jacob. S Congo
Nkhotakota 79 E 2 *var.* Kota Kota.
C Malawi
N'Kongsamba *see* Nkongsamba
Nkongsamba 76 A 4 *var.*
N'Kongsamba. W Cameroon
Nobeoka 131 B 7 Kyūshū, SW
Japan
Noboribetsu 130 D 3 *var.*
Noboribetu. Hokkaidō, NE Japan
Noboribetu *see* Noboribetsu
Nogales 48 B 3 Arizona, SW USA
Nogales 50 B 1 N Mexico
Nogal Valley *see* Dooxo Nugaaleed
Nokia 85 D 5 SW Finland
Nokou 76 B 3 SW Chad
Nola 77 B 5 SW Central African
Republic
Nolinsk 111 D 5 NW Russian
Federation
Nong Chang 137 C 5 W Thailand
Nong Khai 136 D 4 *var.* Mi Chai,
Nongkaya. NE Thailand
Nonouti 145 E 2 *prev.* Sydenham
Island. Island, W Kiribati
Noord-Beveland 86 A 4 *var.* North
Beveland. Island, SW Netherlands
Noordoewer 78 B 4 S Namibia
Noordwijk aan Zee 86 C 3 W
Netherlands
Nora 85 C 6 C Sweden
Norak 123 E 3 *Rus.* Nurek. W
Tajikistan
Nord 83 F 1 N Greenland
Nordaustlandet 83 G 1 island, NE
Svalbard
Norden 94 A 3 NW Germany
Norderstedt 94 B 3 N Germany

Nordfriesische Inseln 94 B 2 *var.*
North Frisian Islands. Island
group, N Germany
Nordhausen 94 C 4 C Germany
Nordhorn 94 A 3 NW Germany
Nordkapp 84 D 1 *Eng.* North Cape.
Headland, N Norway
Nord-Ouest, Territoires du *see*
Northwest Territories
Norfolk 41 F 5 Virginia, NE USA
Norfolk 45 F 3 Nebraska, C USA
Norfolk Ridge 142 D 4 undersea
ridge, W Pacific Ocean
Noril'sk 114 D 3 N Russian
Federation
Normal 40 B 4 Illinois, N USA
Norman 49 G 2 Oklahoma, C USA
Normandes, Iles *see* Channel
Islands
Normandie 90 B 3 *Eng.* Normandy.
Cultural region, N France
Normandy *see* Normandie
Normanton 148 C 3 Queensland,
NE Australia
Norquay 37 F 5 Saskatchewan, S
Canada
Norrköping 85 C 6 S Sweden
Norrtälje 85 C 6 C Sweden
Norseman 147 C 6 Western
Australia, SW Australia
North Albanian Alps 101 D 5 *Alb.*
Bjeshkët e Namuna, *SCr.*
Prokletije. Mountain range,
Albania/Yugoslavia
Northallerton 89 D 5 N England,
UK
Northam 147 B 6 Western Australia,
SW Australia
North America 66 A 3 continent,
North American Basin 66 B 3
undersea basin, W Atlantic Ocean
Northampton 89 D 6 C England,
UK
Northampton 147 A 5 W Australia
North Andaman 133 F 2 island, E
India
North Australian Basin 152 A 3 *Fr.*
Bassin Nord de l' Australie.
Undersea basin, E Indian Ocean
North Bay 38 D 4 Ontario, S
Canada
North Beveland *see* Noord-Beveland
North Cape 150 C 1 headland,
North Island, N New Zealand
North Cape *see* Nordkapp
North Carolina 43 E 1 *off.* State of
North Carolina; *nicknames* Old
North State, Tar Heel State,
Turpentine State. State, SE USA
North Charleston 43 F 2 South
Carolina, SE USA
North Dakota 45 E 1 *off.* State of
North Dakota; *nicknames*
Flickertail State, Peace Garden
State, Sioux State. State, N USA
North Devon Island *see* Devon
Island
Northeim 94 B 4 C Germany
Northern Cook Islands 145 G 4
island group, N Cook Islands
Northern Dvina *see* Severnaya
Dvina
Northern Ireland 88 B 4 *var.* the Six
Counties. Political division, UK
Northern Mariana Islands 144 C 1
US commonwealth territory, W
Pacific Ocean
Northern Territory 148 A 3
territory, N Australia
Northfield 45 G 2 Minnesota, N
USA
North Fiji Basin 152 C 3 undersea
basin, SW Pacific Ocean

North Frisisan Islands *see* Nordfriesische Inseln
North German Plain *see* Norddeutsches Tiefland
North Huvadhu Atoll 132 B 5 *var.* Gaafu Alifu Atoll. Island, S Maldives
North Island 150 B 2 island, North Island, N New Zealand

North Korea 128 E 3 *Kor.* Chosŏn-minjujuǔi-inmin-kanghwaguk. Republic, E Asia

Official name: Democratic People's Republic of Korea **Date of formation:** 1948 **Capital:** Pyongyang **Population:** 23.1 million **Total Area:** 120,540 sq km (46,540 sq miles) **Languages:** Korean*, Chinese **Religions:** Traditional beliefs 16%, Ch'ondogyo 14%, Buddhist 2%, non-religious 68% **Ethnic mix:** Korean 99%, other 1% **Government:** Single-party republic **Currency:** Won = 100 chon

North Las Vegas 47 D 7 Nevada, W USA
North Little Rock 42 B 1 Arkansas, C USA
North Minch *see* Minch, The
North Mole 93 H 4 harbour wall, N Gibraltar
North Platte 45 E 4 Nebraska, C USA
North Platte River 44 D 4 river, N USA
North Pole 155 F 3 pole, Arctic Ocean
North Saskatchewan 37 F 5 river, S Canada
North Scotia Ridge *see* South Georgia Ridge
North Sea 66 D 2 *var.* Mare Germanicum, *Dan.* Nordsøen, *Dut.* Noordzee, *Fr.* Mer du Nord, *Ger.* Nordsee, *Nor.* Nordsjøen; *prev.* German Ocean. Sea, NE Atlantic Ocean
North Siberian Plain 112 D 2 plain, N Russian Federation
North Taranaki Bight 150 D 3 bight, E Tasman Sea
North Uist 88 B 3 island, NW Scotland, UK
Northwest Atlantic Mid-Ocean Canyon 66 B 3 trough, NW Atlantic Ocean
North West Highlands 88 C 3 mountain range, NW Scotland, UK
Northwest Pacific Basin 152 C 2 undersea basin, NW Pacific Ocean
Northwest Providence 54 C 1 channel, N Caribbean Sea
Northwest Territories 37 E 3 *Fr.* Territoires du Nord-Ouest. Territory, NW Canada
Northwind Plain 155 F 2 abyssal plain, Arctic Ocean
Norton Sound 36 C 2 inlet, N Bering Sea

Norway 85 A 5 *Nor.* Norge. Monarchy, N Europe

Official name: Kingdom of Norway **Date of formation:** 1905 **Capital:** Oslo **Population:** 4.3 million **Total area:** 323,900 sq km (125,060 sq miles) **Languages:**

Norwegian (*Bokmal* and *Nynorsk*)*, Lappish, Finnish **Religions:** Evangelical Lutheran 88%, other Christian 12% **Ethnic mix:** Norwegian 95%, Lapp 1%,other 4% **Government:** Constitutional monarchy **Currency:** Krone = 100 øre

Norwegian Basin 66 D 2 undersea basin, NE Atlantic Ocean
Norwegian Sea 66 D 2 *var.* Norske Havet, Norskehavet. Sea, NE Atlantic Ocean
Norwich 89 E 6 E England, UK
Noshiro 130 D 4 *var.* Nosiro; *prev.* Noshirominato. Honshū, C Japan
Nosivka 109 E 1 *Rus.* Nosovka. NE Ukraine
Nosop 78 C 4 *var.* Nossob, Nossop. River, Botswana/Namibia
Nosovka *see* Nosivka
Noşratābād 120 E 3 E Iran
Notabile *see* Mdina
Noteć 98 C 3 *Ger.* Netze. River, NW Poland
Nottingham 89 D 6 C England, UK
Nouâdhibou 74 B 2 *prev.* Port-Étienne. W Mauritania
Nouakchott 74 B 2 country capital, SW Mauritania
Nouméa 144 D 5 dependent territory capital, S New Caledonia
Nouveau-Brunswick *see* New Brunswick
Nouvelle Écosse *see* Nova Scotia
Nova Freixo *see* Cuamba
Nova Gorica 95 D 8 W Slovenia
Nova Gradiška 100 C 3 *Ger.* Neugradisk, *Hung.* Újgradiska. NE Croatia
Nova Iguaçu 63 F 4 SE Brazil
Nova Kakhovka 109 F 4 *Rus.* Novaya Kakhovka. SE Ukraine
Nova Lisboa *see* Huambo
Novara 96 A 2 *anc.* Novaria. NW Italy
Novaria *see* Novara
Nova Scotia 39 F 4 *Fr.* Nouvelle Écosse. Province, SE Canada
Nova Scotia 35 E 5 physical region, E Canada
Novaya Kakhovka *see* Nova Kakhovka
Novaya Sibir', Ostrov 115 F 1 island, Novosibirskiye Ostrova, N Russian Federation
Novaya Zemlya 110 D 1 island group, N Russian Federation
Novgorod 110 B 4 W Russian Federation
Novi Iskăr *see* Novi Iskŭr
Novi Iskŭr 104 C 2 *var.* Novi Iskăr. W Bulgaria
Noviodunum *see* Nevers
Noviomagus *see* Lisieux
Novi Pazar 101 D 5 *Turk.* Yenipazar. C Yugoslavia
Novi Sad 100 D 3 *Ger.* Neusatz, *Hung.* Újvidék. N Yugoslavia
Novoaleksejevka *see* Novoalekseyevka
Novoalekseyevka *see* Novoalekseyevka
Novoazovs'k 109 H 4 *Rus.* Novoazovsk. E Ukraine
Novoazovsk *see* Novoazovs'k
Novocherkassk 111 B 6 SW Russian Federation
Novodvinsk 110 C 3 NW Russian Federation
Novograd-Volynskiy *see* Novohrad-Volyns'kyy
Novohrad-Volyns'kyy 108 D 2 *Rus.* Novograd-Volynskiy. N Ukraine

Novokazalinsk 114 B 4 *Kaz.* Zhangaqazaly. SW Kazakhstan
Novokuznetsk 114 D 4 *prev.* Stalinsk. C Russian Federation
Novolazarevskaya 154 C 2 research station, Antarctica
Novo Mesto 95 E 8 *Ger.* Rudolfswert; *prev. Ger.* Neustadtl. SE Slovenia
Novomoskovsk 111 B 5 W Russian Federation
Novomoskovs'k 109 F 3 *Rus.* Novomoskovsk. C Ukraine
Novomoskovsk *see* Novomoskovs'k
Novopolotsk *see* Navapolatsk
Novoradomsk *see* Radomsko
Novorossiysk 111 A 7 SW Russian Federation
Novoshakhtinsk 111 B 7 SW Russian Federation
Novosibirsk 114 D 4 C Russian Federation
Novosibirskiye Ostrova 115 F 1 *Eng.* New Siberian Islands. Island group, N Russian Federation
Novosokol'niki 110 A 4 W Russian Federation
Novotroitsk 111 D 6 W Russian Federation
Novotroitskoye *see* Novotroyits'ke
Novotroyits'ke 109 F 4 *Rus.* Novotroitskoye. S Ukraine
Novovolyns'k 108 C 1 *Rus.* Novovolynsk. NW Ukraine
Novovolynsk *see* Novovolyns'k
Novy Dvor 107 B 6 *Rus.* Novyy Dvor. W Belorussia
Novyy Bug *see* Novyy Buh
Novyy Buh 109 E 3 *Rus.* Novyy Bug. S Ukraine
Novyy Dvor *see* Novy Dvor
Novyy Uzen' 114 A 4 *Kaz.* Zhangaözen. W Kazakhstan
Nowogard 98 B 3 *var.* Nowógard, *Ger.* Naugard. NW Poland
Nowy Dwór Mazowiecki 98 D 3 C Poland
Nowy Sącz 99 D 5 *Ger.* Neu Sandec. S Poland
Nowy Tomyśl 98 B 3 *var.* Nowy Tomysl. W Poland
Nowy Tomysl *see* Nowy Tomyśl
Noyon 90 C 3 N France
Nsanje 79 E 3 S Malawi
Nsawam 75 E 5 SE Ghana
Ntomba, Lac 77 C 6 *var.* Lac Tumba. Lake, NW Congo
Nubian Desert 72 C 3 desert, NE Sudan
Nu'eima 119 E 7 E West Bank
Nueva Gerona 54 B 2 S Cuba
Nueva Rosita 50 D 2 NE Mexico
Nuevitas 54 C 2 E Cuba
Nuevo, Bajo 53 F 1 reef, NW Colombia
Nuevo Casas Grandes 50 C 1 N Mexico
Nuevo, Golfo 65 C 6 gulf, SW Atlantic Ocean
Nuevo Laredo 51 E 2 NE Mexico
Nûgâtsiaq *see* Nuugaatsiaq
Nui 145 E 3 island, W Tuvalu
Nuku' alofa 145 E 5 country capital, Tongatapu, S Tonga
Nukufetau 145 E 3 island, C Tuvalu
Nukulaelae 145 E 3 *var.* Nukulailai. Island, E Tuvalu
Nukulailai *see* Nukulaelae Atoll
Nukunonu Atoll 145 F 3 island, N Tokelau
Nukus 122 C 3 W Uzbekistan

Nullarbor 147 E 6 South Australia, S Australia
Nullarbor Plain 147 D 6 plateau, S Australia
Nuneaton 89 D 6 C England, UK
Nunivak Island 36 B 2 island, Alaska, NW USA
Nunspeet 86 D 3 E Netherlands
Nuoro 97 A 5 W Italy
Nuquí 58 A 3 W Colombia
Nurakita *see* Niulakita
Nurata *see* Nurota
Nurek *see* Norak
Nuremberg *see* Nürnberg
Nurlat 111 C 6 W Russian Federation
Nurmes 84 E 4 E Finland
Nürnberg 95 C 5 *Eng.* Nuremberg. S Germany
Nurota 123 E 2 *Rus.* Nurata. C Uzbekistan
Nusa Tenggara 139 E 5 *Eng.* Lesser Sunda Islands. Island group, C Indonesia
Nusaybin 117 F 4 *var.* Nisibin. SE Turkey
Nuşayrīyah, Jabal an 118 B 3 mountain range, W Syria
Nuugaatsiaq 82 C 3 *var.* Nûgâtsiaq. W Greenland
Nuuk 82 B 4 *var.* Nûk, *Dan.* Godthåb, Godthaab. Dependent territory capital, SW Greenland
Nuussuaq 82 C 2 *var.* Nûgssuaq, *Dan.* Kraulshavn. N Greenland
Nyainqêntanglha Shan 126 C 5 mountain range, W China
Nyala 72 A 4 W Sudan
Nyamapanda 78 D 3 NE Zimbabwe
Nyamlell 73 B 5 SW Sudan
Nyamtumbo 73 C 8 S Tanzania
Nyandoma 110 C 4 *var.* Njandoma, N'andoma. NW Russian Federation
Nyantakara 73 B 7 NW Tanzania
Nyasa, Lake 79 E 2 *var.* Lake Malawi, *Port.* Lago Niassa; *prev.* Lago Nyassa. Lake, S Africa
Nyasvizh 107 C 6 *Pol.* Nieśwież, *Rus.* Nesvizh. C Belorussia
Nyaunglebin 136 B 4 S Burma
Nyeboe Land 83 E 1 physical region, NW Greenland
Nyeri 73 C 6 C Kenya
Nyima 126 C 5 W China
Nyíregyháza 99 E 6 NE Hungary
Nykøbing 85 B 8 SE Denmark
Nyköping 85 C 6 S Sweden
Nylstroom 78 D 4 NE South Africa
Nyngan 149 C 6 New South Wales, SE Australia
Nyurba 115 F 3 E Russian Federation
Nyzhn'ohirs'kyy 109 F 5 *Rus.* Nizhnegorskiy. S Ukraine
Nzega 73 C 7 NW Tanzania
Nzérékoré 74 C 5 SE Guinea

O

Oahu 47 A 8 *Haw.* O'ahu. Island, Hawaii, W USA
O'ahu *see* Oahu
Oak Harbor 46 B 1 Washington, NW USA
Oakland 47 B 6 California, W USA
Oamaru 151 B 7 South Island, SW New Zealand
Oaxaca 51 F 5 *var.* Oaxaca de Juárez; *prev.* Antequera. SE Mexico

Ob' 114 C 3 river, C Russian Federation
Obal' 107 D 5 *Rus.* Obol'. N Belorussia
Oban 88 B 4 W Scotland, UK
Oban *see* Halfmoon Bay
Obando *see* Puerto Inírida
Oban Hills 75 G 5 hill range, Cameroon/Nigeria
Obdorsk *see* Salekhard
Obeliai 106 C 4 NE Lithuania
Oberhollabrunn *see* Tulln
Ob, Gulf of *see* Obskaya Guba
Obidovichi *see* Abidavichy
Obihiro 130 D 2 Hokkaidō, NE Japan
Obo 76 D 4 E Central African Republic
Obock 72 D 4 E Djibouti
Obol' *see* Obal'
Oborniki 98 B 3 W Poland
Obrovo *see* Abrova
Obskaya Guba 114 D 2 *Eng.* Gulf of Ob. Gulf, S Kara Sea
Ocala 43 E 4 Florida, SE USA
Ocaña 92 D 3 C Spain
Ocaña 58 B 2 N Colombia
Ocean Falls 36 D 5 British Columbia, SW Canada
Ocean Island *see* Banaba
Oceanside 47 C 8 California, W USA
Ochakiv 109 E 4 *Rus.* Ochakov. S Ukraine
Ochakov *see* Ochakiv
Ochamchira *see* Och'amch'ire
Och'amch'ire 117 E 2 *Rus.* Ochamchira. W Georgia
Ocho Rios 54 B 4 C Jamaica
Ocozocuautla 51 G 5 SE Mexico
October Revolution Island *see* Oktyabr'skoy Revolyutsii, Ostrov
Ocú 53 F 5 S Panama
Ōdate 130 D 3 Honshū, C Japan
Ödenburg *see* Sopron
Odenpäh *see* Otepää
Odense 85 B 7 C Denmark
Oder 80 D 3 Cz./Pol. Odra. River, C Europe
Oderhaff 94 D 3 *var.* Stettiner Haff, Zalew Szczeciński. Bay, S Baltic Sea
Odesa 109 E 4 *Rus.* Odessa. SW Ukraine
Odessa 49 E 3 Texas, S USA
Odessa *see* Odesa
Odienné 74 D 4 NW Ivory Coast
Ôdôngk 137 D 6 S Cambodia
Odoorn 86 E 2 NE Netherlands
Odra *see* Oder
Oeiras 92 B 4 N Portugal
Of 117 E 2 NE Turkey
Ofanto 97 D 5 river, S Italy
Offenbach 95 B 5 *var.* Offenbach am Main. W Germany
Offenbach am Main *see* Offenbach
Offenburg 95 B 6 SW Germany
Ōgaki 131 C 6 Honshū, SW Japan
Ogallala 44 D 4 Nebraska, C USA
Ogbomosho 75 F 4 W Nigeria
Ogden 44 B 4 Utah, W USA
Ogulin 100 B 3 NW Croatia
Ohio 40 C 4 *off.* State of Ohio; nickname Buckeye State. State, NE USA
Ohio River 40 D 4 river, N USA
Ohlau *see* Oława
Ohrid 101 D 6 *Turk.* Ochrida, Ohri. SW Macedonia
Ohrid, Lake 101 D 6 *var.* Lake

Ochrida, *Alb.* Liqeni i Ohrit, *Mac.* Ohridsko Ezero. Lake, Albania/Macedonia
Ohura 150 D 3 North Island, C New Zealand
Oildale 47 C 7 California, W USA
Oirschot 87 C 5 S Netherlands
Oise 90 C 3 river, N France
Oistins 55 G 2 S Barbados
Ōita 131 B 7 Kyūshū, SW Japan
Ojinaga 50 D 2 N Mexico
Ojos del Salado, Nevado 64 B 3 mountain, N Chile
Okaihau 150 C 2 North Island, N New Zealand
Okāra 134 C 2 E Pakistan
Okavango 78 C 3 *var.* Cubango, Kavango, Kavengo, Kubango, Okavanggo. River, S Africa
Okavango Delta 78 C 3 wetland, N Botswana
Okayama 131 B 6 Honshū, SW Japan
Okazaki 131 C 6 Honshū, C Japan
Okeechobee, Lake 43 E 4 lake, Florida, SE USA
Okhotsk 115 G 3 SE Russian Federation
Okhotsk, Sea of 152 C 1 sea, NW Pacific Ocean
Okhtyrka 109 F 2 *Rus.* Akhtyrka. NE Ukraine
Okinawa 130 A 3 island, Japan
Okinawa-shotō 130 A 3 island group, Nansei-shotō, S Japan
Oki-shotō 131 B 6 *var.* Oki-guntō. Island group, W Japan
Oklahoma 49 G 2 *off.* State of Oklahoma; nickname Sooner State. State, C USA
Oklahoma City 49 G 1 state capital, Oklahoma, C USA
Okmulgee 49 G 1 Oklahoma, C USA
Oktyabr'skiy 111 D 6 W Russian Federation
Oktyabr'skoy Revolyutsii, Ostrov 115 E 2 *Eng.* October Revolution Island. Island, Severnaya Zemlya, N Russian Federation
Okulovka *see* Uglovka
Okushiri-tō 130 C 3 *var.* Okusiri Tô. Island, Japan
Okusiri Tô *see* Okushiri-tō
Öland 85 C 7 island, S Sweden
Olavarría 65 D 5 E Argentina
Oława 98 C 4 *Ger.* Ohlau. SW Poland
Olbia 97 A 5 *prev.* Terranova Pausania. W Italy
Oldebroek 86 D 3 E Netherlands
Oldenburg 94 C 2 N Germany
Oldenburg 94 B 3 N Germany
Oldenzaal 86 E 3 E Netherlands
Old Harbour 54 B 5 C Jamaica
Olean 41 E 3 New York, NE USA
Olëkminsk 115 F 3 C Russian Federation
Oleksandrivka 109 E 3 *Rus.* Aleksandrovka. C Ukraine
Oleksandriya 109 F 3 *Rus.* Aleksandriya. C Ukraine
Olenegorsk 114 C 2 NW Russian Federation
Olenëk 115 F 3 river, C Russian Federation
Olenyok *see* Olenëk
Oléron, Île d' 91 A 5 island, W France
Olevs'k 108 D 1 *Rus.* Olevsk. N Ukraine

Olevsk *see* Olevs'k
Ölgiy 126 C 2 W Mongolia
Olhão 92 B 5 S Portugal
Olimpo *see* Fuerte Olimpo
Olita *see* Alytus
Oliva 93 F 4 E Spain
Olivet 90 C 4 C France
Olmaliq 123 F 2 *Rus.* Almalyk. E Uzbekistan
Olomouc 99 C 5 *Ger.* Olmütz, *Pol.* Ołomuniec. E Czech Republic
Olonec *see* Olonets
Olonets 110 B 3 *var.* Olonec. NW Russian Federation
Olovyannaya 115 F 4 S Russian Federation
Olpe 94 B 4 W Germany
Olshanka *see* Vil'shanka
Olsnitz *see* Murska Sobota
Olsztyn 98 D 2 *Ger.* Allenstein. N Poland
Olt 108 B 5 *var.* Oltul, *Ger.* Alt. River, S Romania
Oltenița 108 C 5 S Romania
Olvera 92 C 5 S Spain
Ol'viopol' *see* Pervomays'k
Olympia 46 B 2 state capital, Washington, NW USA
Olympic Mountains 46 B 2 mountain range, Washington, NW USA
Ólympos 104 B 4 *var.* Ólimbos, *Eng.* Mount Olympus. Mountain, N Greece
Omagh 89 B 5 *Ir.* An Ómaigh. C Northern Ireland, UK
Omaha 45 F 4 Nebraska, C USA

Oman
121 D 6 *Ar.* Salṭanat 'Umān; *prev.* Muscat and Oman, Sultanat Masqat wah Oman. Monarchy, SW Asia

Official name: Sultanate of Oman
Date of formation: 1650 **Capital:** Muscat **Population:** 1.7 million **Total area:** 212,460 sq km (82,030 sq miles) **Languages:** Arab*, Baluchi **Religions:** Ibadi Muslim 75%, other Muslim 11%, Hindu 14% **Ethnic mix:** Arab 75%, Baluchi 15% **Government:** Monarchy with Consultative Council **Currency:** Rial = 1,000 baizas

Oman, Gulf of 120 E 4 *Ar.* Khalīj 'Umān. Gulf, W Arabian Sea
Omboué 77 A 6 W Gabon
Omdurman 72 B 4 *var.* Umm Durmān. C Sudan
Ometepe, Isla de 52 D 4 island, S Nicaragua
Ōmiya 131 D 5 Honshū, SE Japan
Ommen 86 E 3 E Netherlands
Omsk 114 C 4 C Russian Federation
Ōmuta 131 A 7 Kyūshū, SW Japan
Onda 93 F 3 E Spain
Ondangua *see* Ondangwa
Ondangwa 78 B 3 *var.* Ondangua. N Namibia
Öndörhaan 127 E 2 E Mongolia
Onega 110 C 3 NW Russian Federation
Onega 110 C 4 river, NW Russian Federation
Onega, Lake *see* Onezhskoye Ozero
Onex 95 A 8 SW Switzerland
Onezhskoye Ozero 110 B 3 *Eng.* Lake Onega, Lake, NW Russian Federation
Ongole 132 D 2 E India
Onitsha 75 G 5 S Nigeria

Onon 127 E 2 river, N Mongolia
Onslow 146 A 4 Western Australia, W Australia
Onslow Bay 43 G 2 bay, NW Atlantic Ocean
Ontario 38 B 3 province, S Canada
Ontario, Lake 41 E 3 lake, Canada/USA
Onteniente *see* Ontinyent
Ontinyent 93 F 4 *var.* Onteniente. E Spain
Ontong Java Rise 152 C 3 undersea rise, W Pacific Ocean
Onuba *see* Huelva
Oodeypore *see* Udaipur
Oostakker 87 B 5 NW Belgium
Oostburg 87 B 5 SW Netherlands
Oostende 87 A 5 *Eng.* Ostend, *Fr.* Ostende. NW Belgium
Oosterbeek 86 D 4 SE Netherlands
Oosterhout 86 C 4 S Netherlands
Opatija 100 A 2 *It.* Abbazia. NW Croatia
Opava 99 C 5 *Ger.* Troppau. E Czech Republic
Opelousas 42 B 3 Louisiana, S USA
Opmeer 86 C 2 NW Netherlands
Opochka 110 A 4 *var.* Opočka. W Russian Federation
Opočka *see* Opochka
Opole 98 C 4 *Ger.* Oppeln. SW Poland
Opotiki 150 E 3 North Island, NE New Zealand
Oppeln *see* Opole
Oqtosh 123 E 2 *Rus.* Aktash. C Uzbekistan
Oradea 108 A 3 *prev.* Oradea Mare, *Ger.* Grosswardein, *Hung.* Nagyvárad. NW Romania
Orahovac 101 D 5 *Alb.* Rahovec. S Yugoslavia
Oral *see* Ural'sk
Oran 70 D 2 *var.* Ouahran, Wahran. NW Algeria
Orange 91 D 6 *anc.* Arausio. SE France
Orange 49 H 4 Texas, S USA
Orange 149 D 6 New South Wales, SE Australia
Orangeburg 43 E 2 South Carolina, SE USA
Orange Cone *see* Orange Fan
Orange Fan 67 D 6 *var.* Orange Cone. Undersea fan, SW Indian Ocean
Orange River 78 B 4 *Afr.* Oranjerivier. River, S Africa
Orange Walk 52 C 1 N Belize
Oranienburg 94 D 3 NE Germany
Oranjemund 78 B 4 *var.* Orangemund; *prev.* Orange Mouth. SW Namibia
Oranjerivier *see* Orange River
Oranjestad 55 E 5 dependent territory capital, W Aruba
Orantes 118 B 3 *var.* Oronte, Orontes, *Ar.* Nahr al 'Āṣī, Nahr al 'Āsi Oronte, Nahr el Aassi. River, SW Asia
Orany *see* Varėna
Orašje 100 C 3 N Bosnia & Herzegovina
Oravita 108 A 4 *Ger.* Orawitsa, *Hung.* Oravicabanyá. W Romania
Orbetello 96 B 4 W Italy
Orcadas 154 A 2 research station, Antarctica
Orchard Homes 44 B 1 Montana, NW USA
Ord 146 D 3 river, N Australia
Ordino 91 A 8 NW Andorra

Ordos Desert 127 E 3 *Chin.* Mu Us Shamo. Desert, N China
Ordu 116 D 2 *anc.* Cotyora. N Turkey
Ordzhonikidze 109 F 3 E Ukraine
Orealla 59 G 3 E Guyana
Örebro 85 C 6 C Sweden
Oregon 40 D 3 Ohio, N USA
Oregon 46 B 3 *off.* State of Oregon; *nicknames* Beaver State, Sunset State, Valentine State, Webfoot State. State, NW USA
Oregon City 46 B 3 Oregon, NW USA
Orekhov *see* Orikhiv
Orël 111 B 5 W Russian Federation
Orem 44 B 4 Utah, W USA
Orenburg 111 D 6 *prev.* Chkalov. W Russian Federation
Orestiáda 104 D 3 *prev.* Orestiás NE Greece
Orestiás *see* Orestiáda
Orhei 108 D 3 *var.* Orheiu, *Rus.* Orgeyev. N Moldavia
Orhon Gol 127 E 2 *river*, N Mongolia
Oriental, Cordillera 58 B 3 mountain range, C Colombia
Oriental, Cordillera 61 F 4 mountain range, C Bolivia
Oriental, Cordillera 60 D 3 mountain range, C Peru
Orihuela 93 F 4 E Spain
Orikhiv 109 G 3 *Rus.* Orekhov. SE Ukraine
Orillia 38 D 5 Ontario, S Canada
Orinoco 58 D 3 *river*, Colombia/Venezuela
Orissa 135 F 5 state, NE India
Orissaar *see* Orissaare
Orissaare 106 C 2 *Ger.* Orissaar. Saaremaa, W Estonia
Oristano 97 A 5 W Italy
Orito 58 A 4 SW Colombia
Orkney Islands 88 C 2 *var.* Orkneys, Orkney. Island group, NE Scotland, UK
Orlando 43 E 4 Florida, SE USA
Orléanais 90 C 4 cultural region, C France
Orléans 90 C 4 *anc.* Aurelianum. C France
Orlya 107 B 6 W Belorussia
Örnsköldsvik 84 C 4 C Sweden
Oroluk Atoll 144 C 2 island, C Micronesia
Oromocto 39 F 4 New Brunswick, SE Canada
Orona 145 F 3 *prev.* Hull Island. Island, C Kiribati
Oropeza *see* Cochabamba
Oroqen Zizhiqi 127 G 1 N China
Orsha 107 E 6 NE Belorussia
Orsk 111 D 6 W Russian Federation
Orsova 108 A 5 *Ger.* Orschowa, *Hung.* Orsova. W Romania
Ortelsburg *see* Szczytno
Orthez 91 B 6 SW France
Ortona 96 D 4 C Italy
Oruba *see* Aruba
Orümïyeh, Daryächeh-ye 120 B 2 *var.* Matianus, Sha Hi, Urumi Yeh, *Eng.* Lake Urmia; *prev.* Daryächeh-ye Rezā'īyeh. Lake, NW Iran
Oruro 61 F 4 W Bolivia
Ōsaka 131 C 6 *hist.* Naniwa. Honshū, SW Japan
Osa, Península de 53 E 5 peninsula, S Costa Rica
Osborn Plateau 141 D 5 undersea plateau, E Indian Ocean
Osca *see* Huesca

Osh 123 F 2 SW Kyrgyzstan
Oshawa 38 D 5 Ontario, SE Canada
Oshikango 78 B 3 N Namibia
Ō-shima 131 D 6 island, E Japan
Oshmyany *see* Ashmyany
Osijek 100 C 3 *Ger.* Esseg, Hung, Eszék; *prev.* Osiek, Osjek. E Croatia
Oskaloosa 45 G 4 Iowa, C USA
Oskarshamn 85 C 7 S Sweden
Öskemen *see* Ust'-Kamenogorsk
Oskil *see* Oskol
Oskol 109 G 2 *Ukr.* Oskil. River, Russian Federation/Ukraine
Oslo 85 B 6 *prev.* Christiania, Kristiania. Country capital, S Norway
Osmaniye 116 D 4 S Turkey
Osnabrück 94 B 4 NW Germany
Osogovski Planini 104 B 3 *var.* Osogovske Planine, *Mac.* Osogovski Planini. Mountain range, Bulgaria/Macedonia
Osorno 65 B 5 C Chile
Osprey Reef 148 D 2 reef, NW Coral Sea
Oss 86 D 4 S Netherlands
Ossabaw Island 43 E 3 island, SE USA
Ossa, Serra d' 92 C 4 mountain range, SE Portugal
Ossora 115 H 2 E Russian Federation
Oster 109 E 1 N Ukraine
Östermyra *see* Seinäjoki
Östersund 84 C 4 C Sweden
Ostfriesische Inseln 94 A 3 *Eng.* East Frisian Islands. Island group, NW Germany
Ostiglia 96 C 2 N Italy
Ostrava 99 C 5 E Czech Republic
Ostróda 98 D 2 *Ger.* Osterode, Osterode in Ostpreussen. N Poland
Ostrołęka 98 D 3 *Ger.* Wiesenhof, *Rus.* Ostrolenka. NE Poland
Ostrov 110 A 4 *Latv.* Austrava. W Russian Federation
Ostrowiec Świętokrzyski 98 D 4 *var.* Ostrowiec, Ostrowiec Swiętokrzyski, *Rus.* Ostrovets. SE Poland
Ostrów Mazowiecka 98 D 3 *var.* Ostrów Mazowiecki. NE Poland
Ostrów Mazowiecki *see* Ostrów Mazowiecka
Ostrów Wielkopolski 98 C 4 *var.* Ostrów, Ger. Ostrowo; *prev.* C Poland
Ostyako-Voguls'k *see* Khanty-Mansiysk
Osum *see* Osumit, Lumi i
Ōsumi-shotō 131 A 8 island group, Nansei-shotō, S Japan
Osumit, Lumi i 101 D 7 *var.* Osum. River, SE Albania
Osuna 92 D 5 S Spain
Oswego 41 F 3 New York, NE USA
Otago Peninsula 151 B 7 peninsula, South Island, SW New Zealand
Otaki 150 D 4 North Island, C New Zealand
Otaru 130 C 2 Hokkaidō, NE Japan
Otavalo 60 B 1 N Ecuador
Otavi 78 B 3 N Namibia
Oțelu Roșu 108 A 4 *Ger.* Ferdinandsberg, *Hung.* Nándorhgy. SW Romania
Otepää 106 D 3 *Ger.* Odenpäh. SE Estonia
Otira 151 C 6 South Island, C New Zealand
Otjiwarongo 78 B 3 N Namibia

Otorohanga 150 D 3 North Island, N New Zealand
Otra 85 A 6 *river*, S Norway
Otranto, Canale d' *see* Otranto, Strait of
Otranto, Strait of 103 E 3 *It.* Canale d'Otranto. Strait, Adriatic Sea/Ionian Sea
Otrokovice 99 C 5 *Ger.* Otrokowitz. SE Czech Republic
Otrokowitz *see* Otrokovice
Ōtsu 131 C 6 *var.* Ōtu. Honshū, SW Japan
Ottawa 38 D 5 country capital, Ontario, SE Canada
Ottawa 40 B 3 Illinois, N USA
Ottawa 45 F 5 Kansas, C USA
Ottawa Islands 38 C 1 island group, Northwest Territories, C Canada
Ottignies 87 C 6 C Belgium
Ottobrunn 95 C 6 SE Germany
Ottumwa 45 G 4 Iowa, C USA
Otu *see* Ōtsu
Ouachita Mountains 42 A 1 mountain range, S USA
Ouachita River 42 B 2 river, Arkansas, C USA
Ouâd Nâga 74 B 2 SW Mauritania
Ouagadougou 75 E 4 *var.* Wagadugu. Country capital, C Burkina
Ouahigouya 75 E 3 NW Burkina
Oualata *see* Oualâta
Oualâta 74 D 3 *var.* Oualata. SE Mauritania
Ouanary 59 H 3 E French Guiana
Ouanda Djallé 76 D 4 NE Central African Republic
Ouarâne 74 D 2 physical region, C Mauritania
Ouargla 71 E 2 *var.* Wargla. NE Algeria
Ouarzazate 70 C 3 S Morocco
Oubangui *see* Ubangi
Oudenaarde 87 B 6 *Fr.* Audenarde. SW Belgium
Ouessant, Île d' 90 A 3 *Eng.* Ushant. Island, NW France
Ouésso 77 B 5 NW Congo
Oujda 70 D 2 *Ar.* Ujda, Oudjda. NE Morocco
Oujeft 74 C 2 C Mauritania
Ouled Djellal 71 E 2 *var.* Awled Djellal. N Algeria
Oulu 84 D 4 *Swe.* Uleåborg. C Finland
Oulujärvi 84 D 4 *Swe.* Uleträsk. Lake, C Finland
Oulujoki 84 D 3 *river*, N Finland
Ounianga Kébir 76 C 2 N Chad
Oup *see* Auob
Oupeye 87 D 6 E Belgium
Our 87 D 7 *river*, W Europe
Ourense 92 C 2 *Cast.* Orense; *Lat.* Aurium. NW Spain
Ourique 92 B 4 S Portugal
Ourthe 87 D 7 *river*, E Belgium
Ouse 89 D 5 *river*, N England, UK
Outaouais *see* Ottawa
Outer Hebrides 88 B 2 *var.* Western Isles. Island group, NW Scotland, UK
Outer Islands 79 G 1 island group, SW Seychelles
Outes 92 B 1 NW Spain
Outreau 90 C 2 N France
Ouvéa 144 D 5 island, NE New Caledonia

Ouyen 149 B 6 Victoria, SE Australia
Ovalle 64 B 3 N Chile
Ovar 92 B 2 W Portugal
Overflakkee 86 B 4 island, SW Netherlands
Overijse 87 C 6 C Belgium
Oviedo 92 D 1 *anc.* Asturias. NW Spain
Ovilava *see* Wels
Ovruch 108 D 1 N Ukraine
Owando 77 B 6 *prev.* Fort-Rousset. C Congo
Owase 131 C 6 Honshū, SW Japan
Owatonna 45 F 3 Minnesota, N USA
Owen Fracture Zone 140 B 4 fracture zone, NW Indian Ocean
Owen, Mount 151 C 5 mountain, South Island, C New Zealand
Owensboro 40 B 5 Kentucky, E USA
Owen Stanley Range 144 B 3 mountain range, S Papua New Guinea
Owerri 75 G 5 S Nigeria
Owo 75 F 5 SW Nigeria
Owyhee River 46 C 4 river, NW USA
Oxford 89 D 6 *Lat.* Oxonia. S England, UK
Oxford 151 C 6 South Island, C New Zealand
Oxford 40 C 4 Ohio, N USA
Oxkutzcab 51 H 4 SE Mexico
Oxnard 47 C 7 California, W USA
Oxonia *see* Oxford
Oyama 131 D 5 Honshū, S Japan
Oyem 77 B 5 N Gabon
Oyo 75 F 5 W Nigeria
Oyo 77 B 6 C Congo
Ozark 42 D 3 Alabama, S USA
Ozark Plateau 45 G 5 plain, Missouri, C USA
Ozarks, Lake of the 45 G 5 *Fr.* Lac des Bois. Reservoir, Missouri, C USA
Ózd 99 D 6 NE Hungary
Ozieri 97 A 5 W Italy

P

Paamiut 82 B 4 *var.* Pâmiut, *Dan.* Frederikshåb. SW Greenland
Pa-an 136 B 4 SE Burma
Pābna 135 G 4 W Bangladesh
Pacaraima, Serra 59 F 3 *var.* Pakaraima Mountains. Mountain range, N South America
Pachuca 51 E 4 *var.* Pachuca de Soto. C Mexico
Pachuca de Soto *see* Pachuca
Pacific-Antarctic Ridge 152 D 5 undersea ridge, S Pacific Ocean
Pacific Ocean 152 D 3 ocean
Padang 138 B 4 Sumatera, W Indonesia
Paderborn 94 B 4 NW Germany
Padma *see* Ganges
Padova 96 C 2 *Eng.* Padua; *anc.* Patavium. NE Italy
Padre Island 49 G 5 island, Texas, S USA
Paducah 40 B 5 Kentucky, E USA
Paeroa 150 D 3 North Island, N New Zealand
Pag 100 A 3 *It.* Pago. Island, C Croatia
Page 48 B 1 Arizona, SW USA
Pago *see* Pag
Pago Pago 145 F 4 dependent territory capital, W American Samoa

Pahiatua 150 D 4 North Island, C New Zealand

Paide 106 D 2 *Ger.* Weissenstein. N Estonia

Paihia 150 D 2 North Island, N New Zealand

Päijänne 85 E 5 lake, S Finland

Paine, Cerro 65 B 7 mountain, S Chile

Painted Desert 48 B 1 plain, Arizona, SW USA

Paisley 88 C 4 W Scotland, UK

País Valenciano 93 F 3 cultural region, NE Spain

País Vasco 93 E 1 cultural region, N Spain

Paita 60 B 3 NW Peru

Pakanbaru *see* Pekanbaru

Pakistan
134 A 2 *var.* Islami Jamhuriya e Pakistan. Republic, S Asia

Official name: Islamic Republic of Pakistan **Date of formation:** 1947 **Capital:** Islamabad **Population:** 128.1 million **Total Area:** 796,100 sq km (307,374 sq miles) **Languages:** Urdu*, Punjabi **Religions:** Sunni Muslim 77%, Shi'a Muslim 20%, Hindu 2%, Christian 1% **Ethnic mix:** Punjabi 56%, Sindhi 13%, Pashtun 8%, other 23% **Government:** Multiparty republic **Currency:** Rupee = 100 paisa

Pakokku 136 A 3 W Burma

Pak Phanang 137 C 7 *var.* Ban Pak Phanang. S Thailand

Pakruojis 106 C 4 N Lithuania

Paks 99 C 7 S Hungary

Paksé *see* Pakxé

Pakxé 137 D 5 *var.* Paksé. S Laos

Palafrugell 93 G 2 NE Spain

Palagruža 101 B 5 *It.* Pelagosa. Island, SW Croatia

Palaiá Epídavros 105 C 6 S Greece

Palamós 93 G 2 NE Spain

Palamuse 106 E 2 *Ger.* Sankt-Bartholomäi. E Estonia

Palanka *see* Bačka Palanka

Palapye 78 D 3 SE Botswana

Palatka 43 E 3 Florida, SE USA

Palau
144 A 2 *var.* Belau. Republic, W Pacific Ocean

Official name: Republic of Palau **Date of formation:** 1994 **Capital:** Koror **Population:** 16,000 **Total Area:** 497 sq km (192 sq miles) **Languages:** Palauan*, English **Religions:** Christian 70%, traditional beliefs 30% **Ethnic mix:** Palaun 99%, other 1% **Government:** Multiparty republic **Currency:** US $ = 100 cents

Palawan 139 E 2 island, W Philippines

Palawan Passage 139 E 2 passage, SE South China Sea

Paldiski 106 D 2 *prev.* Baltiski, *Ger.* Baltischport; *prev. Eng.* Baltic Port. NW Estonia

Palembang 138 B 4 Sumatera, W Indonesia

Palencia 92 D 2 *anc.* Palantia, Pallantia. NW Spain

Palermo 97 C 7 *Fr.* Palerme; *anc.* Panormus, Panhormus. SW Italy

Palestine 49 G 3 Texas, S USA

Pāli 134 C 3 N India

Palikir 144 C 2 Country capital, Pohnpei, E Micronesia

Palimé *see* Kpalimé

Palioúri, Ákra 104 C 4 *var.* Akra Kanestron. Headland, N Greece

Palk Strait 132 D 3 strait, N Indian Ocean

Palliser, Cape 151 D 5 headland, North Island, C New Zealand

Palma 93 G 3 *var.* Palma de Mallorca. E Spain

Palma del Río 92 D 4 S Spain

Palma de Mallorca *see* Palma

Palmar Sur 53 E 5 SE Costa Rica

Palma Soriano 54 C 3 E Cuba

Palmdale 47 C 7 California, W USA

Palmer 154 A 2 research station, Antarctica

Palmer Land 154 A 3 physical region, Antarctica

Palmerston 145 G 4 island, S Cook Islands

Palmerston North 150 D 4 North Island, C New Zealand

Palmi 97 D 7 SW Italy

Palmira 58 B 3 W Colombia

Palm Springs 47 D 8 California, W USA

Palmyra Atoll 145 G 2 US unincorporated territory, C Pacific Ocean

Palo Alto 47 B 6 California, W USA

Paloe *see* Denpasar

Paloe *see* Palu

Palu 139 E 4 *prev.* Paloe. Celebes, C Indonesia

Pamiers 91 B 6 S France

Pamir 123 F 3 *var.* Daryā-ye Pāmīr. River, Afghanistan/Tajikistan

Pāmīr, Daryā-ye *see* Pamir

Pamirs 123 F 3 *Pash.* Daryā-ye Pāmīr, *Rus.* Pamir, *Taj.* Daryoi Pomir. Mountain range, C Asia

Pamlico Sound 43 G 1 bay, NW Atlantic Ocean

Pampa 49 F 1 Texas, S USA

Pampa Aullagas, Lago *see* Poopó, Lago

Pampas 64 C 4 plain, C Argentina

Pamplona 93 E 1 *Basq.* Iruñea; *prev.* Pampeluna, *anc.* Pompaelo. N Spain

Pamplona 58 C 2 N Colombia

Panaji 132 B 1 *var.* New Goa, Pangim, Panjim. State capital, W India

Panama
53 G 5 Republic, SE Central America

Official name: Republic of Panama **Date of formation:** 1903 **Capital:** Panama City **Population:** 2.6 million **Total area:** 77,080 sq km (29,761 sq miles) **Languages:** Spanish*, English Creole, Indian languages **Religions:** Roman Catholic 93%, other 7% **Ethnic mix:** *mestizo* 70%, Black 14%, White 10%, Indian 6% **Government:** Multiparty republic **Currency:** Balboa = 100 centesimos

Panamá 53 G 5 *var.* Ciudad de Panamá, *Eng.* Panama City. Country capital, C Panama

Panamá, Bahía de 53 G 5 bay, W Pacific Ocean

Panama Basin 56 A 2 undersea basin, E Pacific Ocean

Panama Canal 53 F 4 canal, E Panama

Panama City 42 D 3 Florida, SE USA

Panama City 35 D 7 country capital, C Panama

Panama City *see* Panamá

Panamá, Golfo de 53 G 5 *var.* Gulf of Panama. Gulf, E Pacific Ocean

Panama, Gulf of *see* Panamá, Golfo de

Panama, Isthmus of *see* Panama, Isthmus of

Panamá, Istmo de 53 G 4 *Eng.* Isthmus of Panama; *prev.* Isthmus of Darien. Isthmus, E Panama

Panama, Republic of *see* Panama

Panay Island 139 E 2 island, C Philippines

Pančevo 100 D 3 *Ger.* Pantschowa, *Hung.* Pancsova. NE Yugoslavia

Pandan, Selat 138 A 2 strait, Indian Ocean/Pacific Ocean

Panevėžys 106 C 4 C Lithuania

Pangkalpinang 138 C 4 Bangka, W Indonesia

Panlong Jiang *see* Lô, Sông

Panopolis *see* Akhmîm

Pánormos 105 C 7 Kriti, SE Greece

Pantanal 63 E 4 *var.* Pantanalmato-Grossense. Wetland, SW Brazil

Pantanalmato-Grossense *see* Pantanal

Pantelleria, Isola di 97 B 7 island, SW Italy

Pánuco 51 E 3 E Mexico

Pao-shan *see* Baoshan

Papagayo, Golfo de 52 D 4 gulf, E Pacific Ocean

Papakura 150 D 3 North Island, N New Zealand

Papantla 51 F 4 *var.* Papantla de Olarte. E Mexico

Papantla de Olarte *see* Papantla

Papatoetoe 150 D 3 North Island, N New Zealand

Papeete 145 H 4 dependent territory capital, Tahiti, W French Polynesia

Paphos *see* Páfos

Papilė 106 B 3 NW Lithuania

Papillion 45 F 4 Nebraska, C USA

Papua, Gulf of 144 B 3 gulf, S Papua New Guinea

Papua New Guinea
144 B 2 *prev.* Territory of Papua and New Guinea. Commonwealth republic, Indian Ocean/Pacific Ocean

Official name: The Independent State of Papua New Guinea **Date of formation:** 1975 **Capital:** Port Moresby **Population:** 4.1 million **Total Area:** 462, 840 sq km (178,700 sq miles) **Languages:** Pidgin English*, Motu*, 750 (est.) native languages **Religions:** Christian 66%, other 34% **Ethnic mix:** Papuan 85%, other 15% **Government:** Parliamentary democracy **Currency:** Kina = 100 toea

Papuk 100 C 3 mountain range, NE Croatia

Pará 63 E 2 *off.* Estado do Pará. State, NE Brazil

Pará *see* Belém

Paracas, Bahía de 60 C 4 bay, W Pacific Ocean

Paracel Islands 138 D 1 disputed territory, N South China Sea

Paracín 100 E 4 C Yugoslavia

Pará, Estado do *see* Pará

Paragua 59 E 3 river, SE Venezuela

Paraguay
64 D 2 country, S South America

Official name: Republic of Paraguay **Date of formation:** 1935 **Capital:** Asunción **Population:** 4.5 million **Total area:** 406,750 sq km (157,046 sq miles) **density:** 11 people per sq km **Languages:** Spanish*, Guaraní **Religions:** Roman Catholic 90%, other 10% **Ethnic mix:** *mestizo* (Euro-Indian) 95%, White 3%, Indian 2% **Government:** Multiparty republic **Currency:** Guaraní = 100 centimos

Paraguay 64 D 2 *Port.* Rio Paraguai. River, S South America

Paraíba 63 G 2 *off.* Estado da Paraíba; *prev.* Parahiba, Parahyba. State, E Brazil

Paraíba *see* João Pessoa

Parakou 75 F 4 C Benin

Paramaribo 59 G 3 country capital, N Surinam

Paramushir, Ostrov 115 H 3 island, E Russian Federation

Paraná 64 E 3 *var.* Alto Paraná. River, S South America

Paraná 64 D 4 E Argentina

Paraná 63 E 4 *off.* Estado do Paraná. State, S Brazil

Paraná, Estado do *see* Paraná

Paranéstio 104 C 3 NE Greece

Paraparaumu 151 D 5 North Island, C New Zealand

Parchim 94 C 3 N Germany

Parczew 98 E 4 E Poland

Pardubice 99 B 5 *Ger.* Pardubitz. C Czech Republic

Pardubitz *see* Pardubice

Parechcha 107 B 5 *Pol.* Porzecze, *Rus.* Porech'ye. W Belorussia

Parecis, Chapada dos 62 D 3 *var.* Serra dos Parecis. Mountain range, W Brazil

Parecis, Serra dos *see* Parecis, Chapada dos

Parenzo *see* Poreč

Parepare 139 E 4 Celebes, C Indonesia

Párga 105 A 5 W Greece

Paria, Golfo de *see* Paria, Gulf of

Paria, Gulf of 59 E 1 *var.* Golfo de Paria. Gulf, W Atlantic Ocean

Parika 59 F 2 N Guyana

Paris 90 C 3 *anc.* Lutetia, Lutetia Parisiorum, Parisii. Country capital, N France

Paris 42 C 1 Tennessee, S USA

Paris 49 G 2 Texas, S USA

Parkent 123 F 2 E Uzbekistan

Parkersburg 40 D 4 West Virginia, NE USA

Parkes 149 C 6 New South Wales, SE Australia

Parkhar *see* Farkhor

Parma 96 B 2 N Italy

Parnahyba *see* Parnaíba

Parnaíba 63 G 2 *var.* Parnahyba. E Brazil

Pärnu 106 D 2 *Ger.* Pernau, *Latv.* Pērnava; *prev. Rus.* Pernov. SW Estonia

Pärnu 106 D 2 *var.* Parnu Jõgi, *Ger.* Pernau. River, SW Estonia

Pärnu-Jaagupi 106 D 2 *Ger.* Sankt-Jakobi. SW Estonia

Pärnu Laht 106 D 2 *Ger.* Pernauer Bucht. Bay, Baltic Sea/Gulf of Riga **Páros** 105 D 6 Páros, SE Greece

Páros 105 D 6 island, Kykládes, SE Greece

Parral 64 B 4 C Chile
Parral see Hidalgo del Parral
Parramatta 149 D 6 New South
  Wales, SE Australia
Parras 50 D 3 var. Parras de la
  Fuente. NE Mexico
Parras de la Fuente see Parras
Parsons 45 F 5 Kansas, C USA
Pasadena 49 H 4 Texas, S USA
Pasadena 47 C 7 California, W USA
Paşcani 108 C 3 Hung. Páskán. NE
  Romania
Pasco 46 C 2 Washington, NW USA
Pasewalk 94 D 3 NE Germany
Pashkeni see Bolyarovo
Pasłęk 98 D 2 Ger. Preußisch
  Holland. N Poland
Pasinler 117 F 3 NE Turkey
Páskán see Paşcani
Pasni 134 A 3 SW Pakistan
Paso de Indios 65 B 6 S Argentina
Paso de los Vientos see Windward
  Passage
Passarowitz see Požarevac
Passau 95 D 6 SE Germany
Passo Fundo 63 E 5 S Brazil
Pastavy 107 C 5 Pol. Postawy, Rus.
  Postawy. NW Belorussia
Pastaza 60 B 2 river, Ecuador/Peru
Pasto 58 A 4 SW Colombia
Pasvalys 106 C 4 N Lithuania
Patagonia 65 B 7 physical region,
  Argentina/Chile
Patani see Pattani
Patea 150 D 4 North Island, C New
  Zealand
Paterson 41 F 4 New Jersey, NE
  USA
Pathein see Bassein
Pátmos 105 D 6 island,
  Dodekánisos, SE Greece
Patna 135 F 3 var. Azimabad. State
  capital, N India
Patnos 117 F 3 E Turkey
Patos, Lagoa dos 63 E 5 lagoon, SW
  Atlantic Ocean
Pátra 105 B 5 Eng. Patras; prev.
  Pátrai. S Greece
Patras see Pátra
Pattani 137 C 7 var. Patani. S
  Thailand
Pattaya 137 C 5 C Thailand
Patuca 52 D 2 river, E Honduras
Pau 91 B 6 SW France
Paulatuk 37 E 3 Northwest
  Territories, NW Canada
Paungde 136 B 4 SW Burma
Pavia 96 B 2 anc. Ticinum. N Italy
Pāvilosta 106 B 3 W Latvia
Pavlikeni 104 D 2 N Bulgaria
Pavlodar 112 C 3 NE Kazakhstan
Pavlograd see Pavlohrad
Pavlohrad 109 G 3 Rus. Pavlograd.
  E Ukraine
Pavlovsk 111 B 6 W Russian
  Federation
Pavlovskaya 111 A 7 SW Russian
  Federation
Pawai, Pulau 138 A 2 island, SW
  Singapore
Pawn 136 B 3 river, C Burma
Pax Augusta see Badajoz
Paxí 105 A 5 island, Iónioi Nísoi, W
  Greece
Pax Julia see Beja
Payakumbuh 138 B 4 Sumatera, W
  Indonesia
Paynes Find 147 B 6 W Australia
Payo Obispo see Chetumal
Paysandú 64 D 4 NW Uruguay
Pazar 117 E 2 NE Turkey

Pazardzhik 104 C 3 var. Pazardžik;
  prev. Tatar Pazardzhik. SW
  Bulgaria
Pearl Islands see Perlas,
  Archipiélago de las
Pearl Lagoon see Perlas, Laguna de
Pearl River 42 B 3 river, S USA
Pearsall 49 F 4 Texas, S USA
Peary Land 83 E 1 physical region,
  Greenland
Peć 101 D 5 Alb. Pejë, Turk. Ipek. C
  Yugoslavia
Pechora 110 E 3 var. Pečora. NW
  Russian Federation
Pechora 110 D 3 var. Pečora. River,
  NW Russian Federation
Pechorskoye More 110 D 2 sea,
  Arctic Ocean/Barents Sea
Pečora see Pechora
Pecos 49 E 3 Texas, SW USA
Pecos Plains 49 E 3 plain, Texas, S
  USA
Pecos River 49 E 3 river, SW USA
Pécs 99 C 7 Ger. Fünfkirchen; Lat.
  Sopianae. SW Hungary
Pedra Lume 74 A 3 NE Cape Verde
Pedro Cays 54 C 3 island group, S
  Jamaica
Pedro Juan Caballero 64 D 2 E
  Paraguay
Peer 87 D 5 NE Belgium
Pegasus Bay 151 C 6 bay, S Pacific
  Ocean
Pegu 136 B 4 var. Bago. S Burma
Pehuajó 64 C 4 E Argentina
Peihai see Beihai
Peine 94 B 4 C Germany
Peiraiás 105 C 6 prev. Piraiévs, Eng.
  Piraeus. C Greece
Pekalongan 138 C 5 Jawa, C
  Indonesia
Pekanbaru 138 B 4 var. Pakanbaru.
  Sumatera, W Indonesia
Pekin 40 B 4 Illinois, N USA
Peking see Beijing
Pelagie, Isole 97 B 8 island group,
  SW Italy
Pelagosa see Palagruža
Pelly Bay 37 F 3 Northwest
  Territories, N Canada
Pelopónnisos 105 B 6 var. Morea,
  Eng. Peloponnese; anc.
  Peloponnesus. Peninsula, S
  Greece
Pematangsiantar 138 B 3 Sumatera,
  W Indonesia
Pemba 73 D 7 island, E Tanzania
Pemba 79 F 2 prev. Port Amelia,
  Porto Amélia. NE Mozambique
Pembroke 38 D 4 Ontario, SE
  Canada
Penderma see Bandırma
Pendleton 46 C 3 Oregon, NW USA
Pend Oreille, Lake 46 D 1 lake,
  Idaho, NW USA
Peng-pu see Bengbu
Peniche 92 B 3 W Portugal
Penn Hills 41 E 4 Pennsylvania, NE
  USA
Pennine Alps 95 A 8 Fr. Alpes
  Pennines, It. Alpi Pennine; Lat.
  Alpes Penninae. Mountain range,
  Italy/Switzerland
Pennine Chain see Pennines
Pennines 89 D 5 var. Pennine
  Chain. Mountain range, NW
  England, UK
Pennsylvania 41 E 4 off.
  Commonwealth of Pennsylvania;
  nickname Keystone State. State,
  NE USA
Penobscot River 41 H 1 river,
  Maine, NE USA

Penong 147 E 6 South Australia, S
  Australia
Penonomé 53 F 5 C Panama
Penrhyn 145 G 3 island, N Cook
  Islands
Penrhyn Basin 152 D 3 undersea
  basin, C Pacific Ocean
Penrith 89 D 5 NW England, UK
Pensacola 42 C 3 Florida, SE USA
Pentecost 144 D 4 Fr. Pentecôte.
  Island, C Vanuatu
Pentecôte see Pentecost
Penza 111 C 6 W Russian
  Federation
Penzance 89 B 8 SW England, UK
Peoria 40 B 4 Illinois, N USA
Perchtoldsdorf 95 E 6 NE Austria
Percival Lakes 146 C 4 lake,
  Western Australia, NW Australia
Pereira 58 B 3 W Colombia
Pergamino 64 D 4 E Argentina
Périgueux 91 B 5 anc. Vesuna. SW
  France
Perito Moreno 65 B 6 S Argentina
Perlas, Archipiélago de las 53 G 5
  Eng. Pearl Islands. Island group,
  SE Panama
Perlas, Laguna de 53 E 3 var. Pearl
  Lagoon. Lagoon, W Caribbean
  Sea
Perleberg 94 C 3 N Germany
Perlepe see Prilep
Perm' 111 D 5 prev. Molotov. NW
  Russian Federation
Pernambuco 63 G 2 off. Estado de
  Pernambuco. State, E Brazil
Pernambuco see Recife
Pernambuco Abyssal Plain see
  Pernambuco Plain
Pernambuco, Estado de see
  Pernambuco
Pernambuco Plain 67 C 5 var.
  Pernambuco Abyssal Plain.
  Abyssal plain, E Atlantic Ocean
Pernauer Bucht see Pärnu Laht
Pernik 104 C 2 prev. Dimitrovo. W
  Bulgaria
Perote 51 F 4 E Mexico
Perpignan 91 C 7 S France
Perryton 49 F 1 Texas, S USA
Perryville 45 H 5 Missouri, C USA
Persian Gulf 120 C 4 var. The Gulf,
  Ar. Khalīj al 'Arabī, Per. Khalīj-e
  Fars. Gulf, W Arabian Sea
Perth 88 C 4 E Scotland, UK
Perth 38 D 5 Ontario, SE Canada
Perth 149 C 8 Tasmania, SE
  Australia
Perth 147 B 6 state capital, Western
  Australia, SW Australia
Perth Basin 141 E 6 undersea basin,
  SE Indian Ocean
Peru see Beru

Peru
  60 C 3 Republic, W South
  America

Official name: Republic of Peru
Date of formation: 1824 **Capital:**
Lima **Population:** 22.9 million
Total area: 1,285,220 sq km
(496,223 sq miles) **Languages:**
Spanish*, Quechua*, Aymará*
Religions: Roman Catholic 95%,
other 5% **Ethnic mix:** Indian 45%,
mestizo 37%, White 15%, other 3%
Government: Multiparty republic
Currency: New sol = 100 centimos

Peru Basin 56 A 4 undersea basin,
  E Pacific Ocean

Peru-Chile Trench 56 A 4 trench, E
  Pacific Ocean
Perugia 96 C 4 Fr. Pérouse; anc.
  Perusia. C Italy
Peru, Republic of see Peru
Péruwelz 87 B 6 SW Belgium
Pervomays'k 109 E 3 prev.
  Ol'viopol'. S Ukraine
Pervyy Kuril'skiy Proliv 115 H 3
  strait, Pacific Ocean/Sea of
  Okhotsk
Pesaro 96 C 3 anc. Pisaurum C Italy
Pescara 96 D 4 anc. Aternum, Ostia
  Aterni. C Italy
Peshāwar 134 C 1 N Pakistan
Peshkopi 101 D 6 var. Peshkopia,
  Peshkopija. NE Albania
Pessac 91 B 5 SW France
Pétange 87 D 8 SW Luxembourg
Peta' Tiqwa 119 A 6 var. Petach-
  Tikva, Petah Tiqva. C Israel
Peterborough 89 E 6 prev.
  Medeshamstede. E England, UK
Peterborough 38 D 5 Ontario, SE
  Canada
Peterborough 149 B 6 South
  Australia, S Australia
Peterhead 88 D 3 NE Scotland, UK
Petersburg 41 E 5 Virginia, NE USA
Peters Mine 59 F 3 var. Peter's
  Mine. N Guyana
Peter's Mine see Peters Mine
Peto 51 H 4 SE Mexico
Petra see Wādī Mūsá
Petrich 104 C 3 SW Bulgaria
Petrikov see Pyetrykaw
Petrinja 100 B 3 C Croatia
Petropavl see Petropavlovsk
Petropavlovsk 114 C 4 Kaz.
  Petropavl. N Kazakhstan
Petropavlovsk-Kamchatskiy 115 H
  3 NE Russian Federation
Petroşani 108 B 4 var. Petroşeni, Ger.
  Petroschen, Hung. Petrozsény. W
  Romania
Petroskoi see Petrozavodsk
Petrovsk 111 C 6 W Russian
  Federation
Petrovsk-Port see Makhachkala
Petrov Val 111 C 6 SW Russian
  Federation
Petrozavodsk 110 B 3 Fin.
  Petroskoi. NW Russian
  Federation
Pevek 115 G 1 NE Russian
  Federation
Pezinok 99 C 6 Ger. Bösing, Hung.
  Bazin. SW Slovakia
Pforzheim 95 B 6 SW Germany
Pfungstadt 95 B 5 W Germany
Phangan, Ko 137 C 6 island, S
  Thailand
Phan Rang-Thap Cham 137 E 6 var.
  Phan Rang, Phanrang, Phan Rang
  Thap Cham. SE Vietnam
Phan Thiêt 137 E 6 S Vietnam
Phatthalung 137 C 7 var. Padalung,
  Patalung. S Thailand
Phayao 136 C 4 var. Muang Phayao.
  N Thailand
Phenix City 42 D 2 Alabama, S
  USA
Phetchaburi 137 C 5 var. Bejraburi,
  Petchaburi, Phet Buri. C Thailand
Philadelphia 41 F 4 Pennsylvania,
  NE USA
Philippeville see Skikda
Philippine Basin 152 B 2 undersea
  basin, W Pacific Ocean

Philippines
  139 F 1 off. Republic of the
  Philippines. Republic, SE Asia

Official name: Republic of the Philippines **Date of formation:** 1946 **Capital:** Manila **Population:** 66.5 million **Total Area:** 300,000 sq km (115,831 sq miles) **Languages:** Pilipino*, English **Religions:** Roman Catholic 83%, Protestant 9%, Muslim 5%, other 3% **Ethnic mix:** Filipino 96%, Chinese 2%, other 2% **Government:** Multiparty republic **Currency:** Peso = 100 centavos

Philippine Sea 152 B 3 sea, W Pacific Ocean

Philippines, Republic of the see Philippines

Philippine Trench 142 A 1 trench, W Pacific Ocean

Phitsanulok 136 C 4 var. Bisnulok, Muang Phitsanulok, Pitsanulok. N Thailand

Phlórina see Flórina

Phnom Penh see Phnum Penh

Phnum Penh 137 D 6 var. Phnom Penh. Country capital, S Cambodia

Phoenix 48 B 2 state capital, Arizona, SW USA

Phoenix Islands 145 F 3 island group, C Kiribati

Phôngsali 136 C 3 var. Phong Saly. N Laos

Phong Saly see Phôngsali

Phrae 136 C 4 var. Muang Phrae, Prae. N Thailand

Phra Nakhon Si Ayutthaya see Ayutthaya

Phra Thong, Ko 137 B 7 island, S Thailand

Phuket 137 B 7 var. Bhuket, Puket, Mal. Ujung Salang; prev. Junkseylon, Salang. S Thailand

Phuket, Ko 137 B 7 island, S Thailand

Phumĭ Kâmpóng Trâlach 137 D 5 C Cambodia

Phumĭ Sâmraông 137 D 5 NW Cambodia

Phu Vinh see Tra Vinh

Piacenza 96 B 2 Fr. Paisance; anc. Placentia. N Italy

Piatra-Neamţ 108 C 3 Hung. Karácsonkő. NE Romania

Piauí 63 F 2 off. Estado do Piauí; prev. Piauhy. State, E Brazil

Picardie 90 C 3 Eng. Picardy. Cultural region, N France

Picardy see Picardie

Picayune 42 C 3 Mississippi, S USA

Pichilemu 64 B 4 C Chile

Pichincha 60 B 1 NE Ecuador

Pico 92 A 5 var. Ilha do Pico. Island, W Portugal

Pico, Ilha do see Pico

Picos 63 G 2 E Brazil

Picsi 60 B 3 W Peru

Picton 151 C 5 South Island, C New Zealand

Piedras Negras 51 E 2 var. Ciudad Porfirio Díaz. NE Mexico

Pielinen 84 E 4 var. Pielisjärvi. Lake, E Finland

Pielisjärvi see Pielinen

Pierre 45 E 3 state capital, South Dakota, N USA

Piešťany 99 C 6 Ger. Pistyan, Hung. Pöstyén. W Slovakia

Pietarsaari see Jakobstad

Pietermaritzburg 78 D 4 var. Maritzburg. E South Africa

Pietersburg 78 D 4 NE South Africa

Pigs, Bay of 54 B 2 Sp. Bahia de Cochinos. Bay, N Caribbean Sea

Pijijiapán 51 G 5 SE Mexico

Pikes Peak 44 C 5 mountain, Colorado, C USA

Pikine 74 B 3 var. Pikini Bougou. W Senegal

Pikini Bougou see Pikine

Pikinni see Bikini Atoll

Piła 98 C 3 Ger. Schneidemühl. NW Poland

Pilar 64 D 3 var. Villa del Pilar. S Paraguay

Pilar 63 G 3 W Brazil

Pilcomayo 64 C 2 river, S South America

Pilos see Pýlos

Pinang, Pulau 138 B 3 var. Penang, Pinang; prev. Prince of Wales Island. Island, W Malaysia

Pinar del Río 54 A 2 W Cuba

Píndos 104 A 4 var. Píndhos Óros, Eng. Pindus Mountains; prev. Pindhos. Mountain range, C Greece

Pindus Mountains see Píndos

Pine Bluff 42 B 2 Arkansas USA

Pine Creek 148 A 2 Northern Territory, N Australia

Pine Dock 37 G 5 Manitoba, S Canada

Pinega 110 C 3 river, NW Russian Federation

Pineiós 104 B 4 var. Piniós; anc. Peneius. River, C Greece

Pine Island Bay 154 A 3 bay, S Pacific Ocean

Pines, Lake O' the 49 H 2 reservoir, Texas, S USA

Pingdingshan 128 C 4 C China

Ping, Mae Nam 136 B 4 river, NW Thailand

Pingyang 128 D 4 E China

Pínnes, Ákra 104 C 4 headland, N Greece

Pinotepa Nacional 51 F 5 var. Santiago Pinotepa Nacional. SE Mexico

Pinsk 107 B 7 Pol. Pińsk. SW Belorussia

Pińsk see Pinsk

Pinta, Isla 60 A 5 var. Abingdon. Island, Galapagos Islands, E Pacific Ocean

Piombino 96 B 3 C Italy

Pionerskiy 106 A 4 Ger. Neukuhren. W Russian Federation

Piotrków Trybunalski 98 D 4 Ger. Petrikau, Rus. Petrokov. C Poland

Piraeus see Peiraiás

Pírgos see Pýrgos

Piripiri 63 G 2 E Brazil

Pirna 94 D 4 E Germany

Pirot 101 E 5 E Yugoslavia

Piryatin see Pyryatyn

Pisa 96 B 3 var. Pisae. C Italy

Pisae see Pisa

Pisaurum see Pesaro

Pisco 60 D 4 SW Peru

Písek 99 A 5 SW Czech Republic

Pishan 126 A 3 var. Guma. NW China

Pistoia 96 B 3 anc. Pistoria, Pistoriæ. C Italy

Pisz 98 D 3 Ger. Johannisburg. NE Poland

Pita 74 C 4 NW Guinea

Pitalito 58 B 4 S Colombia

Pitcairn Islands 143 H 4 UK dependent territory, S Pacific Ocean

Piteå 84 D 4 N Sweden

Piteşti 108 B 5 S Romania

Pitt Island see Makin

Pittsburg 45 F 5 Kansas, C USA

Pittsburgh 41 E 4 Pennsylvania, NE USA

Pittsfield 41 F 3 New York, NE USA

Pituffik 82 C 1 var. Uummannaq; prev. Dundas. NW Greenland

Piura 60 B 3 NW Peru

Pivdennyy Buh 109 E 3 Rus. Yuzhnyy Bug. River, S Ukraine

Placetas 54 B 2 C Cuba

Plainview 49 E 2 Texas, S USA

Planeta Rica 58 B 2 NW Colombia

Planken 94 E 1 C Liechtenstein

Plano 49 G 2 Texas, S USA

Plasencia 92 C 3 W Spain

Plata, Rio de la 64 D 4 estuary, SW Atlantic Ocean

Platinum 36 B 3 Alaska, NW USA

Platte River 45 E 4 river, Nebraska, C USA

Plattsburgh 41 F 2 Vermont, NE USA

Plauen 95 C 5 var. Plauen im Vogtland. E Germany

Plauen im Vogtland see Plauen

Plaviņas 106 D 4 Ger. Stockmannshof. S Latvia

Plây Cu 137 E 5 var. Pleiku. S Vietnam

Pleiku see Plây Cu

Plenty, Bay of 150 E 3 inlet, SW Pacific Ocean

Plérin 90 A 3 NW France

Pleseck see Plesetsk

Plesetsk 110 C 3 var. Pleseck. NW Russian Federation

Pleshchenitsy see Plyeshchanitsy

Pleszew 98 C 4 C Poland

Pleven 104 C 2 prev. Plevna. N Bulgaria

Plevna see Pleven

Pljevlja 100 C 4 prev. Plevlja, Plevlje. N Yugoslavia

Ploče 100 B 4 It. Plocce; prev. Kardeljevo. SE Croatia

Płock 98 D 3 var. Plozk. C Poland

Plöcken Pass 95 C 7 Ger. Plöckenpass, It. Passo di Monte Croce Carnico. Pass, SW Austria

Ploeşti see Ploieşti

Ploieşti 108 C 5 prev. Ploeşti. SE Romania

Plomári 105 D 5 prev. Plomárion. Lésvos, E Greece

Plomárion see Plomári

Plön 94 C 2 N Germany

Płońsk 98 D 3 C Poland

Plovdiv 104 C 3 prev. Eumolpias, anc. Evmolpia, Philippopolis, Lat. Trimontium. C Bulgaria

Plozk see Płock

Plungė 106 B 3 W Lithuania

Plyeshchanitsy 107 D 6 Rus. Pleshchenitsy. N Belorussia

Plymouth 89 C 7 SW England, UK

Plymouth 55 G 3 dependent territory capital, W Montserrat

Plzeň 99 A 5 Ger. Pilsen, Pol. Pilzno. W Czech Republic

Po 96 A 2 river, N Italy

Pobedy, Pik 132 H 2 var. Pobeda Peak, Chin. Tomur Feng. Mountain, China/Kyrgyzstan

Po, Bocche del see Po, Foci del

Pocatello 46 E 4 Idaho, NW USA

Pochinok 111 A 5 W Russian Federation

Pocking 95 D 6 SE Germany

Poděbrady 99 B 5 Ger. Podiebrad. C Czech Republic

Podgorica 101 C 5 prev. Titograd. SW Yugoslavia

Podiebrad see Poděbrady

Podil's'ka Vysochyna 108 D 3 Rus. Podol'skaya Vozvyshennost'. Mountain range, SW Ukraine

Podol'sk 111 B 5 W Russian Federation

Podol'skaya Vozvyshennost' see Podil's'ka Vysochyna

Podravska Slatina 100 C 2 Hung. Szlatina; prev. Slatina. NE Croatia

Podujevo 101 D 5 S Yugoslavia

Po, Foci del 96 C 2 var. Bocche del Po. River, Italy

Pogradec 101 D 6 var. Pogradeci. SE Albania

Pogradeci see Pogradec

Pohnpei 144 C 2 prev. Ponape Ascension Island. Island, E Micronesia

Pohnpei 144 C 2 island group, E Micronesia

Poinsett, Cape 154 D 4 headland, Antarctica

Point Au Fer Island 42 B 4 island, S USA

Point de Galle see Galle

Pointe-à-Pitre 55 G 3 C Guadeloupe

Pointe-Noire 77 A 6 S Congo

Point Lay 36 C 2 Alaska, NW USA

Poitiers 90 B 4 prev. Poictiers, anc. Limonum. W France

Poitou 90 B 4 cultural region, W France

Pokhara 135 F 3 C Nepal

Pok Liu Chau see Lamma Island

Pokrov's'ke 109 G 3 Rus. Pokrovskoye. E Ukraine

Pokrovskoye see Pokrovs'ke

Pola de Lena 92 C 1 N Spain

Poland 98 C 4 var. Polish Republic, Polska Rzeczpospolita Ludowa, Rzeczpospolita Polska, Pol. Polska; prev. The Polish People's Republic. Republic, C Europe

Official name: Republic of Poland **Date of formation:** 1945 **Capital:** Warsaw **Population:** 38.5 million **Total area:** 312,680 sq km (120,720 sq miles) **Languages:** Polish*, German **Religions:** Roman Catholic 95%, other Christian 5% **Ethnic mix:** Polish 98%, other 2% **Government:** Multiparty republic **Currency:** Zloty = 100 groszy

Polatsk 107 D 5 Rus. Polotsk. N Belorussia

Pol-e Khomrī 123 E 4 var. Pul-i-Khumri. NE Afghanistan

Polikraište see Polikrayshte

Polikrayshte 104 D 2 var. Polikraište. N Bulgaria

Pollença 93 G 3 var. Pollensa. E Spain

Pollensa see Pollença

Pologi see Polohy

Polohy 109 G 3 Rus. Pologi. SE Ukraine

Polonne 108 D 2 Rus. Polonnoye. NW Ukraine

Polonnoye see Polonne

Polotsk see Polatsk

Polsko Kosovo 104 D 2 N Bulgaria

Poltava 109 F 2 NE Ukraine

Põlva 106 E 3 *Ger.* Pölwe. SE Estonia
Pölwe *see* Põlva
Polyarnyy 110 C 2 *var.* Pol'arnyj, Poljarny. NW Russian Federation
Polýkastro 104 B 3 *prev.* Políkastron. N Greece
Polynesia 145 G 3 island group, SW Pacific Ocean
Pomeranian Bay 94 D 2 *Ger.* Pommersche Bucht, *Pol.* Zatoka Pomorska. Bay, S Baltic Sea
Pommern 94 D 2 cultural region, NE Germany
Pompano Beach 43 F 5 Florida, SE USA
Ponape Ascension Island *see* Pohnpei
Ponca City 49 G 1 Oklahoma, C USA
Ponce 55 F 3 S Puerto Rico
Pondicherry 132 D 2 *var.* Puduchcheri. SE India
Ponferrada 92 C 1 NW Spain
Poniatowa 98 E 4 E Poland
Pons Vetus *see* Pontevedra
Ponta Delgada 92 A 5 W Portugal
Ponta Grossa 63 E 4 S Brazil
Pontarlier 90 D 4 E France
Pontchartrain, Lake 42 C 3 lake, Louisiana USA
Ponteareas 92 B 2 NW Spain
Ponte da Barca 92 B 2 N Portugal
Pontevedra 92 B 1 *anc.* Pons Vetus. NW Spain
Pontiac 40 D 3 Michigan, N USA
Pontianak 138 C 4 Borneo, C Indonesia
Pontivy 90 A 3 NW France
Pontoise 90 C 3 *anc.* Briva Isarae, Cergy-Pontoise, Pontisarae. N France
Ponton 37 F 5 Manitoba, C Canada
Ponziane, Isole 97 C 5 island, C Italy
Poole 89 D 7 S England, UK
Poona *see* Pune
Poopó, Lago 61 F 4 *var.* Lago Pampa Aullagas. Lake, W Bolivia
Popayán 58 A 4 SW Colombia
Poperinge 87 A 6 W Belgium
Poplar Bluff 45 G 5 Missouri, C USA
Popocatépetl 51 E 4 volcano, S Mexico
Poprad 99 D 5 *Ger.* Popper, *Hung.* Poprád. River, Poland/Slovakia
Poprad 99 D 5 *Ger.* Deutschendorf, *Hung.* Poprád. NE Slovakia
Porbandar 134 B 4 W India
Pordenone 96 C 2 *anc.* Portenau. NE Italy
Poreč 100 A 2 *It.* Parenzo. NW Croatia
Pori 85 D 5 *Swe.* Björneborg. SW Finland
Porirua 151 D 5 North Island, C New Zealand
Porkhov 110 A 4 W Russian Federation
Porlamar 59 E 1 NE Venezuela
Póros 105 C 6 S Greece
Póros 105 A 5 Kefallinía, W Greece
Porsangen 84 D 2 fjord, NE Norway
Porsgrunn 85 B 6 S Norway
Portachuelo 61 G 4 C Bolivia
Portadown 89 B 5 *Ir.* Port An Dúnáin. SE Northern Ireland, UK
Portalegre 92 C 3 *anc.* Ammaia, Amoea. E Portugal

Port Alexander 36 D 4 Alaska, NW USA
Port Alfred 78 D 5 S South Africa
Port An Dúnáin *see* Portadown
Port Angeles 46 B 1 Washington, NW USA
Port Antonio 54 B 5 NE Jamaica
Port Augusta 149 B 6 South Australia, S Australia
Port-au-Prince 54 D 3 country capital, C Haiti
Port Blair 133 F 2 SE India
Port d'Envalira 91 B 8 W Andorra
Port Elizabeth 78 C 5 S South Africa
Portenau *see* Pordenone
Porterville 47 C 7 California, W USA
Port-Étienne *see* Nouâdhibou
Port Florence *see* Kisumu
Port-Francqui *see* Ilebo
Port-Gentil 77 A 6 W Gabon
Port Harcourt 75 G 5 S Nigeria
Port Hardy 36 D 5 Vancouver Island, SW Canada
Port Hedland 146 B 4 Western Australia, W Australia
Port Huron 40 D 3 Michigan, N USA
Portimão 92 B 5 *var.* Vila Nova de Portimão. S Portugal
Port Láirge *see* Waterford
Portland 49 G 5 Texas, S USA
Portland 149 B 7 Victoria, SE Australia
Portland 41 G 2 Maine, NE USA
Portland 46 B 3 Oregon, NW USA
Portland Bight 54 B 5 bay, N Caribbean Sea
Port Laoise 89 B 6 *var.* Portlaoise, *Ir.* Portlaoighise; *prev.* Maryborough. C Ireland
Port Lavaca 49 G 4 Texas, S USA
Port Lincoln 149 A 6 South Australia, S Australia
Port Louis 79 H 3 country capital, NW Mauritius
Port-Lyautey *see* Kénitra
Port Macquarie 149 E 6 New South Wales, SE Australia
Portmore 54 B 5 C Jamaica
Port Moresby 144 B 3 country capital, New Guinea, SW Papua New Guinea
Port Natal *see* Durban
Porto 92 B 2 *Eng.* Oporto; *anc.* Portus Cale. NW Portugal
Pôrto Alegre 63 E 5 *var.* Pôrto Alegre. State capital, S Brazil
Pôrto Alegre 76 E 2 S Sao Tome & Principe
Pôrto Alegre *see* Porto Alegre
Porto Alexandre *see* Tombua
Portobelo 53 G 4 *var.* Porto Bello, Puerto Bello. N Panama
Portoferraio 96 B 4 W Italy
Port-of-Spain 55 H 5 country capital, C Trinidad & Tobago
Portogruaro 96 C 2 NE Italy
Porto-Novo 75 F 5 country capital, S Benin
Porto Santo 70 A 2 *var.* Ilha do Porto Santo. Island, Madeira, Portugal
Porto Torres 97 A 5 W Italy
Porto Velho 62 D 2 *var.* Velho. State capital, W Brazil
Portoviejo 60 A 2 *var.* Puertoviejo. W Ecuador
Port Phillip Bay 149 C 7 bay, SW Tasman Sea

Port Pirie 149 B 6 South Australia, S Australia
Port Said 72 B 1 *Ar.* Bûr Sa'îd. N Egypt
Portsmouth 89 D 7 S England, UK
Portsmouth 40 D 4 Ohio, N USA
Portsmouth 41 G 3 New Hampshire, NE USA
Port Stanley *see* Stanley
Port Sudan 72 C 3 NE Sudan
Port Talbot 89 C 7 S Wales, UK

Portugal
92 B 3 Republic, W Europe

Official name: Republic of Portugal **Date of formation:** 1640 **Capital:** Lisbon **Population:** 9.9 million **Total area:** 92,390 sq km (35,670 sq miles) **Languages:** Portuguese* **Religions:** Roman Catholic 97%, Protestant 1%, other 2% **Ethnic mix:** Portuguese 98%, African 1%, other 1% **Government:** Multiparty republic **Currency:** Escudo = 100 centavos

Port-Vila 144 D 4 *var.* Vila. Country capital, Éfaté, C Vanuatu
Porvenir 65 B 8 S Chile
Porvenir 61 E 3 NW Bolivia
Porvoo 85 E 5 *Swe.* Borgå. S Finland
Posadas 64 D 3 NE Argentina
Posterholt 87 D 5 SE Netherlands
Postojna 95 D 8 *Ger.* Adelsberg, *It.* Postumia. SW Slovenia
Potamós 105 C 7 Andikithira, S Greece
Potentia *see* Potenza
Potenza 97 D 5 *anc.* Potentia. S Italy
P'ot'i 117 F 2 W Georgia
Potiskum 75 G 4 NE Nigeria
Po Toi Island 128 A 2 island, S Hong Kong
Potosí 61 F 4 S Bolivia
Potsdam 94 D 3 NE Germany
Potwar Plateau 134 C 2 plateau, NE Pakistan
Poûthîsăt 137 D 6 *prev.* Pursat. W Cambodia
Po Valley 96 B 2 *It.* Valle del Po. Valley, N Italy
Považská Bystrica 99 C 5 *Ger.* Waagbistritz, *Hung.* Vágbeszterce. NW Slovakia
Poverty Bay 150 E 4 bay, SW Pacific Ocean
Póvoa de Varzim 92 B 2 NW Portugal
Povorino 111 B 6 W Russian Federation
Povungnituk *see* Puvirnituq
Poway 47 C 8 California, W USA
Powder River 44 D 2 river, Montana, NW USA
Powell 44 C 2 Wyoming, C USA
Powell, Lake 44 B 5 lake, Utah, W USA
Požarevac 100 E 4 *Ger.* Passarowitz. E Yugoslavia
Poza Rica 51 F 4 *var.* Poza Rica de Hidalgo. E Mexico
Poza Rica de Hidalgo *see* Poza Rica
Požega 100 D 4 C Yugoslavia
Poznań 98 B 3 *Ger.* Posen, Posnania. W Poland
Pozoblanco 92 D 4 S Spain
Pozzallo 97 C 8 SW Italy
Prachatice 99 A 5 *Ger.* Prachatitz. SW Czech Republic
Prachatitz *see* Prachatice
Prague *see* Praha

Praha 99 B 5 *Eng.* Prague, *Ger.* Prag, *Pol.* Praga. Country capital, NW Czech Republic
Praia 74 A 3 country capital, S Cape Verde
Praslin 55 F 1 E Saint Lucia
Prato 96 B 3 C Italy
Pratt 45 E 5 Kansas, C USA
Prattville 42 D 2 Alabama, S USA
Pravia 92 C 1 N Spain
Preny *see* Prienai
Prenzlau 94 D 3 NE Germany
Prerau *see* Přerov
Přerov 99 C 5 *Ger.* Prerau. E Czech Republic
Prescott 48 B 2 Arizona USA
Preševo 101 D 5 S Yugoslavia
Presidente Epitácio 63 E 4 S Brazil
Presidente Prudente 57 D 5 S Brazil
Prešov 99 D 5 *var.* Preschau, *Ger.* Eperies, *Hung.* Eperjes. NE Slovakia
Prespa, Lake 101 D 7 *var.* Limni Prespa, Prespansko Jezero, *Alb.* Liqen i Prespës, *Gk.* Límni Megáli Préspa, *Mac.* Prespansko Ezero. Lake, SE Europe
Preston 89 C 5 NW England, UK
Prestwick 88 C 4 SW Scotland, UK
Pretoria 78 D 4 *var.* Epitoli, Tshwane. Country capital, NE South Africa
Preussisch Eylau *see* Bagrationovsk
Preussisch-Stargard *see* Starogard Gdański
Preußisch Holland *see* Pasłęk
Préveza 105 A 5 W Greece
Pribilof Islands 36 A 3 island group, Alaska, NW USA
Priboj 100 D 4 W Yugoslavia
Price 44 B 4 Utah, W USA
Prichard 42 C 3 Alabama, S USA
Pridneprovskaya Vozvyshennost' *see* Prydniprovs'ka Vysochyna
Priekulė 106 B 3 *Ger.* Prökuls. W Lithuania
Prienai 107 B 5 *Pol.* Preny. S Lithuania
Prieska 78 C 5 C South Africa
Prijedor 100 B 3 NW Bosnia & Herzegovina
Prijepolje 100 D 4 W Yugoslavia
Prilep 101 D 6 *Turk.* Perlepe. S Macedonia
Priluki *see* Pryluky
Primorsk 106 A 4 *Ger.* Fischhausen. W Russian Federation
Primorsko 104 E 2 *prev.* Keupriya. SE Bulgaria
Prince Albert 37 F 5 Saskatchewan, S Canada
Prince-Édouard, Île-du *see* Prince Edward Island
Prince Edward Island 39 F 4 *Fr.* Île-du Prince-Édouard. Province, SE Canada
Prince Edward Islands 69 E 8 island group, S South Africa
Prince George 37 E 5 British Columbia, SW Canada
Prince of Wales Island 37 F 2 island, NW Canada
Prince of Wales Island 148 B 1 island, Queensland, N Australia
Prince Patrick Island 37 E 2 island, NW Canada
Prince Rupert 36 D 4 British Columbia, SW Canada
Princess Charlotte Bay 148 C 2 bay, W Coral Sea
Princess Elizabeth Land 154 D 3 physical region, Antarctica

Príncipe 76 E 1 *var.* Príncipe Island,
Eng. Prince's Island. Island, N Sao
Tome & Principe
Prinzapolka 53 E 3 NE Nicaragua
Pripet 107 C 7 *Bel.* Prypyats', *Ukr.*
Prypyat'. River,
Belorussia/Ukraine
Pripet Marshes 107 B 7 wetland,
Belorussia/Ukraine
Prishtinë *see* Priština
Priština 101 D 5 *Alb.* Prishtinë. C
Yugoslavia
Privas 91 C 5 E France
Prizren 101 D 5 *Alb.* Prizreni. S
Yugoslavia
Prizreni *see* Prizren
Probolinggo 138 D 5 Jawa, C
Indonesia
Probstberg *see* Wyszków
Progreso 51 H 3 SE Mexico
Prökuls *see* Priekulė
Prome 136 B 4 *var.* Pyè. SW Burma
Promyshlennyy 110 E 3 *var.*
Promŝlennyj, Promyŝlenny. NW
Russian Federation
Prostĕjov 99 C 5 *Ger.* Prossnitz, *Pol.*
Prosciejów. SE Czech Republic
Provence 91 D 6 cultural region, SE
France
Providence 41 G 3 state capital,
Rhode Island, NE USA
Providence *see* Fort Providence
Providencia, Isla de 53 F 3 island,
Colombia
Provo 44 B 4 Utah, W USA
Provost 37 E 5 Alberta, SW Canada
Prudhoe Bay 36 D 2 Alaska, NW
USA
Pruszków 98 D 3 *Ger.* Kaltdorf. C
Poland
Prut 108 D 4 *Ger.* Pruth. River, E
Europe
Pruth *see* Prut
Prużana *see* Pruzhany
Pruzhany 107 B 6 *Pol.* Pruzana. SW
Belorussia
Prychornomors'ka Nyzovyna 109 E
4 *Eng.* Black Sea Lowland.
Physical region, S Ukraine
Prydniprovs'ka Vysochnya 109 G 3
Rus. Pridneprovskaya
Vozvyshennost'. Mountain range,
NW Ukraine
Prydz Bay 154 D 3 bay, S Indian
Ocean
Pryluky 109 E 2 *Rus.* Priluki. NE
Ukraine
Prymors'k 109 G 4 *Rus.* Primorsk;
prev. Primorskoye. SE Ukraine
Przemyśl 99 E 5 *Rus.* Peremyshl. SE
Poland
Przheval'sk *see* Karakol
Psará 105 D 5 island, E Greece
Pskov 110 A 4 *Ger.* Pleskau, *Latv.*
Pleskava. W Russian Federation
Pskov, Lake 106 E 3 *Est.* Pihkva
Järv, *Ger.* Pleskauer See, *Rus.*
Pskovskoye Ozero. Lake,
Estonia/Russian Federation
Ptich' *see* Ptsich
Ptsich 107 C 7 *Rus.* Ptich'. River, SE
Belorussia
Ptsich 107 C 7 *Rus.* Ptich'. SE
Belorussia
Ptuj 95 E 7 *Ger.* Pettau; *anc.*
Poetovio. NE Slovenia
Pucallpa 60 C 3 C Peru
Puck 98 C 2 N Poland
Pudasjärvi 84 E 4 C Finland
Puduchcheri *see* Pondicherry
Puebla 51 F 4 *var.* Puebla de
Zaragoza. S Mexico

Puebla de Zaragoza *see* Puebla
Pueblo 44 D 5 Colorado, C USA
Puerto Acosta 61 E 4 W Bolivia
Puerto Aisén 65 B 6 S Chile
Puerto Arturo 61 G 3 N Bolivia
Puerto Ayacucho 58 D 3 SW
Venezuela
Puerto Bahía Negra 64 D 1 N
Paraguay
Puerto Baquerizo Moreno 60 B 5
var. Baquerizo Moreno. Galapagos
Islands, E Pacific Ocean
Puerto Barrios 52 C 2 E Guatemala
Puerto Berrío 58 B 2 C Colombia
Puerto Cabello 58 D 1 N Venezuela
Puerto Cabezas 53 E 2 *var.* Bilwi.
NE Nicaragua
Puerto Carreño 58 D 3 NE
Colombia
Puerto Casado 64 D 2 C Paraguay
Puerto Cortés 52 C 2 NW
Honduras
Puerto Cumarebo 58 C 1 N
Venezuela
Puerto Deseado 65 C 7 SE
Argentina
Puerto Escondido 51 F 5 W Mexico
Puerto Francisco de Orellana 60 B 1
var. Coca. N Ecuador
Puerto Inírida 58 D 3 *var.* Obando.
E Colombia
Puerto La Cruz 59 E 1 NE
Venezuela
Puerto Lempira 53 E 2 E Honduras
Puerto Limón *see* Limón
Puertollano 92 D 4 SW Spain
Puerto López 58 C 1 N Colombia
Puerto Maldonado 61 E 3 E Peru
Puerto Montt 65 B 5 C Chile
Puerto Natales 65 B 7 S Chile
Puerto Nuevo 58 C 3 N Colombia
Puerto Obaldía 53 H 5 NE Panama
Puerto Plata 55 E 3 *var.* San Felipe
de Puerto Plata. N Dominican
Republic
Puerto Portillo 60 D 3 E Peru
Puerto Princesa 139 E 2 *off.* Puerto
Princesa City. Palawan, W
Philippines
Puerto Princesa City *see* Puerto
Princesa
Puerto Príncipe *see* Camagüey
Puerto Rico 55 F 3 *off.*
Commonwealth of Puerto Rico,
prev. Porto Rico. US
commonwealth territory, N
Caribbean Sea
Puerto Rico Trench 66 B 4 trench,
W Atlantic Ocean
Puerto San José *see* San José
Puerto San Julián 65 B 7 *var.* San
Julián. SE Argentina
Puerto Suárez 61 H 4 E Bolivia
Puerto Supe 60 C 3 W Peru
Puerto Vallarta 50 D 4 SW Mexico
Puerto Varas 65 B 5 C Chile
Puerto Viejo 53 E 4 NE Costa Rica
Puertoviejo *see* Portoviejo
Puerto Williams 65 C 8 S Chile
Puget Sound 46 B 1 inlet, E Pacific
Ocean
Pukaki, Lake 151 B 6 lake, South
Island, SW New Zealand
Pukekohe 150 D 3 North Island, N
New Zealand
Pukhavichy 107 D 6 *Rus.*
Pukhovichi. C Belorussia
Pukhovichi *see* Pukhavichy
Pula 100 A 3 *It.* Pola; *prev.* Pulj. NW
Croatia
Puławy 98 E 4 *Ger.* Neu Amerika. E
Poland

Pul-i-Khumri *see* Pol-e Khomrī
Pullman 46 C 2 Washington, NW
USA
Pułtusk 98 D 3 C Poland
Puná, Isla 60 A 2 island, SW
Ecuador
Pune 134 C 5 *prev.* Poona. W India
Punjab 134 C 2 *prev.* Western
Punjab, West Punjab. Province, E
Pakistan
Puno 61 E 4 SE Peru
Punta Alta 65 C 5 E Argentina
Punta Arenas 65 B 8 *prev.*
Magallanes . S Chile
Punta Gorda 53 E 4 SE Nicaragua
Punta Gorda 52 C 2 SE Belize
Puntarenas 52 D 4 W Costa Rica
Punto Fijo 58 C 1 N Venezuela
Pupuya, Nevado 61 E 4 mountain,
W Bolivia
Puri 135 F 5 *var.* Jagannath. E India
Purmerend 86 C 3 C Netherlands
Pursat *see* Poŭthĭsăt
Purus 62 C 2 *var.* Río Purús. River,
Brazil/Peru
Purús, Río *see* Purus
Pusan 128 E 4 *off.* Pusan-
kwangyŏksi, *var.* Busan, *Jap.*
Fusan. SE South Korea
Püspökladány 99 D 6 E Hungary
Putorana Mountains *see* Putorana,
Plato
Putorana, Plato 115 E 3 *var.*
Putorana Mountains. Mountain
range, N Russian Federation
Puttalam 132 C 3 W Sri Lanka
Puttgarden 94 C 2 N Germany
Putumayo 58 B 5 *var.* Içá. River, N
South America
Putumayo, Río *see* Içá
Puurmani 106 D 2 *Ger.* Talkhof. E
Estonia
Puvirnituq 38 D 1 *prev.*
Povungnituk. Québec, NE
Canada
Puyallup 46 B 2 Washington, NW
USA
Pyatigorsk 111 B 7 SW Russian
Federation
Pyatikhatki *see* P''yatykhatky
P''yatykhatky 109 F 3 *Rus.*
Pyatikhatki. C Ukraine
Pyè *see* Prome
Pyetrykaw 107 C 7 *Rus.* Petrikov.
SE Belorussia
Pyinmana 136 B 4 C Burma
Pýlos 105 B 6 S Greece
P'yŏngyang 128 D 4 *Eng.*
Pyongyang. Country capital, SW
North Korea
Pyramiden 83 G 2 W Svalbard
Pyramid Lake 47 C 5 lake, Nevada,
W USA
Pyrenees 93 F 1 *Fr.* Pyrénées, *Sp.*
Pirineos; *anc.* Pyrenaei Montes.
Mountain range, SW Europe
Pýrgos 105 B 6 *var.* Pirgos. S Greece
Pyritz *see* Pyrzyce
Pyryatyn 109 F 2 *Rus.* Piryatin. N
Ukraine
Pyrzyce 98 B 3 *Ger.* Pyritz. NW
Poland
Pyu 136 B 4 S Burma
Pyuntaza 136 B 4 S Burma

Q

Qāʾ al Jafr 119 C 7 lake, S Jordan
Qaanaaq 82 D 1 *var.* Qânâq, *Dan.*
Thule. N Greenland
Qabatiya 119 E 6 N West Bank

Qābis *see* Gabès
Qābis, Khalīj *see* Gabès, Golfe de
Qafṣah *see* Gafsa
Qaidam Pendi 126 C 4 basin, C
China
Qal'aikhum 123 F 3 *Rus.*
Kalaikhum. S Tajikistan
Qalāt *see* Kalāt
Qal 'at Bishah 121 B 5 SW Saudi
Arabia
Qalqīliya 119 D 7 *var.* Qalqiliya. W
West Bank
Qamdo 126 D 5 S China
Qandahār *see* Kandahār
Qanıx *see* Alazani
Qaqortoq 82 C 5 *Dan.* Julianehåb.
SW Greenland
Qaraghandy *see* Karaganda
Qarataū *see* Karatau
Qarokŭl 123 F 3 *Rus.* Karakul'. E
Tajikistan
Qars *see* Kars
Qarshi 123 E 3 *Rus.* Karshi; *prev.*
Bek-Budi. S Uzbekistan
Qasigiannguit 82 C 3 *var.*
Qasigianguit, *Dan.* Christianshåb.
W Greenland
Qassabah 119 B 5 *var.* Katana. SW
Syria
Qatar
120 D 4 *Ar.* Dawlat Qaṭar.
Monarchy, Qatar
Official name: State of Qatar **Date
of formation:** 1971 **Capital:** Doha
Population: 500,000 **Total area:**
11,000 sq km (4,247 sq miles)
Languages: Arabic*, Farsi (Persian),
Urdu, Hindi, English
Religions: Sunni Muslim 86%,
Hindu 10%, Christian 4% **Ethnic
mix:** Arab 40%, South Asian 35%,
Persian 12%, other 13%
Government: Absolute monarchy
Currency: Riyal = 100 dirhams

Qattara Depression *see* Qaṭṭâra,
Monkhafad el
Qaṭṭâra, Monkhafad el 72 B 1 *var.*
Munkhafaç al Qaddârah, *Eng.*
Qattara Depression. Desert, NW
Egypt
Qazimämmäd 117 H 3 *Rus.* Kazi
Maġomed SE Azerbaijan
Qazris *see* Cáceres
Qazvīn 120 C 2 *var.* Kazvin. NW
Iran
Qena 72 B 2 *var.* Qinā; *anc.* Caene,
Caenepolis. E Egypt
Qeqertarsuaq 82 C 3 *var.*
Qeqertarssuaq, *Dan.* Godhavn. W
Greenland
Qeqertarsuaq 82 C 3 island, W
Greenland
Qeqertarsuatsiaat 82 B 4 *Dan.*
Fiskenæsset. S Greenland
Qeshm 120 D 4 *var.* Jazīreh-ye
Qeshm, Qeshm Island. Island, S
Iran
Qeziʿot 119 A 7 S Israel
Qilian Shan 128 A 3 *var.* Kilien
Mountains. Mountain range, N
China
Qimantag Shan 126 C 4 mountain
range, C China
Qimusseriarsuaq 82 C 2 *Dan.*
Melville Bugt, *Eng.* Melville Bay.
Bay, E Baffin Bay
Qingdao 128 D 4 *var.* Ching-Tao,
Ch'ing-tao, Tsingtao, Tsintao, *Ger.*
Tsingtau. E China
Qinghai 126 D 4 *var.* Chinghai,
Koko Nor, Qing, Tsinghai.
Province, C China

225

Qinghai Hu 126 D 4 *var.* Ch'ing Hai, Tsing Hai, *Mong.* Koko Nor. Lake, C China
Qinghai Nanshan 126 D 4 mountain range, N China
Qinhuangdao 128 D 3 NE China
Qinzhou 129 B 6 SE China
Qiong *see* Hainan
Qiqihar 125 E 1 *var.* Ch'i-ch'i-ha-erh,Tsitsihar; *prev.* Lungkiang. NE China
Qira 126 B 4 NW China
Qita Ghazzah *see* Gaza Strip
Qitai 126 C 3 NW China
Qitaihe 128 E 2 NE China
Qīzān *see* Jīzān
Qizilrabot 123 G 3 *Rus.* Kyzylrabot. SE Tajikistan
Qolleh-ye Damāvand 120 D 3 mountain, N Iran
Qom 120 C 3 *var.* Kum, Qum. N Iran
Qondūz, Daryā-ye 123 E 4 river, NE Afghanistan
Qornet es Saouda 118 B 4 mountain, NE Lebanon
Qorveh 120 C 3 *var.* Qerveh, Qurveh. W Iran
Quang Ngai 137 E 5 *var.* Quangngai, Quang Nghia. E Vietnam
Quanzhou 129 C 6 S China
Quanzhou 129 D 6 *var.* Ch'uanchou, Tsinkiang; *prev.* Chinchiang. SE China
Quarles, Pegunungan 139 E 4 mountain range, Celebes, W Indonesia
Quartu Sant' Elena 97 A 6 W Italy
Quba 117 H 2 *Rus.* Kuba. N Azerbaijan
Qubba *see* Ba'qūbah
Queanbeyan 149 D 7 New South Wales, SE Australia
Quebec *see* Québec
Québec 38 D 3 *var.* Quebec. Province, Québec, SE Canada
Queen Charlotte 36 C 5 Queen Charlotte Islands, SW Canada
Queen Charlotte Islands 36 D 5 *Fr.* Îles de la Reine-Charlotte. Island group, SW Canada
Queen Charlotte Sound 36 D 5 bay, NE Pacific Ocean
Queen Elizabeth Islands 37 F 2 *Fr.* Îles de la Reine-Élisabeth. Island group, N Canada
Queen Maud Land 154 C 2 *var.* Dronning Maud Land. Physical region, Antarctica
Queensland 148 B 4 state, N Australia
Queenstown 151 B 7 South Island, SW New Zealand
Queenstown 149 B 8 Tasmania, SE Australia
Queenstown 78 D 5 S South Africa
Queenstown 138 A 1 S Singapore
Quelimane 79 E 3 *var.* Kilimane, Kilmain, Quilimane. NE Mozambique
Quepos 53 E 5 S Costa Rica
Que Que *see* Kwekwe
Querétaro 51 E 4 C Mexico
Quesada 53 E 4 *var.* Ciudad Quesada, San Carlos. N Costa Rica
Quetta 134 B 2 province capital, SW Pakistan
Quetzaltenango *see* Quezaltenango
Quezaltenango 52 A 2 *var.* Quetzaltenango. W Guatemala

Quezon 139 F 2 *off.* Quezon City. C Philippines
Quezon City *see* Quezon
Quibdó 58 B 3 W Colombia
Quilon 132 C 3 *var.* Kolam, Kollam. SW India
Quimper 90 A 3 *anc.* Quimper Corentin. NW France
Quimper Corentin *see* Quimper
Quimperlé 90 A 3 NW France
Quincy 40 A 4 Illinois, N USA
Quirós Fracture Zone 153 F 4 fracture zone, E Pacific Ocean
Quissico 79 E 4 S Mozambique
Quito 60 B 1 country capital, N Ecuador
Qŭqon 123 F 2 *var.* Khokand, *Rus.* Kokand. E Uzbekistan
Qŭrghonteppa 123 E 3 *Rus.* Kurgan-Tyube. SW Tajikistan
Qurlurtuuq *see* Coppermine
Qūş 72 B 2 *anc.* Apollinopolis Parva. E Egypt
Quy Nhon 137 E 5 *var.* Qui Nhon, Quinhon. SE Vietnam

R

Raab *see* Rába
Raahe 84 D 4 *Swe.* Brahestad. W Finland
Raalte 86 D 3 E Netherlands
Raamsdonksveer 86 C 4 S Netherlands
Raasiku 106 D 2 *Ger.* Rasik. NW Estonia
Raas Xaafuun 72 E 4 *var.* Ras Hafun. Headland, NE Somalia
Rabat 70 C 2 *var.* al Dar al Baida. Country capital, NW Morocco
Rabat *see* Victoria
Rabinal 52 B 2 C Guatemala
Rabka 99 D 5 S Poland
Rabyānah, Ramlat 71 G 3 *var.* Rebiana Sand Sea, Şaḥrā' Rabyānah. Desert, SE Libya
Race, Cape 39 H 4 headland, Newfoundland and Labrador, E Canada
Rach Gia 137 D 6 SW Vietnam
Rach Gia, Vinh 137 D 6 bay, South China Sea/Pacific Ocean
Racine 40 B 3 Wisconsin, N USA
Rădăuţi 108 C 3 *Ger.* Radautz, *Hung.* Rádóc. N Romania
Radom 98 D 4 C Poland
Radomsko 98 C 4 *Rus.* Novoradomsk. C Poland
Radomyshl' 108 D 2 N Ukraine
Radoviš 101 E 6 *prev.* Radovište. E Macedonia
Radovište *see* Radoviš
Radviliškis 106 C 4 N Lithuania
Radzyń Podlaski 98 E 4 E Poland
Rae-Edzo 37 E 4 Northwest Territories, NW Canada
Raeside, Lake 147 C 5 lake, C Australia
Raetihi 150 D 4 North Island, C New Zealand
Rafaela 64 C 3 E Argentina
Rafah 119 A 7 S Israel
Rafḩā' 120 B 4 N Saudi Arabia
Ragged Island Range 54 C 2 island group, S Bahamas
Ragnit *see* Neman
Ragusa 97 C 7 SW Italy
Ragusa *see* Dubrovnik
Rahachow 107 D 7 *Rus.* Rogachëv. SE Belorussia
Rahaeng *see* Tak

Rahīmyār Khān 134 C 3 SE Pakistan
Rahovec *see* Orahovac
Raiatea 145 G 4 island, W French Polynesia
Rāichūr 132 C 1 C India
Rainy Lake 38 B 4 lake, Ontario, S Canada
Raipur 135 E 4 C India
Rājahmundry 135 E 5 E India
Rajang *see* Rajang, Batang
Rajang, Batang 138 D 3 *var.* Rajang. River, Borneo, E Malaysia
Rājapālaiyam 132 C 3 SE India
Rājasthān 134 C 3 state, NW India
Rājkot 134 C 4 W India
Rāj Nāndgaon 135 E 4 C India
Rājshāhi 135 G 4 *prev.* Rampur Boalia. W Bangladesh
Rakahanga 145 F 3 island, N Cook Islands
Rakke 106 E 2 NE Estonia
Rakvere 106 E 2 *Ger.* Wesenberg. N Estonia
Raleigh 43 F 1 state capital, North Carolina, SE USA
Raleigh Bay 43 G 1 bay, NW Atlantic Ocean
Ralik Chain 144 D 1 island group, W Marshall Islands
Ram 119 B 8 SW Jordan
Ramallah 119 E 7 C West Bank
Ramat Gan 119 A 6 C Israel
Râmnicu Sărat 108 C 4 *prev.* Râmnicul-Sărat, Rîmnicu-Sărat. E Romania
Râmnicu Vîlcea 108 B 4 *prev.* Rîmnicu Vîlcea. C Romania
Ramotswa 78 C 4 SE Botswana
Rampur Boalia *see* Rājshāhi
Ramree Island 136 A 4 island, W Burma
Ramtha *see* Ar Ramthā
Rancagua 64 B 4 C Chile
Rānchi 135 F 4 N India
Randers 85 B 7 C Denmark
Rangiora 151 C 6 South Island, C New Zealand
Rangoon *see* Yangon
Rangpur 135 G 3 N Bangladesh
Rankin Inlet 37 G 3 Northwest Territories, C Canada
Rankovićevo *see* Kraljevo
Ranong 137 B 6 SW Thailand
Rantoul 40 B 4 Illinois, N USA
Rapid City 44 D 3 South Dakota, N USA
Räpina 106 E 3 *Ger.* Rappin. SE Estonia
Rapla 106 D 2 *Ger.* Rappel. NW Estonia
Rappel *see* Rapla
Rappin *see* Räpina
Rarotonga 145 F 5 island, S Cook Islands
Ras al'Ayn *see* Ra's al 'Ayn
Ra's al 'Ayn 118 D 1 *var.* Ras al'Ain. N Syria
Ra's an Naqb 119 B 8 S Jordan
Raseiniai 106 B 4 C Lithuania
Ras Hafun *see* Raas Xaafuun
Rasht 120 C 2 *var.* Resht. NW Iran
Rasik *see* Raasiku
Râşnov 108 C 4 *Hung.* Barcarozsnyó; *prev.* Rîşnov, *Hung.* Rozsnyó. C Romania
Rason Lake 147 C 5 lake, C Australia
Ratak Chain 144 D 1 island group, E Marshall Islands
Ratan 85 C 5 C Sweden

Rat Buri *see* Ratchaburi
Ratchaburi 137 C 5 *var.* Rat Buri. C Thailand
Ratlām 134 D 4 *prev.* Rutlam. C India
Ratnapura 132 D 4 S Sri Lanka
Raton 48 D 1 New Mexico, SW USA
Rättvik 85 C 5 C Sweden
Raudhatain *see* Ar Rawḑatayn
Raufarhöfn 83 E 4 NE Iceland
Raukawa *see* Cook Strait
Rauma 85 D 5 *Swe.* Raumo. SW Finland
Raumo *see* Rauma
Raurkela 135 F 4 *prev.* Rourkela. E India
Ravenna 96 C 3 N Italy
Rāvi 134 C 2 river, India/Pakistan
Rāwalpindi 134 C 1 NE Pakistan
Rawa Mazowiecka 98 D 4 C Poland
Rawicz 98 C 4 *Ger.* Rawitsch. W Poland
Rawitsch *see* Rawicz
Rawlins 44 C 3 Wyoming, C USA
Rawson 65 C 6 SE Argentina
Rayak 118 B 4 *var.* Rayaq, Riyāq. E Lebanon
Rayong 137 C 6 C Thailand
Razāzah, Buḩayrat ar 120 B 3 *var.* Baḩr al Milḩ. Lake, C Iraq
Razdolnoye *see* Rozdol'ne
Razelm, Lacul *see* Razim, Lacul
Razgrad 104 D 2 NE Bulgaria
Razim, Lacul 108 D 5 *prev.* Lacul Razelm. Lagoon, W Black Sea
Răznas Ezers 106 D 4 lake, SE Latvia
Reading 89 D 7 S England, UK
Reading 41 F 4 Pennysylvania, NE USA
Realicó 64 C 4 C Argentina
Reăng Kesei 137 D 5 W Cambodia
Rebecca, Lake 147 C 5 lake, Western Australia, C Australia
Rebun-tō 130 C 1 island, NE Japan
Recherche, Archipelago of the 147 C 7 island group, SW Australia
Rechitsa *see* Rechytsa
Rechytsa 107 D 7 *Rus.* Rechitsa. SW Belorussia
Recife 63 G 2 *prev.* Pernambuco. State capital, E Brazil
Recklinghausen 94 A 4 W Germany
Recogne 87 D 7 SE Belgium
Reconquista 64 D 3 NE Argentina
Red Bluff Lake 49 E 3 lake, SW USA
Red Deer 37 E 5 Alberta, SW Canada
Redding 47 B 5 California, W USA
Redon 90 B 4 NW France
Red River 136 C 2 *var.* Yijan Chiang. River, China/Vietnam
Red River 35 C 6 river, S USA
Red River 45 E 1 river, Canada/USA
Red Sea 140 A 3 *var.* Sinus Arabius. Sea, NW Indian Ocean
Red Sea Hills 72 C 3 hill range, NE Sudan
Red Wing 45 G 2 Minnesota, N USA
Reedley 47 C 6 California, W USA
Reefton 151 C 5 South Island, C New Zealand
Reese River 47 C 5 river, Nevada, W USA
Refahiye 117 E 3 C Turkey

Regensburg 95 C 6 *Eng.* Ratisbon, *Fr.* Ratisbonne; *hist.* Ratisbona, *anc.* Castra Regina, Reginum. SE Germany

Regenstauf 95 C 6 SE Germany

Reggane 70 D 3 C Algeria

Reggio di Calabria 97 D 7 *var.* Reggio Calabria, *Gk.* Rhegion; *anc.* Regium, Rhegium. SW Italy

Reggio nell' Emilia 96 B 2 *var.* Reggio Emilia, *abbrev.* Reggio; *anc.* Regium Lepidum. N Italy

Reghin 108 C 4 *Ger.* Sächsisch-Reen, *Hung.* Szászrégen; *prev.* Reghinul Săsesc, *Ger.* Sächsisch-Regen. C Romania

Regina 37 F 5 province capital, Saskatchewan, S Canada

Registan *see* Rīgestān

Rehoboth 78 B 4 C Namibia

Reichenau *see* Bogatynia

Reichenberg *see* Liberec

Reid 147 D 6 Western Australia, S Australia

Reikjavik *see* Reykjavík

Ré, Île de 90 A 4 island, W France

Reims 90 D 3 *Eng.* Rheims; *anc.* Durocortorum, Remi. N France

Reindeer Lake 34 C 4 lake, C Canada

Reine-Charlotte, Îles de la *see* Queen Charlotte Islands

Reine-Élisabeth, Îles de la *see* Queen Elizabeth Islands

Reinosa 92 D 1 N Spain

Reliance 37 F 4 Northwest Territories, C Canada

Rendina *see* Rentina

Rendsburg 94 B 2 N Germany

Rengat 138 B 4 Sumatera, W Indonesia

Reni 108 D 4 SW Ukraine

Rennell 144 C 4 *var.* Mu Nggava. Island, S Solomon Islands

Rennes 90 B 3 *Bret.* Roazon; *anc.* Condate. NW France

Reno 47 C 5 Nevada, W USA

Renqiu 128 C 4 NE China

Rentina 105 B 5 *var.* Rendina. C Greece

Repulse Bay 37 G 3 Northwest Territories, NE Canada

Resht *see* Rasht

Resistencia 64 D 3 NE Argentina

Reşiţa 108 A 4 *Ger.* Reschitza, *Hung.* Resicabánya. W Romania

Resolute 37 F 2 Cornwallis Island, N Canada

Resolution Island 151 A 7 island, South Island, SW New Zealand

Resolution Island 39 E 1 island, Northwest Territories, NE Canada

Réunion 79 H 4 *off.* La Réunion. French overseas department, E Africa

Reus 93 F 2 E Spain

Reutlingen 95 B 6 S Germany

Reuver 87 D 5 SE Netherlands

Revillagigedo Islands *see* Revillagigedo, Islas

Revillagigedo, Islas 50 B 5 *Eng.* Revillagigedo Islands. Island group, SW Mexico

Rexburg 44 E 3 Idaho, NW USA

Reyes 61 F 3 NW Bolivia

Rey, Isla del 53 G 5 island, SE Panama

Reykjanes Basin 66 C 2 undersea basin, N Atlantic Ocean

Reykjavík 83 E 3 *var.* Reikjavik. Country capital, W Iceland

Reynosa 51 E 2 C Mexico

Reza, Gora 122 C 3 *var.* Gora Riza. Mountain, SW Turkmenistan

Rezé 90 B 4 NW France

Rēzekne 106 D 4 *Ger.* Rositten; *prev. Rus.* Rezhitsa. SE Latvia

Rezovo 104 E 3 *Turk.* Rezve. SE Bulgaria

Rezve *see* Rezovo

Rhätikon 95 B 7 mountain range, C Europe

Rheine 94 A 4 *var.* Rheine in Westfalen. NW Germany

Rheine in Westfalen *see* Rheine

Rheinisches Schiefergebirge 95 A 5 *var.* Rhine State Uplands, *Eng.* Rhenish Slate Mountains. Mountain range, W Germany

Rhine 80 D 4 *Dut.* Rijn, *Fr.* Rhin, *Ger.* Rhein. River, W Europe

Rhinelander 40 B 2 Wisconsin, N USA

Rho 96 B 2 N Italy

Rhode Island 41 G 3 *off.* State of Rhode Island and Providence Plantations; *nicknames* Little Rhody, Ocean State. State, NE USA

Rhodes *see* Ródos

Rhodope Mountains 104 C 3 *var.* Rodhópi Óri, *Bul.* Rhodope Planina, Rodopi, *Gk.* Orosirá Rodhópis, *Turk.* Dospad Dagh. Mountain range, Bulgaria/Greece

Rhondda 89 C 7 S Wales, UK

Rhône 80 C 4 river, France/Switzerland

Rhum 88 B 3 *var.* Rum. Island, W Scotland, UK

Ribble 89 D 5 river, NW England, UK

Ribeira 92 B 1 NW Spain

Ribeirão Preto 63 F 4 S Brazil

Riberalta 61 E 2 N Bolivia

Rîbniţa 108 D 3 *var.* Rabniţa, *Rus.* Rybnitsa. NE Moldavia

Richard Toll 74 B 3 N Senegal

Richfield 44 B 4 Utah, W USA

Richland 46 C 2 Washington, NW USA

Richmond 151 C 5 North Island, C New Zealand

Richmond 41 E 5 state capital, Virginia, NE USA

Richmond 40 C 5 Kentucky, C USA

Richmond Range 151 C 5 mountain range, North Island, C New Zealand

Ricomagus *see* Riom

Ridgecrest 47 C 7 California, W USA

Ried *see* Ried im Innkreis

Ried im Innkreis 95 D 6 *var.* Ried. NW Austria

Riemst 87 D 6 NE Belgium

Riesa 94 D 4 E Germany

Rift Valley *see* Great Rift Valley

Riga *see* Rīga

Rīga 106 C 3 *var.* Rīga, *Eng.* Riga. Country capital, C Latvia

Riga, Gulf of 106 C 3 *Est.* Liivi Laht, *Ger.* Rigaer Bucht, *Latv.* Rīgas Jūras Līcis, *Rus.* Rizhskiy Zaliv; *prev.* Riia Laht. Gulf, E Baltic Sea

Rīgān 120 E 4 SE Iran

Rīgestān 122 D 5 *var.* Registan. Physical region, S Afghanistan

Riihimäki 85 D 5 S Finland

Rijeka 100 A 2 *Ger.* Sankt Veit am Flaum, *It.* Fiume, *Slvn.* Reka; *anc.* Tarsatica. NW Croatia

Rijssen 86 E 3 E Netherlands

Rimah, Wādī ar 120 B 4 *var.* Wādí ar Rummah. Dry watercourse, C Saudi Arabia

Rimini 96 C 3 *anc.* Ariminum. N Italy

Rîmnicu Vîlcea *see* Râmnicu Vâlcea

Rimouski 39 E 4 Québec, SE Canada

Rincón del Bonete, Lago Artificial de *see* Río Negro, Embalse del

Ringebu 85 B 5 S Norway

Ringen *see* Rõngu

Ringkøbing Fjord 85 A 7 fjord, E North Sea

Ringsaker 85 B 5 S Norway

Ringvassøy 84 C 2 island, N Norway

Rio *see* Rio de Janeiro

Riobamba 60 B 1 C Ecuador

Río Bravo 51 E 2 C Mexico

Rio Cuarto 64 C 4 C Argentina

Rio de Janeiro 63 F 4 *var.* Rio. State capital, Brazil

Río Gallegos 65 B 7 *var.* Gallegos, Puerto Gallegos. S Argentina

Rio Grande 63 E 5 *var.* São Pedro do Rio Grande do Sul. S Brazil

Rio Grande do Norte 63 G 2 *off.* Estado do Rio Grande do Norte. State, E Brazil

Rio Grande do Norte, Estado do *see* Rio Grande do Norte

Rio Grande do Sul 63 E 5 *off.* Estado do Rio Grande do Sul. State, S Brazil

Rio Grande do Sul, Estado do *see* Rio Grande do Sul

Rio Grande Plateau *see* Rio Grande Rise

Rio Grande Rise 57 E 5 *var.* Rio Grande Plateau. Undersea plateau, SW Atlantic Ocean

Riohacha 58 C 1 N Colombia

Riom 91 C 5 *anc.* Ricomagus. C France

Río Negro, Embalse del 64 D 4 *var.* Lago Artificial de Rincón del Bonete. Reservoir, C Uruguay

Rio Rancho Estates 48 D 2 New Mexico, SW USA

Río Santa Cruz 65 B 7 S Argentina

Ríoverde *see* Río Verde

Río Verde 51 E 4 *var.* Rioverde. C Mexico

Ripoll 93 G 2 NE Spain

Rishiri-tō 130 C 2 *var.* Risiri Tô. Island, Japan

Risiri Tô *see* Rishiri-tō

Risti 106 D 2 *Ger.* Kreuz. W Estonia

Rivas 52 D 3 SW Nicaragua

Rivera 64 D 3 N Uruguay

River Falls 40 A 2 Wisconsin, N USA

Riverside 47 C 8 California, W USA

Riverton 151 A 7 South Island, SW New Zealand

Riverton 44 C 3 Wyoming, C USA

Riviera Beach 43 F 4 Florida, SE USA

Rivière-du-Loup 39 E 4 Québec, SE Canada

Rivne 108 C 1 *Pol.* Równe, *Rus.* Rovno. NW Ukraine

Rivoli 96 A 2 NW Italy

Rixheim 90 E 4 E France

Riyadh *see* Ar Riyāḍ

Riza, Gora *see* Reza, Gora

Rize 117 E 2 NE Turkey

Rizhao 128 D 4 E China

Rkîz, Lac 74 B 3 lake, SW Mauritania

Road Town 55 F 3 dependent territory capital, C British Virgin Islands

Roanne 91 D 5 *anc.* Rodunma. E France

Roanoke 41 E 5 Virginia, NE USA

Roanoke Rapids 43 F 1 North Carolina, SE USA

Roanoke River 43 F 1 river, E USA

Roatán 52 C 2 *var.* Coxen Hole, Coxin Hole. N Honduras

Robinson Ranges 147 B 5 mountain range, Western Australia, W Australia

Robson, Mount 37 E 5 mountain, Alberta, SW Canada

Robstown 49 G 5 Texas, S USA

Roca Partida, Isla 50 B 5 island, W Mexico

Rocas, Atol das 63 H 2 island, E Brazil

Rochefort 91 B 5 *var.* Rochefort sur Mer. W France

Rochefort 87 C 7 SE Belgium

Rochefort sur Mer *see* Rochefort

Rochester 41 E 3 New York, NE USA

Rochester 41 G 2 New Hampshire, NE USA

Rochester 45 G 3 Minnesota, N USA

Rockall Bank 66 C 2 undersea bank, N Atlantic Ocean

Rockford 40 B 3 Illinois, N USA

Rockhampton 148 D 4 Queensland, E Australia

Rock Hill 43 E 1 South Carolina, SE USA

Rockingham 147 B 6 Western Australia, SW Australia

Rock Island 40 B 3 Illinois, N USA

Rock Sound 54 C 1 C Bahamas

Rock Springs 44 B 3 Wyoming, C USA

Rockstone 59 F 3 C Guyana

Rocky Mountains 34 B 4 *var.* Rockies, *Fr.* Montagnes Rocheuses. Mountain range, NW USA

Roden 86 E 2 NE Netherlands

Rodez 91 C 6 *anc.* Segodunum. S France

Ródos 105 E 7 *var.* Ródhos, *Eng.* Rhodes, *It.* Rodi. Ródos, SE Greece

Ródos 105 E 7 *var.* Ródhos, *Eng.* Rhodes, *It.* Rodi; *anc.* Rhodos. Island, Dodekánisos, SE Greece

Rodunma *see* Roanne

Roebuck Bay 146 B 3 bay, E Indian Ocean

Roermond 87 D 5 SE Netherlands

Roeselare 87 A 6 *Fr.* Roulers; *prev.* Rousselaere. W Belgium

Rogachëv *see* Rahachow

Rogers 42 A 1 Arkansas, C USA

Roggeveld Berge 78 C 5 mountain range, S South Africa

Roi Et 137 D 5 *var.* Muang Roi Et, Roi Ed. NE Thailand

Roja 106 C 2 NW Latvia

Rokiškis 106 C 4 NE Lithuania

Rokycany 99 A 5 *Ger.* Rokytzan. W Czech Republic

Rokytzan *see* Rokycany

Rôlas, Ilha das 76 E 2 island, S Sao Tome & Príncipe

Rolla 45 G 5 Missouri, C USA

Röm *see* Rømø

Roma 96 C 4 *Eng.* Rome. Country capital, C Italy

Roma 149 D 5 Queensland, E Australia
Roman 108 C 4 *Hung.* Románvásár. NE Romania
Roman 104 C 2 NW Bulgaria

Romania
108 B 4 *Bul.* Rumŭniya, *Ger.* Romänien, *Hung.* Románia, *Rom.* România, *SCr.* Rumunjska, *Ukr.* Romuniya; *prev.* Republica Socialistă România, Roumania, Rumania, Socialist Republic of Romania, *Rom.* Romînia. Republic, SE Europe

Official name: Romania **Date of formation:** 1947 **Capital:** Bucharest **Population:** 23.4 million **Total area:** 237,500 sq km (91,700 sq miles) **Languages:** Romanian*, Hungarian **Religions:** Romanian Orthodox 70%, Roman Catholic 6%, Protestant 6%, other 18% **Ethnic mix:** Romanian 89%, Hungarian 8%, other (inc. Gypsy) 3% **Government:** Multiparty republic **Currency:** Leu = 100 bani

Románvásár *see* Roman
Rome 42 D 2 Georgia, SE USA
Rome *see* Roma
Romny 109 F 2 NE Ukraine
Rømø 85 A 7 *Ger.* Röm. Island, SW Denmark
Ronda 92 D 5 S Spain
Rondônia 62 D 3 *off.* Território de Rondônia. State, W Brazil
Rondonópolis 63 E 3 W Brazil
Rongelap Atoll 144 D 1 *var.* Rónlap. Island, W Marshall Islands
Rŏngu 106 D 3 *Ger.* Ringen. SE Estonia
RŏnJap *see* Rongelap Atoll
Rønne 85 B 8 E Denmark
Ronne Ice Shelf 154 B 3 ice shelf, Antarctica
Roosendaal 87 C 5 S Netherlands
Roraima 62 D 1 *off.* Território de Roraima; *prev.* Território de Rio Branco. State, N Brazil
Roraima, Mount 59 F 3 mountain, N South America
Røros 85 B 5 S Norway
Rosa, Lake 54 D 2 lake, S Bahamas
Rosario 64 D 4 E Argentina
Rosario 64 D 2 C Paraguay
Rosario *see* Rosarito
Rosarito 50 A 1 *var.* Rosario. NW Mexico
Roscianum *see* Rossano
Roscommon 40 C 2 Michigan, N USA
Roseau 55 G 4 *prev.* Charlotte Town. Country capital, SW Dominica
Roseburg 46 B 4 Oregon, NW USA
Rosenberg 49 G 4 Texas, S USA
Rosengarten 94 B 3 N Germany
Rosenheim 95 C 6 S Germany
Rosia 93 H 5 W Gibraltar
Rosia Bay 93 H 5 bay, NE Atlantic Ocean
Roşiori de Vede 108 B 5 S Romania
Roslavl' 111 A 5 W Russian Federation
Rosmalen 86 D 4 S Netherlands
Ross 151 B 6 South Island, SW New Zealand
Rossano 97 E 6 *anc.* Roscianum. SW Italy
Ross Dependency 154 B 4 dependent territory of New Zealand, Antarctica
Ross Ice Shelf 154 B 4 ice shelf, Antarctica

Rosso 74 B 3 SW Mauritania
Ross Sea 154 B 4 sea, S Pacific Ocean
Rostock 94 C 2 NE Germany
Rostov-na-Donu 111 B 7 *var.* Rostov, *Eng.* Rostov-on-Don. SW Russian Federation
Rostov-on-Don *see* Rostov-na-Donu
Roswell 48 D 2 New Mexico, SW USA
Rota 144 B 1 island, S Northern Mariana Islands
Rotcher Island *see* Tamana
Rothera 154 A 3 research station, Antarctica
Rotomagus *see* Rouen
Rotorua 150 D 3 North Island, NE New Zealand
Rotorua, Lake 150 E 3 lake, North Island, NE New Zealand
Rotterdam 86 C 4 SW Netherlands
Rottweil 95 B 6 S Germany
Rotuma 145 E 4 island, NW Fiji
Roubaix 90 D 2 N France
Rouen 90 C 3 *anc.* Rotomagus. N France
Round Rock 49 G 3 Texas, S USA
Rourkela *see* Raurkela
Roussillon 91 C 7 cultural region, S France
Rouyn-Noranda 38 D 4 Québec, SE Canada
Rovaniemen mlk 84 D 3 N Finland
Rovigno *see* Rovinj
Rovigo 96 C 2 NE Italy
Rovinj 100 A 2 *It.* Rovigno. NW Croatia
Rovuma 69 D 5 *var.* Ruvuma. River, Mozambique/Tanzania
Roxas 139 E 2 Panay Island, C Philippines
Royale, Isle 40 B 1 island, Michigan, N USA
Royan 91 B 5 W France
Rozdol'ne 109 F 4 *Rus.* Razdolnoye. S Ukraine
Rožňava 99 D 6 *Ger.* Rosenau, *Hung.* Rozsnyó. E Slovakia
Ruacana 78 B 3 NW Namibia
Ruapehu, Mount 150 D 4 mountain, North Island, C New Zealand
Ruapuke Island 151 B 8 island, South Island, SW New Zealand
Ruatoria 150 E 3 North Island, NE New Zealand
Rub' al Khali 121 C 6 *Eng.* Empty Quarter, Great Sandy Desert. Desert, SW Asia
Rubezhnoye *see* Rubizhne
Rubizhne 109 H 2 *Rus.* Rubezhnoye. E Ukraine
Ruby Mountains 47 D 5 mountain range, Nevada, W USA
Rucava 106 B 3 SW Latvia
Rudensk *see* Rudzyensk
Rŭdišķes 107 B 5 S Lithuania
Rudnik 104 E 2 E Bulgaria
Rudny *see* Rudnyy
Rudnyy 114 C 4 *var.* Rudny. N Kazakhstan
Rudolf, Lake 68 D 4 *var.* Lake Turkana. Lake, N Kenya
Rudzyensk 107 C 6 *Rus.* Rudensk. C Belorussia
Rufino 64 C 4 C Argentina
Rugāji 106 D 4 E Latvia
Ruggell 94 E 1 N Liechtenstein
Ruhnu 106 C 2 *var.* Ruhnu Saar, *Swe.* Runö. Island, SW Estonia
Rūjiena 106 D 3 *Est.* Ruhja, *Ger.* Rujen. N Latvia

Rukwa, Lake 73 B 7 lake, SE Tanzania
Rum *see* Rhum
Ruma 100 D 3 N Yugoslavia
Rumbek 73 B 5 S Sudan
Rum Cay 54 D 2 island, C Bahamas
Rumia 98 C 2 N Poland
Rummah, Wādī ar *see* Rimah, Wādī ar
Rummelsburg in Pommern *see* Miastko
Runanga 151 B 5 South Island, C New Zealand
Runaway Bay 54 B 4 C Jamaica
Rundu 78 C 3 *var.* Runtu. NE Namibia
Runtu *see* Rundu
Ruoqiang 126 C 3 *var.* Jo-ch'iang, Ruoqiaang, *Uigh.* Charkhlik, Charkhliq, Qarkilik. NW China
Rupea 108 C 4 *Ger.* Reps, *Hung.* Kŏhalom; *prev.* Cohalm. C Romania
Rupel 87 C 5 river, N Belgium
Rupella *see* la Rochelle
Rupert, Rivière de 38 D 3 river, Québec, C Canada
Ruse 104 D 1 *var.* Ruschuk, Rustchuk, *Turk.* Rusçuk. N Bulgaria

Russian Federation
110 B 4 *var.* Russia, *Latv.* Krievija, *Rus.* Rossiyskaya Federatsiya. Republic, Asia/Europe

Official name: Russian Federation **Date of formation:** 1991 **Capital:** Moscow **Population:** 149.2 million **Total area:** 17,075,400 sq km (6,592,800 sq miles) **Languages:** Russian* **Religions:** Russian Orthodox 80%, other (inc. Jewish, Muslim) 20% **Ethnic mix:** Russian 80%, Tartar 4%, Ukrainian 3%, other 13% **Government:** Multiparty republic **Currency:** Rouble = 100 kopeks

Rust'avi 117 G 2 SE Georgia
Rutba *see* Ar Ruţbah
Rutlam *see* Ratlām
Rutland 41 G 2 Vermont, NE USA
Rutog 126 A 4 *var.* Rutok. W China
Rutok *see* Rutog
Ruvuma *see* Rovuma, Rio
Ruwenzori 77 E 5 mountain range, Uganda/Zaire
Ruzhany 107 B 6 SW Belorussia
Ružomberok 99 D 5 *Ger.* Rosenberg, *Hung.* Rózsahegy. N Slovakia

Rwanda
73 B 6 *prev.* Ruanda. Republic, NE Africa

Official name: Republic of Rwanda **Date of formation:** 1962 **Capital:** Kigali **Population:** 7.5 million **Total area:** 26,340 sq km (10,170 sq miles) **Languages:** Kinyarwanda*, French*, Kiswahili **Religions:** Christian 74%, traditional beliefs 25%, other 1% **Ethnic mix:** Hutu 90%, Tutsi 9%, Twa pygmy 1% **Government:** Multiparty republic **Currency:** Franc = 100 centimes

Ryazan' 111 B 5 W Russian Federation
Rybinsk 110 B 4 *prev.* Andropov. W Russian Federation
Rybnik 99 C 5 S Poland

Ryki 98 E 4 E Poland
Rypin 98 D 3 C Poland
Rysy 99 D 5 mountain, S Poland
Ryukyu Islands *see* Nansei-shotō
Ryukyu Trench 152 B 2 *var.* Nansei Syotó Trench. Trench, NW Pacific Ocean
Rzeszów 99 E 5 SE Poland
Ržev *see* Rzhev
Rzhev 110 B 4 *var.* Ržev. W Russian Federation

S

Saalfeld 95 C 5 *var.* Saalfeld an der Saale. C Germany
Saalfeld an der Saale *see* Saalfeld
Saarbrücken 95 A 6 *Fr.* Sarrebruck. SW Germany
Sääre 106 C 2 *var.* Sjar. Saaremaa, W Estonia
Saaremaa 106 C 2 *Ger.* Oesel, Ösel; *prev.* Saare. Island, W Estonia
Saariselkä 84 D 2 *Lapp.* Suoločielgi. N Finland
Sab' Ābār 118 C 4 *var.* Sab'a Biyar, Sa'b Bi'ār. C Syria
Šabac 100 D 3 W Yugoslavia
Sabadell 93 G 2 E Spain
Sabah 138 D 3 cultural region, Borneo, E Malaysia
Sabanalarga 58 B 1 N Colombia
Sabaneta 58 C 1 N Venezuela
Sab'atayn, Ramlat as 121 C 6 desert, C Yemen
Sabaya 61 F 5 S Bolivia
Sabhā 71 F 3 C Libya
Sabi *see* Save, Rio
Sabinas 50 D 2 NE Mexico
Sabinas Hidalgo 51 E 2 NE Mexico
Sabine Lake 49 H 4 lake, SW USA
Sabine River 49 H 3 river, SW USA
Sabkha *see* As Sabkhah
Sable, Cape 39 F 5 headland, Newfoundland and Labrador, SE Canada
Sable Island 39 G 4 island, Nova Scotia, SE Canada
Şabyā 121 B 6 SW Saudi Arabia
Sabzawar *see* Sabzevär
Sabzevär 120 D 2 *var.* Sabzawar. NE Iran
Săcele 108 C 4 *Hung.* Négyfalu; *prev.* Sieben Dörfer, *Hung.* Hétfalu. C Romania
Sachsen 94 D 4 *Eng.* Saxony, *Fr.* Saxe. Cultural region, E Germany
Sachs Harbour 37 E 2 Banks Island, NW Canada
Sächsische Saale 94 C 4 river, C Germany
Sacramento 47 B 6 state capital, California, W USA
Sacramento Mountains 48 D 2 mountain range, New Mexico, SW USA
Sacramento River 47 B 5 river, California, W USA
Sacramento Valley 47 B 5 valley, California, W USA
Sá da Bandeira *see* Lubango
Şa'dah 121 B 6 NW Yemen
Sad Ishträgh 123 F 3 pass, Afghanistan/Pakistan
Sado 131 C 5 *var.* Sadoga-shima. Island, N Japan
Sadoga-shima *see* Sado
Şafāqis *see* Sfax
Säffle 85 B 6 C Sweden
Safford 48 C 3 Arizona, SW USA
Safi 70 B 2 W Morocco

Safīd Kūh, Selseleh-ye 122 D 4 mountain range, NW Afghanistan
Sagaing 136 B 3 C Burma
Sagami-nada 131 D 6 inlet, NW Pacific Ocean
Sāgar 134 D 4 *prev.* Saugor. C India
Saginaw 40 C 3 Michigan, N USA
Saginaw Bay 40 D 2 lake bay, Michigan, N USA
Sagua la Grande 54 B 2 C Cuba
Sagunto 93 F 3 *var.* Sagunt, *Ar.* Murviedro; *anc.* Saguntum. E Spain
Sahara 68 B 3 desert, Algeria/Libya
Sahara el Gharbîya 72 B 2 *var.* AşŞaḥrāʾ al Gharbīyah, *Eng.* Western Desert. Desert, C Egypt
Saharan Atlas *see* Atlas Saharien
Sahel 74 D 3 physical region, N Africa
Sāhīwāl 134 C 2 *prev.* Montgomery. E Pakistan
Sahtinsk *see* Shakhtinsk
Saïda 119 A 5 *var.* Şaydā, Sayida; *anc.* Sidon. W Lebanon
Saidpur 135 G 3 *var.* Syedpur. NW Bangladesh
Sai Kung 128 B 1 E Hong Kong
Saimaa 85 E 5 lake, SE Finland
St.Anthony 39 G 3 Newfoundland and Labrador, SE Canada
St.Catharines 38 D 5 Ontario, S Canada
St.George's 55 H 5 country Capital, SW Grenada
St.John 39 F 4 New Brunswick, SE Canada
St.John's 39 H 3 province capital, Newfoundland and Labrador, E Canada
St.Lawrence 39 E 4 *Fr.* Fleuve St-Laurent. River, Canada/USA
St.Patricks 51 B 5 Barbados
St Albans 89 E 7 *anc.* Verulamium. SE England, UK
Saint Albans 40 D 5 West Virginia, NE USA
St Andrews 88 D 4 E Scotland, UK
St.Ann's Bay 54 B 4 C Jamaica
Saint Augustine 43 E 3 Florida, SE USA
St Austell 89 C 7 SW England, UK
St.Botolph's Town *see* Boston
Saint Catherines Island 43 E 3 island, SE USA
Saint Clair, Lake 40 D 3 lake, Canada/USA
Saint Cloud 45 F 2 Minnesota, N USA
St Croix 55 G 3 island, S Virgin Islands
Saint Croix River 40 A 2 river, N USA
St David's Island 42 B 5 island, E Bermuda
Saintes 91 B 5 *anc.* Mediolanum. W France
St George 42 B 4 N Bermuda
St George 149 D 5 Queensland, E Australia
Saint George 44 A 5 Utah, W USA
Saint George's Channel 89 B 6 channel, Celtic Sea/Irish Sea
St George's Island 42 B 4 island, E Bermuda
St.Gotthard Pass *see* San Gottardo, Passo del
St Helena 67 D 5 island, E Atlantic Ocean
St.Helena Bay 78 B 5 bay, SW South Africa
Saint Helena Sound 43 F 2 bay, NW Atlantic Ocean

Saint Helens, Mount 34 B 4 volcano, Washington, NW USA
St Helier 89 D 8 dependent territory capital, S Jersey, Channel Islands
St.Iago de la Vega *see* Spanish Town
Saint Joe River 46 D 2 river, N USA
St John's 55 G 3 country capital, S Antigua & Barbuda
St Kilda 88 A 3 island, NW Scotland, UK

Saint Kitts & Nevis 55 G 3 *var.* Saint Christopher-Nevis. Commonwealth republic, E Caribbean Sea

Official name: Federation of Saint Christopher and Nevis **Date of formation:** 1983 **Capital:** Basseterre **Population:** 44,000 **Total area:** 360 sq km (139 sq miles) **Languages:** English*, English Creole **Religions:** Protestant 85%, Roman Catholic 10%, other Christian 5% **Ethnic mix:** Black 95%, mixed 5% **Government:** Parliamentary democracy **Currency:** E. Caribbean $ = 100 cents

St.Lawrence, Gulf of 39 F 3 gulf, NW Atlantic Ocean
Saint Lawrence Island 36 C 2 island, Alaska, NW USA
St.Lawrence Seaway 41 F 2 waterway, NW Atlantic Ocean
St Louis 45 G 5 Missouri, C USA

Saint Lucia 55 H 1 Commonwealth republic, E Caribbean Sea

Official name: Saint Lucia **Date of formation:** 1979 **Capital:** Castries **Population:** 156,000 **Total area:** 620 sq km (239 sq miles) **Languages:** English*, French Creole, Hindi, Urdu **Religions:** Roman Catholic 90%, other 10% **Ethnic mix:** Black 90%, mixed European 6%, South Asian 4% **Government:** Parliamentary democracy **Currency:** E. Caribbean $ = 100 cents

St Lucia Channel 55 H 4 channel, E Caribbean Sea
St.Margareth's Bay *see* St.Margareth's Bay
Saint Martin *see* Sint Maarten
St.Matthew's Island *see* Zadetkyi Kyun
Saint Nicholas *see* São Nicolau
Saint-Nicolas *see* Sint-Niklaas
Saint Paul 45 F 2 state capital, Minnesota, N USA
St.Paul Island *see* St-Paul, Île
St Peter Port 89 D 8 dependent territory capital, C Guernsey, Channel Islands
Saint Petersburg 43 E 4 Florida, SE USA
Saint Petersburg *see* Sankt-Peterburg
St Pierre 39 G 4 dependent territory capital, Saint Pierre & Miquelon
Saint Simon Island 43 E 3 island, SE USA
Saint Thomas *see* Charlotte Amalie
Saint Thomas *see* São Tomé
Saint Vincent 55 G 4 island, N Saint Vincent & the Grenadines
Saint Vincent *see* São Vicente

Saint Vincent & the Grenadines 55 H 4 Commonwealth republic, E Caribbean Sea

Official name: St Vincent and the Grenadines **Date of formation:** 1979 **Capital:** Kingstown **Population:** 109,000 **Total area:** 340 sq km (131 sq miles) **Languages:** English*, English Creole **Religions:** Protestant 62% Roman Catholic 19%, other 19% **Ethnic mix:** Black 82%, mixed 14%, White 3%, South Asian 1% **Government:** Parliamentary democracy **Currency:** E. Caribbean $ = 100 cents

Saint Vincent, Cape *see* São Vicente, Cabo de
Saint Vincent Passage 55 H 4 channel, E Caribbean Sea
Saipan 144 B 1 island, S Northern Mariana Islands
Saipan 144 B 1 capital of Northern Mariana Islands, Saipan, S Northern Mariana Islands
Sai Yok 137 B 5 C Thailand
Sajama, Nevado 61 F 4 mountain, W Bolivia
Sajószentpéter 99 D 6 NE Hungary
Sakākah 120 B 4 NW Saudi Arabia
Sakakawea, Lake 44 D 2 reservoir, North Dakota, N USA
Sakata 130 D 4 Honshū, C Japan
Sakhalin *see* Sakhalin, Ostrov
Sakhalin, Ostrov 115 H 4 *var.* Sakhalin. Island, SE Russian Federation
Saki *see* Saky
Şäki 117 G 2 *Rus.* Sheki; *prev.* Nukha. NW Azerbaijan
Sakishima-shotō 130 A 3 *var.* Sakisima Syotō. Island group, Nansei-shotō, S Japan
Sakon Nakhon 136 D 4 *var.* Muang Sakon Nakhon, Sakhon Nakhon. NE Thailand
Saky 109 F 5 *Rus.* Saki. S Ukraine
Sal 74 A 3 island, NE Cape Verde
Sala 85 C 6 C Sweden
Salacgrīva 106 C 3 *Est.* Salatsi. N Latvia
Sala Consilina 97 D 5 S Italy
Salado 64 C 3 river, C Argentina
Şalālah 121 D 6 SW Oman
Salamá 52 B 2 C Guatemala
Salamanca 92 D 2 *anc.* Helmantica, Salmantica. NW Spain
Salamanca 64 B 3 C Chile
Salamīyah 118 B 3 *var.* As Salamīyah. W Syria
Salantai 106 B 3 NW Lithuania
Salatsi *see* Salacgrīva
Salavan 137 E 5 *var.* Saravan, Saravane. SE Laos
Salavat 111 D 6 W Russian Federation
Sala y Gomez 153 F 4 island, E Pacific Ocean
Šalčininkai 107 C 5 SE Lithuania
Saldus 106 B 3 *Ger.* Frauenburg. W Latvia
Sale 149 C 7 Victoria, SE Australia
Salé 70 C 2 NW Morocco
Salekhard 114 D 3 *prev.* Obdorsk. N Russian Federation
Salem 46 B 3 state capital, Oregon, NW USA
Salem 132 C 2 SE India
Salentina, Penisola 97 E 6 peninsula, S Italy
Salerno 97 D 5 *anc.* Salernum. S Italy
Salerno, Golfo di 97 D 5 *Eng.* Gulf of Salerno. Gulf, E Tyrrhenian Sea
Salerno, Gulf of *see* Salerno, Golfo di
Salernum *see* Salerno
Salihorsk 107 C 7 *Rus.* Soligorsk. S Belorussia

Salima 79 E 2 C Malawi
Salina 45 E 5 Kansas, C USA
Salina Cruz 51 F 5 SE Mexico
Salinas 47 B 6 California, W USA
Salinas de Santiago 61 G 4 E Bolivia
Salinas Grandes 64 C 3 wetland, C Argentina
Salisbury 89 D 7 *var.* New Sarum. S England, UK
Salisbury *see* Harare
Sallisaw 49 H 1 Oklahoma, C USA
Sallūm, Khalīj as *see* Salūm, Gulf of
Sallyana *see* Salyan
Salmon Gums 147 C 7 SW Australia
Salmon River 46 D 3 river, Idaho, NW USA
Salmon River Mountains 46 D 3 mountain range, Idaho, NW USA
Salo 85 D 6 SW Finland
Salon-de-Provence 91 D 6 SE France
Salonta 108 A 3 *Hung.* Nagyszalonta. NW Romania
Sal'sk 111 B 7 SW Russian Federation
Salt *see* As Salţ
Salta 64 C 2 NW Argentina
Saltash 89 C 7 SE England, UK
Saltillo 51 E 3 NE Mexico
Salt Lake City 44 B 4 state capital, Utah, W USA
Salto 64 D 4 NW Uruguay
Salton Sea 47 D 8 *var.* Mar de Salton. Lake, California, W USA
Salvador 63 G 3 *prev.* São Salvador. State capital, E Brazil
Salvador, Lake 42 B 3 lake, Louisiana, S USA
Salween 136 B 3 *var.* Nu Jiang, *Bur.* Thanlwin, *Chin.* Nu Chiang. River, SE Asia
Salyan 135 E 3 *var.* Sallyana. W Nepal
Salzburg 95 D 6 *anc.* Juvavum. N Austria
Salzgitter 94 B 4 *prev.* Watenstedt-Salzgitter. C Germany
Salzwedel 94 C 3 N Germany
Samar 139 F 2 island, Visayan Islands, C Philippines
Samara 111 C 6 *prev.* Kuybyshev. W Russian Federation
Samarang *see* Semarang
Samarinda 138 D 4 Borneo, C Indonesia
Samarkand *see* Samarqand
Samarqand 123 E 2 *Rus.* Samarkand. C Uzbekistan
Samawa *see* As Samāwah
Şamaxı 117 H 2 *Rus.* Shemakha. C Azerbaijan
Sambalpur 135 F 4 E India
Sambava 79 G 2 NE Madagascar
Sambir 108 B 2 *Rus.* Sambor. NW Ukraine
Sambor *see* Sambir
Sambre 87 B 7 river, Belgium/France
Samfya 78 D 2 N Zambia
Saminatal 94 E 1 valley, Austria/Liechtenstein
Samnān *see* Semnān
Sam Neua *see* Xam Nua
Samoa Basin 152 D 4 undersea basin, W Pacific Ocean
Sambor 100 B 3 N Croatia
Sámos 105 E 6 *prev.* Limín Vathéos. Sámos, SE Greece
Sámos 105 D 6 island, SE Greece

Samothrace see Samothráki
Samothráki 104 D 4 Samothráki, NE Greece
Samothráki 104 D 4 anc. Samothrace. Island, NE Greece
Sampit 138 D 4 C Indonesia
Samsun 116 D 2 anc. Amisus. N Turkey
Samtredia 117 F 2 W Georgia
Samui, Ko 137 C 6 island, S Thailand
Samut Prakan 137 C 5 var. Muang Samut Prakan, Paknam. C Thailand
San 99 E 5 river, SE Poland
San 74 D 3 C Mali
Sana 100 B 3 river, NW Bosnia & Herzegovina
Şan'ā' 121 B 6 Eng. Sana. Country capital, W Yemen
Sana see Şan'ā'
Saña 60 B 3 NW Peru
Sanae 154 B 2 research station, Antarctica
San Ambrosio Island 153 G 4 var. Isla San Ambrosio. Island, SE Pacific Ocean
San Ambrosio, Isla see San Ambrosio Island
Sanandaj 120 C 3 prev. Sinneh. W Iran
San Andrés, Isla de 53 F 3 island, Colombia
San Andrés Tuxtla 51 F 4 var. Tuxtla. E Mexico
San Angelo 49 F 3 Texas, S USA
San Antonio 64 B 4 C Chile
San Antonio 49 F 4 Texas, S USA
San Antonio 52 B 2 S Belize
San Antonio Bay 49 H 4 bay, Texas, S Gulf of Mexico
San Antonio Oeste 65 C 5 E Argentina
San Antonio River 49 G 4 river, Texas, S USA
Sanāw 121 D 6 var. Sanaw. NE Yemen
Sanaw see Sanāw
San Benedicto, Isla 50 B 5 island, W Mexico
San Benito 49 G 5 Texas, S USA
San Benito 52 B 1 N Guatemala
San Bernardino 47 C 7 California, W USA
San Blas 50 C 3 C Mexico
San Blas, Cordillera de 53 G 4 mountain range, NE Panama
San Carlos de Ancud see Ancud
San Carlos de Bariloche 65 B 5 SW Argentina
San Carlos del Zulia 58 C 2 W Venezuela
San Carlos Reservoir 48 B 2 reservoir, Arizona, SW USA
San Clemente Island 47 C 8 island, California, W USA
San Cristobal 144 C 4 var. Makira. Island, SE Solomon Islands
San Cristóbal 58 C 2 W Venezuela
San Cristóbal see San Cristóbal de Las Casas
San Cristóbal de Las Casas 51 G 5 var. San Cristóbal. SE Mexico
San Cristóbal, Isla 60 B 5 var. Chatham Island. Island, Galapagos Islands, E Pacific Ocean
Sancti Spíritus 54 B 2 C Cuba
Sandakan 139 E 3 Borneo, E Malaysia
Sandanski 104 C 3 prev. Sveti Vrach. SW Bulgaria

Sand Hills 44 D 3 mountain range, Nebraska, C USA
Sandia 48 D 2 New Mexico, SW USA
San Diego 47 C 8 California, W USA
Sandnes 85 A 6 S Norway
Sandomierz 98 D 4 Rus. Sandomir. SE Poland
Sandomir see Sandomierz
Sandoway 136 A 4 W Burma
Sand Springs 49 G 1 Oklahoma, C USA
Sandvika 85 B 6 S Norway
Sandviken 85 C 5 C Sweden
Sandy Bay 93 H 5 bay, W Mediterranean Sea
Sandy City 44 B 4 Utah, W USA
Sandy Desert 134 A 2 physical region, W Pakistan
Sandy Lake 38 B 3 lake, Ontario, C Canada
Sandy Springs 42 D 2 Georgia, SE USA
San Esteban 52 D 2 C Honduras
San Felipe 58 D 1 NW Venezuela
San Felipe de Puerto Plata see Puerto Plata
San Félix Island 153 G 4 Eng. San Felix Island. Island, SE Pacific Ocean
San Fernando 92 C 5 prev. Isla de León. S Spain
San Fernando 55 H 5 S Trinidad & Tobago
San Fernando 64 B 4 C Chile
San Fernando 58 D 2 var. San Fernando de Apure. C Venezuela
San Fernando de Apure see San Fernando
San Fernando del Valle de Catamarca 64 C 3 var. Catamarca. NW Argentina
San Fernando de Monte Cristi see Monte Cristi
San Francisco 64 C 4 C Argentina
San Francisco 47 A 6 California, W USA
San Francisco Bay 47 A 6 bay, California, W Pacific Ocean
San Francisco del Oro 50 C 3 Mexico
San Francisco de Macorís 55 E 3 C Dominican Republic
San Francisco de Selva see Copiapó
San Fructuoso see Tacuarembó
Sanger 47 C 6 California, W USA
Sangihe, Kepulauan 139 F 3 island group, N Indonesia
Sāngli 132 B 1 W India
Sangmélima 77 B 5 S Cameroon
San Gottardo, Passo del 95 B 7 Eng. St.Gotthard Pass. Pass, S Switzerland
Sangre de Cristo Mountains 44 D 5 mountain range, C USA
San Ignacio 52 B 1 prev. Cayo, El Cayo. W Belize
San Ignacio 61 F 3 N Bolivia
San Joaquin Valley 47 B 6 valley, California, W USA
San Jorge, Golfo 65 C 6 var. Gulf of San Jorge. Gulf, SW Atlantic Ocean
San Jorge, Gulf of see San Jorge, Golfo
San Jose 47 B 6 Port. San José. California, W USA
San José 52 B 3 var. Puerto San José. S Guatemala
San José 53 E 4 country capital C Costa Rica

San José 61 G 4 var. San José de Chiquitos. E Bolivia
San José see San José del Guaviare
San José de Chiquitos see San José
San José de Cúcuta see Cúcuta
San José del Guaviare 58 C 4 var. San José. S Colombia
San Juan 55 F 3 dependent territory capital, NE Puerto Rico
San Juan 64 B 4 W Argentina
San Juan 53 E 4 river, Costa Rica/Nicaragua
San Juan see San Juan de los Morros
San Juan Bautista 64 D 3 S Paraguay
San Juan Bautista see Villahermosa
San Juan Bautista Tuxtepec see Tuxtepec
San Juan de Alicante 93 F 4 E Spain
San Juan del Norte 53 E 4 var. Greytown. SE Nicaragua
San Juan del Norte, Bahía de 53 E 4 bay, W Caribbean Sea
San Juan de los Morros 58 D 2 var. San Juan. N Venezuela
San Juan del Río 51 E 4 C Mexico
San Juanito, Isla 50 C 4 island, C Mexico
San Juan Mountains 44 C 5 mountain range, Colorado, C USA
San Juan River 44 B 5 river, C USA
San Julián see Puerto San Julián
Sankt-Bartholomäi see Palamuse
Sankt Gallen 95 F 7 var. St.Gallen, Eng. Saint Gall, Fr. St-Gall. NE Switzerland
Sankt-Jakobi see Pärnu-Jaagupi
Sankt-Petersburg 110 B 4 prev. Leningrad, Petrograd, Eng. Saint Petersburg, Fin. Pietari. NW Russian Federation
Sankt Pölten 95 E 6 N Austria
Sankuru 77 D 7 river, C Zaire
San Lázaro 64 D 2 NE Paraguay
Şanlıurfa 117 E 4 prev. Sanli Urfa, Urfa, anc. Edessa. S Turkey
San Lorenzo 61 G 5 S Bolivia
San Lorenzo 60 A 1 N Ecuador
San Lorenzo, Isla 60 C 4 island, W Peru
Sanlúcar de Barrameda 92 C 5 S Spain
San Luis 64 C 4 C Argentina
San Luis 50 A 1 var. San Luis Río Colorado. NW Mexico
San Luis 52 B 2 NE Guatemala
San Luis Obispo 47 B 7 California, W USA
San Luis Potosí 51 E 3 C Mexico
San Luis Río Colorado see San Luis
San Marcos 49 G 4 Texas, S USA
San Marcos 52 A 2 W Guatemala
San Marcos 60 C 3 W Peru
San Marcos de Arica see Arica
San Marino 96 E 1 country capital, C San Marino

San Marino
96 D 1 Marino. Republic, S Europe

Official name: Republic of San Marino **Date of formation:** AD 301 **Capital:** San Marino **Population:** 23,000 **Total area:** 61 sq km (24 sq miles) **Languages:** Italian* **Religions:** Roman Catholic 96%, Protestant 2%, other 2% **Ethnic mix:** Sammarinese 95%, Italian 4%, other 1% **Government:** Multiparty republic

Currency: Italian lira = 100 centesimi

San Martín 154 A 3 research station, Antarctica
San Mateo 47 B 6 California, W USA
San Mateo 59 E 2 NE Venezuela
San Matías 61 H 3 E Bolivia
San Matías, Golfo 65 C 6 gulf, SW Atlantic Ocean
Sanmenxia 128 C 4 var. Shan Xian. C China
San Miguel 52 C 3 SE El Salvador
San Miguel 61 G 3 river, Colombia/Ecuador
San Miguel de Allende 51 E 4 C Mexico
San Miguel de Ibarra see Ibarra
San Miguel de Tucumán 64 C 3 var. Tucumán. N Argentina
San Miguelito 53 G 4 C Panama
Sannär see Sennar
San Nicolás, Bahía 60 D 4 bay, E Pacific Ocean
San Nicolas Island 47 C 8 island, California, W USA
Sânnicolau Mare 108 A 4 var. Sânnicolaul-Mare, Hung. Nagyszentmiklós; prev. Sânmiclăus Mare, Sînnicolau Mare. W Romania
Sanok 99 E 5 SE Poland
San Pablo 61 F 5 S Bolivia
San Pedro 50 D 3 var. San Pedro de las Colonias. NE Mexico
San Pedro 52 C 1 NE Belize
San-Pédro 74 D 5 S Ivory Coast
San Pedro de las Colonias see San Pedro
San Pedro de Lloc 60 B 3 NW Peru
San Pedro Mártir, Sierra 50 A 1 mountain range, NW Mexico
San Pedro Sula 52 C 2 NW Honduras
San Rafael 64 B 4 W Argentina
San Rafael Mountains 47 B 7 mountain range, California, W USA
San Ramón de la Nueva Orán 64 C 2 N Argentina
San Remo 96 A 3 NW Italy
San Salvador 54 D 1 prev. Watlings I. Island, E Bahamas
San Salvador 52 B 3 country capital, SW El Salvador
San Salvador de Jujuy 64 C 2 var. Jujuy. N Argentina
Sansanné-Mango 75 E 4 var. Mango. N Togo
Sansepolcro 96 C 3 C Italy
San Severo 97 D 5 SE Italy
Santa 60 C 3 W Peru
Santa Ana 52 B 3 NW El Salvador
Santa Ana 47 C 8 California, W USA
Santa Ana 61 F 3 N Bolivia
Santa Ana de Coro see Coro
Santa Barbara 50 C 2 N Mexico
Santa Barbara 47 C 7 California, W USA
Santa Catalina, Gulf of 47 B 8 gulf, W USA
Santa Catalina Island 47 C 8 island, California, W USA
Santa Catarina 63 E 5 off. Estado de Santa Catarina. State, S Brazil
Santa Catarina, Estado de see Santa Catarina
Santa Clara 54 B 2 C Cuba
Santa Clara 47 B 6 California, W USA
Santa Comba 92 B 1 NW Spain

Santa Cruz 65 B 7 river, S Argentina
Santa Cruz 47 B 6 California, W USA
Santa Cruz 76 E 2 var. São João. São Tomé, SE Sao Tome & Principe
Santa Cruz 61 G 4 var. Santa Cruz de la Sierra. C Bolivia
Santa Cruz Barillas see Barillas
Santa Cruz de la Sierra see Santa Cruz
Santa Cruz del Quiché 52 B 2 W Guatemala
Santa Cruz de Tenerife 70 A 3 regional capital, Tenerife, SW Spain
Santa Cruz, Isla 60 B 5 var. Indefatigable Island, Isla Chávez. Island, Galapagos Islands, E Pacific Ocean
Santa Cruz Islands 144 D 4 island group, E Solomon Islands
Santa Elena 64 D 3 NE Argentina
Santa Elena 52 B 1 W Belize
Santa Fe 64 D 4 NE Argentina
Santa Fe 48 D 1 state capital, New Mexico, SW USA
Santa Inês 63 F 2 NE Brazil
Santa Isabel 144 C 3 var. Bughotu. Island, N Solomon Islands
Santa Isabel see Malabo
Santa Lucia Range 47 B 6 mountain range, California, W USA
Santa Margarita, Isla 50 B 3 island, W Mexico
Santa Maria 92 A 5 island, W Portugal
Santa Maria 63 E 5 S Brazil
Santa Maria 47 B 7 California, W USA
Santa Maria del Buen Aire see Buenos Aires
Santa María del Orinoco 58 D 2 C Venezuela
Santa María, Isla 60 A 5 var. Charles Island, Isla Floreana. Island, Galapagos Islands, E Pacific Ocean
Santa Marta 58 B 1 N Colombia
Santana 76 E 2 São Tomé, C Sao Tome & Principe
Santander 92 D 1 N Spain
Santanilla, Islas 53 E 1 Eng. Swan Islands. Island, NE Honduras
Santarém 92 B 3 anc. Scalabis. W Portugal
Santarém 63 E 2 N Brazil
Santa Rosa 65 C 5 C Argentina
Santa Rosa 47 B 6 California, W USA
Santa Rosa see Santa Rosa de Copán
Santa Rosa de Copán 52 C 2 var. Santa Rosa. W Honduras
Santa Rosa Island 47 B 8 island, California, W USA
Sant Carles de la Rápida see Sant Carles de la Ràpita
Sant Carles de la Ràpita 93 F 3 var. Sant Carles de la Rápida. NE Spain
Santiago 92 B 1 var. Santiago de Compostela, Eng. Compostella; anc. Campus Stellae. NW Spain
Santiago 55 E 3 var. Santiago de los Caballeros. N Dominican Republic
Santiago 64 B 4 var. Gran Santiago. Country capital, C Chile
Santiago 74 A 3 var. São Tiago. Island, S Cape Verde
Santiago 53 F 5 S Panama
Santiago 60 B 2 river, N Peru
Santiago see Santiago de Cuba

Santiago de Cuba 54 C 3 var. Santiago. E Cuba
Santiago de Guayaquil see Guayaquil
Santiago del Estero 64 C 3 C Argentina
Santiago de los Caballeros see Santiago
Santiago, Isla 60 A 5 var. Isla San Salvador, James Island. Island, Galapagos Islands, E Pacific Ocean
Santiago Mountains 49 E 4 mountain range, Texas, S USA
Santiago Pinotepa Nacional see Pinotepa Nacional
Sant Julià de Lòria 91 A 8 SW Andorra
Santo see Espiritu Santo
Santo André 63 F 4 S Brazil
Santo Antão 74 A 2 island, N Cape Verde
Santo António 76 E 1 var. São António Príncipe, N Sao Tome & Principe
Santo Domingo 55 E 3 prev. Ciudad Trujillo. Country capital, SE Dominican Republic
Santo Domingo de Los Colorados 60 B 1 NW Ecuador
Santo Domingo Tehuantepec see Tehuantepec
San, Tônle 137 E 5 var. San, Sé. River, Cambodia/Vietnam
Santos 63 F 4 S Brazil
Santos Plateau 57 D 5 undersea plateau, SW Atlantic Ocean
Santo Tomé 64 D 3 NE Argentina
San Valentín, Cerro 65 B 7 mountain, S Chile
San Vicente 52 C 3 C El Salvador
São António see Santo António
São Francisco 63 F 3 river, E Brazil
Sao Hill 73 C 7 S Tanzania
São João see São Tomé
São João da Madeira 92 B 2 W Portugal
São Jorge 92 A 5 island, W Portugal
São Luís 63 F 2 state capital, NE Brazil
São Marcos, Baía de 63 F 1 bay, W Atlantic Ocean
Saona, Isla 55 E 3 island, SE Dominican Republic
Saône 91 D 5 river, E France
São Nicolau 74 A 3 Eng. Saint Nicholas. Island, N Cape Verde
São Paulo 63 F 4 state capital, S Brazil
São Paulo 63 E 4 off. Estado de São Paulo. State, S Brazil
São Paulo, Estado de see São Paulo
São Pedro do Rio Grande do Sul see Rio Grande
São Salvador see Salvador
São Tiago see Santiago
São Tomé 76 E 2 Eng. Saint Thomas. Island, S Sao Tome & Principe
São Tomé 76 E 2 country capital, São Tomé, S Sao Tome & Principe

Sao Tome & Principe 76 D 1 off. Sao Tome and Principe, Port. São Tomé e Príncipe. Republic, C Africa

Official name: Democratic Republic of Sao Tome and Principe **Date of formation:** 1975 **Capital:** São Tomé **Population:** 121,000 **Total area:** 964 sq km (372 sq miles) **Languages:** Portuguese*, Portuguese Creole

Religions: Roman Catholic 90%, other Christian 10% **Ethnic mix:** Black 90%, Portuguese and Creole 10% **Government:** Multiparty republic **Currency:** Dobra = 100 centimos

São Tomé, Pico de 76 E 2 mountain, São Tomé, S Sao Tome & Principe
São Vicente 74 A 3 Eng. Saint Vincent. Island, N Cape Verde
São Vicente, Cabo de 92 B 5 Eng. Cape Saint Vincent. Headland, SW Portugal
Sápai see Sápes
Sapele 75 F 5 S Nigeria
Sápes 104 D 3 var. Sápai. NE Greece
Sa Pobla 93 G 3 var. La Puebla. E Spain
Sapporo 130 D 2 Hokkaidō, NE Japan
Sapri 97 D 6 Italy
Sapulpa 49 G 1 Oklahoma, C USA
Saqqez 120 C 2 var. Saghez, Sakiz, Saqqiz. NW Iran
Sara Buri 137 C 5 var. Saraburi. C Thailand
Saraburi see Sara Buri
Saragt see Serakhs
Saraguro 60 B 2 S Ecuador
Sarajevo 101 A 8 country capital, SE Bosnia & Herzegovina
Sarakhs 120 E 2 NE Iran
Saraktash 111 D 6 W Russian Federation
Saran' 114 C 4 Kaz. Saran. C Kazakhstan
Saran see Saran'
Sarandë 101 C 7 var. Saranda, It. Porto Edda; prev. Santi Quaranta. S Albania
Saransk 111 C 5 W Russian Federation
Sarasota 43 E 4 Florida, SE USA
Saratov 111 C 6 W Russian Federation
Sarawak 138 D 3 cultural region, Borneo, E Malaysia
Sarawak see Kuching
Sardegna 97 A 5 Eng. Sardinia. Island, W Italy
Sardinia see Sardegna
Sar-e Pol see Sar-e Pol-e Žaháb
Sargasso Sea 66 B 4 sea, N Atlantic Ocean
Sargodha 134 C 2 NE Pakistan
Sarh 76 C 4 prev. Fort-Archambault. S Chad
Saría 105 E 7 island, Dodekánisos, SE Greece
Sarıkamış 117 F 3 NE Turkey
Sarikol Range 123 G 3 mountain range, China/Tajikistan
Sark 89 D 8 Fr. Sercq. Island , C Channel Islands
Şarkışla 116 D 3 C Turkey
Sarmiento 65 B 6 S Argentina
Sarnia 38 C 5 Ontario, S Canada
Sarny 108 C 1 NW Ukraine
Sarochyna 107 D 5 Rus. Sorochino. N Belorussia
Sarpsborg 85 B 6 S Norway
Sarrebruck see Saarbrücken
Sartène 91 E 7 SE France
Sarthe 90 B 4 cultural region, NW France
Sárti 104 C 4 N Greece
Sary-Tash 123 F 3 SW Kyrgyzstan
Sasebo 131 A 7 Kyūshū, SW Japan
Saskatchewan 37 F 5 province, SW Canada
Saskatchewan 37 F 5 river, C

Canada
Saskatoon 37 F 5 Saskatchewan, S Canada
Sasovo 111 B 5 W Russian Federation
Sassandra 74 D 5 S Ivory Coast
Sassandra 74 D 5 var. Ibo, Sassandra Fleuve. River, S Ivory Coast
Sassari 97 A 5 W Italy
Sassenheim 86 C 3 W Netherlands
Sassnitz 94 D 2 NE Germany
Sátoraljaújhely 99 E 6 NE Hungary
Sātpura Range 134 D 4 mountain range, C India
Satsunan-shotō 130 A 3 var. Satunan Syotō. Island group, Nansei-shotō, S Japan
Sattanen 84 D 3 NE Finland
Satu Mare 108 B 3 Ger. Sathmar, Hung. Szatmárrnémeti. NW Romania

Saudi Arabia 121 B 5 Ar. Al 'Arabīyah as Su'ūdīyah, Al Mamlakah al 'Arabīyah as Su'ūdīyah. Monarchy, SW Asia

Official name: Kingdom of Saudi Arabia **Date of formation:** 1932 **Capital:** Riyadh **Population:** 16.5 million **Total area:** 2,149,690 sq km (829,995 sq miles) **Languages:** Arabic* **Religions:** Sunni Muslim 85%, Shi'a Muslim 14%, Christian 1% **Ethnic mix:** Arab 90%, Yemeni 8%, other Arab 1%, other 1% **Government:** Absolute monarchy **Currency:** Riyal = 100 malalah

Sauer see Sûre
Saugor see Sāgar
Saulkrasti 106 C 3 C Latvia
Sault Ste.Marie 38 C 4 Ontario, S Canada
Sault Ste Marie 40 C 2 Michigan, N USA
Saumarez Reef 148 E 4 reef, S Coral Sea
Saumur 90 B 4 NW France
Saurimo 78 C 1 var. Henrique de Carvalho, Port. Vila Henrique de Carvalho. NE Angola
Sava 100 B 3 river, SE Europe
Sava 107 E 6 E Belorussia
Savá 52 D 2 N Honduras
Savai'i 145 E 4 island, NW Western Samoa
Savannah 43 E 2 Georgia, SE USA
Savannah River 43 E 2 river, SE USA
Savannakhét 136 D 4 S Laos
Savanna-La-Mar 54 A 5 W Jamaica
Save, Rio 79 E 3 var. Sabi. River, Mozambique/Zimbabwe
Saverne 90 E 3 var. Zabern; anc. Tres Tabernae. NE France
Savigliano 96 A 2 NW Italy
Savigsivik see Savissivik
Savinski see Savinskiy
Savinskiy 110 C 3 var. Savinski. NW Russian Federation
Savissivik 82 D 1 var. Savigsivik. NW Greenland
Savoie 91 D 5 cultural region, SE France
Savona 96 A 2 NW Italy
Sävsjö 85 B 7 S Sweden
Savu Sea see Sawu, Laut
Sawakin see Suakin

Şawqirah 121 E 6 *var.* Suqrah. S Oman

Sawu, Laut 139 E 5 *Eng.* Savu Sea. Sea, E Indian Ocean

Sayaboury *see* Xaignabouli

Sayat 122 D 3 E Turkmenistan

Sayaxché 52 B 2 N Guatemala

Sayhūt 121 D 6 E Yemen

Saylac 72 D 4 *var.* Zeila. NW Somalia

Saynshand 127 E 2 S Mongolia

Say 'ūn 121 C 6 *var.* Saywūn. C Yemen

Saywūn *see* Say 'ūn

Scalabis *see* Santarém

Scandinavia 66 D 2 geophysical region, NW Europe

Scania *see* Skåne

Scarborough 89 D 5 NE England, UK

Scarborough 38 D 5 Ontario, S Canada

Schaan 94 E 1 W Liechtenstein

Schaerbeek 87 C 6 C Belgium

Schaffhausen 95 B 7 *Fr.* Schaffhouse. N Switzerland

Schaffhouse *see* Schaffhausen

Schagen 86 C 2 NW Netherlands

Schaulen *see* Šiauliai

Schaumburg 40 B 3 Illinois, N USA

Schebschi Mountains *see* Shebshi Mountains

Scheessel 94 B 3 NW Germany

Schefferville 39 E 2 Québec, E Canada

Scheldt 87 B 5 *Dut.* Schelde, *Fr.* Escaut. River, W Europe

Schell Creek Range 47 D 5 mountain range, Nevada, W USA

Schenectady 41 F 3 New York, NE USA

Scherrebek *see* Skærbæk

Schertz 49 G 4 Texas, S USA

Schiedam 86 C 4 SW Netherlands

Schiermonnikoog 86 D 1 *Fris.* Skiermûntseach. Island, N Netherlands

Schijndel 86 D 4 S Netherlands

Schivelbein *see* Świdwin

Schleswig 94 B 2 N Germany

Schleswig-Holstein 94 B 2 cultural region, N Germany

Schlettstadt *see* Sélestat

Schlochau *see* Człuchów

Schneekoppe *see* Sněžka

Schneidemühl *see* Piła

Schönebeck 94 C 4 C Germany

Schönlanke *see* Trzcianka

Schooten *see* Schoten

Schoten 87 C 5 *var.* Schooten. N Belgium

Schouwen 86 B 4 island, SW Netherlands

Schwäbische Alb 95 B 6 *var.* Schwabenalb, *Eng.* Swabian Jura. Mountain range, S Germany

Schwandorf 95 C 5 SE Germany

Schwarzwald 95 B 6 *Eng.* Black Forest. Mountain range, SW Germany

Schwaz 95 C 7 W Austria

Schweidnitz *see* Świdnica

Schweinfurt 95 B 5 SE Germany

Schwerin 94 C 3 N Germany

Schwertberg *see* Świecie

Schwiebus *see* Świebodzin

Scilly, Isles of 89 B 8 island group, SW England, UK

Scoresby Sund *see* Kangertittivaq

Scotia Ridge 154 A 1 undersea ridge, S Atlantic Ocean

Scotia Sea 67 B 7 sea, SW Atlantic Ocean

Scotland 88 C 3 national region, UK

Scott Base 154 C 4 research station, Antarctica

Scott Island 154 B 5 island, Antarctica

Scottsbluff 44 D 3 Nebraska, C USA

Scottsdale 48 B 2 Arizona, SW USA

Scranton 41 F 3 Pennsylvania, NE USA

Scrobesbyrig' *see* Shrewsbury

Scutari, Lake 101 C 5 *Alb.* Liqeni i Shkodrës; *SCr.* Skadarsko Jezero. Lake, Albania/Yugoslavia

Seaside 47 B 6 California, W USA

Seattle 46 B 2 Washington, NW USA

Sébaco 52 D 3 W Nicaragua

Sebago Lake 41 G 2 lake, Maine, NE USA

Sebastián Vizcaíno, Bahía 50 A 2 bay, E Pacific Ocean

Sebastopol *see* Sevastopol'

Sebenico *see* Šibenik

Sebta *see* Ceuta

Sechura, Bahía de 60 A 3 bay, W Pacific Ocean

Secunderābād 132 C 1 *var.* Sikandarabad. C India

Sedan 90 D 3 N France

Seddon 151 D 5 South Island, C New Zealand

Seddonville 151 C 5 South Island, C New Zealand

Sédhiou 74 B 4 SW Senegal

Sedona 48 B 2 Arizona, SW USA

Seesen 94 B 4 C Germany

Segeža *see* Segezha

Segezha 110 B 3 *var.* Segeža. NW Russian Federation

Segodunum *see* Rodez

Ségou 74 D 3 *var.* Segu. C Mali

Segovia 92 D 2 C Spain

Segu *see* Ségou

Séguédine 75 H 2 NE Niger

Seguin 49 G 4 Texas, S USA

Segura 93 E 4 river, S Spain

Seinäjoki 85 D 5 *Swe.* Östermyra. W Finland

Seine 100 C 3 river, N France

Seine, Baie de la 90 B 3 bay, E English Channel

Sekondi *see* Sekondi-Takoradi

Sekondi-Takoradi 75 E 5 *var.* Sekondi. S Ghana

Sélestat 90 E 4 *Ger.* Schlettstadt. N France

Seleucia *see* Silifke

Selfoss 83 E 5 SW Iceland

Sélibaby *see* Sélibabi

Selibi Phikwe 78 D 3 E Botswana

Selima Oasis 72 B 3 oasis, N Sudan

Selma 47 C 6 California, W USA

Selvagens, Ilhas 70 A 2 island group, Madeira, E Atlantic Ocean

Selway River 46 D 2 river, Idaho, NW USA

Selwyn Range 148 B 3 mountain range, Queensland, NW Australia

Selzaete *see* Zelzate

Semara 70 B 3 N Western Sahara

Semarang 138 C 5 *var.* Samarang. Jawa, C Indonesia

Sembé 77 B 5 NW Congo

Semendria *see* Smederevo

Semey *see* Semipalatinsk

Semezhevo *see* Syemyezhava

Seminole 49 E 3 Texas, S USA

Seminole, Lake 42 D 3 reservoir, SE USA

Semipalatinsk 114 D 4 *Kaz.* Semey. E Kazakhstan

Semna 72 B 3 N Sudan

Semnān 120 D 3 *var.* Samnān. N Iran

Semois 87 C 8 river, SE Belgium

Senatobia 42 C 2 Mississippi, S USA

Sendai 130 D 4 Honshū, C Japan

Sendai 131 A 8 Kyūshū, SW Japan

Sendai-wan 130 D 4 bay, NW Pacific Ocean

Senec 99 C 6 *Ger.* Wartberg, *Hung.* Szenc; *prev.* Szempcz. W Slovakia

Senegal 74 C 3 *Fr.* Sénégal. River, W Africa

Senegal
74 B 3 *Fr.* Sénégal. Republic, W Africa

Official name: Republic of Senegal **Date of formation:** 1960 **Capital:** Dakar **Population:** 7.9 million **Total area:** 196,720 sq km (75,950 sq miles) **Languages:** French*, Wolof, Fulani **Religions:** Muslim 92%, traditional beliefs 6%, Christian 2% **Ethnic mix:** Wolof 46%, Fulani 25%, Serer 16%, other 13% **Government:** Multiparty republic **Currency:** CFA franc = 100 centimes

Senftenberg 94 D 4 E Germany

Sengkang 139 E 4 *var.* Singkang. Celebes, C Indonesia

Senica 99 C 6 *Ger.* Senitz, *Hung.* Szenice. W Slovakia

Seniça *see* Sjenica

Senj 100 A 3 *Ger.* Zengg, *It.* Segna; *anc.* Senia. NW Croatia

Senja 84 C 2 *prev.* Senjen. Island, N Norway

Senjen *see* Senja

Senkaku-shotō 130 A 3 island group, Nansei-shotō, S Japan

Senlis 90 C 3 N France

Sennar 72 C 4 *var.* Sannār. C Sudan

Sens 90 C 4 *anc.* Agendicum, Senones. C France

Sên, Stœng 137 D 5 river, N Cambodia

Senta 100 D 2 *Hung.* Zenta. N Yugoslavia

Sentosa 138 A 2 island, S Singapore

Sept-Îles 39 E 3 Québec, SE Canada

Seraing 87 D 6 E Belgium

Serakhs 122 D 3 *var.* Saragt. S Turkmenistan

Seram, Laut 139 F 4 *Eng.* Ceram Sea. Sea, W Pacific Ocean

Seram, Pulau 139 F 4 *var.* Serang, *Eng.* Ceram. Island, Maluku, E Indonesia

Serang 138 C 5 Jawa, C Indonesia

Serasan, Selat 138 C 3 strait, W Pacific Ocean

Serbia 100 D 4 *Ger.* Serbien, *Serb.* Srbija. Constituent republic of Yugoslavia, Yugoslavia. *See also* Yugoslavia

Sercq *see* Sark

Serdo 72 D 4 N Ethiopia

Seremban 138 B 3 W Malaysia

Serenje 78 D 2 E Zambia

Sérifos 105 C 6 *anc.* Seriphos. Island, Kykládes, SE Greece

Seriphos *see* Sérifos

Serov 114 C 3 C Russian Federation

Serowe 78 D 3 SE Botswana

Serpent's Mouth, The 59 F 2 *Sp.* Boca de la Serpiente. Strait, W Atlantic Ocean

Serpiente, Boca de la *see* Serpent's Mouth, The

Serpukhov 111 B 5 W Russian Federation

Serravalle 96 E 1 N San Marino

Sérres 104 C 3 *var.* Seres; *prev.* Sérrai. NE Greece

Sesto San Giovanni 96 B 2 N Italy

Sesvete 100 B 2 N Croatia

Sète 91 C 6 *prev.* Cette. S France

Sétif 71 E 2 *var.* Stif. N Algeria

Setté Cama 77 A 6 SW Gabon

Setúbal 92 B 4 *Eng.* Saint Ubes, Saint Yves. W Portugal

Setúbal, Baía de 92 B 4 bay, NE Atlantic Ocean

Seul, Lac 38 B 3 lake, Ontario, S Canada

Sevan 117 G 2 C Armenia

Sevana Lich 117 G 3 *Eng.* Lake Sevan, *Rus.* Ozero Sevan. Lake, E Armenia

Sevastopol' 109 F 5 *Eng.* Sebastopol. S Ukraine

Severn 89 D 7 *Wel.* Hafren. River, England/Wales, UK

Severn 38 B 2 river, Ontario, S Canada

Severnaya Dvina 110 C 4 *var.* Northern Dvina. River, NW Russian Federation

Severnaya Zemlya 115 E 2 *var.* Nicholas II Land, North Land. Island group, N Russian Federation

Severnyy 110 E 3 *var.* Severny, Severnyj. NW Russian Federation

Severodonetsk *see* Syeverodonets'k

Severodvinsk 110 C 3 *prev.* Molotov, Sudostroy. NW Russian Federation

Severomorsk 110 C 2 NW Russian Federation

Sevier Lake 44 A 4 lake, Utah, W USA

Sevier River 44 B 5 river, W USA

Sevilla 92 C 5 *Eng.* Seville; *anc.* Hispalis, SW Spain

Seville *see* Sevilla

Sevlievo 104 D 2 C Bulgaria

Seychelles
79 G 1 E Africa

Official name: Republic of the Seychelles **Date of formation:** 1976 **Capital:** Victoria **Population:** 69,000 **Total area:** 280 sq km (108 sq miles) **Languages:** Creole*, French, English **Religions:** Roman Catholic 90%, other 10% **Ethnic mix:** Seychellois (mixed African, South Asian and European) 95%, Chinese and South Asian 5% **Government:** Multiparty republic **Currency:** Rupee = 100 cents

Seydhisfjördhur 83 E 5 E Iceland

Seydi 122 D 2 *prev.* Neftezavodsk. E Turkmenistan

Seyhan *see* Adana

Şeytan Deresi 116 D 4 river, NW Turkey

Sfákia 105 C 8 Kríti, SE Greece

Sfântu Gheorghe 108 C 4 *Ger.* Sankt-Georgen, *Hung.* Sepsiszentgyörgy; *prev.* Sepsi-Sângeorz, Sfîntu Gheorghe. C Romania

Sfax 71 F 2 *var.* Şafāqis. E Tunisia

's-Gravenhage 86 B 4 *var.* Den Haag, *Eng.* The Hague, *Fr.* La Haye. Seat of government, W Netherlands

's-Gravenzande 86 B 4 W Netherlands

Shaanxi 129 B 5 *var.* Shaan, Shanhsi, Shenshi, Shensi. Province, C China

Shabani *see* Zvishavane

Shache 126 A 3 *var.* Yarkant. NW China

Shackleton Ice Shelf 154 D 3 ice shelf, Antarctica

Shafer, Mount 154 C 4 mountain, Antarctica

Shahr-e Kord 120 C 3 *var.* Shahr Kord. C Iran

Shahr Kord *see* Shahr-e Kord

Shakawe 78 C 3 NW Botswana

Shakhtinsk 114 C 4 C Kazakhstan

Shaluli Shan 129 A 5 mountain range, S China

Shandi *see* Shendi

Shandong 128 C 4 *var.* Lu, Shantung. Province, E China

Shanghai 129 D 5 *var.* Shang-hai. E China

Shang-hai *see* Shanghai

Shangrao 129 D 5 E China

Shannon 89 A 6 C Ireland

Shannon 89 A 6 *Ir.* An tSionainn. River, W Ireland

Shan Plateau 136 B 3 plateau, C Burma

Shantar Islands *see* Shantarskiye Ostrova

Shantarskiye Ostrova 115 G 3 *Eng.* Shantar Islands. Island group, SE Russian Federation

Shantou 129 D 6 *var.* Shan-t'ou, Swatow. SE China

Shanxi 128 C 4 *var.* Jin, Shan-hsi, Shansi. Province, NE China

Shan Xian *see* Sanmenxia

Shaoguan 129 C 6 *var.* Shao-kuan, *Cant.* Kukong; *prev.* Ch'u-chiang. SE China

Shaqrā' 120 C 4 C Saudi Arabia

Shaqrā *see* Shuqrah

Shari *see* Chari

Shari 130 D 2 Hokkaidō, NE Japan

Sharif 135 F 3 N India

Sharīngol 127 E 2 N Mongolia

Shark Bay 147 A 5 bay, E Indian Ocean

Sharqī, Jazīrat ash *see* Chergui, Île

Shashe 78 D 3 *var.* Shashi. River, Botswana/Zimbabwe

Shashi *see* Shashe

Shasta Lake 47 B 5 reservoir, California, W USA

Shawnee 49 G 1 Oklahoma, C USA

Shaykh, Jabal ash *see* Hermon, Mount

Shchadryn 107 D 7 *Rus.* Shchedrin. SE Belorussia

Shchedrin *see* Shchadryn

Shcheglovsk *see* Kemerovo

Shchekino 111 B 5 W Russian Federation

Shchigry 111 B 5 W Russian Federation

Shchors 109 E 1 N Ukraine

Shchuchinsk 114 C 4 *prev.* Shchuchye. N Kazakhstan

Shchuchye *see* Shchuchinsk

Shchuchyn 107 B 5 *Pol.* Szczuczyn Nowogródzki, *Rus.* Shchuchin. W Belorussia

Shebekino 111 A 6 W Russian Federation

Shebeli 73 D 5 *Amh.* Wabē Shebelē Wenz, *It.* Scebeli, *Som.* Webi Shabeelle. River, Ethiopia/Somalia

Sheberghān 123 E 3 *var.* Shibarghan, Shibarghān, Shiberghan, Shiberghān. N Afghanistan

Sheboygan 40 B 3 Wisconsin, N USA

Shebshi Mountains 75 H 4 *var.* Schebschi Mountains. Mountain range, E Nigeria

Sheffield 89 D 6 N England, UK

Shelburne 39 F 5 Ontario, S Canada

Shelburne Bay 148 C 1 bay, NW Coral Sea

Shelby 44 B 1 Montana, NW USA

Shelbyville, Lake 40 B 4 reservoir, Illinois, N USA

Sheldon 45 F 3 Iowa, C USA

Shelekhov Gulf *see* Shelikhova, Zaliv

Shelikhova, Zaliv 115 H 2 *Eng.* Shelekhov Gulf. Gulf, N Sea of Okhotsk

Shemakha *see* Şamaxı

Shendi 72 C 3 *var.* Shandī. NE Sudan

Shenyang 128 D 3 *Chin.* Shen-yang, *Eng.* Moukden, Mukden; *prev.* Fengtien. Province capital, NE China

Shepetivka 108 D 2 *Rus.* Shepetovka. NW Ukraine

Shepetovka *see* Shepetivka

Shepparton 149 C 7 Victoria, SE Australia

Sherbrooke 39 E 4 Québec, SE Canada

Shereik 72 C 3 N Sudan

Shergui, Shatt al- *see* Ech Chergui, Chott

Sheridan 44 C 2 Wyoming, C USA

Sherman 49 G 2 Texas, S USA

's-Hertogenbosch 86 D 4 *Fr.* Bois-le-Duc, *Ger.* Herzogenbusch. S Netherlands

Shetland Islands 88 D 1 island group, NE Scotland, UK

Shibushi-wan 131 B 8 bay, NW Pacific Ocean

Shihezi 126 C 2 NW China

Shiichi *see* Shyichy

Shijiazhuang 128 C 4 *var.* Shih-chia-chuang, Shihkiachwang; *prev.* Shihmen. Province capital, NE China

Shikārpur 134 B 3 SE Pakistan

Shikoku 131 C 7 *var.* Sikoku. Island, Japan

Shikoku Basin 152 B 2 *var.* Sikoku Basin. Undersea basin, NE Pacific Ocean

Shiliguri 135 F 3 *prev.* Siliguri. NE India

Shilka 115 F 4 river, C Russian Federation

Shimbir Berris *see* Shimbiris

Shimbiris 72 E 4 *var.* Shimbir Berris. Mountain, N Somalia

Shimoga 132 C 2 W India

Shimonoseki 131 A 7 *var.* Simonoseki; *hist.* Akamagaseki, Bakan. Honshū, SW Japan

Shinano-gawa 131 C 5 *var.* Sinano Gawa. River, Honshū, C Japan

Shindand 122 D 4 W Afghanistan

Shingū 131 C 7 *var.* Singū. Honshū, SW Japan

Shinjō 130 D 4 *var.* Sinzyô. Honshū, C Japan

Shinyanga 73 C 7 NW Tanzania

Shiprock 48 C 1 New Mexico, SW USA

Shiquanhe 126 A 4 W China

Shīrāz 120 D 4 *var.* Shīrāz. S Iran

Shīrāz *see* Shīrāz

Shishchitsy *see* Shyshchytsy

Shivpuri 134 D 3 C India

Shizugawa 130 D 4 Honshū, NE Japan

Shizuoka 131 D 6 *var.* Sizuoka. Honshū, S Japan

Shklov *see* Shklow

Shklow 107 E 6 *Rus.* Shklov. E Belorussia

Shkodër 101 C 5 *var.* Shkodra, *It.* Scutari, *SCr.* Skadar. NW Albania

Shkumbinit, Lumi i 101 D 6 *var.* Shkumbī, Shkumbin. River, C Albania

Shoal Lake 37 F 5 Manitoba, S Canada

Sholāpur *see* Solapur

Shostka 109 F 1 NE Ukraine

Show Low 48 B 2 Arizona, SW USA

Shpola 109 E 3 N Ukraine

Shreveport 42 A 2 Louisiana, S USA

Shrewsbury 89 C 6 *hist.* Scrobesbyrig'. W England, UK

Shūlgareh 123 E 3 N Afghanistan

Shumagin Islands 36 B 3 island group, Alaska, NW USA

Shumen 104 D 2 *var.* Šumen. NE Bulgaria

Shumerlya 111 C 5 W Russian Federation

Shumilina 107 E 5 *Rus.* Shumilino. NE Belorussia

Shumilino *see* Shumilina

Shunsen *see* Ch'unch'ŏn

Shuqrah 121 C 7 *var.* Shaqrā. SW Yemen

Shwebo 136 B 3 N Burma

Shyichy 107 C 7 *Rus.* Shiichi. SE Belorussia

Shymkent 114 B 5 *var.* Čimkent; *prev.* Chimkent. S Kazakhstan

Shyshchytsy 107 C 6 *Rus.* Shishchitsy. C Belorussia

Sīāh Kūh 122 D 4 mountain range, Afghanistan/Iran

Šiauliai 106 B 4 *Ger.* Schaulen. N Lithuania

Siazan' *see* Siyäzän

Sibay 111 D 6 W Russian Federation

Šibenik 100 A 4 *It.* Sebenico. S Croatia

Siberia 115 E 3 *var.* Sibir'. Physical region, C Russian Federation

Siberoet *see* Siberut, Pulau

Siberut, Pulau 138 A 4 *prev.* Siberoet. Island, Kepulauan Mentawai, W Indonesia

Sibi 134 B 2 SW Pakistan

Sibiu 108 B 4 *Ger.* Hermannstadt, *Hung.* Nagyszeben. C Romania

Sibolga 138 B 3 Sumatera, N Indonesia

Sibu 138 D 3 Borneo, E Malaysia

Sibut 76 C 4 *prev.* Fort-Sibut. S Central African Republic

Sibuyan Sea 139 E 2 sea, W Pacific Ocean

Sichon 137 C 7 *var.* Ban Sichon, Si Chon. S Thailand

Sichuan 129 B 5 *var.* Chuan, Ssu-ch'uan, Szechuan, Szechwan. Province, C China

Sichuan Pendi 129 B 5 depression, C China

Sicilia 97 C 7 *Eng.* Sicily; *anc.* Trinacria. Island, S Italy

Sicilian Channel *see* Sicily, Strait of

Sicily *see* Sicilia

Sicuani 61 E 4 S Peru

Sidári 104 A 4 Kérkyra, W Greece

Siderno 97 D 7 SW Italy

Sidhirókastron *see* Sidirókastro

Sidi Barrâni 72 A 1 NW Egypt

Sidi Bel Abbès 70 D 2 *var.* Sidi bel Abbès, Sidi-Bel-Abbès. NW Algeria

Sidirókastron 104 C 3 *prev.* Sidhirókastron. NE Greece

Sidley, Mount 154 B 4 mountain, Antarctica

Sidney 40 C 4 Ohio, N USA

Sidney 44 D 1 Nebraska, C USA

Sidney 44 D 4 Missouri, C USA

Siedlce 98 E 4 *Ger.* Sedlez, *Rus.* Sesdlets. E Poland

Siegen 94 B 4 W Germany

Siemiatycze 98 E 3 E Poland

Siena 96 C 3 *Fr.* Sienne; *anc.* Saena Julia. C Italy

Sieradz 98 C 4 C Poland

Sierpc 98 D 3 C Poland

Sierra de Soconusco *see* Sierra Madre

Sierra Leone 74 C 4 Leone. Republic, W Africa

Official name: Republic of Sierra Leone **Date of formation:** 1961 **Capital:** Freetown **Population:** 4.5 million **Total area:** 71,740 sq km (27,699 sq miles) **Languages:** English*, Krio (Creole) **Religions:** Traditional beliefs 52%, Muslim 40%, Christian 8% **Ethnic mix:** Mende 34%, Temne 31%, Limba 9%, Kono 5%, other 21% **Government:** Military regime **Currency:** Leone = 100 cents

Sierra Leone Basin 66 C 4 undersea basin, E Atlantic Ocean

Sierra Leone Rise 66 C 4 *var.* Sierra Leone Ridge, Sierra Leone Schwelle. Undersea rise, E Atlantic Ocean

Sierra Madre 52 A 2 *var.* Sierra de Soconusco. Mountain range, Guatemala/Mexico

Sierra Nevada 47 C 6 mountain range, California, W USA

Sierra Nevada de Mérida *see* Mérida, Cordillera de

Sierra Vieja 48 D 4 mountain range, Texas, SW USA

Sierra Vista 48 B 3 Arizona, SW USA

Sífnos 105 C 6 *anc.* Siphnos. Island, Kykládes, SE Greece

Sigli 138 A 3 W Indonesia

Siglufjördhur 83 E 4 N Iceland

Signy 154 A 2 research station, Antarctica

Sigsbee Deep *see* Mexico Basin

Siguatepeque 52 C 2 W Honduras

Siguiri 74 D 4 NE Guinea

Siilinjärvi 84 E 4 C Finland

Siirt 117 F 4 *var.* Sert; *anc.* Tigranocerta. SE Turkey

Sikainana *see* Stewart Island

Sikandarabad *see* Secunderābād

Sikasso 74 D 4 S Mali

Sikeston 45 H 5 Iowa, C USA

Sikhote-Alin', Khrebet 115 G 4 mountain range, SE Russian Federation

Siklós 99 C 7 SW Hungary

Sikoku *see* Shikoku
Sikoku Basin *see* Shikoku Basin
Šilalė 106 B 4 W Lithuania
Silchar 135 G 3 NE India
Silifke 116 C 4 *anc.* Seleucia. S Turkey
Siliguri *see* Shiliguri
Siling Co 126 C 5 lake, W China
Silistra 104 E 1 *var.* Silistria; *anc.* Durostorum. NE Bulgaria
Sillamäe 106 E 2 *Ger.* Sillamäggi. NE Estonia
Sillamäggi *see* Sillamäe
Silsbee 49 H 3 Texas, S USA
Šilutė 106 B 4 *Ger.* Heydekrug. W Lithuania
Silvan 117 E 4 SE Turkey
Silva Porto *see* Kuito
Silverek 117 E 4 SE Turkey
Simanichy 107 C 7 *Rus.* Simonichi. SE Belorussia
Simav 116 B 3 W Turkey
Simav 116 A 3 river, NW Turkey
Simbirsk *see* Ul'yanovsk
Simeto 97 C 7 river, SW Italy
Simeulue, Pulau 138 A 3 island, NW Indonesia
Simferopol' 109 F 5 S Ukraine
Simitli 104 C 3 SW Bulgaria
Šimleu Silvaniei 108 B 3 *Hung.* Szilágysomlyo; *prev.* Simlăul Silvaniei, Şimleul Silvaniei. NW Romania
Simonichi *see* Simanichy
Simpang 138 B 4 W Indonesia
Simpelveld 87 D 6 SE Netherlands
Simplon Pass 95 B 8 pass, S Switzerland
Simplon Tunnel 95 B 8 tunnel, Italy/Switzerland
Simpson *see* Fort Simpson
Simpson Desert 148 B 4 desert, C Australia
Sînā' *see* Sinai
Sinai 72 C 2 *Ar.* Shibh Jazīrat Sīnā', Sīnā'. Physical region, NE Egypt
Sinaia 108 C 4 SE Romania
Sinano Gawa *see* Shinano-gawa
Sincelejo 58 B 2 NW Colombia
Sind 134 B 3 *var.* Sindh. Province, SE Pakistan
Sindelfingen 95 B 6 SW Germany
Sindh *see* Sind
Sindi 106 D 2 *Ger.* Zintenhof. SW Estonia
Sinegorskiy 111 B 7 SW Russian Federation
Sinel'nikovo *see* Synel'nykove
Sines 92 B 4 S Portugal

Singapore
138 A 1 Singapore. Republic, SE Asia

Official name: Republic of Singapore **Date of formation:** 1965 **Capital:** Singapore City **Population:** 2.8 million **Total Area:** 620 sq km (239 sq miles) **Languages:** Malay*, Chinese **Religions:** Buddhist 30%, Christian 20%, Muslim 17%, other 33% **Ethnic mix:** Chinese 76%, Malay 15%, South Asian 7%, other 2% **Government:** Multiparty democracy **Currency:** Singapore $ = 100 cents

Singapore, Republic of *see* Singapore
Singapore, Strait of 138 A 2 strait, W Pacific Ocean
Singen 95 B 7 S Germany

Singida 73 C 7 C Tanzania
Singkang *see* Sengkang
Singkawang 138 C 4 Borneo, C Indonesia
Singû *see* Shingū
Siniscola 97 A 5 W Italy
Sinj 100 B 4 SE Croatia
Sinnamarie *see* Sinnamary
Sinnamary 59 H 3 *var.* Sinnamarie. N French Guiana
Sinneh *see* Sanandaj
Sinoe, Lacul *see* Sinoie, Lacul
Sinoie, Lacul 108 D 5 *prev.* Lacul Sinoe. Lagoon, W Black Sea
Sinop 116 D 2 *anc.* Sinope. N Turkey
Sinope *see* Sinop
Sinsheim 95 B 6 SW Germany
Sint Maarten 55 G 3 *Eng:* Saint Martin. Island, N Netherlands Antilles
Sint-Michielsgestel 86 D 4 S Netherlands
Sint-Niklaas 87 B 5 *Fr.* Saint-Nicolas. N Belgium
Sint-Pieters-Leeuw 87 B 6 C Belgium
Sintra 92 B 4 *prev.* Cintra. W Portugal
Sinujiif 73 E 5 NE Somalia
Sinus Arabious *see* Red Sea
Sinzyô *see* Shinjō
Siorapaluk 82 D 1 NW Greenland
Sioux City 45 F 3 South Dakota, N USA
Sioux Falls 45 F 3 South Dakota, N USA
Siphnos *see* Sífnos
Siping 128 D 3 *var.* Ssu-p'ing, Szeping; *prev.* Ssu-p'ing-chieh NE China
Siple, Mount 154 A 4 mountain, Antarctica
Siquirres 53 E 4 E Costa Rica
Siracusa 97 D 7 *Eng.* Syracuse. SW Italy
Sir Charles Forbes Island *see* Kau-Ye Kyun
Sir Edward Pellew Islands 148 B 2 island group, Northern Territory, NE Australia
Siret 108 C 3 *var.* Siretul, Ger. Sereth, *Rus.* Seret, *Ukr.* Siret. River, Romania/Ukraine
Sirikit Reservoir 136 C 4 lake, N Thailand
Sirna *see* Sýrna
Sirte, Gulf of 103 E 4 *var.* Khalīj Surt, *Eng.* Gulf of Sidra, Gulf of Sirti, Sidra. Gulf, S Mediterranean Sea
Sisak 100 B 3 *var.* Siscia, Ger. Sissek, *Hung.* Sziszek; *anc.* Segestica. C Croatia
Sisimiut 82 C 3 *var.* Holsteinborg, Holsteinsborg, Holstenborg, Holstensborg. W Greenland
Sīstān, Daryācheh-ye 122 D 5 *var.* Daryācheh-ye Hāmūn, Hāmūn-e flāberī. Lake, E Iran
Siteía 105 D 8 *var.* Sitía. Kríti, SE Greece
Sitges 93 G 2 NE Spain
Sitía *see* Siteía
Sittang 136 B 4 *var.* Sittoung. River, C Burma
Sittard 87 D 5 SE Netherlands
Sittoung *see* Sittang
Sittwe 136 A 3 *var.* Akyab. W Burma
Siuna 52 D 3 NE Nicaragua
Sivas 116 D 3 *anc.* Sebaste, Sebastia. C Turkey

Siwa Oasis 72 A 2 oasis, NW Egypt
Six Counties, The *see* Northern Ireland
Six-Fours-les-Plages 91 D 6 SE France
Siyäzän 117 H 2 *Rus.* Siazan'. NE Azerbaijan
Sizuoka *see* Shizuoka
Sjar *see* Säare
Sjælland 85 B 8 *Eng.* Zealand, Ger. Seeland. Island, E Denmark
Sjenica 101 D 5 *Turk.* Seniça. SW Yugoslavia
Skagerrak 85 A 6 *var.* Skagerak, Skag-e-rak. Channel, Baltic Sea/North Sea
Skagit River 46 B 1 river, Washington, NW USA
Skalka 84 C 3 lake, N Sweden
Skåne 85 B 7 *prev.* Eng. Scania. Cultural region, S Sweden
Skaudvilė 106 B 4 SW Lithuania
Skegness 89 E 6 E England, UK
Skeleton Coast 78 A 3 physical region, NW Namibia
Skellefteå 84 D 4 N Sweden
Skellefteälven 84 C 4 river, N Sweden
Ski 85 B 6 S Norway
Skíathos 105 C 5 Vóreioi Sporádes, E Greece
Skidal' 107 B 5 *Rus.* Skidel'. W Belorussia
Skidel' *see* Skidal'
Skiermûntseach *see* Schiermonnikoog
Skíros *see* Skýros
Skópelos 105 C 5 Vóreioi Sporádes, E Greece
Skopje 101 D 6 *var.* Üsküb, Turk. Üsküp; *prev.* Skoplje, *anc.* Scupi. Country capital, N Macedonia
Skovorodino 115 F 4 SE Russian Federation
Skrīveri 106 C 4 S Latvia
Skuodas 106 B 3 *Ger.* Schoden, Pol. Szkudy. NW Lithuania
Skye, Isle of 88 B 3 island, W Scotland, UK
Skylge *see* Terschelling
Skýros 105 C 5 *var.* Skíros. Skýros, E Greece
Skýros 105 C 5 *var.* Skíros; *anc.* Scyros. Island, Vóreioi Sporádes, E Greece
Slagelse 85 B 7 E Denmark
Slatina 108 B 4 S Romania
Slave Coast 75 F 5 coastal region, W Africa
Slavgorod *see* Slawharad
Slavonska Požega 100 C 3 *Ger.* Poschega, *Hung.* Pozsega; *prev.* Požega. NE Croatia
Slavonski Brod 100 C 3 *Ger.* Brod, Hung. Bród; *prev.* Brod, Brod na savi. NE Croatia
Slavuta 108 C 2 NW Ukraine
Slavyansk *see* Slov''yans'k
Slawharad 107 E 7 *Rus.* Slavgorod. E Belorussia
Sławno 98 B 2 NW Poland
Sléibhte Chill Mhantáin *see* Wicklow Mountains
Sligeach *see* Sligo
Sligo 89 A 5 *Ir.* Sligeach. NW Ireland
Sliven 104 D 2 *var.* Slivno. E Bulgaria
Slivnitsa 104 C 2 W Bulgaria
Slivno *see* Sliven
Slobozia 108 D 5 SE Romania
Slonim 107 B 6 *Pol.* Słonim, *Rus.* Slonim. W Belorussia

Slovakia
99 D 6 *Ger.* Slowakei, *Hung.* Szlovákia, *Slvk.* Slovensko. Republic, C Europe

Official name: Slovak Republic **Date of formation:** 1993 **Capital:** Bratislava **Population:** 5.3 million **Total area:** 49,500 sq km (19,100 sq miles) **Languages:** Slovak*, Hungarian (Magyar), Czech **Religions:** Roman Catholic 80%, Protestant 12%, other 8% **Ethnic mix:** Slovak 85%, Hungarian 9%, Czech 1%, other (inc. Gypsy) 5% **Government:** Multiparty republic **Currency:** Koruna = 100 halierov

Slovenia
95 D 8 *Ger.* Slowenien, *Slvn.* Slovenija. Republic, C Europe

Official name: Republic of Slovenia **Date of formation:** 1991 **Capital:** Ljubljana **Population:** 2 million **Total area:** 20,250 sq km (7,820 sq miles) **Languages:** Slovene*, Serbian, Croatian **Religions:** Roman Catholic 96%, Muslim 1%, other 3% **Ethnic mix:** Slovene 92%, Croat 3%, Serb 1%, other 4% **Government:** Multiparty republic **Currency:** Tolar = 100 stotins

Slovenské Rudohorie 99 D 6 *var.* Ungarisches Erzgebirge, *Eng.* Slovak Ore Mountains, *Ger.* Slowakisches Erzgebirge. Mountain range, C Slovakia
Slov''yans'k 109 G 3 *Rus.* Slavyansk. E Ukraine
Słubice 98 B 3 *Ger.* Frankfurt. W Poland
Sluch 108 D 1 river, NW Ukraine
Słupsk 98 C 2 *Ger.* Stolp. NW Poland
Slutsk 107 C 6 S Belorussia
Småland 85 B 7 cultural region, S Sweden
Smallwood Reservoir 39 F 2 lake, Newfoundland and Labrador, E Canada
Smarhon' 107 C 5 *Pol.* Smorgonie, *Rus.* Smorgon'. W Belorussia
Smederevo 100 E 4 *Ger.* Semendria. N Yugoslavia
Smela *see* Smila
Smila 109 E 2 *Rus.* Smela. C Ukraine
Smilten *see* Smiltene
Smiltene 106 D 3 *Ger.* Smilten. N Latvia
Smithton 149 C 8 Tasmania, SE Australia
Smoky Cape 149 E 6 headland, New South Wales, SE Australia
Smøla 84 A 4 island, W Norway
Smolensk 111 A 5 W Russian Federation
Smyrna *see* İzmir
Snake River 46 C 3 river, NW USA
Snake River Plain 46 D 4 plain, Idaho, NW USA
Sneek 86 D 2 N Netherlands
Sněžka 98 B 4 *Ger.* Schneekoppe. Mountain, N Czech Republic
Sniečkus *see* Visaginas
Snina 99 E 5 *Hung.* Szinna. E Slovakia
Snowdonia 89 C 6 mountain range, N Wales, UK
Snowdrift *see* Lutsel'k'e
Snyder 49 F 3 Texas, S USA
Sobradinho, Barragem de *see* Sobradinho, Represa de

Sobradinho, Represa de 63 F 2 *var.* Barragem de Sobradinho. Reservoir, E Brazil

Socabaya 61 E 4 SE Peru

Sochi 111 A 7 SW Russian Federation

Société, Archipel de la 145 G 4 *var.* Îles de la Société, *Eng.* Society Islands. Island group, W French Polynesia

Society Islands *see* Leeward Islands

Socorro, Isla 50 B 5 island, W Mexico

Socotra 121 D 7 *var.* Sokotra. Island, SE Yemen

Soc Trăng 137 D 6 *var.* Khanh Hung. S Vietnam

Socuéllamos 93 E 3 C Spain

Sodankylä 84 D 3 N Finland

Söderhamn 85 C 5 C Sweden

Södertälje 85 C 6 C Sweden

Sodiri 72 B 4 *var.* Sawdirī, Sodari. C Sudan

Soekaboemi *see* Sukabumi

Sofia *see* Sofiya

Sofiya 104 C 2 *var.* Sofija, Sophia, *Eng.* Sofia; *Lat.* Serdica . Country capital, W Bulgaria

Sogamoso 58 B 3 C Colombia

Sognefjorden 85 A 5 fjord, NE North Sea

Sohâg 72 B 2 *var.* Sawhâj, Suliag. C Egypt

Sohar *see* Şuḩār

Sokal' 108 C 2 *Rus.* Sokal. NW Ukraine

Sokal *see* Sokal'

Söke 116 A 4 SW Turkey

Sokhumi 117 E 1 *Rus.* Sukhumi. NW Georgia

Sokodé 75 F 4 C Togo

Sokol 110 C 4 NW Russian Federation

Sokolov 99 A 5 *Ger.* Falkenau an der Eger; *prev.* Falknov nad Ohří. W Czech Republic

Sokoto 75 F 4 State capital NW Nigeria

Sokotra *see* Socotra

Solapur 132 C 1 *prev.* Sholāpur. SW India

Solca 108 C 3 *Ger.* Solka. N Romania

Sol, Costa del 92 D 5 coastal region, S Spain

Soldeu 91 B 8 NE Andorra

Solec Kujawski 98 C 3 W Poland

Soledad 58 B 1 N Colombia

Soledad *see* East Falkland

Soligorsk *see* Salihorsk

Solikamsk 110 D 4 NW Russian Federation

Sol'-Iletsk 111 D 6 W Russian Federation

Solin 100 B 4 *It.* Salona; *anc.* Salonae. S Croatia

Solingen 94 A 4 W Germany

Solka *see* Solca

Sollentuna 85 C 6 C Sweden

Solok 138 B 4 W Indonesia

Solomon Islands 144 D 3 *prev.* British Solomon Islands Protectorate. Commonwealth republic, SW Pacific Ocean

Official name: Solomon Islands
Date of formation: 1978
Capital: Honiara **Population:** 400,000 **Total Area:** 289,000 sq kms (111,583 sq miles) **Languages:** English*, 87 (est.) native languages

Religions: Christian 91%, other 9% **Ethnic mix:** Melanesian 94%, other 6% **Government:** Parliamentary democracy **Currency:** Solomon Is $ = 100 cents

Solomon Sea 144 B 3 sea, SW Pacific Ocean

Soltau 94 B 3 NW Germany

Sol'tsy 110 A 4 *var.* Solcy,Sol'cy. W Russian Federation

Solwezi 78 D 2 NW Zambia

Sōma 130 D 4 Honshū, C Japan

Somalia 73 E 5 *Som.* Jamuuriyada Demuqraadiga Soomaaliyeed, Soomaaliya; *prev.* Italian Somaliland, Somaliland Protectorate. Republic, NE Africa

Official name: Somali Democratic Republic **Date of formation:** 1960 **Capital:** Mogadishu **Population:** 9.5 million **Total area:** 637,660 sq km (246,200 sq miles) **Languages:** Somali,* Arabic **Religions:** Sunni Muslim 99%, other (inc. Christian) 1% **Ethnic mix:** Somali 98%, Bantu, Arab and other 2% **Government:** Transitional **Currency:** Shilling = 100 cents

Somali Basin 140 B 4 undersea basin, W Indian Ocean

Somali Peninsula 68 E 4 coastal feature, NE Somalia

Sombor 100 D 3 *Hung.* Zombor. NW Yugoslavia

Someren 87 D 5 SE Netherlands

Somerset 42 A 5 *var.* Somerset Village. W Bermuda

Somerset 40 C 5 Massachusetts, NE USA

Somerset Island 37 F 2 island, NW Canada

Somerset Island 42 A 5 island, W Bermuda

Somerset Village *see* Somerset

Somerton 48 A 3 Arizona, SW USA

Somerville Lake 49 G 3 reservoir, Texas, S USA

Somes 108 B 3 *var.* Someşul, Szamos, *Ger.* Samosch, Somesch. River, Hungary/Romania

Somme 90 C 2 river, N France

Sommerfeld *see* Lubsko

Somotillo 52 C 3 NW Nicaragua

Somoto 52 D 3 NW Nicaragua

Sonaguera 52 D 2 N Honduras

Sondre Strømfjord *see* Kangerlussuaq

Songea 73 C 8 S Tanzania

Sŏngjin *see* Kimch'aek

Songkhla 137 C 7 *var.* Songkla, *Mal.* Singora. S Thailand

Sông Srepok *see* Srêpôk, Tônle

Sonsonate 52 B 3 W El Salvador

Sop Hao 136 D 3 NE Laos

Sopot 98 C 2 *Ger.* Zoppot. N Poland

Sopron 99 B 6 *Ger.* Ödenburg. NW Hungary

Sorgues 91 D 6 SE France

Sorgun 116 D 3 C Turkey

Soria 93 E 2 N Spain

Soroca 108 D 3 *Rus.* Soroki. N Moldavia

Sorocaba 57 D 5 S Brazil

Sorochino *see* Sarochyna

Soroki *see* Soroca

Sorong 139 G 4 New Guinea, E Indonesia

Sørøy *see* Sørøya

Sørøya 84 C 2 *var.* Sørøy. Island, N Norway

Sortavala 110 B 3 NW Russian Federation

Sosnogorsk 110 D 4 NW Russian Federation

Sotavento, Ilhas de 74 A 3 *var.* Leeward Islands. Island group, S Cape Verde

Sotkamo 84 E 4 C Finland

Souanké 77 B 5 NW Congo

Souflí 104 D 3 *prev.* Souflíon. NE Greece

Souflíon *see* Souflí

Soufrière 55 F 2 W Saint Lucia

Soufrière 71 F 2 *var.* Sûsah. NE Tunisia

South Africa 78 C 4 Africa, *Afr.* Suid-Afrika. Republic, S Africa

Official name: Republic of South Africa **Date of formation:** 1910 **Capitals:** Pretoria, Cape Town, Bloemfontein **Population:** 37.4 million **Total area:** 1,221,040 sq km (471,443 sq miles) **Languages:** Afrikaans*, English, 11 African languages **Religions:** Protestant 55%, Roman Catholic 9%, Hindu 1%, Muslim 1%, other 34% **Ethnic mix:** Black 75%, White 14%, mixed 9%, South Asian 2% **Government:** Multiparty republic **Currency:** Rand = 100 cents

South America 67 B 5 continent

Southampton 89 D 7 *hist.* Hamwih, *Lat.* Clausentum. S England, UK

Southampton Island 37 G 3 island, NE Canada

South Andaman 133 F 2 island, SE India

South Australia 149 A 5 state, S Australia

South Australian Basin 152 B 4 undersea basin, SW Indian Ocean

South Bend 40 C 3 Indiana, N USA

South Beveland *see* Zuid-Beveland

South Carolina 43 E 2 off. State of South Carolina; nickname Palmetto State. State, SE USA

South China Basin 152 A 3 undersea basin, E Pacific Ocean

South China Sea 152 A 2 *Chin.* Nan Hai, *Ind.* Laut Cina Selatan, *Vtn.* Biển fông. Sea, E Pacific Ocean

South Dakota 45 E 2 off. State of South Dakota; nicknames Coyote State, Sunshine State. State, N USA

South East Cape 149 C 7 headland, Victoria, S Australia

Southeast Indian Ridge 141 D 6 undersea ridge, S Indian Ocean

Southeast Pacific Basin 153 F 5 *var.* Belling Hausen Mulde. Undersea basin, SE Pacific Ocean

Southend-on-Sea 89 E 6 SE England, UK

Southern Alps 151 B 6 mountain range, South Island, SW New Zealand

Southern Cook Islands 145 F 5 island group, S Cook Islands

Southern Cross 147 B 6 Western Australia, SW Australia

Southern Ocean 152 C 5 ocean

Southern Uplands 88 C 4 mountain range, S Scotland, UK

Southesk Tablelands 146 D 3 plain, NW Australia

South Fiji Basin 152 C 4 undersea basin, S Pacific Ocean

South Georgia 154 A 1 island, SW Atlantic Ocean

South Georgia Ridge 57 C 8 *var.* North Scotia Ridge. Undersea ridge, SW Atlantic Ocean

South Huvadhu Atoll 132 B 5 *var.* Gaafu Dhaalu Atoll. Island, S Maldives

South Indian Basin 141 D 7 undersea basin, S Indian Ocean

South Indian Lake 37 F 4 Manitoba, C Canada

South Indian Lake 38 A 2 lake, Manitoba, C Canada

South Island 151 C 6 island, South Island, S New Zealand

South Island *see* Auk Bok

South Korea 128 E 4 *Kor.* Taehan Min'guk. Republic, E Asia

Official name: Republic of Korea **Date of formation:** 1948 **Capital:** Seoul **Population:** 44.5 million **Total Area:** 99,020 sq km (38,232 sq miles) **Languages:** Korean*, Chinese **Religions:** Mahayana Buddhist 47%, Protestant 38%, Roman Catholic 11%, Confucianist 3%, other 1% **Ethnic mix:** Korean 99.9% other 0.1% **Government:** Multiparty republic **Currency:** Won = 100 chon

South Lake Tahoe 47 C 5 California, W USA

South Magnetic Pole 154 D 5 pole, Antarctica

South Orkney Islands 154 A 2 island group, Antarctica

South Ossetia 117 F 2 region, C Georgia

South Pacific Basin *see* Southwest Pacific Basin

South Platte River 44 D 4 river, C USA

South Pole 154 B 3 pole, Antarctica

South Portland 41 G 2 Maine, NE USA

South Sandwich Islands 154 A 1 island group, S Atlantic Ocean

South Sandwich Trench 154 A 1 trench, SW Atlantic Ocean

South Shetland Islands 154 A 2 island group, Antarctica

South Shields 88 D 4 N England, UK

South Sioux City 45 F 3 Nebraska, C USA

South Taranaki Bight 150 C 4 bight, E Tasman Sea

South Tasmania Plateau *see* Tasman Plateau

South Uist 88 B 3 island, W Scotland, UK

South Wellesley Islands 148 B 3 island group, Northern Territory, N Australia

Southwest Indian Ocean Ridge *see* Southwest Indian Ridge

Southwest Indian Ridge 141 A 6 *var.* Southwest Indian Ocean Ridge. Undersea ridge, SW Indian Ocean

South West Island 148 D 3 island,
E Australia
Southwest Pacific Basin 152 D 4
var. South Pacific Basin. Undersea
basin, SE Pacific Ocean
Soweto 78 D 4 NE South Africa

Spain
92-93 0 *Sp.* España; *anc.* Hispania,
Iberia, *Lat.* Hispana. Monarchy,
SW Europe

Official name: Kingdom of Spain
Date of formation: 1492 **Capital:**
Madrid **Population:** 39.2 million
Total area: 504,780 sq km
(194,900 sq miles) **Languages:**
Castilian Spanish*, Catalan*,
Galician*, Basque*
Religions: Roman Catholic 99%,
other 1% **Ethnic mix:** Castilian
Spanish 72%, Catalan 16%, Galician
7%, other 5% **Government:**
Constitutional monarchy
Currency: Peseta = 100 céntimos

Spalato *see* Split
Spaldings 54 B 5 C Jamaica
Spanish Town 54 B 5 *hist.* St.Iago
de la Vega. C Jamaica
Spanish Wells 54 C 1 C Bahamas
Sparks 47 C 5 Nevada, W USA
Sparta *see* Spárti
Spartanburg 43 E 1 South Carolina,
SE USA
Spárti 105 B 6 *Eng.* Sparta. S Greece
Spearfish 44 D 3 South Dakota, N
USA
Speightstown 55 G 1 W Barbados
Spencer 45 F 3 Iowa, C USA
Spencer Gulf 149 B 6 gulf, E Indian
Ocean
Spenser Mountains 151 C 5
mountain range, South Island, C
New Zealand
Spey 88 C 3 river, NE Scotland, UK
Spijkenisse 86 B 4 SW Netherlands
Spíli 105 C 8 Kríti, SE Greece
Spīn Būldak 123 E 5 S Afghanistan
Spitsbergen 83 G 2 island, NW
Svalbard
Split 101 A 8 *It.* Spalato. S Croatia
Spogi 106 D 4 SE Lithuania
Spokane 46 C 2 Washington, NW
USA
Spratly Islands 125 E 4 island
group, S South China Sea
Spratly Islands 138 D 2 *Chin.*
Nansha Qundao. Disputed
territory, S South China Sea
Spree 94 D 4 river, E Germany
Springfield 40 C 4 Ohio, NE USA
Springfield 41 G 3 state capital,
Illinois, N USA
Springfield 46 B 3 Oregon, NW
USA
Springfield 45 G 5 Missouri, C
USA
Spring Garden 59 F 2 NE Guyana
Spring Hill 43 E 4 Florida, SE USA
Springsure 148 D 4 Queensland, E
Australia
Sprottau *see* Szprotawa
Srbobran 100 D 3 *var.*
Bácsszenttamás, *Hung.*
Szenttamás. N Yugoslavia
Srebrenica 100 C 4 E Bosnia &
Herzegovina
Sredets 104 E 2 *var.* Sredec; *prev.*
Syulemeshlii. C Bulgaria
Srednesibirskoye Ploskogor'ye 115
E 3 *var.* Central Siberian Uplands,
Eng. Central Siberian Plateau.

Mountain range, C Russian
Federation
Sremska Mitrovica 100 D 3 *Ger.*
Mitrowitz; *prev.* Mitrovica. NW
Yugoslavia
Srêpôk, Tônle 137 E 5 *var.* Sông
Srepok. River,
Cambodia/Vietnam
Sri Aman 138 C 3 *var.* Bandar Sri
Aman, Simanggang. Borneo, E
Malaysia
Srīkākulam 135 F 5 E India

Sri Lanka
132 D 3 Republic of Sri Lanka;
prev. Ceylon. Republic, S Asia

Official name: Democratic Socialist
Republic of Sri Lanka **Date of
formation:** 1948 **Capital:** Colombo
Population:17.9 million **Total area:**
65,610 sq km (25,332 sq miles)
Languages: Sinhala*, Tamil, English
Religions: Buddhist 70%, Hindu
15%, Christian 8%, Muslim 7%
Ethnic mix: Sinhalese 74%, Tamil
18%, other 8% **Government:**
Multiparty republic
Currency: Rupee = 100 cents

Srinagarind Reservoir 137 C 5 lake,
W Thailand
Stabroek 87 C 5 N Belgium
Stade 94 B 3 NW Germany
Stadskanaal 86 F 2 NE Netherlands
Stafford 89 D 6 W England, UK
Staicele 106 D 3 N Latvia
Stakhanov 109 H 3 E Ukraine
Stalinsk *see* Novokuznetsk
Stalinski Zaliv *see* Varnenski Zaliv
Stalowa Wola 98 E 4 SE Poland
Stamford 41 F 3 Connecticut, NE
USA
Stanley 65 D 7 *var.* Port Stanley.
Dependent territory capital, E
Falkland Islands
Stanley *see* Chek Chue
Stanleyville *see* Kisangani
Stann Creek *see* Dangriga
Stanovoy Khrebet 115 F 4
mountain range, E Russian
Federation
Stanthorpe 149 D 5 Queensland, SE
Australia
Staphorst 86 D 3 E Netherlands
Starachowice 98 D 4 SE Poland
Stara Pazova 100 D 3 *Ger.* Altpasua,
Hung. Ópazova. N Yugoslavia
Stara Planina *see* Balkan Mountains
Stara Zagora 104 D 2 *Lat.* Augusta
Trajana. C Bulgaria
Starbuck Island 145 G 3 *prev.*
Volunteer Island. Island, E
Kiribati
Stargard in Pommern *see* Stargard
Szczeciński
Stargard Szczeciński 98 B 3 *Ger.*
Stargard in Pommern. NW
Poland
Starobel'sk *see* Starobil's'k
Starobil's'k 109 H 2 *Rus.*
Starobel'sk. E Ukraine
Starobin *see* Starobyn
Starobyn 107 C 7 *Rus.* Starobin. S
Belorussia
Starogard Gdański 98 C 2 *Ger.*
Preussisch-Stargard. N Poland
Starokonstantinov *see*
Starokostyantyniv
Starokostyantyniv 108 D 2 *Rus.*
Starokonstantinov. NW Ukraine
Starominskaya 111 A 7 SW Russian
Federation

Starry Oskol 111 B 6 W Russian
Federation
Staryya Darohi 107 C 7 *Rus.*
Staryye Dorogi. C Belorussia
Staryye Dorogi *see* Staryya Darohi
Staten Island *see* Estados, Isla de los
State of Eritrea *see* Eritrea
Statesboro 43 E 2 Georgia, SE USA
Staunton 41 E 5 Virginia, NE USA
Stavanger 85 A 6 S Norway
St-Avertin 90 B 4 W France
Stavropol' 111 B 7 *prev.*
Voroshilovsk. SW Russian
Federation
Stavropol' *see* Tol'yatti
St-Brieuc 90 A 3 NW France
St-Chamond 91 D 5 E France
St-Claude 91 D 5 *anc.* Condate. E
France
St-Denis 90 C 3 N France
St-Denis 79 H 4 dependent
territory capital, N Réunion
St-Dié 90 E 4 NE France
Steamboat Springs 44 C 4
Colorado, C USA
Steenwijk 86 D 2 N Netherlands
St-Egrève 91 D 5 E France
Steier *see* Steyr
Steinkjer 84 B 4 C Norway
Stejarul *see* Karapelit
Stendal 94 C 3 C Germany
Stephenville 49 G 3 Texas, S USA
Sterling 40 B 3 Illinois, N USA
Sterling 44 D 4 Colorado, C USA
Sterling Heights 40 D 3 Michigan,
N USA
Sterlitamak 111 D 6 W Russian
Federation
St-Étienne 91 C 5 E France
Stettin *see* Szczecin
Stevenage 89 E 6 SE England, UK
Stevens Point 40 B 2 Wisconsin, N
USA
Stewart 36 D 4 British Columbia, W
Canada
Stewart Island 151 A 8 *var.*
Sikainana. Island, South Island, S
New Zealand
Steyr 95 D 6 *var.* Steier. N Austria
St-Flour 91 C 5 C France
St-Gaudens 91 B 6 S France
St-Georges 39 E 4 Québec, SE
Canada
St-Georges 59 H 3 E French Guiana
Stif *see* Sétif
Stillwater 49 G 1 Oklahoma, C USA
Štip 101 E 6 E Macedonia
Stirling 88 C 4 S Scotland, UK
St-Jean-de-Luz 91 A 6 SW France
St-Jean, Lac 39 E 4 lake, Québec, SE
Canada
Stjørdal 84 B 4 C Norway
St-Laurent *see* St-Laurent-du-Maroni
St-Laurent-du-Maroni 59 H 3 *var.*
St-Laurent. NW French Guiana
St-Lô 90 B 3 *anc.* Briovera, Laudus.
N France
St-Louis 90 E 4 NE France
St-Louis 74 B 3 NW Senegal
St-Malo 90 B 3 NW France
St-Malo, Golfe de 90 B 3 inlet, C
English Channel
St-Max 90 D 3 NE France
St-Nazaire 90 A 4 NW France
Stockach 95 B 6 S Germany
Stockholm 85 C 6 country capital,
C Sweden
Stockmannshof *see* Pļaviņas
Stockton 47 B 6 California, W USA
Stœng Trêng 137 D 5 *prev.* Stung
Treng. N Cambodia
Stoke *see* Stoke-on-Trent

Stoke-on-Trent 89 C 6 *var.* Stoke. W
England, UK
Stolp *see* Słupsk
Stolpmünde *see* Ustka
St-Omer 90 C 2 N France
Stómio 104 B 4 C Greece
Storebælt 85 B 7 *var.* Store Bælt,
Storebelt, *Eng.* Great Belt.
Channel, Baltic Sea/North Sea
Støren 85 B 5 S Norway
Storfjorden 83 G 2 fjord, Barents
Sea/Norwegian Sea
Storhammer *see* Hamar
Stornoway 88 B 2 island authority
area capital, NW Scotland, UK
Storsjön 85 B 5 lake, C Sweden
Storuman 84 C 4 lake, N Sweden
Storuman 84 C 4 N Sweden
Stowbtsy 107 C 6 *Pol.* Stolbce, *Rus.*
Stolbtsy. C Belorussia
St-Paul, Île 141 C 6 *var.* St.Paul
Island. Island, NE French
Southern & Antarctic Territories
St-Pierre & Miquelon 39 G 4 *Fr.*
Îles St-Pierre et Miquelon. French
Territorial Collectivity, NW
Atlantic Ocean
St-Pierre et Miquelon, Îles *see* St-
Pierre and Miquelon
St-Quentin 90 D 3 N France
Strabane 89 B 5 *Ir.* An Srath Bán. C
Northern Ireland, UK
Strakonice 99 A 5 *Ger.* Strakonitz.
SW Czech Republic
Strakonitz *see* Strakonice
Stralsund 94 D 2 NE Germany
Stranraer 89 B 5 SW Scotland, UK
Strasbourg 90 E 3 *Ger.* Strassburg;
anc. Argentoratum. NE France
Strǎșeni 108 D 4 *var.* Strasheny. C
Moldavia
Strasheny *see* Strǎșeni
Stratford 150 D 4 North Island, C
New Zealand
Straubing 95 C 6 SE Germany
Streaky Bay 149 A 6 bay, SE Indian
Ocean
Strehaia 108 B 5 SW Romania
Strelka 114 D 4 C Russian
Federation
Strofiliá *see* Strofyliá
Strofyliá 105 C 5 *var.* Strofilia.
Évvoia, C Greece
Stromboli, Isola 97 D 6 island, S
Italy
Stromeferry 88 B 3 NW Scotland,
UK
Strömstad 85 B 6 S Sweden
Strömsund 84 C 4 C Sweden
Struga 101 D 6 SW Macedonia
Struma 104 C 3 *Gk.* Strymónas.
River, Bulgaria/Greece
Strumica 101 E 6 E Macedonia
Strumyani 104 C 3 SW Bulgaria
Stryy 108 B 2 NW Ukraine
Studholme 151 B 7 South Island,
SW New Zealand
Stung Treng *see* Stœng Trêng
Stupino 111 B 5 W Russian
Federation
Sturgis 44 D 3 South Dakota, N
USA
Stuttgart 95 B 6 SW Germany
Stykkishólmur 83 E 5 W Iceland
Styr 108 C 1 river, NW Ukraine
Suakin 72 C 3 *var.* Sawakin. NE
Sudan
Subačius 106 C 4 NE Lithuania
Subotica 100 D 2 *Ger.* Maria-
Theresiopel, *Hung.* Szabadka. N
Yugoslavia

Suceava 108 C 3 *Ger.* Suczawa, *Hung.* Szucsava. NE Romania

Sucre 61 F 4 *hist.* Chuquisaca, La Plata. Country capital, S Bolivia

Sudan 74 C 4 physical region, W Africa

Sudan
72 A 4 *Ar.* Jamhuryat es-Sudan, Jumhuriyat as-Sudan; *prev.* Anglo-Egyptian *Sudan.* Republic, NE Africa

Official name: Republic of Sudan **Date of formation:** 1956 **Capital:** Khartoum **Population:** 27.4 million **Total area:** 2,505,815 sq km (967,493 sq miles) **Languages:** Arabic* **Religions:** Muslim 70%, traditional beliefs 20%, Christian 5%, other 5% **Government:** Military regime **Currency:** Pound = 100 piastres

---

Sudbury 38 C 4 Ontario, S Canada

Sudd 73 B 5 wetland, S Sudan

Suddie 59 F 2 NE Guyana

Sudeten 99 C 5 *var.* Sudetes, Sudetic Mountains, Cz./Pol. Sudety. Mountain range, Czech Republic/Poland

Sudong, Pulau 138 A 2 island, SW Singapore

Sueca 93 F 3 E Spain

Sue Wood Bay 42 B 5 bay, W Atlantic Ocean

Suez 72 B 1 *Ar.* As Suways, El Suweis. NE Egypt

Suez Canal 72 C 1 *Ar.* Qanāt as Suways. Canal, NE Egypt

Suez, Gulf of 72 B 1 *Ar.* Khalīj as Suways. Gulf, NW Red Sea

Suffolk 41 F 5 Virginia, NE USA

Sugla Gölü 116 C 4 lake, SW Turkey

Sühbaatar 127 E 1 N Mongolia

Suhl 95 C 5 C Germany

Şuḥār 121 D 5 *var.* Sohar. N Oman

Suixi 129 C 7 S China

Sukabumi 138 C 5 *prev.* Soekaboemi. Jawa, C Indonesia

Sukagawa 131 D 5 Honshū, C Japan

Sukhumi *see* Sokhumi

Sukkur 134 B 3 SE Pakistan

Sukumo 131 B 7 Shikoku, SW Japan

Sulaimān Range 134 C 2 mountain range, C Pakistan

Sula, Kepulauan 139 F 4 *prev.* Soela, Xulla Islands. Island group, E Indonesia

Sulawesi 139 E 4 island, C Indonesia

Sulawesi, Laut *see* Celebes Sea

Sullana 60 B 2 NW Peru

Sullivan Island *see* Lanbi Kyun

Sulphur 42 A 3 Louisiana, S USA

Sulphur Springs 49 G 2 Texas, S USA

Sultānābād *see* Arāk

Sulu Archipelago 139 E 3 island group, SW Philippines

Sülüktü *see* Sulyukta

Sulu, Laut *see* Sulu Sea

Sulu Sea 139 E 2 *var.* Laut Sulu. Sea, W Pacific Ocean

Sulyukta 123 F 2 *Kir.* Sülüktü. SW Kyrgyzstan

Sulz *see* Sulz am Neckar

Sulz am Neckar 95 B 6 *var.* Sulz. SW Germany

Sumatera 138 A 4 *Eng.* Sumatra. Island, W Indonesia

Sumatra *see* Sumatera

Sumba, Pulau 139 E 5 *Eng.* Sandalwood Island; *prev.* Soemba. Island, Nusa Tenggara, C Indonesia

Sumba, Selat 138 D 5 strait, Indian Ocean/Savu Sea

Sumbawanga 73 B 7 W Tanzania

Sumbay 61 E 4 SE Peru

Sumbe 78 B 2 *var.* N'Gunza, *Port.* Novo Redondo. W Angola

Şumen *see* Shumen

Sumgait *see* Sumqayıt

Summer Lake 46 B 4 lake, Oregon, NW USA

Sumqayıt 117 H 2 *Rus.* Sumgait. E Azerbaijan

Sumy 109 F 1 NE Ukraine

Suna 73 C 5 NE Tanzania

Sunbury 149 C 7 Victoria, SE Australia

Sun City 48 B 2 Arizona, SW USA

Sunda, Selat 138 B 5 strait, Indian Ocean/Pacific Ocean

Sunda Shelf 140 E 4 continental shelf, W Pacific Ocean

Sunda Trench 140 D 4 trench, NE Indian Ocean

Sunderland 88 D 4 *var.* Wearmouth. N England, UK

Sundsvall 85 C 5 C Sweden

Sunne 85 B 6 C Sweden

Sunnyside 46 C 2 Washington, NW USA

Sunnyvale 47 B 6 California, W USA

Suntar 115 F 3 E Russian Federation

Sunyani 75 E 5 W Ghana

Suoločielgi *see* Saariselkä

Suomussalmi 84 E 4 E Finland

Suŏng 137 D 6 SE Cambodia

Suoyarvi 110 B 3 NW Russian Federation

Supérieur, Lac *see* Superior, Lake

Superior 40 A 1 Wisconsin, N USA

Superior, Lake 40 B 1 *Fr.* Lac Supérieur. Lake, Canada/USA

Suqrah *see* Şawqirah

Şūr 121 E 5 NE Oman

Surabaya 138 D 5 *prev.* Soerabaja, Surabaja. Jawa, C Indonesia

Surakarta 138 C 5 *Eng.* Solo; *prev.* Soerakarta. Jawa, C Indonesia

Šurany 99 C 6 *Hung.* Nagysurány. SW Slovakia

Sūrat 134 C 4 W India

Suratdhani *see* Surat Thani

Surat Thani 137 C 7 *var.* Suratdhani. S Thailand

Surazh 107 E 5 NE Belorussia

Surdulica 101 E 5 SE Yugoslavia

Sûre 87 D 7 *var.* Sauer. River, W Europe

Surendranagar 134 C 4 W India

Surin 137 D 5 E Thailand

Surinam
59 G 3 *var.* Suriname; *prev.* Dutch Guiana, Netherlands Guiana. Republic, NE South America

Official name: Republic of Surinam **Date of formation:** 1975 **Capital:** Paramaribo **Population:** 400,000 **Total area:** 163,270 sq km (63,039 sq miles) **Languages:** Dutch*, Pidgin English (Taki-Taki), Hindi, Javanese, Carib **Religions:** Christian 48%, Hindu 27%, Muslim 20%, other 5% **Ethnic mix:** South Asian 37%, Creole 31%, Javanese 15%, other 17% **Government:** Multiparty republic **Currency:** Guilder = 100 cents

---

Surkhob 123 F 3 river, C Tajikistan

Surt 71 G 2 *var.* Sidra, Sirte. N Libya

Surtsey 83 E 5 island, S Iceland

Suruga-wan 131 D 6 bay, NW Pacific Ocean

Susa 96 A 2 NW Italy

Sūsah *see* Sousse

Susitna 36 C 3 Alaska, NW USA

Susteren 87 D 5 SE Netherlands

Susuman 115 G 3 E Russian Federation

Sutlej 134 C 2 river, India/Pakistan

Suur Munamägi 106 D 3 *var.* Munamägi, *Ger.* Eier-Berg. Mountain, SE Estonia

Suur Väin 106 C 2 *Ger.* Grosser Sund. Strait, E Baltic Sea

Suva 145 E 4 country capital, Viti Levu, W Fiji

Suwałki 98 E 2 *Lith.* Suvalkai, *Rus.* Suvalki. NE Poland

Suwannee River 43 E 3 river, SE USA

Şuwār 118 D 2 E Syria

Suways, Khalīj as *see* Suez, Gulf of

Suways, Qanāt as *see* Suez Canal

Suzhou 129 D 5 *var.* Soochow, Su-chou, Suchow; *prev.* Wuhsien, China

Svalbard 83 G 2 Norwegian dependency, Svalbard

Svartisen 84 C 3 glacier, C Norway

Svay Riĕng 137 D 6 SE Cambodia

Sveg 85 C 5 C Sweden

Svenstavik 85 C 5 C Sweden

Sverdlovsk *see* Yekaterinburg

Sveti Vrach *see* Sandanski

Svetlogorsk *see* Svyetlahorsk

Svetlograd 111 B 7 SW Russian Federation

Svetlovodsk *see* Svitlovods'k

Svetozarevo 100 E 4 *var.* Jadodina. C Yugoslavia

Svilengrad 104 D 3 *prev.* Mustafa-Pasha. SE Bulgaria

Svisloch' *see* Svislach

Svitlovods'k 109 E 2 *Rus.* Svetlovodsk. C Ukraine

Svobodnyy 115 G 4 SE Russian Federation

Svyataya Anna Trough 155 H 4 trough, Arctic Ocean

Svyetlahorsk 107 D 7 *Rus.* Svetlogorsk. SE Belorussia

Swakopmund 78 B 3 W Namibia

Swan Islands *see* Santanilla, Islas

Swansea 89 C 7 *Wel.* Abertawe. S Wales. UK

Swarzędz 98 C 3 W Poland

Swaziland
78 D 4 S Monarchy, S Africa

Official name: Kingdom of Swaziland **Date of formation:** 1968 **Capital:** Mbabane **Population:** 800,000 **Total area:** 17,360 sq km (6,703 sq miles) **Languages:** Siswati*, English*, Zulu **Religions:** Christian 60%, traditional beliefs 40% **Ethnic mix:** Swazi 95%, other 5% **Government:** Executive monarchy **Currency:** Lilangeni = 100 cents

---

Sweden
84 B 4 *Swe.* Sverige. Monarchy, N Europe

Official name: Kingdom of Sweden **Date of formation:** 1905 **Capital:** Stockholm **Population:** 8.7 million **Total area:** 449,960 sq km (173,730 sq miles) **Languages:**

Swedish*, Finnish, Lappish **Religions:** Evangelical Lutheran 94%, Roman Catholic 2%, other 4% **Ethnic mix:** Swedish 87%, Finnish and Lapp 1%, other European 12% **Government:** Constitutional monarchy **Currency:** Krona = 100 öre

---

Sweetwater 49 F 3 Texas, S USA

Świdnica 98 B 4 *Ger.* Schweidnitz. SW Poland

Świdwin 98 B 2 *Ger.* Schivelbein. NW Poland

Świebodzice 98 B 4 *Ger.* Freiburg in Schlesien, Swiebodzice. SW Poland

Świebodzin 98 B 3 *Ger.* Schwiebus. W Poland

Świecie 98 C 3 *Ger.* Schwertberg. N Poland

Swindon 89 D 7 S England, UK

Swinemünde *see* Świnoujście

Świnoujście 98 A 2 *Ger.* Swinemünde. NW Poland

Switzerland
95 A 7 *Fr.* La Suisse, *Ger.* Schweiz, *It.* Svizzera; *anc.* Helvetica. Federal republic, C Europe

Official name: Swiss Confederation **Date of formation:** 1815 **Capital:** Bern **Population:** 6.9 million **Total area:** 41,290 sq km (15,940 sq miles) **Languages:** German*, French*, Italian* **Religions:** Roman Catholic 48%, Protestant 44%, other 8% **Ethnic mix:** German 65%, French 18%, Italian 10%, other 7% **Government:** Federal republic **Currency:** Franc = 100 centimes

---

Syas'stroy 110 B 4 *var.* S'as'stroj, Sjasstroj. NW Russian Federation

Sydenham Island *see* Nonouti

Sydney 39 G 4 Nova Scotia, SE Canada

Sydney 149 D 6 state capital, New South Wales, SE Australia

Sydney Island *see* Manra

Sydney Mines 39 G 4 Nova Scotia, SE Canada

Syedpur *see* Saidpur

Syemyezhava 107 C 6 *Rus.* Semezhevo. C Belorussia

Syeverodonets'k 109 H 3 *Rus.* Severodonetsk. E Ukraine

Syktyvkar 110 D 4 *var.* Sysol'sk. NW Russian Federation

Sylacauga 42 D 2 Alabama, S USA

Sylhet 135 G 3 NE Bangladesh

Synel'nykove 109 G 3 *var.* Sinel'nikovo. E Ukraine

Syowa 154 C 2 research station, Antarctica

Syracuse 41 F 3 New York, NE USA

Syracuse *see* Siracusa

Syr Darya 114 C 5 *var.* Sai Hun, Sir Darya, Syrdarya, *Kaz.* Syrdariya, *Rus.* Syrdar'ya, *Uzb.* Sirdaryo; *anc.* Jaxartes. River, C Asia

Syrdar'ya 123 E 2 E Uzbekistan

Syria
118 B 3 *var.* Siria, Syrie, *Ar.* Al-Jumhūrīyah al-'Arabīyah as-Sūrīyah, Jumhuriya al-Arabya as-Suriya, Sūrīya. Republic, SW Asia

Official name: Syrian Arab Republic **Date of formation:** 1946 **Capital:** Damascus **Population:** 13.8 million **Total area:** 185,180 sq km (71,500 sq miles) **Languages:**

Arabic*, French, Kurdish, Armenian
Religions: Sunni Muslim 74%, other
Muslim 16%, Christian 10%
Ethnic mix: Arab 90%, other 10%
Government: Single-party republic
Currency: Pound = 100 piastres

Syriam 136 B 4 S Burma
Syrian Desert 119 D 5 *Ar.* Ādiyat
ash Sham, Al Hamad, Bādiyat ash
Shām. Desert, SW Asia
Sýrna 105 E 7 *var.* Sirna. Island,
Dodekánisos, SE Greece
Syvash, Zatoka 109 F 4 *Rus.* Zaliv
Syvash. Inlet, W Sea of Azov
Syzran' 111 C 6 W Russian
Federation
Szamotuły 98 B 3 W Poland
Szczecin 98 B 3 *Eng./Ger.* Stettin.
NW Poland
Szczecinek 98 C 2 *Ger.* Neustettin.
NW Poland
Szczytno 98 D 3 *Ger.* Ortelsburg.
NE Poland
Szeged 99 D 7 *Ger.* Szegedin, *Rom.*
Seghedin. SE Hungary
Székesfehérvár 99 C 7 *Ger.*
Stuhlweissenberg; *anc.* Alba
Regia. W Hungary
Szekszárd 99 C 7 S Hungary
Szinna *see* Snina
Szolnok 99 D 7 C Hungary
Szombathely 99 B 6 *Ger.*
Steinamanger; *anc.* Sabaria,
Savaria. W Hungary
Szprotawa 98 B 4 *Ger.* Sprottau. W
Poland

T

Ṭabaqah 118 D 2 N Syria
Tabasará, Serranía de 53 F 5
mountain range, W Panama
Tábor 99 B 5 SW Czech Republic
Tabora 73 B 7 W Tanzania
Tabrīz 120 C 2 *var.* Tauris, Tebriz.
NW Iran
Tabuaeran 145 G 2 *prev.* Fanning
Island. Island, E Kiribati
Tabūk 120 A 4 NW Saudi Arabia
Täby 85 C 6 C Sweden
Tachau *see* Tachov
Tachov 99 A 5 *Ger.* Tachau. W
Czech Republic
Tacloban 139 F 2 *off.* Tacloban City.
Leyte, C Philippines
Tacloban City *see* Tacloban
Tacna 61 E 4 SE Peru
Tacoma 46 B 2 Washington, NW
USA
Tacuarembó 64 D 4 *prev.* San
Fructuoso. N Uruguay
Tademaït, Plateau du 70 D 3
plateau, C Algeria
Tādpatri 132 C 2 E India
Taegu 128 E 4 *off.* Taegu-
kwangyŏksi, *var.* Daegu, *Jap.*
Taikyū. SE South Korea
Taejŏn 128 E 4 *off.* Taejŏn-
kwangyŏksi, *Jap.* Taiden. C South
Korea
Tafí Viejo 64 C 3 NW Argentina
Taganrog 111 A 7 SW Russian
Federation
Taganrog, Gulf of 109 G 4 *Rus.*
Taganrogskiy Zaliv, *Ukr.*
Tahanroz'ka Zatoka. Gulf, Black
Sea/Sea of Azov
Taguatinga 63 F 3 C Brazil
Tagus 92 C 3 *Port.* Rio Tejo, *Sp.* Río
Tajo. River, Portugal/Spain
Tahat 71 E 4 mountain, SE Algeria

Tahiti 145 H 4 island, W French
Polynesia
Tahlequah 49 G 1 Oklahoma, C
USA
Tahoe, Lake 47 B 5 lake, W USA
Tahoua 75 F 3 W Niger
T'aichung 129 D 6 *Jap.* Taichou,
Taichū; *prev.* Taiwan. W Taiwan
Taieri 151 B 7 river, South Island, S
SW New Zealand
Taihape 150 D 4 North Island, C
New Zealand
T'ainan 129 D 6 *Jap.* Tainan; *prev.*
Dainan. SW Taiwan
Tai Pak Wan *see* Discovery Bay
T'aipei 129 D 6 *Jap.* Taihoku; *prev.*
Daihoku. Country capital, N
Taiwan
Taiping 138 B 3 W Malaysia
Tai Po 128 A 1 N Hong Kong

Taiwan
129 D 6 *var.* Formosa, Formo'sa.
Republic, E Asia

Official name: Republic of China
(Taiwan) **Date of formation:** 1949
Capital: Taipei **Population:** 20.8
million **Total Area:** 36,179 sq km
(13,969 sq miles) **Languages:**
Mandarin* **Religions:** Buddhist,
Confucianist, Taoist 93%, other 7%
Ethnic mix: Taiwanese 84%,
mainland Chinese 14%, other 2%
Government: Multiparty republic
Currency: New Taiwan $ = 100 cents

Taiwan Strait 125 E 3 *var.* Formosa
Strait, *Chin.* T'aiwan Haihsia,
Taiwan Haixia. Strait, East China
Sea/South China Sea
Taiyuan 128 C 4 *var.* T'ai-yuan, T'ai-
yüan; *prev.* Yangku. Province
capital, N China
Tai Yue Shan *see* Lantau Island
Ta'izz 121 B 7 SW Yemen

Tajikistan
123 E 3 *Rus.* Tadzhikistan, *Taj.*
Jumhurii Tojikiston; *prev.* Tajik
SSR. Republic, C Asia

Official name: Republic of
Tajikistan **Date of formation:** 1991
Capital: Dushanbe **Population:** 5.7
million **Total Area:** 143,100 sq km
(55,251 sq miles) **Languages:** Tajik*,
Uzbek, Russian **Religions:**
Sunni Muslim 85%, Shi'a Muslim
5%, other 10% **Ethnic mix:** Tajik
62%, Uzbek 24%, Russian 4%, Tartar
2%, other 8% **Government:**
Single-party republic
Currency: Tajik rouble = 100 kopeks

Tak 136 C 4 *var.* Rahaeng. W
Thailand
Takaoka 131 C 5 Honshū, SW Japan
Takapuna 150 D 2 North Island, N
New Zealand
Takengon 138 A 3 W Indonesia
Takhiatash *see* Takhiatosh
Takhiatosh 122 C 2 *Rus.* Takhiatash.
W Uzbekistan
Takhtakŭpir 122 D 1 *Rus.*
Takhtakupyr. NW Uzbekistan
Takhtakupyr *see* Takhtakŭpir
Takikawa 130 D 2 Hokkaidō, NE
Japan
Takli Makan Desert *see* Taklimakan
Shamo
Taklimakan Shamo 126 B 3 *Eng.*
Takli Makan Desert. Desert, NW
China
Takutea 145 G 5 island, S Cook
Islands

Talabriga *see* Aveiro
Talachyn 107 D 6 *Rus.* Tolochin. NE
Belorussia
Talamanca, Cordillera de 53 E 5
mountain range, C Costa Rica
Talara 60 B 2 NW Peru
Talas 123 F 2 NW Kyrgyzstan
Talaud, Kepulauan 139 F 3 island
group, E Indonesia
Talavera de la Reina 92 D 3 *anc.*
Caesarobriga, Talabriga. C Spain
Talca 64 B 4 C Chile
Talcahuano 65 B 5 C Chile
Taldykorgan 114 C 5 *Kaz.*
Taldyqorghan; *prev.* Taldy-
Kurgan. SE Kazakhstan
Taliq-an *see* Tālōqān
Tal'ka 107 D 6 C Belorussia
Talkhof *see* Puurmani
Tallahassee 42 D 3 *prev.*
Muskogean. State capital, Florida,
SE USA
Tall Fadghāmī 118 E 2 *var.*
Fadghāmī. NE Syria
Tallinn 106 D 2 *Ger.* Reval, *Rus.*
Tallin; *prev.* Revel. Country
capital, NW Estonia
Tall Kalakh 118 B 4 *var.* Tell Kalakh.
W Syria
Tallulah 42 B 2 Louisiana, S USA
Tal'ne 109 E 3 *Rus.* Tal'noye. C
Ukraine
Tal'noye *see* Tal'ne
Tālōqān 123 E 3 *var.* Taliq-an. NE
Afghanistan
Talsen *see* Talsi
Talsi 106 C 3 *Ger.* Talsen. NW
Latvia
Taltal 64 B 2 N Chile
Talvik 84 D 2 N Norway
Tamale 75 E 4 C Ghana
Tamana 145 E 3 *prev.* Rotcher
Island. Island, W Kiribati
Tamanrasset 71 E 4 *var.*
Tamenghest. S Algeria
Tamar 89 C 7 river, SW England, S
UK
Tamatave *see* Toamasina
Tamazunchale 51 E 4 C Mexico
Tambacounda 74 C 3 SE Senegal
Tambo 148 C 4 Queensland, C
Australia
Tambov 111 B 6 W Russian
Federation
Tambura 73 B 5 SW Sudan
Tamchaket *see* Tâmchekkeṭ
Tâmchekkeṭ 74 C 3 *var.* Tamchaket.
S Mauritania
Tamenghest *see* Tamanrasset
Tamiahua, Laguna de 51 F 4 coastal
lagoon, SW Gulf of Mexico
Tam Ky 137 E 5 E Vietnam
Tammerfors *see* Tampere
Tampa 43 E 4 Florida, SE USA
Tampa Bay 43 E 4 bay, Florida, SE
Gulf of Mexico
Tampere 85 D 5 *Swe.* Tammerfors.
SW Finland
Tampico 51 E 3 C Mexico
Tamshiyacu 60 C 1 N Peru
Tamworth 149 D 6 New South
Wales, SE Australia
Tana 84 D 2 *var.* Tenojoki, *Fin.* Teno,
Lapp. Dealnu. River,
Finland/Norway
Tana 84 D 2 N Norway
Tanabe 131 C 7 Honshū, SW Japan
Tanaga Island 36 A 3 island,
Alaska, NW USA
T'ana Hāyk' 72 C 4 *var.* Lake Tana.
Lake, NW Ethiopia

Tana, Lake *see* T'ana Hāyk'
Tanami Desert 146 E 3 desert,
Northern Territory, N Australia
Tananarive *see* Antananarivo
Ţăndărei 108 D 5 SE Romania
Tandil 65 D 5 E Argentina
Tando Ādam 134 B 3 *var.* Adam-jo-
Tando. S Pakistan
Tanega-shima 131 B 8 island,
Ōsumi-shotō, SW Japan
Tanen Taunggyi *see* Tane Range
Tane Range 136 B 4 *Bur.* Tanen
Taunggyi. Mountain range, N
Thailand
Tanezrouft 70 D 4 desert,
Algeria/Mali
Tanga 73 C 7 E Tanzania
Tanganyika, Lake 73 B 7 lake, E
Africa
Tanger 70 C 2 *var.* Tangier, Tangiers,
Fr./Ger. Tanger, *Sp.* Tánger; *anc.*
Tingis. NW Morocco
Tanggula Shan 126 C 4 *var.* Dangla,
Tangla Range. Mountain range, W
China
Tangier *see* Tanger
Tangiers *see* Tanger
Tangra Yumco 126 B 5 *var.* Tangro
Tso. Lake, W China
Tangro Tso *see* Tangra Yumco
Tangshan 128 D 3 *var.* T'angshan,
T'ang-shan. NE China
Tanimbar, Kepulauan 139 G 5
island group, Maluku, E
Indonesia
Tanjungkarang 138 C 4 Sumatera,
W Indonesia
Tanna 144 D 5 island, S Vanuatu
Tansen 135 E 3 C Nepal
Tan-Tan 70 B 3 SW Morocco

Tanzania
73 C 7 Swa.Jamhuri ya
Muungano wa Tanzania; *prev.*
German East Africa, Tanganyika
and Zanzibar. Republic, NE
Africa

Official name: United Republic of
Tanzania **Date of formation:** 1964
Capital: Dodoma **Population:** 28.8
million **Total area:** 945,090 sq km
(364,900 sq miles) **Languages:**
English*, Swahili* **Religions:**
Traditional beliefs 42%, Muslim
31%, Christian 27% **Ethnic mix:** 120
Ethnic Bantu groups 99%, other 1%
Government: Single-party republic
Currency: Shilling = 100 cents

Tao, Ko 137 C 6 island, C Thailand
Taoudenit *see* Taoudenni
Taoudenni 75 E 2 *var.* Taoudenit. N
Mali
Tapa 106 E 2 *Ger.* Taps. NE Estonia
Tapachula 51 G 5 SE Mexico
Tapaiu *see* Gvardeysk
Tapajós 63 E 2 *var.* Tapajóz. River,
NW Brazil
Tapajóz *see* Tapajós
Taps *see* Tapa
Ţarābulus 71 F 2 *var.* Ţarābulus al
Gharb; *Eng.* Tripoli. Country
capital, NW Libya
Taraclia 108 D 4 *Rus.* Tarakilya. S
Moldavia
Tarakilya *see* Taraclia
Taranaki, Mount 150 D 4 *var.*
Egmont. Mountain, North Island,
C New Zealand
Tarancón 93 E 3 C Spain
Taranto 97 E 5 *var.* Tarentum. SE
Italy

Taranto, Golfo di 97 E 6 *Eng.* Gulf of Taranto. Gulf, N Ionian Sea
Taranto, Gulf of *see* Taranto, Golfo di
Tarapoto 60 C 2 N Peru
Tarare 91 D 5 E France
Tarascon 91 D 6 SE France
Tarawa Atoll 144 D 2 island, W Kiribati
Tarazona 93 E 2 NE Spain
Tarbes 91 B 6 *anc.* Bigorra. S France
Tarcoola 149 A 6 South Australia, S Australia
Taree 149 D 6 New South Wales, SE Australia
Tarentum *see* Taranto
Târgoviște 108 C 5 *prev.* Tîrgoviște. S Romania
Targu Jui 108 B 4 *prev.* Tîrgu Jiu. W Romania
Târgu Mureș 108 B 4 *Ger.* Neumarkt, *Hung.* Marosvásárhely; *prev.* Oșorhei, Tîrgu Mures. C Romania
Târgu-Neamț 108 C 3 *var.* Târgul-Neamt; *prev.* Tîrgu-Neamţ. NE Romania
Târgu Ocna 108 C 4 *Hung.* Aknavásár; *prev.* Tîrgu Ocna. E Romania
Târgu Secuiesc 108 C 4 *Ger.* Neumarkt, Szekler Neumarkt, *Hung.* Kezdivásárhely; *prev.* Chezdi-Oșorheiu, Târgul-Săcuiesc, Tîrgu Secuiesc. E Romania
Tarija 61 G 5 S Bolivia
Tarim 121 C 6 C Yemen
Tarim Basin 126 B 3 *var.* Tarim Pendi. Basin, NW China
Tarim He 126 B 3 river, NW China
Tarim Pendi *see* Tarim Basin
Tarma 60 C 3 C Peru
Tarn 91 C 6 cultural region, S France
Tarn 91 C 6 river, S France
Târnăveni 108 B 4 *Ger.* Marteskirch, Martinskirch, *Hung.* Dicsőszentmárton; *prev.* Sînmartin, Tîrnăveni. C Romania
Tarnobrzeg 98 D 4 SE Poland
Tarnów 99 D 5 SE Poland
Taroom 149 D 5 Queensland, SE Australia
Tarraco *see* Tarragona
Tarragona 93 G 2 *anc.* Tarraco. E Spain
Tarran Hills 149 C 6 hill range, New South Wales, C Australia
Tarrasa *see* Terrassa
Tàrrega 93 F 2 *var.* Tarrega. NE Spain
Tarsus 116 C 4 S Turkey
Tartu 106 E 3 *Ger.* Dorpat; *prev. Rus.* Yurev, Yurýev. SE Estonia
Ţarţūs 118 B 4 *Fr.* Tartouss; *anc.* Tortosa. W Syria
Tarutao, Ko 137 C 7 island, S Thailand
Tarvisio 96 D 2 NE Italy
Tarvisium *see* Treviso
Tashkent *see* Toshkent
Tash-Kömür *see* Tash-Kumyr
Tash-Kumyr 123 F 2 *Kir.* Tash-Kömür. W Kyrgyzstan
Tasikmalaja *see* Tasikmalaya
Tasikmalaya 138 C 5 *prev.* Tasikmalaja. Jawa, Indonesia
Tasiusaq 82 C 2 *var.* Tasiusak, Tasiussaq. W Greenland

Tasman Basin 152 C 5 *var.* East Australian Basin. Undersea basin, SW Pacific Ocean
Tasman Bay 151 C 5 inlet, E Tasman Sea
Tasmania 149 B 8 *prev.* Van Diemen's Land. State, SE Australia
Tasman Plateau 142 C 5 *var.* South Tasmania Plateau. Undersea plateau, S Tasman Sea
Tasman Sea 152 C 5 sea, SW Pacific Ocean
Tassili N'Ajjer 71 E 4 *var.* Hamada du Tinghert. Plateau, E Algeria
Tatabánya 99 C 6 NW Hungary
Tathlīth 121 B 6 S Saudi Arabia
Tatra Mountains 99 D 5 *Ger.* Tatra, *Hung.* Tátra, Pol./Slvk. Tatry. Mountain range, Poland/Slovakia
Tatvan 117 F 3 SE Turkey
Tau 145 F 4 *var.* Ta'ú. Island, E American Samoa
Taumarunui 150 D 4 North Island, C New Zealand
Taungdwingyi 136 B 3 W Burma
Taunggyi 136 B 3 C Burma
Taunton 89 C 7 SW England, UK
Taupo 150 D 3 North Island, N New Zealand
Taupo, Lake 150 D 3 lake, North Island, N New Zealand
Tauragė 106 B 4 *Ger.* Tauroggen. SW Lithuania
Tauranga 150 D 3 North Island, NE New Zealand
Tauroggen *see* Tauragė
Taurus Mountains *see* Toros Dağları
Tavas 116 B 4 SW Turkey
Tavastehus *see* Hämeenlinna
Tavira 92 C 5 SE Portugal
Tavoy 137 B 5 *var.* Dawei. SE Burma
Tavoy Island *see* Mali Kyun
Ta Waewae Bay 151 A 7 bay, S Pacific Ocean
Tawakoni, Lake 49 G 2 reservoir, Texas, S USA
Tawau 138 D 3 Borneo, E Malaysia
Ţawkar *see* Tokar
Tawzar *see* Tozeur
Taxco 51 E 4 *var.* Taxco de Alarcón. S Mexico
Taxco de Alarcón *see* Taxco
Tay 88 C 3 river, C Scotland, UK
Taylor 49 G 3 Texas, S USA
Taymā' 120 A 4 NW Saudi Arabia
Taymyr, Ozero 115 E 2 lake, N Russian Federation
Taymyr, Poluostrov 115 E 2 peninsula, N Russian Federation
Tayshet 115 E 4 S Russian Federation
Taz 114 D 3 river, N Russian Federation
Tbilisi 117 G 2 *Eng.* Tiflis. Country capital, SE Georgia
Tchad, Lac *see* Chad, Lake
Tchien *see* Zwedru
Tczew 98 C 2 *Ger.* Dirschau. N Poland
Te Anau 151 A 7 South Island, SW New Zealand
Te Anau, Lake 151 A 7 lake, South Island, SW New Zealand
Teapa 51 G 5 SE Mexico
Teate *see* Chieti
Tebingtinggi 138 B 3 Sumatera, N Indonesia
Teboe Top 59 G 3 SE Surinam
Techirghiol 108 D 5 E Romania
Tecomán 50 D 4 SW Mexico
Tecpan 51 E 5 *var.* Tecpan de Galeana. S Mexico

Tecpan de Galeana *see* Tecpan
Tecuci 108 D 4 E Romania
Tedzhen 122 D 3 *Turkm.* Tejen. S Turkmenistan
Tees 89 D 5 river, N England, UK
Tefé 62 D 2 N Brazil
Tegal 138 C 4 Jawa, C Indonesia
Tegelen 87 D 5 SE Netherlands
Tegucigalpa 52 C 3 country capital, SW Honduras
Tehama *see* Tihāmah
Teheran *see* Tehrān
Tehrān 120 C 3 *var.* Teheran. Country capital, N Iran
Tehuacán 51 F 4 S Mexico
Tehuantepec 51 F 5 *var.* Santo Domingo Tehuantepec. SE Mexico
Tehuantepec, Golfo de 51 G 5 *var.* Gulf of Tehuantepec. Gulf, E Pacific Ocean
Tehuantepec, Gulf of *see* Tehuantepec, Golfo de
Tehuantepec, Isthmus of *see* Tehuantepec, Istmo de
Tehuantepec, Istmo de 51 F 5 *var.* Isthmus of Tehuantepec. Isthmus, SE Mexico
Tejen *see* Tedzhen
Te Kao 150 C 1 North Island, N New Zealand
Tekax 51 H 4 *var.* Tekax de Álvaro Obregón. SE Mexico
Tekax de Álvaro Obregón *see* Tekax
Tekeli 114 C 5 SE Kazakhstan
Tekirdağ 116 A 2 *It.* Rodosto; *anc.* Bisanthe, Raidestos, Rhaedestus. NW Turkey
Tekong, Pulau 138 B 1 island, E Singapore
Te Kuiti 150 D 3 North Island, N New Zealand
Tela 52 C 2 NW Honduras
Tel Aviv-Jaffa *see* Tel Aviv-Yafo
Tel Aviv-Yafo 119 A 6 *var.* Tel Aviv-Jaffa. C Israel
Telish 104 C 2 *var.* Teliš; *prev.* Azizie. NW Bulgaria
Tell Atlas *see* Atlas Tellien
Tell Kalakh *see* Tall Kalakh
Telschen *see* Telšiai
Telšiai 106 B 3 *Ger.* Telschen. NW Lithuania
Teluk Intan 138 B 3 *var.* Telok Anson, Telok Intan, Teluk Anson. W Malaysia
Tema 75 E 5 SE Ghana
Temerin 100 D 3 N Yugoslavia
Temirtau 114 C 4 *prev.* Samarkandski, Samarkandskoye. C Kazakhstan
Tempe 48 B 2 Arizona, SW USA
Tempio Pausania 97 A 5 W Italy
Temple 49 G 3 Texas, S USA
Temple Bay 148 C 2 bay, NW Coral Sea
Temryuk 111 A 7 SW Russian Federation
Temuco 65 B 5 C Chile
Temuka 151 B 6 South Island, SW New Zealand
Téna Kourou 74 D 4 mountain, SW Burkina
Tenasserim Range 137 C 6 mountain range, S Burma
Ténenkou 74 D 3 C Mali
Ténéré 75 G 2 desert, Algeria/Niger
Ténéré du Tafassâsset 75 G 2 desert, N Niger
Tenerife 70 A 3 island, Islas Canarias, SW Spain

Tengger Shamo 127 E 3 desert, N China
Tengréla 74 D 4 *var.* Tingréla. N Ivory Coast
Tenkodogo 75 E 4 S Burkina
Tennant Creek 148 A 3 Northern Territory, C Australia
Tennessee 42 C 1 *off.* State of Tennessee; nickname Volunteer State. State, SE USA
Tenos *see* Tínos
Tenterfield 149 D 5 New South Wales, SE Australia
Ten Thousand Islands 43 E 5 island, Florida, SE USA
Tepelenë 101 C 7 *var.* Tepelena, *It.* Tepeleni. S Albania
Tepic 50 D 4 C Mexico
Teplice 98 A 4 *Ger.* Teplitz; *prev.* Teplice-Šanov, Teplitz-Schönau. NW Czech Republic
Tequila 50 D 4 SW Mexico
Teraina 145 G 2 *prev.* Washington Island. Island, E Kiribati
Teramo 96 D 4 *anc.* Interamna. C Italy
Tercan 117 E 3 NE Turkey
Terceira 92 A 5 *var.* Ilha Terceira. Island, W Portugal
Terceira, Ilha *see* Terceira
Terekhovka *see* Tsyerakhowka
Teresina 63 F 2 *var.* Therezina. State capital, NE Brazil
Termez *see* Termiz
Términos, Laguna de 51 G 4 lagoon, SE Gulf of Mexico
Termiz 123 E 3 *Rus.* Termez. S Uzbekistan
Termoli 96 D 4 C Italy
Terneuzen 87 B 5 *var.* Neuzen. SW Netherlands
Terni 96 C 4 *anc.* Interamna Nahars. C Italy
Ternopil' 108 C 2 *Pol.* Tarnopol, *Rus.* Ternopol'. W Ukraine
Terrace Bay 38 B 4 Ontario, S Canada
Terracina 97 C 5 W Italy
Terranova di Sicilia *see* Gela
Terranova Pausania *see* Olbia
Terrassa 93 G 2 *Cast.* Tarrasa. E Spain
Terre Adélie 154 C 4 French dependent territory, Antarctica
Terre Neuve *see* Newfoundland and Labrador
Terre-Neuve *see* Newfoundland
Terschelling 86 C 1 *Fris.* Skylge. Island, N Netherlands
Teruel 93 F 3 *anc.* Turba. E Spain
Tervel 104 E 1 *prev.* Kurtbunar, *Rom.* Curtbunar. NE Bulgaria
Tervueren *see* Tervuren
Tervuren 87 C 6 *var.* Tervueren. C Belgium
Teseney 72 C 4 *var.* Tessenei. N Eritrea
Tessalit 75 E 2 NE Mali
Tessaoua 75 G 3 S Niger
Tessenderlo 87 C 5 NE Belgium
Tessenei *see* Teseney
Tete 79 E 2 NW Mozambique
Teterow 94 C 3 NE Germany
Tetouan 70 C 2 *var.* Tétouan, Tetuán. N Morocco
Tetovo 101 D 6 *Alb.* Tetova, Tetovë, *Turk.* Kalkandelen. NW Macedonia
Tetschen *see* Děčín
Tevere 96 C 4 *Eng.* Tiber. River, C Italy

Teverya 119 B 5 *var.* Tiberias. N
Israel
Texarkana 42 A 2 Arkansas, C USA
Texarkana 49 H 2 Texas, S USA
Texas 49 G 3 *off.* State of Texas;
nickname Lone Star State. State, S
USA
Texas City 49 H 4 Texas, S USA
Texel 86 C 2 island, NW
Netherlands
Texoma, Lake 49 G 2 reservoir, SW
USA
Teziutlán 51 F 4 S Mexico
Thai Binh 136 D 3 N Vietnam

Thailand
137 C 5 *Th.* Prathet Thai; *prev.*
Siam. Monarchy, SE Asia

Official name: Kingdom of
Thailand **Date of formation:** 1882
Capital: Bangkok **Population:** 56.9
million **Total Area:** 513,120 sq km
(198,116 sq miles) **Languages:** Thai*,
Chinese, Malay **Religions:** Buddhist
95%, Muslim 4%, other 1% **Ethnic
mix:** Thai 75%, Chinese 14%, Malay
4%, other 7% **Government:**
Constitutional monarchy
Currency: Baht = 100 stangs

Thailand, Gulf of 137 C 6 *var.* Gulf
of Siam, *Th.* Ao Thai, *Vtn.* Vinh
Thai Lan. Gulf, Pacific
Ocean/South China Sea
Thai Nguyên 136 D 3 N Vietnam
Thakhek *see* Thakhèk
Thames 89 D 7 river, S England,
UK
Thames 150 D 3 North Island, N
New Zealand
Thãna *see* Thãne
Thãne 134 C 5 *prev.* Thãna. W India
Thanh Hoa 136 D 4 N Vietnam
Thap Put 137 B 7 S Thailand
Thar Desert 134 C 3 *var.* Great
Indian Desert, Indian Desert.
Desert, India/Pakistan
Thásos 104 C 4 Thásos, E Greece
Thásos 104 C 4 island, E Greece
Thaton 136 B 4 SE Burma
Thatta 134 B 3 SE Pakistan
Thayetmyo 136 A 4 W Burma
The Dalles 46 B 3 Oregon, NW
USA
The Flatts Village *see* Flatts Village
The Hague *see* 's-Gravenhage
The Pas 37 F 5 Manitoba, C Canada
Therezina *see* Teresina
Thérma 105 D 6 Ikaría, SE Greece
Thermaïkós Kólpos 104 B 4 *Eng.*
Thermaic Gulf; *anc.* Thermaicus
Sinus. Gulf, NW Aegean Sea
Thérmo 105 B 5 C Greece
The Rock 93 H 4 E Gibraltar
Thessaloníki 104 B 4 *Eng.* Salonica,
Salonika, *SCr.* Solun, *Turk.*
Selânik. N Greece
The Valley 55 G 3 dependent
territory capital, E Anguilla
The Village 49 G 1 Oklahoma, C
USA
The Woodlands 49 H 4 Texas, S
USA
Thiamis *see* Thýamis
Thief River Falls 45 F 1 Minnesota,
N USA
Thiers 91 C 5 C France
Thiès 74 B 3 W Senegal
Thikombia *see* Cikobia
Thimphu 135 G 3 *var.* Thimbu; *prev.*
Tashi Chho Dzong. Country
capital, W Bhutan
Thionville 90 D 3 *Ger.*
Diedenhofen. NE France

Thíra 105 D 7 Thíra, SE Greece
Thíra 105 D 7 *prev.* Santorin,
Santoríni, *anc.* Thera. Island,
Kykládes, SE Greece
Thiruvanathapuram *see* Trivandrum
Tholen 86 B 4 island, SW
Netherlands
Thomasville 42 D 3 Georgia, SE
USA
Thompson 37 G 5 Manitoba, C
Canada
Thompson 148 C 4 river, E
Australia
Thon Buri 137 C 5 C Thailand
Thonon-les-Bains 91 D 5 E France
Thonze 136 B 4 SW Burma
Thorlákshöfn 83 E 5 SW Iceland
Thorn *see* Toruń
Thornton Island *see* Caroline Island
Thorshavn *see* Tórshavn
Thouars 90 B 4 W France
Thoune *see* Thun
Thracian Sea 104 D 4 *Gk.* Thrakikó
Pélagos; *anc.* Thracium Mare. Sea,
N Aegean Sea
Thrakikó Pélagos *see* Thracian Sea
Three Kings Island 150 C 1 island,
North Island, N New Zealand
Thrissur *see* Trichūr
Thuin 87 B 7 S Belgium
Thun 95 A 7 *Fr.* Thoune. W
Switzerland
Thunder Bay 38 B 4 Ontario, S
Canada
Thuner See 95 A 7 lake, C
Switzerland
Thung Song 137 C 7 *var.* Cha Mai.
S Thailand
Thüringer Wald 95 C 5 *Eng.*
Thuringian Forest. Mountain
range, C Germany
Thuringian Forest *see* Thüringer
Wald
Thurso 88 C 2 N Scotland, UK
Thýamis 104 A 4 *var.* Thiamis.
River, W Greece
Tianjin 128 D 4 NE China
Tianshui 128 B 4 C China
Tiba *see* Chiba
Tiber *see* Tevere
Tiber *see* Tivoli
Tiberias *see* Teverya
Tiberias, Lake 119 B 5 *var.*
Chinnereth, Sea of Bahr Tabariya,
Sea of Galilee, *Ar.* Bahrat
Tabariya, *Heb.* Yam Kinneret.
Lake, N Israel
Tibesti 76 C 2 *var.* Tibesti Massif,
Ar. Tibīstī. Mountain range, N
Africa
Tibet, Plateau of 126 C 5 plateau, S
Asia
Tibnī *see* At Tibnī
Tiburón, Isla 50 B 2 *var.* Isla del
Tiburón. Island, NW Mexico
Tiburón, Isla del *see* Tiburón, Isla
Tichau *see* Tychy
Tîchît 74 D 2 *var.* Tichitt. C
Mauritania
Tichitt *see* Tîchît
Tichvin *see* Tikhvin
Ticinum *see* Pavia
Ticul 51 H 4 SE Mexico
Tiel 86 C 4 C Netherlands
Tienen 87 C 6 *var.* Thienen, *Fr.*
Tirlemont. C Belgium
Tien Shan 123 G 2 *Chin.* Thian
Shan, Tian Shan, T'ien Shan, *Rus.*
Tyan Shan , Tyan'-Shan'.
Mountain range,
China/Kyrgyzstan
Tierp 85 C 6 C Sweden
Tierra del Fuego 65 B 8 island,
Argentina/Chile

Tiflis *see* T'bilisi
Tifton 43 E 3 Georgia, SE USA
Tighina 108 D 4 *Rus.* Bendery; *prev.*
Bender. E Moldavia
Tigris 120 B 2 *Ar.* Dijlah, *Turk.* Dicle.
River, Iraq/Turkey
Tihāmah 121 B 6 *var.* Tehama. Plain,
Saudi Arabia/Yemen
Tijuana 50 A 1 NW Mexico
Tikhoretsk 111 A 7 SW Russian
Federation
Tikhvin 110 B 4 *var.* Tichvin. NW
Russian Federation
Tiki Basin 153 E 3 undersea basin,
S Pacific Ocean
Tiksi 115 F 2 N Russian Federation
Tilburg 86 C 4 S Netherlands
Tillabéri 75 F 3 *var.* Tillabéry. W
Niger
Tillabéry *see* Tillabéri
Tílos 105 E 7 island, Dodekánisos,
SE Greece
Timah, Bukit 138 B 1 hill, C
Singapore
Timaru 151 B 6 South Island, SW
New Zealand
Timbedgha 74 D 3 *var.* Timbédra.
SE Mauritania
Timbédra *see* Timbedgha
Timbuktu *see* Tombouctou
Timétrine 75 E 2 mountain range, C
Mali
Timiş 108 A 4 river, W Romania
Timişoara 108 A 4 *Ger.*
Temeschwar, Temeswar, *Hung.*
Temesvár; *prev.* Temeschberg. W
Romania
Timmins 38 C 4 Ontario, S Canada
Timor 139 F 5 island, Nusa
Tenggara, C Indonesia
Timor Sea 152 A 3 sea, E Indian
Ocean
Timor Trench *see* Timor Trough
Timor Trough 125 F 5 *var.* Timor
Trench. Trough, N Timor Sea
Timrå 85 C 5 C Sweden
Tindouf 70 C 3 W Algeria
Tineo 92 C 1 N Spain
Tinghert, Hamada du *see* Tassili
N'Ajjer
Tingo María 60 C 3 C Peru
Tingréla *see* Tengréla
Tinhosa Grande 76 E 2 island, C
Sao Tome & Principe
Tinhosa Pequena 76 E 1 island, C
Sao Tome & Principe
Tinian 144 B 1 island, S Northern
Mariana Islands
Tínos 105 D 6 Tínos, SE Greece
Tínos 105 D 6 *anc.* Tenos. Island,
Kykládes, SE Greece
Tinrhert, Hamada de 71 E 3 *var.*
Plateau du Tinghert. Plateau, W
Algeria
Tipitapa 52 D 3 W Nicaragua
Tirana *see* Tiranë
Tiranë 101 D 6 *var.* Tirana. Country
capital, C Albania
Tirasberge 78 B 4 mountain range,
SW Namibia
Tiraspol 108 D 4 *Rus.* Tiraspol'. E
Moldavia
Tiraspol' *see* Tiraspol
Tiree 88 B 3 island, W Scotland, UK
Tîrgoviste *see* Târgovişte
Tîrgu Jiu *see* Targu Jui
Tírnavos *see* Týrnavos
Tirol 95 C 7 *var.* Tyrol, *It.* Tirolo.
Cultural region, W Austria
Tirreno, Mare *see* Tyrrhenian Sea
Tiruchchirāppalli 132 C 3 *prev.*
Trichinopoly. SE India
Tiruntán 60 C 3 C Peru
Tiruppattūr 132 C 2 SE India

Tisza 81 E 4 *var.* Tisa, Tysa, *Rus.*
Tissa. River, E Europe
Tiszakécske 99 D 7 Hungary
Tit 70 D 3 C Algeria
Titano, Monte 96 E 1 mountain, C
San Marino
Titicaca, Lake 61 E 4 lake,
Bolivia/Peru
Titograd *see* Podgorica
Titose *see* Chitose
Titovo Užice *see* Užice
Titov Veles 101 E 6 C Macedonia
Titu 108 C 5 S Romania
Titule 77 D 5 N Zaire
Tiverton 89 C 7 SW England, UK
Tivoli 96 C 4 *anc.* Tibur. C Italy
Tizimín 51 H 3 SE Mexico
Tizi Ouzou 71 E 1 *var.* Tizi-Ouzou.
N Algeria
Tizi-Ouzou *see* Tizi Ouzou
Tiznit 70 B 3 SW Morocco
Tjilatjap *see* Cilacap
Tjirebon *see* Cirebon
Tlaquepaque 50 D 4 C Mexico
Tlaxcala 51 E 4 *var.* Tlascala,
Tlaxcala de Xicohténcatl. C
Mexico
Tlemcen 70 D 2 *var.* Tilimsen,
Tlemsen. NW Algeria
Tmassah 71 G 3 C Libya
Toamasina 79 G 3 *var.* Tamatave. E
Madagascar
Toba, Danau 138 B 3 lake,
Sumatera, W Indonesia
Tobago 55 H 5 island, NE Trinidad
& Tobago
Toba Kākar Range 134 B 2
mountain range, NW Pakistan
Tobol 114 C 4 *Kaz.* Tobyl. River,
Kazakhstan/Russian Federation
Tobol'sk 114 C 3 C Russian
Federation
Tobyl *see* Tobol
Tocantins 63 F 3 river, N Brazil
Tocoa 52 D 2 N Honduras
Tocopilla 64 B 2 N Chile
Todi 96 C 4 C Italy
Todos os Santos, Baía de 63 G 3
bay, W Atlantic Ocean
Toetoes Bay 151 B 8 bay, SW Pacific
Ocean
Tofua 145 E 5 island, C Tonga

Togo
75 E 4 *prev.* French Togoland.
Republic, W Africa

Official name: Togolese Republic
Date of formation: 1960 **Capital:**
Lomé **Population:** 3.9 million **Total
area:** 56,790 sq km (21,927 sq miles)
Languages: French*, Ewe, Kabye,
Gurma **Religions:** Traditional beliefs
70%, Christian 20%, Muslim 10%
Ethnic mix: Ewe 43%, Kabye 26%,
Gurma 16%, other 15%
Government: Multiparty republic
Currency: CFA franc = 100 centimes

Toiyabe Range 47 C 5 mountain
range, Nevada, W USA
Tokanui 151 B 8 South Island, SW
New Zealand
Tokar 72 C 3 *var.* Ţawkar. NE Sudan
Tokat 116 D 3 N Turkey
Tokelau 145 F 3 New Zealand
overseas territory, C Pacific Ocean
Tōketerebes *see* Trebišov
Tokio *see* Tōkyō
Tokmak 109 G 4 *var.* Velykyy
Tokmak. SE Ukraine
Tokmak 123 G 2 *Kir.* Tokmok. N
Kyrgyzstan
Tokmok *see* Tokmak

Tokoroa 150 D 3 North Island, N New Zealand
Tokuno-shima 130 A 3 island, Amami-shotō, SW Japan
Tokushima 131 C 7 *var.* Tokusima. Shikoku, SW Japan
Tokusima *see* Tokushima
Tōkyō 131 D 5 country capital, Honshū, S Japan
Tōkyō Bay 130 A 1 bay, NW Pacific Ocean
Toledo 92 D 3 *anc.* Toletum. C Spain
Toledo 40 D 3 Ohio, N USA
Toledo 61 F 4 W Bolivia
Toledo Bend Reservoir 49 H 3 reservoir, SW USA
Toletum *see* Toledo
Toliara 79 F 4 *var.* Toliary; *prev.* Tuléar. SW Madagascar
Tolmin 95 D 8 *Ger.* Tolmein, *It.* Tolmino. W Slovenia
Tolna 99 C 7 *Ger.* Tolnau. S Hungary
Tolnau *see* Tolna
Tolochin *see* Talachyn
Tolo Harbour 128 B 1 NE Hong Kong
Tolosa 93 E 1 N Spain
Tolosa *see* Toulouse
Toluca 51 E 4 *var.* Toluca de Lerdo. S Mexico
Toluca de Lerdo *see* Toluca
Tol'yatti 111 C 6 *prev.* Stavropol'. W Russian Federation
Tomakomai 130 D 2 Hokkaidō, NE Japan
Tomar 92 B 3 W Portugal
Tomaschow *see* Tomaszów Lubelski
Tomaszów Lubelski 98 E 4 *Ger.* Tomaschow. SE Poland
Tomaszów Mazowiecki 98 D 4 *var.* Tomaszów Mazowiecka; *prev.* Tomaszów, *Ger.* Tomaschow. C Poland
Tombigbee River 42 C 3 river, SE USA
Tombouctou 75 E 3 *Eng.* Timbuktu. N Mali
Tombua 78 A 2 *Port.* Porto Alexandre. SW Angola
Tomelloso 93 E 3 C Spain
Tomini, Teluk 139 E 4 *prev.* Teluk Gorontalo. Bay, N Molucca Sea
Tomsk 114 D 4 C Russian Federation
Tonezh *see* Tonyezh

Tonga 145 E 4 *var.* Friendly Islands. Monarchy, S Pacific Ocean

Official name: Kingdom of Tonga
Date of formation: 1970 **Capital:** Nuku'alofa **Population:** 101,000
Total Area: 750 sq km (290 sq miles) **Languages:** Tongan*, English **Religions:** Protestant 82% Roman Catholic 18% **Ethnic mix:** Tongan 98% other 2% **Government:** Constitutional monarchy **Currency:** Pa'anga = 100 seniti

Tongatapu 145 E 5 island, S Tonga
Tongatapu Group 145 E 5 island group, S Tonga
Tonga Trench 152 D 4 trench, S Pacific Ocean
Tongchuan 128 C 4 C China
Tongeren 87 D 6 *Fr.* Tongres. NE Belgium
Tong Fuk 128 A 2 SW Hong Kong
Tongking, Gulf of 136 E 4 *Chin.* . Beibu Wan, *Vtn.* Vinh Bắc Bộ. Gulf, Pacific Ocean/South China Sea
Tongliao 127 G 2 N China

Tongres *see* Tongeren
Tongtian He 126 C 4 river, C China
Tonj 73 B 5 SW Sudan
Tônlé Sap 137 D 5 *Eng.* Great Lake. Lake, W Cambodia
Tonyezh 107 C 7 *Rus.* Tonezh. SE Belorussia
Tooele 44 B 4 Utah, W USA
Toowoomba 149 E 5 Queensland, E Australia
Topeka 45 F 4 state capital, Kansas, C USA
Topliţa 108 C 3 *Ger.* Töplitz, *Hung.* Maroshévíz; *prev.* Oláh-Toplicza, Toplicza, Topliţa Română. C Romania
Topolčany 99 C 6 *Hung.* Nagytapolcsány. W Slovakia
Topolovgrad 104 D 3 *prev.* Kavakli. SE Bulgaria
Top Springs 146 E 3 Northern Territory, N Australia
Torbalı 116 A 4 W Turkey
Torez 109 H 3 SE Ukraine
Torgau 94 D 4 E Germany
Torhout 87 A 5 W Belgium
Torino 96 A 2 *Eng.* Turin. NW Italy
Torneå *see* Tornio
Torneträsk 84 C 3 lake, N Sweden
Tornio 84 D 3 *Swe.* Torneå. NW Finland
Tornionjoki 84 D 3 *var.* Torniojoki, *Swe.* Torneälven. River, Finland/Sweden
Toro 92 D 2 N Spain
Toronto 38 D 5 province capital, Ontario, S Canada
Toropec *see* Toropets
Toropets 110 A 4 *var.* Toropec. W Russian Federation
Toros Dağları 116 C 4 *Eng.* Taurus Mountains. Mountain range, S Turkey
Torquay 89 C 7 SW England, UK
Torre, Alto da 92 C 3 mountain, C Portugal
Torre del Greco 97 D 5 S Italy
Torrejón de Ardoz 93 E 3 C Spain
Torrejón, Embalse de 92 C 3 reservoir, W Spain
Torrelavega 92 D 1 N Spain
Torrens, Lake 149 B 5 salt lake, South Australia, S Australia
Torrente 93 F 3 *var.* Torrent, Torrent de l'Horta. E Spain
Torreón 50 D 3 C Mexico
Torres Strait 148 C 1 strait, Queensland, Arafura Sea/Coral Sea
Torres Vedras 92 A 3 W Portugal
Torrington 44 D 3 Wyoming, C USA
Tórshavn 83 F 5 *Dan.* Thorshavn. Dependent territory capital, N Faeroe Islands
Tortosa 93 F 2 *anc.* Dertosa. E Spain
Tortue, Montagne 59 H 3 mountain range, C French Guiana
Tortuga, Isla *see* La Tortuga, Isla
Toruń 98 C 3 *Ger.* Thorn. C Poland
Tõrva 106 D 3 *Ger.* Tõrwa. S Estonia
Tõrwa *see* Tõrva
Torzhok 110 B 4 *var.* Toržok. W Russian Federation
Toržok *see* Torzhok
Tosa-wan 131 B 7 bay, NW Pacific Ocean
Toscano, Archipelago 96 B 4 *Eng.* Tuscan Archipelago. Island group, C Italy
Toshkent 123 E 2 *Rus.* Tashkent. Country capital, E Uzbekistan
Totana 93 E 4 SE Spain
Totness 59 G 3 N Surinam

Tottori 131 B 6 Honshū, SW Japan
Touba 74 B 3 W Senegal
Touboro 76 B 4 NE Cameroon
Touggourt 71 E 2 NE Algeria
Toukoto 74 C 3 W Mali
Toul 90 D 3 NE France
Toulon 91 D 6 *anc.* Telo Martius, Tilio Martius. SE France
Toulouse 91 B 6 *anc.* Tolosa. S France
Toungoo 136 B 4 S Burma
Touraine 90 B 4 cultural region, C France
Tourane *see* Đà Nẵng
Tourcoing 90 D 2 N France
Tournai 87 B 6 *var.* Tournay, *Dut.* Doornik; *anc.* Tornacum. SW Belgium
Tournavista 60 C 3 C Peru
Tours 90 B 4 *anc.* Caesarodunum, Turoni. C France
Tovarkovskiy 111 B 5 W Russian Federation
Tower Island *see* Genovesa, Isla
Townshend Island 148 D 4 island, Queensland, E Australia
Townsville 148 D 3 Queensland, NE Australia
Towoeti Meer *see* Towuti, Danau
Towraghoudī 122 D 4 NW Afghanistan
Towson 41 F 4 Maryland, NE USA
Towuti, Danau 139 E 4 *Dut.* Towoeti Meer. Lake, Celebes, C Indonesia
Toxkan He 126 A 3 *var.* Aksay. River, China/Kyrgyzstan
Toyama 131 C 5 Honshū, SW Japan
Toyama-wan 131 B 5 bay, E Sea of Japan
Toyota 131 C 6 Honshū, SW Japan
Tozeur 71 E 2 *var.* Tawzar. W Tunisia
Trabzon 117 E 2 *Eng.* Trebizond; *anc.* Trapezus. NE Turkey
Traiskirchen 95 E 6 NE Austria
Trajectum ad Rhenum *see* Utrecht
Trakai 107 C 5 *Ger.* Traken, *Pol.* Troki. SE Lithuania
Tralee 89 A 6 *Ir.* Trá Lí. SW Ireland
Trá Lí *see* Tralee
Trang 137 C 7 S Thailand
Transantarctic Mountains 154 C 3 mountain range, Antarctica
Transylvania 108 B 4 *Eng.* Ardeal, Transilvania, *Ger.* Siebenbürgen, *Hung.* Erdély. Cultural Region, NW Romania
Trapani 97 B 7 *anc.* Drepanum. SW Italy
Traralgon 149 C 7 Victoria, SE Australia
Trasimeno, Lago 96 B 3 *Eng.* Lake of Perugia, *Ger.* Trasimenischersee. Lake, C Italy
Traù *see* Trogir
Traunsee 95 D 6 *var.* Gmundner See, *Eng.* Lake Traun. Lake, N Austria
Traunstein 95 C 6 SE Germany
Traverse City 40 C 2 Michigan, N USA
Tra Vinh 137 E 6 *var.* Phu Vinh. S Vietnam
Travis, Lake 49 F 4 reservoir, Texas, S USA
Travnik 100 C 4 C Bosnia & Herzegovina
Trbovlje 95 E 8 *Ger.* Trifail. C Slovenia
Třebíč 99 B 5 *Ger.* Trebitsch. S Czech Republic
Trebinje 101 C 5 S Bosnia & Herzegovina

Trebišov 99 E 6 *Hung.* Tőketerebes. E Slovakia
Trebitsch *see* Třebíč
Trebnitz *see* Trzebnica
Trélazé 90 B 4 NW France
Trelew 65 C 6 SE Argentina
Tremelo 87 C 6 C Belgium
Trenčín 99 C 6 *Ger.* Trentschin, *Hung.* Trencsén. W Slovakia
Trenque Lauquen 64 C 4 E Argentina
Trento 96 C 2 *Eng.* Trent, *Ger.* Trient; *anc.* Tridentum. N Italy
Trenton 41 F 4 state capital, New Jersey, NE USA
Tres Arroyos 65 D 5 E Argentina
Treskavica 100 C 4 mountain range, SE Bosnia & Herzegovina
Treviso 96 C 2 *anc.* Tarvisium. NE Italy
Trg *see* Feldkirchen in Kärnten
Trichinopoly *see* Tiruchchirāppalli
Trichūr 132 C 3 *var.* Thrissur. SW India
Trier 95 A 5 *Eng.* Treves, *Fr.* Trèves; *anc.* Augusta Treverorum. SW Germany
Triesen 94 E 2 SW Liechtenstein
Triesenberg 94 E 2 SW Liechtenstein
Trieste 96 D 2 *Slvn.* Trst. NE Italy
Trifail *see* Trbovlje
Tríkala 104 B 4 *prev.* Trikkala. C Greece
Trikkala *see* Tríkala
Trincomalee 132 D 3 *var.* Trinkomali. NE Sri Lanka
Trinidad 55 H 5 island, C Trinidad & Tobago
Trinidad 64 D 4 SW Uruguay
Trinidad 44 D 5 Colorado, C USA
Trinidad 61 F 3 N Bolivia

Trinidad & Tobago 55 H 5 *var.* Tobago. Republic, SE Caribbean Sea

Official name: Republic of Trinidad and Tobago **Date of formation:** 1962 **Capital:** Port-of-Spain **Population:** 1.3 million **Total area:** 5,130 sq km (1,981 sq miles) **Languages:** English* **Religions:** Christian 58%, Hindu 30%, Muslim 8%, other 4% **Ethnic mix:** Black 43%, South Asian 40%, mixed 14%, other 3% **Government:** Multiparty republic **Currency:** Trin. & Tob. $ = 100 cents

Trinité, Montagnes de la 59 H 3 mountain range, C French Guiana
Trinity River 49 G 3 river, Texas, S USA
Trinkomali *see* Trincomalee
Tripoli 118 B 4 *var.* Ţarābulus, Ţarābulus ash Shām, Trâblous; *anc.* Tripolis. N Lebanon
Tripoli *see* Ţarābulus
Trípoli 105 B 6 *prev.* Trípolis. S Greece
Trípolis *see* Trípoli
Tristan da Cunha 69 A 7 *var.* Tristan da Cunha Islands. Island group, S Atlantic Ocean
Tristan da Cunha 67 C 6 island, S Atlantic Ocean
Tristan da Cunha Islands *see* Tristan da Cunha
Trivandrum 132 C 3 *var.* Thiruvanathapuram. State capital, SW India
Trnava 99 C 6 *Ger.* Tyrnau, *Hung.* Nagyszombat. W Slovakia
Trobriand Islands *see* Kiriwina Islands
Trogir 100 B 4 *It.* Traù. S Croatia

Troglav 100 B 4 mountain, Bosnia & Herzegovina/Croatia
Troía Peninsula 92 B 4 peninsula, W Portugal
Troisdorf 95 A 5 W Germany
Trois-Rivières 39 E 4 Québec, SE Canada
Trojan see Troyan
Trollhättan 85 B 6 S Sweden
Tromsø 84 C 2 *Fin.* Tromssa. N Norway
Tromssa see Tromsø
Trondheim 84 B 4 *Ger.* Drontheim; *prev.* Nidaros, Trondhjem. S Norway
Trondheimsfjorden 84 A 4 fjord, E North Sea
Troodos Mountains see Troódos
Troppau see Opava
Troy 42 D 3 Alabama, S USA
Troy 41 F 3 New York, NE USA
Troyan 104 C 2 *var.* Trojan. C Bulgaria
Troyes 90 D 4 *anc.* Augustobona Tricassium. N France
Trst see Trieste
Trstenik 100 D 4 C Yugoslavia
Trujillo 92 C 3 W Spain
Trujillo 52 D 2 NE Honduras
Trujillo 60 B 3 NW Peru
Trŭn 104 B 2 W Bulgaria
Trung Phán 137 E 5 physical region, S Vietnam
Truro 89 C 7 SW England, UK
Truro 39 F 4 Nova Scotia, SE Canada
Trzcianka 98 B 3 *Ger.* Schönlanke. NW Poland
Trzebnica 98 C 4 *Ger.* Trebnitz. SW Poland
Tsafjördhur 83 E 4 NW Iceland
Tsalka 117 F 2 SE Georgia
Tsaochuang see Zaozhuang
Tsarevo 104 E 2 *var.* Mičurin; *prev.* Michurin. E Bulgaria
Tschaslau see Čáslav
Tsetserleg 126 D 2 W Mongolia
Tshela 77 B 6 W Zaire
Tshikapa 77 C 7 SW Zaire
Tshuapa 77 D 6 river, C Zaire
Tsodilo Hills 78 C 3 mountain range, NW Botswana
Tsu 131 C 6 *var.* Tu. Honshū, SW Japan
Tsuen Wan 128 A 1 W Hong Kong
Tsugaru-kaikyō 130 C 3 strait, Pacific Ocean/Sea of Japan
Tsumeb 78 B 3 N Namibia
Tsuruga 131 C 6 *var.* Turuga. Honshū, SW Japan
Tsuruoka 130 D 4 *var.* Turuoka. Honshū, C Japan
Tsushima 131 A 7 *var.* Tsushima-tö, Tusima. Island group, Japan
Tsyerakhowka 107 D 8 *Rus.* Terekhovka. SE Belorussia
Tsyurupinsk see Tsyurupyns'k
Tsyurupyns'k 109 F 4 *Rus.* Tsyurupinsk. S Ukraine
Tu see Tsu
Tuamotu, Îles 145 H 4 *var.* Tuamotu Islands. Island group, N French Polynesia
Tuamotu Islands see Tuamotu, Îles
Tuapi 53 E 2 NE Nicaragua
Tuapse 111 A 7 SW Russian Federation
Tuba City 48 B 1 Arizona, SW USA
Tubbergen 86 E 3 E Netherlands
Tubeke see Tubize
Tubize 87 B 6 *Dut.* Tubeke. C Belgium

Tubmanburg 74 C 5 county capital, NW Liberia
Tucker's Town 42 B 5 E Bermuda
Tuckum see Tukums
Tucson 48 B 3 Arizona, SW USA
Tucumán see San Miguel de Tucumán
Tucupita 59 E 2 NE Venezuela
Tucuruí 63 F 2 NE Brazil
Tucuruí, Represa de 63 F 2 reservoir, NE Brazil
Tudela 93 E 2 *Basq.* Tutera; *anc.* Tutela. N Spain
Tudmur 118 C 3 *var.* Tadmur, Tamar, *Gk.* Palmyra; *Bibl.* Tadmor. C Syria
Tuen Mun 128 A 1 W Hong Kong
Tuguegarao 139 E 1 Luzon, N Philippines
Tuktoyaktuk 37 E 3 Northwestern Territories, NW Canada
Tukums 106 C 3 *Ger.* Tuckum. W Latvia
Tula 111 B 5 W Russian Federation
Tulancingo 51 E 4 C Mexico
Tulare 47 C 7 California, W USA
Tulcán 60 B 1 N Ecuador
Tulcea 108 D 5 E Romania
Tul'chin see Tul'chyn
Tul'chyn 108 D 3 *Rus.* Tul'chin. C Ukraine
Tulia 49 E 2 Texas, S USA
Tulkarm 119 D 7 NW West Bank
Tullahoma 42 D 1 Tennessee, S USA
Tulle 91 C 5 *anc.* Tutela. C France
Tulln 95 E 6 *var.* Oberhollabrunn. NE Austria
Tully 148 D 3 Queensland, NE Australia
Tulsa 49 G 1 Oklahoma, C USA
Tuluá 58 B 3 W Colombia
Tulun 115 E 4 S Russian Federation
Tumaco 58 A 4 SW Colombia
Tumba, Lac see Ntomba, Lac
Tumbes 60 B 2 NW Peru
Tumkūr 132 C 2 W India
Tumuc-Humac Mountains 63 E 1 *var.* Serra Tumucumaque, *Port.* Serra Tumuc-Humac. Mountain range, N South America
Tunca Nehri see Tundzha
Tunduru 73 C 8 S Tanzania
Tundzha 104 D 3 *Turk.* Tunca Nehri. River, Bulgaria/Turkey
Tungabhadra Reservoir 132 C 2 lake, S India
Tungsten 37 E 4 Northwestern Territories, W Canada
Tung-t'ing Hu see Dongting Hu
Tunis 71 E 1 *var.* Tūnis. Country capital, NE Tunisia

Tunisia
71 E 2 *Ar.* Al Jumhūrīyah at Tūnisīyah, *Fr.* République Tunisienne. Republic, N Africa

Official name: Republic of Tunisia **Date of formation:** 1956 **Capital:** Tunis **Population:** 8.6 million **Total area:** 163,610 sq km (63,170 sq miles) **Languages:** Arabic*, French **Religions:** Muslim 98%, Christian 1%, other 1% **Ethnic mix:** Arab and Berber 98%, European 1%, other 1% **Government:** Multiparty republic **Currency:** Dinar = 1,000 millimes

Tūnis, Khalīj see Tunis, Golfe de
Tunja 58 B 3 C Colombia
Tuong Buong see T,ong Ð,ong

Tương Đương 136 D 4 *var.* Tuong Buong. N Vietnam
Tüp see Tyup
Tupelo 42 C 2 Mississippi, S USA
Tupiza 61 G 5 S Bolivia
Turabah 121 B 5 W Saudi Arabia
Turangi 150 D 4 North Island, N New Zealand
Turan Lowland 122 C 2 *var.* Turan Plain, *Rus.* Turanskaya Nizmennost'. Plain, C Asia
Turan Plain see Turan Lowland
Turayf 120 A 3 NW Saudi Arabia
Turba see Teruel
Turda 108 B 4 *Ger.* Thorenburg, *Hung.* Torda. NW Romania
Turin see Torino
Turkana, Lake 73 C 6 *Eng.* Lake Rudolf. Lake, E Africa
Turkestan 114 B 5 *Kaz.* Türkistan. S Kazakhstan

Turkey
116 B 3 *Turk.* Türkiye Cumhuriyeti. Republic, SW Asia

Official name: Republic of Turkey **Date of formation:** 1923 **Capital:** Ankara **Population:** 59.6 million **Total area:** 779,450 sq km (300,950 sq miles) **Languages:** Turkish*, Kurdish, Arabic **Religions:** Muslim 99%, other 1% **Ethnic mix:** Turkish 80%, Kurdish 17%, other 3% **Government:** Multiparty republic **Currency:** Turkish lira = 100 krural

Turkish Republic of Northern Cyprus 116 C 5 country, SW Asia
Türkistan see Turkestan
Türkmen Aylagy see Turkmenskiy Zaliv
Turkmenbashi 122 B 2 *prev.* Krasnovodsk. W Turkmenistan

Turkmenistan
122 B 2 *prev.* Turkmenskaya Soviet Socialist Republic. Republic, C Asia

Official name: Republic of Turkmenistan **Date of formation:** 1991 **Capital:** Ashgabat **Population:** 4 million **Total Area:** 488,100 sq km (188,455 sq miles) **Languages:** Turkmen*, Russian, Uzbek **Religions:** Muslim 85%, Eastern Orthodox 10%, other 5% **Ethnic mix:** Turkmen 72%, Russian 9%, Uzbek 9%, other 10% **Government:** Single-party republic **Currency:** Manat = 100 tenge

Turkmenskiy Zaliv 122 B 2 *Turkm.* Türkmen Aylagy. Inlet, S Caspian Sea
Turks & Caicos Islands 55 E 2 UK dependent territory, N Caribbean Sea
Turku 85 D 6 *Swe.* Åbo. SW Finland
Turlock 47 B 6 California, W USA
Turnau see Turnov
Turnhout 87 C 5 N Belgium
Turnov 98 B 4 *Ger.* Turnau. N Czech Republic
Turnu Măgurele 108 B 5 *var.* Turnu-Măgurele. S Romania
Turnu Severin see Drobeta-Turnu Severin
Turpan 126 C 3 *var.* Turfan. NW China
Turpan Depression 124 C 2 depression, NW China
Turpan Pendi 126 C 3 *Eng.* Turpan Depression. Depression depth, NW China

Türtkül 122 D 2 *prev.* Petroaleksandrovsk, *Rus.* Turtkul'. W Uzbekistan
Turuga see Tsuruga
Turuoka see Tsuruoka
Tuscaloosa 42 C 2 Alabama, S USA
Tuscan Archipelago see Toscano, Archipelago
Tutela see Tulle
Tuticorin 132 C 3 SE India
Tutrakan 104 D 1 NE Bulgaria
Tutuila 145 F 4 Island, W American Samoa

Tuvalu
145 E 4 *prev.* The Ellice Islands. Commonwealth republic, C Pacific Ocean

Official name: Tuvalu **Date of formation:** 1978 **Capital:** Fongafale **Population:** 9,000 **Total Area:** 26 sq km (10 sq miles) **Languages:** Tuvaluan*, Kiribati **Religions:** Protestant 97%, other 3% **Ethnic mix:** Tuvaluan 95% other 5% **Government:** Constitutional monarchy **Currency:** Australian $ = 100 cents

Tuxpan 50 D 4 C Mexico
Tuxpán 51 F 4 *var.* Tuxpán de Rodríguez Cano. E Mexico
Tuxpán de Rodríguez Cano see Tuxpán
Tuxtepec 51 F 4 *var.* San Juan Bautista Tuxtepec. S Mexico
Tuxtla 51 G 5 *var.* Tuxtla Gutiérrez. SE Mexico
Tuxtla see San Andrés Tuxtla
Tuxtla Gutiérrez see Tuxtla
Tuy Hoa 137 E 5 SE Vietnam
Tuz Gölü 116 C 3 lake, C Turkey
Tuzla 100 C 3 NE Bosnia & Herzegovina
Tuz, Lake see Tuz Gölü
Tver' 110 B 4 *prev.* Kalinin. W Russian Federation
Twante 136 B 4 S Burma
Twin Falls 46 D 4 Idaho, NW USA
Two Thumbs Range 151 B 6 mountain range, South Island, SW New Zealand
Tychy 99 C 5 *Ger.* Tichau. S Poland
Tyler 49 H 3 Texas, S USA
Tynda 115 F 4 SE Russian Federation
Tyne 88 D 4 river, N England, UK
Tyôsi see Chōshi
Týrnavos 104 B 4 *var.* Tírnavos. C Greece
Tyrrhenian Sea 97 B 6 *It.* Mare Tirreno. Sea, C Mediterranean Sea
Tyumen' 114 C 3 C Russian Federation
Tyup 123 G 2 *Kir.* Tüp. NE Kyrgyzstan
Tywyn 89 C 6 W Wales, UK
Tzekung see Zigong

U

Uaco Cungo 78 B 2 *var.* Waku Kungo, *Port.* Santa Comba. C Angola
UAE see United Arab Emirates
Uaupés, Rio see Vaupés, Río
Ubangi 77 C 5 *Fr.* Oubangui. River, C Africa
Ube 131 B 7 Honshū, SW Japan
Ubeda 93 E 4 S Spain
Uberaba 63 F 4 SE Brazil

Uberlândia 63 F 4 SE Brazil
Ubin, Pulau 138 B 1 island, NE Singapore
Ubon Ratchathani 137 D 5 var. Muang Ubon, Ubol Rajadhani, Ubol Ratchathani, Udon Ratchathani. E Thailand
Ubrique 92 C 5 S Spain
Ubsu-Nur, Ozero see Uvs Nuur
Ucayali 60 D 3 river, C Peru
Uchiura-wan 130 D 3 bay, NW Pacific Ocean
Uchkuduk see Uchquduq
Uchquduq 122 D 2 Rus. Uchkuduk. N Uzbekistan
Udaipur 134 C 4 prev. Oodeypore. C India
Uddevalla 85 B 6 S Sweden
Udine 96 D 2 anc. Utina. NE Italy
Udipi see Udupi
Udon Thani 136 D 4 var. Ban Mak Khaeng, Udorndhani. N Thailand
Udupi 132 B 2 var. Udipi. SW India
Ueckermünde 94 D 3 NE Germany
Ueda 131 C 5 var. Uyeda. Honshū, S Japan
Uele 77 D 5 var. Welle. River, N Zaire
Uelzen 94 C 3 N Germany
Ufa 111 D 6 W Russian Federation
Ugāle 106 C 3 NW Latvia

Uganda
73 C 6 Republic, NE Africa

Official name: Republic of Uganda **Date of formation:** 1962 **Capital:** Kampala **Population:** 19.2 million **Total area:** 235,880 sq km (91,073 sq miles) **Languages:** English*, Luganda, Nkole, Chiga **Religions:** Christian 66%, traditional beliefs 18%, Muslim 16% **Ethnic mix:** Buganda 18%, Banyoro 14%, Teso 9%, other 59% **Government:** Multiparty republic **Currency:** Shilling = 100 cents

Uglovka 110 B 4 var. Okulovka. W Russian Federation
Uíge 78 B 1 Port. Carmona, Vila Marechal Carmona. NW Angola
Uinta Mountains 44 B 4 mountain range, Utah, W USA
Uitenhage 78 C 5 S South Africa
Uithoorn 86 C 3 C Netherlands
Ujelang Atoll 144 C 1 var. Wujlān. Island, W Marshall Islands
Ujungpandang 139 E 4 var. Macassar, Makassar; prev. Makasar. Celebes, C Indonesia
UK 89 B 5 off. UK of Great Britain and Northern Ireland. Monarchy, NW Europe
Ukhta 110 D 4 var. Uchta, Uhta. NW Russian Federation
Ukiah 47 B 5 California, W USA
Ukmergé 106 C 4 Pol. Wiłkomierz. C Lithuania

Ukraine
108 C 2 Rus. Ukraina, Ukr. Ukrayina; prev. Ukrainian Soviet Socialist Republic, Ukrainskaya S.S.R. Republic, E Europe

Official name: Ukraine **Date of formation:** 1991 **Capital:** Kiev **Population:** 52.2 million **Total area:** 603,700 sq km (223,090 sq miles) **Languages:** Ukrainian*, Russian, Tartar **Religions:** mostly Ukrainian Orthodox, with Roman Catholic, Protestant and Jewish minorities

Ethnic mix: Ukrainian 73%, Russian 22%, other (inc. Tartar) 5% **Government:** Multiparty republic **Currency:** Karbovanets (coupons)

Ulaanbaatar 127 E 2 Eng. Ulan Bator. Country capital, C Mongolia
Ulaangom 126 C 2 NW Mongolia
Ulan Bator see Ulaanbaatar
Ulanhad see Chifeng
Ulan-Ude 115 E 4 prev. Verkhneudinsk. C Russian Federation
Uldz 127 F 1 river, NE Mongolia
Uleåborg see Oulu
Uleälv see Oulujoki
Uleträsk see Oulujärvi
Ulft 86 E 4 E Netherlands
Ullapool 88 B 3 N Scotland, UK
Ulm 95 B 6 S Germany
Ulsan 128 E 4 Jap. Urusan. SE South Korea
Ulster 89 B 5 cultural region, N Ireland
Ulungur Hu 126 C 2 lake, NW China
Uluru 146 E 5 var. Ayers Rock. Rock, Northern Territory, C Australia
Ulyanivka 109 E 3 Rus. Ul'yanovka. C Ukraine
Ul'yanovka see Ulyanivka
Ul'yanovsk 111 C 5 prev. Simbirsk. W Russian Federation
Uman' 109 E 3 Rus. Uman. C Ukraine
Uman see Uman'
Umán 51 G 3 SE Mexico
'Umān, Khalīj see Oman, Gulf of
Umbrian-Michigian Mountains see Umbro-Marchigiano, Appennino
Umbro-Marchigiano, Appennino 96 C 4 Eng. Umbrian-Michigian Mountains. Mountain range, C Italy
Umeå 84 D 4 N Sweden
Umeälven 84 C 4 river, N Sweden
Umiat 36 D 2 Alaska, NW USA
Umm al Ḥayt, Wādī 121 D 6 var. Wādi Amilíayt. River, SW Oman
Umm Durmān see Omdurman
Umm Ruwaba 72 B 4 var. Umm Ruwābah, Um Ruwāba. C Sudan
Umnak Island 36 A 3 island, Alaska, NW USA
Umtata 78 D 5 SE South Africa
Una 100 B 3 river, Bosnia & Herzegovina/Croatia
Unalaska Island 36 A 3 island, Alaska, NW USA
'Unayzah 120 B 4 C Saudi Arabia
Uncompahgre Peak 44 C 5 mountain, Colorado, C USA
Ungama Bay see Formosa Bay
Ungava Bay 39 E 1 bay, W Labrador Sea
Ungava, Péninsule d' 38 D 1 peninsula, Québec, SE Canada
Ungeny see Ungheni
Ungheni 108 D 3 Rus. Ungeny. W Moldavia
Unguja see Zanzibar
Üngüz Angyrsyndaky Garagum see Zaunguzskiye Karakumy
Unimak Island 36 B 3 island, Alaska, NW USA
Union 43 E 1 South Carolina, SE USA
Union City 42 C 1 Tennessee, S USA

United Arab Emirates
121 E 5 Ar. Al Imārāt al 'Arabīyah Muttaḥidah, abbrev. UAE; prev. Trucial States. Federation, SW Asia

Official name: United Arab Emirates **Date of formation:** 1971 **Capital:** Abu Dhabi **Population:** 1.7 million **Total area:** 83,600 sq km (32,278 sq miles) **Languages:** Arabic*, Farsi (Persian), Urdu, Hindi **Religions:** Sunni Muslim 77%, Shi'a Muslim 19%, other 4% **Ethnic mix:** South Asian 50%, Emirian 19%, other Arab 23%, other 8% **Government:** Federation of monarchs **Currency:** Dirham = 100 fils

UnitedKingdom
89 B 5 Monarchy, NW Europe

Official name: United Kingdom of Great Britain and Northern Ireland **Date of formation:** 1921 **Capital:** London **Population:** 57.8 million **Total area:** 244,880 sq km (94,550 sq miles) **Languages:** English* **Religions:** Protestant 52%, Roman Catholic 9%, Muslim 3%, other 36% **Ethnic mix:** English 81%, Scottish 10%, Welsh 2%, other 7% **Government:** Constitutional monarchy **Currency:** Pound sterling = 100 pence

United States of America
var. America, The States abbrev. USA, U.S, U.S.A. Federal Republic, North America

Official name: United States of America **Date of formation:** 1959 **Capital:** Washington DC **Population:** 257.8 million **Total area:** 9,372,610 sq km (3,681,760 sq miles) **Languages:** English*, Spanish **Religions:** Protestant 56%, Roman Catholic 28%, Jewish 2%, other 14% **Ethnic mix:** White (inc. Hispanic) 83%, Black 13%, other 4% **Government:** Multiparty republic **Currency:** US $ = 100 cents

Unst 88 D 1 island, NE Scotland, UK
Ünye 116 D 2 W Turkey
Upala 52 D 4 NW Costa Rica
Upata 59 E 2 E Venezuela
Upemba, Lake 77 D 7 lake, SE Zaire
Upernavik 82 C 2 var. Upernivik. W Greenland
Upernivik see Upernavik
Upington 78 C 4 W South Africa
'Upolu 145 F 4 island, SE Western Samoa
Upper Darby 41 F 4 Pennsylvania, NE USA
Upper Klamath Lake 46 B 4 lake, Oregon, NW USA
Upper Lough Erne 89 B 5 lake, S Northern Ireland, UK
Upper Red Lake 45 F 1 lake, Minnesota, N USA
Uppsala 85 C 6 C Sweden
Ural 114 B 3 Kaz. Zayyq. River, , Kazakhstan/Russian Federation
Ural Mountains see Ural'skiye Gory
Ural'sk 114 B 3 Kaz. Oral. NW Kazakhstan
Ural'skiye Gory 114 C 3 var. Ural'skiy Khrebet, Eng. Ural Mountains. Mountain range, Kazakhstan/Russian Federation
Uraricoera 62 D 1 N Brazil
Ura-Tyube see Úroteppa

Urbandale 45 F 4 Iowa, C USA
Ureki 117 F 2 W Georgia
Uren' 111 C 5 W Russian Federation
Urganch 122 D 2 Rus. Urgench; prev. Novo-Urgench. W Uzbekistan
Urgut 123 E 3 C Uzbekistan
Uroševac 101 D 5 Alb. Ferizaj. S Yugoslavia
Úroteppa 123 E 2 Rus. Ura-Tyube. NW Tajikistan
Uruapan 51 E 4 var. Uruapan del Progreso. SW Mexico
Uruapan del Progreso see Uruapan
Uruguai, Rio see Uruguay
Uruguay 64 D 3 river, NE Uruguay
Uruguay 64 D 4 off. Oriental Republic of Uruguay; prev. La Banda Oriental. Republic, S South America
Urumaco 58 C 1 NW Venezuela
Ürümqi 126 C 3 var. Tihwa, Urumchi, Urumqi, Urumtsi, Wu-lu-k'o-mu-shi, Wu-lu-mu-ch'i; prev. Ti-hua. NW China
Urup, Ostrov 115 H 4 island, Kuril'skiye Ostrova, SE Russian Federation
Urusan see Ulsan
Urziceni 108 C 5 SE Romania
Usa 110 E 3 river, NW Russian Federation
Uşak 116 B 3 prev. Ushak. W Turkey
Ushak see Uşak
Ushant see Ouessant, Île d'
Ushuaia 65 B 8 S Argentina
Usinsk 110 E 3 NW Russian Federation
Usmas Ezers 106 B 3 lake, NW Latvia
Usol'ye-Sibirskoye 115 E 4 C Russian Federation
Ussel 91 C 5 C France
Ussuriysk 115 G 5 prev. Nikol'sk, Nikol'sk-Ussuriyskiy, Voroshilov. SE Russian Federation
Ustica, Isola d' 97 B 6 island, S Italy
Ústí nad Labem 98 A 4 Ger. Aussig. N Czech Republic
Ustinov see Izhevsk
Ustka 98 B 2 Ger. Stolpmünde. NW Poland
Ust'-Kamchatsk 115 H 2 NE Russian Federation
Ust'-Kamenogorsk 114 D 5 Kaz. Öskemen. E Kazakhstan
Ust'-Sysol'sk see Syktyvkar
Ustyurt Plateau 122 C 4 var. Ust Urt, Uzb. Ustyurt Platosi. Plateau, Kazakhstan/Uzbekistan
Usulután 52 C 3 SE El Salvador
Usumacinta 52 A 1 river, Guatemala/Mexico
Usumbura see Bujumbura
Utah 44 B 4 off. State of Utah; nicknames Beehive State, Mormon State. State, W USA
Utah Lake 44 B 4 lake, Utah, W USA
'Uta Vava'u 145 F 4 island, C Tonga
Utena 106 C 4 E Lithuania
Utica 41 F 3 New York, NE USA
Utina see Udine
Utrecht 86 C 3 Lat. Trajectum ad Rhenum. C Netherlands
Utsunomiya 131 D 5 var. Utunomiya. Honshū, S Japan
Uttar Pradesh 135 E 3 prev. United Provinces, United Provinces of Agra and Oudh. State, N India
Utunomiya see Utsunomiya
Uulu 106 D 2 SW Estonia

Uummannaq 82 C 3 *var.* Umanak, Umanaq. Greenland
Uummannarsuaq 82 B 5 *var.* Nunap Isua, *Dan.* Kap Farvel, *Eng.* Cape Farewell. Headland, S Greenland
Uvalde 49 F 4 Texas, S USA
Uvaravichy 107 D 7 *Rus.* Uvarovichi. SE Belorussia
Uvarovichi *see* Uvaravichy
Uvea, Île 145 E 4 island, S Wallis & Futuna
Uvs Nuur 126 C 1 *var.* Ozero Ubsu-Nur. Lake, Mongolia/Russian Federation
Uyeda *see* Ueda
Uyuni 61 F 5 W Bolivia

Uzbekistan
122 C 1 Republic, C Asia

Official name: Republic of Uzbekistan **Date of formation:** 1991 **Capital:** Tashkent **Population:** 21.9 million **Total Area:** 1,138,910 sq km (439,733 sq miles) **Languages:** Uzbek*, Russian **Religions:** Muslim 88%, other (mostly Eastern Orthodox) 12% **Ethnic mix:** Uzbek 71%, Russian 8%, Tajik 5%, Kazakh 4%, other 12% **Government:** Single-party republic **Currency:** Sum = 100 teen

Uzhhorod 108 B 2 *Rus.* Uzhgorod; *prev.* Ungvár. W Ukraine
Užice 100 D 4 *prev.* Titovo Užice. W Yugoslavia
Vaal 78 D 4 river, C South Africa
Vaals 87 D 6 SE Netherlands
Vaasa 84 D 4 *Swe.* Vasa; *prev.* Nikolainkaupunki. W Finland
Vaassen 86 D 3 E Netherlands
Vác 99 C 6 *Ger.* Waitzen. N Hungary
Vacaville 47 B 6 California, W USA
Vadodara 134 C 4 *prev.* Baroda W India
Vaduz 94 E 2 country capital, W Liechtenstein
Váh 99 C 5 *Ger.* Waag, *Hung.* Vág. River, W Slovakia
Väinameri 106 C 2 *Ger.* Moon-Sund; *prev.* Muhu Väin. Sea, E Baltic Sea
Vaiņode 106 B 3 SW Latvia
Valdaj *see* Valday
Valday 110 B 4 *var.* Valdaj. W Russian Federation
Valdecañas, Embalse de 92 D 3 reservoir, W Spain
Valdepeñas 93 E 4 C Spain
Valdés, Península 65 C 6 peninsula, SE Argentina
Valdez 36 C 3 Alaska, NW USA
Valdivia 65 B 5 C Chile
Val-d'Or 38 D 4 Québec, SE Canada
Valdosta 43 E 3 Georgia, SE USA
Valence 91 D 5 *anc.* Valentia, Valentia Julia, Ventia. E France
Valencia 93 F 3 E Spain
Valencia 58 D 2 N Venezuela
Valencia, Golfo de 93 G 3 *var.* Gulf of Valencia. Gulf, W Mediterranean Sea
Valencia, Gulf of *see* Valencia, Golfo de
Valenciennes 90 D 2 N France
Valera 58 C 2 NW Venezuela
Valetta *see* Valletta
Valga 106 D 3 *Ger.* Walk, *Latv.* Valka. S Estonia
Valira 91 A 8 river, Andorra/Spain
Valjevo 100 D 4 W Yugoslavia

Valjok 84 D 2 N Norway
Valka 106 D 3 *Ger.* Walk. N Latvia
Valkenswaard 87 D 5 S Netherlands
Valladolid 92 D 2 NW Spain
Valladolid 51 H 3 SE Mexico
Vall d'Uxó 93 F 3 E Spain
Valle de La Pascua 58 D 2 N Venezuela
Valle del Po *see* Po Valley
Valledupar 58 B 1 N Colombia
Vallejo 47 B 6 California, W USA
Vallenar 64 B 3 N Chile
Valletta 80 D 5 *prev.* Valetta. Country capital, E Malta
Valley City 45 E 2 North Dakota, N USA
Valls 93 F 2 NE Spain
Valmiera 106 D 3 *Est.* Volmari, *Ger.* Wolmar. N Latvia
Valona Bay *see* Vlorës, Gjiri i
Valozhyn 107 C 5 *Pol.* Wołożyn, *Rus.* Volozhin. C Belorussia
Valparaiso 40 C 3 Indiana, N USA
Valparaíso 64 B 4 C Chile
Valverde del Camino 92 B 4 S Spain
Van 117 F 3 E Turkey
Vanadzor 117 F 2 *prev.* Kirovakan. N Armenia
Vancouver 37 E 5 British Columbia, SW Canada
Vancouver 46 B 2 Washington, NW USA
Vancouver Island 36 D 5 island, SW Canada
Vanda *see* Vantaa
Van Diemen Gulf 146 E 2 gulf, SW Arafura Sea
Van Diemen's Land *see* Tasmania
Vänern 85 B 6 *Eng.* Lake Vaner; *prev.* Lake Vener. Lake, S Sweden
Vangaindrano 79 G 4 S Madagascar
Van Gölü 117 F 3 *var.* Thospitis, *Eng.* Van Lake. Salt lake, E Turkey
Van, Lake *see* Van Gölü
Vannes 90 A 4 *anc.* Dariorigum. NW France
Vantaa 85 D 6 *Swe.* Vanda. S Finland
Vanua Levu 145 E 4 island, N Fiji

Vanuatu
144 C 4 *prev.* New Hebrides. Republic, S Pacific Ocean

Official name: Republic of Vanuatu **Date of formation:** 1980 **Capital:** Port-Vila **Population:** 155,000 **Total Area:** 12,190 sq km (4,706 sq miles) **Languages:** Bislama*, English*, French* **Religions:** Protestant 77%, Roman Catholic 15%, traditional beliefs 8% **Ethnic mix:** Ni-Vanuatu 98%, other 2% **Government:** Multiparty republic **Currency:** Vatu - 100 centimes

Vapincum *see* Gap
Varakļani 106 D 4 C Latvia
Vārānasi 135 E 3 *prev.* Banaras, Benares, *hist.* Kasi. N India
Varangerfjorden 84 E 2 fjord, SW Barents Sea
Varangerhalvøya 84 E 1 peninsula, N Norway
Varaždin 100 B 2 *Ger.* Warasdin, *Hung.* Varasd. N Croatia
Varberg 85 B 7 S Sweden
Vardar 101 E 6 *Gk.* Axiós. River, Greece/Macedonia
Varde 85 A 7 W Denmark
Varéna 107 B 5 *Pol.* Orany. S Lithuania

Varese 96 B 2 N Italy
Vârful Moldoveanu 108 B 4 *var.* Moldoveanul; *prev.* Vîrful Moldoveanu. Mountain, C Romania
Varkaus 85 E 5 C Finland
Varna 104 E 2 *prev.* Stalin, *anc.* Odessus. NE Bulgaria
Varnenski Zaliv 104 E 2 *prev.* Stalinski Zaliv. Bay, NW Black Sea
Vasilikí 105 A 5 Kríti, SE Greece
Vasilishki 107 B 5 *Pol.* Wasiliszki. W Belorussia
Vasil'kov *see* Vasyl'kiv
Vaslui 108 D 4 C Romania
Västerås 85 C 6 C Sweden
Vasyl'kiv 109 E 2 *var.* Vasil'kov. N Ukraine

Vatican City
97 A 7 Papal state, S Europe

Official name: Vatican City State **Date of formation:** 1929 **Capital:** Not applicable **Population:** 1,000 **Total area:** 0.44 sq km (0.17 sq miles) **Languages:** Italian*, Latin* **Religions:** Roman Catholic 100% **Ethnic mix:** Italian 90%, Swiss 10% (including the Swiss Guard, which is responsible for papal security) **Government:** Papal Commission **Currency:** Italian lira = 100 centesimi

Vatican City State *see* Vatican City
Vatnajökull 83 E 5 glacier, SE Iceland
Vättern 85 B 6 *Eng.* Lake Vatter; *prev.* Lake Vetter. Lake, S Sweden
Vaupés 58 C 4 *var.* Rio Uaupés. River, Brazil/Colombia
Vava'u Group 143 E 3 island group, N Tonga
Vavuniya 132 D 3 N Sri Lanka
Vawkavysk 107 B 6 *Pol.* Wołkowysk, *Rus.* Volkovysk. W Belorussia
Växjö 85 C 7 *var.* Vexiö. S Sweden
Vaygach, Ostrov 110 E 2 Island, NW Russian Federation
Veendam 86 E 2 NE Netherlands
Veenendaal 86 D 4 C Netherlands
Vega 84 B 4 island, C Norway
Veisiejai 107 B 5 S Lithuania
Vejer de la Frontera 92 C 5 S Spain
Veldhoven 87 D 5 S Netherlands
Velebit 100 A 3 mountain range, C Croatia
Velenje 95 E 7 *Ger.* Wöllan. N Slovenia
Velho *see* Porto Velho
Velika Gorica 100 B 2 N Croatia
Velika Morava 100 E 4 *var.* Glavn'a Morava, Morava, *Ger.* Grosse Morava. River, C Yugoslavia
Velika Plana 100 E 4 C Yugoslavia
Velikaya 115 H 2 river, NE Russian Federation
Velike-Luki *see* Velikiye Luki
Velikij Ust'ug *see* Velikiy Ustyug
Velikiye Luki 110 A 4 *var.* Velike-Luki. W Russian Federation
Velikiy Ustyug 110 C 4 *var.* Velikij Ust'ug. NW Russian Federation
Veliko Tŭrnovo 104 D 2 *var.* Veliko Tărnovo; *prev.* Tirnovo, Trnovo, Tŭrnovo. N Bulgaria
Velingrad 104 C 3 SW Bulgaria
Vel'ký Krtíš 99 D 6 S Slovakia
Vellore 132 C 2 SE India
Velsen *see* Velsen-Noord
Velsen-Noord 86 C 3 *var.* Velsen. W Netherlands

Vel'sk 110 C 4 *var.* Velsk. NW Russian Federation
Velsk *see* Vel'sk
Velvendos *see* Velvendós
Velvendós 104 B 4 *var.* Velvendos. N Greece
Velykyy Tokmak *see* Tokmak
Vendée 90 B 4 cultural region, W France
Vendôme 90 B 4 C France
Venezia 96 C 2 *Eng.* Venice, *Fr.* Venise, *Ger.* Venedig; *anc.* Venetia. NE Italy

Venezuela
58 D 2 *prev.* Estados Unidos de Venezuela, United States of Venezuela. Republic, N South America

Official name: Republic of Venezuela **Date of formation:** 1830 **Capital:** Caracas **Population:** 20.6 million **Total area:** 912,050 sq km (352,143 sq miles) **Languages:** Spanish*, Indian languages **Religions:** Roman Catholic 96%, Protestant 2%, other 2% **Ethnic mix:** *mestizo* 67%, White 21%, Black 10%, Indian 2% **Government:** Multiparty republic **Currency:** Bolívar = 100 centimos

Venezuela, Golfo de 58 C 1 *Eng.* Gulf of Maracaibo, Gulf of Venezuela. Gulf, E Caribbean Sea
Venezuelan Basin 66 B 4 undersea basin, N Atlantic Ocean
Venice 43 E 4 Florida, SE USA
Venice 42 C 4 Louisiana, S USA
Venice *see* Venezia
Venice, Gulf of 96 D 2 *It.* Golfo di Venezia, *Slvn.* Beneški Zaliv. Gulf, N Adriatic Sea
Venlo 87 D 5 *prev.* Venloo. SE Netherlands
Venloo *see* Venlo
Venta 106 B 3 *Ger.* Windau. River, Latvia/Lithuania
Ventimiglia 96 A 3 NW Italy
Ventspils 106 B 2 *Ger.* Windau. NW Latvia
Ventura 47 C 7 California, W USA
Vera 64 D 3 NE Argentina
Veracruz 51 F 4 *var.* Veracruz Llave. E Mexico
Veracruz Llave *see* Veracruz
Vercellae *see* Vercelli
Vercelli 96 A 2 *anc.* Vercellae. NW Italy
Verdalsøra 84 B 4 C Norway
Verde, Costa 92 D 1 coastal region, N Spain
Verden 94 B 3 NW Germany
Verkhnedvinsk *see* Vyerkhnyadzvinsk
Verkhneudinsk *see* Ulan-Ude
Verkhoyanskiy Khrebet 115 F 3 mountain range, E Russian Federation
Vermillion 45 F 3 South Dakota, N USA
Vermont 41 F 2 *off.* State of Vermont; nickname Green Mountain State. State, NE USA
Vernal 44 B 4 Utah, W USA
Vernon 49 F 2 Texas, SW USA
Vero Beach 43 F 4 Florida, SE USA
Véroia 104 B 4 *var.* Veria, Vérroia, *Turk.* Karaferiye. N Greece
Verona 96 B 2 NE Italy
Versailles 90 C 3 N France
Verulamium *see* St Albans

Verviers 87 D 6 E Belgium
Veselinovo 104 E 2 E Bulgaria
Vesoul 90 D 4 *anc.* Vesulium, Vesulum. E France
Vesterålen 84 B 2 island group, N Norway
Vestfjorden 84 C 3 fjord, E Norwegian Sea
Vestmannaeyjar 83 E 5 S Iceland
Vesuna *see* Périgueux
Vesuvio 97 D 5 *Eng.* Vesuvius. Volcano, S Italy
Vesuvius *see* Vesuvio
Veszprém 99 C 7 *Ger.* Veszprim. W Hungary
Veszprim *see* Veszprém
Vetrino 104 E 2 NE Bulgaria
Vetrino *see* Vyetryna
Veurne 87 A 5 *var.* Furnes. W Belgium
Vexiö *see* Växjö
Vhuru Peak *see* Kilimanjaro
Viacha 61 F 4 W Bolivia
Viana do Castelo 92 B 2 *var.* Viana de Castelo; *anc.* Velobriga. NW Portugal
Vianden 87 D 7 NE Luxembourg
Vianen 86 C 4 C Netherlands
Viangchan 136 D 4 *Eng./Fr.* Vientiane. Country capital, C Laos
Viangphoukha 136 C 3 *var.* Vieng Pou Kha. NW Laos
Viareggio 96 B 3 C Italy
Viborg 85 A 7 NW Denmark
Vic 93 G 2 *var.* Vich; *anc.* Ausa, Vicus Ausonensis. NE Spain
Vicentia *see* Vicenza
Vicenza 96 C 2 *anc.* Vicentia. NE Italy
Vichy 91 C 5 C France
Victor Harbor 149 B 7 South Australia, S Australia
Victoria 36 D 5 province capital, Vancouver Island, SW Canada
Victoria 65 B 5 C Chile
Victoria 49 G 4 Texas, S USA
Victoria 149 B 7 state, SE Australia
Victoria 146 D 3 river, Western Australia, N Australia
Victoria 79 H 1 country capital, NE Seychelles
Victoria de Durango *see* Durango
Victoria de las Tunas *see* Las Tunas
Victoria Falls 78 C 3 W Zimbabwe
Victoria Falls 78 C 3 waterfall, Zambia/Zimbabwe
Victoria Harbour 128 A 1 harbour, S Hong Kong
Victoria Island 37 F 3 island, NW Canada
Victoria, Lake 73 B 6 *var.* Victoria Nyanza. Lake, NE Africa
Victoria Land 154 C 4 physical region, Antarctica
Victoria Nyanza *see* Victoria, Lake
Victoria Peak 128 A 2 mountain, S Hong Kong
Victorville 47 C 7 California, W USA
Vicus Elbii *see* Viterbo
Vidalia 43 E 2 Georgia, SE USA
Vidin 104 B 1 *anc.* Bononia. NW Bulgaria
Vidzeme 106 C 3 *Eng.* Livonia. Cultural region, NE Latvia
Vidzy 107 C 5 NW Belorussia
Viedma 65 C 5 E Argentina
Vieng Pou Kha *see* Viangphoukha
Vienna *see* Vienne
Vienna *see* Wien

Vienne 91 D 5 *anc.* Vienna. E France
Vienne 91 B 5 river, W France
Vientiane *see* Viangchan
Vierwaldstätter See 95 B 7 *Eng.* Lake of Lucerne. Lake, C Switzerland
Vierzon 90 C 4 C France
Viesïte 106 C 4 *var.* Viesīte, *Ger.* Eckengraf. S Latvia

Vietnam 136 D 4 *Vtn.* Công Hoa Xa Hôi Chu Nghia Viêt Nam, Công Hôa Xã Hôi Chu Nghĩa Viêt Nam. Republic, SE Asia

Official name: Socialist Republic of Viet-Nam **Date of formation:** 1976 **Capital:** Hanoi **Population:** 70.9 million **Total Area:** 329,560 sq km (127,243 sq miles) **Languages:** Vietnamese* **Religions:** Buddhist 55%, Roman Catholic 7%, Muslim 1%, other 37% **Ethnic mix:** Vietnamese 88%, Chinese 4%, Thai 2%, other 6% **Government:** Single-party republic **Currency:** Dong = 10 hao = 100 xu

Viêt Tri 136 D 3 *var.* Vietri. N Vietnam
Vieux Fort 55 F 2 S Saint Lucia
Vigo 92 B 2 NW Spain
Viipuri *see* Vyborg
Vijayawāda 132 D 1 *prev.* Bezwada. SE India
Vila *see* Port-Vila
Vila de Mocímboa da Praia *see* Mocímboa da Praia
Vila do Conde 92 B 2 NW Portugal
Vila do Zumbo 78 D 2 *prev.* Vila do Zumbu, Zumbo. NW Mozambique
Vilafranca del Penedès 93 F 2 *var.* Villafranca del Panadés. NE Spain
Vijaka 106 D 4 *Ger.* Marienhausen. NE Latvia
Vilalba 92 C 1 NW Spain
Vila Nova de Gaia 92 B 2 NW Portugal
Vila Nova de Portimão *see* Portimão
Vila Real 92 B 2 *var.* Vila Rial. N Portugal
Vila-real de los Infantes 93 F 3 *var.* Villarreal. E Spain
Vila Rial *see* Vila Real
Vilhelmina 84 C 4 N Sweden
Vilhena 62 D 3 W Brazil
Vília 105 C 5 C Greece
Viljandi 106 D 2 *Ger.* Fellin. S Estonia
Vilkaviškis 106 B 4 *Pol.* Wyłkowyszki. SW Lithuania
Villa Acuña *see* Ciudad Acuña
Villacarrillo 93 E 4 S Spain
Villa Cecilia *see* Ciudad Madero
Villach 95 D 7 *Slvn.* Beljak. S Austria
Villacidro 97 A 5 W Italy
Villa Concepción *see* Concepción
Villa del Pilar *see* Pilar
Villafranca de los Barros 92 C 4 W Spain
Villafranca del Panadés *see* Vilafranca del Penedès
Villahermosa 51 G 4 *prev.* San Juan Bautista. SE Mexico
Villajoyosa 93 F 4 *var.* La Vila Jojosa. E Spain
Villalcampo, Embalse de 92 C 2 reservoir, NW Spain
Villa María 64 C 4 C Argentina
Villa Martín 61 F 5 SW Bolivia

Villanueva 50 D 4 C Mexico
Villanueva de la Serena 92 C 4 W Spain
Villanueva de los Infantes 93 E 4 C Spain
Villa Ojo de Agua 64 C 3 Argentina
Villarreal *see* Vila-real de los Infantes
Villarrica 64 D 2 SE Paraguay
Villavicencio 58 B 3 C Colombia
Villaviciosa 92 D 1 N Spain
Villazón 61 G 5 S Bolivia
Villena 93 E 4 E Spain
Villeneuve d'Ascq 90 D 2 NE France
Villeurbanne 91 D 5 E France
Villingen-Schwenningen 95 B 6 S Germany
Villmanstrand *see* Lappeenranta
Vilnius 107 C 5 *Ger.* Wilna, *Pol.* Wilno; *prev. Rus.* Vilna. Country capital, SE Lithuania
Vil'shanka 109 E 3 *Rus.* Olshanka. C Ukraine
Vilvoorde 87 C 6 *Fr.* Vilvorde. C Belgium
Vilvorde *see* Vilvoorde
Vilyeyka 107 C 5 *Pol.* Wilejka, *Rus.* Vileyka. NW Belorussia
Vilyuy 115 F 3 river, C Russian Federation
Viña del Mar 64 B 4 C Chile
Vinarós 93 F 3 E Spain
Vincennes 40 B 4 Indiana, N USA
Vindhya Mountains *see* Vindhya Range
Vindhya Range 134 D 4 *var.* Vindhya Mountains. Mountain range, N India
Vineland 41 F 4 Delaware, NE USA
Vinh 136 D 4 N Vietnam
Vinh Loi *see* Bac Liêu
Vinishte 104 B 2 *var.* Viniśte. NW Bulgaria
Viniśte *see* Vinishte
Vinita 49 G 1 Oklahoma, C USA
Vinkovci 100 C 3 *Ger.* Winkowitz, *Hung.* Vinkovce. E Croatia
Vinnitsa *see* Vinnytsya
Vinnytsya 108 D 2 *Rus.* Vinnitsa. C Ukraine
Vinson Massif 154 B 3 mountain, Antarctica
Viranşehir 117 E 4 SE Turkey
Virginia 41 E 5 *off.* Commonwealth of Virginia; *nicknames* Old Dominion, Mother of Presidents, Mother of States. State, E USA
Virginia 45 G 1 Minnesota, N USA
Virginia Beach 41 F 5 Virginia, NE USA
Virgin Islands 55 F 3 *var.* Virgin Islands of the United States; *prev.* Danish West Indies. US unincorporated territory, E Caribbean Sea
Virgin Islands *see* British Virgin Islands
Virôchey 137 E 5 NE Cambodia
Virovitica 100 C 2 *Ger.* Virovititz, *Hung.* Verôcze. E Croatia
Virton 87 D 8 SE Belgium
Virtsu 106 D 2 *Ger.* Werder. W Estonia
Vis 100 B 4 *It.* Lissa; *anc.* Issa. Island, S Croatia
Vis *see* Fish
Visaginas 106 C 4 *prev.* Sniečkus. E Lithuania
Visäkhapatnam 132 D 1 SE India

Visalia 47 C 7 California, W USA
Visby 85 C 7 *Ger.* Wisby. SE Sweden
Viscount Melville Sound 37 F 2 *prev.* Melville Sound. Sound, Arctic Ocean
Visé 87 D 6 E Belgium
Viseu 92 C 3 *prev.* Vizeu. N Portugal
Vişeu de Sus 108 B 3 *var.* Vişeul de Sus, *Ger.* Oberwischau, *Hung.* Felsővisó. N Romania
Visoko 100 C 4 C Bosnia & Herzegovina
Vista 47 C 8 California, W USA
Vistula *see* Wisła
Vistula Lagoon 98 C 2 *Ger.* Frisches Haff, *Pol.* Zalew Wiślany, *Rus.* Vislinskiy Zaliv. Lagoon, S Baltic Sea
Vitebsk *see* Vitsyebsk
Viterbo 96 C 4 *anc.* Vicus Elbii. C Italy
Viti Levu 145 E 4 island, C Fiji
Vitim 115 F 4 river, C Russian Federation
Vitória 63 G 4 state capital, SE Brazil
Vitória da Conquista 63 G 3 E Brazil
Vitoria-Gasteiz 93 E 1 *var.* Vitoria, *Eng.* Vittoria. N Spain
Vitré 90 B 3 NW France
Vitsyebsk 107 E 5 *Rus.* Vitebsk. NE Belorussia
Vittoria 97 C 7 SW Italy
Vizeu *see* Viseu
Vizianagaram 132 D 1 *var.* Vizianagram. E India
Vizianagram *see* Vizianagaram
Vjosës, Lumi i 101 C 7 *var.* Vijosa, Vijosë, *Gk.* Aóos. River, Albania/Greece
Vlaardingen 86 C 4 SW Netherlands
Vladikavkaz 111 B 8 *prev.* Dzaudzhikau, Ordzhonikidze. SW Russian Federation
Vladimir 111 B 5 W Russian Federation
Vladivostok 115 G 5 SE Russian Federation
Vlagtwedde 86 E 2 NE Netherlands
Vlasotince 101 E 5 SE Serbia
Vlieland 86 C 1 *Fris.* Flylân. Island, N Netherlands
Vlijmen 86 C 4 S Netherlands
Vlissingen 87 B 5 *Eng.* Flushing, *Fr.* Flessingue. SW Netherlands
Vlodava *see* Włodawa
Vlorë 101 C 7 *It.* Valona, Vlora; *prev.* Vlonë. SW Albania
Vlorës, Gjiri i 101 C 6 *var.* Valona Bay. S Adriatic Sea
Vlotslavsk *see* Włocławek
Vöcklabruck 95 D 6 NW Austria
Vogel Peak *see* Dimlang
Voiron 91 D 5 E France
Vojvodina 100 D 3 *Ger.* Wojwodina. Cultural region, N Yugoslavia
Volga 111 C 7 river, W Russian Federation
Volgograd 111 B 7 *prev.* Stalingrad, Tsaritsyn. SW Russian Federation
Volkhov 111 B 4 *var.* Volchov, Volnov, NW Russian Federation
Volnovakha 109 G 3 SE Ukraine
Volodymyr-Volyns'kyy 108 C 1 *Pol.* Włodzimierz, *Rus.* Vladimir-Volynskiy. NW Ukraine
Vologda 110 B 4 W Russian Federation

Volokonovka 111 A 6 W Russian Federation
Vólos 105 B 5 C Greece
Vol'sk 111 C 6 W Russian Federation
Volta 75 E 4 river, SE Ghana
Volta, Lake 75 E 4 reservoir, SE Ghana
Volturno 97 D 5 river, S Italy
Volunteer Island see Starbuck Island
Volzhsk 111 C 5 W Russian Federation
Volzhskiy 111 B 6 SW Russian Federation
Võnnu 106 E 3 Ger. Wendau. SE Estonia
Voorst 86 D 3 E Netherlands
Voranava 107 C 5 Pol. Werenów, Rus. Voronovo. W Belorussia
Vorderrhein 95 B 7 river, SE Switzerland
Vóreioi Sporádes 105 C 5 var. Vórioi Sporádhes, Eng. Northern Sporades. Island group, E Greece
Vorkuta 110 E 3 NW Russian Federation
Vormsi 106 D 2 var. Vormsi Saar, Ger. Worms, Swe. Ormsö. Island, W Estonia
Voronezh 111 B 6 W Russian Federation
Voroshilovsk see Stavropol'
Vorskla 109 F 2 river, C Ukraine
Võrtsjärv 106 D 3 Ger. Wirz-See. Lake, SE Estonia
Võru 106 D 3 Ger. Werro. SE Estonia
Vosges 90 E 4 mountain range, NE France
Vostochno-Sibirskoye More 115 G 1 Eng. East Siberian Sea. Sea, Arctic Ocean
Vostok 154 C 3 research station, Antarctica
Vostok Island 145 G 3 var. Vostock Island; prev. Stavers Island. Island, E Kiribati
Voznesens'k 109 E 3 Rus. Voznesensk. S Ukraine
Voznesensk see Voznesens'k
Vraca see Vratsa
Vrangelya, Ostrov 115 G 1 Eng. Wrangel Island. Island, NE Russian Federation
Vranje 101 E 5 SE Yugoslavia
Vranov nad Topl'ou 99 E 5 var. Vranov, Hung. Varannó. E Slovakia
Vratsa 104 C 2 var. Vraca. NW Bulgaria
Vrbas 100 C 3 river, N Bosnia & Herzegovina
Vrbas 100 D 3 N Yugoslavia
Vršac 100 E 3 Ger. Werschetz, Hung. Versecz. NE Yugoslavia
Vsetín 99 C 5 Ger. Wsetin. E Czech Republic
Vučitrn 101 D 5 C Yugoslavia
Vukovar 100 D 3 Hung. Vukovár. E Croatia
Vukovár see Vukovar
Vulcan 37 E 5 Alberta, SW Canada
Vulcan 108 B 4 Ger. Wulkan, Hung. Zsilyvajdevulkán; prev. Crivadia Vulcanului, Vaidei, Hung. Sily-Vajdej, Vajdej. W Romania
Vulcano, Isola 97 C 7 island, S Italy
Vung Tau 137 E 6 prev. Fr. Cap Saint-Jacques, Eng. Cape Saint Jacques. S Vietnam
Vyatka 111 C 5 var. V'atka, Viatka. River, NW Russian Federation
Vyatka see Kirov

Vyborg 110 B 3 Fin. Viipuri. NW Russian Federation
Vyerkhnyadzvinsk 107 D 5 Rus. Verkhnednisk. N Belorussia
Vyetryna 107 D 5 Rus. Vetrino. N Belorussia
Vynohradiv 108 B 3 Cz. Sevluš, Hung. Nagyszöllös, Rus. Vinogradov; prev. Sevlyush. W Ukraine
Vytegra 110 B 4 NW Russian Federation

W

Wa 75 E 4 NW Ghana
Waal 86 D 4 river, S Netherlands
Wabash River 40 B 5 river, NE USA
Waco 49 G 3 Texas, S USA
Waddān 71 F 3 NW Libya
Waddeneilanden 86 C 1 Eng. West Frisian Islands. Island group, N Netherlands
Waddenzee 86 C 2 var. Wadden Zee, Eng. Wadden Sea. Sea, E North Sea
Waddington, Mount 36 D 5 mountain, SW Canada
Wādī as Sīr 119 B 6 var. Wadi es Sir. NW Jordan
Wadi es Sir see Wādī as Sīr
Wadi Halfa 72 B 3 var. Wādī Ḥalfā'. N Sudan
Wādī Ḥalfā' see Wadi Halfa
Wādī Mūsā 119 B 7 var. Petra. S Jordan
Wad Madanī see Wad Medani
Wad Medani 72 C 4 var. Wad Madanī. C Sudan
Wagadugu see Ouagadougou
Wagga Wagga 149 C 7 New South Wales, SE Australia
Wagin 147 B 7 Western Australia, SW Australia
Wāh 134 C 1 NE Pakistan
Wahai 139 F 4 Pulau Seram, E Indonesia
Wahiawa 47 A 8 Haw. Wahiawā. Hawaii, W USA
Wahiawā see Wahiawa
Wahpeton 45 F 2 North Dakota, N USA
Waiau 151 C 5 river, South Island, New Zealand
Waigeo, Pulau 139 G 4 island, Maluka, E Indonesia
Waikaremoana, Lake 150 E 4 lake, North Island, E New Zealand
Wailuku 47 B 8 Hawaii, W USA
Waimate 151 B 7 South Island, SW New Zealand
Waiouru 150 D 4 North Island, C New Zealand
Waipara 151 C 6 South Island, C New Zealand
Waipawa 150 E 4 North Island, NE New Zealand
Waipukurau 150 E 4 North Island, NE New Zealand
Wairau 151 C 5 river, South Island, C New Zealand
Wairoa 150 D 2 river, North Island, N New Zealand
Wairoa 150 E 4 North Island, NE New Zealand
Waitaki 151 B 7 river, South Island, SW New Zealand
Waitara 150 D 4 North Island, C New Zealand
Waitzen see Vác
Waiuku 150 D 3 North Island, N New Zealand

Wakasa-wan 131 C 6 bay, SE Sea of Japan
Wakatipu, Lake 151 A 7 lake, South Island, SW New Zealand
Wakayama 131 C 6 Honshū, SW Japan
Wake Island 142 D 1 US unincorporated territory, W Pacific Ocean
Wakkanai 130 C 1 Hokkaidō, NE Japan
Wałbrzych 98 B 4 Ger. Waldenburg, Waldenburg in Schlesien. SW Poland
Walcourt 87 C 7 S Belgium
Wałcz 98 B 3 Ger. Deutsch Krone. NW Poland
Wales 89 C 6 Wel. Cymru. National region, UK
Wales 36 C 2 Alaska, NW USA
Walgett 149 D 5 New South Wales, SE Australia
Walk see Valka
Walker Lake 47 C 6 lake, Nevada, W USA
Wallaby Island 148 C 2 island, Queensland, N Australia
Wallachia 108 B 5 var. Walachia, Ger. Walachei, Rom. Valachia. Cultural region, S Romania
Wallal Downs 146 B 3 W Australia
Walla Walla 46 C 2 Washington, NW USA
Wallis & Futuna 145 F 4 Fr. Territoire de Wallis et Futuna. French overseas territory, S Pacific Ocean
Wallis et Futuna, Territoire de see Wallis and Futuna
Walnut Ridge 42 B 1 Arkansas, C USA
Walvisbaai see Walvis Bay
Walvis Bay 78 B 4 Afr. Walvisbaai. W Namibia
Walvis Bay 78 B 4 bay, W Atlantic Ocean
Walvish Ridge see Walvis Ridge
Walvis Ridge 67 D 6 var. Walvish Ridge. Undersea ridge, E Atlantic Ocean
Wanaka 151 B 7 South Island, SW New Zealand
Wanaka, Lake 151 B 6 lake, South Island, SW New Zealand
Wandel Sea 83 F 1 sea, Arctic Ocean
Wanganui 150 D 4 North Island, C New Zealand
Wangaratta 149 C 7 Victoria, SE Australia
Wankie see Hwange
Wanlaweyn 73 D 6 var. Wanle Weyn, It. Uanle Uen. SW Somalia
Wanxian 129 B 5 C China
Warburg 94 B 4 W Germany
Ware 37 E 4 British Columbia, W Canada
Waremme 87 C 6 E Belgium
Waren 94 C 3 NE Germany
Wargla see Ouargla
Warnemünde 94 C 2 NE Germany
Warnes 61 G 4 C Bolivia
Warrego 149 D 5 river, New South Wales/Queensland, E Australia
Warrego Range 148 D 4 mountain range, E Australia
Warren 40 D 4 Ohio, N USA
Warren 40 D 3 Michigan, N USA
Warri 75 F 5 S Nigeria
Warrnambool 149 B 7 Victoria, SE Australia
Warsaw see Warszawa

Warszawa 98 D 3 Eng. Warsaw, Ger. Warschau, Rus. Varshava. Country capital, C Poland
Warta 98 C 4 Ger. Warthe. River, W Poland
Warthe see Warta
Warwick 149 D 5 Queensland, E Australia
Washington 40 D 4 Pennsylvania, NE USA
Washington 46 B 2 off. State of Washington; nicknames Chinook State, Evergreen State. State, NW USA
Washington D.C. 41 E 4 country capital, District of Columbia, NE USA
Washington Island see Teraina
Washington Land 82 D 1 physical region, NW Greenland
Wash, The 89 E 6 inlet, SW North Sea
Waspam 53 E 2 var. Waspán. NE Nicaragua
Waspán see Waspam
Watampone 139 E 4 var. Bone. Sulawesi, C Indonesia
Watenstedt-Salzgitter see Salzgitter
Waterbury 41 G 3 Connecticut, NE USA
Waterford 89 B 6 Ir. Port Láirge. S Ireland
Waterloo 45 G 3 Iowa, C USA
Watertown 41 F 2 New York, NE USA
Watertown 45 E 2 South Dakota, N USA
Waterville 41 G 2 Maine, NE USA
Watford 89 E 7 SE England, UK
Watlings Island see San Salvador
Watsa 77 E 5 NE Zaire
Watsonville 47 B 6 California, W USA
Wau 73 B 5 var. Wāw. S Sudan
Waukegan 40 B 3 Illinois, N USA
Waukesha 40 B 3 Wisconsin, N USA
Wausau 40 B 2 Wisconsin, N USA
Wave Hill 146 E 3 N Australia
Waverly 45 G 3 Iowa, C USA
Wavre 87 C 6 C Belgium
Wāw see Wau
Wawa 38 C 4 Ontario, S Canada
Waycross 43 E 3 Georgia, SE USA
Wearmouth see Sunderland
Weatherford 49 F 1 Oklahoma, C USA
Webster City 45 F 3 Iowa, C USA
Weddell Plain 154 A 2 abyssal plain, SW Atlantic Ocean
Weddell Sea 154 B 2 sea, SW Atlantic Ocean
Weener 94 A 3 NW Germany
Weert 87 D 5 SE Netherlands
Weesp 86 C 3 C Netherlands
Węgorzewo 98 D 2 Ger. Angerburg. NE Poland
Weimar 94 C 4 C Germany
Weissenburg 95 C 6 SE Germany
Weissenstein see Paide
Wejherowo 98 C 2 NW Poland
Welchman Hall 55 G 1 C Barbados
Weldiya 72 C 4 var. Waldia, It. Valdia. N Ethiopia
Welkom 78 D 4 C South Africa
Welle see Uele
Wellesley Islands 148 B 2 island group, N Australia
Wellington 151 D 5 country capital, North Island, C New Zealand
Wellington 45 F 5 Kansas, C USA

Wellington *see* Wellington, Isla
Wellington, Isla 65 B 7 *var.*
 Wellington. Island, S Chile
Wellsford 150 D 2 North Island, N
 New Zealand
Wells, Lake 147 C 5 lake, Western
 Australia, C Australia
Wels 95 D 6 *anc.* Ovilava. N Austria
Wemmel 87 B 6 C Belgium
Wenatchee 46 C 2 Washington, NW
 USA
Wenchi 75 E 4 W Ghana
Wen-chou *see* Wenzhou
Wendau *see* Võnnu
Wenden *see* Cēsis
Wenmen Island *see* Wolf, Isla
Wentworth 149 B 6 New South
 Wales, SE Australia
Wenzhou 129 D 5 *var.* Wen-chou. E
 China
Werda 78 C 4 S Botswana
Werder *see* Virtsu
Werkendam 86 C 4 S Netherlands
Werro *see* Võru
Wesenberg *see* Rakvere
Wessel Islands 148 B 1 island
 group, N Australia
West Antarctica *see* Lesser
 Antarctica
West Australian Basin *see* Wharton
 Basin
West Bank 119 D 6 disputed region,
 SW Asia
West Bend 40 B 3 Wisconsin, N
 USA
West Bengal 135 F 4 state, NE India
West Caroline Basin 152 B 3
 undersea basin, SW Pacific Ocean
West Caroline Islands 144 B 2
 island group, C Micronesia
West Des Moines 45 F 4 Iowa, C
 USA
Westerland 94 B 2 N Germany
Western Australia 146 C 4 state, W
 Australia
Western Carpathians *see* Carpaţii
 Occidentali
Western Dvina 106 D 4 *Bel.* Dzvina,
 Ger. Düna, *Latv.* Daugava, *Rus.*
 Zapadnaya Dvina. River,
 Asia/Europe
Western Ghats 132 B 1 mountain
 range, SW India
Western Isles *see* Outer Hebrides
Western Punjab *see* Punjab
Western Sahara 70 B 4 territory of
 NW Africa, occupied by Morocco
 from 1976

Western Samoa
 145 F 4 *Sam.* Smoa-i-Sisifo.
 Monarchy, S Pacific Ocean

Official name: Independent State of
 Western Samoa **Date of formation:**
 1962 **Capital:** Apia
 Population: 162,000 **Total Area:**
 2,840 sq km (1,027 sq miles)
 Languages: Samoan*, English
 Religions: Protestant 74%, Roman
 Catholic 26% **Ethnic mix:** Samoan
 93%, other 7% **Government:**
 Parliamentary state
 Currency: Tala = 100 sene

Western Sayans *see* Zapadnyy
 Sayan
Western Sierra Madre *see* Madre
 Occidental, Sierra
Westerschelde 87 B 5 *Eng.* Western
 Scheldt; *prev.* Honte. Channel, S
 North Sea
Westerville 40 C 4 Ohio, N USA

West European Basin 66 C 3
 undersea basin, N Atlantic Ocean
Westfalen 94 A 4 cultural region, W
 Germany
West Falkland 65 C 7 *var.* Gran
 Malvina. Island, W Falkland
 Islands
West Fargo 45 F 2 North Dakota, N
 USA
West Frisian Islands *see*
 Waddeneilanden
West Indies 66 A 4 island group, W
 Atlantic Ocean
Westliche Morava *see* Zapadna
 Morava
Weston-super-Mare 89 D 7 SW
 England, UK
West Palm Beach 43 F 5 Florida, SE
 USA
Westport 151 C 5 South Island, C
 New Zealand
West Punjab *see* Punjab
West Siberian Plain *see* Zapadno-
 Sibirskaya Ravnina
West Virginia 40 D 4 *off.* State of
 West Virginia; nickname
 Mountain State. State, E USA
Wetar, Pulau 138 D 5 island, E
 Indonesia
Wetzlar 95 B 5 W Germany
Wevok 36 C 2 *var.* Wewuk. Alaska,
 NW USA
Wewuk *see* Wevok
Wexford 89 B 6 *Ir.* Loch Garman. SE
 Ireland
Weyburn 37 F 5 Saskatchewan, S
 Canada
Weymouth 89 D 7 S England, UK
Weymouth 41 G 3 Massachusetts,
 NE USA
Weymouth, Cape 148 C 2 headland,
 Queensland, NE Australia
Wezep 86 D 3 E Netherlands
Whakatane 150 E 3 North Island,
 NE New Zealand
Whale Cove 37 G 4 Northwest
 Territories, C Canada
Whangarei 150 D 2 North Island, N
 New Zealand
Wharton Basin 141 D 5 *var.* West
 Australian Basin. Undersea basin,
 E Indian Ocean
Whataroa 151 B 6 South Island, SW
 New Zealand
Wheatland 44 D 3 Wyoming, C
 USA
Wheeling 40 D 4 West Virginia, NE
 USA
Whitby 89 D 5 N England, UK
Whitefish 44 B 1 Montana, NW
 USA
Whitehaven 89 C 5 NW England,
 UK
Whitehorse 36 D 4 territory capital,
 Yukon Territory, W Canada
White Lake 42 A 3 lake, Louisiana,
 S USA
White Mountains 41 G 2 mountain
 range, USA
White Nile 72 B 4 *Ar.* Al Baḥr al
 Abyaḍ, An Nīl al Abyaḍ, Bahr el
 Jebel. River, SE Sudan
White River 44 D 3 river, South
 Dakota, N USA
White Sea *see* Beloye More
White Volta 75 F 4 *var.* Nakambé,
 Fr. Volta Blanche. River,
 Burkina/Ghana
Whitewater Bay 43 E 5 bay, Florida,
 SE Gulf of Mexico
Whitianga 150 D 2 North Island, N
 New Zealand

Whitney, Mount 47 C 6 mountain,
 California, W USA
Whitsunday Island 148 D 3 island,
 Queensland, E Australia
Whyalla 149 A 6 South Australia, S
 Australia
Wichita 45 F 5 Kansas, C USA
Wichita Falls 49 F 2 Texas, S USA
Wichita River 49 F 2 river, Texas, S
 USA
Wicklow Mountains 89 B 6 *Ir.*
 Sléibhte Chill Mhantáin.
 Mountain range, E Ireland
Wiehl 94 A 4 W Germany
Wieliczka 99 D 5 S Poland
Wieluń 98 C 4 C Poland
Wien 95 E 6 *Eng.* Vienna, *Hung.*
 Bécs, *Slvk.* Vídeň, *Slvn.* Dunaj;
 anc. Vindobna, Vindobona.
 Country capital, NE Austria
Wiener Neustadt 95 E 6 E Austria
Wierden 86 E 3 E Netherlands
Wiesbaden 95 B 5 W Germany
Wight, Isle of 89 D 7 island, S
 England, UK
Wigorna Ceaster *see* Worcester
Wijchen 86 D 4 SE Netherlands
Wijk bij Duurstede 86 D 4 C
 Netherlands
Wilberforce, Cape 148 B 1
 headland, Northern Territory, N
 Australia
Wilcannia 149 C 6 New South
 Wales, SE Australia
Wilhelm, Mount 144 B 3 mountain,
 New Guinea, C Papua New
 Guinea
Wilhelm-Pieck-Stadt *see* Guben
Wilhelmshaven 94 B 3 NW
 Germany
Wilkes Barre 41 F 3 Pennsylvania,
 NE USA
Wilkes Fracture Zone 153 F 3
 fracture zone, E Pacific Ocean
Wilkes Land 154 D 4 physical
 region, Antarctica
Wilkes Rise *see* Wilkes Guyot
Wiłkomierz *see* Ukmergė
Willebroek 87 C 5 C Belgium
Willemstad 55 E 5 dependent
 territory capital, C Netherlands
 Antilles
Willeroo 146 E 2 N Australia
Williston 44 D 1 North Dakota, N
 USA
Wilmington 43 F 2 North Carolina,
 SE USA
Wilmington 41 F 4 Delaware, NE
 USA
Wilrijk 87 C 5 N Belgium
Winchester 89 D 7 *hist.*
 Wintanceaster, *Lat.* Venta
 Belgarum. S England, UK
Winchester 41 E 4 Virginia, NE
 USA
Windau *see* Venta
Windau *see* Ventspils
Windhoek 78 B 3 *Ger.* Windhuk.
 Country capital, C Namibia
Windhuk *see* Windhoek
Windsor 89 D 7 S England, UK
Windsor 38 C 5 Ontario, S Canada
Windsor 41 G 3 Connecticut, NE
 USA
Windward Islands 55 H 4 island
 group, SE Caribbean Sea
Windward Islands *see* Barlavento,
 Ilhas de
Windward Passage 54 D 3 *Sp.* Paso
 de los Vientos. Channel, N
 Caribbean Sea
Winisk 38 C 2 river, Ontario, S
 Canada

Winisk 38 C 2 Ontario, C Canada
Winnebago, Lake 40 B 2 lake,
 Wisconsin, N USA
Winning 146 A 4 W Australia
Winnipeg 37 G 5 province capital,
 Manitoba, S Canada
Winnipeg, Lake 37 G 5 lake,
 Manitoba, C Canada
Winnipesaukee, Lake 41 G 2 lake,
 New Hampshire, NE USA
Winona 45 G 3 Minnesota, N USA
Winschoten 86 E 2 NE Netherlands
Winsen 94 B 3 N Germany
Winslow 48 B 2 Arizona, SW USA
Winston Salem 43 E 1 North
 Carolina, SE USA
Winsum 86 D 1 NE Netherlands
Winter Haven 43 E 4 Florida, SE
 USA
Winterswijk 86 E 4 E Netherlands
Winterthur 95 B 7 NE Switzerland
Winton 151 A 7 South Island, SW
 New Zealand
Winton 148 C 4 Queensland, E
 Australia
Wirz-See *see* Võrtsjärv
Wisby *see* Visby
Wisconsin 40 A 2 *off.* State of
 Wisconsin; nickname Badger
 State. State, N USA
Wisconsin Rapids 40 B 2
 Wisconsin, N USA
Wisconsin River 40 B 3 river,
 Wisconsin, N USA
Wisła 98 D 4 *Eng.* Vistula, *Ger.*
 Weichsel. River, C Poland
Wismar 94 C 2 N Germany
Wittenberge 94 C 3 N Germany
Wittlich 95 A 5 SW Germany
Wittstock 94 C 3 NE Germany
W.J.van Blommesteinmeer 59 G 3
 reservoir, E Surinam
Władysławowo 98 C 2 N Poland
Włocławek 98 C 4 *Ger./Rus.*
 Vlotslavsk. C Poland
Włodawa 98 E 4 *Rus.* Vlodava. SE
 Poland
Wodonga 149 C 7 Victoria, SE
 Australia
Wodzisław Śląski 99 C 5 *Ger.*
 Loslau. S Poland
Wōjjā *see* Wotje Atoll
Wojwodina *see* Vojvodina
Woking 89 E 7 SE England, UK
Wolf, Isla 60 A 4 *var.* Wenmen
 Island. Island, Galapagos Islands,
 E Pacific Ocean
Wolfsburg 94 C 3 N Germany
Wolgast 94 D 2 NE Germany
Wöllan *see* Velenje
Wollaston Lake 37 F 4
 Saskatchewan, C Canada
Wollongong 149 D 6 New South
 Wales, SE Australia
Wolvega 86 D 2 *Fris.* Wolvegea. N
 Netherlands
Wolvegea *see* Wolvega
Wolverhampton 89 C 6 W England,
 UK
Wonowon 37 E 4 British Columbia,
 W Canada
Wŏnsan 128 E 3 SE North Korea
Woodburn 46 B 3 Oregon, NW
 USA
Woodland 47 B 5 California, W
 USA
Woodruff 40 B 2 Wisconsin, N USA
Woods, Lake of the 38 B 3 *Fr.* Lac
 des Bois. Lake, Canada/USA
Woodville 150 D 4 North Island, C
 New Zealand

Woodward 49 F 1 Oklahoma, C USA
Wooramel 147 A 5 W Australia
Worb 95 A 7 C Switzerland
Worcester 89 D 6 *hist.* Wigorna Ceaster. W England, UK
Worcester 41 G 3 Massachusetts, NE USA
Worcester 78 C 5 SW South Africa
Workington 89 C 5 NW England, UK
Worland 44 C 3 Wyoming, C USA
Worms 95 B 5 *anc.* Augusta Vangionum, Borbetomagus, Wormatia. SW Germany
Worthington 45 F 3 Minnesota, N USA
Wotje Atoll 144 D 1 *var.* Wōjjā. Island, E Marshall Islands
Woudrichem 86 C 4 S Netherlands
Wrangel Island *see* Vrangelya, Ostrov
Wrangel Plain 155 G 2 abyssal plain, Arctic Ocean
Wreck Reef 148 F 4 reef, W Coral Sea
Wrocław 98 C 4 *Eng./Ger.* Breslau. SW Poland
Września 98 C 3 C Poland
Wsetin *see* Vsetín
Wuday 'ah 121 C 6 S Saudi Arabia
Wuhai 127 E 3 N China
Wuhan 129 C 5 *var.* Han-kou, Han-k'ou, Hanyang, Wuchang, Wu-han; *prev.* Hankow. Province capital, C China
Wuhu 129 D 5 *var.* Wu-na-mu. E China
Wujlān *see* Ujelang Atoll
Wukari 75 G 5 E Nigeria
Wuliang Shan 129 A 6 mountain range, S China
Wu-na-mu *see* Wuhu
Wuppertal 94 A 4 *prev.* Barmen-Elberfeld. W Germany
Würzburg 95 B 5 SW Germany
Wuxi 129 D 5 *var.* Wuhsi, Wu-hsi, Wusih. E China
Wye 89 C 6 *Wel.* Gwy. River, England/Wales, UK
Wyłkowyszki *see* Vilkaviškis
Wyndham 146 D 2 Western Australia, N Australia
Wyoming 40 C 3 Michigan, N USA
Wyoming 44 B 3 *off.* State of Wyoming; nickname Equality State. State, C USA
Wyszków 98 D 3 *Ger.* Probstberg. NE Poland

X

Xaçmaz 117 H 2 *Rus.* Khachmas. N Azerbaijan
Xai-Xai 79 E 4 *prev.* João Belo, Vila de João Bel. S Mozambique
Xam Nua 136 D 3 *var.* Sam Neua. NE Laos
Xankändi 117 G 3 *Rus.* Khankendi; *prev.* Stepanakert. SW Azerbaijan
Xánthi 104 C 3 NE Greece
Xátiva 93 F 4 *var.* Jativa; *anc.* Setabis. E Spain
Xiaguan 129 A 6 S China
Xiamen 129 D 6 *var.* Hsia-men; *prev.* Amoy. China
Xi'an 128 C 4 *var.* Changan, Hsi-an Sian, Sian, Signan, Siking,Singan, Xian. Province capital, C China
Xiang *see* Hunan
Xiangkhoang 136 D 4 *var.* Xieng Khouang. E Laos
Xiangtan 129 C 5 *var.* Hsiang-t'an, Siangtan. S China
Xianning 129 C 5 E China
Xiao Hinggan Ling 128 E 2 *Eng.* Lesser Khingan Range. Mountain range, NE China
Xichang 129 B 5 C China
Xieng Khouang *see* Pèk
Xieng Ngeun *see* Muong Xiang Ngeun
Xifeng 128 B 4 N China
Xigazè 126 C 5 *var.* Jih-k'a-tse, Shigatse, Xigaze. W China
Xi Jiang 124 D 3 *var.* Hsi Chiang, *Eng.* West River. River, S China
Xilin Hot 127 F 2 *var.* Abagnar Qi. NE China
Xilokastro *see* Xylókastro
Xingu 63 E 2 river, C Brazil
Xingxingxia 126 D 3 C China
Xining 127 E 4 *var.* Hsining, Hsi-ning, Sining. C China
Xinjiang Uygur Zizhiqu 126 B 3 *var.* Sinkiang, Sinkiang Uighur, Sinkiang Uighur Autonomous Region, Xin, Xinjiang. Autonomous region, NW China
Xinpu *see* Lianyungang
Xinxiang 128 C 4 NE China
Xinyang 129 C 5 *var.* Hsin-yang, Sinyang. C China
Xinzo de Limia 92 C 2 NW Spain
Xizang Zizhiqu 126 B 4 *var.* Thibet, Xizang, *Chin.* Sitsang, *Eng.* Tibet. Autonomous region, W China
Xolotlán *see* Managua, Lago de
Xuguit Qi 127 F 1 *var.* Yakeshi. N China
Xuwen 129 C 7 S China
Xuzhou 128 D 4 *var.* Hsu-chou, Suchow, Tongshan; *prev.* T'ung-shan. E China
Xylókastro 105 B 6 *var.* Xilokastro. S Greece

Y

Ya'an 129 B 5 *var.* Yaan. C China
Yaan *see* Ya'an
Yabēlo 73 C 5 S Ethiopia
Yablis 53 E 2 NE Nicaragua
Yablonovyy Khrebet 115 F 4 mountain range, C Russian Federation
Yafran 71 F 2 NW Libya
Yaghan Basin 67 B 7 undersea basin, SE Pacific Ocean
Yagotin *see* Yahotyn
Yahualica 50 D 4 SW Mexico
Yakeshi *see* Xuguit Qi
Yakima 46 B 2 Washington, NW USA
Yakima River 46 B 2 river, Washington, NW USA
Yakoruda 104 C 3 SW Bulgaria
Yaku-shima 131 B 8 island, Ōsumi-shotō, SW Japan
Yakutat 36 C 4 Alaska, NW USA
Yakutsk 115 F 3 E Russian Federation
Yakymivka 109 F 4 SE Ukraine
Yala 137 C 7 S Thailand
Yalizava 107 D 6 *Rus.* Yelizovo. E Belorussia
Yalong Jiang 129 A 5 river, C China
Yalova 116 B 3 NW Turkey
Yalpug, Ozero *see* Yalpuh, Ozero
Yalpuh, Ozero 108 D 4 *Rus.* Ozero Yalpug. Lake, SW Ukraine
Yalta 109 F 5 S Ukraine
Yalu 125 E 2 *Chin.* Yalu Jiang, *Jap.* Oryokko, *Kor.* Amnok-kang. River, China/North Korea
Yamaguchi 131 B 7 *var.* Yamaguti. Honshū, SW Japan
Yamaguti *see* Yamaguchi
Yamal, Poluostrov 114 D 2 peninsula, N Russian Federation
Yambio 73 B 5 *var.* Yambiyo. S Sudan
Yambiyo *see* Yambio
Yambol 104 D 2 *var.* Jambol, *Turk.* Yanboli. E Bulgaria
Yamdena, Pulau 139 G 5 *prev.* Jamdena. Island, Kepulauan Tanimbar, E Indonesia
Yamoussoukro 74 D 5 country capital, C Ivory Coast
Yana 115 F 2 river, N Russian Federation
Yanaul 111 D 5 W Russian Federation
Yanbu' al Baḥr 121 A 5 W Saudi Arabia
Yangambi 77 D 5 N Zaire
Yangchow *see* Yangzhou
Yangiyūl 123 E 2 *Rus.* Yangiyul'. E Uzbekistan
Yangiyul' *see* Yangiyūl
Yangon 136 B 4 *var.* Rangoon. Country capital, S Burma
Yangtze 129 B 5 *var.* Chang Jiang, Yangtze Kiang. River, C China
Yangzhou 129 D 4 *Chin.* Yangchow. NE China
Yankton 45 E 3 South Dakota, N USA
Yantai 128 D 4 *var.* Yan-t'ai; *prev.* Chefoo, Chih-fu. E China
Yaoundé 77 B 5 *var.* Yaunde. Country capital, S Cameroon
Yap 144 A 1 state, W Micronesia
Yapanskoye More *see* Japan, Sea of
Yapen, Pulau 139 G 4 *prev.* Japen. Island, E Indonesia
Yap Trough *see* Yap Trench
Yaqui, Río 50 B 2 river, NW Mexico
Yaransk 111 C 5 *var.* Jaransk. NW Russian Federation
Yarega 110 D 4 *var.* Jarega. NW Russian Federation
Yarkant *see* Shache
Yarmouth 39 F 5 Nova Scotia, SE Canada
Yarmouth *see* Great Yarmouth
Yaroslavl' 110 B 4 *var.* Jaroslavl. W Russian Federation
Yarumal 58 B 2 NW Colombia
Yasyel'da 107 B 7 river, SW Belorussia
Yatsushiro 131 A 7 *var.* Yatusiro. Kyūshū, SW Japan
Yatusiro *see* Yatsushiro
Yaunde *see* Yaoundé
Yavari 56 B 3 *var.* Javari. River, C Brazil
Yavarí *see* Javari
Yaviza 53 H 5 SE Panama
Yavoriv 108 B 2 *Pol.* Jaworów, *Rus.* Yavorov. NW Ukraine
Yazd 120 D 3 *var.* Yezd. C Iran
Yazd-e Khvāst 120 D 3 Iran
Yazoo City 42 B 2 Mississippi, S USA
Yding Skovhøj 85 A 7 hill, C Denmark
Ýdra 105 C 6 *var.* Ídhra. S Greece
Ye 137 B 5 SE Burma
Yecheng 126 A 3 *var.* Kargilik. NW China
Yeeda 146 C 3 NW Australia
Yefremov 111 B 5 W Russian Federation
Yei 73 B 5 S Sudan
Yekaterinburg 114 C 3 *prev.* Sverdlovsk. C Russian Federation
Yekaterinodar *see* Krasnodar
Yelets 111 B 5 W Russian Federation
Yelizovo *see* Yalizava
Yell 88 D 1 island, NE Scotland, UK
Yellowknife 37 E 4 territory capital, Northwest Territories, W Canada
Yellow River 124 D 2 river, C China
Yellow River *see* Huang He
Yellow Sea 128 D 4 *Chin.* Huang Hai, *Kor.* Hwang-Hae. Sea, NW Pacific Ocean
Yellowstone River 44 C 2 river, NW USA
Yel'sk 107 C 8 SE Belorussia
Yelwa 75 F 4 W Nigeria
Yemassee 43 E 2 South Carolina, SE USA

Yemen 121 C 7 *Ar.* Al Jumhuriyah al Yamaniyah, Al Yaman. Republic, SW Asia

Official name: Republic of Yemen
Date of formation: 1990
Capital: Sana **Population:** 13 million (203,849 sq miles) **Languages:** Arabic* **Religions:** Sunni Muslim 55%, Shi'a Muslim 42%, other 3% **Ethnic mix:** Arab 95%, Afro-Arab 3%, South Asian, African, European 2% **Government:** Multi-party republic **Currency:** Rial (North), Dinar (South) - both are legal currency

---

Yemva 110 D 4 *var.* Železnodorožny, Zeleznodorožnyj; *prev.* Zheleznodorozhnyy. NW Russian Federation
Yenakiyeve 109 G 3 *Rus.* Yenakiyevo; *prev.* Ordzhonikidze, Rykovo. E Ukraine
Yenangyaung 136 A 3 W Burma
Yendi 75 E 4 NE Ghana
Yengisar 126 A 3 NW China
Yenisey 114 D 3 river, Mongolia/Russian Federation
Yeovil 89 D 7 S England, UK
Yeppon 148 D 4 Queensland, E Australia
Yerevan 117 G 3 *var.* Erevan, *Eng.* Erivan. Country capital, C Armenia
Yerushalayim *see* Jerusalem
Yeu, Île d' 90 A 4 island, NW France
Yevlakh *see* Yevlax
Yevlax 117 G 2 *Rus.* Yevlakh. C Azerbaijan
Yevpatoriya 109 F 5 S Ukraine
Yezd *see* Yazd
Yezerishche *see* Yezyaryshcha
Yezyaryshcha 107 E 5 *Rus.* Yezerishche. NE Belorussia
Yiannitsá *see* Giannitsá
Yichang 129 C 5 C China
Yıldızeli 116 D 3 N Turkey
Yinchuan 128 B 4 *var.* Yinch'uan, Yin-ch'uan, Yinchwan. Autonomous region capital N China

Yingcheng 128 E 3 C China
Yining 126 B 2 *var.* I-ning, *Uigh.*
Gulja, Kuldja. NW China
Yin Shan 127 E 3 mountain range,
N China
Yof 74 B 3 W Senegal
Yogyakarta 138 C 5 *prev.*
Djokjakarta, Jogjakarta,
Jokyakarta. Jawa, C Indonesia
Yokohama 131 D 5 Honshū, S
Japan
Yokote 130 D 4 Honshū, C Japan
Yola 75 H 4 E Nigeria
Yonago 131 B 6 Honshū, SW Japan
Yong'an 129 D 6 *var.* Yongan. SE
China
Yongan *see* Yong'an
Yonkers 41 F 4 New York, NE USA
Yonne 90 C 4 river, C France
Yopal 58 C 3 *var.* El Yopal. C
Colombia
York 89 D 5 *anc.* Eboracum,
Eburacum. N England, UK
York 45 E 4 Nebraska, C USA
York, Cape 148 C 1 headland,
Queensland, NE Australia
Yorkton 37 F 5 Saskatchewan, S
Canada
Yoro 52 C 2 C Honduras
Yoshkar-Ola 111 C 5 W Russian
Federation
Youngstown 40 D 4 Ohio, N USA
Ypres *see* Ieper
Yssel *see* IJssel
Yuba City 47 B 5 California, W USA
Yucatán, Canal de *see* Yucatan
Channel
Yucatan Channel 54 A 2 *Sp.* Canal
de Yucatán. Channel Caribbean
Sea/Gulf of Mexico
Yucatan Peninsula *see* Yucatán,
Península de
Yucatán, Península de 51 H 4 *Eng.*
Yucatan Peninsula. Peninsula,
Guatemala/Mexico
Yuci 128 C 2 C China
Yuen Long 128 A 1 NW Hong
Kong
Yueyang 129 C 5 S China

Yugoslavia
100 D 4 *SCr.* Jugoslavija, Savezna
Republika Jugoslavija. Federal
republic, SE Europe. See also
Serbia, Montenegro

Official name: Federal Republic of
Yugoslavia **Date of formation:** 1992
Capital: Belgrade **Population:** 10.6
million **Total area:** 102,173 sq km
(39,449 sq miles) **Languages:**
Serbian*, Croatian* **Religions:**
Orthodox Catholic 65%, Muslim
19%, other 16% **Ethnic mix:** Serb
63%, Albanian 14%, Montenegrin
6%, other 17% **Government:**
Multiparty republic
Currency: Dinar = 100 para

Yukhavichy 107 D 5 *Rus.*
Yukhovichi. N Belorussia
Yukhovichi *see* Yukhavichy
Yukon River 36 D 3 river,
Canada/USA
Yukon Territory 36 D 3 *var.* Yukon,
Fr. Territoire du Yukon. Territory,
NW Canada
Yulin 129 C 6 S China
Yuma 48 A 2 Arizona, SW USA
Yumen 128 A 4 *var.* Lao-chin-miao,
Laojunmiao, Yümen. N China
Yunjinghong *see* Jinghong

Yunnan 129 A 6 *var.* Yun, Yünna,
Yun-nan. Province, SW China
Yuruá, Río *see* Juruá
Yushu 126 D 4 C China
Yuty 64 D 3 S Paraguay
Yuzhno-Sakhalinsk 115 H 4 *Jap.*
Toyohara; *prev.* Vladimirovka.
Ostrov Sakhalin, SE Russian
Federation
Yuzhnyy Bug *see* Pivdennyy Buh
Yylanly *see* Il'yaly

Z

Zaandam *see* Zaanstad
Zaanstad 86 C 3 *prev.* Zaandam. C
Netherlands
Zabaykal'sk 115 F 5 S Russian
Federation
Zabīd 121 B 7 W Yemen
Ząbkowice Śląskie 98 C 4 *var.*
Ząbkowice, *Ger.* Frankenstein,
Frankenstein in Schlesien. SW
Poland
Zábřeh 99 B 5 *Ger.* Hohenstadt. E
Czech Republic
Zacapa 52 B 2 E Guatemala
Zacatecas 50 D 3 C Mexico
Zacatepec 51 E 4 S Mexico
Zacháro 105 B 6 *var.* Zakháro. S
Greece
Zadar 100 A 3 *It.* Zara; *anc.* Iader. W
Croatia
Zadetkyi Kyun 137 B 6 island, S
Burma
Zafra 92 C 4 W Spain
Zagazig 72 B 1 *var.* Az Zaqāzīq. N
Egypt
Zagreb 100 B 2 *Ger.* Agram, *Hung.*
Zágráb. Country capital, N
Croatia
Zāgros, Kuhhā-ye 120 C 3 *Eng.*
Zagros Mountains. Mountain
range, W Iran
Zagros Mountains *see* Zāgros,
Kūhhā-ye
Zāhedān 120 E 4 *var.* Zahidan; *prev.*
Duzdab. SE Iran
Zaḩlah *see* Zaḩlé
Zaḩlé 118 B 4 *var.* Zaḩlah. C
Lebanon
Záhony 99 E 6 NE Hungary

Zaire
77 D 6 *prev.* Belgian Congo,
Congo (Kinshasa). Republic,
C Africa

Official name: Republic of Zaire
Date of formation: 1960 **Capital:**
Kinshasa **Population:** 41.2 million
Total area: 2,345,410 sq km
(905,563 sq miles) **Languages:**
French*, Kiswahili, Tshiluba
Religions: Christian 70%, traditional
beliefs 20%, Muslim 10% **Ethnic
mix:** Bantu 23%, Hamitic 23%, other
54% **Government:** Transitional
Currency: New zaire = 100 makuta

Zaire 78 C 1 *prev.* Congo. Province,
NW Angola
Zaječar 100 E 4 E Yugoslavia
Zakataly *see* Zaqatala
Zākhō 120 B 2 *var.* Zākhū. N Iraq
Zākhū *see* Zākhō
Zákynthos 105 A 5 *var.* Zákinthos,
It. Zante. Island, W Greece
Zalaegerszeg 98 E 3 W Hungary
Zalantun *see* Butha Qi
Zalău 108 B 3 *Ger.* Waltenberg,
Hung. Zilah; *prev.* Zillenmarkt.
NW Romania

Zalim 121 B 5 W Saudi Arabia
Zaliv Syvash *see* Syvash, Zatoka
`Zalni Pjašaci` *see* Zlatni Pyasûtsi
Zambezi Canyon *see* Zambezi
Canyon
Zambezi 78 D 2 *var.* Zambesi, *Port.*
Zambeze. River, S Africa
Zambezi 78 C 2 W Zambia

Zambia
78 C 2 *prev.* Northern Rhodesia.
Republic, S Africa

Official name: Republic of Zambia
Date of formation: 1964 **Capital:**
Lusaka **Population:** 8.9 million **Total
area:** 752,610 sq km (290,563 sq
miles) **Languages:** English*, Bemba,
Tonga, Nyanja **Religions:** Christian
63%, traditional beliefs 35%, other
2% **Ethnic mix:** Bemba 36%, Maravi
18%, Tonga 15%, other 31%
Government: Multiparty republic
Currency: Kwacha = 100 ngwee

Zamboanga 139 E 3 *off.* Zamboanga
City. Mindanao, S Philippines
Zamboanga City *see* Zamboanga
Zambrów 98 E 3 E Poland
Zamora 92 D 2 NW Spain
Zamora de Hidalgo 50 D 4 SW
Mexico
Zamość 98 E 4 *Rus.* Zamostye. SE
Poland
Zamostye *see* Zamość
Zanda X 126 A 4 W China
Zanjān 120 C 2 *var.* Zenjan, Zinjan.
NW Iran
Zanthus 147 C 6 S Australia
Zanzibar 73 D 7 *Swa.* Unguja.
Island, E Tanzania
Zanzibar 73 D 7 E Tanzania
Zaozhuang 128 D 4 *var.*
Tsaochuang. E China
Zapadna Morava 100 D 4 *Ger.*
Westliche Morava. River, C
Yugoslavia
Zapadnaya Dvina 110 A 4 W
Russian Federation
Zapadno-Sibirskaya Ravnina 114 D
3 *Eng.* West Siberian Plain. Plain,
Kazakhstan/Russian Federation
Zapadnyy Sayan 114 D 4 *Eng.*
Western Sayans. Mountain range,
C Russian Federation
Zapala 65 B 5 W Argentina
Zapiola Ridge 67 B 6 undersea
ridge, SW Atlantic Ocean
Zapolyarnyy 110 C 2 *var.*
Zapol'arnyj, Zapoljarny. NW
Russian Federation
Zaporizhzhya 109 G 3 *Rus.*
Zaporozh'ye; *prev.*
Aleksandrovsk. SE Ukraine
Zapotiltic 50 D 4 SW Mexico
Zaqatala 117 G 2 *Rus.* Zakataly. NW
Azerbaijan
Zara 116 D 3 C Turkey
Zarafshan *see* Zarafshon
Zarafshon 122 D 2 *Rus.* Zarafshan.
N Uzbekistan
Zarafshon *see* Zeravshan
Zaragoza 93 F 2 *Eng.* Saragossa; *anc.*
Caesaraugusta, Salduba. NE
Spain
Zarand 120 D 3 C Iran
Zaranj 122 D 5 SW Afghanistan
Zarasai 106 C 4 E Lithuania
Zárate 64 D 4 *prev.* General José
F.Uriburu. E Argentina
Zaravitz 93 E 1 *var.* Zarauz. N Spain
Zarauz *see* Zaravitz
Zaraza 59 E 2 N Venezuela

Zarghūn Shahr 122 D 5 SE
Afghanistan
Zaria 75 G 4 C Nigeria
Zarós 105 D 8 Kríti, SE Greece
Zarqa *see* Az Zarqā'
Żary 98 B 4 *Ger.* Sorau, Sorau in der
Niederlausitz. W Poland
Zaunguzskiye Karakumy 122 C 2
Turkm. Ungüz Angyrsyndak
Garagum. Desert, N
Turkmenistan
Zavertse *see* Zawiercie
Zavet 104 D 1 NE Bulgaria
Zavidovići 100 C 3 N Bosnia &
Herzegovina
Zawiercie 98 C 4 *Rus.* Zavertse. S
Poland
Zaysan Köl *see* Zaysan, Ozero
Zaysan, Ozero 114 D 5 *Kaz.* Zaysan
Köl. Lake, E Kazakhstan
Zayyq *see* Ural
Zbarazh 108 C 2 W Ukraine
Zduńska Wola 98 C 4 C Poland
Zēbāk 123 F 3 NE Afghanistan
Zeebrugge 87 A 5 NW Belgium
Zeewolde 86 D 3 C Netherlands
Zefat 119 B 5 *var.* Safed, *Ar.* Safad.
N Israel
Zeila *see* Saylac
Zeist 86 C 4 C Netherlands
Zele 87 B 5 NW Belgium
Zelenoborski *see* Zelenoborskiy
Zelenoborskiy 110 C 2 *var.*
Zelenoborski. NW Russian
Federation
Zelenodol'sk 111 C 5 W Russian
Federation
Zelenograd 111 B 5 W Russian
Federation
Zelenogradsk 106 A 4 *var.* Kranz,
Ger. Cranz. W Russian Federation
Železnodorožny *see* Yemva
Zelle *see* Celle
Zel'va 107 B 6 *Pol.* Zelwa. W
Belorussia
Zelwa *see* Zel'va
Zelzate 87 B 5 *var.* Selzaete. NW
Belgium
Žemaičių Aukštumas 106 B 3
physical region, W Lithuania
Zemst 87 C 6 C Belgium
Zemun 100 D 3 N Yugoslavia
Zenica 100 C 4 C Bosnia &
Herzegovina
Zenta *see* Senta
Žepa 100 C 4 SE Bosnia &
Herzegovina
Zeravshan 123 E 3 Taj./Uzb.
Zarafshon. River,
Tajikistan/Uzbekistan
Zevenaar 86 D 4 SE Netherlands
Zevenbergen 86 C 4 S Netherlands
Zgierz 98 C 4 *Ger.* Neuhof, *Rus.*
Zgerzh. C Poland
Zgorzelec 98 B 4 *Ger.* Görlitz. SW
Poland
Zhabinka 107 A 6 *Pol.* Żabinka. SW
Belorussia
Zhambyl 114 C 5 *prev.* Aulie
Ataprev, Auliye-Ata, Džambul,
Dzhambul. S Kazakhstan
Zhangaözen *see* Novyy Uzen'
Zhangaqazaly *see* Novokazalinsk
Zhangjiakou 128 C 3 *var.*
Changkiakow, Zhang-chia-k'ou,
Eng. Kalgan; *prev.* Wanchuan. NE
China
Zhangzhou 129 D 6 SE China
Zhanjiang 129 C 7 *var.* Chanchiang,
Chan-chiang, *Cant.* Tsamkong, *Fr.*
Fort-Bayard. S China

MAP FINDER

NORTH & WEST ASIA 112-113

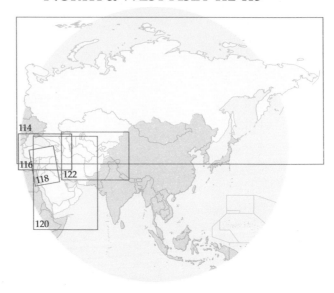

SOUTH & EAST ASIA 124-125

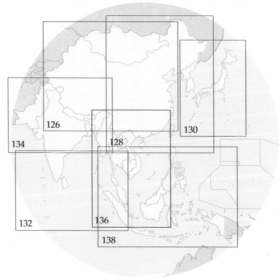